AN Irish Literature READER

Poetry, Prose, Drama

SECOND EDITION

Edited by
Maureen O'Rourke Murphy
and
James MacKillop

SYRACUSE UNIVERSITY PRESS

First Edition 1987
Second Edition 2006
06 07 08 09 10 11   6 5 4 3 2 1

The paper used in this publication meets the minimum requirements of American
National Standard for Information Sciences—Permanence of Paper for Printed
Library Materials, ANSI Z39.48–1984.∞™

Library of Congress Cataloging-in-Publication Data
An Irish literature reader : poetry, prose, drama / edited by Maureen O'Rourke Murphy
and James MacKillop.— 2nd ed.
p.   cm.—(Irish studies)
Rev. ed. of: Irish literature. 1st ed. 1987.
Includes bibliographical references and index.
ISBN 0–8156–3046–8 (pbk. : alk. paper)
1. Irish literature—Translations into English. 2. English literature—Irish authors.
3. Ireland—Literary collections. I. Murphy, Maureen O'Rourke. II. MacKillop, James.
III. Irish literature. IV. Series: Irish studies (Syracuse, N.Y.)
PB1421.I76 2006   891.6'208—dc22
2006001865

Manufactured in the United States of America

For DON MURPHY
(1934–1986)

Do chodladh san gcillse thuas
dod charaid ní cuimse an cás;
do ré níor fionnadh a raon
do thaobh gur bioradh re bás.

Maureen O'Rourke Murphy of Hofstra University is past president of the American Conference for Irish Studies and has been cited by *Irish America* as one of the one hundred most prominent Irish Americans. She is the author of *The Great Irish Famine Curriculum* (2001) for New York State, and among her many other publications on Irish language, history, folklore, and literature is the new edition of Asenath Nicholson's *Ireland's Welcome to the Stranger* (2002), a vivid portrayal of prefamine life.

James MacKillop is series editor for the Irish Studies series of Syracuse University Press and a former president of the American Conference for Irish Studies. He has written several books in the field of Irish studies, most recently the *Dictionary of Celtic Mythology* (1998) and *Myths and Legends of the Celts* (2005). Among his earlier works published by Syracuse University Press are *Contemporary Irish Cinema: From* The Quiet Man *to* Dancing at Lughnasa (1999) and *Fionn mac Cumhaill: Celtic Myth in English Literature*. His theater reviews and art features appear regularly in the *Syracuse New Times*.

Contents

Preface to the Second Edition

In the nineteen years since the first edition of *Irish Literature: A Reader,* our intentions have changed only slightly, and that in response to readers' reactions. Our first goal remains to introduce the immense variety and richness of literature written in Ireland. Initially we thought that our typical reader might be in an undergraduate classroom. We have learned, instead, that this volume has been reaching many independent readers, sampling what is to be found on their own. This knowledge, added to the gratifying wider acceptance of *Irish Literature: A Reader,* means we have sought to add more living writers to the collection. We have also increased the size of writers' primary and secondary bibliographies with the thought that any poem, short story, or drama has more resonance when placed against other works by the same author.

Once again, we do not segregate works written in English from those in the Irish (or Gaelic) language. Mac Giolla Meidhre's *Cúirt an Mheadhon Oídhche* was written during the youth of Maria Edgeworth and is found a few pages away from her *Castle Rackrent.* So too for the poetry of Thomas Moore and Anthony Raftery or the short stories of Pádraic Ó Conaire and George Moore. Included also without categorization are women and men, Protestants, Catholics, Jews, and secularists, northerners and southerners, urban sophisticates and rough-hewn country people.

The first criterion for inclusion is that the work should be significant in itself; the second, that it be representative of an author, a style, or a movement. Consequently, our organization is not thematic, and such as we do impose can easily be ignored. Many readers will make their own links within the text. The story of the Children of Lir from early Ireland invites comparison with Katharine Tynan Hinkson's treatment of the story in the early twentieth century. Discerning readers will find many common threads: nature and the importance of landscape; the use of Irish tradition; exile.

This collection contains no stealthy plan for canon formation. Some of the greatest Irish writers—Swift, Wilde, Yeats, Joyce, O'Casey, and Beckett, among others—are not found here. Their works are readily available elsewhere. Neither is there room for writers whose genius is expressed primarily in longer forms, like dramatist Brian Friel or novelist Francis Stuart. But the sampling is wide, from the premedieval *Táin Bó Cuailnge* to poet Greg Delanty, born in 1958.

MO'RM, Sea Cliff

JMK, Syracuse
Spring 2006

Acknowledgments

Boland, Eavan. "Athene's Song," "Child of Our Time," "After a Childhood Away from Ireland." By kind permission of the author.

Cannon, Moya. "Night." By permission of The Gallery Press.

Carson, Ciarán. "The Bomb Disposal," "Gate," "Last Orders." By permission of Wake Forest University Press and The Gallery Press.

Clarke, Austin. "Aisling," "The Straying Student," "Irish-American Dignitary," "Burial of an Irish President (Dr. Douglas Hyde)." By permission of R. Dardis Clarke, 17 Oscar Square, Dublin 8, Ireland.

Corkery, Daniel. "Solace." Copyright © 1916, Executor of Daniel Corkery. Reprinted by kind permission of Mercier Press Ltd., Cork.

Delanty, Greg. "The Heritage Centre, Cobh 1993," "To President Mary Robinson." By kind permission of the author.

Dillon, Éilis. Translation of *Caoineadh Airt Uí Laoghaire*. By kind permission of Eiléan Ní Chuilleanáin and Cormac Ó Cuilleanáin.

Fallon, Peter. "The Lost Field," "Fostering." By permission of The Gallery Press.

Flower, Robin. Translations, "Pangur Ban," "He That Never Read a Line." From *The Irish Tradition*. Dublin: Lilliput Press, 1995. By permission of Lilliput Press.

Heaney, Seamus. "Digging," "Traditions," "Mossbawn," "Act of Union," "Exposure," "Punishment," from "Station Island, XII," "Sweeney Redivivus," "A Brigid's Girdle," "Tollund," "Postscript." North American rights, by permission of Farrar, Straus and Giroux, LLC. United Kingdom and world rights by permission of Faber and Faber.

Hewitt, John. "The Glens," "An Irishman in Coventry." By kind permission of the author.

Hyde, Douglas. "The Necessity for De-Anglicising Ireland," selections from *The Love Songs of Connacht* by permission of Mrs. Christopher (Joan) Sealy of Co. Wicklow, Ireland.

Kavanagh, Patrick. "Shancoduff," "Epic," "Pegasus," "In Memory of My Mother," "Canal Bank Walk," "Lines Written on a Seat on the Grand

Canal, Dublin . . ." The six poems by Patrick Kavanagh, reprinted from *Collected Poems,* edited by Antoinette Quinn (Penguin Books, 2004), are reprinted by kind permission of the trustees of the estate of the late Katherine B. Kavanagh, through the Jonathan Williams Literary Agency.

Keefe, Joan. Translations: "Valentine Browne," "Friend of My Heart," "Sean O'Dwyer of the Glen." By kind permission of the author.

Kelleher, John V. "Cú Chuimne." By kind permission of the author.

Kinsella, Thomas. "Kilcash," "In the Ringwood," "The Poet Egan O'Rahilly, Homesick in Old Age," "Handclasp at Euston," "Sisters." By kind permission of the author. Translations from *An Duanaire: Poems of the Dispossessed* (Dublin: Dolmen Press, i gComhar le Bord na Gaeilge, 1981) and poems from *Collected Poems* (Manchester, UK: Carcanet, 2001).

Lavin, Mary, "Happiness." By the kind permission of Caroline Walsh, Dublin.

Longley, Michael, "Emily Dickinson," "The Linen Industry," "In Memoriam." By kind permission of the author.

MacKillop, James. Translation: "Táin Bó Cuailnge," "Deirdre," "Oidheadh Chlainne Lir," "The Frenzy of Suibne." By permission of the translator.

MacNeill, Máire. Translation: "The Scribe in the Woods," "The Blackbird by Belfast Loch," "Liádan Tells of Her Love for Cuirithir," "News of Winter," "Eve." By the kind permission of Dr. John Donovan Coyle, Louise Farrell, Maribel MacNeill, Dr. Anthony McDowell, Michael McDowell, Muiris O'Dwyer, Nora Smyth, Martin Tierney, Michael Tierney, and Dr. Niall Tierney.

Mahon, Derek. "A Disused Shed in Co. Wexford," "The Snow Party," "Imbolc: JBY." By permission of The Gallery Press. "To Mrs. Moore at Inishannon." By permission of Wake Forest University Press.

Marcus, David. Translation of "Cúirt an Mheadhon Oidhche." By permission of the author.

Maude, Caitlín. "Untitled" [*I m'ait dhúchais ó thuiadh*]. Irish text by permission of Cathal Ó Luain, trans. Maureen Murphy.

McGahern, John. "Korea." From the *Collected Stories* by John McGahern. Copyright © 1993, John McGahern. Used by permission of Alfred A. Knopf, a division of Random House, Inc. World rights by permission of Faber and Faber Ltd.

McGuckian, Medbh. "The Mast Year," "The Soil Map," "Vanessa's Bower." By permission of The Gallery Press.

Meehan, Paula. "The Statue of the Virgin at Granard Speaks." By permission of The Gallery Press.

Mhac an tSaoi, Máire. "Inquisitio 1584," "For Sheila," "Finit," "Lament for Séamus Ennis." By kind permission of the author.

Montague, John. "Like Dolmens Round My Childhood, the Old People," "A Grafted Tongue." By permission of The Gallery Press and Wake Forest University Press. "The Flight of the Earls," also known as "Lament for the O'Neills," from *The Rough Field*, is reprinted from *John Montague: Collected Poems*, by permission of Wake Forest University Press and The Gallery Press.

Muldoon, Paul. "Mules," "The Boundary Commission," "Moy Sand and Gravel," "The Ancestor," "The Stoic," "One Last Draw of the Pipe," "The Breather," "The Ancestor" from *Moy Sand and Gravel* by Paul Muldoon. Copyright © 2002, Paul Muldoon. "The Boundary Commission" and "Mules" from *Poems: 1968–1998* by Paul Muldoon. Copyright © 2001, Paul Muldoon. For United States and Canada, reprinted by permission of Farrar, Straus and Giroux, LLC. World rights by kind permission of the author.

Murphy, Gerard. Translations: "The Bird-Crib" (Poem XLI from *Duanaire Finn*, Vol. 2), "A Blue Eye Will Look Back," "The Three Best-Beloved Places," "Derry," "My Hand Is Weary With Writing." By permission of Oxford University Press.

Murphy, Tom/Thomas. "On the Outside." By permission of the author and Alexandra Cann, Representation, London.

Ní Chuilleanáin, Eiléan. "Waterfall," "The Second Voyage," "Old Roads," "J'ai Mal à nos Dents," "St. Mary Magdalene Preaching at Marseilles." By permission of The Gallery Press and Wake Forest University Press.

Ní Dhomhnaill, Nuala. "The Language Issue," "Deepfreeze," "Inside Out." By permission of Wake Forest University Press. "Annunciations," "Marvellous Grass," "The Great Queen Speaks. Cú Chulainn Listens," "Muirghil Castigates Sweeny," "Parthenogenesis," "The Shannon Estuary Welcoming the Fish." By kind permission of the author.

Ní Dhuibhne, Éilís. "Love, Hate and Friendship." By kind permission of the author.

O'Brien, Flann [pseud. of Brian O'Nolan] Selections from *At Swim-Two-Birds*, copyright © 1939, Brian O'Nolan. Selections from *An Béal Bocht*, copyright © 1941, Brian O'Nolan; translated as *The Poor Mouth*, copyright © Patrick C. Power. Reprinted by permission of HarperCollins Publishers Ltd., London.

O'Connor, Frank [pseud. of Michael O'Donovan]. "The Long Road to Ummera." From *The Collected Stories of Frank O'Connor,* copyright © Harriet O'Donovan Sheehy, executrix of the Estate of Frank O'Connor. Used by permission of Alfred A. Knopf, a division of Random House, Inc. World rights by permission of the Permissions Company, High Bridge, N.J.

Ó Direáin, Máirtín. "Honesty," "The Dignity of Sorrow," "Memories." By permission of An Clóchomhar, Teo.

O'Faolain, Sean. "The Fur Coat," copyright © 1957, Sean O'Faolain. Reproduced by permission of the author, c/o Rogers, Coleridge & White Ltd., 20 Powis Mews, London, W11 1JN.

O'Flaherty, Liam. "Going Into Exile." "Going Into Exile" from *Spring Sowing* by Liam O'Flaherty, published by Jonathan Cape. Used by permission of the Random House Group Ltd., London. Copyright © 1924, The Estate of Liam O'Flaherty. Reproduced in the United States by permission of PFD (www.pfd.uk) on behalf of the estate of Liam O'Flaherty.

Ó Ríordáin, Seán. "The Back of the House," "Frozen," "My Mother's Burying," translated by Valentine Iremonger. By permission of Sairséal agus Ó Marcaigh.

Ó Searcaigh, Cathal. "The Well," "Beyond." "The Well" originally published in Irish as "An Tobar (do Mháire Mhac an tSaoi)," in *Homecoming/An Bealach 'na Bhaile* (Indreabhán, Co. Galway, Ireland: Cló Iar-Chonnachta, 1993).

Stephens, James. Extracts from *The Insurrection in Dublin* and *Irish Fairy Tales.* By permission of the Society of Authors as the literary representative of the Estate of James Stephens.

Trevor, William [pseud. of William Trevor Cox]. "The Ballroom of Romance." From *The Ballroom of Romance* by William Trevor, copyright © 1965, 1966, 1969, 1971, 1972, William Trevor. Used by permission of Viking Penguin, a division of Penguin Group (USA) Inc. UK and Canada rights by permission of Sll/Sterling Lord Literistic, Inc.

PART ONE

Eighth Century to the Irish Literary Renaissance

Early and Medieval Irish Literature

With a manuscript tradition dating to the sixth century, Irish literature—the oldest vernacular literature in Western Europe—is remarkable for its range: law texts, genealogies, scholarly treatises, devotional tracts, and especially imaginative literature. Battles and burnings, feasts and forays, amours and elopements, voyages and visions are some of the themes of the tales that scholars have organized into four great cycles of stories: the Mythological, the Ulster, the Fenian, and the Historical. (We might say that cattle rustling is the theme of the *Táin Bó Cuailgne,* Ireland's *Aeneid!*) Ours is only a summary of the action, but there is a splendid modern translation by Thomas Kinsella.

Deirdre's story, first seen as a preliminary to the *Táin,* tells the tale of a young woman betrothed to an old man who elopes with a young lover. It introduced the Tristan and Iseult theme into European literature. One of the most popular sources for later Irish writers, Deirdre's story has appeared in a score of modern versions, notably those of John Millington Synge and William Butler Yeats.

The following tale, *Oidheadh Chlainne Lir* (The Story of the Children of Lir), is often linked thematically to Deirdre's story as one of the "Three Sorrows of Storytelling." No matter that the two are from different cycles, the former from the Mythological, the latter from the Ulster. Elsewhere in this anthology, readers will find that Thomas Moore's "The Song of Fionnuala" treats with the most vocal of Lir's children. *See* (PS. 106 [handwritten])

See Greene text [handwritten margin note]

Early Irish poetry also speaks of the sorrow of exile: first, the self-imposed exile of such early monks as St. Columcille, who left Ireland in the sixth century to found a monastery at Iona; later, involuntary political or economic exile. Love, too, is tragic, being variously unlucky, unrealized, or unfulfilled. Scholars have commented on the freshness, intensity, and compression of Early Irish poetry. Many of the little poems found in the margins of manuscripts were written by monks who looked up from copying scripture to celebrate their surroundings. Comparing them to haiku, Kuno Meyer, who translated many of the lyrics, said: "Like the Japanese, the Celts were always quick to take an artistic hint; they avoid the obvious and the commonplace; the half said thing to them is dearest." The importance of landscape, embracing at once nature, place, and mythology, is a theme that has come down from the old hermit poets to their medieval counterparts, and later to modern and contemporary Irish poetry. It is a special feature of Middle Irish tales, such as those told about Fionn mac Cumhaill. [*Finn mac Cool*]

Since the eleventh century, the name of Fionn mac Cumhaill (Finn mac Cool) has been preserved in manuscript as well as in oral tradition. Fionn is the most popular Irish mythological hero. Contemporary storytellers include tales of Fionn and his warrior band, the Fianna, in their repertoires, while place-names and field monuments further testify to his place in folk memory. Like all cultural heroes, Fionn performs precocious feats as a boy, while as a man he leads the Fianna in hunting, in feasting, and in warfare. However, a darker side is revealed in *Tóraidheacht Dhiarmada agus Ghráinne* (The Pursuit of Diarmait and Gráinne), the Fenian parallel to "The Exile of the Children of Uisnech," where Fionn is the injured older man responsible for the death of Diarmait. The interested reader is directed to James MacKillop's *Fionn mac Cumhaill: Celtic Myth in English Literature,* which traces the figure of Fionn from Macpherson's *Ossian* to Joyce's *Finnegans Wake.*

Buile Shuibhne (The Madness of Sweeney), the Middle-Irish romance translated by J. G. O'Keeffe, is another important source for Irish writers. Dating back to the second half of the twelfth century, there are earlier references to Suibne Geilt ("Mad Sweeney") at the Battle of Mag Rath (637). Some of the best poems in the text are those in praise of the trees of Ireland, Suibne's leafy home as he wanders in his frenzy through the country.

Ferguson used Suibne's story in *Congal,* and he became Yeats's King Goll; Flann O'Brien used Suibne for the Mad Sweeney versus Jem Casey episode in *At Swim Two Birds.* Suibne appears in the title poem of the first collection of Donegal poet Cathal Ó Searcaigh, *Súile Shuibhne* (Sweeney's Eye), and Austin Clarke has translated part of the romance. Finally, Trevor Joyce published a translation called *The Poems of Sweeny Peregrine,* and Seamus Heaney's adaptation appeared under the title *Sweeney Astray.*

Old Irish Prose

Táin Bó Cuailnge

[*On one level "The Táin" is pure adventure, on another it's an examination of men + women — both sexes equally regarded, equally imbued with wit + intelligence*]

For wealth of detail, richness of characterization, enumeration of episode, not to mention sheer length, the *Táin Bó Cuailnge* can stand comparison with the national epics of Europe. It is not, however, a highly finished work. To begin with, it lacks a unifying narrative tone. Successive episodes do not advance continuing themes.

[*geis = not acceptable behavior, a faux pas*]

[audio Tape]

Scant motivation appears for abrupt shifts in character. Some have derisively called it an "epic-like saga" rather than an epic. What we have survives in two versions that differ in both character and specifics. Internal linguistic evidence implies that narratives within the epic *Táin Bó Cuailnge* began to form as early as the seventh century, but the two versions that come down to us are of later date. The oldest rescension, found in *Lebor na hUidre* (Book of the Dun Cow), exhibits lean prose and sharp humor but is somewhat disjoined. The text in *Lebor Buide Lecáin* (Yellow Book of Lecan), completed c. 1390, is clearly copied from the *Lebor na hUidre*. The second version, found in *Lebor Laignech* (Book of Leinster), completed c. 1150, can be more literary at best but is also given to florid alliteration and sentimentality. The *Lebor Laignech* version includes the *remscéla* or foretales, such as the Deirdre story, that are now usually cited as anticipations of the central narrative, even when Cúchulainn or Medb do not appear in them.

Táin Bó Cuailnge is often referred to as "the *Táin*" for short, although that is a bit misleading. The words *Táin Bó* (cattle raid) follow a storyteller's device of categorizing in the first word of the title the kind of action what is about to be told. Several other early Irish stories have titles beginning Táin . . . , such as the *Táin Bó Flidais* or *Táin Bó Fraích*. David Greene suggested the title of the epic is inappropriate and may have been influenced by analogy with the others. The motive in the action is a quest for a single bull, not a herd of cattle. The English title, The Cattle Raid of Cooley, is not usually cited in learned commentary.

The first of the *rémscéla* is a ninth-century anecdote giving the purported origin of the story. Fergus mac Róich returns from the dead and recites the entire text to the chief poet Senchán Torpéist. Internal evidence indicates that the *Táin* is the work of many hands, but the creation of Senchán Torpéist, whose name does not appear elsewhere, suggests that the compilers wished for a native equivalent of Homer.

In other *remscéla* we learn of Macha's curse on the Ulstermen, of Conchobar's birth, his struggle to gain the kingship, and his ill-fated love for Deirdre. Three stories of Cúchulainn tell of his birth, his courtship of Emer and training by Scáthach, and the tragic combat with his son Connla. The final foretale is a story of magical transformation with comic undertones, explaining how the two great bulls, the Brown and the Whitehorned, came to be. Two swineherds, Friuch (boar's bristle) and Rucht (boar's grunt), are good friends, but their masters and everyone around them try to incite trouble between them. Friuch keeps pigs in the household of Bodb, king of the Munster *sídh,* while Rucht labors at the Connacht *sídh* of Ochall Ochne, bitter enemy of Bodb. Each plays a trick on the other as a test of power, which ends their friendship and sets them against one another. Dismissed for damage to the herds from their trickery, the pig-keepers spend two years transformed into birds of prey before returning to human form to tell of war-wailing and heaps of corpses. By now their enmity seethes through each change of form. Off again, they become, successively, two water creatures, warriors, stags, phantoms, dragons, and, finally, maggots or water worms, each transformation bringing them different names. When a cow belonging to Dáire mac Fiachna in Ulster drinks water containing one of the insects, Medb's cow in Connacht swallows the other. Both cows beget bulls. Rucht is then Finnbennach, the Whitehorned Bull of Connacht, and Friuch is Dub (dark) or Donn Cuailnge, the Brown Bull of Ulster.

The body of the *Táin Bó Cuailnge* embraces fourteen episodes of varying lengths, of which the fourth is clearly interpolated. It tells of the boyhood deeds of Cúchulainn, not included here. The other thirteen depict the collisions of Connacht and Ulster, Medb and Cúchulainn.

Action begins in disarming quiet, with "pillow talk," a dispute between Medb and her husband Ailill mac Máta in their bedroom at Cruachain (now Rathcrogan, Co. Roscommon). Romance is not the issue; power, as measured by possessions, is. Medb's luxuries give her an initial edge, but Ailill seems to win the contest by laying claim to the great white-horned bull, Finnbennach. Possession of cattle was the standard of wealth in early Ireland, a herding society; in pre-Christian culture they had been worshipped. Sealing his superiority with a gibe, Ailill reminds his wife that the prized Finnbennach was born into her herds but left them because it did not wish to be ruled by a woman. All her possessions are thus diminished because she does not possesses a bull to equal the great whitehorned one of her husband. What should she do? Through her courtier (and lover), Fergus mac Róich, Medb learns how she can win advantage. The greatest bull in all of Ireland is living now in the cantred (region) of Cuailnge in Ulster, and she must have it. (Cuailnge is now the Cooley Peninsula in northeastern County Louth in the Republic of Ireland, but was then a part of Ulster.) Medb sends representatives to bargain with the owner, Dáire mac Fiachna, offering many treasures, including access to her "friendly thighs" (a phrase that will reappear in the text). Dáire rebuffs her offer.

Enraged when the news is delivered, Medb resolves to take the bull by force and calls up the armies of Connacht and Leinster, as well as Ulster exiles Cormac Connloinges, son of Conchobar mac Nessa, and Fergus mac Róich. Convincing Ailill that any insult to her is shared by the household, she gains him as an ally in the quest to assert her claim to superior wealth. Before the army decamps Medb consults two seers about what it is to face. One is the mysterious prophetess known only as Fedelm, who weaves a fringe with a gold staff as she rides on the shaft of a chariot. Asked what she sees, Fedelm answers with the word "Crimson." When she is challenged by Medb and others, she repeats "Crimson" and adds a description of the formidable deeds of Cúchulainn. The second seer, a druid, is more consoling; he tells Medb that she will return alive.

As the driving force of a huge army, Medb is attentive to the discipline and deportment of individual troops. Her judgment, however, sometimes appears impetuous. Noticing that the Leinster soldiers are more adept than the Connachtmen, she fears that they will outshine her own people, demoralizing them. Such allies could betray her. She thinks of sending them home or even of killing them. Dissuaded from such rashness, Medb agrees to distribute the crack Leinster fighters among her own soldiers, shoring up weaker regiments and reducing the threat that her allies will win more glory.

Fergus mac Róich, though an Ulsterman, takes command in the field. Why he has joined the enemies of his country is not always clear. He may be jealous of Conchobar mac Nessa, who is king in his place, or he may have exiled himself after his role in the murder of the sons of Uisnech, as told in the Deirdre story. He is uneasy about opposing his countrymen. Ulster is virtually defenseless, as the warriors there still suffer under Macha's curse, binding them in the pain of a woman in labor—all, that is, except Sualtam and his son Cúchulainn.

In his first encounter with Medb's army, Cúchulainn merely leaves a posted, written warning. This happens at Iraird Cuillen (now Crossakeel, Co. Meath), when the party is two-thirds of the way to Cuailnge. The hero cuts an oak sapling into the ring shape of a spancel, which could be used as a fetter for a cow or goat, an item common to the Irish landscape at that time. On this Cúchulainn writes a threatening message in ogham: "Come no further, unless you have a man who can make a hoop like this one, with one hand, out of one piece." At this point Cúchulainn sends his mortal father Sualtam to warn the rest of the Ulstermen.

Cúchulainn himself is far removed when the army reads his warning, as he is enjoying a tryst with a young woman, possibly Fedelm Noíchrothach, daughter of Conchobar, or her bondswoman. This Fedelm is married to Ailill's elder brother, Cairbre Nia Fer, whom Cúchulainn kills in a story outside the *Táin*. Cairbre's son Erc is destined to make Cúchulainn suffer vengeance for this particular killing, even though it is only one of thousands.

On the next night Cúchulainn's message is more compelling. After cutting the fork of a tree with a single stroke, he thrusts two thirds of the trunk into the earth. Then he decorates the branches with the severed heads of four Connachtmen who had strayed from the rest of the forces. In horror Fergus *[handwritten margin notes: "Men of Ireland" / Connacht vs Ulster / Poor form (taboo)]*

reminds his men that it would violate a *geis* to pass the tree without pulling it out. Medb asks him to do this, and it takes him seven tries to succeed. When asked who could have slaughtered the four and had the strength to drive the tree so far into the ground, Fergus replies that it could only be his foster-son Cúchulainn. He then gives a long account of Cúchulainn's boyhood deeds.

[handwritten margin note: tell of some deeds]

As the Connacht army advances further toward Cuailnge, it faces only one enemy fighter. Cúchulainn taunts and terrorizes, usually targeting only one soldier at a time. Yet he can show disarming mercy. He assures one trembling Connacht charioteer that he has no quarrel with him and seeks his master instead. That master turns out to be Orlám, a son of Medb and Ailill. Cúchulainn instantly decapitates him, knowing that the head will be returned to headquarters. As the grieving parents examine it, Cúchulainn uses his long slingshot to crush the head of Fertedil, Orlám's charioteer, because he had disobeyed Cúchulainn's order to carry Orlám's head all the way to Medb and Ailill's camp. When the occasion presents itself, Cúchulainn also employs his sling to kill the pet squirrel on Medb's warm neck, as well as the bird perched on Ailill's shoulder. Three arrogant brothers try to avenge Orlám's death, but Cúchulainn makes short work of them.

[handwritten margin note: Kills Maeve's son + pets]

Meanwhile, in Cuailnge, Donn the Brown Bull begins to sniff the distant bloodletting. Hovering near him, croaking encouragement, is the many-shaped goddess of war Mórrígan, who is sometimes a woman, sometimes a beast, a bird, or the wind. Now she is a raven on the bull's shoulder, decrying death and slaughter. Rampaging, Donn Cuailnge lowers his head and levels everything in front of him, plowing a deep furrow in the earth and frightening everyone within earshot.

[handwritten margin note: shape shifter]

The Connachman's first encounter with Donn Cuailnge goes badly when the bull gores the herdsman who tries to capture him. With a retinue of fifty heifers, Donn tramples through Medb and Ailill's camp, killing fifty warriors before bounding into the countryside. Such mishaps do not keep Medb from leaving the camp for amorous meetings with Fergus. A charioteer reports these indiscretions to Ailill, who accepts them but with rancor.

[handwritten margin note: Donn the bull's destruction]

With the Ulstermen still debilitated by Macha's curse, Cúchulainn alone faces the western army. Each night he makes devastating raids, smashing heads by the skillful use of his slingshot, leaving hundreds dead. Even with this cost, however, the army advances. Events put Fergus in a tight corner, as Medb and the Connachtmen expect him to strike a blow for their side. In a parley with Cúchulainn, Fergus negotiates an agreement committing both sides to single combat each day; the duration of the combat will be the only time the army advances. With Fergus at this meeting is Etarcomol, the headstrong foster-son

[handwritten margin note: single combat plan]

Savage violence

of Medb and Ailill. Staring insolently at Cúchulainn, he sneers at him and boasts that he will be the first westerner to face the Ulster champion the next day. Etarcomol persists in baiting Cúchulainn until the Ulster hero in exasperation slices the young man in two, from crown to navel. After the rebuff of Fergus's claim that Cúchulainn has already violated the agreement, there is nothing left to do but drag Etarcomol's body back to Medb's camp.

In an unexpected turn of events Medb and her entourage head north, away from the path east to Cuailnge, taking a bead on Dún Sobairche (now Dunseverick, Co. Antrim). This temporarily confounds Cúchulainn, as he wishes to track the queen but also wants to protect his own territory on the eastern coast. As he is doubling back he encounters Buide mac Báin and twenty-four followers, who most unexpectedly are driving none other than Donn Cuailnge and twenty-four cows. Cúchulainn kills Buide easily, but in the fracas the great Brown Bull is driven off, plunging the hero into deep disappointment and dismay. Recovering, he resumes the slaughter of the enemy. One prey is Medb and Ailill's satirist Redg, who first asks for the Ulsterman's javelin. Cúchulainn responds by putting it through the satirist's head. In his death throes, Redg answers gamely, "Now, that is a stunning gift." The remark inspires the early Irish place name for the site of this combat, *Áth Tolam Sét* (Ford of the Overwhelming Gift). Dozens of Cúchulainn's other combats are described as explaining names of places, some real and others probably imaginary, on the medieval map of Ireland. In the meantime, Medb plunders Dún Sobairche to the north, a diversion from her principal mission.

Again and again, Cúchulainn is the superior in all encounters, even when Medb's side reneges on the agreement by sending as many as a hundred fighters, hoping to extend the length of the combat so that her army will have more time to advance. As this is happening, Cúchulainn must also face another resourceful female opponent, the supernatural Mórrígan, goddess of war, who is adept at shapeshifting. Usually taking the form of a huge raven, she may also appear as an eel that coils around the hero's legs, a she-wolf, and a red-eared (i.e., otherworldly) heifer. Once when he fights her off, wounding her in the process, she comes before him as a crone milking a cow with three teats, one for each of the wounds he has inflicted on her. So tired that he does not perceive her ruse, Cúchulainn asks for drink. When he blesses the teats for nourishing him, he inadvertently heals the wounds he had inflicted on Mórrígan.

Another supernatural figure serves Cúchulainn's efforts to defend Ulster. It is the hero's divine father, Lug Lámfhota, who appears gloriously clad in brilliantly colored clothes, carrying lethal weapons and invisible to everyone except his son. To give the young man respite, he stands guard for three days

M & A's satirist killed

humor (!?)

Place name

Cuch. vs Morrigan

Cuchulainn's father Lug too supernatural

Lug tends
to C.'s wounds
10 | *Eighth Century to the Irish Literary Renaissance*

and nights, allowing time for restorative sleep. Lug also attends to his son's wounds, washing them and applying healing oils. On the fourth day Cúchulainn awakes to the fitness and strength of his first day in combat.

Cúchulainn receives mortal assistance from an unexpected source, the boy troop of Emain Macha, younger counterparts of the youthful corps that the hero had joined when he went to the capital. One hundred and fifty of them fight because they have been spared Macha's debilitating curse, delivered only to grown men. Their initial foray yields costly success, as each boy takes down a single Connachtman before falling himself. But the greater numbers in Medb's army mean that the boy troop is eventually depleted, with only one boy escaping. When he makes a final dash to kill Ailill, he too is brought down, this time by the king's bodyguards.

News of the boy troop calamity sends Cúchulainn into an extreme *ríastrad* or battle fury (sometimes warp-spasm), with a red mist like a fog of vaporized blood rising from him. To avenge the boy soldiers who had honored him, Cúchulainn lays into the Connacht army with even greater intensity than before. Mounting his chariot he drives around the perimeter of the massed armies, slaughtering the hapless westerners six deep in a standing. Soon five hundred are gone, then dozens of petty kings, scores of animals, even women and children. The huge pile of corpses means that no one can keep count of the massacre. But Cúchulainn and his chariot sustain not a scratch.

Fergus, Medb, and Ailill rethink the principle of single combat. After some false starts (including a deceitful attempt by Medb to send twenty-nine selected warriors in a fruitless attack against Cúchulainn), the Connacht leadership is ready to comply. The question is to select the right champion for their side. Though his name has not been mentioned earlier in the *Táin*, only Ferdiad, foster-brother of Cúchulainn and former pupil of Scáthach, is judged worthy of the challenge. *Ferdiad*

Getting the combatants to square off takes some doing. Ferdiad is initially reluctant to face his beloved foster-brother. To push him, the Connacht forces threaten him with disgrace if he refuses but offer rich rewards if he consents, including the pledged troth of Medb's beautiful, fair-haired daughter Finnabair and access to Medb's lovemaking as well. Ferdiad responds that this will be a fight to the death and warns that if he must kill his own foster-brother, he will return to camp and finish off Medb. Yet Ferdiad has to be Connacht's man because he is the only one who could possibly match the Ulster hero. In his camp Cúchulainn admits he dreads the looming duel, not because he fears Ferdiad but rather because he loves him.

Ferdaid
C's foster bro. whom he loves

Ferdiad's duel with Cúchulainn, the climax of the *Táin* for many readers, is often cited as "the combat at the ford," as if it were the only one. In a herding society like early Ireland's, a society without modern bridges, all paths must eventually cross shallow passages of rivers and streams. Armed men and the cattle they drive are at their most vulnerable at such crossings. Not surprisingly, then, many battles take place at the fords of rivers, not only in the *Táin* but also in other early Irish literature. So while there is no foreshadowing for the person of Ferdiad, his battle with Cúchulainn at Áth Fhirdiad (now Ardee, Co. Louth), on the Dee River fourteen miles north of Drogheda, is the culmination of a long series.

In a battle that rages for four days, the combatants boast and taunt one another as well as engaging in constant hand-to-hand combat. Pieces of flesh the size of a baby's head are hacked away, leaving wounds that gape so wide birds can fly through them. Each night Cúchulainn sends Ferdiad leeches and herbs to heal his wounds; the Ulsterman does not wish to have the advantage of better medical treatment. Ferdiad responds by sharing his food. For the first three days, as they fight with darts, slender spears, heavy spears, and heavy swords, neither can gain an advantage. On the fourth day Cúchulainn calls for his Gáe Bulga, the mysterious and powerful weapon whose use he had learned from the amazonian Scáthach. It is a spear that enters the body at one point but opens to make thirty wounds within. Before he can act, Ferdiad plunges his sword into Cúchulainn's chest, but Cúchulainn still manages to cast his spear through Ferdiad's heart and halfway out his back. But the *coup de grâce* is just now coming. With Láeg the charioteer helping him, Cúchulainn thrusts the Gáe Bulga against Ferdiad, killing him. Immediately Cúchulainn begins to lament the passing of his foster-brother and friend, but he is prostrate from his own wounds.

The Ulstermen have little to celebrate in Ferdiad's death because their own hero lies so weakened. Into the breech steps another champion, who achieves some Cúchulainn-like deeds. White-haired Cethern mac Fintain, known for his generosity and his bloody blade, flies into the camp of the western army, inflicting great damage. He, too, is severely wounded. Returned to the Ulster camp he makes a poor patient. Cethern kills the healers—fifteen or as many as fifty—who attempt to treat him because he does not like their unfavorable diagnoses. At the same time he tells stories of how he acquired his wounds, one of which has come from Medb herself. Cúchulainn gathers bone marrow and animal ribs to help restore him, and Cethern returns to battle, felling many of the enemy before he himself is struck down.

Other single champions come forth from Ulster while Cúchulainn lies exhausted, but their futile efforts serve only to disturb Sualtam, the hero's mortal father. Frightened, he thinks that either the sky is falling or his son is continuing against unequal odds and so seeks him out on the battlefield. Unable to rise, Cúchulainn sends Sualtam back to Emain Macha to rouse the rest of the troops. Taking this call most seriously, Sualtam rushes to the palace shouting with all the fury he can muster: "Men murdered! Women stolen! Cattle plundered!" Three times he calls out, but there is no answer. A geis forbids a commoner to speak before the king, and a king to speak before the druid. Cathbad asks about the meaning of Sualtam's cry, and, learning that Cúchulainn has broken protocol by speaking before the king, refuses any help. Angered by the response, Sualtam shouts even louder, and in so doing loses his footing and trips on his scallop-edged but razor-sharp shield, instantly separating his head from his shoulders. The severed head is brought before Conchobar, where Sualtam still shouts the same warnings.

In death Sualtam achieves what he could not in life. Conchobar rouses the men of Ulster, and, at long last, the debilities of Macha's curse begin to fall away from the fighting men. The charioteer Láeg, speaking for Cúchulainn, joins in the call to arms. The narrative now recognizes that immense forces are hurtling toward each other. As the armed companies advance, the text lavishes more than five hundred lines on descriptions of color and armaments, all in anticipation of the massed assembly at Gáirech and Irgairech, southwest of Mullingar in what is now Co. Westmeath. During the night before what must be the final encounter, Mórrígan incites both armies against each other. As the battle begins, the Connacht forces under Fergus's command break through the lines. In Cúchulainn's absence, Conall Cernach rises to the fore and taunts Fergus for betraying his own kind for "the sake of a whore's backside." Undeterred, Fergus makes his way to Conchobar and almost succeeds in killing him but pulls back when he remembers the king is a fellow Ulsterman. Word of the assault on Conchobar reaches the still-recovering Cúchulainn, driving him from his bed and thrusting him into his battle frenzy. This is enough to drive Fergus from the field; as he had earlier promised, there would be no duel with Ulster's prime hero.

Except for the Brown Bull, which accompanies them, Ailill and Medb are now alone on the battlefield. Suddenly, and to Ailill's displeasure, Medb announces that she has to relieve herself and withdraws. This is the time of her period, and the massive flow of her menstrual blood digs three great channels, each big enough to take a household. An alternative reading depicts her urine. This occurs just as Cúchulainn, restored from his bed of pain, comes upon her. He refrains from taking her when she is at a disadvantage. And when she

C, spares Medb

pleads to be spared, he answers that it would be right to execute her, but he is not a killer of women. Thus he allows her to escape, taking the prized Donn Cuailnge with her. In anger Cúchulainn slices off the tops of three nearby hills. The human battle is over.

Surveying the carnage, Fergus observes: "We followed the rump of a misguiding woman." (The pun *tóin* [rump] and *táin* [cattle raid] disappears in translation.) And Fergus adds, "It is the usual thing for a herd led by a mare to stray and be destroyed."

women are dissed

Once Donn Cuailnge is led to Cruachain, Ailill and Medb's residence, he gives out three mighty bellows, challenging Finnbennach the white-horned bull, which is grazing nearby. Finnbennach rises to the call, charging toward Cruachain, attracting a huge crowd. As Donn Cuailnge is tired from the trek across Ireland, Finnbennach gains an initial advantage. Briccriu Neimthegna, known for equanimity as well as his bitter tongue, is called in as judge, but the raging beasts trample him under their hooves. In a reversal, Donn Cuailnge stamps his hoof on Finnbennach's horn, pinning him the ground. Standing nearby, Fergus goads the Brown Bull, saying too many men have died to let the White-horned Bull throw away his honor so easily. Thus released, the two bulls continue the battle all over Ireland until, at dawn, Donn Cuailnge emerges at Cruachain with Finnbennach's bloody remains dangling from his horns. With the battle decided, Donn Cuailnge begins a circuitous route home, leaving Finnbennach's body parts thither and yon. The loins are memorably dropped at the principal ford of the Shannon, Áth Lúain (ford of the loins, modern Athlone). When Donn Cuailnge reaches Ulster at last, he falls at Druim Tairb (ridge of the bull), victim of his own bursting heart.

Bull fight bet. brown + white bulls

Ailill and Medb make peace with Ulster and with Cúchulainn, but their beautiful daughter stays with the former enemy. The men of Ulster return to Emain Macha in triumph.

Medb meets an absurd death in an eleventh-century story. In it, Furbaide Ferbend, son of her murdered sister, punctures her skull with a hardened piece of cheese on an island in Lough Ree, County Roscommon. Her prowess and resilience fail her at the end.

Medb killed by Cheese

Cúchulainn, though his life is short, is destined for many more adventures.

Deirdre

Two beautiful young Irish women escape from dominating men and pay heavy prices for their independence. They flee the aging, powerful men to whom they were betrothed and assert their own form of honor by cleaving to younger lovers they select for themselves. They are Deirdre (or Derdriu, etc.) from the Ulster Cycle and Gráinne from the Fenian Cycle. While their tales share striking parallels, they are also separated by profound differences that depict Deirdre as the more complex personality. Certainly her adventures and subsequent downfall have been portrayed more often in English language adaptation since 1870, poetry, drama, fiction, even opera, so that Deirdre is now popularly the best-known name of any from early Celtic traditions.

Deirdre's story was widely known over many centuries. It is found in two medieval versions, a third from the early nineteenth century and several folk variants from both Ireland and Gaelic Scotland.

Fedlimid, the chief bard of Ulster at the court of King Conchobar mac Nessa, becomes the father of a baby girl, Deirdre. Even before her birth, the court druid, Cathbad, prophesies that the girl-child will grow to be a woman of wonderful beauty, but that she will also cause great enmity, leading to the destruction of Ulster. On hearing the druid's words, several courtiers demand that she be killed, but Conchobar (anglicized Conor) does not wish to. Instead, he fosters her secretly until she is of marriageable age so that he might then take her as his wife.

The girl is raised in isolation from society, with only the company of a few women, notably Leborcham, a poet and confidante. One day the two of them observe a visiting Conchobar skinning a recently killed calf in the snow. A raven perches nearby, drinking the calf's blood. Deirdre exclaims at the juxtaposition of the three colors: white snow, red blood, and black raven. She declares that the man she marries will have this coloring, and Leborcham responds that such a man—one with white skin, red cheeks, and black hair—lives nearby, by name Noíse (also Naoise, etc.), a nephew of Conchobar and a son of Uisnech.

After Leborcham arranges that the two meet, Noíse remarks, "Fair is the heifer that goes past me." Deirdre responds, "Heifers are wont to be big where there is no bull." To which Noíse replies, "You have the bull of the province, the king of Ulster." And then Deirdre admits, "I will choose between the two of you, and I will choose a young bull like you." Shortly thereafter Deirdre and Noíse elope, fleeing first across Ireland with Conchobar in pursuit and later to Scotland. Noíse's brothers Ardan and Ainnle go with them—thus the title of the best-known version in Irish, *Longas* (or *Longes*) *mac nUislenn* (*The Exile of the Sons of Uisnech*). It is a *rémscél* or prologue of the *Táin Bó Cuailnge* (*The Cattle Raid of Cooley*) and is often bound with the

Conchobar's treachery

epic. When a host king in Scotland begins to lust after Deirdre, the party flees. Soon news of pardon from Conchobar reaches them. Wanting the young people back in the Ulster capital of Emain Macha, he sends the heroes Fergus mac Róich with pledges of good faith to the fugitives. The brothers are willing to accept the invitation to return, but Deirdre perceives the falsity of the offer and fears Conchobar's treachery. Deirdre sings the verses of "Farewell to Alba" (Scotland), before joining the others in the boat.

When they land in Ulster, Conchobar employs a ruse to separate Fergus from Deirdre and the brothers. The king's men, led by Eógan mac Durthacht, then attack quickly, killing all but Deirdre. For the next year she lives subject to Conchobar, never smiling, frequently berating him for killing what was dear to her. No longer wishing to mate with her himself, Conchobar contrives to increase Deirdre's humiliation by having her marry the hated Eógan, Noíse's murderer and possibly also a member of a lower social order. To exacerbate her predicament, Conchobar makes Deirdre the butt of a crude sexual joke. Deirdre then commits suicide. In the earlier of the medieval texts she does this by throwing herself against a stone and smashing her head into fragments. She does this outside her residence but before she reaches the assembly of Macha, where her treatment by Conchobar and Eógan would have invited more shame and ridicule. Like a male hero, she chooses death before dishonor.

Deirdre Commits Suicide

The later medieval version, *Oided Mac n Uisnig* (*Death of the Sons of Uisnech*), provides details preferred in modern retellings of the story. Here she falls from the chariot into the sea, dashing her head on a rock, her blood leaving a red streak on the foam. The last Irish-language version, perhaps reflecting an unease about suicide influenced by Christianity, has her falling upon her lover's grave, overcome by grief.

In the Fenian parallel story of Gráinne, the young beauty runs off with the handsome Diarmait, who is killed in a boar hunt. At the end of that tale, Gráinne is reunited with old Fionn mac Cumhaill, to whom she had been betrothed at the beginning of the action.

The Deirdre story in different texts is often classed as one of the "Three Sorrows of Storytelling," along with *Oidheadh Chlainne Tuireann* (*The Tragic Story of the Children of Tuireann*), and *Oidheadh Chlainne Lir* (*The Tragic Story of the Children of Lir*), whose summary follows.

—*Summary by James MacKillop*

Children of Lir

Oidheadh Chlainne Lir

See Thomas Moore's The Song of Fionnuala

The story of the four children of Lir who are magically transformed into swans by their cruel stepmother Aífe could easily be mistaken for a fairy tale. When we put the story into a larger context, however, we can see that it carries much cultural and religious resonance. Lir, his children, and their stepmother are all members of the Tuatha Dé Danann, the mythical, semidivine early invaders of Ireland. A fuller account of their story as well as tales of several other invaders appears in the twelfth-century pseudohistory *Lebor Gabála Érenn* (known in English as *The Book of Invasions*). In this account, the Tuatha Dé Danann are the second-to-last invaders, a magical people who are succeeded by the mortal and somewhat prosaic Milesians, the progenitors of ordinary mortals. The action of *Oidheadh Chlainne Lir* (*The Tragic Story of the Children of Lir*) takes place just as the Tuatha Dé Danann are giving away to mere morals. The anonymous author who put the story in final form about 1500 hoped to interpolate or interleave these episodes within the general framework of events set out in the *Lebor Gabála Érenn*. He allows that the Tuatha Dé Danann would have survived long enough to encounter Christian evangelists, a faith absent from the *Lebor Gabála*.

Events in *Oidheadh Chlainne Lir* were not much celebrated in oral tradition but more recently have become among the best known from early tradition through the efforts of cultural revivalists and educators. Oisin Kelly's huge sculpture of the children changing back from swans into elderly humans is the focal point of the Garden of Remembrance in Parnell Square, Dublin. *Oidheadh Chlainne Lir* is one of the "Three Sorrows of Storytelling," along with the Deirdre story and *Oidheadh Chlainne Tuireann* (*The Tragic Story of the Children of Tuireann*). *Also statue in Eire Sq Galway*

Lir loses his b.d to King

When the Tuatha Dé Danann are defeated by the Milesians at the battle of Tailtiu, they seek out a new king so they will not be ruled by their conquerors. Two of the five candidates are Bodb Derg of Connacht and Lir of what is now County Armagh; the latter is not the Lir of Manannán's patronymic, mac Lir. Bodb Derg's selection disappoints Lir, who retreats to his *sídh* of Finnachad, where his unhappiness is compounded by the death of his wife. Magnanimously, Bodb offers Lir the hand of one of his foster-daughters, and Lir chooses the eldest, usually named Áeb. In quick succession she bears two sets of twins, first a daughter, Finnguala, and a son, Áed, and then two more sons, Fiachra and Conn, after which Áeb dies. To compensate Lir for this loss, Bodb Derg offers the hand of a second daughter, Aífe, who cherishes her stepchildren—at least at first. *Finnuala*

Proving childless in her own marriage, however, Aífe's attitude toward the four children takes a dark turn. Overcome with a debilitating jealousy, she takes to her bed, pretending sickness for a year. Brusquely pronouncing herself cured, she declares she will visit her father in Killaloe, in what is now County Clare, taking the children with her. A wary Finnguala, who has seen evil portents in a dream, resists. On the way to the west, Aífe begins to rant against the children on patently false charges, claiming that they are depriving her of her husband's love. She orders her servants to butcher them on the spot—Lough Derraverragh (Ir. Dairbhreach, meaning "with an oak plantation") in what is now County Westmeath. When the retainers refuse, Aífe shoves the children into the water and produces a druidical wand (or sword) to transform the children into swans. Finnguala, who like all the children has retained the power of speech, protests, asserting their blamelessness and asking Aífe how long their unjust punishment will last. The stepmother answers harshly. They will suffer nine hundred years in three sentences of increasing misery: three hundred years here at Lough Derraverragh; three hundred years in the North Channel, the narrowest passage between Ireland and the Mull of Kintyre in Scotland, sometimes called the Sea of Moyle; and a final three hundred years on the stormy west coast of Ireland between Erris and the small island of Inishglora, County Mayo. The spell on the children will end, Aífe explains, when a woman from the south, Deoch, daughter of Fingen, king of Munster, unites with a man of the north, Lairgnéan, son of Colmán of Connacht. Now that Finnguala has asked the terms of the curse, any power of the Tuatha Dé Danann to lift it has been nullified. Aífe does allow the transformed children, however, to retain along with their power of speech their human senses and faculties, as well as an ability to sing supreme among mortals. Leaving the children at Lough Derraverragh, Aífe proceeds to Bodb Derg's palace, where her treachery is soon discovered and she is punished by being transformed into a demon (sometimes vulture) of the wind, condemned to wander through air until the end of time.

In the midst of their pain and sorrow, the child-swans find that they can indeed sing, and with eloquence, poetry, and fine speech. People from all over Ireland flock to Lough Derravaragh to hear them. Bodb, Lir, and other prominent figures attend. The text includes many verse passages of their songs. At the end of each three-hundred-year term, Finnguala reminds her three brothers to move on. During their second exile they encounter a party of horsemen, including two other sons of Bodb Derg, near an estuary of the River Bann. The men had been looking for the children and give them news of the Tuatha Dé Danann. Such fleeting gestures of good will are of little avail. Eventually the people of Ireland forget about Lir's off-spring.

In their third exile the children's songs reach the ears of a character new to the story. The young man, Áebhric by name, appears to be a well-born cleric living by his own hand in isolation near Erris (Ir. Irrus Domnann, Iorras Domhnann). Like all the others, he is entranced by the children's singing, but he decides to write down their story so that we may read it now. Their nine-hundred-year exile complete, the children return to the *sídh* of Finnachad only to find it abandoned and desolate. Their only hope now is to wait at Inishglora (Ir. Inis Gluaire, meaning "island of brightness") until Mo Cháemóc, a disciple of St. Patrick, brings the gospel of Christianity to the island. Hearing the evangelist's bell, the swan children begin to sing with it, making themselves known to him. To help the children forget their suffering, Mo Cháemóc brings them into his household and there links them together with a silver chain.

Without the children's knowing it, meanwhile, Aífe's prophecy is fulfilled. South and north are united with Deoch of Munster's marriage to Lairgnéan, and they now reign in Connacht. Once introduced to the reader, Deoch proves vain and grasping. She covets the singing swans for herself and demands that the king secure them for her. Bowing to her command, Lairgnéan tries to pull them away from Mo Cháemóc by yanking their silver chain, and in so doing unwittingly returns them to human form. That form is no longer childlike, of course. After nine hundred years of exile the four off-spring of Lir are virtually pillars of dust. Mo Cháemóc baptizes them immediately, just in time to save their immortal souls.

—*Summary by James MacKillop*

Old Irish Poetry

News of Winter

Found in a late sixth century life of St. Columcille, this poem—a gloss on the word for "sea"—is attributed to Fionn.

News for you:
The stag roars,
Winter pours,
Summer's end.

High cold wind,
Low lies sun,
Short its run,
Sea waves pound.

Bracken browns,
Clumps are bare,
In grey air
Wild goose cries.

Cold has seized
Song bird's wing,
Ice is King.
This is my news.
trans. Máire MacNeill

[handwritten: Sounds, colors, movement of environment]

The Blackbird by Belfast Loch

In his edition of the poem, Gerard Murphy suggests the blackbird was singing from a gorse bush. Loch Lee (Loch Loígh) is Belfast Lough.

[handwritten: Lake]

The small bird
lets a trill
from bright tip
of yellow bill.

The shrill chord
by Loch Lee
of blackbird
from yellow tree.
trans. Máire MacNeill

[handwritten: gorse]

Líadan Tells of Her Love for Cuirithir

[handwritten: she visited him in his cloister and he had to sail away from her. Later to avoid her. She died praying upon the stone which he used to pray.]

These early seventh-century lovers were the subject of a ninth-century poem that describes how Líadan promised to marry Cuirithir but became a nun instead. Cuirithir entered a monastery in the Déisi (Waterford); Líadan followed him there, but he fled. The poem attributed to Líadan is the earliest known of the Irish women's laments. Líadan and Cuirithir anticipate a later fascinating and tragic clerical couple—Héloïse and Abelard.

[handwritten note: From Liadan pov a Lament]

Void of joy
what I have done:
the one I loved I crossed.

Crazed I was
to take that vow
and outlaw his desire.

Not pain he sought
but a quiet road
to Paradise.

For small cause
I hurt him most
whom I would hurt the least.

I Líadan
loved Cuirithir:
Nothing is more true.

A short time
we were together
Cuirithir and I.

Forest music
sang to us
and the sound of the sea.

I thought then
nothing I would do
could vex Cuirithir.

No secret now:
I loved him
as I loved no other.

A roar of fire
has split my heart;
without him I die.
　　　trans. Máire MacNeill

The Scribe in the Woods

This ninth-century lyric was found in the margin of Priscian's treatise on Latin grammar in the monastery of St. Gall, near Lake Constance, Switzerland, a monastery famous for its library of Irish manuscripts. The Irish St. Gall (d. 645) is the Swiss patron
saint.

Over me green branches hang
A blackbird leads the loud song;
Above my pen-lined booklet
I hear a fluting bird-throng.

The cuckoo pipes a clear call
Its dun cloak hid in deep dell:
Praise to God for this goodness
That in woodland I write well.
　　　trans. Máire MacNeill

The Viking Terror

plundered the monesturies

Another St. Gall manuscript poem mentions the Vikings, who began to raid Ireland
in the ninth century.

Bitter is the wind tonight,
It tosses the ocean's white hair:
Tonight I fear not the fierce warriors of Norway
Coursing on the Irish Sea.
　　　trans. Kuno Meyer

Pangur Ban

Another ninth-century poem, found in a miscellany of notes on grammar, astron-
omy, and Latin poetry in the monastery of St. Paul in Carinthia (southern

Austria), suggests that the monk-poet must have been a kindred spirit to the monk-scribe whose playful white cats arrest their own mice on the Chi-Rho page of *The Book of Kells.* Pangur is a Welsh name. Ban (Ir. *bán, bawn*) means "white."

show this

I and Pangur Ban, my cat,
'Tis a like task we are at;
Hunting mice is his delight,
Hunting words I sit all night.

> identification

Better far than praise of men
'Tis to sit with book and pen;
Pangur bears me no ill will,
He too plies his simple skill.

'Tis a merry thing to see
At our tasks how glad are we,
When at home we sit and find
Entertainment to our mind.

Oftentimes a mouse will stray
In the hero Pangur's way;
Oftentimes my keen thought set
Takes a meaning in its net.

'Gainst the wall he sets his eye
Full and fierce and sharp and sly;
'Gainst the wall of knowledge I
All my little wisdom try.

When a mouse darts from its den,
O how glad is Pangur then!
O what gladness do I prove
When I solve the doubts I love!

So in peace our tasks we ply,
Pangur Ban, my cat, and I;
In our arts we find our bliss,
I have mine and he has his.

Practice every day has made
Pangur perfect in his trade;
I get wisdom day and night
Turning darkness into light. *illumination*

    trans. Robin Flower

Three Ninth-Century Poems for Students and Pilgrims

He That Never Read a Line

"Son of learning" is a literal translation of *mac léinn* (pron. mac lay in), the Irish word for a student.

'Tis sad to see the Sons of learning
In everlasting Hellfire burning
While he that never read a line
Doth in eternal glory shine.

    trans. Robin Flower

The Pilgrim at Rome

To go to Rome
Is much of trouble, little of profit:
The King whom thou seekest here,
Unless thou bring Him with thee, thou wilt not find.

    trans. Kuno Meyer

Ref. to absence Christ's from Rome. (Rome had no domination over Ireland)

Cú Chuimne   *coo Kvam*

A poem from the Annals of Ulster, A.D. 747

Cú Chuimne in youth
Read his way through half the Truth   *scripture*
He let the other half lie
While he gave women a try.

Well for him in old age,
He became a holy sage.

He gave women the laugh.
He read the other half.

trans. John V. Kelleher

From the Late Tenth or Eleventh Century

Eve

I am Eve, great Adam's wife;
I doomed Jesus from far off;
I lost Eden for my kind;
'Tis I should hang on the cross.

I had a king's house to rule.
Evil the choice that ruined me,
Evil the withering penalty.
Alas! my hand is foul.

'Twas I plucked the apple down,
Losing mastery to greed;
For that, women while they live
Will be captive to folly.

No ice would be anywhere,
No glistening windy winter,
No hell would be, no terror
Nor any sorrow but for me.

trans. Máire MacNeill

[handwritten annotations: "medieval idea enters Irish lit. — that women are intrinsically evil — daughters of Eve"]

[handwritten annotation: "If Fall had not occurred"]

[handwritten annotation: "Columcille defended the fili class of Ireland from being banished for overcharging for their work. He brought about reform in the fili ranks"]

Columcille's Poems

These poems are attributed to St. Columcille—after St. Patrick, Ireland's most beloved saint. A member of the royal Uí Neill family, Columcille was born in Gartan, in Tír Luigdech, now the parish of Kilmacrenan, County Donegal, in 521 (d. 597). He founded monasteries at Derry (546) and Durrow (551) before he left

[handwritten annotations: "colum-chill"   "became saint Columba"   "Refer to Battle of The Book"]

[handwritten: scotland]

Ireland in 563 to establish a foundation at Iona. (From its summit he could still see Ireland.)

Adamnán's *Life of Columcille* describes Irish monastic life in the sixth century. Columcille's poems provide other insights: the identification with place, the loneliness of exile, and the tedium of the scribe's life. The *Cathach,* a manuscript of the Psalter believed to have been written by Columcille, is in the Royal Irish Academy.

The Three Best-Beloved Places

[handwritten: Triad   see contemp. Triad pg. 404]

The three best-beloved places I have left in the peopled world are Durrow, Derry (noble angel-haunted city), and Tír Luigdech.

[handwritten: Lu Deck]

[handwritten: C. writes with a depth of sadness of what he is not only his leaving behind ... earthly kin, family]

Derry

Many wonders and miracles did God work for Columcille in Derry. And because he loved that city greatly Columcille said:

This is why I love Derry, it is so calm and bright; for it is all full of white angels from one end to the other.

[handwritten: irony — later history]

A Blue Eye Will Look Back

[handwritten: and friends & security of a close-knit community that bonded them. It is also the non-human — the land itself. Each leaf of the oaks & the angels of wh. Derry is full.]

Columcille about to leave Ireland, A.D. 563:

There is a blue eye which will look back at Ireland; never more shall it see the men of Ireland nor her women.

My Hand Is Weary with Writing

My hand is weary with writing; my sharp great point is not thick; my slender-beaked pen juts forth a beetle-hued draught of bright blue ink.

[handwritten: Difficulty & tedium of illuminating mss.]

A steady stream of wisdom springs from my well-coloured neat fair hand; on the page it pours its draught of ink of the green-skinned holly.

[handwritten: plant produced ink]

[handwritten: Name 7 The Rose Umberto Ecco]

I send my little dripping pen unceasingly over an assem-
blage of books of great beauty, to enrich the possessions
of men of art—whence my hand is weary with writing.

> trans. Gerard Murphy

Belief that every embellishment the scribe/monk will be rewarded in heaven

From *Duanaire Finn*

The Bird-Crib

(Bird trap) *Finnegan's wake based on Finn*

This poem about Fionn, one of a collection called the *Duanaire Finn* (*Poem Book of Fionn*), was probably written in the fifteenth century. Gerard Murphy, who edited the poem, describes similar bird-cribs or bird-traps that were used in the Irish countryside when he was a boy. The question marks indicate unclear entries in the text.

Christianity has entered Patrick interested in the ancient Tale

St. Patrick asks the question

1 "A hazel bird-crib: who made one, tell,
   ancient men: and tell which of you first
   played the jerking(?) trick upon birds." *) Patrick's voice*

2 "Dost thou hear, thou ancient man, the
   question which the Táilgheann puts? Answer,
   according to thy knowledge, the question
   Patrick asks." *Another voice asks the bard to tell the Tale*

3 One day when Fionn was on Sliabh Luachra
   of the full glens he chanced to be apart
   from the Fian with three score willing *30 warriors only*
   warriors.

4 Although we were strong we were uneasy
   and ignorant, beneath a dark magic mist,
   till we decided on a plan.

5 As Fionn, son of Cumhall, prince of the
   Fianna, glanced out towards the west,
   he sees
   a tall roving warrior clad in a handsome
   red suit.

[handwritten: Trickery]

6   On the big man's right hand was a beautifully coloured bird-crib of red gold: he caught as he wished what birds went past him.

7   The warrior came towards us on the fairsided heavy hill, and indeed greeted us in polished pure words.

8   "If thou and all thy band come with me, O Fionn of the truly brave Fianna, I shall give you what is old in every drink and what is new in every ancient food."

9   We, the people of Fionn of the unsheathed weapons, rose up quickly: although no good came of it to us, we were not slow to rise.

10 The big man went before us: we followed him (and it was sad) to the stronghold of Inbhear dhá Shál where the crib was prepared.

11 When the big man had gone out from us beyond the gate of the stronghold, without delay he closed a door of rough iron upon us.

[handwritten: Biblical number]

12 For seven days and nights we were in the high-ditched earthen fortress without food; and no one came to see us from far or near.

13 In imitation of the jerking (?) crib, to secure sufficient birdcatching for every man, Fionn made a hazel crib (the lesson was not neglected[?] by us), that we might get from the jerking (?) crib sufficient birdcatching for every man of us.

[handwritten marginal notes: This cycle was composed by the common people. It tells of Fionn's wily means of keeping himself & his men from starving when an enemy trapped by / Note, Fionn's the "red man" should have impressed Patrick]

[handwritten: Fionn's wisdom / Bird meat sustained them]

14 At the end of seven days spent thus the
son of Troghan comes to see us: he thought
we were not alive, and came to behead us
all on one day.

[handwritten: Severed head motif]
[handwritten: Fionna attack him]

15 We come from all sides about the son of
Troghan then: when we came round
him in fury his magic availed him nothing.

16 Fionn bore the red man away, though
our anger was great against him; and he
sent him safe to his house, although we did
not so will it, O cleric.

[handwritten: speaking to Patrick]

17 The best act of clemency ever done by
the good son of Cumhall, prince of the
Fiana, was to conduct the red man safe
and to ward us off.

18 There, O cleric of the jewelled croziers,
is an act of clemency done by Fionn,
the man who practised all valour: by
him was the crib prepared.

19 O Caoilte, although I am weak, do not let
it pass if I speak a lie: any person as good
as Fionn sawest thou ever in thy time?

[handwritten: In praise of fionn by Patrick]

20 "As regards his soul and his body (though
tonight my appearance is gloomy) no man
living in his age had nobility equal to
that of Fionn."

[handwritten: Blend of pagan & Christian belief]

From *Buile Shuibhne* [The Madness of Sweeney]

[handwritten: Popular Irish legend of the wild man]
[handwritten: King vs clergy]

The Frenzy of Suibne

Suibne or Suibhne, the antecedent of Sweeney, was a common enough name in
early Ireland, but there is no indication that Suibne, the cursed king who went mad,

[handwritten: Popular subj. S. Heaney writes about him]

ever existed. He does not appear in the genealogies of the people he is supposed to have ruled. The setting of his three-part story is linked to the Battle of Mag Rath (or Moira) of A.D. 637, the culmination of a momentous dynastic struggle in what is today County Down. Citations for *Suibne Geilt* (*Mad Sweeney*) appear in a ninth-century law tract, but his main story, *Buile Shuibhne* (*The Frenzy of Suibne*), did not take its present form until the twelfth century, surviving in three manuscripts written five centuries later. Redactors of his narrative are careful to present the Church most favorably, especially as a repository of native learning. The two stories preceding *Buile Shuibhne* are *Fled Dúin na nGéd* (*The Feast of Dún na nGéd*), which deals with events leading up to the battle, and *Cath Maige Rátha* (*The Battle of Mag Rath*), a description of the carnage there.

Although the names are changed, Suibne is unmistakably the model for Goll in William Butler Yeats's early poem, "The Madness of King Goll" (1887).

Action begins in the petty kingdom of Dál nAraide, which straddled the border of Counties Antrim and Down in what is now eastern Northern Ireland. King Suibne, son of Colmán, seeks to expel the evangelizing St. Rónán from his realm, but his wife Eórann tries to temper her husband's anger. Enraged by the sound of Rónán's proselytizing bell, Suibne is dashing out the front door of his castle when Eórann tries to stop him by grabbing his coat. This leaves the pagan king stark naked but still carrying weapons, like the ancient Gaulish warriors described by Posidonius. In a fit of fury, Suibne hurls Rónán's psalter into a lake and is about to give the saint what for when his kingly responsibility calls him to the Battle of Mag Rath. Piously the saint gives thanks to God for being spared, but he also curses King Suibne, asking that he be made to wander through the world naked, just as he came naked into Rónán's presence.

The king's second encounter with the saint has a more lasting effect. After an otter magically restores Rónán's psalter, so that it appears it was never dropped in water, the saint approaches the Mag Rath battlefield, hoping to bring peace. He fails. As he blesses the armies, his sprinkling of holy water irks Suibne so severely that he thrusts a spear through an attendant, killing him. He hurls another at the saint himself, only to see it break against Rónán's bell, its shaft flying into the air. Thus the saint curses the king a second time, declaring not only that Suibne should fly through the air like the shaft of his spear but that he should perish of a cast spear. Initially unconcerned, Suibne rejoins the battle, but finds himself increasingly disoriented amid the clamor of bloodletting. Seized with trembling like a wild bird, he flees the battlefield. As he races madly, his feet barely touch the ground until he alights in a yew tree. Meanwhile, at the battle, Suibne's withdrawal opens the way for a victory by his opponents. After a kinsman fails to restore the king to his senses, Suibne flees to a remote corner of Ireland, perching on a tree in Tír Chonaill (Donegal). Passages filled with arrays of poetic place-names describe the wanderings of the tormented Suibne, who often wishes that he had been killed in battle. His lamentations come in long verse narratives, or lays. While not a member of the privileged, powerful caste of poets, a *fili* (pl. *filid*), Suibne is a king who speaks poetry. He describes himself as a mad man, and as he is naked, shivering in the trees, he looks like one. Eventually he finds respite in the valley of the lunatics, Glen Bolcáin. This appears to have been an actual place, usually sited at what is now Glenbuck, near Rasharkin, County Antrim. (A Fenian text places the valley on the Dingle Peninsula, in County Kerry, but that may have been another such retreat.)

At some of his stops Suibne gives cryptic advice. Reaching the lyrically named church of Snám Dá Én (Swim Two Birds) on the Shannon, near the monastery of Clonmacnoise, the mad king observes the clerics reciting their Friday canonical prayers, the nones. Nearby, women are beating flax, and one of them is giving birth to a child. Unsettled by what he sees, Suibne announces that it is unseemly for women to violate the Lord's fast-day, which is how he views the miracle of childbirth. Then he compares the beating of the flax with the bloody beating his folk had taken at Mag Rath. Hearing the vesper bell, he complains, "Sweeter indeed were it to me to hear the voices of the cuckoos on the banks of the Bann from every side than the cacophony of this bell, which I hear tonight." His lay that follows repeats this theme, praises the beauty of nature, and ends with a plea to Christ not to sever Suibne from His sweetness.

Throughout this torment, Suibne's one faithful friend is Loingsechán, perhaps a foster-brother or a half-brother sharing the same mother. On three occasions Loingsechán rescues Suibne and keeps him informed about his family. In his mental state Suibne sometimes does not wish to be approached, so on one occasion Loingsechán has to take on the guise of a mill-hag; she had won his confidence by giving the king food.

Led by Loingsechán, Suibne speaks of his desire to be with his wife Eórann, who has gone to live with a friend of the king, Guaire. At first he reproaches his wife for this, but when she says that she would rather live with him, even in misery, he takes pity on her and recommends that she stay with her new lover.

When a crowd gathers, Suibne flees again to the wilderness, coming to rest in a tree. On Loingsechán's second visit the subject to turns to Suibne's kingdom. The sad news is that the king's father, mother, and brother have died. So has his only daughter, a needle to the heart. When he learns that his son, too, has died, Suibne is so overcome by grief that he falls from his tree. At this Loingsechán grabs Suibne, ties him up, and tells him that his family is actually alive after all. The news shocks the king back to sanity, at which Loingsechán takes him back to Dál nAriade and helps reinstall him as king.

Sanity and lucidity do not last long. When Suibne is alone in his palace, he is approached by the once-helpful mill-hag, whom Loingsechán impersonated. She reminds him of her period of madness and persuades him to jump, as he had often done in his former state. Maliciously, she competes with him, and they both jump into the wilderness, where Suibne falls back into his lunacy. The mill-hag and her contest reappear in Irish oral tradition and probably originate there. Arriving at the northern cliff-edge fortress of Dún Sobairche (Dunseverick, Co. Antrim), Suibne clears the battlements in a single bound. Trying to equal his feat, the mill-hag falls from a cliff and is killed. Following this Suibne migrates to Britain and keeps company with a madman, who had been cursed by his people for sending soldiers into battle dressed in satin. This man eventually drowns himself in a waterfall, but his presence underscores the links with the Welsh-Arthurian figure Merlin, called Myrddin (G)wyllt in his madness, perhaps an anticipation of Suibne Geilt.

Returning to Ireland once again, Suibne is afraid to enter his own house for fear of capture. His wife Eórann complains that she is now ashamed of his madness and as long as he does not chose to live with her, she wishes he would depart forever. Crestfallen, Suibne departs, bewailing the fickleness of women.

More torments beset Suibne in his wanderings around Ireland before he can find deliverance. A severely wet and cold night brings another interval of lucidity, in which he seeks to return to Dál nAraide. But when this news is miraculously transmitted to St. Rónán, he prays that the mad king be prevented from persecuting the Church again. Following this, a horde of fiendish phantoms vex and harry Suibne, sending him deliriously in every direction. At last, finding forgiveness for his many misdeeds, Suibne comes to the monastery of St. Moling, Tech Moling (now St. Mullins, County Carlow). Moling, or Mo Ling, is an historical figure (d. 697), whom the eleventh-century writer and cleric Giraldus Cambrensis called "one of the Four Prophets of Ireland." This saint takes pity on the wandering madman and allows him to return to the monastery each evening for a meal. More importantly, Moling also writes down his adventures. Reception from the saint's household takes a different tone. The monastery cook, Muirghil, delivers sustenance by poking a hole in a cowdung with her foot and then filling it with milk for Suibne to lap. Even this demeaning favor is too much for the cook's husband, who runs Suibne through with his spear. Fainting in weakness from the wound, Suibne confesses his sins to St. Moling and is given last rites. Taking the forgiving saint's hand, Suibne is led to the door of the church where he collapses and dies, freed from his double curse.

—*Summary by James MacKillop*

Further Readings for Early and Medieval Irish Literature

Translations

Carney, James. *Medieval Irish Lyrics.* Dublin: Dolmen Press, 1967.

Cross, Tom Peete, and Clark Harris Slover, eds. *Ancient Irish Tales.* Revised bibliography by C. W. Dunn. 1936. Reprint, New York: Barnes and Noble, 1969.

Doan, James. *The Romance of Cearbhall and Fearbhlaidh.* Mountrath, Republic of Ireland: Dolmen Press; Atlantic Highlands, N.J.: Humanities Press, 1985.

Flower, Robin. *Poems and Translations.* London: Constable and Co., 1931.

Gantz, Jeffrey. *Early Irish Myths and Sagas.* Harmondsworth: Penguin, 1981.

Gregory, Augusta. *Cuchulain of Muirthemne.* Introduction by Daniel Murphy. 1902. Reprint, Gerrards Cross, UK: Colin Smythe, 1984.

———. *Gods, Heroes and Fighting Men.* edited by T. R. Henn and Colin Smythe. 1904. Reprint, Gerrards Cross, UK: Colin Smythe, 1970.

Heaney, Seamus. *Sweeney Astray.* New York: Farrar, Straus and Giroux, 1984.

Jackson, Kenneth. *A Celtic Miscellany.* 1951. Rev. ed., Harmondsworth: Penguin, 1971.

Keefe, Joan. *Irish Poems: from Cromwell to the Famine.* Lewisburg, Pa.: Bucknell University Press, 1977.

Kelleher, John V. *Too Small for Stove Wood, Too Big for Kindling. Collected Verse and Translations.* Dublin: Dolmen Press, 1979.

Kinsella, Thomas. *The Tain.* Dublin: Dolmen, 1970.

MacNeill, Eoin, ed. *Duanaire Finn: The Book of the Lays of Finn,* Part 1. Irish Texts Society, 7. 1908. Reprint, London: David Nutt, 1948.

Meyer, Kuno. *Selections from Ancient Irish Poetry.* 1911. Reprint, London: Constable, 1959.

Murphy, Gerard, ed. *Duanaire Finn: The Book of the Lays of Finn,* Part 2, Irish Texts Society, 28. London: Simpkin and Marshall, 1933; Part 3, Irish Texts Society, 43. Dublin: Educational Company of Ireland, 1953.

———. *Early Irish Lyrics: Eighth to Twelfth Century.* Oxford: Clarendon Press, 1956.

Ní Shéaghdha, Nessa. *Tóruigheacht Dhiarmada agus Ghráinne* [The Pursuit of Diamuid and Gráinne]. Irish Texts Society, 47. Dublin: Educational Company of Ireland, 1967.

O'Connor, Frank. *Kings, Lords and Commons.* New York: Alfred Knopf, 1959.

———, and David Greene, eds. *A Golden Treasury of Irish Poetry,* A.D. *600–1200.* London: Macmillan, 1967.

O'Faoláin, Seán. *The Silver Branch. A Collection of the Best Old Irish Lyrics Variously Translated.* London: Jonathan Cape, 1938.

O'Keeffe, J. G. *Buile Suibhne* [The Frenzy of Suibhne]. Irish Texts Society, 12. London: David Nutt, 1913.

Criticism

Bergin, Osborn. *Irish Bardic Poetry.* Dublin: Dublin Institute for Advanced Studies, 1970.

Carney, James, ed. *Early Irish Poetry.* Cork: Mercier, 1965.

———. *The Irish Bardic Poet.* Dublin: Dolmen Press, 1967.

Delargy, J. G. *The Gaelic Story-teller.* London: The Sir John Rhys Memorial Lecture, British Academy, 1945.

Dillon, Myles, ed. *Early Irish Literature.* Chicago: University of Chicago Press, 1948.

———. *Early Irish Society.* Dublin: At the Sign of the Three Candles, 1954.

———. *Irish Sagas.* Dublin: Stationery Office, 1959.

Flower, Robin. *The Irish Tradition.* 1947. Oxford: Clarendon Press, 1963.

Knott, Eleanor. *Irish Classical Poetry.* Rev. ed. Cork: Mercier Press, 1973.

MacCana, Proinsias. *The Learned Tales of Medieval Ireland.* Dublin: Dublin Institute for Advanced Studies, 1980.

———. *Literature in Irish.* Dublin: Department of Foreign Affairs, 1980.

MacKillop, James. *Fionn mac Cumhaill: Celtic Myth in English Literature.* Syracuse, N.Y.: Syracuse University Press, 1986.

Murphy, Gerard. *The Ossianic Lore and Romantic Tales of Medieval Ireland.* Dublin: At the Sign of the Three Candles, 1955.

———.*Saga and Myth in Ancient Ireland.* Dublin: At the Sign of the Three Candles, 1955.

Nagy, Joseph Falaky. *The Wisdom of the Outlaw: The Boyhood Deeds of Finn in Gaelic Narrative Tradition.* Berkeley: University of California Press, 1985.

Rees, Alwyn, and Brinley Rees. *Celtic Heritage: Ancient Tradition in Ireland and Wales.* New York: Grove Press, 1961.

Early Modern Irish Poetry

Loss is a major theme of early modern Irish poetry: political exile, lost or abandoned love, laments for the dead, nostalgia for a lost way of life. Much of the poetry reflects the times: the Flight of the Earls—the term for the migration of the great Earls of Tirconnell (O'Donnell) and Tyrone (O'Neill) and their followers, who left Ireland for the continent in 1607; the subsequent "plantation" of Ulster, when English and Scottish Protestants were brought in ("planted") to settle Ulster and displace the native Irish; and the further dispossession that resulted from the Cromwellian land confiscations of 1652–53. *(see Yeats (Cromwell poem)*

One of the most poignant expressions of loss is the anonymous poem "Kilcash," which marks the passing of the house of one of the Butler family of County Tipperary.

landless noble family driven into exile

Anonymous

Cill Chais (Kilcash)

British strip land of trees

Now what will we do for timber,
    with the last of the woods laid low?
There's no talk of Cill Chais or its household
    and its bell will be struck no more.
That dwelling where lived the good lady
    most honoured and joyous of women
—earls made their way over wave there
    and the sweet Mass once was said.

Ducks' voices nor geese do I hear there,
    nor the eagle's cry over the bay,
nor even the bees at their labour
    bringing honey and wax to us all.

18th cent. estates of the earls were declared forfeit to the crown

No birdsong there, sweet and delightful,
    as we watch the sun go down,
nor cuckoo on top of the branches
    settling the world to rest.

A mist on the boughs is descending
    neither daylight nor sun can clear.
A stain from the sky is descending
    and the waters receding away.
No hazel nor holly nor berry
    but boulders and bare stone heaps,
not a branch in our neighbourly haggard,
    and the game all scattered and gone.

Then a climax to all of our misery:
    the prince of the Gael is abroad
oversea with that maiden of mildness
    who found honour in France and Spain.
Her company now must lament her,
    who would give yellow money and white
—she who'd never take land from the people
    but was friend to the truly poor.

I call upon Mary and Jesus
    to send her safe home again:
dances we'll have in long circles
    and bone-fires and violin music;
that Cill Chais, the townland of our fathers,
    will rise handsome on high once more
and till doom—or the Deluge returns—
    we'll see it no more laid low.
    trans. Thomas Kinsella

Séathrún Céitinn (Geoffrey Keating) (1580–c. 1644)

This seventeenth-century priest-poet wrote one of the greatest of Irish love poems, a poem Seán Ó Tuama called "the most human and realistic renunciation of courtly love that I know."

[handwritten annotations: "Erings up theme again like that of Laidan tells of her love of Cuirithir"]

O Woman Full of Wile

[handwritten annotation: "Priest rejects a woman for spiritual reasons"]

O woman full of wile,
Keep from me thy hand:
I am not a man of the flesh,
Tho' thou be sick for my love.

[handwritten annotation: "Typical of work of early 17th cent. in its deeply personal qualities — passionate & sincere rather than conventional —"]

See how my hair is grey!
See how my body is powerless!
See how my blood hath ebbed!
For what is thy desire?

Do not think me besotted:
Bend not again thy head,
Let our love be without act
Forever, O slender witch.

[handwritten annotation: "ref to women's temptation (Eve)"]

Take thy mouth from my mouth,
Graver the matter so;
Let us not be skin to skin:
From heat cometh will.

[handwritten annotation: "sensual language"]

'Tis thy curling ringleted hair,
Thy grey eye bright as dew,
Thy lovely round white breast,
That draw the desire of eyes.

Every deed but the deed of the flesh
And to lie in thy bed of sleep
Would I do for thy love,
O woman full of wile!

   trans. Padraic Pearse

[handwritten annotation: "native of Inishbofin"]

Thomas Flavell (fl. late seventeenth century)

The historian James Hardiman published Thomas Flavell's "The County of Mayo" in *Irish Minstrelsy* (1831), characterizing the song as a favorite one in the west of Ireland. Flavell was a native of Inisbofin, the island off the Galway coast associated with the contemporary Irish poet Richard Murphy.

The County of Mayo *(Song)*

On the deck of Patrick Lynch's boat I sat in woeful plight,
Through my sighing all the weary day and weeping all the night.
Were it not that full of sorrow from my people forth I go,
By the blessed sun, 'tis royally I'd sing thy praise, Mayo.

When I dwelt at home in plenty, and my gold did much abound,
In the company of fair young maids the Spanish ale went round. *exile*
'Tis a bitter change from those gay days that now I'm forced to go,
And must leave my bones in Santa Cruz, far from my own Mayo. *spain?*

They're altered girls in Irrul now; 'tis proud they're grown and high,
With their hair-bags and their top-knots—for I pass their buckles by.
But it's little now I heed their airs, for God will have it so,
That I must depart for foreign lands, and leave my sweet Mayo.

'Tis my grief that Patrick Loughlin is not Earl in Irrul still, *dispossessed*
And that Brian Duff no longer rules as Lord upon the Hill; *by*
And that Colonel Hugh MacGrady should be lying dead and low, *Brits.*
And I sailing, sailing swiftly from the county of Mayo.

trans. George Fox

Donnchadh Rua Mac Conmara (1715–1810)

another poem of exile

Fair Hills of Eire

Donnchadha Rua wrote "The Fair Hills of Eire" while in Hamburg. His other well-known poem written in exile (in Newfoundland), "Eachtra Ghiolla an Amaráin" (The Adventures of a Luckless Fellow), has been put into a lively modern translation by Arland Ussher. Born in Cratloe, County Clare, Mac Conmara spent much of his life in Waterford, where he was associated with the poets of the Sliabh gCua district.

Take my heart's blessing over to dear Eire's strand—
    Fair Hills of Eire O!
To the Remnant that love her—Our Forefathers' Land!
    Fair Hills of Eire O!

How sweet sing the birds, o'er mount there and vale,
Like soft-sounding chords, that lament for the Gael,—
And I, o'er the surge, far, far away must wail
    The Fair Hills of Eire O.

[handwritten: name for Ireland]

How fair are the flowers on the dear daring peaks,
    Fair Hills of Eire O!
Far o'er foreign bowers I love her barest reeks,
    Fair Hills of Eire O!

Triumphant her trees, that rise on ev'ry height,
Bloom-kissed, the breeze comes odorous and bright,
The love of my heart!—O my very soul's delight!
    The Fair Hills of Eire O!

Still numerous and noble her sons who survive,
    Fair Hills of Eire O!

[handwritten: mother Ireland]

Ah, 'tis this makes my grief, my wounding and my woe
To think that each chief is now a vassal low,
And my Country divided amongst the Foreign Foe—
    The Fair Hills of Eire O!

In purple they gleam, like our H: . . . 'ings of yore,
    The Fair Hills of Eire C . . .
With honey and cre . . . . ing o'er,
    Fair Hills . . .
Once m . . .
To the . . . . Gael,
Than kin . . . . ng sail—
    For the . . .

[handwritten: Bright most Bright]

The dew-drop . . . . nds on the corn,
    Fair Hills o . . .
Where green bou . . . . arkle the bright apples burn
    Fair Hills of Eire O!
Behold, in the valley, cress and berries bland,
Where the streams love to dally, in that Wondrous Land,
While the great River-voices roll their music grand
    Round the Fair Hills of Eire O!

Oh, 'tis welcoming, wide-hearted, that dear land of love!
    Fair Hills of Eire O!

New life unto the martyred is the pure breeze above
   The Fair Hills of Eire O!
More sweet than tune flowing o'er the chords of gold
Comes the kine's soft lowing, from the mountain fold,—
   Oh, the Splendor of the Sunshine on them all,—
   Young and Old.
   'Mid the Fair Hills of Eire O!
trans. Dr. George Sigerson (1836–1925)

Aogán Ó Rathaille (c. 1675–1729)

Aogán Ó Rathaille's poetry reflects the turbulence of Ireland in the late seventeenth century: the dispossession, the lack of leadership, and—for poets who were part of the households of the great Gaelic families—the loss of their hereditary prerogatives. Ó Rathaille lived during the period of the penal laws, laws enacted after the Treaty of Limerick (1691) that maintained the transfer of Catholic lands to Protestant settlers and barred Catholics from Parliament, government, and the professions.

The MacCarthys would have been the chiefs of the mountainous Sliabh Lu-achra region of Kerry where Ó Rathaille was born. They were succeeded by the Anglo-Irish Brownes, the first of whom—Sir Nicholas Browne—was a Catholic him-self and sympathetic to the Irish. Ó Rathaille welcomes Sir Nicholas's son Sir Valen-tine with a poem celebrating the latter's marriage; however, Ó Rathaille later wrote the bitter "Valentine Browne." Bitterness had given way to despair—for himself, for Ireland—by his last poem, "No Help I'll Call."

Ó Rathaille's other poetic response to the broken world around him was the *aislingí,* or vision poems, a form he perfected in *aislingí* such as "Mac an Cheannaí" (The Merchant's Son) and "Gile na Gile" (Brightness Most Bright). An *aisling* is a po-litical allegory, an interview between the poet and a *spéir-bhean* (literally, "sky woman") who is Ireland. The poet asks her why she mourns; she tells him her beloved is in exile, but that he will return and bring relief. The *aisling* is a virtuoso piece with elaborate descriptions of place and of the *spéir-bhean,* as well as with many allusions to Irish, classical, and Christian mythology.

Brightness Most Bright

The Brightness of Brightness I saw in a lonely path,
Crystal of crystal, her blue eyes tinged with green,
Melody of melody, her speech not morose with age,
The ruddy and white appeared in her glowing cheeks.

Plaiting of plaiting in every hair of her yellow locks,
That robbed the earth of its brilliancy by their full sweeping,
An ornament brighter than glass on her swelling breast,
Which was fashioned at her creation in the world above.

A tale of knowledge she told me, all lonely as she was,
News of the return of HIM to the place which is his by kingly descent,
News of the destruction of the bands who expelled him,
And other tidings which, through sheer fear, I will not put in my lays.

Oh, folly of follies for me to go up close to her!
By the captive I was bound fast a captive;
As I implored the Son of Mary to aid me, she bounded from me,
And the maiden went off in a flash to the fairy mansion of Luachair.

I rush in mad race running with a bounding heart,
Through margins of a morass, through meads, through a barren
    moorland,
I reach the strong mansion—the way I came I know not—
That dwelling of dwellings, reared by wizard sorcery.

They burst into laughter, mockingly—a troop of wizards
And a band of maidens, trim, with plaited locks;
In the bondage of fetters they put me without much respite,
While to my maiden clung a clumsy, lubberly clown.

I told her then, in words the sincerest,
How it will become her to be united to an awkward, sorry churl,
While the fairest thrice over of all the Scotic race
Was waiting to receive her as his beauteous bride.

As she hears my voice she weeps through wounded pride,
The streams run down plenteously from her glowing cheeks,
She sends me with a guide for my safe conduct from the mansion,
She is the Brightness of Brightness I saw upon a lonely path.

THE BINDING.

O my sickness, my misfortune, my fall, my sorrow, my loss!
The bright, fond, kind, fair, soft-lipped, gentle maiden,

(Transfer of Catholic lands to Protestant settlers)

Held by a horned, malicious, croaking, yellow clown, with a black troop!
While no relief can reach her until the heroes come back across the main.

trans. Patrick S. Dinneen

Valentine Brown

an English educated Catholic who came into the possession of O'Rahilly's fathers estate

return of earls

Darkness spreading over my age-crusted heart
As the foreign devils march through the green fields of Conn,
A cloud on the western sun whose right was Munster's throne,
—The reason I turn to you, Valentine Brown.

(He had to humble himself to make this supplication)

Cashel without company or horses, overgrown,
Brian's palace swamped with a black flood of otters,
No royal son of Munster ruling his own acres,
—The reason I turn to you, Valentine Brown.

The deer discarding the graceful shape by which she's known
Since the alien crow nested in the thick woods of Ross,
Fish leaving sunlit pools and hidden silent streams,
—The reason I turn to you, Valentine Brown.

Protestants

Dar-Inish in the west mourning her earl of high renown,
In Hamburg, alas, our exiled noble lord,
An old gray eye weeping hard for all that is gone.
—The reason I turn to you, Valentine Brown.

trans. Joan Keefe

The Geraldine's Daughter

Conglomerate name of a grp. of interconnecting Catholic families who led The "Geraldine rebellion" vs English rule 1565-83

A beauty all stainless, a pearl of a maiden,
    Has plunged me in trouble, and wounded my heart.
With sorrow and gloom are my soul overladen;
    An anguish is there that will never depart.
I could voyage to Egypt across the deep water,
    Nor care about bidding dear Eire farewell,
So I only might gaze on the Geraldine's daughter,
    And sit by her side in some green, pleasant dell!

Her curling locks wave round her figure of lightness,
    All dazzling and long, like the purest of gold;

Ireland portrayed as a beautiful woman.

Her blue eyes resemble twin stars in their brightness,
And her brow is like marble or wax to behold!
The radiance of heaven illumines her features
 Where the snows and the rose have erected their throne;
It would seem that the sun had forgotten all creatures,
 To shine on the Geraldine's daughter alone!

Her bosom is swan-white, her waist smooth and slender;
 Her speech is like music, so sweet and so free;
The feelings that glow in her noble heart lend her
 A mien and a majesty lovely to see.
Her lips, red as berries, but riper than any,
 Would kiss away even a sorrow like mine.
No wonder such heroes and nobleman many
 Should cross the blue ocean to kneel at her shrine.

She is sprung from the Geraldine race, the great Grecians,
 Niece of Mileadh's sons of the Valorous Bands,
Those heroes, the seed of the olden Phenicians,
 Though now trodden down, without fame, without lands!
Of her ancestors flourished the Barrys and Powers,
 To the Lords of Bunratty she too is allied;
And not a proud noble near Cashel's high towers
 But is kin to this maiden—the Geraldine's Pride!

Of Saxon or Gael there are none to excel in
 Her wisdom, her features, her figure, this fair;
In all she surpasses the far-famed Helen,
 Whose beauty drove thousands to death and despair.
Whoe'er could but gaze on her aspect so noble
 Would feel from thenceforward all anguish depart,
Yet for me 'tis, alas! my worst woe and my trouble,
 That her image must always abide in my heart!
 trans. James Clarence Mangan

Further Readings on Aogán Ó Rathaille

Selected Works

Hartnett, Michael. *Ó Rathaille* [translations]. Loughcrew, Ireland: Gallery Press, 1998.
Ua Duinnín, An tAthair Pádraig. *Dánta Aodhagáin Uí Rathaille*. Rev. ed.

Ó Donnchadha, Tadhg. Irish Texts Society, 3A. London: Simpkin, Marshall, 1909.

Biography and Criticism

Breatnach, R. "The Lady and the King." *Studies* 42: 321–36. A study of the *aisling* form.
Corkery, Daniel. *The Hidden Ireland: A Story of Gaelic Munster in the Eighteenth Century*, 160–92. 1925. Reprint, Dublin: Gill and Macmillan, 1975.
Heaney, Seamus. "The Glamoured" [translation of *Gile na gile*, with commentary]. *Index on Censorship* 27, no. 5:131–32.
Jordan, John. "Aogán Ó Rathaille." In *The Pleasures of Gaelic Poetry*, edited by Seán MacReamoinn, 81–91. Dublin: Allen Lane, 1982.
Ó Tuama, Seán. "Aogán O'Rathaille." In *File faoi Sceimhle*, 87–124. Dublin: Oifig an tSoláthair, 1978.

Eoghan Rua Ó Suilleabháin (1748–1784)

Eoghan Rua ("Red Owen") or Eoghan an Bheóil Bhínn ("Owen of the Sweet Mouth") was born near Killarney, not far from where Aogán Ó Rathaille spent his life. Schooled in English, Irish, and probably a little Latin, he was by turns a schoolmaster and a *spalpín fánach* (wandering laborer) who left Kerry to work the harvest in neighboring counties, returning in November or December.

Superficially, Eoghan Rua's poem to his friend, the blacksmith Séamus Fitzgerald, is a request for a new spade to take on the road, but it is in effect a statement about the migrant laborer's life: hard work by day, hard drinking by night. He is perhaps best remembered for his *aislingí* written in the classical manner. Eoghan Rua continues to be a popular and romantic figure in Irish-speaking Munster; the contemporary composer Seán Ó Riada wrote a play based on Eoghan Rua.

Friend of My Heart

Friend of my heart, Seamus, loving and witty,
Of Geraldine blood, Greek-tinged and poetic,
Make me a clean smooth handle to fit my spade
And add a nice crook as a crowning elegance.

Then I'll shoulder my tool and go on my way
Since my thirst for adventure has not been quenched

Without stop with my spade as far off as Galway
Where daily my pay will be breakfast and sixpence.

Before the day's end if my tired bones give out
And the steward says my grip of the spade is in doubt,
Then calmly I will tell him of the adventure of death
And of classical battles that left heroes weak.

Of Samson and high deeds I will talk for a while,
Of strong Alexander eager for enemies,
Of the Caesars' dictatorship, powerful and wise,
Or of Achilles who left many dead in the field,

Of the fall of the Fenians with terrible slaughter,
And the heartbreaking story of ravishing Deirdre.
And then with sweet coaxing I will sing songs,
An account of my day you have there now, Seamus.

After my labor I'll take my pay in a lump
And tie it with hemp in the breast of my shirt,
Still with a high heart I will head straight for home,
Not parting with sixpence till I come to your forge.

You are a man like me tormented with thirst,
So we will briskly set off for the inn down the road,
Ale and drams I will order to be arrayed on the table
And no ha'penny of hard-earned money will be spared.

    trans. Joan Keefe

Further Readings on Eoghan Rua Ó Suilleabháin

Selected Works

Ó Suilleabháin, Eoghan Rua. *Na hAislingí: Vision Poems.* Edited and translated by Pat
    Muldowney. Aubane, Millstreet, Co. Cork : Aubane Historical Society, 2002.
Rosenstock, Gabriel, ed. *Dánta duitse!: scothvéarsai do dhaoine óga.* Béal an Daingin,
    Ireland: Cló Iar-Chonnachta, 1988.
Ua Duinnín, an tAthair Pádraig. *Amhráin Eoghain Ruaidh Uí Súilleabháin.* Dublin:
    Connradh na Gaeilge, 1923.

Biography and Criticism

Corkery, Daniel. *The Hidden Ireland: A Study of Gaelic Munster in the Eighteenth Century*, 193—236. 1925. Reprint, Dublin: Gill and Macmillan, 1975.

O'Broin, Padraig. "The Wandering Spadesmen." *Éire-Ireland* 1:64—69.

Eibhlín Dhubh Ní Chonaill (Eileen O'Connell) (c. 1770)

"Caoineadh Airt Uí Laoghaire" (The Lament for Art O'Leary) is at once the best example of the *caoine* (keen), that unique expression of Irish grief, and one of the most passionate love poems in modern Irish. Daniel O'Connell's aunt, Eibhlín Dhubh Ní Chonaill, made the song for her outlawed husband, a captain in the Hungarian Hussars, who returned from the Continent, quarreled with the high sheriff of Cork and tried to kill him, but was shot himself instead.

In his edition of the poem, Seán Ó Tuama identified a number of traditional elements: the address to the deceased, the use of formulaic language, the plea to rise up from the dead, the recital of praise, the description of the effect of the death on all nature, the singer's premonition of death, the curse laid on those responsible, and the dispute between the wife and her sister-in-law about whose is the greater loss. These elements suggest something of the community's values: family pedigrees, family relationships, physical grace, valor, and generosity—values reinforced by the *caoine* itself.

Caoineadh Airt Uí Laoghaire (Lament for Art O'Leary)

I

HIS WIFE:
My love forever!
The day I first saw you
At the end of the market-house,
My eye observed you,
My heart approved you,
I fled from my father with you,
Far from my home with you.

II

I never repented it:
You whitened a parlour for me,

Painted rooms for me,
Reddened ovens for me,
Baked fine bread for me,
Basted meat for me,
Slaughtered beasts for me;
I slept in ducks' feathers
Till midday milking-time
Or more if it pleased me.

[handwritten annotation: Here she recollects how she has fled with him & how he received her in his mansion]

[handwritten annotation: He cooked! He pampered her]

III

My friend forever!
My mind remembers
That fine spring day
How well your hat suited you,
Bright gold-banded,
Sword silver-hilted—
Right hand steady—
Threatening aspect—
Trembling terror
On treacherous enemy—
You poised for a canter
On your slender bay horse.
The Saxons bowed to you,
Down to the ground to you,
Not for love of you
But for deadly fear of you,
Though you lost your life to them,
Oh my soul's darling.

[handwritten annotation: addresses the deceased]

[handwritten annotation: Recital of details suggesting his nobility]

IV

Oh white-handed rider!
How fine your brooch was
Fastened in cambric,
And your hat with laces
When you crossed the sea to us,
They would clear the street for you,

And not for love of you
But for deadly hatred.

he is hated

V

My friend you were forever!
When they will come home to me,
Gentle little Conor
And Farr O'Leary, the baby,
They will question me so quickly,
Where did I leave their father.
I'll answer in my anguish
That I left him in Killnamartyr.
They will call out to their father:
And he won't be there to answer.

children ask where father is.

VI

My friend and my love!
Of the blood of Lord Antrim,
And of Barry of Allchoill,
How well your sword suited you,
Hat gold-banded,
boots of fine leather,
Coat of broadcloth,
Spun overseas for you.

VII

My friend you were forever!
I knew nothing of your murder
Till your horse came to the stable
With the reins beneath her trailing,
And your heart's blood on her shoulders
Staining the tooled saddle
Where you used to sit and stand.
My first leap reached the threshold,
My second reached the gateway,
My third leap reached the saddle.

Eileen's first signs that her husband was murdered

VIII

I struck my hands together
And I made the bay horse gallop
As fast as I was able,
Till I found you dead before me
Beside a little furze-bush.
Without Pope or bishop,
Without priest or cleric
To read the death-psalms for you,
But a spent old woman only
Who spread her cloak to shroud you—
Your heart's blood was still flowing;
I did not stay to wipe it
But filled my hands and drank it.

IX

My love you'll be forever!
Rise up from where you're lying
And we'll be going homewards.
We'll have a bullock slaughtered,
We'll call our friends together,
We'll get the music going.
I'll make a fine bed ready
With sheets of snow-white linen,
And fine embroidered covers
That will bring the sweat out through you
Instead of the cold that's on you!

X

ART'S SISTER: My friend and my treasure!
There's many a handsome woman
From Cork of the sails
To the bridge of Toames
With a great herd of cattle
And gold for her dowry,

That would not have slept soundly
On the night we were waking you.

XI

EIBHLÍN
DHUBH:

My friend and my lamb;
You must never believe it,
Nor the whisper that reached you,
Nor the venomous stories
That said I was sleeping.
It was not sleep was on me,
But your children were weeping,
And they needed me with them
To bring their sleep to them

she gives her reason for not attending the wake

XII

Now judge, my people,
What woman in Ireland
That at every nightfall
Lay down beside him,
That bore his three children,
Would not lose her reason
After Art O'Leary
That's here with me vanquished
Since yesterday morning?

XIII

ART'S FATHER:

Bad luck to you, Morris!—
May your heart's blood poison you!
With your squint eyes gaping!
And your knock-knees breaking!—
That murdered my darling,
And no man in Ireland
To fill you with bullets.

Curse laid on those responsible for his death!

XIV

Plea (again) to rise from dead

pathos

My friend and my heart!
Rise up again now, Art,
Leap up on your horse,
Make straight for Macroom town,
Then to Inchigeela back,
A bottle of wine in your fist,
The same as you drank with your dad.

XV

EIBHLÍN
DHUBH:

she would have given her life for him

My bitter, long torment
That I was not with you
When the bullet came towards you,
My right side would have taken it
Or a fold of my tunic,
And I would have saved you
Oh smooth-handed rider.

XVI

ART'S SISTER:

His sister would also have given her life for him (competition)

My sore sharp sorrow
That I was not behind you
When the gun-powder blazed at you,
My right side would have taken it,
Or a fold of my gown,
And you would have gone free then
Oh grey-eyed rider,
Since you were a match for them.

XVII

EIBHLÍN
DHUBH:

My friend and my treasure!
It's bad treatment for a hero
To lie hooded in a coffin,
The warm-hearted rider
That fished in bright rivers,
That drank in great houses

With white-breasted women,
My thousand sorrows
That I've lost my companion.

XVIII

Bad luck and misfortune
Come down on you, Morris!
That snatched my protector,
My unborn child's father:
Two of them walking
And the third still within me,
And not likely I'll bear it.

she has 2 children + is pregnant with 3rd when her husband is murdered

XIX

My friend and my pleasure!
When you went out through the gateway
You turned and came back quickly,
You kissed your two children,
You kissed me on the forehead,
You said: 'Eileen, rise up quickly,
Put your affairs in order
With speed and with decision.
I am leaving home now
And there's no telling if I'll return.'
I mocked this way of talking,
He had said it to me so often.

Prophetic

XX

My friend and my dear!
Oh bright-sworded rider,
Rise up this moment,
Put on your fine suit
Of clean, noble cloth,
Put on your black beaver,
Pull on your gauntlets.
Up with your hip;

Plea t. rise again

Outside your mare is waiting.
Take the narrow road east,
Where the trees thin before you,
Where men and women will bow before you,
If they keep their old manners—
But I fear they have lost them.

XXI

My love and my treasure!
Not my dead ancestors,
Nor the deaths of my three children,
Nor Domhnall Mór O'Connell,
Nor Connall that drowned at sea,
Nor the twenty-six years woman
Who went across the water
And held kings in conversation—
It's not on all of them I'm calling
But on Art who was slain last night
At the inch of Carriganima!—
The brown mare's rider
That's here with me only—
With no living soul near him
But the dark little women of the mill,
And my thousand sorrows worsened
That their eyes were dry of tears.

XXII

My friend and my lamb!
Arthur O'Leary,
Of Connor, of Keady,
Of Louis O'Leary,
From west in Geeragh
And from east in Caolchnoc,
Where berries grow freely
And gold nuts on branches
And great floods of apples
All in their seasons.

[handwritten margin note:] Ancestry & place names listed

Would it be a wonder
If Ive Leary were blazing
Besides Ballingeary
And Guagán of the saint
For the firm-handed rider
That hunted the stag down,
All out from Grenagh
When slim hounds fell behind?
And Oh clear-sighted rider,
What happened last night?
For I thought to myself
That nothing could kill you
Though I bought your habit.

XXIII

ART'S SISTER: My friend and my love!
Of the country's best blood,
That kept eighteen wet-nurses at work,
And each received her pay—
A heifer and a mare,
A sow and her litter,
A mill at the ford,
Yellow gold and white silver,
Silks and fine velvets,
A holding of land—
To give her milk freely
To the flower of fair manhood.

XXIV

My love and my treasure
And my love, my white dove!
Though I did not come to you,
Nor bring my troops with me,
That was no shame to me
For they were all enclosed
In shut-up rooms,

[handwritten margin note:] Vengeance for Art's death is made impossible + poor attendance at funeral due to epidemics + plagues

In narrow coffins,
In sleep without waking.

XXV

Were it not for the small-pox
And the black death
And the spotted fever,   *Epidemics*
That powerful army
Would be shaking their harness
And making a clatter
On their way to your funeral,
Oh white-breasted Art.

XXVI

My love you were and my joy!
Of the blood of those rough horsemen
That hunted in the valley,
Till you turned them homewards
And brought them to your hall,
Where knives were being sharpened,
Pork laid out for carving
And countless ribs of mutton,
The red-brown oats were flowing
To make the horses gallop—
Slender, powerful horses
And stable-boys to care them
Who would not think of sleeping
Nor of deserting their horses
If their owners stayed a week,
Oh brother of many friends.

Art was Captain of Hungarian Hussars

XXVII

My friend and my lamb!
A cloudy vision   *Vision*
Came last night to me

In Cork at midnight
Alone in my bed:
That our white court fell,
That the Geeragh withered,
That your slim hounds were still
And the birds without sweetness
When you were found vanquished
On the side of the mountain,
Without priest or cleric
But an old shrivelled woman
That spread her cloak over you,
Arthur O'Leary,
While your blood flowed freely
On the breast of your shirt.

XXVIII

My love and my treasure!
And well they suited you,
Five-ply stockings,
Boots to your knees,
A three-cornered Caroline,
A lively whip,
On a frisky horse—
Many a modest, mannerly maiden
Would turn to gaze after you.

His vitality + physical beauty

XXIX

EIBHLÍN
DHUBH:

My love forever!
And when you went in cities,
Strong and powerful,
The wives of the merchants
All bowed down to you
For they knew in their hearts
What a fine man in bed you were,
And what a fine horseman
And father for children.

His manly qualities

XXX

Jesus Christ knows
I'll have no cap on my head,
Nor a shift on my back,
Nor shoes on my feet,
Nor goods in my house,
Nor the brown mare's harness
That I won't spend on lawyers;
That I'll cross the seas
And talk to the king,
And if no one listens
That I'll come hack
To the black-blooded clown
That took my treasure from me.

[handwritten margin note: Promise to bring his murder to justice]

[handwritten note: Morris]

XXXI

My love and my darling!
If my cry were heard westwards
To great Derrynane
And to gold-appled Capling,
Many swift, hearty riders
And white-kerchiefed women
Would be coming here quickly
To weep at your waking,
Beloved Art O'Leary.

[handwritten margin note: Women to keen]

XXXII

My heart is warming
To the fine women of the mill
For their goodness in lamenting
The brown mare's rider.

XXXIII

May your black heart fail you,
Oh false John Cooney!

[handwritten note: John Cooney ?]

 If you wanted a bribe,
You should have asked me.
I'd have given you plenty:
A powerful horse
That would carry you safely
Through the mob
When the hunt is out for you,
Or a fine herd of cattle,
Or ewes to bear lambs for you,
Or the suit of a gentleman
With spurs and top-boots—
Though it's sorry I'd be
To see you done up in them,
For I've always heard
You're a piddling lout.

XXXIV

Oh white-handed rider,
Since you are stuck down,
Rise and go after Baldwin,
The ugly wretch
With the spindle shanks,
And take your revenge
For the loss of your mare—
May he never enjoy her.
May his six children wither!
But no bad wish to Máire
Though I have no love for her,
But that my own mother
Gave space in her womb to her
For three long seasons.

XXXV

My love and my dear!
Your stooks are standing,
Your yellow cows milking;
On my heart is such sorrow

That all Munster could not cure it,
Nor the wisdom of the sages.
Till Art O'Leary returns
There will be no end to the grief
That presses down on my heart,
Closed up tight and firm
Like a trunk that is locked
And the key is mislaid.

XXXVI

All you women out there weeping,
Wait a little longer;
We'll drink to Art son of Connor
And the souls of all the dead,
Before he enters the school—
Not learning wisdom or music
But weighted down by earth and stones.

trans. Éilís Dillon

acceptance of his death

Further Readings on Caoineadh Airt Uí Laoghaire

Selected Works

Dillon, Éilís. "Laoineadh Airt Uí: Lament for Art O'Leary." *Irish University Review* 1:198–210.

O'Connor, Frank. *A Lament for Art O'Leary: Translated from the Irish by Frank O'Connor.* Illustrated by Jack B. Yeats. Dublin: Cuala Press, 1940. Reprinted in *Kings, Lords and Commons,* 110–19. New York: Alfred A. Knopf, 1959.

Ó Tuama, Seán, ed. *Caione Airt Uí Laoghaire.* Baile Átha Cliath: An Clóchomar, 1961.

Biography and Criticism

Bromwich, Rachel. "The Keen for Art O'Leary, Its Background and Its Place in the Tradition of Gaelic Keening." *Éigse* 5:236–52.

Murphy, Gerard, "The Gaelic Background." In *Daniel O'Connell: Nine Centenary Essays,* 1–24. Dublin: Browne and Nolan, 1948.

Brian Mac Giolla Meidhre (Brian Merriman)

(1749?–1805)

[handwritten: Chaucer's CT composed in 1385]

The author of this ribald poem in the Irish language was born in Ennistymon, County Clare, about 1749. He farmed and taught in the village of Feakle in east Clare before settling in Limerick. The notice of his death in 1805 described him as a "teacher of mathematics, etc." "The Midnight Court," Merriman's long poem of some thousand lines, was not written in the classical literary language of eighteenth-century Munster, but rather in vigorous Clare Irish. It is one of the most frequently translated Irish poems, existing in versions by Arland Ussher, Frank O'Connor, Lord Longford, David Marcus, Patrick Power, and Cosslett Ó Cuinn. In addition, Brendan Behan and Thomas Kinsella have made partial translations of the poem.

The Midnight Court of Aeval, queen of the Munster fairies, is convened to hear an assembly of unmarried women complain about their difficulties finding husbands. An old man charges that his wife presented him with a bastard on their wedding night; a young woman rebuts that the girl was forced into marrying him and that handsome young priests, who would make better mates, ought to be allowed to marry, Aeval leaves the priests to Rome, but rules that all other young men must marry or be tortured by women. *[handwritten: on the view of THE WIFE OF BATH]*

Cúirt an Mheadhon Oidhche (The Midnight Court)

[handwritten: The poet narrates]

FROM PART ONE

[handwritten: Satire on an aisling (vision of a beautiful woman — (hilarious + grotesque)]

Then, drowsy, dull and half-asleep,
I rested where the grass was deep
Along a tree-lined, shady ditch
Where there was room for me to stretch.
No sooner had I closed my eyes,
My face being covered from the flies,
And settled for a peaceful doze
Than in my dreams the flies arose
And swarmed about me in attack
While I, asleep, could not hit back.

Brief was my rest when, it appeared,
With shocks and shakes the mountains reared,

[handwritten: Celibacy is criticized unmercifully + priests are not spared in any way]

[handwritten: Written originally in octosyllabic couplets which have a vivacity + swing — suitable to them for the theme]

[handwritten: Turns courtly Love tradition upside down]

The north was numbed with thunder-crash,
The waves were laced with lightning-flash;
Whatever look I chanced to take
I saw, approaching by the lake,
A hellish, hairy, haggard hank,
Bearded, bony, long and lank;

an anti-aisling

Her height I'd estimate for sure
At twenty feet, and maybe more,
For yards behind she dragged her coat
Through all the muck and mire and mud;
It took some nerve merely to glance
Upon that ghoulish countenance
For with her ghastly, toothless grin
She'd frighten the life out of anyone.
To top it all, in a mighty paw
Was the biggest staff I ever saw
And in letters of brass the information
That she had a bailiff's qualification.

Then, with a gruff and angry shout,
"Get up!" she snarled, "you lazy lout;
A nice, bloody thing: you're stretched in state
While the Court's convened and thousands wait."

. . . .

"The Court considered the country's crisis,
And what do you think its main advice is—
That unless there's a spurt in procreation
We can bid goodbye to the Irish nation;
It's growing smaller year by year—
And don't pretend that's not your affair.
Between death and war and ruin and pillage
The land is like a deserted village;
Our best are banished, but you, you slob,
Have you ever hammered a single job?
What use are you to us, you cissy?
We have thousands of women who'd keep you busy,
With breasts like balloons or small as a bud
Buxom of body and hot in the blood,

the dire circumstances of the Irish

Virgins or whores—whatever's your taste—
At least don't let them go to waste;
It's enough to make us broken-hearted—
Legs galore—and none of them parted.
They're ready and willing for any endeavour—
But you can't expect them to wait forever.

"And as the Court has recommended
That all this nonsense must be ended,
A judge was chosen without delay
To hear what both sides have to say.
'Twas Munster's friend and Craglee's queen,
Aeval, of heart and spirit clean,
Who has been picked to try and see
If she can find a remedy.
And she has solemnly sworn and vowed
That no exceptions will be allowed;
She'll stand by the poor and the weak she'll save,
And see to it that the rich behave,
She won't take long to curb the strong
And Right won't have to give way to Wrong.
She's an eye on the fellows who think they're smart:
No spiv or pimp or painted tart
Will treat the law as a thing of sport
While Aeval rules the Midnight Court.
It's assembled in Feakle this very day
And she'd like to hear what you've to say,
So up with you now or else you'll find
My boot disturbing your fat behind."
Then suiting her action to her words
She lofted me like a sack of spuds
And over the hills I was jet-propelled
Till we reached Moinmoy where the Court was held.

. . . .

Then there appeared a majestic maid,
Slender, silky, soft, and sad,
With skin as tanned as the golden sand
And she took her place on the witness-stand.

Her hair was flowing loose and free
But her face was a picture of misery;
Her eyes were fierce and flashed with hate
And she'd worked herself up into such a state
That she moaned and heaved and sobbed and sighed
But couldn't speak, though hard she tried.
You could see from the flood of tears she shed
That she'd much prefer to have dropped down dead
Than to stand in the witness-box alone
Exposing her grief to everyone.
After a while, as her sobs grew weak,
She made a determined attempt to speak,
And finding her passion at last was spent,
She spoke, and this was her argument:

Speaker
 # 1

"O Aeval, greetings from my heart
To you, who Craglee's ruler art;
Our sun by day, our moon by night,
Our only comfort and delight,
O strong protector, firm and true,
Munster and Ireland depend on you;
The start of my story, the source of my strain,
The reason I'm senseless and almost insane,
The thing that has taken and torn me in twain
And has pricked me with pangs and has plagued me with pain—
Is the number of women, old and young,
For whom no wedding-bells have rung,
Who become in time mere hags and crones
Without man or money to warm their bones.
Thousands will back my evidence,
And I speak, alas, from experience;
Like me, I can swear, there's many another
Aching to be a wife and mother,
But the way we're ignored you'd think we're wrecks
Possessed of gender but not of sex;
At night with longing I'm lacerated,
Alone in bed I lie frustrated
And damned with dreams of desire denied
My hunger goes unsatisfied.

O Aeval, you must find a way
To save our women without delay,
For if the men are allowed to shirk
We'll have to force them to do their work.
By the time they're ready to take a wife
They're not worth taking to save their life,
They're stiff and shrunken and worn and weak
And when they mount you they wheeze and creak."

. . . .

FROM PART TWO

"Let every unmarried man take heed
And avoid being hooked by one of her breed,
Or he'll spend his life being bullied and bossed,
You can take it from me—for I know to my cost.
I remember when I was a bachelor
And I wonder now what I married for;
I had health and wealth and a reputation,
My name was a golden recommendation,
Treated by the Law with unction,
Asked to every high-class function,
People listened when I spoke
And laughed whenever I cracked a joke.
What more could I want? I thought I knew:
So I married—and landed in a stew.
I claimed at the time I did well to win her—
Plenty of eating and drinking in her,
Hair that was curled and soft to touch,
A look in her eye that promised much,
A laugh that was laced with implication,
A figure that offered an invitation—
All I craved was to be wed
And then to get her into bed;
But the bigger they are the harder they fall,
And Fate has fixed me for good and all;
My prayers were answered—to be sure—
But I got much more than I bargained for.

Begs Aeval to bring salvation in form of marriageable men

Speaker #2 Voice of male defending himself

What marriage promised & what it delivered are contrasted

"I saw that all was rightly done:
The clergy blessed our union,
I threw a party I'll never forget
And didn't leave a single debt;
And—fair is fair—there's none can say
That anyone was turned away.
The priest, who received a handsome fee,
Was as pleased as Punch—and why wouldn't he be?
The guzzling crowds around the table
Sounded like the Tower of Babel;
And the drink it took to stock the bar
Was enough to float a man-o'-war!
A pity indeed that I wasn't drowned
At birth, or at least before I found
The urge to marry that old crock —
And make myself a laughing-stock.
Not that I wasn't tipped the wink
About the name she had for drink
And how she'd sleep with anyone—
Married or single, father or son.
For long I wouldn't believe a word
And laughed at everything I heard
Till people wondered what I'd do
When I'd find their tales were true.
How right they were—but none can be
As blind as him who will not see.
I said it was gossip that couldn't be proved—
Until her corset was removed,
And I saw that they hadn't exaggerated—
To be frank, the position was understated—
For, contrary to orthodoxy,
Someone had made me a father by proxy!"
. . . .

FROM PART THREE

"Another thing I'd like to mention
That's beyond my comprehension—

Whatever made the Church create
A clergy that is celibate?
The lack of men is a cruel curse
Just now when things were never worse;
I'd give my eyes to have a lover
The ripest, though, are under cover.
It's such a bitter pill to swallow
For one like me, who hasn't a fellow,
To see them big and strong of stature,
Full of charm and bright good-nature,
Each one seems a fresh young stripling,
Hard of bone and muscles rippling,
Backs as straight as a sergeant-major's,
And desires as keen as razors.
They live in the lap of luxury,
And, what's more, it's all tax-free;
Well-dressed, well-treated, and well-fed,
With warming-pans to heat their bed.
Man for man they'd beat the best,
And they're human like the rest.
I'd skip the ones who don't pass muster,
Raddled ancients who lack lustre,
But I'd soon shake up the one
Who snores while work is left undone!
Perhaps you'd find that quite a share
Would play their part, and those I'd spare,
For, after all, it wouldn't do
To damn the many for the few,
A sturdy ship should not be sunk
Because one sailor has no spunk!
We know that some are tough old terrors
Who would never mend their errors,
Frozen fogeys who believe
God blundered when he fashioned Eve;
But others secretly admit
They think her nature's choicest bit!
There's many a house that didn't begin
To prosper and smile till the priest dropped in,
And many a woman could toss her head

And boast of the time he blessed her bed;
Throughout the land there's ample proof
The Church is anything but aloof,
And many a man doesn't know that he
Has a son with a clerical pedigree.
But it's a shame the strength and time
They waste on women past their prime,
While others miss the best in life
Because a priest can't take a wife;
Just think of the massive population
This rule has cost the Irish nation!

"It's for Your Honour to decide *aeval*
What's mainly needed: priest or bride.
It seems to me a priest should know
Life's ups and downs; is that not so?
Tell us, that we may understand,
What was the Holy Book's command.
When was it the Creator said
That bodily appetites mustn't be fed?
Lust, said Paul, and not a wife
Was something man should shun for life,
For indeed he advocated
Men and women should be mated.
Ah, but who am I to jaw—
You're the one who knows the law;
That's what got you your degrees,
For you can recollect with ease
Every sentence, every word
Of all the sayings of the Lord;
They should be in our favour, for
The Lord Himself was no bachelor."

. . . .

FROM PART FOUR

Aeval arose, all charm and grace,
And sunshine seemed to fill the place.
Her features had the glow of youth,

Her voice was strong—the voice of truth.
The bailiff rapped to stop the talk
And glared and glowered like a hawk;
The chatter slowly died, until
She spoke, and then the Court was still:—

Speaker #4

"My girl," she said, "I must declare
Your treatment has been far from fair.
I cannot but be shocked to know
Our women's plight has sunk so low,
Unwanted, haggard, tired, sore,
Turned away from every door;
And that the country's on its ear
Exploited by each racketeer.

"So grab each male who's still unmarried
At twenty-one, and have him carried
And tied unto the nearest tree,
And make quite sure he can't break free;
Strip him of his coat and shirt
And flay him till he's really hurt.

Aevel's declaration

. . . .

"There's some dark mystery unknown
That's made this blackguard live alone,
For lords salute him when they pass
And he has friends in every class;
At high-tone functions he's a guest,
And when he's there they serve the best;
He's had enough of selfish pleasure,
Now at last we have his measure.
His name is one we must applaud:
"Merriman," but it's a fraud; ——
He must have been baptised in haste—
For though he's old he still is chaste.
I'll teach the likes of him a lesson
And I'll suffer no digression;
His race provides a full admission:
Thirty years without coition!

The Poet appears

"Now, my hearties, be prepared,
No endeavour must be spared;
Recall the times that we were spurned,
But here, at last, the worm has turned.
All hands now! Help! Hold down the pup!
Run, Una! Rope him! Tie him up!
Push, Anne! You can do better surely!
Mary, tie his hands securely!
Sheila, Sal, don't stand and stare
Hurry now, and do your share,
You heard his punishment announced
So see he's well and truly trounced,
Lay into him each time you hit,
His bottom's broad enough for it;
Just keep on striking where he bends,
You'll soon reduce his fat, my friends,
Don't weaken, don't be faint of heart,
You're not to miss a single part.
Beat hard so that his screams and cries
Will freeze the other nancy-boys.
No better day than this could be,
It should go down in history.
So write it out, and don't forget
We may be all quite famous yet—"

She took her pen; I gave a moan;
Her threats bad chilled me to the bone;
And as she scribbled in a book
And eyed me with a dreadful look,
I took a breath that was long and deep,
And opened my eyes—I had been asleep.

Further Readings on Brian Mac Giolla Meidhre

Standard Edition

Ó hUaithne, Dáithí, edited by *Cúirt an Mheán Oíche*. Foreword by Seán Ó Tuama. Dublin: Dolmen Press, 1969.

Selected Translations

Egan, Bowes. *On Trial at Midnight.* Killybegs, Ireland: Brehon Press, 1985.

Heaney, Seamus. *The Midnight Verdict.* 1993. Oldcastle, Ireland: Gallery Press, 2000.

Marcus, David. *The Midnight Court.* 1953. Reprint, Dublin: Dolmen Press, 1967.

O'Connor, Frank. *The Midnight Court: A Rhythmical Bacchanalia from the Irish of Bryan Merryman.* London: Maurice Fridberg, 1945.

Power, Patrick C. *The Midnight Court/Cúirt an mheán oíche.* 1971. Cork: Mercier Press, 1999.

Ussher, Percy Arland. *The Midnight Court and the Adventures of a Luckless Fellow.* Introduction by W. B. Yeats. New York: Boni and Liveright, 1926. Reprint, Folcraft, Pa.: Folcraft Library Editions, 1974.

Selected Criticism

Heaney, Seamus. "Orpheus in Ireland: Merriman's *The Midnight Court.*" *Southern Review* [Baton Rouge] 31, no. 3:786–806.

Ó Cuinn, Cosslett. "Merriman's Court." In *The Pleasures of Gaelic Poetry,* edited by Seán Mac Réamoinn, 111–26. London: Allen Lane, 1982.

Irish Folk Songs

Like all folk songs, these Irish songs have been transmitted and perpetuated by oral tradition. While most are anonymous, some, like Padraic Colum's "She Moved Through the Fair" and Dion Boucicault's "The Wearin' o' the Green" have passed into folk tradition. "Shule Aroon" even emigrated to America, where "Johnny Has Gone for a Soldier" is often substituted for the Irish refrain.

Our selection offers some sense of the range of folk-song themes. Many of the best are love lyrics like "The Grief of a Girl's Heart," an example of the genre of laments of abandoned girls that Seán Ó Tuama has described as unique in European love literature. "Mary from Dungloe" is an emigration song, while "Sean O'Dwyer of the Glens" is a farewell to one of the O'Dwyers of Kilnamanagh, County Tipperary, who served with Colonel Edmund O'Dwyer and shared his fate after the defeat in the Cromwellian wars: exile to the Continent and service in the Spanish army.

"The Sorrowful Lamentation of Callaghan, Greally, and Mullen," a nineteenth-century street ballad, describes the faction fight (or politicized fisticuffs) at the fair of Darrynaclougherg in 1843. The fight led to a confrontation with the police and the death of the lamented trio. The Mr. Brew who ordered the police to fire was the local magistrate; he died before he could stand trial.

These street ballads are an important source for social historians, and—with the patriotic ballads—are part of the Anglo-Irish ballad tradition rather than the Gaelic song tradition. "The Rising of the Moon" celebrates the 1798 Rising, especially in its promise of another rising. The song, often attributed to John Keegan Casey, gives its title to Lady Gregory's famous play. Some readers consider "Nell Flaherty's Drake" to be an allegorical song, promising ruin not only to "the monster that murdered" the unfortunate drake but to Ireland's oppressors as well.

The last three songs are of more literary interest. "The Star of Slane" is an *aisling* written in English, though preserving the Gaelic rhyme scheme based on assonance or vowel rhyme: "muses/refuses/infuses; favors/endeavours/labours." "The Night Before Larry Was Stretched" is a pungent example of Irish gallows humor. Finally, "Finnegan's Wake," possibly of American origin but widely known in Ireland, provided James Joyce with the title of his novel (although he misplaced the apostrophe). In both the song and the novel, a man thought dead comes back to life.

The Grief of a Girl's Heart

[handwritten: "Lament of girls unique about abandoned love in European literature"]

[handwritten: translated by Lady Gregory]

O Donall óg, if you go across the sea, bring myself with you and do not forget it; and you will have a sweetheart for fair days and market days, and the daughter of the King of Greece beside you at night. *[handwritten: animal imagery]*

It is late last night the dog was speaking of you; the snipe was speaking of you in her deep marsh. It is you are the lonely bird through the woods; and that you may be without a mate until you find me.

You promised me, and you said a lie to me, that you would be before me where the sheep are flocked; I gave a whistle and three hundred cries to you, and I found nothing there but a bleating lamb. *[handwritten: Promises]*

You promised me a thing that was hard for you, a ship of gold under a silver mast; twelve towns with a market in all of them, and a fine white court by the side of the sea.

You promised me a thing that is not possible, that you would give me gloves of the skin of a fish; that you would give me shoes of the skin of a bird; and a suit of the dearest silk in Ireland.

O Donnall óg, it is I would be better to you than a high, proud, spendthrift lady: I would milk the cow; I would bring help to you; and if you were hard pressed. I would strike a blow for you. *[handwritten: Her love for him]*

O, ochone, and it's not with hunger or with wanting food, or drink, or sleep, that I am growing thin, and my life is shortened; but it is the love of a young man has withered me away.

It is early in the morning that I saw him coming, going along the road on the back of a horse; he did not come to me; he made nothing of me; and it is on my way home that I cried my fill.

When I go by myself to the Well of Loneliness, I sit down and I go through my trouble; when I see the world and do not see my boy, he that has an amber shade in his hair.

It was on that Sunday I gave my love to you; the Sunday that is last before Easter Sunday. And myself on my knees reading the Passion; and my two eyes giving love to you for ever. *[handwritten: Palm Sunday]*

O, aya! my mother, give myself to him; and give him all that you have in the world; get out yourself to ask for alms, and do not come back and forward looking for me.

My mother said to me not to be talking with you to-day, or tomorrow, or on the Sunday; it was a bad time she took for telling me that: it was shutting the door after the house was robbed.

My heart is as black as the blackness of the sloe, or as the black coal that is on the smith's forge; or as the sole of a shoe left in white halls; it was you put that darkness over my life.

You have taken the east from me; you have taken the west from me: you have taken what is before me and what is behind me; you have taken the moon, you have taken the sun from me. and my fear is great that you have taken God from me!

trans. Lady Gregory

Bríghidín Bán Mo Stóre
(Bridget, My Treasure)

I am a wand'ring minstrelman,
    And Love my only theme:
I've strayed beside the pleasant Bann.
    And eke the Shannon's stream;
I've piped and played to wife and maid
    By Barrow, Suir, and Nore,
But never met a maiden yet
    Like *Bríghidín bán mo stóre.*

My girl hath ringlets rich and rare,
    By Nature's fingers wove—
Loch-Carra's swan is not so fair
    As is her breast of love;
And when she moves, in Sunday sheen,
    Beyond our cottage door,
I'd scorn the high-born Saxon queen
    For Bríghidín bán mo stóre.

It is not that thy smile is sweet,
    And soft thy voice of song—

It is not that thou fleest to meet
    My comings lone and long:
But that doth rest beneath thy breast
    A heart of purest core,
Whose pulse is known to me alone,
    My Bríghidín bán mo stóre.
      trans. Edward Walsh

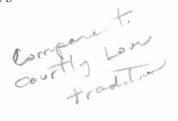

Have You Been at Carrick?

Have you been at Carrick, and saw you my true-love there,
And saw you her features, all beautiful, bright and fair?
Saw you the most fragrant, flowery, sweet apple-tree?
Oh! saw you my loved one, and pines she in grief like me?

"I have been at Carrick, and saw thy own true-love there;
And saw, too, her features, all beautiful, bright and fair;
And saw the most fragrant, flowering, sweet apple-tree—
I saw thy loved one—she pines *not* in grief like thee."

Five guineas would price every tress of her golden hair—
Then think what a treasure her pillow at night to share!
These tresses thick-clust'ring and curling around her brow—
O Ringlet of Fairness! I'll drink to thy beauty now.

When, seeking to slumber, my bosom is rent with sighs—
I toss on my pillow till morning's blest beams arise;
No aid, bright beloved! can reach me save God above.
For a blood-lake is formed of the light of my eyes with love.

Until yellow autumn shall usher the Paschal day,
And Patrick's gay festival come in its train alway—
Until through my coffin the blossoming boughs shall grow,
My love on another I'll never in life bestow!

Lo! yonder the maiden illustrious, queen-like, high.
With long-flowing tresses adown to her sandal-tie—
Swan, fair as the lily, descended of high degree,
A myriad of welcomes, dear mind of my heart, to thee!
    trans. Edward Walsh

Shule Aroon

A BRIGADE BALLAD

[handwritten: woman whose love is fighting for France (soldier of fortune?)]

I would I were on yonder hill,
'T is there I'd sit and cry my fill,
And every tear would turn a mill,
Is go d-teidh tú, a mhúrnín, slán!

> Refrain: *Siubhail, siubhail, siubhail, a rúin!*
> *Siubhail go socair, agus siubhail go ciúin,*
> *Siubhail go dtí an doras agus eulaigh liom,*
> *Is go d-teidh tú, a mhúrnín, slán!*

I'll sell my rock, I'll sell my reel,
I'll sell my only spinning-wheel,
To buy for my love a sword of steel,
Is go d-teidh tú, a mhúrnín, slán!

I'll dye my petticoats, I'll dye them red,
And round the world I'll beg my bread,
Until my parents shall wish me dead,
Is go d-teidh tú, a mhúrnín, slán!

REFRAIN

I wish, I wish, I wish in vain,
I wish I had my heart again,
And vainly think I'd not complain,
Is go d-teidh tú, a mhúrnín, slán!

REFRAIN

But now my love has gone to France,
To try his fortune to advance;
If he e'er come back, 't is but a chance,
Is go d-teidh tú, a mhúrnín, slán!

REFRAIN

Mary from Dungloe

[handwritten: Emigration Song. Voice of young male emigree]

Oh, then, fare ye well, sweet Donegal, the Rosses and Gweedore
I'm crossing the main ocean, where the foaming billows roar.
It breaks my heart from you to part, where I spent many happy days
Farewell to kind relations, I'm bound for Amerikay.

Oh, my love is tall and handsome and her age is scarce eighteen
She far exceeds all other fair maids when she trips over the green
Her lovely neck and shoulders are fairer than the snow
Till the day I die I'll ne'er deny my Mary from Dungloe.

If I was at home in sweet Dungloe a letter I would write
Kind thoughts would fill my bosom for Mary my delight
'Tis in her father's garden, the fairest violets grow
And 'twas there I came to court the maid, my Mary from Dungloe.

Ah then, Mary you're my heart's delight my pride and only care
It was your cruel father, would not let me stray there.
But absence makes the heart grow fond and when I'm o'er the main
May the Lord protect my darling girl till I return again.

[handwritten: Mary's father not cooperating]

And I wished I was in sweet Dungloe and seated on the grass
And by my side a bottle of wine and on my knee a lass.
I'd call for liquor of the best and I'd pay before I would go
And I'd roll my Mary in my arms in the town of sweet Dungloe.

Sean O'Dwyer of the Glen

Rising in the morning
The summer sun shining,
I have heard the chant weaving
And the sweet songs of birds,
Badgers and small creatures,
The woodcock with his long beak,
The sounding of echoes,
The firing of strong guns,
The red fox on the crag.
Thousand yells of huntsmen

[handwritten: a farewell to one of the O'Dwyers. one of the defeated in Cromwell, was exile. Fate was the Continent & ser- view in the Spanish army.]

[handwritten: animal imagery]

And a woman glumly in the pathway
Counting her flock of geese,
But now the woods are being cut
We will cross over the sea
And, Sean O'Dwyer of the Glen,
You are left weak.

This is my long loneliness,
the shelter for my head being cut,
The North wind lashing me
And death in the sky;
My happy dog being tied up
With no right to move or gambol
Who would take bad temper from a child
In the bright noon day;
The hearts of nobles on the rock
Capering, proud, prancing,
Who would climb up beyond the furze
Until their final day.
So if I get a little peace soon
From the gentry of the town
I will make my way to Galway
And leave the rout behind.

Meadows in stream-cut valleys
Have no vigor, no strength of men,
No glass or cup is raised
To health or happy life;
My bare hills! loss of hedges
From low field to mountain stacks
Leaves the hare on thickets' edges,
A vagrant on the plain.
What is this raid of strangers
But long-drawn cutting and clearing?
Sweet-whistled thrush and blackbird
Without branches for their singing,
An omen of coming troubles
Burdened priest and people
Adrift in empty harbors
Of deep mountain glens.

This is my daily bitterness,
To have lived to the age of sin,
To see this heavy scandal fall
On my people, my own kind.
How often on those long fine days
There were apples on the trees,
Green leaves on the oak,
Fresh dew on the grass;
Now I am driven from my acres,
In lonely cold without friends,
Hiding sadly in holes
And hollows of the mountain.
If I don't get some peace soon
And the right to stay at home
I must give up my own ground,
My country and my life.

trans. Joan Keefe

The Sorrowful Lamentation of Callaghan, Greally, and Mullen

"Come, tell me, dearest mother, what makes my father stay,
Or what can be the reason that he's so long away?"
"Oh! hold your tongue, my darling son, your tears do grieve me sore;
I fear he has been murdered in the fair of Turloughmore."

Come, all you tender Christians, I hope you will draw near;
It's of this dreadful murder I mean to let you hear,
Concerning those poor people whose loss we do deplore
The Lord have mercy on their souls they died at Turloughmore.

It is on the First of August, the truth I will declare,
Those people they assembled that day all at the fair;
But little was their notion what evil was in store,
All by the bloody Peelers at the fair of Turlouglmore.

Were you to see that dreadful sight 'twould grieve your heart, I know,
To see the comely women and the men all lying low;

God help their tender parents, they will never see them more,
For cruel was their murder at the fair of Turloughmore.

It's for that base bloodthirsty crew, remark the word I say,
The Lord He will reward them against the judgment day;
The blood they have taken innocent, for it they'll suffer sore,
And the treatment that they gave to us that day at Turloughmore.

The morning of their trial as they stood up in the dock,
The words they spoke were feeling, the people round them flock;
"I tell you, Judge and Jury, the truth I will declare,
It was Brew that ordered us to fire that evening at the fair."

Now to conclude and finish this sad and doleful fray,
I hope their souls are happy against the judgment day;
It was little time they got, we know, when they fell like new-mowed hay,
May the Lord have mercy on their souls against the judgment day.

The Rising of the Moon

"Tell me, tell me, Seán O'Farrell, tell me why you hurry so."
"Hush, a bhuachaill, hush and listen," and his cheeks were all aglow.
"I bear orders from the Captain, get you ready quick and soon,
For the pikes must be together at the rising of the moon."

"Oh! then, tell me. Seán O'Farrell, where the gatherin' is to be?"
"In the old spot by the river, right well-known to you and me.
One word more, for signal token whistle up the marchin' tune,
With your pike upon your shoulder at the rising of the moon."

Out from many a mud-wall cabin eyes were watching thro' the night.
Many a manly heart was throbbing for that blessed warning light;
Murmurs passed along the valley, like the banshee's lonesome croon,
And a thousand blades were flashing at the rising of the moon.

There beside the singing river that dark mass of men was seen,
High above their shining weapons flew their own beloved green,
"Death to every foe and traitor! forward! strike the marchin' tune!
And hurra! my boys, for freedom; 'tis the rising of the moon!"

Well they fought for poor old Ireland, and full bitter was their fate;
Oh! what glorious pride and sorrow fill the name of 'Ninety-eight. [1798]
But, thank God, there still are beating strong young hearts in
    manhood's bloom,
Who will follow in their footsteps at the rising of the moon.

The Wearin' o' the Green

Oh, Paddy dear! an' did ye hear the news that's goin' round?
The shamrock is by law forbid to grow on Irish ground.
No more St. Patrick's Day we'll keep, his color can't be seen,
For there's a cruel law agin the wearin' o' the green!

I met wid Napper Tandy, and he took me by the hand.
And he said, "How's poor Ould Ireland, and how does she stand?"
She's the most disthressful country that iver yet was seen,
For they're hangin' men and women there for wearin' o' the green.

An' if the color we must wear is England's cruel red,
Let it remind us of the blood that Ireland has shed;
Then pull the shamrock from your hat, and throw it on the sod,—
And never fear, 'twill take root there, tho' under foot 'tis trod!

When law can stop the blades of grass from growin' as they grow,
And when the leaves in summer-time their color dare not show,
Then I will change the color, too, I wear in my caubeen,
But till that day, plaze God, I'll stick to wearin' o' the green.
    Dion Boucicault

Nell Flaherty's Drake

My name it is Nell, quite candid I tell,
    That I live near Coote hill, I will never deny;
I had a fine drake, the truth for to spake,
    That my grandmother left me and she going to die;
He was wholesome and sound, he would weigh twenty pound,
    The universe round I would rove for his sake—
Bad wind to the robber—be he drunk or sober—
    That murdered Nell Flaherty's beautiful drake.

His neck it was green—most rare to be seen,
    He was fit for a queen of the highest degree;
His body was white—and would you delight—
    He was plump, fat and heavy, and brisk as a bee.
The dear little fellow, his legs they were yellow,
    He would fly like a swallow and dive like a hake,
But some wicked savage, to grease his white cabbage,
    He murdered Nell Flaherty's beautiful drake.

May his pig never grunt, may his cat never hunt,
    May a ghost ever haunt him at dead of the night;
May his hen never lay, may his ass never bray,
    May his goat fly away like an old paper kite.
That the flies and the fleas may the wretch ever tease,
    And the piercing north breeze make him shiver and shake,
May a lump of a stick raise bumps fast and thick
    On the monster that murdered Nell Flaherty's drake.

May his cradle ne'er rock, may his box have no lock,
    May his wife have no frock for to cover her back;
May his cock never crow, may his bellows ne'er blow,
    And his pipe and his pot may he evermore lack.
May his duck never quack, may his goose turn black,
    And pull down his turf with her long yellow beak;
May the plague grip the scamp, and his villainy stamp
    On the monster that murdered Nell Flaherty's drake.

May his pipe never smoke, may his teapot be broke,
    And to add to the joke, may his kettle ne'er boil;
May he keep to the bed till the hour that he's dead,
    May he always be fed on hogwash and boiled oil.
May he swell with the gout, may his grinders fall out,
    May he roll, howl and shout with the horrid toothache;
May the temples wear horns, and the toes many corns,
    Of the Monster that murdered Nell Flaherty's drake.

May his spade never dig, may his sow never pig,
    May each hair in his wig be well thrashed with a flail;

May his door have no latch, may his house have no thatch,
 May his turkey not hatch, may the rats eat his meal.
May every old fairy, from Cork to Dunleary,
 Dip him snug and airy in river or lake,
Where the eel and the trout may feed on the snout
 Of the monster that murdered Nell Flaherty's drake.

May his dog yelp and howl with the hunger and cold.
 May his wife always scold till his brains go astray;
May the curse of each hag that e'er carried a bag
 Alight on the vag, till his hair turns gray.
May monkeys affright him, and mad dogs still bite him,
 And everyone slight him, asleep or awake;
May weasels still gnaw him, and jackdaws still claw him—
 The monster that murdered Nell Flaherty's drake.

The only good news that I have to infuse
 Is that old Peter Hughes and blind Peter McCrake,
And big-nosed Bob Manson, and buck-toothed Ned Hanson,
 Each man had a grandson of my lovely drake.
My treasure had dozens of nephews and cousins,
 And one I must get or my heart it will break;
To keep my mind easy, or else I'll run crazy—
 This ends the whole song of my beautiful drake.

The Star of Slane

Ye brilliant muses, who ne'er refuses,
 But still infuses in the poet's mind,
Your kind sweet favors to his endeavors.
 That his ardent labors should appear sublime;
Preserve my study from getting muddy,
 My idea's ready, so inspire my brain;
My quill refine, as I write each line,
 On a nymph divine called the Star of Slane.

In beauteous Spring, when the warblers sing,
 And their carols ring through each fragrant grove;

Bright Sol did shine, which made me incline
    By the river Boyne for to go to rove.
I was ruminating and meditating
    And contemplating as I paced the plain,
When a charming fair, beyond compare,
    Did my heart ensnare near the town of Slane.

Had Paris seen this young maid serene,
    The Grecian queen he would soon disdain,
And straight embrace this virgin chaste,
    And peace would grace the whole Trojan plain.
If Ancient Caesar could on her gaze, sir,
    He'd stand amazed for to view this dame;
Sweet Cleopatra he would freely part her.
    And his crown he'd barter for the Star of Slane.

There's Alexander, that famed commander,
    Whose triumphant standard it did conquer all,
Who proved a victor over crowns and scepters,
    And great warlike structures did before him fall;
Should he behold her, will uphold, sir,
    From pole to pole he would then proclaim,
For the human race in all that wide space,
    To respect the chaste blooming Star of Slane.

To praise her beauty then is my duty,
    But alas! I'm footy in this noble part,
And to my sorrow, sly Cupid's arrow
    Full deep did burrow in my tender heart;
In pain and trouble yet I will struggle,
    Though sadly hobbled by my stupid brain,
Yet backed by Nature I can tell each feature
    Of this lovely creature called the Star of Slane.

Her eyes it's true are an azure blue,
    And her cheeks the hue of the crimson rose;
Her hair behold it does shine like gold,
    And is finely rolled and so nicely grows;
Her skin is white as the snow by night,
    Straight and upright is her supple frame;

The chaste Diana, or fair Susanna,
    Are eclipsed in grandeur by the Star of Slane.

Her name to mention it might cause contention,
    And it's my intention for to breed no strife;
For me to woo her I am but poor,
    I'm deadly sure she won't be my wife;
In silent anguish I here must languish
    Till time does banish all my love-sick pain,
And my humble station I must bear with patience,
    Since great exaltation suits the Star of Slane.

The Night Before Larry Was Stretched

The night before Larry was stretched,
    The boys they all paid him a visit;
A bait in their sacks, too, they fetched;
    They sweated their duds till they riz it:
for Larry was ever the lad,
    When a boy was condemned to the squeezer,
Would fence all the duds that he had
    To help a poor friend to a sneezer,
    And warm his gob 'fore he died.

The boys they came crowding in fast,
    They drew all their stools round about him,
Six glims round his trap-case were placed,
    He couldn't be well waked without 'em,
When one of us asked could he die
    Without having duly repented,
Says Larry, "That's all in my eye;
    And first by the clargy invented,
    To get a fat bit for themselves."

"I'm sorry, dear Larry," says I,
    "To see you in this situation;
And, blister my limbs if I lie,
    I'd as lieve it had been my own station."

"Ochone! it's all over," says he,
    "For the neckcloth I'll be forced to put on
And by this time to-morrow you'll see
    Your poor Larry as dead as a mutton,"
    Because, why, his courage was good.

"And I'll be cut up like a pie,
    And my nob from my body be parted."
"You're in the wrong box, then," says I,
    "For blast me if they're so hard-hearted:
A chalk on the back of your neck
    Is all that Jack Ketch dares to give you;
Then mind not such trifles a feck,
    For why should the likes of them grieve you?
    And now, boys, come tip us the deck."

The cards being called for, they played,
    Till Larry found one of them cheated;
A dart at his napper he made
    (The boy being easily heated):
"Oh, by the hokey, you thief,
    I'll scuttle your nob with my daddle!
You cheat me because I'm in grief,
    But soon I'll demolish your noddle,
    And leave you your claret to drink."

Then the clergy came in with his book,
    He spoke him so smooth and so civil;
Larry tipped him a Kilmainham look,
    And pitched his big wig to the devil;
Then sighing, he threw back his head
    To get a sweet drop of the bottle,
And pitiful sighing, he said:
    "Oh, the hemp will be soon round my throttle
    And choke my poor windpipe to death.

"Though sure it's the best way to die,
    Oh, the devil a betther a-livin'!
For, sure, when the gallows is high
    Your journey is shorter to Heaven:

But what harasses Larry the most,
    And makes his poor soul melancholy,
Is to think of the time when his ghost
    Will come in a sheet to sweet Molly—
    Oh, sure it will kill her alive!"

So moving these last words he spoke,
    We all vented our tears in a shower;
For my part, I thought my heart broke,
    To see him cut down like a flower,
On his travels we watched him next day;
    Oh, the throttler! I thought I could kill him;
But Larry not one word did say,
    Nor changed till he come to "King William"—
Then, *musha!* his color grew white.

When he came to the nubbling chit,
    He was tucked up so neat and so pretty,
The rumbler jogged off from his feet,
    And he died with his face to the city;
He kicked, too—but that was all pride,
    For soon you might see 't was all over;
Soon after the noose was untied,
    And at darky we waked him in clover,
    And sent him to take a ground sweat.

Finnegan's Wake

Tim Finnegan liv'd in Walkin Street
    a gentleman Irish mighty odd.
He had a tongue both rich and sweet,
    an' to rise in the world he carried a hod.
Now Tim had a sort of a tipplin' way,
    with the love of the liquor he was born,
An' to help him on with his work each day
    he'd a drop of the craythur ev'ry morn.

    Chorus: Whack fol the dah,
        dance to your partner

Welt the flure yer trotters shake
Wasn't it the truth I told you,
Lots of fun at Finnegan's wake.

One morning Tim was rather full,
    His head felt heavy which made him shake,
He fell from the ladder and broke his skull,
    So they carried him home his corpse to wake,
They rolled him up in a nice clean sheet
    And laid him out upon the bed,
With a gallon of whiskey at his feet,
    And a barrel of porter at his head.

His friends assembled at the wake,
    And Mrs. Finnegan called for lunch,
First they brought in tay and cake,
    The pipes, tobacco, and whiskey punch.
Miss Biddy O'Brien began to cry,
    "Such a neat clean corpse, did you ever see,
Arrah, Tim avourneen, why did you die?"
    "Ah, hould your gab," said Paddy McGee.

Then Biddy O'Connor took up the job,
    "Biddy," says she, "you're wrong, I'm sure,"
But Biddy gave her a belt in the gob,
    And left her sprawling on the floor;
Oh, then the war did soon enrage;
    'Twas woman to woman and man to man,
Shillelagh law did all engage,
    And a row and a ruction soon began.

Then Micky Maloney raised his head,
    When a noggin of whiskey flew at him,
It missed and falling on the bed,
    The liquor scattered over Tim;
Bedad he revives, see how he rises,
    And Timothy rising from the bed,
Says, "Whirl your liquor round like blazes,
    Thanam o'n dhoul, do ye think I'm dead?"

Further Readings on Irish Folk Songs

Collections

Ó Lochlainn, Cólm, ed. *The Bunting Collection of Irish Folk Music and Songs* 1–6. Journal of the Irish Folk Song Society, 22–29, 1927–39.
———. *Irish Street Ballads*. Appreciation by Frank O'Connor. Dublin: At the Sign of the Three Candles, 1939; New York; Corinth Books, 1960.
———. *More Irish Street Ballads*. Dublin: At the Sign of the Three Candles, 1965.
Ó Sullivan, Donal. *Songs of the Irish*. Dublin: Browne and Nolan, 1960.

Studies

Golden, Sean V. "Traditional Irish Music in Contemporary Irish Literature." *MOSAIC* 12:1–23.
Ó Canainn, Tomás. *Traditional Music in Ireland*. London: Routledge and Kegan Paul, 1978.
Ó Riada, Seán. *Our Musical Heritage*. Edited by Tomas Kinsella. Music edited by Tomás Ó Canainn. Dublin: Dolmen Press, 1982.
O'Sullivan, Donal. *Irish Folk Music and Song*. Rev. ed., Dublin: The Cultural Relations Committee, 1961.
Ó Tuama, Seán. *An Grá in Amhráin na nDaoine*. Dublin: An Clóchomhar, 1960.
Zimmerman, George-Denis. *Songs of the Irish Rebellion*. Reprint, Detroit: Gale, 1967.

[handwritten annotation at top:] Imp. historically because it presents a sympathetic view of Irish peasants as seen by an Anglo-Irish Protestant outsider & establishes the peasant/landlord relationship as a continuing theme in Anglo-Irish fiction. She remains an outsider, viewing the peasant from the window of the Big House.

Nineteenth-Century Prose

Maria Edgeworth (1767–1849)

There are those who date the beginning of Anglo-Irish literature with the publication of Maria Edgeworth's *Castle Rackrent* (1800). Certainly, it was she who first cultivated the untilled field of the regional novel, and in so doing inspired Sir Walter Scott, William Makepeace Thackeray, James Fenimore Cooper—perhaps even Ivan Turgenev.

The eldest daughter and favorite child among Richard Lovell Edgeworth's twenty children, Maria Edgeworth helped run her father's estate at Edgeworthtown (Mostrim), County Longford, and collaborated with her father on a series of educational and moral tales. It was while her father was taken up with the Act of Union that she published, anonymously at first, her novel *Castle Rackrent*.

Using their steward John Langan as a model, she created the narrator Thady Quirk, the first of a line of family retainers that would become a standard feature of nineteenth-century Irish fiction. Thady's ironic account of three generations of Rackrents opens with a description of Sir Patrick Rackrent, whom Thady's grandfather served and from whom Thady learned the facts of life in the Big House: lavish entertainment, hard drinking, and debt. The litigious Sir Kit follows, and then Thady's favorite, Sir Condy, who finally loses the estate to Thady's shrewd son Jason, *Castle Rackrent* is a cautionary tale, as strong a statement of the failure of responsibility of the landlord class as exists in Irish literature.

Edgeworth's own notes follow the narrative.

From *Castle Rackrent*

[handwritten annotation:] narrated by Thady Quirk

Monday Morning.[1]

Having, out of friendship for the family, upon whose estate, praised be Heaven! I and mine have lived rent-free, time out of mind, voluntarily undertaken to publish the memoirs of the Rackrent Family, I think it my duty to say a few words, in the first place, concerning myself. My real name is Thady Quirk, though in the family I have always been known by no other than "hon-

est Thady,"—afterward, in the time of Sir Murtagh, deceased, I remember to hear them calling me *"old Thady,"* and now I'm come to "poor Thady"; for I wear a long great coat winter and summer, which is very handy, as I never put my arms into the sleeves; they are as good as new, though come Holantide next I've had it these seven years; it holds on by a single button round my neck, cloak fashion. To look at me, you would hardly think "poor Thady" was the father of attorney Quirk; he is a high gentleman, and never minds what poor Thady says, and having better than fifteen hundred a year, landed estate, looks down upon honest Thady; but I wash my hands of his doings, and as I have lived so will I die, true and loyal to the family. The family of the Rackrents is, I am proud to say, one of the most ancient in the kingdom. Every body knows this is not the old family name, which was O'Shaughlin, related to the kings of Ireland—but that was before my time. My grandfather was driver to the great Sir Patrick O'Shaughlin, and I heard him, when I was a boy, telling how the Castle Rackrent estate came to Sir Patrick; Sir Tallyhoo Rackrent was cousin-german to him, and had a fine estate of his own, only never a gate upon it, it being his maxim that a car was the best gate, Poor gentleman! he lost a fine hunter and his life, at last, by it, all in one day's hunt. But I ought to bless that day, for the estate came straight into *the* family, upon one condition, which Sir Patrick O'Shaughlin at the time took sadly to heart, they say, but thought better of it afterwards, seeing how large a stake depended upon it, that he should, by act of parliament, take and bear the surname and arms of Rackrent.

Now it was that the world was to see what was *in* Sir Patrick. On coming into the estate, he gave the finest entertainment ever was heard of in the country; not a man could stand after supper but Sir Patrick himself, who could sit out the best man in Ireland, let alone the three kingdoms itself.[2] He had his house, from one year's end to another, as full of company as ever it could hold, and fuller; for rather than be left out of the parties at Castle Rackrent, many gentlemen, and those men of the first consequence and landed estates in the country, such as the O'Neills of Ballynagrotty, and the Moneygawls of Mount Juliet's Town, and O'Shannons of New Town Tullyhog, made it their choice, often and often, when there was no room to be had for love nor money, in long winter nights, to sleep in the chickenhouse, which Sir Patrick had fitted up for the purpose of accommodating his friends and the public, in general, who honoured him with their company unexpectedly at Castle Rackrent; and this went on, I can't tell you how long. The whole country rang with his praises!—Long life to him! I'm sure I love to look upon his picture, now opposite to me; though I never saw him, he must have been a portly gentleman his neck something short, and remarkable for the largest pimple on his nose, which, by his particular desire, is still extant in his picture, said to be a striking likeness, though taken when young. He is said also to be the inventor of raspberry whiskey, which is very likely, as nobody has ever appeared to dispute it with him, and as there still exists a broken punch-bowl at Castle Rackrent, in the garret, with an inscription to that effect—a great curiosity. A few days before his death he was very merry; it being his honour's birth-day, he called my grandfather in, God bless him! to drink the company's health, and filled a bumper himself, but could not carry it to his head, on account of the great shake in his hand; on this he cast his joke, saying, "What would my poor father say to me if he was to pop out of the grave, and see me now? I remember when I was a little boy, the first bumper of claret he gave me after dinner, how he praised me for carrying it so steady to my mouth. Here's my thanks to him— a bumper toast." Then he fell to singing the favourite song he learned from his father—for the last time, poor gentleman—he sung it that night as loud and as hearty as ever with a chorus:

> He that goes to bed, and goes to bed sober,
> Falls as the leaves do, falls as the leaves do, and dies in October;
> But he that goes to bed, and goes to bed mellow,
> Lives as he ought to do, lives as he ought to do, and dies an honest fellow.

Sir Patrick died that night: just as the company rose to drink his health with three cheers, he fell down in a sort of fit, and was carried off; they sat it out, and were surprised, on inquiry, in the morning, to find that it was all over with poor Sir Patrick. Never did any gentleman live and die more beloved in the country by rich and poor. His funeral was such a one as was never known before or since in the country! All the gentlemen in the three counties were at it; far and near, how they flocked! my great grandfather said, that to see all the women even in their red cloaks, you would have taken them for the army drawn out. Then such a fine whillaluh![3] you might have heard it to the farthest end of the county, and happy the man who could get but a sight of the hearse! But who'd have thought it? Just as all was going on right, through his own town they were passing, when the body was seized for debt—a rescue was apprehended from the mob; but the heir who attended the funeral was against that, for fear of consequences, seeing that those villains who came to serve acted under the disguise of the law: so, to be sure, the law must take its course, and little gain had the creditors for their pains. First and foremost, they had the curses of the country: and Sir Murtagh Rackrent, the new heir, in the next place, on account of this affront to the body, refused to pay a shilling of the debts, in which he was countenanced by all the best gentlemen of property, and others of his acquaintance; Sir Murtagh alleging in all companies, that he all along meant to pay his father's debts of honour, but the moment the law was taken of him, there was an end of honour to be sure. It was whispered (but none but the enemies of the family believe it), that this was all a sham seizure to get quit of the debts, which he had bound himself to pay in honour.

[handwritten: Patrick was in debt]

Notes

1. *Monday morning.*—Thady begins his memoirs of the Rackrent Family by dating *Monday morning*, because no great undertaking can be auspiciously commenced in Ireland on any morning but *Monday morning*. "Oh, please God we live till Monday morning, we'll set the slater to mend the roof of the house. On Monday morning we'll fall to, and cut the turf. On Monday morning we'll see and begin mowing. On Monday morning, please your honour, we'll begin and dig the potatoes," &c.

All the intermediate days, between the making of such speeches and the ensuing Monday, are wasted: and when Monday morning comes, it is ten to one that the business is deferred to *the next* Monday morning. The Editor knew a gentleman, who, to counteract this prejudice, made his workmen and labourers begin all new pieces of work upon a Saturday.

2. *Let alone the three kingdoms itself.*—*Let alone, in this sentence, means put out of consideration*. The phrase, *let alone*, which is now used as the imperative of a verb, may in time become a conjunction, and may exercise the ingenuity of some future etymologist. The celebrated Horne Tooke has proved most satisfactorily, that the conjunction *but* comes from the imperative of the Anglo-Saxon verb (*beoutan*) *to be out;* also, that *if* comes from *gif*, the imperative of the Anglo-Saxon verb which signifies to *give*, &c.

3. *Whillaluh.*—Ullaloo, Gol, or lamentation over the dead *[handwritten: ✳ Keen]*

"Magnoque ululante tumultu."—VIRGIL.
"Ululatibus omne / Implevere nemus."—OVID.

A full account of the Irish Gal, or Ullaloo, and of the Caoinan or Irish funeral song, with its first semichorus, second semichorus, full chorus of sighs and groans, together with the Irish words and music, may be found in the fourth volume of the transactions of the Royal Irish Academy. For the advantage of *lazy* readers, who would rather read a page than walk a yard, and from compassion, not to say sympathy, with their infirmity, the Editor transcribes the following passages:

The Irish have been always remarkable for their funeral lamentations; and this peculiarity has been noticed by almost every traveller who visited them; and it seems derived from their Celtic ancestors, the primæval inhabitants of this isle. . . .

It has been affirmed of the Irish, that to cry was more natural to them than to any other nation, and at length the Irish cry became proverbial. . . .

Cambrensis in the twelfth century says, the Irish then musically expressed their griefs; that is, they applied the musical art, in which they excelled all others, to the orderly celebration of funeral obsequies, by dividing the mourners into two bodies, each alternately singing their part, and the whole at times joining in full chorus. . . . The body of the deceased, dressed in grave clothes, and ornamented with flowers, was placed on a bier, or some elevated spot. The relations and keepers *(singing mourners)* ranged themselves in two divisions, one at the head, and the other at the feet of the corpse. The bards and croteries had before prepared the funeral Caoinan. The chief bard of the head chorus began by singing the first stanza, in a low, doleful tone, which was softly accompanied by the harp: at the conclusion, the foot semichorus began the lamentation, or Ullaloo, from the final note of the preceding stanza, in which they were answered by the head semichorus; then both united in one general chorus. The chorus of the first stanza being ended, the chief bard of the foot semichorus began the second Gol or lamentation, in which he was answered by that of the head; and then, as before, both united in the general full chorus. Thus alternately were the song and cho- ruses performed during the night. The genealogy, rank, possessions, the virtues and vices of the dead were rehearsed, and a number of interrogations were addressed to the deceased; as, Why did he die? If married, whether his wife was faithful to him, his sons dutiful, or good hunters or warriors? If a woman, whether her daughters were fair or chaste? If a young man, whether he had been crossed in love; or if the blue-eyed maids of Erin treated him with scorn?

We are told, that formerly the feet (the metrical feet) of the Caoinan were much attended to; but on the decline of the Irish bards these feet were gradually neglected, and the Caoinan fell into a sort of slipshod metre amongst women. Each province had different Caoinans, or at least differ- ent imitations of the original. There was the Munster cry, the Ulster cry, &c. It became an extem- pore performance, and every set of keepers varied the melody according to their own fancy.

It is curious to observe how customs and ceremonies degenerate. The present Irish cry, or howl, cannot boast of such melody, nor is the funeral procession conducted with much dignity. The crowd of people who assemble at these funerals sometimes amounts to a thousand, often to four or five hundred. They gather as the bearers of the hearse proceed on their way, and when they pass through any village, or when they come near any houses, they begin to cry—Oh! Oh! Oh! Oh! Oh! Agh! Agh! raising their notes from the first *Oh!* to the last *Ah!* in a kind of mournful howl. This gives notice to the inhabitants of the village that a *funeral is passing,* and immediately they flock out to follow it. In the province of Munster it is a common thing for the women to fol- low a funeral, to join in the universal cry with all their might and main for some time, and then to turn and ask—"Arrah! who is it that's dead?—who is it we're crying for?" Even the poorest peo- ple have their own burying-places, that is, spots of ground in the church-yards where they say that their ancestors have been buried ever since the wars of Ireland; and if these burial-places are ten miles from the place where a man dies, his friends and neighbours take care to carry his corpse thither. Always one priest, often five or six priests, attend these funerals; each priest repeats a mass, for which he is paid, sometimes a shilling, sometimes half-a-crown, sometimes half-a-guinea, or a guinea, according to their circumstances, or, as they say, according to the *ability* of the deceased. After the burial of any very poor man, who has left a widow or children, the priest makes what is called *a collection* for the widow; he goes round to every person present, and each contributes six- pence or a shilling, or what they please.

Certain old women, who cry particularly loud and well, are in great request, and, as a man said to the Editor, "Everyone would wish and be proud to have such at his funeral, or at that of his friends." The lower Irish are wonderfully eager to attend the funerals of their friends and relations, and they make their relationships branch out to a great extent. The proof that a poor man has been well beloved during his life is his having a crowded funeral. To attend a neighbour's funeral is a cheap proof of humanity, but it does not, as some imagine, cost nothing. The time spent in attending funerals may be safely valued at half a million to the Irish nation; the Editor thinks that double that sum would not be too high an estimate. The habits of profligacy and drunkenness which are acquired at *wakes,* are here put out of the question. When a labourer, a carpenter, or a smith, is not at his work, which frequently happens, ask where he is gone, and ten to one the answer is—"Oh, faith, please your honour, he couldn't do a stroke to-day, for he's gone to *the* funeral."

Even beggars, when they grow old, go about begging *for their own funerals;* that is, begging for money to buy a coffin, candles, pipes, and tobacco.

Those who value customs in proportion to their antiquity, and nations in proportion to their adherence to ancient customs, will doubtless, admire the Irish *Ullaloo,* and the Irish nation, for persevering in this usage from time immemorial. The Editor, however, has observed some alarming symptoms, which seem to prognosticate the declining taste for the Ullaloo in Ireland. In a comic theatrical entertainment, represented not long since on the Dublin stage, a chorus of old women was introduced, who set up the Irish howl round the relics of a physician, who is supposed to have fallen under the wooden sword of Harlequin. After the old women have continued their Ullaloo for a decent time, with all the necessary accompaniments of wringing their hands, wiping or rubbing their eyes with the corners of their gowns or aprons, &c. one of the mourners suddenly suspends her lamentable cries, and, turning to her neighbour, asks, "Arrah now, honey, who is it we're crying for?"

Further Readings on Maria Edgeworth

Bibliography

Butler, Marilyn, *Maria Edgeworth: A Literary Biography,* 501–9. Oxford: Clarendon Press, 1972.
Newcomber, James, *Maria Edgeworth,* 88–94. Lewisburg, Pa: Bucknell University Press, 1973.
Slade, Bertha Coolidge. *Maria Edgeworth: A Bibliographical Tribute.* London: Constable, 1937.

Selected Works

The Absentee. Edited by Kim Walker. London: Penguin, 1999.
The Absentee. Edited by W. J. McCormack. Oxford: Oxford University Press, 1988.
Belinda. Edited by Eiléan Ní Chuilleanáin. London: J. M. Dent, 1993.
Belinda. Edited by Kathryn L. Kirkpatrick. Oxford: Oxford University Press, 1994.
Castle Rackrent. Edited by George Watson. 1800. Reprint, London: Oxford University Press, 1964.

Castle Rackrent; and, Ennui. Edited by Marilyn Butler. London: Penguin, 1992.

Helen. London, New York: Pandora, 1987.

Helen. Edited by Susan Manly and Cliona Ó Gallchoir. London: Pickering and Chatto, 1999.

Leonore; Harrington. Edited by Susan Manly and Marilyn Butler. London: Pickering and Chatto, 1999.

Letters for Literary Ladies, etc. 1795. Reprint, London: J. M. Dent, 1993.

The Lottery. London: Phoenix, 1996.

Manoeuvring; Vivian. Edited by Claire Connolly and Marilyn Butler. London: Pickering and Chatto, 1999.

Memoirs of Richard Lovell Edgeworth, Esq., Begun by Himself and Concluded by his Daughter, Maria Edgeworth. 2 vols. Introduction by Desmond Clarke. 1820. Reprint, Shannon: Irish University Press, 1970.

Ormond. Edited by Claire Connolly. London: Penguin Books, 2000.

Ormond. Introduction by A. Norman Jeffares. 1817. Reprint, Shannon: Irish University Press, 1972.

Ormond: A Tale. Edited by John Banville. Dublin: Appletree Press, 1992.

Patronage. Edited by W. J. McCormack. London: Pickering and Chatto, 1999.

Tales and Novels of Maria Edgeworth. 1893. Reprint, New York: AMS, 1967.

Tour in Connemara and the Martins of Ballinahinch. Edited by Harold Edgeworth Butler. London: Constable and Co., 1950.

Biography and Criticism

Bilger, Audrey. *Laughing Feminism: Subversive Comedy in Frances Brunei, Maria Edgeworth, and Jane Austin.* Detroit: Wayne State University Press, 1998.

Butler, Marilyn. *Maria Edgeworth: A Literary Biography.* Oxford: Clarendon Press, 1972.

Clarke, Desmond. *The Ingenious Mr. Edgeworth.* London: Oldbourne, 1965.

Clarke, Isabel C. *Maria Edgeworth: Her Family and Friends.* London: Hutchinson and Co., 1950.

Flanagan, Thomas J. *The Irish Novelists, 1800–1850,* 53–106. New York: Columbia University Press, 1959.

Gilmartin, Sophie. *Ancestry and Narrative in Nineteenth-Century British Literature: Blood Relations from Edgeworth to Hardy.* Cambridge, N.Y.: Cambridge University Press, 1998.

Gonda, Caroline. *Reading Daughters' Fictions, 1709–1834: Novels and Society from Manley to Edgeworth.* Cambridge, N.Y.: Cambridge University Press, 1996.

Harden, O. Elizabeth. *Maria Edgeworth.* Boston: Twayne Publishers, 1984.

———. *Maria Edgeworth's Art of Prose Fiction*. The Hague: Mouton, 1971.

Hare, Augustus J. C. *The Life and Letters of Maria Edgeworth*. 2 vols. 1894. Reprint, Freeport, N.Y.: Books for Libraries Press, 1971.

Hawthorne, Mark D. *Doubt and Dogma in Maria Edgeworth*. Gainesville: University of Florida Press, 1967.

Hollingworth, Brian. *Maria Edgeworth's Irish Writing: Language, History, and Politics*. Basingstoke, UK: Macmillan, 1997.

Inglis-Jones, Elisabeth, *The Great Maria*. London: Faber and Faber, 1959.

Kowaleski-Wallace, Elizabeth. *Their Father's Daughters: Hannah More, Maria Edgeworth, and Patriarchal Complicity*. New York: Oxford University Press, 1991.

McHugh, Roger. "Maria Edgeworth's Irish Novels." *Studies* 27:556–70.

Murray, Patrick. *Companion to Castle Rackrent*. Dublin: Educational Company, 1991.

Newcomber, James. *Maria Edgeworth*. Lewisburg, Pa: Bucknell University Press, 1973.

———. *Maria Edgeworth the Novelist, 1767–1849: A Bicentennial Study*. Fort Worth: Texas Christian University Press, 1967.

Owens, Cóilín. *Family Chronicles: Maria Edgeworth's Castle Rackrent*. Dublin: Wolfhound Press, 1987.

Tracy, Robert. "Maria Edgeworth and Lady Morgan: Legality versus Legitimacy." *Nineteenth Century Fiction* 40:1–22.

Woolf, Virginia. "The Taylors and the Edgeworths." In *The Common Reader*. New York: Harcourt, Brace and World, 1953.

William Carleton (1794–1869)

William Carleton's fiction is unique for its description of Irish rural life in the early nineteenth century—especially the world of the tenant farmer and landless laborer, a world destroyed by the famine of 1845–48. W. B. Yeats judged him a great Irish historian: "The history of a nation is not parliaments and battle-fields, but in what the people say to each other on fair-days and high days, and in how they farm, and quarrel, and go on pilgrimage. These things has Carleton recorded." Carleton himself realized the value of this work. He introduced *Tales of Ireland* (1834) as follows:

> I found them a class unknown in literature, unknown by their landlords, and unknown by those in whose hands much of their destiny was placed. If I became the historian of their habits and manners, their feelings, their prejudices, their superstitions and their crimes, if I have attempted to delineate their moral, religious and physical state, it was because I saw no person willing to undertake a task which surely must be looked on as an important one.

He was one of their own, too. Son of a tenant farmer and a mother celebrated locally as a singer, Carleton was born in Prillisk, Clogher parish, County Tyrone, was steeped in oral tradition in both Irish and English. Like Jemmy M'Evoy, the hero of "The Poor Scholar," Carleton set off to Munster; however, he quickly returned home. Later, he went to Dublin where his struggle with poverty was responsible for his uneven career—much of his output consisted of potboilers and propaganda—and for his broken health.

Jemmy was more fortunate. His first bit of luck was meeting the hospitable farmer who took him home for the night. The passage illustrates Carleton's adroit use of language—a combination of authentic dialect and rich dialogue that anticipates Synge and O'Casey.

From "The Poor Scholar" *use of dialect*

There is no country on the earth in which either education, or the desire to procure it, is so much reverenced as in Ireland. Next to the claims of the priest and schoolmaster come those of the poor scholar for the respect of the people. It matters not how poor or how miserable he may be; so long as they see him struggling with poverty in the prosecution of a purpose so laudable, they will treat him with attention and kindness. Here there is no danger of his being sent to the workhouse, committed as a vagrant—or passed from parish to parish until he reaches his own settlement. Here the humble lad is not met by the sneer of purse-proud insolence, or his simple tale answered only by the frown of heartless contempt. No—no—no. The best bit and sup are placed before him; and whilst his poor, but warm-hearted entertainer can afford only potatoes and salt to his own half-starved family, he will make a struggle to procure something better for the poor scholar; *"Bekase he's far from his own, the crathur!* An' sure the intintion in him is good, any how: the Lord prosper him, an' every one that has the heart set upon the larnin'!"

As Jemmy proceeded, he found that his satchel of books and apparel gave as clear an intimation of his purpose, as if he had carried a label to that effect upon his back.

"God save you, a bouchal!" said a warm, honest-looking countryman, whom he met driving home his cows in the evening, within a few miles of the town in which he purposed to sleep.

"God save you kindly!"

"Why, thin, 'tis a long journey you have before you, alanna, for I know well it's for Munster you're bound."

"Thrue for you, 'tis there wid the help of God I'm goin'. A great scarcity of larnin' was in my own place, or I wouldn't have to go at all," said the boy, whilst his eyes filled with tears.

" 'Tis no discredit in life," replied the countryman, with untaught natural delicacy, for he perceived that a sense of pride lingered about the boy which made the character of poor scholar sit painfully upon him; " 'tis no discredit, dear, nor don't be cast down. I'll warrant you that God will prosper you; an' that He may, avick, I pray this day!" and as he spoke, he raised his hat in reverence to the Being whom he invoked, "An' tell me, dear—where do you intend to sleep to-night?"

"In the town forrid here," replied Jemmy. "I'm in hopes I'll be able to reach it before dark."

"Pooh! asy you will. Have you any friends or acquaintances there that'ud welcome you, *a bouchal dhas* [my handsome boy]?"

"No, indeed," said Jemmy, "they're all strangers to me; but I can stop in 'dhry lodgin',' for it's chaper."

"Well, alanna, I believe you; but *I'm no stranger to you*—so come home wid me to-night; where you'll get a good bed, and betther thratement nor in any of their dhry lodgins. Give me your books, and I'll carry them for you. Ethen, but you have a great batch o' them entirely. Can you make any hand o' the Latin at all yet?"

"No, indeed," replied Jemmy, somewhat sorrowfully; "I didn't ever open a Latin book, at all at all."

"Well, acushla, everything has a beginnin';—you won't be so, An' I know by your face that you'll be bright at it, an' a credit to them that owes you. There's my house in the fields beyant, where you'll be well kept for one night, any way, or for twinty, or for ten times twinty, if you wanted them."

The honest farmer then commenced the song of *Colleen dhas Crotha na Mho,* which he sang in a clear mellow voice, until they reached the house.

"Alley," said the man to his wife, on entering, "here's a stranger I've brought you."

"Well," replied Alley, "he's welcome sure, any way; *Kead millia failta ghud,* alanna! sit over to the fire. Brian, get up, dear," said she to one of the children, "an' let the stranger to the hob."

"He's goin' on a good errand, the Lord bless him!" said the husband, "up the country for the larnin', Put thim books over on the settle; an' whin the *girshas* are done milkin', give him a brave dhrink of the sweet milk; it's the stuff to thravel on."

"Troth, an' I will, wid a heart an' a half, wishin' it was better I had to give him. Here, Nelly, put down a pot o' wather, an' lave soap an' a *praskeen,* afore you go to milk, till I bathe the dacent boy's feet. Sore an' tired they are afther his journey, poor young crathur."

When Jemmy placed himself upon the hob, he saw that some peculiarly good fortune had conducted him to so comfortable a resting-place. He considered this as a good omen, and felt, in fact, much relieved, for the sense of loneliness among strangers was removed.

The house evidently belonged to a wealthy farmer, well to do in the world; the chimney was studded with sides upon sides of yellow smoke-dried bacon, hams, and hung beef in abundance. The kitchen tables were large, and white as milk; and the dresser rich in its shining array of delf and pewter. Everything, in fact, was upon a large scale. Huge meal chests were ranged on one side, and two or three settle beds on the other, conspicuous, as I have said, for their uncommon cleanliness; "whilst hung from the ceiling were the *glaiks*, a machine for churning; and beside the dresser stood an immense churn, certainly too unwieldy to be managed except by machinery/ The farmer was a ruddy-faced Milesian, who wore a drab frieze coat, with a velvet collar, buff waistcoat, corduroy small-clothes, and top-boots well greased from the tops down. He was not only an agriculturist, but a grazier—remarkable for shrewdness and good sense, generally attended fairs and markets, and brought three or four large droves of fat cattle to England every year. From his fob hung the brass chain and almost rusty key of a watch, which he kept certainly more for use than ornament.

"A little sup o' this," said he, "won't take your life," approaching Jemmy with a bottle of as good poteen as ever escaped the eye of an exciseman; "it'll refresh you—for you're tired, or I wouldn't offer it, by rason that one bint on what you're bint on, oughtn't to be makin' freedoms wid the same dhrink. But there's a time for everything, an' there's a time for this.—Thank you, agra," he added, in reply to Jemmy, who had drunk his health. "Now, don't be frettin'—but make yourself as aisy as if you were at your own father's hearth. You'll have everything to your heart's contint for this night; the carts are goin' in to the market to-morrow airly—you can sit upon them, an' maybe you'll get somethin' more nor you expect: sure the Lord has given it to me, an' why wouldn't I share it wid them that wants it more nor I do?"

[Jemmy is given his dinner and later the local schoolmaster arrives.]

As she spoke, a short thickset man, with black twinkling eyes and ruddy cheeks entered. This personage was no other than the schoolmaster of that district, who circulated, like a newspaper, from one farmer's house to another, in order to expound for his kind entertainers the news of the day, his own learning, and the very evident extent of their ignorance.

The moment he came in, the farmer and his wife rose with an air of much deference, and placed, a chair for him exactly opposite the fire, leaving a respectful distance on each side, within which no illiterate mortal durst presume to sit.

"Misther Corcoran," said the farmer, presenting Jemmy's satchel, through which the shapes of the books were quite plain, *"thig in thu shinn?"* and as he spoke he looked significantly at its owner.

"Ah;" replied the man of letters, *"thigum, thigum.* God be wid the day when I carried the likes of it. 'Tis a badge of polite genius, that no boy need be ashamed of. So my young suckling of litherature, you're bound for Munster?—for that counthry where the swallows fly in conic sections—where the magpies and the turkeys confab in Latin, and the cows and bullocks will roar you Doric Greek—bo-a-o—clamo. What's your pathronymic? *quo nomine gowdes, Domine doctissime?"*

The lad was silent; but the farmer's wife turned up the whites of her eyes with an expression of wonder and surprise at the erudition of the "masther."

"I persave you are as yet uninitiated into the elementary *principia* of the languages; well—the honour is still before you. What's your name?"

"James M'Evoy, Sir."

Just now the farmer's family began to assemble round the spacious hearth; the yound lads, whose instruction the worthy teacher claimed as his own peculiar task, came timidly forward, together with two or three pretty bashful girls with sweet flashing eyes, and countenances full of feeling and intelligence. Behind on the settles, half-a-dozen servants of both sexes sat in pairs—each boy placing himself beside his favourite girl. These *appeared* to be as strongly interested in the learned conversation which the master held, as if they were masters and mistresses of Munster Latin and Doric Greek themselves; but an occasional thump cautiously bestowed by no slender female hand upon the sturdy shoulder of her companion, or a dry cough from one of the young men, fabricated to drown the coming blow, gave slight indications that they contrived to have a little amusement among themselves, altogether independent of Mr. Corcoran's erudition.

When the latter came in, Jemmy was taking the tumbler of punch which the farmer's wife had mixed for him; on this he fixed an expressive glance, which instantly reverted to the *vanithee,* and from her to the large bottle which stood in a window to the right of the fire. It is a quick eye, however, that Gill anticipate Irish hospitality.

"Sure, I am," she replied, "an' will have it for you in less than no time."

She accordingly addressed herself to the bottle, and in a few minutes handed a reeking jug of punch to the *Farithee,* or good man.

"Come, Masthter, by the hand o' my body, I don't like dhry talk so long as I can get anything to moisten the discoorse. Here's your health, Masthter," continued the farmer, winking at the rest, "and a speedy conclusion to what you know! In throth, she's the pick of a good girl—not to mintion what she has for her portion. I'm a friend to the same family, an' will put a spoke in your wheel, Masthter, that'll sarve you."

"Oh, Mr. Lanigan, very well, Sir—very well—you're becoming quite facetious upon me," said the little man, rather confused; "but upon my credit and reputation, except the amorous inclination in regard to me is on *her* side," and he looked sheepishly at his hands, "I can't say that the arrows of Cupid have as yet pinethrated the sintimintal side of *my* heart. It is not with me as it was wid Dido—hem— *allusion to Aeneid*

Non 'hæret lateri lethalis arundo,'

as Virgil says. Yet I can't say, but if a friend were to become spokesman for me, and insinuate in my behalf a small taste of amorous sintimintality, why—hem, hem, hem! The company's health! Lad, James M'Evoy, *your* health, and success to you, my good boy!—hem, hem!"

"Here's wishin' him the same!" said the farmer.

"James," said the schoolmaster, "you are goin' to Munsther, an' I can say that I have travelled it from end to end, not to a bad purpose, I hope—hem! Well, a bouchal, there are hard days and nights before you, so keep a firm heart. If you have money, as 'tis likely you have, don't let a single rap of it into the hands of the schoolmaster, although the first thing he'll do will be to bring you home to his own house, an' palaver you night an' day, till he succeeds in persuading you to leave it in his hands for security. You might, if not duly pre-adominished, surrender it to his solicitations, for—

advice vs corrupt schoolmaster

'Nemo mortalium omnibus horis sapit.'

Michael, what case is *mortalium*?" added he, suddenly addressing one of the farmer's sons: "come now, Michael, where's your brightness? What case is *mortalium*?"

The boy was taken by surprise, and for a few minutes could not reply.

"Come man," said the father, "be sharp, spake out bravely, an' don't be afeard; nor don't be in a hurry aither, we'll wait for you."

Schoolmaster quizzes children.

"Let him alone—let him alone," said Corcoran; "I'll face the same boy agin the county for *cuteness*. If he doesn't expound that, I'll never consthre a line of Latin, or Greek, or Masoretic, while I'm livin'."

His cunning master knew right well that the boy, who was only confused at the suddenness of the question, would feel no difficulty in answering it to his satisfaction. Indeed, it was impossible for him to miss it, as he was then reading the seventh book of Virgil, and the fourth of Homer. It is, however, a trick with such masters to put simple questions of that nature to their pupils, when at the houses of their parents, as knotty and difficult, and when they are answered, to assume an air of astonishment at the profound reach of thought displayed by the pupil.

When Michael recovered himself, he instantly replied, "*Mortalium* is the genitive case of *nemo*, by '*Nomina Partitiva.*'"

Corcoran laid down the tumbler, which he was in the act of raising to his lips, and looked at the lad with an air of surprise and delight, then at the farmer and his wife, alternately, and shook his head with much mystery. "Michael," said he to the lad, "will you go out, and tell us what the night's doin'."

The boy accordingly went out—"Why," said Corcoran, in his absence, "if ever there was a phanix, and that boy will be an the bird—an Irish phanix he will be, a

Phoenex

Rara avis in terris, nigorque simillima cygno!

There is no batin' him at anything he undhertakes. Why, there's thim that are makin' good bread by their larnin', that couldn't resolve that; and you all saw how he did it widout the book! Why, if he goes on at this rate, I'm afraid he'll soon be too many for myself—hem!"

"Too many for yourself! Fill the masther's tumbler, Alley. Too many for yourself! No, no! I doubt he'll never see that day, bright as he is, an' cute, That's it—put a hape upon it. Give me your hand, masther. I thank you for your attintion to him, an' the boy is a credit to us. Come over, Michael, avourneen. Here, take what's in this tumbler, an' finish it. Be a good boy, an' mind your lessons, an' do everything the masther here—the Lord bless him!—bids you; an' you'll never want a frind, masther, nor a dinner, nor a bed, nor a guinea, while the Lord spares me aither the one or the other."

"I know it, Mr. Lanigan, I know it; and I will make that boy the pride of Ireland, if I'm spared. I'll show him *cramboes* that would puzzle the great Scaliger himself; and many other difficulties I'll let him into, that I have never let out yet, except to Tim Kearney, that bate them all at Thrinity College in Dublin up, last June."

"Arrah, how was that, Masther?"

"Tim, you see, went in to his Entrance Examinayshuns, and one of the Fellows came to examine him, but divil a long it was till Tim sacked him.

" 'Go back agin,' says Tim, 'and sind some one that's *able* to tache me, for you're *not.*'

"So another greater scholar agin came to thry Tim, and *did* thry him, and Tim made a hare of *him,* before all that was in the place—five or six thousand ladies and gintlemen, at laste!

"The great learned Fellows thin began to look odd enough; so they picked out the best scholar among them but one, and slipped him at Tim: but well becomes Tim, the never a long it was still he had *him,* too, as dumb as a post. The fellow went back—

" 'Gintlemen,' says he to the rest, 'we'll be disgraced all out,' says he, 'for except the Prowost sacks that Munsther spalpeen, he'll bate us all, an' we'll never be able to hould up our heads afther.'

"Accordingly, the Prowost attacks Tim; and such a meetin' as they had, never was seen in Thrinity College since its establishment. At last when they had been nine hours and a half at it, the Prowost put one word to him that Tim couldn't expound, so he lost it by *one* word only. For the last two hours the Prowost carried an the examinashun in Hebrew, thinking, you see, he *had* Tim there; but he was mistaken for Tim answered him in good Munsther Irish, and it so happened that they understood each other, for the two languages are first cousins, or, at all evints, close blood relations. Tim was then pronounced to be the best scholar in Ireland except the Prowost; though among ourselves they might have thought of the man that *taught* him. That, however, wasn't all. A young lady fell in love wid Tim, and is to make him a present of herself and her great fortune (three estates) the moment he becomes a counsellor; and in the meantime she allows him thirty pounds a year to bear his expenses, and live like a gintleman.

"Now to return to the youth in the corner: *Nemo mortalium omnibus horis sapit,* Jemmy keep your money, or give it to the priest to keep, and it will be safest; but by no means let the Hyblean honey of the schoolmaster's blarney deprive you of it, otherwise it will be a *vale, vale, longum vale* between you."

master brags about having taught Tim

Further Readings on William Carleton

Bibliography

Hayley, Barbara. *The William Carleton Bibliography.* Gerrards Cross, UK: Colin Smythe, 1985.

Selected Works

The Autobiography. London: MacGibbon and Kee, 1968.
The Autobiography. Belfast: White Row Press, 1996.
The Black Prophet. 1847. Reprint, New York: Garland Press, 1979.
The Black Prophet. Poole, UK: Woodstock Books, 1996.
Denis O'Shaughnessy Going to Maynooth. Introduction by Maurice Harmon. Cork: Mercier Press, 1973.
The Emigrants of Ahadarra. 1848. Reprint, New York: Garland Publishing, 1979.
Inside the Margins: A Carleton Reader. Edited by Tess Hurson. Belfast: Lagan Press, 1992.
The Life of William Carleton. 2 vols. Edited by David J. O'Donoghue. Introduction by Mrs. Cashel Hoey. 1896. Reprint, New York: Garland Publishing, 1979.
Stories from Carleton. Edited and with an introduction by William Butler Yeats. 1889. Reprint, New York: Lemma, 1973.
Traits and Stories of the Irish Peasantry. 1830. Reprint, New York: Garland Publishing, 1979.
Valentine M'Clutchy, The Irish Agent. 1847. Reprint, New York: Garland Publishing, 1979.
Works of William Carleton. 1881. Reprint, Freeport, N.Y.: Books for Libraries, 1970.

Biography and Criticism

Bell, Sam Hanna. "William Carleton and his Neighbors." *Ulster Folk Life* 7:37–40.
Boué, André. *William Carleton, romancier irlandais (1794–1869).* Lille: Université de Lille, III, 1973. Reprint, Paris: Publications de la Sorbonne, 1978.
Flanagan, Thomas. *The Irish Novelists, 1800–1850,* 255–330. New York: Columbia University Press, 1958.
Hayley, Barbara. *Carleton's "Traits and Stories" and the Nineteenth Century Anglo-Irish Tradition.* Gerrards Cross, UK: Colin Smythe, 1983.
Kiely, Benedict. *Poor Scholar. A Study of the Works and Days of William Carleton (1794–1869).* New York: Sheed and Ward, 1948. Reprint, Dublin: Wolfhound Press, 1997.

Krause, David. *Revisionary Views: Some Counter-Statements about Irish Life and Literature.* Dublin: Maunsel and Co., 2002.

———. *William Carleton, the Novelist: His Carnival and Pastoral World of Tragicomedy.* Lanham, Md.: University Press of America, 2000.

Ó hAinle, Cathal G. "The Gaelic Background of Carleton's *Traits and Stories.*" *Éire-Ireland* 18:6–19.

Shaw, Rose. *Carleton Country.* Introduction by Shane Leslie. Dublin: Talbot Press, 1930.

Sullivan, Eileen. *William Carleton.* Boston: Twayne Publishers, 1983.

Wolff, Robert Lee. *William Carleton, Irish Peasant Novelist: A Preface to His Fiction.* New York: Garland, 1980.

The tradition of sentimental propaganda's patriotic verse was later challenged by Yeats.

Moore established certain poetic conventions:
"chains" of oppression
"tears" of suffering
The "shadow of death"
the "sword of valor"
the "smile of freedom"
and the harp representing national culture

Later parodied in work of Shaw, Joyce & O'Casey

Nineteenth-Century Poetry

Thomas Moore (1779–1852)

Lionized in his own day, popular still in 1879, the year of his centenary, Thomas Moore's bicentenary passed with scant attention; yet, some would argue he is Ireland's national poet. People have sung Moore's *Irish Melodies* with great feeling for more than one hundred and fifty years, and while it may be true that other, less sentimental music better embodies Irish identity today, generations of Irish at home and abroad have found an expression of national aspiration in Moore's imagery.

Born to a middle-class Dublin family, Moore attended Trinity College, Dublin, where Robert Emmet became a good friend. Here, too, he discovered Edward Bunting's *Irish Airs,* and first conceived the idea to provide lyrics for that music. He left Ireland to spend the required terms at the Middle Temple to become a barrister; however, he abandoned law after he published his translation of the Greek poet Anacreon. Moore's patron, the Earl of Moira, arranged for him to be the Registrar of the court of Admiralty at Bermuda in 1803. Leaving a deputy in charge there, Moore traveled in the United States. He was taken with the country's natural beauty but disapproved of American democracy, prophesying that it would not succeed.

Eventually, Moore returned to London, to the drawing-room society where his vivacious personality, his wit, and his ability to entertain made him, in Byron's words, "the poet of all circles and the idol of his own." Byron himself made Moore the custodian of his memoirs, which Moore published in 1830 as *Letters and Journals of Lord Byron: with Notes of His Life.* Despite his popularity and his commercial successes—his Oriental romance *Lalla Rookh* (1816) brought him a 3,000-guinea advance—his last years were darkened by the death of his children and his own mental deterioration.

Moore found the story of the children of Lir among the Irish manuscripts belonging to the Countess of Moira. Noting that the entire narrative would require more verses "than anyone is authorized to inflict upon an audience at once," Moore offered the two-stanza "Song of Fionnuala," which suggests that Lir's children were a metaphor for Ireland, since both were enchanted and both waited for heaven to deliver them.

The Minstrel Boy

The minstrel boy to the war is gone,
    In the ranks of death you'll find him,
His father's sword he has girded on,
    And his wild harp slung behind him.
"Land of song!" said the warrior bard,
    "Though all the world betrays thee,
One sword, at least, thy rights shall guard,
    One faithful harp shall praise thee!"

The minstrel fell!—but the foeman's chain
    Could not bring his proud soul under;
The harp he loved ne'er spoke again,
    For he tore its chords asunder;
And said, "No chains shall sully thee,
    Thou soul of love and bravery!
Thy songs were made for the pure and free,
    They shall never sound in slavery!"

The Song of Fionnuala

Silent, O Moyle! be the roar of thy water,
    Break not, ye breezes, your chain of repose,
While, murmuring mournfully, Lir's lonely daughter
    Tells to the night-star her tale of woes.
When shall the swan, her death-note singing,
    Sleep, with wings in darkness furled?
When will heaven, its sweet bell ringing,
    Call my spirit from this stormy world?

Sadly, O Moyle! to thy winter wave weeping,
    Fate bids me languish long ages away!
Yet still in her darkness doth Erin lie sleeping,
    Still doth the pure light its dawning delay!
When will that day-star, mildly springing,

Warm our isle with peace and love?
When will heaven, its sweet bell ringing,
Call my spirit to the fields above?

Further Readings on Thomas Moore

Bibliography

MacManus, M. J. *A Bibliographical Hand-List of the First Editions of Thomas Moore.* Dublin: Alex. Thom, 1934.

Selected Works

A Centenary Selection of Moore's Melodies. Edited by David Hammond. Introduction by Seamus Heaney. Dublin: Gilbert Dalton, 1979.
Dear Harp of My Country: The Irish Melodies of Thomas Moore. Edited by James Flannery. Nashville: J. S. Sanders, 1997.
Harp That Once Through Tara's Halls. Champagne, Ill.: Project Gutenberg Net Library, 1990.
Lalla Rookh: An Oriental Romance. London: Darf, 1986.
Letters and Journals of Lord Byron: with Notes of His Life. London: John Murray, 1830.
The Letters of Thomas Moore. 2 vols. Edited by Wilfred S. Dowden. Oxford: Clarendon Press, 1964.
The Memoirs, Journal and Correspondence of Thomas Moore. Edited by Lord John Russell. London: Longmans, 1853–56.
Moore's Irish Melodies: The Illustrated 1846 Edition. Mineola, N.Y.: Dover, 2000.
Poetical Works of the Late Thomas Little, esq. 1801. Reprint, Oxford: Woodstock Books, 1990.
The Poetical Works of Thomas Moore. Edited by A. D. Godley. London: Henry Frowde, 1910.
Political and Historical Writings on Irish and British Affairs. Belfast: Athol Books, 1993.

Biography and Criticism

de Ford, Miriam Allen. *Thomas Moore.* New York: Twayne, 1967.
Jordan, Hoover. *Bolt Upright: The Life of Thomas Moore.* 2 vols. Salzburg: Salzburg Institut für Englische Sprache und Literatur, 1975.
Tessier, Therese. *The Bard of Erin. A Study of Thomas Moore's "Irish Melodies," 1808–1834.* Atlantic Highlands, N.J.: Humanities Press, 1981.
White, Terence de Vere. *Tom Moore: The Irish Poet.* London: Hamish Hamilton, 1977.

Anthony Raftery (1784–1835)

One still hears Raftery's songs sung in the west of Ireland—love songs like "An Pósae Glégeal" (The bright flower), written to celebrate Mary Hynes, a local beauty, or "Anach-Cuain" (Annaghdown), which commemorates a local tragedy: the drowning in Lough Corrib of nineteen young people on their way to a fair in Galway. One cannot compare Raftery with such sophisticated and accomplished Munster poets as Aogán Ó Rathaille and Eoghan Rua Ó Suilleabháin; nevertheless, Raftery's songs share the simplicity and passion of the best of Irish folk songs and ballads.

Raftery was born in Lias Ard, County Mayo, near Killedan, the house of his landlord Frank Taafe, He received some education at a local hedge school, but left when he was blinded by smallpox at the age of nine. He was encouraged to take up music by Mrs. Taafe, but—though he was said to have been "taught by the fairies"—he was only a poor fiddler. After Taafe banished him in connection with the accidental death of a favorite horse, Raftery went to South Galway, where he remained a wandering minstrel until his death on Christmas Eve, 1835. Raftery was something of a cult figure for Hyde, Yeats, and Lady Gregory. Indeed, the latter arranged for a stone to mark his grave in Killeenin, near Craughwell; it was dedicated at a *feis* in August, 1900.

Douglas Hyde published two collections of Raftery's poems, the first with help from Lady Gregory. Hyde's play "An Posadh" (The Marriage) is based on an account of Raftery at the wedding of a poor pair near Cappaghtagle, Yeats cited Raftery's "Antoine Ó Dalaigh" and "An Pósae Glégeal" in his essays "The Literary Movement in Ireland" and "Dust Hath Closed Helen's Eye," and alludes to Raftery in both section 2 of "The Tower" and "Coole Park and Ballylee, 1931." A number of writers have made their own translations or adaptations of Raftery's work, including Padraic Fallon, Lady Gregory, Thomas Kinsella, Donagh MacDonagh, and Desmond O'Grady. Finally, he is a figure in three of Austin Clarke's poems: "A Centenary Tribute," "F. R. Higgins," and "Paupers."

Scholars have concluded that the language, rhyme, and thought in "Mise Raifterí" strongly suggest it was written by someone else (perhaps Hyde himself), although based on a genuine tradition that owes much of its flavor, at the very least, to the poet. James Stephens made another translation of it, while Derek Mahon's "I Am Raftery" is a modern parody.

[handwritten: Loss of filid identity]

I Am Raftery

[handwritten: Translation by Lady Gregory + Douglas Hyde]

Said to have been Raftery's response to someone who asked who he was.

I am Raftery the poet,
Full of hope and love,
With eyes that have no light, — *[handwritten: blinded by small pox]*
With gentleness that has no misery.

[handwritten: Became a wandering minstrel — farmers became his patrons]

Going west upon my pilgrimage
By the light of my heart,
Feeble and tired
To the end of my road.

Behold me now,
And my face to a wall,
A-playing music
Unto empty pockets.

trans. Douglas Hyde

Raftery's Praise of Mary Hynes

[handwritten: Love song tradition developed in this poem; Mary Hynes invites the poet in for a drink]

Going to Mass by the will of God, the day came wet and the wind rose; I met Mary Hynes at the cross of Kiltartan, and I fell in love with her there and then. I spoke to her kind and mannerly, as by report was her own way; and she said "Raftery, my mind is easy; you may come to-day to Ballylee."

When I heard her offer I did not linger; when only talk went to my heart my heart rose. We have only to go across the three fields; we had daylight with us to Ballylee.

The table was laid with glasses and a quart measure; she had fair hair and she sitting beside me; and she said "drink, Raftery, and a hundred welcomes; there is a strong cellar in Ballylee,"

O star of light and O sun in harvest; O amber hair, O my share of the world! Will you come with me on the Sunday, till we agree together before all the people?

I would not begrudge you a song every Sunday evening; punch on the table or wine if you would drink it. But O King of Glory, dry the roads before me till I find the way to Ballylee.

There is sweet air on the side of the hill, when you are looking down upon Ballylee; When you are walking in the valley picking nuts and blackberries, there
is music of the birds in it and music of the Sidhe.

What is the worth of greatness till you have the light of the flower of the
branch that is by your side? There is no good to deny it or to try and hide it;
she is the sun in the heavens who wounded my heart.

There was no part in Ireland I did not travel, from the rivers to the tops of the
mountains; to the edge of Lough Greine whose mouth is hidden, and I saw no
beauty but was behind hers.

Her hair was shining and her brows were shining too; her face was like herself,
her mouth pleasant and sweet; She is the pride and I give her the branch: she
is the shining flower of Ballylee.

It is Mary Hynes, the calm and easy woman, has beauty in her mind and in her
face. If a hundred clerks were gathered together, they could not write down a
half of her ways.

trans. Lady Gregory

Lake Corrib 19 youth
drowning on the way
on the Galway
fair

Anach-Cuain (The Drowning of Annach Doon)

If I get health, it is long there shall be talk,
    Of all who were drowned at Annach Down,
And my grief: on the morrow each father and mother,
    Wife and child a-shedding eyes;
O, King of the Graces, who hast shaped Heaven and Paradise
    Were it not small the grief to us two or three,
But a day so fine as it was, without wind, without rain,
    To sweep away the full of a boat of them!

Was it not great the wonder, forenent the people,
    To see them stretched on the backs of their heads,
Screaming and crying that would terrify people,
    Hair a-dishevelling, and the spoil being divided?
Pathos
There were young boys there on the coming of harvest,
    Being stretched on the bier and being taken to the churchyard,
And sure it was the materials for their wedding that served for their
        wake,
    And, O God of Glory, is it not great the pity!

It was on Friday you would hear the keening
    Coming on every side, and the clapping of hands together,
And numbers of people, after the night, heavy, weary, overthrown,
    With nothing for them to do but to lay-out corpses.
O God, and O Christ, who suffered as an offering (?),
    Who hast purchased truly the poor and the naked,
To holy Paradise, mayest Thou bring free with Thee
    Each creature of them who has fallen beneath the lot,

A bitter blame to be on the same place [where they died],
    That star may never shine on it and that sun may never rise on it!
Which has drowned all those who journeyed together
    To Galway, to the fair, early a-Thursday.
The men who used to get-ready harrow and plough,
    Who used to turn-up fallows and scatter seed,
And the women according, who would make everything
    Who would spin freize and then linen.

Ballyclare was nigh hand,
    But the luck did not suffer them to go up to it;
Death was so strong that he gave no respite
    To a single mother's son of all that were ever born.
Unless it be a thing that was decreed for them, on this day of their
        drowning,
    O King of Graces! was it not a poor thing!
But to lose them all, without (their being on) lake or brine,
    Through a vile old boat, and they close to land!

O King of Graces, who hast created Heaven and Paradise,
    And O God! what were the grief to us, two or three,
But on a day so fine, without wind, without rain,
    And the full of the boat of them to go to the bottom.
The boat broke and the people were drowned,
    The sheep scattered over in the water;
And O God, is it not there the great slaughter was made
    Of eleven men and of eight women.

There were fathers and mothers there, women and children.
    Crying and calling and shedding tears,
Women accordingly, who would make anything,
    Who would spin freize and then linen.

O Thomas O'Cahill, you were the great pity;
    You would plough the fallow-land and you would scatter seed,
And the numbers of boys who used to shake hands with you!
    My grief, and you drowned in Annaghdown!

O John O Cosgair [Cosgrave] you were the great pity
    That you ever stood in ship or boat,
And all the vigorous steps you travelled
    From London over to Beltra.
When you thought to make a swimming
    The young women caught hold of you on this side and that,
And sure your little-mother thought though a hundred men might be
        drowned
    That yourself [at least] would come home to her safe.

There was Mary Ruane there, a bright young-shoot,
    The sky-like girl that we had in the place;
She dressed herself up, early a Wednesday,
    To go to the fair from Knock Delain.
She had a coat upon her of choice cloth,
    A lace cap, and white ribbons,
And she has left her little-mother sorrowful, ruined,
    Shedding the tears again for ever.

A mountain-burning and a scalding breast
    Be on the place where they expired, and a hard reproach,
For it is many is the creature it has left bitterly-weeping,
    Shedding tears, and lamenting each Monday morning.
It was no lack of knowledge that sent them out of their right-direction.
    But great misfortune that was in Caislean-Nuadh,
And the finishing of the song is—that many were drowned,
    Which has left cause of grief to Annach Doon.

                    trans. Douglas Hyde

*J. Clarence Mangan — wore outlandish
clothes inc. a huge cloak, green
spectacles pointed hat (a notable
Dublin figure) He admired De Quincey
who also experimented w/drugs.*

Further Readings on Anthony Raftery

Selected Works

Abhráin atá Leagtha ar an Reachtúire: Songs Ascribed to Raftery, Being the Fifth Chapter of the Songs of Connacht. Translated by Douglas Hyde. 1903. Reprint, Shannon: Irish University Press, 1973.

Blind Raftery: Selected Poems. Edited by Criostóir Ó Floinn. Indreabhán, Ireland: Cló Iar-Chonnachta, 1998.

Biography and Criticism

Gregory, Augusta, "Raftery," "The Poet Raftery," "Raftery's Repentance"; "A Red-Letter Day in Killeenan." In *Poets and Dreamers*. Foreword by T. R. Henn. 1903. Reprint, Gerrards Cross, UK: Colin Smythe, 1974.

Ní Cheannain, Áine. *Raifteirí an File*. Dublin: Foilseacháin Náisiúnta, 1984.

O'Rourke, Brian. "County Mayo in Gaelic Folksong." In *Mayo: Aspects of its Heritage*, edited by Bernard O'Hara, 153–56, 291–96. Galway: Corrib, 1982.

[handwritten: (Poets of real merit in 19th cont. Ireland were essentially non-political)]

James Clarence Mangan (1803–1849)

Mangan is often cited as the most significant poetic precursor of the Irish Renaissance: no less than Yeats and Joyce became his champions in later generations. Born to an impoverished Dublin Catholic grocer, Mangan led a life of unrelieved misery and died, perhaps of starvation or malnutrition, during a cholera epidemic. He was a lonely, sickly, eccentric character, addicted either to alcohol or to opium. Much in his life and work invite comparisons with Poe: both were fascinated by extreme states of psychic distress and both experimented in verse techniques. Despite his isolation, Mangan was published in the leading Dublin journals, including the first edition of *The Nation* (1842), the organ of Young Ireland, and *The Dublin University Review*. Many of Mangan's best works are "translations" from languages he had not studied. His translations from the Irish, for example, rely on the prose paraphrases of intermediaries.

His "translations" from Arabic and Persian, such as "To the Ingleezee Khafir," were once dismissed but recently have been cited in discussions of colonialism and imperialism. At question is how a colonized Irishman like Mangan viewed exotic Orientals beyond the British Empire.

"Dark Rosaleen" is Mangan's version of *Róisín Dubh,* a seventeenth-century poem ascribed to Owen Roe MacWard. Mangan produced three versions, of which the best-known, from *The Nation* of May 30, 1846, appears here; a later version, though less favored by critics, is arguably closer to the original text. The phrases *Róisín Dubh* and "Dark Rosaleen" both indicate a personification of Ireland.

Dark Rosaleen

O my Dark Rosaleen,
    Do not sigh, do not weep!
The priests are on the ocean green,
    They march along the Deep.
There's wine . . . from the royal Pope
    Upon the ocean green;
And Spanish ale shall give you hope,
    My Dark Rosaleen!
    My own Rosaleen!
Shall glad your heart, shall give you hope,
Shall give you health, and help, and hope,
    My Dark Rosaleen.

Over hills and through dales
    Have I roamed for your sake;
All yesterday I sailed with sails
    On river and on lake.
The Erne . . . at its highest flood
    I dashed across unseen,
Fen there was lightning in my blood,
    My Dark Rosaleen!
    My own Rosaleen!
Oh! there was lightning in my blood,
Red lightning lightened through my blood,
    My Dark Rosaleen!

All day long in unrest
    To and fro do I move
The very soul within my breast
    Is wasted for you, love!

The heart . . . in my bosom faints
    To think of you, my Queen,
My life of life, my saint of saints,
      My Dark Rosaleen!
      My own Rosaleen!
To hear your sweet and sad complaints,
My life, my love, my saint of saints,
      My Dark Rosaleen!

Woe and pain, pain and woe,
    Are my lot night and noon,
To see your bright face clouded so,
    Like to the mournful moon.
But yet . . . will I rear your throne
    Again in golden sheen;
'Tis you shall reign, shall reign alone,
      My Dark Rosaleen!
      My own Rosaleen!
'Tis you shall have the golden throne,
'Tis you shall reign, and reign alone,
      My Dark Rosaleen!

Over dews, over sands
    Will I fly for your weal;
Your holy delicate white hands
    Shall girdle me with steel.
At home . . . in your emerald bowers,
    From morning's dawn till e'en,
You'll pray for me, my flower of flowers,
      My Dark Rosaleen!
      My fond Rosaleen!
You'll think of me through daylight's hours,
My virgin flower, my flower of flowers,
      My Dark Rosaleen!

I could scale the blue air,
    I could plough the high hills,
Oh, I could kneel all night in prayer,
    To heal your many ills!

And one . . . beamy smile from you
    Would float like light between
My toils and me, my own, my true,
    My Dark Rosaleen!
    My fond Rosaleen!
Would give me life and soul anew,
A second life, a soul anew,
    My Dark Rosaleen!

O! the Erne shall run red
    With redundance of blood,
The earth shall rock beneath our tread,
    And flames wrap hill and wood,
And gun-peal, and slogan cry,
    Wake many a glen serene,
Ere you shall fade, ere you shall die,
    My Dark Rosaleen!
    My own Rosaleen!
The Judgement Hour must first be nigh,
Ere you can fade, ere you can die,
    My Dark Rosaleen!

The Nameless One

Roll forth, my song, like the rushing river,
    That sweeps along to the mighty sea;
God will inspire me while I deliver
    My soul of thee!

Tell thou the world, when my bones lie whitening
    Amid the last homes of youth and eld.
That there was once one whose veins ran lightning
    No eye beheld.

Tell how his boyhood was one drear night-hour,
    How shone for *him*, through is griefs and gloom,
No star of all heaven sends to light our
    Path to the tomb.

Roll on, my song, and to after ages
    Tell how, disdaining all earth can give,
He would have taught men, from wisdom's pages,
    The way to live.

And tell how trampled, derided, hated,
    And worn by weakness, disease, and wrong,
He fled for shelter to God, who mated
    His soul with song—

With song which alway, sublime or vapid,
    Flowed like a rill in the morning beam,
Perchance not deep, but intense and rapid—
    A mountain stream.

Tell how this Nameless, condemned for years long
    To herd with demons from hell beneath,
Saw things that made him, with groans and tears, long
    For even death.

Go on to tell how, with genius wasted,
    Betrayed in friendship, befooled in love,
With spirit shipwrecked, and young hopes blasted,
    He still, still strove.

Till, spent with toil, dreeing death for others,
    And some whose hands should have wrought for him
(If children live not for sires and mothers),
    His mind grew dim.

And he fell far through that pit abysmal
    The gulf and grave of Maginn and Burns,
And pawned his soul for the devil's dismal
    Stock of returns

But yet redeemed it in days of darkness
    And shapes and signs of the final wrath.
When death, in hideous and ghastly starkness,
    Stood on his path.

And tell how now, amid wreck and sorrow,
   And want, and sickness, and houseless nights.
He bides in calmness the silent morrow,
   That no ray lights.

And lives he still, then? Yes! Old and hoary
   At thirty-nine, from despair and woe,
He lives enduring what future story
   Will never know.

Him grant a grave to, yet pitying noble,
   Deep in your bosoms! There let him dwell!
He, too, had tears for all souls in trouble,
   Here and in hell.

Shapes and Signs

I see black dragons mount the sky,
   I see earth yawn beneath my feet—
   I feel within the asp, the worm
That will not sleep and cannot die,
   Fair though may show the winding-sheet!
   I hear all night as through a storm
   Hoarse voices calling, calling
   My name upon the wind—
   All omens monstrous and appalling
   Affright my guilty mind.

I exult alone in one wild hour—
   That hour in which the red cup drowns
   The memories it anon renews
In ghastlier guise, in fiercer power—
   Then Fancy brings me golden crowns,
   And visions of all brilliant hues
   Lap my lost soul in gladness,
   Until I wake again,
   And the dark lava-fires of madness
   Once more sweep through my brain.

To the Ingleezee Khafir, Calling Himself Djaun Bool Djenkinzun

Thus writeth Meer Djafrit—
    I hate thee, Djaun Bool,
Worse than Márid or Afrit,
    Or corpse-eating Ghool.
I hate thee like Sin,
    For thy mop-head of hair,
Thy snub nose and bald chin,
    And thy turkeycock air.
Thou vile Ferindjee!
    That thou thus shouldst disturb an
Old Moslim like me,
    With my Khizzilbash turban,
Old fogy like me,
    With my Khizzilbash turban.

I spit on thy clothing,
    That garb for baboons
I eye with deep loathing
    Thy tight pantaloons!
I curse the cravat
    That encircles thy throat,
And thy cooking-pot hat,
    And thy swallow-tailed coat!
Go, hide thy thick sconce
    In some hovel suburban;
Or else don at once
    The red Moosleman turban.
Thou dog, don at once
    The grand Khizzilbash turban!

Further Readings on James Clarence Mangan

Bibliography

Chuto, Jacques. *James Clarence Mangan: A Bibliography.* Dublin: Irish Academic Press, 1999.

Holzapfel, Rudi P. *James Clarence Mangan: A Checklist of Printed and Other Sources.* Dublin: Scepter, 1969.

———. "Mangan's Poetry in the *Dublin University Magazine:* A Bibliography." *Hermathena* 105:40–54.

Selected Works

Autobiography. Edited by James Kilroy. Dublin: Dolmen, 1968.

Collected Works of James Clarence Mangan. Edited by Jacques Chuto. *Poems,* 4 vols. *Prose,* 2 vols. *General Index.* Dublin: Irish Academic Press, 1996–2002.

James Clarence Mangan: His Selected Poems. Edited and with a study by L. I. Guiney. Boston: Lamson-Wolfe, 1897.

Poems. Edited and with preface and notes by D. J. O'Donoghue. Dublin: O'Donoghue and Co., 1903.

Poems. Edited by David Wheatley. Oldcastle, Ireland: Gallery Press, 2003.

The Prose Writings. Edited by D. J. O'Donoghue. Essay by Lionel Johnson. Dublin: O'Donoghue and Co., 1904.

Selected Poems. Edited by Jacques Chuto. Dublin: Irish Academic Press, 2002.

Biography and Criticism

Clifford, Brendan. *The Dubliner: The Lives, Times and Writings of James Clarence Mangan.* Belfast: Athol Books, 1988.

D'Alton, Louis. *The Man in the Cloak: A Play About James Clarence Mangan.* In *Two Plays.* London: Macmillan, 1938. Reprint, Dublin: Bourke, 1971.

Donaghy, Henry J. *James Clarence Mangan.* New York: Twayne, 1974.

Joyce, James. "James Clarence Mangan." 1902. Reprinted in *James Joyce: The Critical Writings,* edited by Ellsworth Mason and Richard Ellmam, 73–83. New York: Viking, 1959.

Kilroy, James. *James Clarence Mangan.* Lewisburg, Pa.: Bucknell University Press, 1970.

Lloyd, David. *Nationalism and Minor Literature: James Clarence Mangan and the Emergence of Irish Cultural Nationalism.* Berkeley: University of California Press, 1987.

MacCarthy, Anne. *James Clarence Mangan, Edward Walsh, and Nineteenth Century Irish Literature in English.* Lewiston, N.Y.: Edwin Mellen, 2000.

O'Donoghue, D. J. *The Life and Writings of J. C. Mangan.* Edinburgh: P. Geddes, 1897.

Shannon-Mangan, Ellen. *James Clarence Mangan: A Biography*. Blackrock, Ireland: Irish Academic Press, 1996.

Sheridan, Desmond. *James Clarence Mangan*. Dublin: Talbot, 1936.

Yeats, William Butler. "Clarence Mangan." *Irish Fireside*. Reprinted in *Uncollected Prose*. Vol. 1, 114–19. Edited by John Frayne. New York: Columbia University Press, 1970.

[handwritten: Basically a dull poet with important intentions]

Samuel Ferguson (1810–1886)

Samuel Ferguson was one of the first writers to realize the possibilities of a national literature based on Irish myth and legend. Born in Belfast and educated at the Belfast Academical Institute and at Trinity College, Dublin, Ferguson was trained as a lawyer and called to the Irish bar in 1838. However, he gave up his practice to become the first deputy keeper of records in 1869, and was knighted for his service to the state in 1878.

Ferguson's poetry was informed by his knowledge of Irish antiquarianism. More than a keen amateur, though, he was elected president of the Royal Irish Academy in 1881. The Ordnance Survey project (1828), which brought together such brilliant scholars as John O'Donovan, Eugene O'Curry, and Sir Charles Petrie to collect place-names and topographical lore, stimulated Ferguson's interest in antiquities. O'Donovan's translation of the *Battle of Magh Rath* inspired Ferguson's *Congal* (written 1861, published 1872), an epic describing the conflict between Congal and Donald, which is to say, between paganism and Christianity. Yeats later drew upon *Congal* as a source for *On Baile's Strand* (1904) and *The Herne's Egg* (1938).

Ferguson turned to translating when he reviewed James Hardiman's *Irish Minstrelsy or Bardic Remains of Ireland* (1831) in a series of essays for the *Dublin University Review* in 1834. He judged Hardiman's translations to be too artificial, and offered instead his own, which were more faithful to the original and which retained their Irish rhythms. Indeed, poems like "Cashel of Munster" and "Dear Dark Head" demonstrated the potential for Irish metrics in Anglo-Irish poetry to such distinguished successors as Yeats and Austin Clarke.

Cashel of Munster *[handwritten: a translation]*   *[handwritten: Love poems (conflicted)]*

I'd wed you without herds, without money, or rich array,
And I'd wed you on a dewy morning at day-dawn gray;
My bitter woe it is, love, that we are not far away
In Cashel town, though the bare deal board were our marriage bed this
    day!

Oh, fair maid, remember the green hill side,
Remember how I hunted about the valleys wide;
Time now has worn me; my locks are turned to gray,
The year is scarce and I am poor, but send me not, love, away!

Oh, deem not my blood is of base strain, my girl, *[handwritten: Class difference]*
Oh, deem not my birth was as the birth of the churl;
Marry me, and prove me, and say soon you will,
That noble blood is written on my right side still!

My purse holds no red gold, no coin of the silver white,
No herds are mine to drive through the long twilight!
But the pretty girl that would take me, all bare though I be and lone,
Oh, I'd take her with me kindly to the county Tyrone.

Oh, my girl, I can see 'tis in trouble you are,
And, oh, my girl, I see 'tis your people's reproach you bear;
[handwritten: voice of the lover (female)] "I am a girl in trouble for his sake with whom I fly,
And, oh, may no other maiden know such reproach as I!"

Dear Dark Head   *[handwritten: translation]*

Put your head, darling, darling, darling,
    Your darling black head my heart above;
Oh, mouth of honey, with the thyme for fragrance,
    Who, with heart in breast, could deny you love?
Oh, many and many a young girl for me is pining,
    Letting her locks of gold to the cold wind free,
For me, the foremost of our gay young fellows;
    But I'd leave a hundred, pure love, for thee!
Then put your head, darling, darling, darling,
    Your darling black head my heart above;
Oh, mouth of honey, with the thyme for fragrance,
    Who, with heart in breast, could deny you love?

Further Readings on Samuel Ferguson

Bibliography

Ferguson, Lady Mary Catherine. *Sir Samuel Ferguson in the Ireland of His Day.* Vol. 2, 369–74. Edinburgh: William Blackwood and Sons, 1896.

Selected Works

Congal. London: G. Bell and Sons, 1872.
Lays of the Western Gael. London: Bell, 1862.
Lays of the Western Gael. 1865. Reprint, Otley, UK: Woodstock, 2001.
Poems. Edited by Padraic Colum. Dublin: Hodges, Figgis, 1963.
The Poetry of Sir Samuel Ferguson. Edited by John O'Hagan. Dublin: Gill, 1887.

Biography and Criticism

Brown, Malcolm. *Sir Samuel Ferguson.* Lewisburg, Pa.: Bucknell University Press, 1973.
Denman, Peter. *Samuel Ferguson: The Literary Achievement.* Gerrards Cross, UK: Colin Smythe, 1990.
Ferguson, Lady Mary Catherine. *Sir Samuel Ferguson in the Ireland of His Day.* 2 vols. Edinburgh: William Blackwood and Sons, 1896.
O'Driscoll, Robert. *An Ascendancy of the Heart: Ferguson and the Beginnings of Modern Irish Literature.* Dublin: Dolmen, 1976.
———. "Sir Samuel Ferguson and the Idea of an Irish National Literature." *Éire-Ireland* 6:82–95.
Yeats, William Butler. "The Poetry of Sir Samuel Ferguson—I," "The Poetry of Sir Samuel Ferguson—II," edited by John P. Frayne. In *Uncollected Prose by W. B. Yeats.* Vol. I: *First Reviews and Articles, 1886–1896,* 81–87; 87–104. 1886. Reprint, New York: Columbia University Press, 1970.

Thomas Davis (1814–1845)

[handwritten annotation: mediocre poet but brilliant leader & patriot & essayist]

Thomas Davis was to nineteenth-century Irish cultural unity what Daniel O'Connell was to nineteenth-century Irish political unity. His 1840 valedictory speech to the Historical Society of Trinity College, Dublin, can be compared with Ralph Waldo Emerson's 1837 Phi Beta Kappa address, "The American Scholar," in its call for cultural autonomy.

[handwritten annotation: Ireland's call for cultural autonomy]

In September 1842, Davis founded *The Nation* with John Blake Dillon and Charles Gavan Duffy. The paper's nationalist ideals informed Irish politics for the rest of the century, and on into our own time. When *The Nation* proposed compiling a ballad history of Ireland, Davis wrote that such a project would ". . . make Irish history familiar to the minds, pleasant to the ears, dear to the passions and powerful over the taste and conduct of Irish people in times to come." His own contributions, especially ballads like the "Lament for the Death of Eoghan Ruadh O'Neill," awaken in the Irish people a sense of the nobility of the Irish past. (The death of O'Neill, who had been responsible for a brilliant victory at Benburb in 1649, removed the only Irish leader who could have challenged Cromwell.) "The West's Asleep" alludes to the familiar Barbarossa legend of the sleeping hero who will awaken to help his people in their hour of need.

"Our National Language" (1843), one of a series of essays about the relationships between Irish cultural and national identity, anticipates the work of the Gaelic League fifty years later. His admonition, "Educate that you may be free," has been commemorated in the Thomas Davis Lectures, long a feature of Radio Éireann.

David died suddenly on September 16, 1845—just one week after the first reports of a potato blight in Ireland.

Lament for the Death of Eoghan Ruadh O'Neill

TIME—*10th November, 1649.* SCENE—*Ormond's Camp, County Waterford.*
SPEAKERS—*A veteran of Eoghan O'Neill's clan, and one of the horsemen, just arrived with an account of his death.*

I

"Did they dare, did they dare, to slay Eoghan Ruadh O'Neill?"
"Yes, they slew with poison him, they feared to meet with steel."
"May God wither up their hearts! May their blood cease to flow!
"May they walk in living death, who poisoned Eoghan Ruadh!

II

"Though it break my heart to hear, say again the bitter words."
"From Derry, against Cromwell, he marched to measure swords:
But the weapon of the Sassanach met him on his way,
And he died at Cloch Uachtar, upon St. Leonard's day.

III

"Wail, wail ye for the Mighty One! Wail, wail, ye for the Dead!
Quench the hearth, and hold the breath—with ashes strew the head.
How tenderly we loved him! How deeply we deplore!
Holy Saviour! but to think we shall never see him more.

IV

"Sagest in the council was he, kindest in the hall!
Sure we never won a battle—'twas Eoghan won them all
Had he lived—had he lived—our dear country had been free;
But he's dead, but he's dead, and 'tis slaves we'll ever be.

[handwritten marginal note: a last hope for Ireland]

V

"O'Farrell and Clanrickarde, Preston and Red Hugh,
Audley, and MacMahon, ye are valiant, wise, and true;
But—what, what are ye all to our darling who is gone?
The Rudder of our Ship was he, our Castle's corner stone!

VI

"Wail, wail him through the Island! Weep, weep, for our pride!
Would that on the battle-field our gallant chief had died!
Weep the Victor of Beann-bhorb—weep him, young men and old;
Weep for him, ye women—your Beautiful lies cold!

[handwritten marginal note: Title for Plunkett's short story]

VII

"We thought you would not die—we were sure you would not go,
And leave us in our utmost need to Cromwell's cruel blow—
Sheep without a shepherd, when the snow shuts out the sky—
Oh! why did you leave us, Eoghan? Why did you die?

[handwritten marginal note: what Eoghan suffered at the hands of the British? now Peter suffer at the hands of his own people]

VIII

"Soft as woman's was your voice, O'Neill! bright was your eye,
Oh! why did you leave us, Eoghan? Why did you die?

Your troubles are all over, you're at rest with God on high,
But we're slaves, and we're orphans, Eoghan!—why didst thou die?"

The West's Asleep

*Ballad
(Davis had a
good heart
but a "cloth ear"*

AIR—*The Brink of the White Rocks.*

I

*alludes to
Barbarossa
legend of
sleeping)
The hero who will
awaken & help
his people in
Their hour of
need.*

When all beside a vigil keep,
The West's asleep, the West's asleep—
Alas! and well may Erin weep,
When Connacht lies in slumber deep.
There lake and plain smile fair and free,
'Mid rocks—their guardian chivalry—
Sing oh! let man learn liberty
From crashing wind and lashing sea.

II

That chainless wave and lovely land
Freedom and Nationhood demand—
Be sure, the great God never planned,
For slumbering slaves, a home so grand.
And, long, a brave and haughty race
Honoured and sentinelled the place—
Sing oh! not even their sons' disgrace
Can quite destroy their glory's trace.

III

For often, in O'Connor's van,
To triumph dashed each Connacht clan—
And fleet as deer the Normans ran
Through Corlieu's Pass and Ardrahan.
And later times saw deeds as brave;
And glory guards Clanrickarde's grave—
Sing oh! they died their land to save,
At Aughrim's slopes and Shannon's wave.

IV

And if, when all a vigil keep,
The West's asleep, the West's asleep—
Alas! and well may Erin weep,
That Connacht lies in slumber deep.
But, hark! some voice like thunder spake:
"The West's awake! the West's awake!"—
"Sing oh! hurra! let England quake,
We'll watch till death for Erin's sake!"

From "Our National Language," Part I
(*The Nation*, April 1, 1843)

[handwritten: Time of famine beginning]

Men are ever valued most for peculiar and original qualities.

A man who can only talk common-place, and act according to routine, has little weight. To speak, look, and do what your own soul from its depths orders you, are credentials of greatness which all men understand and acknowledge. Such a man's dictum has more influence than the reasoning of an imitative or common-place. He fills his circle with confidence. He is self-possessed, firm, accurate, and daring. Such men are the pioneers of civilization, and the rulers of the human heart.

Why should not nations be judged thus? Is not a full indulgence of its natural tendencies essential to a people's greatness? Force the manners, dress, language, and constitution of Russia, on Italy, or Norway, or America, and you instantly stunt and distort the whole mind of either people.

The language, which grows up with a people, is conformed to their organs, descriptive of their climate, constitution, and manners, mingled inseparably with their history, and their soil, fitted beyond any other language to express their prevalent thoughts in the most natural efficient way.

To impose another language on such a people is to send their history adrift among the accidents of translation—'tis to tear their identity from all places—'tis to substitute arbitrary signs for picturesque and suggestive names—'tis to cut off the entail of feeling, and separate the people from their forefathers by deep gulf—'tis to corrupt their very organs, and abridge their power of expression.

The language of a nation's youth is the only easy and full speech for its manhood and for its age. And when the language of its cradle goes, itself craves a tomb.

What business has a Russian for the rippling language of Italy or India? How could a Greek distort his organs and his soul to speak Dutch upon the sides of the Hymettus, or the beach of Salamis, or on the waste where once was Sparta? And is it befitting the fiery, delicate-organed Celt to abandon his beautiful tongue, docile and spirited as an Arab, "sweet as music, strong as the wave"—is it befitting in him to abandon this wild liquid speech for the mongrel of a hundred breeds called English, which, powerful though it be, creaks, and bangs about the Celt who tries to use it?

We lately met a glorious thought in the *Triads of Mochmed,* printed in one of the Welsh codes by the Record Commission. "There are three things without which there is no country—common language, common judicature, and co-tillage land—for without these a country cannot support itself in peace and social union."

A people without a language of its own is only half a nation. A nation should guard its language more than its territories—'tis a surer barrier, and more important frontier, than fortress or river.

And in good times it has ever been thought so. Who had dared to propose the adoption of Persian or Egyptian in Greece?—how had Pericles thundered at the barbarian! How had Cato scourged from the forum him who would have given the Attic or Gallic speech to men of Rome! How proudly and how nobly Germany stopped "the incipient creeping" progress of French! And no sooner had she succeeded than her genius, which had tossed in a hot trance, sprung up fresh and triumphant.

Had Pyrrhus quelled Italy, or Xerxes subdued Greece for a time long enough to impose new languages, where had been the literature which gives a pedigree to human genius? Even liberty recovered had been sickly and insecure without the language with which it had hunted in the woods, worshipped at the fruit-strewn altar, debated on the council-hill, and shouted in the battle-charge.

There is a fine song of the Frisians which describes *"language linked to liberty."* To lose your native tongue, and learn that of an alien, is the worst badge of conquest—it is the chain on the soul. To have lost entirely the national language is death; the fetter has worn through. So long as the Saxon held to his German speech he could hope to resume his land from the Norman; now, if he is to be free and locally governed, he must build himself a new home. There is hope for Scotland—strong hope for Wales—sure hope for Hungary. The speech of the alien is not universal in the one; is gallantly held at bay in the other; is nearly expelled from the third.

How unnatural—how corrupting—'tis for us, three-fourths of whom are of Celtic blood, to speak a medley of Teutonic dialects. If we add the Celtic Scots, who came back here from the thirteenth to the seventeenth centuries, and the Celtic Welsh, who colonised many parts of the Wexford and other Leinster counties, to the Celts who never left Ireland, probably five-sixths, or more of us are Celts. What business have we with the Norman-Sasanach?

Nor let any doubt these proportions because of the number of English names in Ireland. With a politic cruelty, the English of the Pale passed an Act compelling every Irishman within English jurisdiction, "to go like to one Englishman in apparel, and shaving off his beard above the mouth," "and shall take to him an English sirname of one town, as Sutton, Chester, Trym, Skyrne, Corke, Kinsale; or colour, as White, Blacke, Browne; or art of science, as Smith, or Carpenter; or office, as Cook, Butler; and that he and his issue shall use this name under pain of forfeiting his goods yearly."

And just as this parliament before the Reformation, so did another after the Reformation. By the 28th Henry VII, the dress and language of the Irish were insolently described as barbarous by the minions of that ruffian king, and were utterly forbidden and abolished under many penalties and incapacities. These laws are still in force; but whether the Archaeological Society, including Peel and O'Connell, will be prosecuted, seems doubtful.

There was also, 'tis to be feared, an adoption of English names, during some periods, from fashion, fear, or meanness, Some of our best Irish names, too, have been so mangled as to require some scholarship to identify them. For these and many other reasons, the members of the Celtic race here are immensely greater than at first appears.

But this is not all; for even the Saxon and Norman colonist, notwithstanding these laws, melted down into the Irish, and adopted all their ways and language. For centuries upon centuries Irish was spoken by men of all bloods in Ireland, and English was unknown, save to a few citizens and nobles of the Pale. 'Tis only within a very later period that the majority of the people learned English.

But, it will be asked, how can the language be restored now?

We shall answer this partly by saying that, through the labours of the Archaeological and many lesser societies, it is being revived rapidly.

Nothing can make us believe that it is natural or honourable for the Irish to speak the speech of the alien, the invader, the Sasanach tyrant, and to abandon the language of our kings and heroes. What! give up the tongue of Ollamh Fodhla and Brian Boru, the tongue of M'Carthy, and the O'Neills, the tongue of Sarsfield's, Curran's, Mathew's, and O'Connell's boyhood, for that of Strafford and Poynings, Sussex, Kirk, and Cromwell!

call to embrace Gaelic

No! oh, no! the "brighter days shall surely come," and the green flag shall wave on our towers, and the sweet old language be heard once more in college, mart, and senate.

But, even should the effort to save it as the national language fail, by the attempt we will rescue its old literature, and hand down to our descendants proofs that we had a language as fit for love, and war, and business, and pleasure, as the world ever knew, and that we had not the spirit and nationality to preserve it!

Had Swift known Irish he would have sowed its seed by the side of that nationality which he planted, and the close of the last century would have seen the one as flourishing as the other. Had Ireland used Irish in 1782, would it not have impeded England's re-conquest of us? But 'tis not yet too late.

Further Readings on Thomas Davis

Bibliography

Moody, T. W. "Thomas Davis and the Irish Nation." *Hermathena* 102:5–31.

Selected Works

Essays. 1914. Reprint, New York: Lemma, 1974.
Essays and Poems with a Centenary Memoir: 1845–1945. Introduction by Eamon de Valera. Dublin: M. H. Gill and Sons, 1945.
Literary and Historical Essays. 1846. Reprint, Washington, D.C.: Woodstock, 1998.
Prose Writings. 1890. Reprint, Freeport, N.Y.: Books for Libraries, 1972.
Thomas Davis, Selections from His Prose and Poetry. 1914. Reprint, New York: AMS Press, 1982.

Biography and Criticism

Duffy, Charles Gavan. *Thomas Davis: The Memoirs of an Irish Patriot, 1840–1846.* London: T. Fisher Unwin, 1890.
———. *Young Ireland: A Fragment of Irish History, 1840–1845.* 2 vols. London: T. Fisher Unwin, 1896.
Molony, John N. *A Soul Came into Ireland: Thomas Davis, 1814–1845: A Biography.* Dublin: Geography Publications, 1995.
Moody, T. W. *Thomas Davis, 1814–1815.* Dublin: The Stationery Office, 1945.
Mulvey, Helen F. *Thomas Davis and Ireland: A Biographical Study.* Washington, D.C.: Catholic University Press, 2003.

O'Sullivan, T. F. *The Young Irelanders*. Tralee: The Kerryman, 1944.

Sullivan, Eileen. *Thomas Davis*. Lewisburg, Pa.: Bucknell, 1977.

Yeats, William Butler. *A Tribute to Thomas Davis*, etc. 1947. Reprint, Folcroft, Pa.: Folcroft Library Editions, 1977.

Yeats, William Butler, and Thomas Kinsella. *Davis, Mangan, Ferguson?* 15–20. Dublin: Dolmen Press, 1970.

PART TWO

The Irish Literary Renaissance

PART II
THE IRISH LITERARY RENAISSANCE
1885 — 1940

Celtic Revival

Matt Arnold named 4 basic charactistics of the Celtic imagination (for English readers)

① A sense of natural magic & the mystery of life

② melancholy titanism coupled with a love for brightness & lightness

Yeats 1865 — 1939

③ generousity

④ continuing rebellion vs despotism of fact

most imp. collection of folklore – The Celtic Twilight (1893) – set of short sketches of Irish story-tellers & their tales – many of. them having to do with magic & the supernatural

The Celtic Twilight is significant in the following ways ① a sort of fragmented autobiography of Yeats own discovery of himself as an Irish writer & his discovery of his affinities with the illiterate storytellers he met around Sligo & elsewhere ② Yeats's was the first popular book of Irish folklore to take seriously the beliefs of the peasant in the supernatural ③ The subject & tone of the C.T did much to create the popular impression of what Ireland & Irish writing could & should be like.

Douglas Hyde
(1860–1949)

Douglas Hyde wrote prolifically in both English and Irish, sometimes using the pseudonym "An Craoibhín Aoibhínn" (The Pleasant [or Delightful] Little Branch). He was by turns a poet, scholar, translator, folklorist, playwright, academic, and Ireland's president. His *Leabhar Sgéulaigheachta* (1889), a collection of folklore, was the first of its kind in the Irish language. He helped to found the Gaelic League (1893), which was dedicated to the revival of the Irish language, and became its first president. In response to the criticism that there was little to read in the native language, he produced *A Literary History of Ireland* (1899). His contribution to the revived theater movement that began under Yeats and Lady Gregory was *Casadh an tSúgáin* (The Twisting of the Rope) (1901), the first drama in the Irish language to be performed in modern times. He served as a professor of the Irish language at University College, Dublin, and in 1938 won unopposed election as president of Ireland.

The Love Songs of Connacht, begun serially in 1890, showed a generation of younger poets the means of finding a new tone and idiom in English. Using materials he had collected from unlettered peasants, Hyde gave side-by-side translations that attempted to carry the Irish vowel sounds and meters into English. The *Love Songs* served as a handbook for poetic diction as well as a dual-language learning text.

"The Necessity for De-Anglicising Ireland" (1892), Hyde's declaration of cultural and linguistic independence, predates the Easter Rising by more than twenty-three years. Writing at a time when the Irish language was disparaged and fast disappearing, Hyde saw seeds of renewal in what others saw as a language of poverty.

In his 70's he took office as president of Eire under de Valera

135

used material collected from illiterate peasants & translated them trying to stay true to the idiom

Selections from *The Love Songs of Connacht*

My Grief on the Sea

My grief on the sea,
    How the waves of it roll!
For they heave between me
    And the love of my soul!

Abandoned, forsaken,
    To grief and to care,
Will the sea ever waken
    Relief from despair?

My grief, and my trouble!
    Would he and I were
In the province of Leinster,
    Or county of Clare.

Were I and my darling—
    Oh, heart-bitter wound!—
On board of the ship
    For America bound.

On a green bed of rushes
    All last night I lay,
And I flung it abroad
    With the heat of the day.

And my love came behind me—
    He came from the South;
His breast to my bosom,
    His mouth to my mouth.

sensuality of early poetry in Ireland.

Ringleted Youth of My Love

Ringleted youth of my love,
    With thy locks bound loosely behind thee,
You passed by the road above,
    But you never came in to find me;

Where were the harm for you
    If you came for a little to see me,
Your kiss is a wakening dew
    Were I ever so ill or so dreamy.

If I had golden store
    I would make a nice little boreen — *path*
To lead straight up to his door,
    The door of the house of my storeen;
Hoping to God not to miss
    The sound of his footfall in it,
I have waited so long for his kiss
    That for days I have slept not a minute.

I thought, O my love! you were so—
    As the moon is, or sun on a fountain,
And I thought after that you were snow,
    The cold snow on top of the mountain;
And I thought after that, you were more
    Like God's lamp shining to find me,
Or the bright star of knowledge before,
    And the star of knowledge behind me.

JM Synge uses this in Christy Mahon's dialogue (directed toward Pegeen)

You promised me high-heeled shoes,
    And satin and silk, my storeen,
And to follow me, never to lose,
    Though the ocean were round us roaring;
Like a bush in a gap in a wall
    I am now left lonely without thee,
And this house I grow dead of, is all
    That I see around or about me.

My Love, Oh, She Is My Love

unrequited love

She casts a spell, oh, casts a spell,
    Which haunts me more than I can tell.
    Dearer, because she makes me ill,
    Than who would will to make me well.

She is my store, oh, she my store,
    Whose grey eye wounded me so sore,

Who will not place in mine her palm,
Who will not calm me any more.

She is my pet, oh, she my pet,
    Whom I can never more forget;
    Who would not lose by me one moan,
    Nor stone upon my cairn set. *grave site*

She is my roon, oh, she my roon,
    Who tells me nothing, leaves me soon;
    Who would not lose by me one sigh,
    Were death and I within one room.

She is my dear, oh, she my dear,
    Who cares not whether I be here.
    Who would not weep when I am dead,
    Who makes me shed the silent tear.

Hard my case, oh, hard my case,
    How have I lived so long a space,
    She does not trust me any more,
    But I adore her silent face.

She is my choice, oh, she my choice,
    Who never made me to rejoice;
    Who caused my heart to ache so oft,
    Who put no softness in her voice.

Great my grief, oh, great my grief,
    Neglected, scorned beyond belief,
    By her who looks at me askance.
    By her who grants me no relief.

She's my desire, oh, my desire,
    More glorious than the bright sun's fire;
    Who were than wind-blown ice more cold,
    Had I the boldness to sit by her.

She it is who stole my heart,
    But left a void and aching smart,
    And if she soften not her eye   *) Romeo*
    Then life and I shall shortly part.   *complex*

The Necessity for De-Anglicising Ireland

When we speak of "The Necessity for De-Anglicising the Irish Nation," we mean it, not as a protest against imitating what is *best* in the English people, for that would be absurd, but rather to show the folly of neglecting what is Irish, and hastening to adopt, pell-mell, and indiscriminately, everything that is English, simply because it *is* English.

This is a question which most Irishmen will naturally look at from a National point of view, but it is one which ought also to claim the sympathies of every intelligent Unionist, and which, as I know, does claim the sympathy of many.

If we take a bird's-eye view of our island to-day, and compare it with what it used to be, we must be struck by the extraordinary fact that the nation which was once, as everyone admits, one of the most classically learned and cultured nations in Europe, is now one of the least so; how one of the most reading and literary peoples has become one of the *least* studious and most *un*-literary, and how the present art products of one of the quickest, most sensitive, and most artistic races on earth are now only distinguished for their hideousness.

I shall endeavour to show that this failure of the Irish people in recent times has been largely brought about by the race diverging during this century from the right path, and ceasing to be Irish without becoming English. I shall attempt to show that with the bulk of the people this change took place quite recently, much more recently than most people imagine, and is, in fact, still going on. I should also like to call attention to the illogical position of men who drop their own language to speak English, of men who translate their euphonious Irish names into English monosyllables, of men who read English books, and know nothing about Gaelic literature, nevertheless protesting as a matter of sentiment that they hate the country which at every hand's turn they rush to imitate.

I wish to show you that in Anglicising ourselves wholesale we have thrown away with a light heart the best claim which we have upon the world's recognition of us as a separate nationality. What did Mazzini say? What is Goldwin Smith never tired of declaiming? What do the *Spectator* and *Saturday Review* harp on? That we ought to be content as an integral part of the United Kingdom because we have lost the notes of nationality, our language and customs.

It has always been very curious to me how Irish sentiment sticks in this half-way house—how it continues to apparently hate the English, and at the same time continues to imitate them; how it continues to clamour for recognition as a distinct nationality, and at the same time throws away with both hands what would make it so. If Irishmen only went a little farther they would become good Englishmen in sentiment also. But—illogical as it appears—there seems not the slightest sign or probability of their taking that step. It is the curious certainty that come what may Irishmen will continue to resist English rule, even though it should be for their good, which prevents many of our nation from becoming Unionists upon the spot. It is a fact, and we must face it as a fact, that although they adopt English habits and copy the English in every way, the great bulk of Irishmen and Irishwomen over the whole world are known to be filled with a dull, ever-abiding animosity against her, and—right or wrong—to grieve when she prospers, and to joy when she is hurt. Such movements as Young Irelandism, Fenianism, Land Leagueism, and Parliamentary obstruction seem always to gain their sympathy and support. It is just because there appears no earthly chance of their becoming good members of the Empire that I urge that they should not remain in the anomalous position they are in, but since they absolutely refuse to become the one thing, that they become the other; cultivate what they have rejected, and build up an Irish nation on Irish lines.

But you ask, why should we wish to make Ireland more Celtic than it is—why should we de-Anglicise it at all?

I answer because the Irish race is at present in a most anomalous position, imitating England and yet apparently hating it. How can it produce anything good in literature, art, or institutions as long as it is actuated by motives so contradictory? Besides I believe it is our Gaelic past which, though the Irish race does not recognise it just at present, is really at the bottom of the Irish heart, and prevents us becoming citizens of the Empire, as, I think, can be easily proved.

To say that Ireland has not prospered under English rule is simply a truism; all the world admits it, England does not deny it. But the English retort is ready. You have not prospered, they say, because you would not settle down contentedly, like the Scotch, and form part of the Empire. "Twenty years of good, resolute, grandfatherly government," said a well-known Englishman, will solve the Irish question. He possibly made the period too short, but let us suppose this. Let us suppose for a moment—which is impossible—that there were to arise a series of Cromwells in England for the space of one hundred years, able administrators of the Empire, careful rulers of Ireland, developing to the utmost our national resources, whilst they unremittingly stamped out every spark of national feeling, making Ireland a land of wealth and factories, whilst they extinguished every thought and every idea that was Irish, and left us, at last, after a hundred years of good government, fat, wealthy, and populous, but with all our characteristics gone, with every external that at present differentiates us from the English lost or dropped; all our Irish names of places and people turned into English names; the Irish language completely extinct; the O's and the Macs dropped; our Irish intonation changed, as far as possible, by English schoolmasters into something English; our history no longer remembered or taught; the names of our rebels and martyrs blotted out; our battlefields and traditions forgotten; the fact that we were not of Saxon origin dropped out of sight and memory, and let me now put the question—How many Irishmen are there who would purchase material prosperity at such a price? It is exactly such a question as this and the answer to it that shows the difference between the English and Irish race. Nine Englishmen out of ten would jump to make the exchange, and I as firmly believe that nine Irishmen out of ten would indignantly refuse it.

And yet this awful idea of complete Anglicisation, which I have here put before you in all its crudity, is, and has been, making silent inroads upon us for nearly a century.

Its inroads have been silent, because, had the Gaelic race perceived what was being done, or had they been once warned of what was taking place in their own midst, they would, I think, never have allowed it. When the picture of complete Anglicisation is drawn for them in all its nakedness Irish sentimentality becomes suddenly a power and refuses to surrender its birthright.

What lies at the back of the sentiments of nationality with which the Irish millions seem so strongly leavened, what can prompt them to applaud such sentiments as:

> They say the British Empire owes much to Irish hands,
> That Irish valour fixed her flag o'er many conquered lands;
> And ask if Erin takes no pride in these her gallant sons,
> Her Wolseleys and her Lawrences, her Wolfes and Wellingtons.

> Ah! these were of the Empire—we yield them to her fame,
> And ne'er in Erin's orisons are heard their alien name;
> But those for whom her heart beats high and benedictions swell,
> They died upon the scaffold and they pined within the cell.

Of course it is a very composite feeling which prompts them; but I believe that what is largely behind it is the half unconscious feeling that the race which at one time held possession of more than half Europe, which established itself in Greece, and burned infant Rome, is now—almost extirpated and absorbed elsewhere—making its last stand for independence in this island of Ireland; and do what they may the race of to-day cannot wholly divest itself from the mantle of its own past. Through early Irish literature, for instance, can we best form some conception of what that race really was, which, after overthrowing and trampling on the primitive peoples of half of Europe, was itself forced in turn to yield its speech, manners, and independence to the victorious eagles of Rome. We alone of the nations of Western Europe escaped the claws of those birds of prey; we alone developed ourselves naturally upon our own lines outside of and free from all Roman influence; we alone were thus able to produce an early art and literature, *our* antiquities can best throw light upon the pre-Romanised inhabitants of half Europe, and—we are our father's sons.

There is really no exaggeration in all this, although Irishmen are sometimes prone to overstating as well as to forgetting. Westwood himself declares that, were it not for Irishmen these islands would possess no primitive works of art worth the mentioning; Jubainville asserts that early Irish literature is that which best throws light upon the manners and customs of his own ancestors the Gauls; and Zimmer, who has done so much for Celtic philology, has declared that only a spurious criticism can make an attempt to doubt about the historical character of the chief persons of our two epic cycles, that of Cuchullain and that of Finn. It is useless elaborating this point; and Dr. Sigerson has already shown in his opening lecture the debt of gratitude which in many respects Europe owes to ancient Ireland. The dim consciousness of this is one of those things which are at the back of Irish national sentiment, and our business, whether we be Unionists or Nationalists, should be to make this dim consciousness an active and potent feeling, and thus increase our sense of self-respect and of honour.

What we must endeavour to never forget is this, that the Ireland of to-day is the descendant of the Ireland of the seventh century, then the school of Europe and the torch of learning. It is true that Northmen made some minor settlements in it in the ninth and tenth centuries, it is true that the Normans made extensive settlements during the succeeding centuries, but none of those broke the continuity of the social life of the island. Dane and Norman drawn to the kindly Irish breast issued forth in a generation or two fully Irishised, and more Hibernian than the Hibernians themselves, and even after the Cromwellian plantation the children of numbers of the English soldiers who settled in the south and midlands, were, after forty years' residence, and after marrying Irish wives, turned into good Irishmen, and unable to speak a word of English, while several Gaelic poets of the last century have, like Father English, the most unmistakably English names. In two points only was the continuity of the Irishism of Ireland damaged. First, in the north-east of Ulster, where the Gaelic race was expelled and the land planted with aliens, whom our dear mother Erin, assimilative as she is, has hitherto found it difficult to absorb, and in the ownership of the land, eight-ninths of which belongs to people many of whom always lived, or live, abroad, and not half of whom Ireland can be said to have assimilated.

During all this time the continuation of Erin's national life centred, according to our way of looking at it, not so much in the Cromwellian or Williamite landholders who sat in College Green, and governed the country, as in the mass of the people whom Dean Swift considered might be entirely neglected, and looked upon as hewers of wood and drawers of water; the men who, nevertheless, constituted the real working population, and who were living on in the hopes of better days; the men who have since made America, and have within the last ten years proved what an important factor they may be in wrecking or in building the British Empire. These are the men of whom our merchants, artisans, and farmers mostly consist, and in whose hands is to-day the making or marring of an Irish nation. But, alas, *quantum mutatus ab illo!* What the battleaxe of the Dane, the sword of the Norman, the wile of the Saxon were unable to perform, we have accomplished ourselves. We have at last broken the continuity of Irish life, and just at the moment when the Celtic race is presumably about to largely recover possession of its own country, it finds itself deprived and stript of its Celtic characteristics, cut off from the past, yet scarcely in touch with the present. It has lost since the beginning of this century almost all that connected it with the era of Cuchullain and of Ossian, that connected it with the Christianisers of Europe, that connected it with Brian Boru and the heroes of Clontarf, with the O'Neills and O'Donnells, with Rory O'More, with the Wild Geese, and even to some extent with the men of '98. It has lost all that they had—language, traditions, music, genius, and ideas. Just when we should be starting to build up anew the Irish race and the Gaelic nation—as within our own recollection Greece has been built up anew—we find ourselves despoiled of the bricks of nationality. The old bricks that lasted eighteen hundred years are destroyed; we must now set to, to bake new ones, if we can, on other ground and of other clay. Imagine for a moment the restoration of a German-speaking Greece.

The bulk of the Irish race really lived in the closest contact with the traditions of the past and the national life of nearly eighteen hundred years, until after the beginning of this century. Not only so, but during the whole of the dark Penal times they produced amongst themselves a most vigorous literary development. Their schoolmasters and wealthy farmers, unwearied scribes, produced innumerable manuscripts in beautiful writing, each letter separated from another as in Greek, transcripts both of the ancient literature of their sires and of the more modern literature produced by themselves. Until the beginning of the present century there was no county, no barony, and, I may almost say, no town land which did not boast of an Irish poet, the people's representative of those ancient bards who died out with the extirpation of the great Milesian families. The literary activity of even the eighteenth century among the Gaels was very great, not in the South alone, but also in Ulster— the number of poets it produced was something astonishing. It did not, however, produce many works in Gaelic prose, but it propagated translations of many pieces from the French, Latin, Spanish, and English. Every well-to-do farmer could read and write Irish, and many of them could understand even archaic Irish. I have myself heard persons reciting the poems of Donogha More O'Daly, Abbot of Boyle, in Roscommon, who died sixty years before Chaucer was born. To this very day the people have a word for archaic Irish, which is much the same as though Chaucer's poems were handed down amongst the English peasantry, but required a special training to understand. This training, however, nearly every one of fair education during the Penal times possessed, nor did they begin to lose their Irish training and knowledge until the establishment of Maynooth and the rise of O'Connell. These two events made an end of the Gaelicism of the Gaelic race, although a great number of poets and scribes existed even down to the forties and fifties of the present century, and a few may linger on yet in remote localities. But it may be said, roughly speaking, that the ancient Gaelic civilisation died with O'Connell, largely, I am afraid, owing to his example and his neglect of inculcating the necessity of keeping alive racial customs, language, and traditions, in which with the one notable exception of our scholarly idealist, Smith O'Brien, he has been followed until a year ago by almost every leader of the Irish race.

Thomas Davis and his brilliant band of Young Irelanders came just at the dividing of the line, and tried to give to Ireland a new literature in English to replace the literature which was just being discarded. It succeeded and it did not succeed. It was a most brilliant effort, but the old bark had been too recently stripped off the Irish tree, and the trunk could not take as it might have done to a fresh one. It was a new departure, and at first produced a violent effect. Yet in the long run it failed to properly leaven our peasantry who might, perhaps, have been reached upon other lines. I say they *might* have been reached upon other lines because it is quite certain that even well on into the

Loss of tradition of reading of mss of antiquity

beginning of this century, Irish poor scholars and schoolmasters used to gain the greatest favour and applause by reading out manuscripts in the people's houses at night, some of which manuscripts had an antiquity of a couple of hundred years or more behind them, and which, when they got illegible from age, were always recopied. The Irish peasantry at that time were all to some extent cultured men, and many of the better off ones were scholars and poets. What have we now left of all that? Scarcely a trace. Many of them read newspapers indeed, but who reads, much less recites, an epic poem or chants an elegiac or even a hymn?

Wherever Irish throughout Ireland continued to be spoken, there the ancient MSS. continued to be read, there the epics of Cuchullain, Conor Mac-Nessa, Deirdre, Finn, Oscar, and Ossian continued to be told, and there poetry and music held sway. Some people may think I am exaggerating in asserting that such a state of things existed down to the present century, but it is no exaggeration. I have myself spoken with men from Cavan and Tyrone who spoke excellent Irish. Carleton's stories bear witness to the prevalence of the Irish language and traditions in Ulster when he began to write. My friend Mr. Lloyd has found numbers in Antrim who spoke good Irish. And, as for Leinster, my friend Mr. Cleaver informed me that when he lived in Wicklow a man came by from the County Carlow in search of work who could not speak a word of English. Old labourers from Connacht, who used to go to reap the harvest in England and take shipping at Drogheda, told me that at that time, fifty years ago, Irish was spoken by everyone round that town. I have met an old man in Wicklow, not twenty miles from Dublin, whose parents always repeated the Rosary in Irish. My friend Father O'Growney, who has done and is doing so much for the Irish language and literature at Maynooth, tells me that there, within twenty miles of Dublin, are three old people who still speak Irish. O'Curry found people within seven miles of Dublin city who had never heard English in their youth at all, except from the car-drivers of the great town. I gave an old man in the street who begged from me, a penny, only a few days ago, saying, '*Sin pighin agad*' (Here's a penny for you), and when he answered in Irish I asked him where he was from, and he said from *Newna (n' Eamhain)*, i.e., Navan. Last year I was in Canada and out hunting with some Red Indians. and we spent a night in the last white man's house in the last settlement on the brink of the primeval forest; and judging from a peculiarly Hibernian physiognomy that the man was Irish. I addressed him in Gaelic, and to the intense astonishment both of whites and Indians we entered into a conversation which none of them understood; and it turned out that he was from within three miles of Kilkenny, and he had been forty years in that country without forgetting the language he had spoken as a child, and I, although from the centre of Connacht, understood him perfectly. When my father was a young boy in the county Leitrim, not far from Longford, he seldom heard the farm labourers and tenants speak anything but Irish amongst themselves. So much for Ulster and Leinster, but Connacht and Munster were until quite recently completely Gaelic. In fact, I may venture to say, that, up to the beginning of the present century, neither man, woman, nor child of the Gaelic race, either of high blood or low blood, existed in Ireland who did not either speak Irish or understand it. But within the last ninety years we have, with an unparalleled frivolity, deliberately thrown away our birthright and Anglicised ourselves. None of the children of those people of whom I have spoken know Irish, and the race will from henceforth be changed; for as Monsieur Jubainville says of the influence of Rome upon Gaul, England "has definitely conquered us, she has even imposed upon us her language, that is to say, the form of our thoughts during every instant of our existence." It is curious that those who most fear West Britonism have so eagerly consented to imposing upon the Irish race what, according to Jubainville, who in common with all the great scholars of the continent, seems to regret it very much, is "the form of our thoughts during every instant of our existence."

So much for the greatest stroke of all in our Anglicisation, the loss of our language. I have often heard people thank God that if the English gave us nothing else they gave us at least their language. In this way they put a bold face upon the matter, and pretend that the Irish language is not worth knowing, and has no literature. But the Irish language *is* worth knowing, or why would the greatest philologists of Germany, France, and Italy be emulously studying it, and it *does* possess a literature, or why would a German savant have made the calculation that the books written in Irish between the eleventh and seventeenth centuries, and still extant, would fill a thousand octavo volumes.

I have no hesitation at all in saying that every Irish-feeling Irishman, who hates the reproach of West-Britonism, should set himself to encourage the efforts which are being made to keep alive our once great national tongue. The losing of it is our greatest blow, and the sorest stroke that the rapid Anglicisation of Ireland has inflicted upon us. In order to de-Anglicise ourselves we must at once arrest the decay of the language. We must bring pressure upon our politicians not to snuff it out by their tacit discouragement merely because they do not happen themselves to understand it. We must arouse some spark of patriotic inspiration among the peasantry who still use the language, and put an end to the shameful state of feeling—a thousand-tongued reproach to our leaders and statesmen—which makes young men and women blush and hang their heads when overheard speaking their own language. Maynooth has at last come splendidly to the front, and it is now incumbent upon every clerical student to attend lectures in the Irish language and history during the first three years of his course. But in order to keep the Irish language alive where it is still spoken—which is the utmost we can at present aspire to— nothing less than a house-to-house visitation and exhortation of the people themselves will do, something—though with a very different purpose—analogous to the procedure that James Stephens adopted throughout Ireland when he found her like a corpse on the dissecting table, This and some system of giving medals or badges of honour to every family who will guarantee that they have always spoken Irish amongst themselves during the year. But, unfortunately, distracted as we are and torn by contending factions, it is impossible to find either men or money to carry out this simple remedy, although to a dispassionate foreigner—to a Zeuss, Jubainville, Zimmer, Kuno Meyer, Windisch, or Ascoli, and the rest—this is of greater importance than whether Mr. Redmond or Mr. MacCarthy lead the largest wing of the Irish party for the moment, or Mr. So-and-So succeed with his election petition. To a person taking a birds-eye view of the situation a hundred or five hundred years hence, believe me, it will also appear of greater importance than any mere temporary wrangle, but, unhappily, our countrymen cannot be brought to see this.

* As an instance of this, I mention the case of a young man I met on the road coming from the fair of Tuam, some ten miles away. I saluted him in Irish, and he answered me in English, "Don't you speak Irish," said I. "Well, I declare to God, sir," he said, "My father and mother hasn't a word of English, but still, I don't speak Irish." This was absolutely true for him. There are thousands upon thousands of houses all over Ireland to-day where the old people invariably use Irish in addressing the children, and the children as invariably answer in English, the children understanding Irish but not speaking it, the parents understanding their children's English but unable to use it themselves. In a great many cases, I should almost say most, the children are not conscious of the existence of two languages. I remember asking a gossoon a couple of miles west of Ballaghaderreen in the Co. Mayo, some questions in Irish and he answered them in English. At last I said to him, *"Nach labhrann tú Gaedheilg?"* (i.e., "Don't you speak Irish?") and his answer was, "And isn't it Irish I'm spaking?" No *a-chuisle*," said I, "it's not Irish you're speaking, but English." "Well, then," said he, "that's how I spoke it ever!" He was quite unconscious that I was addressing him in one language and he answering in another. On a different occasion I spoke Irish to a little girl in a house near Kilfree Junction, Co. Sligo, into which I went while waiting for a train. The girl answered me in Irish until her brother came in. "Arrah now, Mary," said he, with what was intended to be a most bitter sneer; "and isn't that a credit to you!" And poor Mary— whom I had with difficulty persuaded to begin—immediately hung her head and changed to English. This is going on from Malin Head to Galway, and from Galway to Waterford, with the exception possibly of a few spots in Donegal and Kerry, where the people are wiser and more national.

⑤

We can, however, insist, and we *shall* insist if Home Rule be carried, that the Irish language, which so many foreign scholars of the first calibre find so worthy of study, shall be placed on a par with—or even above—Greek, Latin, and modern languages, in all examinations held under the Irish Government. We can also insist, and we *shall* insist, that in those baronies where the children speak Irish, Irish shall be taught, and that Irish-speaking schoolmasters, petty sessions clerks, and even magistrates be appointed in Irish-speaking districts. If all this were done, it should not be very difficult, with the aid of the foremost foreign scholars, to bring about a tone of thought which would make it disgraceful for an educated Irishman—especially of the old Celtic race, Mac-Dermotts, O'Conors, O'Sullivans, MacCarthys, O'Neills—to be ignorant of his own language—would make it at least as disgraceful as for an educated Jew to be quite ignorant of Hebrew.

Further Readings on Douglas Hyde

Bibliography

de Bhaldraithe, Tomás. "Agusín le clár saothair An Craoibhín." *Galvia* 4:18–24.

Kersnowski, Frank L., C. W. Spinks, and Laird Loomis. *A Bibliography of Modern Irish and Anglo-Irish Literature,* 54–60. San Antonio, Tex.: Trinity University Press, 1976.

O'Hegarty, P. S. *A Bibliography of Dr. Douglas Hyde.* Dublin: Alex Thorn, 1939.

Selected Works

Beside the Fire. 1890. Reprint, New York: Lemma, 1973.

Casadh an tSugáin. Drama, first performed 21 October 1901. Translated by Lady Gregory as *The Twisting of the Rope.* In Gregory's *Poets and Dreamers.* 1903. Reprint, Gerrards Cross, UK: Colin Smythe, 1974.

Language, Lore and Lyrics: Essays and Lectures. Edited by Breandan Ó Conaire. Blackrock, Ireland: Irish Academic Press, 1985.

Leabhar Sgéulaighteachta. 1889. Reprinted, with additions, Dublin: Oifig Díolta Foillseacháin Rialtais, 1931.

The Literary History of Ireland from the Earliest Times to the Present. 1899. Reprinted, with revisions by Brian Ó Cuiv, London: Ernest Benn, 1967.

The Love Songs of Connacht. 1893. Reprint, Shannon: Irish University Press, 1969.

Selected Plays of Douglas Hyde. Edited by Gareth W. Dunleavy and Janet Egleson. Gerrards Cross, UK: Colin Smythe, 1988.

The Story of Early Gaelic Literature. 1895. Rev. ed., London: Unwin, 1920.

Biography and Criticism

Coffey, Diarmid. *Douglas Hyde: President of Ireland*. Dublin: Talbot, 1938.

Daly, Dominic. *The Young Douglas Hyde: The Dawn of the Irish Revolution and Renaissance, 1874–1893*. Totowa, N.J.: Rowman and Littlefield, 1974.

Dunleavy, Gareth W. *Douglas Hyde*. Lewisburg, Pa.: Bucknell University Press, 1974.

Dunleavy, Janet Egleson, and Gareth W. Dunleavy. *Douglas Hyde: A Maker of Modern Ireland*. Berkeley: University of California Press, 1991.

Isabella Augusta, Lady Gregory

(1852–1932)

The godmother of the Irish Literary Renaissance was born of a landed, Protestant, Unionist, and nonliterary family. Lady Gregory did not begin an active career in literature until she was widowed and past forty. Once awakened, however, she gave of herself tirelessly, usually as a champion of the traditions and culture of the Catholic peasant underclass. She worked as a folklorist, recording narratives and beliefs in her own poetic version of folk language, called "Kiltartanese" after the region around her estate, Coole Park, in County Galway. With William Butler Yeats she founded the Irish Literary Theatre in 1899, and then the Abbey Theatre five years later. When the works of others failed to draw crowds, she wrote her own plays, many in Kiltartanese, and these were often highly popular with audiences. Her two retellings (in Kiltartanese) of Old Irish heroic literature, *Cuchulain of Muirthemne* (1902) and *Gods and Fighting Men* (1904), fusing disparate narratives into a continuous whole, have been compared to Thomas Malory's work with the Arthurian legends. Lady Gregory was a prudent manager of the Abbey Theatre, where she promoted the careers of many younger playwrights, notably Sean O'Casey.

"The Only Son of Aoife," from her *Cuchulain,* adapts an Irish variant of an international tale sometimes known by its Persian title, "Sohrub and Rustum." (The title of the Irish text is *Aided Oenfir Aífe.*) Yeats used versions of the narrative in his poem "Cuchulain's Fight with the Sea" (1892), and in his play *On Baile's Strand* (1904). In other texts, the name of the main characters may be spelled differently: Aoife/Aífe, Conlaoch/Connla, and Cuchulain/Cúchulainn.

The Rising of the Moon, one of Lady Gregory's best-known short plays, was published in 1904 but not performed until 1907. Alluding to the 1798 revolution, the title of the play is taken from the patriotic ballad of the same name, attributed to John Keegan Casey (1846–1870). An adaptation of Lady Gregory's play appears in John Ford's film (1958), again of the same title.

The Only Son of Aoife

written in Kiltartanese after region around her estate

The time Cuchulain came back from Alban, after he had learned the use of arms under Scathach, he left Aoife, the queen he had overcome in battle, with child.

And when he was leaving her, he told her what name to give the child, and he gave her a gold ring, and bade her keep it safe till the child grew to be a lad, and till his thumb would fill it; and he bade her to give it to him then, and to send him to Ireland, and he would know he was his son by that token. She promised to do so, and with that Cuchulain went back to Ireland.

gold ring · identification as his son

It was not long after the child was born, word came to Aoife that Cuchulain had taken Emer to be his wife in Ireland. When she heard that, great jealousy came on her, and great anger, and her love for Cuchulain was turned to hatred; and she remembered her three champions that he had killed, and how he had overcome herself, and she determined in her mind that when her son would come to have the strength of a man, she would get her revenge through him. She told Conlaoch her son nothing of this, but brought him up like any king's son; and when he was come to sensible years, she put him under the teaching of Scathach, to be taught the use of arms and the art of war. He turned out as apt a scholar as his father, and it was not long before he had learnt all Scathach had to teach.

under teaching of Scathach

Then Aoife gave him the arms of a champion, and bade him go to Ireland, but first she laid three commands on him: the first, never to give way to any living person, but to die sooner than be made turn back; the second, not to refuse a challenge from the greatest champion alive, but to fight him at all risks, even if he was sure to lose his life; the third, not to tell his name on any account, though he might be threatened with death for hiding it. She put him under *geasa*, that is, under bonds, not to do these things.

Then the young man, Conlaoch, set out, and it was not long before his ship brought him to Ireland, and the place he landed at was Baile's Strand, near Dundealgan.

It chanced that at that time Conchubar, the High King, was holding court there, for it was a convenient gathering-place for his chief men, and they were settling some business that belonged to the government of that district.

Title of play

When word was brought to Conchubar that there was a ship come to the strand, and a young lad in it armed as if for fighting, and armed men with him, he sent one of the chief men of his household to ask his name, and on what business he was come.

The messenger's name was Cuinaire, and he went down to the strand, and when he saw the young man he said: "A welcome to you, young hero from the east, with the merry face. It is likely, seeing you come armed as if for fighting, you are gone astray on your journey; but as you are come to Ireland, tell me your name and what your deeds have been, and your victories in the eastern bounds of the world."

"As to my name," said Conlaoch, "it is of no great account; but whatever it is, I am under bonds not to tell it to the stoutest man living."

"It is best for you to tell it at the king's desire," said Cuinaire, "before you get your death through refusing it, as many a champion from Alban and from Britain has done before now." "If that is the order you put on us when we land here, it is I will break it," said Conlaoch, "and no one will obey it any longer from this out."

So Cuinaire went back and told the king what the young lad had said. Then Conchubar said to his people: "Who will go out into the field, and drag the name and the story out of this young man?" "I will go," said Conall, for his hand was never slow in fighting. And he went out, and found the lad angry and destroying, handling his arms, and they attacked one another with a great noise of swords and shouts, and they were gripped together, and fought for a while, and then Conall was overcome, and the great name and the praise that was on Conall, it was on the head of Conlaoch it was now.

Word was sent then to where Cuchulain was, in pleasant, bright-faced Dundealgan. And the messenger told him the whole story, and he said: "Conall is lying humbled, and it is slow the help is in coming; it is a welcome there would be before the Hound."

Cuchulain rose up then and went to where Conlaoch was, and he still handling his arms. And Cuchulain asked him his name and said: "It would be well for you, young hero of unknown name, to loosen yourself from this knot, and not to bring down my hand upon you, for it will be hard for you to escape death." But Conlaoch said: "If I put you down in the fight, the way I put down your comrade, there will be a great name on me; but if I draw back now, there will be mockery on me, and it will be said I was afraid of the fight. I will never give in to any man to tell the name, or to give an account of myself. But if I was not held with a command," he said, "there is no man in the world I would sooner give it to than to yourself, since I saw your face. But do not think, brave champion of Ireland, that I will let you take away the fame I have won, for nothing."

With that they fought together, and it is seldom such a battle was seen, and all wondered that the young lad could stand so well against Cuchulain.

Pathos

Battle of vs. father son

So they fought a long while, neither getting the better of the other, but at last Cuchulain was charged so hotly by the lad that he was forced to give way, and although he had fought so many good fights, and killed so many great champions, and understood the use of arms better than any man living, he was pressed very hard.

And he called for the Gae Bulg, and his anger came on him, and the flames of the hero-light began to shine about his head, and by that sign Conlaoch knew him to be Cuchulain, his father. And just at that time he was aiming his spear at him, and when he knew it was Cuchulain, he threw his spear crooked that it might pass beside him. But Cuchulain threw his spear, the Gae Bulg, at him with all his might, and it struck the lad in the side and went into his body, so that he fell to the ground.

And Cuchulain said; "Now, boy, tell your name and what you are, for it is short your life will be, for you will not live after that wound."

And Conlaoch showed the ring that was on his hand, and he said: "Come here where I am lying on the field, let my men from the east come round me. I am suffering for revenge. I am Conlaoch, son of the Hound, heir of dear Dundealgan; I was bound to this secret in Dun Scathach, the secret in which I have found my grief."

And Cuchulain said: "It is a pity your mother not to be here to see you brought down. She might have stretched out her hand to stop the spear that wounded you." And Conlaoch said: "My curse be on my mother, for it was she put me under bonds; it was she sent me here to try my strength against yours." And Cuchulain said: "My curse be on your mother, the woman that is full of treachery; it is through her harmful thoughts these tears have been brought on us." And Conlaoch said: "My name was never forced from my mouth till now; I never gave an account of myself to any man under the sun. But, O Cuchulain of the sharp sword, it was a pity you not to know me the time I threw the slanting spear behind you in the fight."

And then the sorrow of death came upon Conlaoch, and Cuchulain took his sword and put it through him, sooner than leave him in the pain and the punishment he was in.

And then great trouble and anguish came on Cuchulain, and he made this complaint:

"It is a pity it is, O son of Aoife, that ever you came into the province of Ulster, that you ever met with the Hound of Cuailgne.

"If I and my fair Conlaoch were doing feats of war on the one side, the men of Ireland from sea to sea would not be equal to us together. It is no wonder I to be under grief when I see the shield and the arms of Conlaoch. A pity it is there is no one at all, a pity there are not hundreds of men on whom I could get satisfaction for his death.

"If it was the king himself had hurt your fair body, it is I would have shortened his days.

"It is well for the House of the Red Branch, and for the heads of its fair army of heroes, it was not they that killed my only son.

"It is well for Laegaire of Victories it is not from him you got your heavy pain.

"It is well for the heroes of Conall they did not join in the killing of you; it is well that travelling across the plain of Macha they did not fall in with me after such a fight.

"It is well for the tall, well-shaped Forbuide; well for Dubthach, your Black Beetle of Ulster.

"It is well for you, Cormac Conloingeas, you I share of arms gave no help, that it is not from your weapons he got his wound, the hard-skinned shield or the blade.

"It is a pity it was not one on the plains of Munster, or in Leinster of the sharp blades, or at Cruachan of the rough fighters, that struck down my comely Conlaoch.

"It is a pity it was not in the country of the Cruithne, of the fierce Fians, you fell in a heavy quarrel, or in the country of the Greeks, or in some other place of the world, you died, and I could avenge you.

"Or in Spain, or in Sorcha, or in the country of the Saxons of the free armies; there would not then be this death in my heart.

"It is very well for the men of Alban it was not they that destroyed your fame; and it is well for the men of the Gall.

"Och! It is bad that it happened; my grief! it is on me is the misfortune, O Conlaoch of the Red Spear, I myself to have spilled your blood.

"I to be under defeat, without strength. It is a pity Aoife never taught you to know the power of my strength in the fight.

"It is no wonder I to be blinded after such a fight and such a defeat.

"It is no wonder I to be tired out, and without the sons of Usnach beside me.

"Without a son, without a brother, with none to come after me; without Conlaoch, without a name to keep my strength.

"To be without Naoise, without Ainnle, without Ardan; is it not with me is my fill of trouble?

"I am the father that killed his son, the fine green branch; there is no hand or shelter to help me.

"I am a raven that has no home; I am a boat going from wave to wave; I am a ship that has lost its rudder; I am the apple left on the tree; it is little I thought of falling from it; grief and sorrow will be with me from this time."

Then Cuchulain stood up and faced all the men of Ulster. "There is trouble on Cuchulain," said Conchubar; "he is after killing his own son, and if I and all my men were to go against him, by the end of the day he would destroy every man of us. Go now," he said to Cathbad, the Druid, "and bind him to go down to Baile's Strand, and to give three days fighting against the waves of the sea, rather than to kill us all."

So Cathbad put an enchantment on him, and bound him to go down. And when he came to the strand, there was a great white stone before him, and he took his sword in his right hand, and he said: "If I had the head of the woman that sent her son to his death, I would split it as I split this stone." And he made four quarters of the stone.

Then he fought with the waves three days and three nights, till he fell from hunger and weakness, so that some men said he got his death there. But it was not there he got his death, but on the plain of Muirthemne.

The Rising of the Moon

Persons

SERGEANT.
POLICEMAN X.
POLICEMAN B.
A RAGGED MAN.

SCENE. *Side of a quay in a seaport town. Some posts and chains. A large barrel. Enter three policemen. Moonlight.*

(SERGEANT, *who is older than the others, crosses the stage to right and looks down steps. The others put down a pastepot and unroll a bundle of placards.*)

POLICEMAN B. I think this would be a good place to put up a notice. (*He points to barrel.*)

POLICEMAN X. Better ask him. (*Calls to* SERGEANT) Will this be a good place for a placard?

(*No answer.*)

POLICEMAN B. Will we put up a notice here on the barrel?

(*No answer.*)

SERGEANT. There's a flight of steps here that leads to the water. This is a place that should be minded well. If he got down here, his friends might have a boat to meet him; they might send it in here from outside.

POLICEMAN B. Would the barrel be a good place to put a notice up?

SERGEANT. It might; you can put it there.

(*They paste the notice up.*)

SERGEANT (*reading it*). Dark hair—dark eyes, smooth face, height five feet five—there's not much to take hold of in that—It's a pity I had no chance of seeing him before he broke out of gaol. They say he's a wonder, that it's he makes all the plans for the whole organization. There isn't another man in Ireland would have broken gaol the way he did. He must have some friends among the gaolers.

POLICEMAN B. A hundred pounds is little enough for the Government to offer for him. You may be sure any man in the force that takes him will get promotion.

SERGEANT. I'll mind this place myself. I wouldn't wonder at all if he came this way. He might come slipping along there (*points to side of quay*), and his friends might be waiting for him there (*points down steps*), and once he got away it's little chance we'd have of finding him; it's maybe under a load of kelp he'd be in a fishing boat, and not one to help a married man that wants it to the reward.

POLICEMAN X. And if we get him itself, nothing but abuse on our heads for it from the people, and maybe from our own relations.

SERGEANT. Well, we have to do our duty in the force. Haven't we the whole country depending on us to keep law and order? It's those that are down would be up and those that are up would be down, if it wasn't for us. Well, hurry on, you have plenty of other places to placard yet, and come back here then to me. You can take the lantern. Don't be too long now, It's a very lonesome here with nothing but the moon.

POLICEMAN B. It's a pity we can't stop with you. The Government should have brought more police into the town, with *him* in gaol, and at assize time too. Well, good luck to your watch.

(*They go out.*)

SERGEANT (*walks up and down once or twice and looks at placard*). A hundred pounds and promotion sure. There must be a great deal of spending in a hundred pounds. It's a pity some honest man not to be better of that.

(A RAGGED MAN *appears at left and tries to slip past.* SERGEANT *suddenly turns.*)

SERGEANT. Where are you going?

MAN. I'm a poor ballad-singer, your honour. I thought to sell some of these *(holds out bundle of ballads)* to the sailors.

(He goes on.)

SERGEANT. Stop! Didn't I tell you to stop? You can't go on there.

MAN. Oh, very well. It's a hard thing to be poor. All the world's against the poor!

SERGEANT. Who are you?

MAN. You'd be as wise as myself if I told you, but I don't mind. I'm one Jimmy Walsh, a ballad-singer.

SERGEANT. Jimmy Walsh? I don't know that name.

MAN. Ah, sure, they know it well enough in Ennis. Were you ever in Ennis, sergeant?

SERGEANT. What brought you here?

MAN. Sure, it's to the assizes I came, thinking I might make a few shillings here or there. It's in the one train with the judges I came.

SERGEANT. Well, if you came so far, you may as well go farther, for you'll walk out of this.

MAN. I will, I will; I'll just go on where I was going.

(Goes towards steps.)

SERGEANT. Come back from those steps; no one has leave to pass down them to-night.

MAN. I'll just sit on the top of the steps till I see will some sailor buy a ballad off me that would give me my supper. They do be late going back to the ship. It's often I saw them in Cork carried down the quay in a hand-cart.

SERGEANT. Move on, I tell you. I won't have anyone lingering about the quay to-night.

MAN. Well, I'll go. It's the poor have the hard life! Maybe yourself might like one. sergeant. Here's a good sheet now. *(Turns one over.)* "Content and a pipe"—that's not much. "The Peeler and the goat"—you wouldn't like that. "Johnny Hart"—that's a lovely song.

SERGEANT. Move on.

MAN. Ah, wait till you hear it. *(Sings:)*

There was a rich farmer's daughter lived near the town of Ross;
She courted a Highland soldier, his name was Johnny Hart;
Says the mother to her daughter, "I'll go distracted mad
If you marry that Highland soldier dressed up in Highland plaid."

SERGEANT. Stop that noise.

(MAN *wraps up his ballads and shuffles towards the steps.*)

SERGEANT. Where are you going?

MAN. Sure you told me to be going, and I am going.

SERGEANT. Don't be a fool. I didn't tell you to go that way; I told you to go back to the town.

MAN. Back to the town, is it?

SERGEANT (*taking him by the shoulder and shoving him before him*). Here, I'll show you the way. Be off with you. What are you stopping for?

MAN (*who has been keeping his eye on the notice, points to it*). I think I know what you're waiting for, sergeant.

SERGEANT. What's that to you?

MAN. And I know well the man you're waiting for—I know him well—I'll be going.

(*He shuffles on.*)

SERGEANT. You know him? Come back here. What sort is he?

MAN. Come back is it, sergeant? Do you want to have me killed?

SERGEANT. Why do you say that?

MAN. Never mind. I'm going. I wouldn't be in your shoes if the reward was ten times as much. (*Goes on off stage to left.*) Not if it was ten times as much.

SERGEANT (*rushing after him*). Come back here, come back. (*Drags him back.*) What sort is he? Where did you see him?

MAN. I saw him in my own place, in the County Clare. I tell you you wouldn't like to be looking at him. You'd be afraid to be in the one place with him. There isn't a weapon he doesn't know the use of, and as to strength, his muscles are as hard as that board (*slaps barrel*).

SERGEANT. Is he as bad as that?

MAN. He is then.

SERGEANT. Do you tell me so?

MAN. There was a poor man in our place, a sergeant from Bally-vaughan.—It was with a lump of stone he did it.

SERGEANT. I never heard of that.

MAN. And you wouldn't, sergeant. It's not everything that happens gets into the papers. And there was a policeman in plain clothes, too . . . It is in Limerick he was. . . . It was after the time of the attack on the police barrack at Kilmallock. . . . Moonlight . . . just like this . . . waterside. . . . Nothing was known for certain.

SERGEANT. Do you say so? It's a terrible county to belong to.

MAN. That's so, indeed! You might be standing there, looking out that way, thinking you saw him coming up this side of the quay (*points*), and might be coming up this other side *(points)*, and he'd be on you before you knew where you were.

SERGEANT. It's a whole troop of police they ought to put here to stop a man like that.

MAN. But if you'd like me to stop with you, I could be looking down this side. I could be sitting up here on this barrel.

SERGEANT. And you know him well, too?

MAN. I'd know him a mile off, sergeant.

SERGEANT. But you wouldn't want to share the reward?

MAN. Is it a poor man like me, that has to be going the roads and singing in fairs, to have the name on him that he took a reward? But you don't want me. I'll be safer in the town.

SERGEANT. Well, you can stop.

MAN *(getting up on barrel)*. All right, sergeant. I wonder, now, you're not tired out, sergeant, walking up and down the way you are.

SERGEANT. If I'm tired I'm used to it.

MAN. You might have hard work before you to-night yet. Take it easy while you can. There's plenty of room up here on the barrel, and you see farther when you're higher up.

SERGEANT. Maybe so. *(Gets up beside him on barrel, facing right. They sit back to back, looking different ways.)* You made me feel a bit queer with the way you talked.

MAN. Give me a match, sergeant *(He gives it and man lights pipe)*; take a draw yourself? It'll quiet you. Wait now till I give you a light, but you needn't turn round. Don't take your eye off the quay for the life of you.

SERGEANT. Never fear, I won't. *(Lights pipe. They both smoke.)* Indeed it's a hard thing to he in the force, out at night and no thanks for it, for all the danger we're in. And it's little we get but abuse from the people, and no choice but to obey our orders, and never asked when a man is sent into danger, if you are a married man with a family.

MAN *(sings)*—

As through the hills I walked to view the hills and shamrock plain,
I stood awhile where nature smiles to view the rocks and streams,
On a matron fair I fixed my eyes beneath a fertile vale,
And she sang her song it was on the wrong of poor old Granuaile.

SERGEANT. Stop that; that's no song to be singing in these times.

MAN. Ah, sergeant. I was only singing to keep my heart up. It sinks when I think of him. To think of us two sitting here, and he creeping up the quay, maybe, to get to us.

SERGEANT. Are you keeping a good lookout?

MAN. I am; and for no reward too. Amn't I the foolish man? But when I saw a man in trouble, I never could help trying to get him out of it. What's that? Did something hit me?

(Rubs his heart.)

SERGEANT *(patting him on the shoulder)*. You will get your reward in heaven.

MAN. I know that, I know that, sergeant, but life is precious.

SERGEANT. Well, you can sing if it gives you more courage,

MAN *(sings)*—

Her head was bare, her hands and feet with iron bands were bound,

Her pensive strain and plaintive wail mingles with the evening gale,

And the song she sang with mournful air, I am old Granuaile.

Her lips so sweet that monarchs kissed . . .

SERGEANT. That's not it. . . . "Her gown she wore was stained with gore." . . . That's it—you missed that.

MAN. You're right, sergeant, so it is; I missed it. *(Repeats line.)* But to think of a man like you knowing a song like that.

SERGEANT. There's many a thing a man might know and might not have any wish for.

MAN. Now, I daresay, sergeant, in your youth, you used to be sitting up on a wall, the way you are sitting up on this barrel now, and the other lads beside you, and you singing "Granuaile"? . . .

SERGEANT. I did then.

MAN. And the "Shan Van Vocht"? . . .

SERGEANT. I did then.

MAN. And the "Green on the Cape"?

SERGEANT. That was one of them.

MAN. And maybe the man you are watching, for to-night used to be sitting on the wall, when he was young, and singing those same songs. . . . It's a queer world. . . .

SERGEANT. Whisht! . . . I think I see something coming. . . . It's only a dog.

MAN. And isn't it a queer world? . . . Maybe it's one of the boys you used to be singing with that time you will be arresting to-day or to-morrow, and sending into the dock. . . .

The man wins over the sergeant with his words of wisdom

SERGEANT. That's true indeed.

MAN. And maybe one night, after you had been singing, if the other boys had told you some plan they had, some plan to free the country, you might have joined with them . . . and maybe it is you might be in trouble now.

SERGEANT. Well, who knows but I might? I had a great spirit in those days.

MAN. It's a queer world, sergeant, and it's little any mother knows when she sees her child creeping on the floor what might happen to it before it has gone through its life, or who will be who in the end.

SERGEANT. That's a queer thought now, and a true thought. Wait now till I think it out. . . . If it wasn't for the sense I have, and for my wife and family, and for me joining the force the time I did, it might be myself now would be after breaking gaol and hiding in the dark, and it might be him that's hiding in the dark and that got out of gaol would be sitting up here where I am on this barrel. . . . And it might be myself would be creeping up trying to make my escape from himself, and it might be himself would be keeping the law, and myself would be breaking it, and myself would be trying to put a bullet in his head, or to take up a lump of stone the way you said he did . . . no, that myself did. . . . Oh! (*Gasps. After a pause*) What's that? (*Grasps man's arm.*)

MAN (*jumps off barrel and listens, looking over the water*). It's nothing, sergeant.

SERGEANT. I thought it might be a boat. I had a notion there might be friends of his coming about the quays with a boat.

MAN. Sergeant, I am thinking it was with the people you were, and not with the law you were, when you were a young man.

SERGEANT. Well, if I was foolish then, that time's gone.

MAN. Maybe, sergeant, it comes into your head sometimes, in spite of your belt and your tunic, that it might have been as well for you to have followed Granuaile.

SERGEANT. It's no business of yours what I think.

MAN. Maybe, sergeant, you'll be on the side of the country yet.

SERGEANT (*gets off barrel*). Don't talk to me like that. I have my duties and I know them. (*Looks round.*) That was a boat; I hear the oars.

(*Goes to the steps and looks down.*)

MAN (*sings*)—

O, then, tell me, Shawn O'Farrell,
    Where the gathering is to be.

In the old spot by the river
    Right well known to you and me!

SERGEANT. Stop that! Stop that, I tell you!
MAN *(sings louder)*—
One word more, for signal token.
    Whistle up the marching tune,
With your pike upon your shoulder,
    At the Rising of the Moon.

sings "The praises of The Moon".

SERGEANT. If you don't stop that, I'll arrest you.
(A whistle from below answers, repeating the air.)
SERGEANT. That's a signal. *(Stands between him and steps.)* You must not pass this way. . . . Step farther back. . . . Who are you? You are no ballad-singer.
    MAN. You needn't ask who I am; that placard will tell you. *(Points to placard.)*
SERGEANT. You are the man I am looking for.
Removes disguise
MAN *(takes off hat and wig.* SERGEANT *seizes them)*. I am. There's a hundred pound on my head. There is a friend of mine below in a boat. He knows a safe place to bring me to.
SERGEANT *(looking still at hat and wig)*. It's a pity! It's a pity! You deceived me. You deceived me well.
    MAN. I am a friend of Granuaile. There is a hundred pounds on my head.
    SERGEANT. It's a pity, it's a pity!
    MAN. Will you let me pass, or must I make you let me?
    SERGEANT. I am in the force. I will not let you pass.
    MAN. I thought to do it with my tongue. *(Puts hand in breast.)* What is that?
    (Voice of POLICEMAN X *outside)*. Here, this is where we left him.
    SERGEANT. It's my comrades coming.
    MAN. You won't betray me . . . the friend of Granuaile. *(Slips behind barrel.)*
    (Voice of POLICEMAN B.*)*. That was the last of the placards.
    POLICEMAN X. *(as they come in)*. If he makes his escape it won't be unknown he'll make it.
    *(*SERGEANT *puts hat and wig behind his back.)* — hides the man's disguise
    POLICEMAN B. Did anyone come this way?
    SERGEANT. *(after a pause)*. No one.

POLICEMAN B. No one at all?

SERGEANT. No one at all.

POLICEMAN B. We had no orders to go back to the station; we can stop along with you.

SERGEANT. I don't want you. There is nothing for you to do here.

POLICEMAN B. You bade us to come back here and keep watch with you.

SERGEANT. I'd sooner be alone. Would any man come this way and you making all that talk? It is better the place to be quiet.

POLICEMAN B. Well, we'll leave you the lantern anyhow.

(Hands it to him.)

SERGEANT. I don't want it. Bring it with you.

POLICEMAN B. You might want it. There are clouds coming up and you have the darkness of the night before you yet. I'll leave it over here on the barrel. *(Goes to barrel.)*

SERGEANT. Bring it with you I tell you. No more talk.

POLICEMAN B. Well, I thought it might be a comfort to you. I often think when I have it in my hand and can be flashing it about into every dark corner *(doing so)* that it's the same as being beside the fire at home, and the bits of bogwood blazing up now and again.

(Flashes it about, now on the barrel, now on SERGEANT.*)*

SERGEANT *(furious)*. Be off the two of you, yourselves and your lantern!

(They go out. MAN *comes from behind barrel. He and* SERGEANT *stand looking at one another.)*

SERGEANT. What are you waiting for?

MAN. For my hat, of course, and my wig. You wouldn't wish me to get my death of cold?

*(*SERGEANT *gives them.)*

MAN *(going towards steps)*. Well, good-night, comrade, and thank you. You did me a good turn to-night, and I'm obliged to you. Maybe I'll be able to do as much for you when the small rise up and the big fall down . . . when we all change places at the Rising *(waves his hand and disappears)* of the Moon.

SERGEANT *(turning his back to audience and reading placard)*. A hundred pounds reward! A hundred pounds! *(Turns toward audience.)* I wonder, now, am I as great a fool as I think I am?

Further Readings on Isabella Augusta, Lady Gregory

Bibliography

Carens, James F. "Lady Gregory." In *Anglo-Irish Literature: A Review of Research,* edited by R. J. Finneran, 437–46. New York: Modern Language Association, 1976.

Selected Works

Collected Works of Lady Gregory. The Coole Edition. Edited by T. R. Henn and Colin Smythe. 21 vols. Gerrards Cross, UK: Colin Smythe, 1969–76.
Cuchulain of Muirthemne: The Story of the Men of the Red Branch of Ulster. 1902. Reprint, Gerrards Cross, UK: Colin Smythe, 1970.
Gods and Fighting Men: The Story of the Tuatha de Danaan and of the Fianna of Ireland. 1904. Reprint, Gerrards Cross, UK: Colin Smythe, 1970.
Irish Myths and Legends. 1910. Reprint, Philadelphia: Courage Books, 1998.
Lady Gregory's Diaries, 1892–1902. Edited by James Pethica. New York: Oxford University Press, 1995.
The Rising of the Moon. First published in *Samhain* (December 1904). Reprinted in *Collected Plays.* vol. 1. Gerrards Cross, UK: Colin Smythe, 1971.
Selected Plays of Lady Gregory. Edited by Mary FitzGerald. Gerrards Cross, UK: Colin Smythe, 1983.
Selected Writings. Edited by Lucy McDiarmid and Maureen Waters. London: Penguin Books, 1995.

Biography and Criticism

Adams, Hazard. *Lady Gregory.* Irish Writers Series. Lewisburg, Pa.: Bucknell University Press, 1973.
Coxhead, Elizabeth. *Lady Gregory: A Literary Portrait.* London: Macmillan, 1961.
Kohfeldt, Mary Lou. *Lady Gregory, The Woman Behind the Irish Literary Renaissance.* London: Andre Deutsch, 1985.
Kopper, Richard A., Jr. *Lady Isabella Persse Gregory.* Boston: Twayne, 1976.
Saddlemyer, Ann. *In Defence of Lady Gregory, Playwright.* Dublin: Dolmen Press, 1966.
———, and Colin Smythe. *Lady Gregory, Fifty Years Later.* Gerrards Cross, UK: Colin Smythe, 1987.
Tóibín, Colm. *Lady Gregory's Toothbrush.* Dublin: Lilliput, 2002.

Lyric Voices of the Irish Renaissance

Although William Butler Yeats was the dominant Irish poet to emerge in the Irish Literary Renaissance (1895–1916), the movement allowed many distinctive talents to speak. Many, though not all, defined themselves in relation to Yeats, accepting or rejecting his visions of the Irish tradition, of nature, and of a world beyond the senses.

[margin note: Yeats influence]

T[homas] W[illiam] Rolleston (1857–1920) was better known in his lifetime as scholar and translator than as poet. He championed Walt Whitman, wrote commentaries on ancient philosophers, translated the works of Richard Wagner, and popularized Old Irish heroic narratives. His "Clonmacnoise" contemplates the Irish past at the monastic ruin on east bank of the Shannon in County Offaly, a seat of learning in the golden age of the Celtic church, c. A.D. 700–1100.

[margin note: golden age of the Celtic Church]

Katharine Tynan, or Tynan Hinkson (1861–1931), was a close friend of Yeats from her youth. At first a poet of nationalist sympathies, she became an astoundingly prolific prose writer with pro-British views. She published 105 novels, 18 collections of poetry, and 38 other volumes, including a valuable memoir of the beginnings of the Irish Renaissance, *Twenty-Five Years* (1913). Her poem "The Children of Lir" draws on an Old Irish story, much invested with mythological symbolism, in which the children of the sea god Lir are transformed by a cruel stepmother into swans, and remain so for nine hundred years when they finally return to human form.

George W. Russell (1867–1935) was an early friend and rival of Yeats, as well as a fellow-mystic who was later eclipsed by him. Russell—whose pseudonym, "AE," came from a printer's misunderstanding of an earlier pen-name, Aeon—was, like Yeats, a man of action as well of words. He edited several publications, fostered the careers of many younger writers, and became an authority on agricultural economy. A career of more than forty years produced many volumes of poetry, drama, and journalistic gleanings, as well as several distinguished paintings. "The Winds of Angus" alludes to the Old Irish god of poetry and love. "Terence MacSwiney" concerns the real man of that name, who served as lord mayor of Cork from 1879 to

1920 but died as a result of a hunger strike protesting his imprisonment by the British.

Padraic Colum (1881–1972) produced sixty-one books in sixty years, achieving distinction in every genre: drama, short and long fiction, biography, folklore, and children's literature. Born before James Joyce but outliving Brendan Behan, Colum the poet had many styles, including the spareness of modernism in his last collection, *Images of Departure* (1969), but he is best remembered for the pastoralism of his youth in the midland counties, as seen in "She Moved Through the Fair."

Francis Ledwidge (1887–1917) was a self-educated farm laborer who wrote nature poetry in evocation of Thomas Gray and Keats. Befriended by the fantasy-fiction writer Lord Dunsany (1878–1957), Ledwidge was introduced to Yeats's literary circle. Although a nationalist and a labor activist, he volunteered for the British Army and survived the disastrous invasion at Gallipoli, only to be killed in action in Belgium.

T. W. Rolleston (1857–1920)

Clonmacnoise

In a quiet water'd land, a land of roses,
  Stands Saint Kieran's city fair;
And the warriors of Erin in their famous generations
  Slumber there.

There beneath the dewy hillside sleep the noblest
  Of the clan of Conn,
Each below his stone with name in branching Ogham
  And the sacred knot thereon.

There they laid to rest the seven Kings of Tara,
  There the sons of Cairbré sleep—
Battle-banners of the Gael that in Kieran's plain of crosses
  Now their final hosting keep.

And in Clonmacnoise they laid the men of Teffia,
  And right many a lord of Breagh;
Deep the sod above Clan Creidé and Clan Conaill,
  Kind in hall and fierce in fray

[Handwritten annotations: "Great center of learning & burial place of kings. St. Kieran. Dermot, a local prince, helped him erect the first posts for his Church & when Dermot became High King, shortly afterwards he richly endowed the monastery. The monastery was plundered 6 times bet. 834–1012, burned 26 times bet 841–1204" / "SEAT OF Learning during golden age of the celtic church 700–1100 AD" / "Care-brea"]

Many and many a son of Conn the Hundred-fighter
    In the red earth lies at rest;
Many a blue eye of Clan Colman the turf covers,
    Many a swan-white breast.

Katharine Tynan Hinkson (1861–1931)

The Children of Lir

[handwritten: Lush visual imagery]

Out upon the sand-dunes thrive the coarse long grasses,
    Herons standing knee-deep in the brackish pool.
Overhead the sunset fire and flame amasses,
    And the moon to eastward rises pale and cool:
Rose and green about her, silver-grey and pearly
    Chequered with the black rooks flying home to bed:
For, to wake at daybreak, birds must couch them early,
    And the day's a long one since the dawn was red.

On the chilly lakelet, in that pleasant gloaming,
    See the sad swans sailing: they shall have no rest:
Never a voice to greet them save the bittern's booming
    Where the ghostly sallows sway against the West.
"Sister," saith the grey swan, "Sister, I am weary,"
    Turning to the white swan wet, despairing eyes;
"Oh," she saith, "my young one, oh," she saith, "my dearie,"
    Casts her wings about him with a storm of cries.

[handwritten: Aoife]

Woe for Lir's sweet children whom their vile stepmother
    Glamoured with her witch-spells for a thousand years;
Died their father raving, on his throne another,
    Blind before the end came from the burning tears.
Long the swans have wandered over lake and river.
    Gone is all the glory of the race of Lir,
Gone and long forgotten like a dream of fever:
    But the swans remember the sweet days that were.

Dews are in the clear air, and the roselight paling,
    Over sands and sedges shines the evening star,

And the moon's disc lonely high in heaven is sailing,
  Silvered all the spear-heads of the rushes are,—
Housed warm are all things as the night grows colder,
  Water-fowl and sky-fowl dreamless in the nest;
But the swans go drifting, drooping wing and shoulder
  Cleaving the still water where the fishes rest.

George W. Russell ["AE"] (1867–1935)

The Great Breath

Its edges foamed with amethyst and rose,
Withers once more the old blue flower of day:
There where the ether like a diamond glows
  Its petals fade away.

A shadowy tumult stirs the dusky air:
Sparkle the delicate dews, the distant snows;
The great deep thrills, for through it everywhere
  the breath of Beauty blows.

I saw how all the trembling ages past,
Moulded to her by deep and deeper breath,
Neared to the hour when Beauty breathes her last
  And knows herself in death.

Parting

As from our dream we died away
Far off I felt the outer things;
Your wind-blown tresses round me play,
Your bosom's gentle murmurings.

And far away our faces met
As on the verge of the vast spheres;
And in the night our cheeks were wet,
I could not say with dew or tears.

As one within the Mother's heart
In that hushed dream upon the height
We lived, and then we rose to part,
Because her ways are infinite.

The Winds of Angus

The grey road whereupon we trod became as holy ground:
The eve was all one voice that breathed its message with no sound:
And burning multitudes pour through my heart, too bright, too blind,
Too swift and hurried in their flight to leave their tale behind.
Twin gates unto that living world, dark honey-coloured eyes,
The lifting of whose lashes flushed the face with Paradise,
Beloved, there I saw within their ardent rays unfold
The likeness of enraptured birds that flew from deeps of gold
To deeps of gold within my breast to rest, or there to be
Transfigured in the light, or find a death to life in me.
So love, a burning multitude, a seraph wind that blows
From out the deep of being to the deep of being goes.
And sun and moon and starry fires and earth and air and sea.
Are creatures from the deep let loose, who pause in ecstasy,
Or wing their wild and heavenly way until again they find
The ancient deep, and fade therein, enraptured, bright, and blind.

Immortality

We must pass like smoke or live within the spirit's fire;
For we can no more than smoke unto the flame return
If our thought has changed to dream, our will unto desire,
    As smoke we vanish though the fire may burn.

Lights of infinite pity star the grey dusk of our days:
Surely here is soul: with it we have eternal breath:
In the fire of love we live, or pass by many ways,
    By unnumbered ways of dream to death.

Terence MacSwiney

[handwritten: he died protesting imprisonment by British]

[handwritten: Sonnet form]

See, though the oil below more purely still and higher
The flame burns in the body's lamp! The watchers still
Gaze with unseeing eyes while the Promethean Will,
The Uncreated Light, the Everlasting Fire
Sustains itself against the torturer's desire
Even as the fabled Titan chained upon the hill.
Burn on, shine on, thou immortality, until
We, too, have lit our lamps at the funereal pyre;
Till we, too, can be noble, unshakable, undismayed:
Till we, too, can burn with the holy flame, and know
There is that within us can triumph over pain,
And go to death, alone, slowly, and unafraid.
The candles of God are already burning row on row:
Farewell, lightbringer, fly to thy heaven again!

[handwritten: Gk. myth allusion]
[handwritten: MacSwiney compared to Prometheus]

Padraic Colum (1881–1972)

[handwritten: Pastoral quality]

She Moved Through the Fair

My young love said to me, "My brothers won't mind,
And my parents won't slight you for your lack of kind."
Then she stepped away from me, and this she did say,
"It will not be long, love, till our wedding day."

[handwritten: Lack of means / $]

She stepped away from me and she moved through the fair,
And fondly I watched her go here and go there,
Then she went her way homeward with one star awake,
As the swan in the evening moves over the lake.

The people were saying no two were e're wed
But one had a sorrow that never was said, — *[handwritten: narrator?]*
And I smiled as she passed with her goods and her gear,
And that was the last that I saw of my dear.

I dreamt it last night that my young love came in,
So softly she entered, her feet made no din;
She came close beside me, and this she did say,
"It will not be long, love, till our wedding day."

Francis Ledwidge (1887–1917)   *Best one*

June

Broom out the floor now, lay the fender by,
And plant this bee-sucked bough of woodbine there,
And let the window down. The butterfly
Floats in upon the sunbeam, and the fair
Tanned face of June, the nomad gipsy, laughs
Above her widespread wares, the while she tells
The farmer's fortunes in the fields, and quaffs
The water from the spider-peopled wells.

The hedges are all drowned in green grass seas,
And bobbing poppies flare like Elmo's light,
While siren-like the pollen-stainèd bees
Drone in the clover depths. And up the height
The cuckoo's voice is hoarse and broke with joy.
And on the lowland crops the crows make raid,
Nor fear the clappers of the farmer's boy,
Who sleeps, like drunken Noah, in the shade.   *allusion*

And loop this red rose in that hazel ring
That snares your little ear, for June is short
And we must joy in it and dance and sing,
And from her bounty draw her rosy worth.
Ay! soon the swallows will be flying south,
The wind wheel north to gather in the snow,
Even the roses split on youth's red mouth
Will soon blow down the road all roses go.

Thomas MacDonagh

[handwritten: Died in the Easter Rising — a poet & playwright]

He shall not hear the bittern cry
In the wild sky, where he is lain,
Nor voices of the sweeter birds
Above the wailing of the rain.

Nor shall he know when loud March blows
Thro' slanting snows her fanfare shrill,
Blowing to flame the golden cup
Of many an upset daffodil.

But when the Dark Cow leaves the moor,
And pastures poor with greedy weeds,
Perhaps he'll hear her low at morn
Lifting her horn in pleasant meads.

[handwritten: Ulster cycle ref]

Further Reading on Lyric Voices of the Irish Renaissance

Bibliography

Carens, James F. "AE (George W. Russell)." In *Anglo-Irish Literature: A Review of Research,* edited by R. J. Finneran, 446–52. New York: Modern Language Association, 1976.

Denson, Alan. *Printed Writings by George W. Russell (AE): A Bibliography.* 1961. Reprint, Gerrards Cross, UK: Colin Smythe, 1975.

Selected Works

Colum, Padraic. *Collected Poems.* New York: Devin-Adair, 1953.

———. *Images of Departure.* Dublin: Dolmen Press, 1969.

———. *Selected Poems.* Edited by Sanford Sternlicht. Syracuse, N.Y.: Syracuse University Press, 1989.

Ledwidge, Francis. *Complete Poems.* Edited by A. Curtayne. London: Martin Brian and O'Keefe, 1974; Dublin: Poolbeg, 1998.

———. *Complete Poems.* Edited by Liam O'Meara. Newbridge, Ireland: Goldsmith, 1997.

———. *Selected Poems.* Edited by Dermot Bolger. Dublin: New Island Books, 1992.

Rolleston, T. W. *The High Deeds of Finn MacCool.* London: Harrap, 1910.

———. *Myths and Legends of the Celtic Race.* 1911. Reprint, New York: Dover, 1990.

———. *Sea Spray: Verses and Translations.* Dublin: Maunsel, 1909.

Russell, George W. *Collected Poems.* 1913. Reprint, St. Clair Shores, Mich.: Scholarly Press, 1970.

Tynan Hinkson, Katharine. *Collected Poems.* London: Macmillan, 1930.

———. *Twenty-Five Years.* London: Smith Elder, 1913.

———. *Twenty One Poems.* Shannon: Irish University Press, 1970.

Biography and Criticism

Bowen, Zack. *Padraic Colum: A Biographical-Critical Introduction.* Carbondale, Ill.: Southern Illinois University Press, 1970.

Boyd, Ernest A. *Ireland's Literary Renaissance.* Rev. ed. New York: Knopf, 1922. Reprint, New York: Barnes and Noble, 1968.

Curtayne, Alice. *Francis Ledwidge: A Life of the Poet.* 1972. Reprint, Dublin: New Island Books, 1998.

Davis, Robert B. *George William Russell* ("AE"). Boston: Twayne, 1977.

Fallis, Richard. *The Irish Renaissance.* Syracuse, N.Y.: Syracuse University Press, 1977.

Fallon, Ann Connerton. *Katherine Tynan.* Boston: Twayne, 1979.

Figgis, Darrell. *AE, George Russell: A Study of a Man and a Nation.* 1916. Reprint, Port Washington, N.Y.: Kennikat Press, 1970.

Hall, Wayne E. *Shadowy Heroes: Irish Literature of the 1890s.* Syracuse, N.Y.: Syracuse University Press, 1980.

Howarth, Herbert. *Irish Writers, 1880–1940.* New York: Hill and Wang, 1958.

Journal of Irish Literature 2, no.1 (January 1973). Special issue on Padraic Colum, edited by Zack Bowen and Gordon Henderson.

Kain, Richard M., and J. H. O'Brien. *George Russell ("AE").* Lewisburg, Pa.: Bucknell University Press, 1976.

Kuch, Peter. *Yeats and AE.* Gerrards Cross, UK: Colin Smythe, 1986.

Marcus, Phillip L. *Yeats and the Beginning of the Irish Renaissance.* Ithaca, N.Y.: Cornell University Press, 1970.

O'Meara, Liam. *A Lantern on the Wave: Francis Ledwidge, Poet, Activist and Soldier.* Dublin: Riposte Books, 1999.

Rolleston, Charles H. *Portrait of an Irishman* [T. W. Rolleston]. London: Methuen, 1939.

Rose, Marilyn Gaddis. *Katharine Tynan.* Lewisburg, Pa.: Bucknell University Press, 1973.

Sommerfield, Henry. *That Myriad-Minded Man: A Biography of George William Russell.* Gerrards Cross, UK: Colin Smythe, 1975.

Sternlicht, Sanford. *Padraic Colum.* Boston: Twayne, 1985.

John Millington Synge

(1871–1909)

John Millington Synge (pronounced "sing") is the author of *The Playboy of the Western World* (1907), the most admired of all Irish dramas. The child of a Protestant family of the professional classes, Synge had a diverse cultural education in addition to his degree from Trinity College. He studied the violin in Germany and literature in Paris, and he knew Hebrew, German, French, and Irish. An oft-repeated, but inaccurate, story has it that Synge was struggling as a translator in Paris when Yeats suggested he find his theme for writing in the Aran Islands on Ireland's remote west coast. In fact, Synge had visited the islands before this time, and in the four years after Yeats is supposed to have advised him he spent only four and a half months on the islands but forty-three months in Paris! Nevertheless, the inaccurate story is instructive, since Synge indeed took his most important themes from the Irish peasantry—of the Aran Islands and the western counties of Mayo, Galway, Clare, and Kerry, as well as Wicklow, whose glens he had walked in his youth.

Synge described his travelogue-memoir *The Aran Islands*—completed in 1901 but not published until 1907—as his "first serious piece of work." He continued to produce essays, translations, and poetry, but his greatest contribution would be his plays. His first tentative effort was *When the Moon Has Set* (1900), but more successful works followed: *In the Shadow of the Glen* (1903), *Riders to the Sea* (1904), *The Well of the Saints* (1905), *The Playboy of the Western World* and *The Tinker's Wedding* (both 1907), and *Deirdre of the Sorrows* (posthumously published in 1910). Although Synge was the most significant playwright to emerge from the efforts of Yeats and Lady Gregory to found a national theater, controversy often followed his work. The riots that greeted the opening of *Playboy* in January, 1907, for example, marked one of the most infamous (and most widely reported) episodes in Irish literary history. Similarly, his outrageous farce *The Tinker's Wedding* was thought to be "too dangerous to be performed in Dublin" for almost fifty years.

As early as 1897, when he was only twenty-six, Synge had the first indications of the Hodgkins disease that would eventually kill him, but mercifully he was not in pain until 1907, two years before he died. Many of the poems included here date from those later years, when he knew that his own death was as imminent as that of the fishermen in *Riders to the Sea*.

Based on a story he had heard in the Aran Islands, *Riders to the Sea* embodies an important theme in Synge's writing: that people living at the edge of life and death know life more fully. Often described as the "only one-act tragedy in the English language," *Riders to the Sea* has an international reputation among non-Irish readers and theater-goers. The English composer Ralph Vaughan Williams turned it into an opera in 1936.

Riders to the Sea

MAURYA (*an old woman*)
BARTLEY (*her son*)
CATHLEEN (*her daughter*)
NORA (*a younger daughter*)
MEN and WOMEN

SCENE. *An Island off the West of Ireland. (Cottage kitchen, with nets, oilskins, spinning wheel, some new boards standing by the wall, etc. Cathleen, a girl of about twenty, finishes kneading cake, and puts it down in the pot-oven by the fire; then wipes her hands, and begins to spin at the wheel. Nora, a young girl, puts her head in at the door.)*

NORA (*in a low voice*). Where is she?

CATHLEEN. She's lying down, God help her, and may be sleeping, if she's able.

(NORA *comes in softly, and takes a bundle from under her shawl.*)

CATHLEEN (*spinning the wheel rapidly*). What is it you have?

NORA. The young priest is after bringing them. It's a shirt and a plain stocking were got off a drowned man in Donegal.

(CATHLEEN *stops her wheel with a sudden movement, and leans out to listen.*)

NORA. We're to find out if it's Michael's they are, some time herself will be down looking by the sea.

CATHLEEN. How would they be Michael's, Nora. How would he go the length of that way to the far north?

NORA. The young priest says he's known the like of it. "If it's Michael's they are," says he, "you can tell herself he's got a clean burial by the grace of God, and if they're not his, let no one say a word about them, for she'll be getting her death," says he, "with crying and lamenting."

(*The door which* NORA *half closed is blown open by a gust of wind.*)

CATHLEEN (*looking out anxiously*). Did you ask him would he stop Bartley going this day with the horses to the Galway fair?

NORA. "I won't stop him," says he, "but let you not be afraid. Herself does be saying prayers half through the night, and the Almighty God won't leave her destitute," says he, "with no son living."

CATHLEEN. Is the sea bad by the white rocks, Nora?

NORA. Middling bad, God help us. There's a great roaring in the west, and it's worse it'll be getting when the tide's turned to the wind.

(*She goes over to the table with the bundle.*)

Shall I open it now?

CATHLEEN. Maybe she'd wake up on us, and come in before we'd done. (*Coming to the table.*) It's a long time we'll be, and the two of us crying.

NORA (*goes to the inner door and listens*). She's moving about on the bed. She'll be coming in a minute.

CATHLEEN. Give me the ladder, and I'll put them up in the turf-loft, the way she won't know of them at all, and maybe when the tide turns she'll be going down to see would he be floating from the east.

(*They put the ladder against the gable of the chimney;* CATHLEEN *goes up a few steps and hides the bundle in the turf-loft.* MAURYA *comes from the inner room.*)

MAURYA (*looking up at* CATHLEEN *and speaking querulously*). Isn't it turf enough you have for this day and evening?

CATHLEEN. There's a cake baking at the fire for a short space (*throwing down the turf*) and Bartley will want it when the tide turns if he goes to Connemara.

(NORA *picks up the turf and puts it round the pot-oven.*)

MAURYA (*sitting down on a stool at the fire*). He won't go this day with the wind rising from the south and west. He won't this day, for the young priest will stop him surely.

NORA. He'll not stop him, mother, and I heard Eamon Simon and Stephen Pheety and Colum Shawn saying he would go.

MAURYA. Where is he itself?

NORA. He went down to see would there be another boat sailing in the week, and I'm thinking it won't be long till he's here now, for the tide's turning at the green head, and the hooker's tacking from the east.

CATHLEEN. I hear some one passing the big stones.

NORA (*looking out*). He's coming now, and he in a hurry.

BARTLEY (*comes in and looks round the room. Speaking sadly and quietly*). Where is the bit of new rope, Cathleen, was bought in Connemara?

CATHLEEN (*coming down*). Give it to him, Nora; it's on a nail by the white boards, I hung it up this morning, for the pig with the black feet was eating it.

NORA (*giving him a rope*). Is that it, Bartley?

MAURYA. You'd do right to leave that rope, Bartley, hanging by the boards. (BARTLEY *takes the rope*.) It will be wanting in this place, I'm telling you, if Michael is washed up to-morrow morning, or the next morning, or any morning in the week, for it's a deep grave we'll make him by the grace of God.

BARTLEY (*beginning to work with the rope*). I've not halter the way I can ride down on the mare, and I must go now quickly. This is the one boat going for two weeks or beyond it, and the fair will be a good fair for horses I heard them saying below.

MAURYA. It's a hard thing they'll be saying below if the body is washed up and there's no man in it to make the coffin, and I after giving a big price for the finest white boards you'd find in Connemara.

Pride in burial

(*She looks round at the boards.*)

BARTLEY. How would it be washed up, and we after looking each day for nine days, and a strong wind blowing a while back from the west and south?

MAURYA. If it wasn't found itself, that wind is raising the sea, and there was a star up against the moon, and it rising in the night. If it was a hundred horses, or a thousand horses you had itself, what is the price of a thousand horses against a son where there is one son only?

Tide lore (super stition)

BARTLEY (*working at the halter, to* CATHLEEN). Let you go down each day, and see the sheep aren't jumping in on the rye, and if the jobber comes you can sell the pig with the black feet if there is a good price going.

MAURYA. How would the like of her get a good price for a pig?

BARTLEY (*to* CATHLEEN). If the west wind holds with the last bit of the moon let you and Nora get up weed enough for another cock for the kelp. It's hard set we'll be from this day with no one in it but one man to work.

MAURYA. It's hard set we'll be surely the day you're drownd'd with the rest. What way will I live and the girls with me, and I an old woman looking for the grave?

Prophetic

(BARTLEY *lays down the halter, takes off his old coat, and puts on a newer one of the same flannel.*)

boat

BARTLEY (*to* NORA). Is she coming to the pier?

NORA (*looking out*). She's passing the green head and letting fall her sails.

BARTLEY (*getting his purse and tobacco*). I'll have half an hour to go down, and you'll see me coming again in two days, or in three days, or maybe in four days if the wind is bad.

MAURYA (*turning round to the fire, and putting her shawl over her head*).

Isn't it a hard and cruel man won't hear a word from an old woman, and she holding him from the sea?

CATHLEEN. It's the life of a young man to be going on the sea, and who would listen to an old woman with one thing and she saying it over?

BARTLEY (*taking the halter*). I must go now quickly. I'll ride down on the red mare, and the gray pony 'll run behind me. . . . The blessing of God on you.

(*He goes out.*)   *identification*

MAURYA (*crying out as he is in the door*). He's gone now, God spare us, and we'll not see him again. He's gone now, and when the black night is falling I'll have no son left me in the world. (*She knows*)

CATHLEEN. Why wouldn't you give him your blessing and he looking round in the door? Isn't it sorrow enough is on everyone in this house without your sending him out with an unlucky word behind him, and a hard word in his ear?

Import of her blessing

(MAURYA *takes up the tongs and begins raking the fire aimlessly without looking around.*)

NORA (*turning towards her*). You're taking away the turf from the cake.

CATHLEEN (*crying out*). The Son of God forgive us, Nora, we're after forgetting his bit of bread.

(*She comes over to the fire.*)

NORA. And it's destroyed he'll be going till dark night, and he after eating nothing since the sun went up.

CATHLEEN (*turning the cake out of the oven*). It's destroyed he'll be, surely. There's no sense left on any person in a house where an old woman will be talking for ever.

(MAURYA *sways herself on her stool.*)

CATHLEEN (*cutting off some of the bread and rolling it in a cloth; to* MAURYA). Let you go down now to the spring well and give him this and he passing. You'll see him then and the dark word will be broken, and you can say, "God speed you," the way he'll be easy in his mind.

MAURYA (*taking the bread*). Will I be in it as soon as himself?

CATHLEEN. If you go now quickly.

MAURYA (*standing up unsteadily*). It's hard set I am to walk.

CATHLEEN (*looking at her anxiously*). Give her the stick, Nora, or maybe she'll slip on the big stones.

NORA. What stick?

CATHLEEN. The stick Michael brought from Connemara.

MAURYA (*taking a stick* NORA *gives her*). In the big world the old people *unnatural*

do be leaving things after them for their sons and children, but in this place it
is the young men do be leaving things behind for them that do be old.

(*She goes out slowly.* NORA *goes over to the ladder.*)

CATHLEEN. Wait, Nora, maybe she'd turn back quickly. She's that sorry,
God help her, you wouldn't know the thing she'd do.

NORA. Is she gone round by the bush?

CATHLEEN (*looking out*). She's gone now. Throw it down quickly, for the
Lord knows when she'll be out of it again.

NORA (*getting the bundle from the loft*). The young priest said he'd be
passing to-morrow, and we might go down and speak to him below if it's
Michael's they are surely.

CATHLEEN (*taking the bundle*). Did he say what way they were found?

NORA (*coming down*). "There were two men," says he, "and they rowing
round with poteen before the cocks crowed, and the oar of one of them
caught the body, and they passing the black cliffs of the north."

CATHLEEN (*trying to open the bundle*). Give me a knife, Nora, the string's
perished with the salt water, and there's a black knot on it you wouldn't
loosen in a week.

NORA (*giving her a knife*). I've heard tell it was a long way to Donegal.

CATHLEEN (*cutting the string*). It is surely. There was a man in here a
while ago—the man sold us that knife—and he said if you set off walking from
the rocks beyond, it would be seven days you'd be in Donegal.

NORA. And what time would a man take, and he floating?

(*Cathleen opens the bundle and takes out a bit of a stocking. They look at
them eagerly.*)

CATHLEEN (*in a low voice*). The Lord spare us, Nora! isn't it a queer hard
thing to say if it's his they are surely?

NORA. I'll get his shirt off the hook the way we can put the one flannel on
the other. (*She looks through some clothes hanging in the corner.*) It's not with
them, Cathleen, and where will it be? *Bartley wears the dead man's shirt*

CATHLEEN. I'm thinking Bartley put it on him in the morning, for his
own shirt was heavy with the salt in it (*pointing to the corner*). There's a bit of
a sleeve was of the same stuff. Give me that and it will do.

(NORA *brings it to her and they compare the flannel.*)

CATHLEEN. It's the same stuff, Nora; but if it is itself aren't there great
rolls of it in the shops of Galway, and isn't it many another man may have a
shirt of it as well as Michael himself?

NORA (*who has taken up the stocking and counted the stitches, crying out*).

identified by knitted pattern

It's Michael, Cathleen, it's Michael; God spare his soul, and what will herself say when she hears this story, and Bartley on the sea?

CATHLEEN *(taking the stocking)*. It's a plain stocking.

NORA. It's the second one of the third pair I knitted, and I put up three score stitches, and I dropped four of them.

CATHLEEN *(counts the stitches)*. It's that number is in it *(crying out)*. Ah, Nora, isn't it a bitter thing to think of him floating that way to the far north, and no one to keen him but the black hags that do be flying on the sea?   Superstition

NORA *(swinging herself round, and throwing out her arms on the clothes)*. And isn't it a pitiful thing when there is nothing left of a man who was a great rower and fisher, but a bit of an old shirt and a plain stocking?

CATHLEEN *(after an instant)*. Tell me is herself coming, Nora? I hear a little sound on the path.

NORA *(looking out)*. She is, Cathleen. She's coming up to the door.

CATHLEEN. Put these things away before she'll come in. Maybe it's easier she'll be after giving her blessing to Bartley, and we won't let on we've heard anything the time he's on the sea.

NORA *(helping CATHLEEN to close the bundle)*. We'll put them here in the corner.

(They put them into a hole In the chimney corner. CATHLEEN goes back to the spinning-wheel.)

NORA. Will she see it was crying I was?

CATHLEEN. Keep your back to the door the way the light'll not be on you.

(NORA sits down at the chimney corner, with her back to the door. MAURYA comes in very slowly, without looking at the girls, and goes over to her stool at the other side of the fire. The cloth with the bread is still in her hand. The girls look at each other, and NORA points to the bundle of bread.)

CATHLEEN *(after spinning for a moment)*. You didn't give him his bit of bread?

(MAURYA begins to keen softly, without turning round.)

CATHLEEN. Did you see him riding down?

(MAURYA goes on keening.)

CATHLEEN *(a little impatiently)*. God forgive you; isn't it a better thing to raise your voice and tell what you seen, than to be making lamentation for a thing that's done? Did you see Bartley, I'm saying to you.

MAURYA *(with a weak voice)*. My heart's broken from this day.

CATHLEEN *(as before)*. Did you see Bartley?

MAURYA. I seen the fearfulest thing.

CATHLEEN *(leaves her wheel and looks out)*. God forgive you; he's riding the mare now over the green head, and the gray pony behind him.

MAURYA *(starts, so that her shawl falls back from her head and shows her white tossed hair. With a frightened voice)*. The gray pony behind him.

CATHLEEN *(coming to the fire)*. What is it ails you, at all?

MAURYA *(speaking very slowly)*. I've seen the fearfulest thing any person has seen, since the day Bride Dara seen the dead man with the child in his arms. *a vision*

CATHLEEN and NORA. Uah.

(They crouch down in front of the old woman at the fire.)

NORA. Tell us what it is you seen.

MAURYA. I went down to the spring well, and I stood there saying a prayer to myself. Then Bartley came along, and he riding on the red mare with the gray pony behind him. *(She puts up her hands, as if to hide something from her eyes.)* The Son of God spare us, Nora!

CATHLEEN. What is it you seen?

MAURYA. I seen Michael himself. *M. Has a vision of Michael on grey pony*

CATHLEEN *(speaking softly)*. You did not, mother; It wasn't Michael you seen, for his body is after being found in the far north, and he's got a clean burial by the grace of God.

MAURYA *(a little defiantly)*. I'm after seeing him this day, and he riding and galloping. Bartley came first on the red mare; and I tried to say "God speed you," but something choked the words in my throat. He went by quickly; and "the blessing of God on you," says he, and I could say nothing. I looked up then, and I crying, at the gray pony, and there was Michael upon it—with fine clothes on him, and new shoes on his feet.

CATHLEEN *(begins to keen)*. It's destroyed we are from this day. It's destroyed, surely.

NORA. Didn't the young priest say the Almighty God wouldn't leave her destitute with no son living? *indictment of young priest*

MAURYA *(in a low voice, but clearly)*. It's little the like of him knows of the sea. . . . Bartley will be lost now, and let you call in Eamon and make me a good coffin out of the white boards, for I won't live after them. I've had a husband, and a husband's father, and six sons in this house—six fine men, though it was a hard birth I had with everyone of them and they coming to the world—and some of them were found and some of them were not found, but they're gone now the lot of them. . . . There were Stephen, and Shawn, were *Litany of loss* lost in the great wind, and found after in the Bay of Gregory of the Golden Mouth, and carried up the two of them on the one plank, and in by that door.

(She pauses for a moment, the girls start as if they heard something through the door that is half open behind them.)

NORA *(in a whisper)*. Did you hear that, Cathleen? Did you hear a noise in the north-east?

CATHLEEN *(in a whisper)*. There's some one after crying out by the seashore.

MAURYA *(continues without hearing anything)*. There was Sheamus and his father, and his own father again, were lost in a dark night, and not a stick or sign was seen of them when the sun went up. There was Patch after was drowned out of a curragh that turned over. I was sitting here with Bartley, and he a baby, lying on my two knees, and I seen two women, and three women, and four women coming in, and they crossing themselves, and not saying a word. I looked out then, and there were men coming after them, and they holding a thing in the half of a red sail, and water dripping out of it—it was a dry day, Nora—and leaving a track to the door.

(She pauses again with her hand stretched out towards the door. It opens softly and old women begin to come in, crossing themselves on the threshold, and kneeling down in front of the stage with red petticoats over their heads.)

MAURYA *(half in a dream, to* CATHLEEN*)*. Is it Patch, or Michael, or what is it at all?

CATHLEEN. Michael is after being found in the far north, and when he is found there how could he be here in this place?

MAURYA. There does be a power of young men floating round in the sea, and what way would they know if it was Michael they had, or another man like him, for when a man is nine days in the sea, and the wind blowing, it's hard set his own mother would be to say what man was it.

CATHLEEN. It's Michael. God spare him, for they're after sending us a bit of his clothes from the far north.

(She reaches out and hands MAURYA *the clothes that belonged to Michael.* MAURYA *stands up slowly and takes them in her hands.* NORA *looks out.)*

NORA. They're carrying a thing among them and there's water dripping out of it and leaving a track by the big stones.

CATHLEEN *(in a whisper to the women who have come in)*. Is it Bartley it is?

ONE OF THE WOMEN. It is surely, God rest his soul.

(Two younger WOMEN *come in and pull out the table. Then men carry in the body of* BARTLEY, *laid on a plank, with a bit of a sail over it, and lay it on the table.)* Bartley's body

CATHLEEN (*in a whisper to the women who have come in*). What way was he drowned?

vision realized

ONE OF THE WOMEN. The gray pony knocked him into the sea, and he was washed out where there is a great surf on the white rocks.

(MAURYA *has gone over and knelt down at the head of the table. The women are keening softly and swaying themselves with a slow movement.* CATHLEEN *and* NORA *kneel at the other end of the table. The* MEN *kneel near the door.*)

famous speech

MAURYA (*raising her head and speaking as if she did not see the people around her*). They're all gone now, and there isn't anything more the sea can do to me. . . . I'll have no call now to be up crying and praying when the wind breaks from the south, and you can hear the surf is in the east, and the surf is in the west, making a great stir with the two noises, and they hitting one on the other. I'll have no call now to be going down and getting Holy Water in the dark nights after Samhain, and I won't care what way the sea is when the other women will be keening. (*To* NORA.) Give me the Holy Water, Nora, there's a small sup still on the dresser.

(NORA *gives it to her.*)

MAURYA (*drops* MICHAEL'S *clothes across* BARTLEY'S *feet, and sprinkles the Holy Water over him.*) It isn't that I haven't prayed for you, Bartley, to the Almighty God. It isn't that I haven't said prayers in the dark night till you wouldn't know what I'ld be saying; but it's a great rest I'll have now, and great sleeping in the long nights after Samhain, if it's only a bit of wet flour we do have to eat, and maybe a fish that would be stinking.

(*She kneels down again, crossing herself, and saying prayers under her breath.*)

CATHLEEN (*to an old man*). Maybe yourself and Eamon would make a coffin when the sun rises. We have fine white boards herself bought, God help her, thinking Michael would be found, and I have a new cake you can eat while you'll be working. (*had been for Bartley*)

THE OLD MAN (*looking at the boards*). Are there nails with them?

CATHLEEN. There are not, Colum; we didn't think of the nails.

ANOTHER MAN. It's a great wonder she wouldn't think of the nails, and all the coffins she's seen made already.

CATHLEEN. It's getting old she is, and broken.

(MAURYA *stands up again very slowly and spreads out the pieces of* MICHAEL'S *clothes beside the body, sprinkling them with the last of the Holy Water.*)

NORA (*in a whisper to* CATHLEEN). She's quiet now and easy; but the day

Michael was drowned you could hear her crying out from this to the spring well. It's fonder she was of Michael, and would any one have thought that?

CATHLEEN (*slowly and clearly*). An old woman will be soon tired with anything she will do, and isn't it nine days herself is after crying and keening, and making great sorrow in the house? *gesture*

MAURYA (*puts the empty cup mouth downwards on the table, and lays her hands together on* BARTLEY'S *feet*). They're all together this time, and the end is come. May the Almighty God have mercy on Bartley's soul, and on Michael's soul, and on the souls of Sheamus and Patch, and Stephen and Shawn (*bending her head*); and may He have mercy on my soul, Nora, and on the soul of every one is left living in the world.

(*She pauses, and the keen rises a little more loudly from the women, then sinks away.*)

MAURYA (*continuing*). Michael has a clean burial in the far north, by the grace of the Almighty God. Bartley will have a fine coffin out of the white boards, and a deep grave surely. What more can we want than that? No man at all can be living for ever, and we must be satisfied.

(*She kneels down again and the curtain falls slowly.*)

[handwritten margin note: Somewhat like a Greek chorus finale]

Prelude

Still south I went and west and south again.
Through Wicklow from the morning till the night,
And far from cities, and the sites of men,
Lived with the sunshine and the moon's delight.

I knew the stars, the flowers, and the birds,
The grey and wintry sides of many glens,
And did but half remember human words,
In converse with the mountains, moors, and fens.

[handwritten margin note: Synge believed that poetry of his time needed to learn to be brutal in order to become human again]

On an Anniversary

AFTER READING THE DATES IN A BOOK OF LYRICS

With Fifteen-ninety or Sixteen-sixteen
We end Cervantes, Marot, Nashe or Green:
Then Sixteen-thirteen till two score and nine,
Is Crashaw's niche, that honey-lipped divine.
And so when all my little work is done

They'll say I came in Eighteen-seventy-one,
And died in Dublin. . . . What year will they write
For my poor passage to the stall of Night?

Queens

Seven dog-days we let pass
Naming Queens in Glenmacnass,
All the rare and royal names
Wormy sheepskin yet retains,
Etain, Helen, Maeve, and Fand,
Golden Deirdre's tender hand,
Bert, the big-foot, sung by Villon,
Cassandra, Ronsard found in Lyon.
Queens of Sheba, Meath and Connaught,
Coifed with crown, or gaudy bonnet,
Queens whose finger once did stir men,
Queens were eaten of fleas and vermin,
Queens men drew like Monna Lisa,
Or slew with drugs in Rome and Pisa,
We named Lucrezia Crivelli,
And Titian's lady with amber belly,
Queens acquainted in learned sin,
Jane of Jewry's slender shin:
Queens who cut the bogs of Glanna,
Judith of Scripture, and Gloriana,
Queens who wasted the East by proxy,
Or drove the ass-cart, a tinker's doxy,
Yet these are rotten—I ask their pardon—
And we've the sun on rock and garden,
These are rotten, so you're the Queen
Of all are living, or have been.

The Passing of the Shee—

AFTER LOOKING AT ONE OF A.E.'S PICTURES

Adieu, sweet Angus, Maeve and Fand,
Ye plumed yet skinny Shee,

That poets played with hand in hand
To learn their ecstasy.

We'll search in Red Dan Sally's ditch,
And drink in Tubber fair,
Or poach with Red Dan Philly's bitch
The badger and the hare.

On an Island

You've plucked a curlew, drawn a hen,
Washed the shirts of seven men,
You've stuffed my pillow, stretched the sheet,
And filled the pan to wash your feet,
You've cooped the pullets, wound the clock,
And rinsed the young men's drinking crock;
And now we'll dance to jigs and reels,
Nailed boots chasing girls' naked heels,
Until your father'll start to snore,
And Jude, now you're married, will stretch on the floor.

Is It a Month

Is it a month since I and you
In the starlight of Glen Dubh
Stretched beneath a hazel bough
Kissed from ear and throat to brow,
Since your fingers, neck, and chin
Made the bars that fenced me in,
Till Paradise seemed but a wreck
Near your bosom, brow, and neck
And stars grew wilder, growing wise,
In the splendour of your eyes!
Since the weasel wandered near
Whilst we kissed from ear to ear
And the wet and withered leaves
Blew about your cap and sleeves,
Till the moon sank tired through the ledge

Of the wet and windy hedge?
And we took the starry lane
Back to Dublin town again.

Beg-Innish

Bring Kateen-beug and Maurya Jude
To dance in Beg-Innish,
And when the lads (they're in Dunquin)
Have sold their crabs and fish,
Wave fawny shawls and call them in,
And call the little girls who spin,
And seven weavers from Dunquin,
To dance in Beg-Innish.

I'll play you jigs, and Maurice Kean,
Where nets are laid to dry,
I've silken strings would draw a dance
From girls are lame or shy;
Four strings I've brought from Spain and France
To make your long men skip and prance,
Till stars look out to see the dance
Where nets are laid to dry.

We'll have no priest or peeler in
To dance in Beg-Innish;
But we'll have drink from M'riarty Jim
Rowed round while gannets fish,
A keg with porter to the brim,
That every lad may have his whim,
Till we up sails with M'riarty Jim
And sail from Beg-Innish.

To the Oaks of Glencree

My arms are round you, and I lean
Against you, while the lark

[handwritten marginalia: Refers to subjects of Celtic Twilight that were finished for any real creative purpose. Synge was ahead of his time as he was poetry as his plays in his vision of Ireland, this. He had no use for what he saw as nationalistic nonsense about his country]

[handwritten marginalia: Synge is very ill at this point]

Sings over us, and golden lights, and green
Shadows are on your bark.

There'll come a season when you'll stretch
Black boards to cover me:
Then in Mount Jerome I will lie, poor wretch,
With worms eternally.

The Curse

TO A SISTER OF AN ENEMY OF THE AUTHOR'S WHO
DISAPPROVED OF "THE PLAYBOY"

Lord, confound this surly sister,
Blight her brow with blotch and blister,
Cramp her larynx, lung, and liver,
In her guts a galling give her.
Let her live to earn her dinners
In Mountjoy with seedy sinners:
Lord, this judgment quickly bring,
And I'm your servant, J. M. Synge.

In Kerry

We heard the thrushes by the shore and sea,
And saw the golden stars' nativity,
Then round we went the lane by Thomas Flynn,
Across the church where bones lie out and in;
And there I asked beneath a lonely cloud
Of strange delight, with one bird singing loud,
What change you'd wrought in graveyard, rock and sea,
This new wild paradise to wake for me . . .
Yet knew no more than knew these merry sins
Had built this stack of thigh-bones, jaws and shins.

On a Birthday

Friend of Ronsard, Nashe, and Beaumont,
Lark of Ulster, Meath and Thomond,
Heard from Smyrna and Sahara

To the surf of Connemara,
Lark of April, June, and May,
Sing loudly this my Lady-day.

A Question

I asked if I got sick and died, would you
With my black funeral go walking too,
If you'd stand close to hear them talk or pray
While I'm let down in that steep bank of clay.
And, No, you said, for if you saw a crew
Of living idiots, pressing round that new
Oak coffin—they alive, I dead beneath
That board,—you'd rave and rend them with your teeth.

Further Readings on John Millington Synge

Bibliography

Levitt, Paul. *John Millington Synge: A Bibliography of Published Criticism*. New York: Barnes and Noble, 1973.
Mikhail, E. H. *John Millington Synge: A Bibliography of Criticism*, Totowa, N.J.: Rowman and Littlefield, 1975.
Thornton, Weldon. "J. M. Synge." In *Anglo-Irish Literature: A Review of Research,* edited by R. J. Finneran, 315–65. New York: Modern Language Association, 1976.

Selected Works

Collected Works. Edited by Robin Skelton and Ann Saddlemyer. 4 vols. London: Oxford University Press, 1962–68. Reprint, Washington, D.C.: Catholic University Press, 1983.
Complete Plays. New York: Vintage, 1960.
Letters to Molly: John Millington Synge to Máire O'Neill, 1906–1909. Edited by Ann Saddlemyer. Cambridge: Harvard University Press, 1971.

Biography and Criticism

Benson, Eugene. *J. M. Synge*. London: Macmillan, 1983.
Bushrui, Suheil B., ed. *Sunshine and the Moon's Delight: A Centenary Tribute to John Millington Synge, 1871–1909*. Gerrards Cross, UK: Colin Smythe, 1972.

Casey, Daniel, ed. *Critical Essays on John Millington Synge.* New York: G. K. Hall, 1994.

Castle, Gregory. *Modernism and the Celtic Revival.* Cambridge: Cambridge University Press, 2001.

Corkery, Daniel. *Synge and Anglo-Irish Literature: A Study.* 1931. Reprint, Cork: Mercier Books, 1966.

Coxhead, Elizabeth. *J. M. Synge and Lady Gregory.* London: Longmans, 1962.

Fleming, Deborah. *The Man Who Does Not Exist: The Irish Peasant in the Work of W. B. Yeats and J. M. Synge.* Ann Arbor: University of Michigan Press, 1995.

Gerstenberger, Donna. *John Millington Synge.* New York: Twayne, 1964.

Greene, David Herbert, and Edward M. Stephens. *J. M. Synge, 1871–1909.* New York: Macmillan, 1959.

Grene, Nicholas. *Synge: A Critical Interpretation of the Plays.* London: Macmillan, 1975.

Harmon, Maurice, ed. *J. M. Synge Centenary Papers, 1971.* Dublin: Dolmen Press, 1972.

Johnson, Toni O'Brien. *Synge: The Medieval and the Grotesque.* Gerrards Cross, UK: Colin Smythe, 1982.

Johnston, Denis. *John Millington Synge.* New York: Columbia University Press, 1965.

Kiberd, Declan. *Synge and the Irish Language.* Totowa, N.J.: Rowman and Littlefield, 1979.

Kiely, David M. *John Millington Synge: A Biography.* New York: St. Martin's Press, 1994.

Kilroy, James. *The "Playboy" Riots.* Dublin: Dolmen Press, 1971.

King, Mary C. *The Drama of J. M. Synge.* Syracuse, N.Y.: Syracuse University Press, 1986.

Krause, David. *The Regeneration of Ireland.* Bethesda, Md.: Academica Press, 2001.

McCormack, W. J. *Fool of the Family: A Life of J. M. Synge.* London: Weinfeld and Nicolson, 2000.

———. *The Silence of Barbara Synge.* Manchester: Manchester University Press, 2002.

Price, Alan Frederick. *Synge and Anglo-Irish Drama.* London: Methuen, 1961.

Saddlemyer, Ann. *J. M. Synge and Modern Comedy.* Dublin: Dolmen Press, 1968.

Skelton, Robin. *J. M. Synge.* Lewisburg, Pa.: Bucknell University Press, 1972.

———. *J. M. Synge and His World.* New York: Viking, 1971.

———. *The Writings of J. M. Synge.* London: Thames and Hudson, 1971.

Thornton, Weldon. *J. M. Synge and the Western Mind.* New York: Harper and Row, 1979.

Whitaker, Thomas R., ed. *Twentieth Century Interpretations of "The Playboy of the Western World."* Englewood Cliffs, N.J.: Prentice-Hall, 1969.

[handwritten: See Irish Writers DVD]

[handwritten: He encouraged Yeats to write his autobiography Reveries Over childhood + youth 1914]

[handwritten: — born in Connemara, entertained Gogarty]

George Moore
(1852–1933)

[handwritten: Inventor of the Irish literary autobiography. Mod. Irish Lit. is rich in autobiog. writing e.g. Frank O'Connor's An Only Child + Patrick Kavanagh The Green Fool]

[handwritten: Behan's Borstal Boy]

George Moore was one of the most cosmopolitan Irish authors of any generation. Born in County Mayo to landed gentry, he was equally at home in Paris, where he studied art from 1873 to 1880, and in London, where he was something of a literary lion. From 1901 to 1911 he resided in Dublin, where he was active in the Irish literary revival, and where he served as an adviser and sometime collaborator of Yeats. His memoir of the years in Dublin, the three-volume *Hail and Farewell* (*Ave* [1911]; *Salve* [1912]; and *Vale* [1914]), is one of the most personal (if mordant) retellings of those glory years. Moore achieved distinction as novelist, short-story writer, dramatist, essayist, art critic, and poet. His best-known (if not best) work, *Esther Waters* (1894), is set in England. A symbolic novel set in rural Ireland, *The Lake*, has been praised by critic John V. Kelleher as the finest of all Irish novels excepting *Ulysses*. As a dramatist, he was a disciple of Ibsen in his *Strike at Arlingford* (1893). Yet he also co-wrote *Diarmuid and Grania* with Yeats in 1901.

"Julia Cahill's Curse" comes from Moore's collection *The Untilled Field* (1903), based on perceptions of a homeland revisited in middle age. In his own words, the stories were written . . . "out of no desire of self-expression, but in the hope of furnishing the young Irish of the future with models." The collection was translated into the Irish language and published in 1902, with the thought that the English originals would be burned. But when sales for the Irish language volume were disappointing, *The Untilled Field* was issued in its present form. In the collection, Moore draws from such Continental writers as Dostoevski, Zola, and Turgenev, and anticipates an Irish one: James Joyce.

[handwritten: Moore believed the future of Irish lit. lay not in English, but in the old tongue.]

Julia Cahill's Curse

"And what has become of Margaret?"

"Ah, didn't her mother send her to America as soon as the baby was born? Once a woman is waked here she has to go. Hadn't Julia to go in the end, and she the only one that ever said she didn't mind the priest?"

"Julia who?" said I.

Recall priest in Ballroom of Romance

"Julia Cahill."

Infamous

The name struck my fancy, and I asked the driver to tell me her story.

"Wasn't it Father Madden who had her put out of the parish, but she put her curse on it, and it's on it to this day."

"Do you believe in curses?"

"Bedad I do, sir. It's a terrible thing to put a curse on a man, and the curse that Julia put on Father Madden's parish was a bad one, the divil a worse. The sun was up at the time, and she on the hilltop raising both her hands. And the curse she put on the parish was that every year a roof must fall in and a family go to America. That was the curse, your honour, and every word of it has come true. You'll see for yourself as soon as we cross the mearing."

"And what became of Julia's baby?"

"I never heard she had one, sir."

He flicked his horse pensively with his whip, and it seemed to me that the disbelief I had expressed in the power of the curse disinclined him for further conversation.

"But," I said, "who is Julia Cahill, and how did she get the power to put a curse upon the village?"

Power from fairies

"Didn't she go into the mountains every night to meet the fairies, and who else could've given her the power to put a curse on the village?"

"But she couldn't walk so far in one evening."

"Them that's in league with the fairies can walk that far and as much farther in an evening, your honour. A shepherd saw her; and you'll see the ruins of the cabins for yourself as soon as we cross the mearing, and I'll show you the cabin of the blind woman that Julia lived with before she went away."

"And how long is it since she went?"

"About twenty year, and there hasn't been a girl the like of her in these parts since. I was only a gossoon at the time, but I've heard tell she was as tall as I'm myself and as straight as a poplar. She walked with a little swing in her walk, so that all the boys used to be looking after her, and she had fine black eyes, sir, and she was nearly always laughing. Father Madden had just come to the parish; and there was courting in these parts then, for aren't we the same as other people—we'd like to go out with a girl well enough if it was the custom of the country. Father Madden put down the ball alley because he said the boys stayed there instead of going into Mass, and he put down the cross-road dances because he said dancing was the cause of many a bastard, and he wanted none in his parish. Now there was no dancer like Julia; the boys used to gather about to see her dance, and who ever walked with her under the hedges in the summer could never think about another woman. The village

courtship

→ Fr. Madden's restrictions

was cracked about her. There was fighting, so I suppose the priest was right: he had to get rid of her. But I think he mightn't have been as hard on her as he was.

"One evening he went down to the house. Julia's people were well-to-do people, they kept a grocery-store in the village; and when he came into the shop who should be there but the richest farmer in the country, Michael Moran by name, trying to get Julia for his wife. He didn't go straight to Julia, and that's what swept him. There are two counters in that shop, and Julia was at the one on the left hand as you go in. And many's the pound she had made for her parents at that counter. Michael Moran says to the father, 'Now, what fortune are you going to give with Julia?' And the father says there was many a man who would take her without any; and that's how they spoke, and Julia listening quietly all the while at the opposite counter. For Michael didn't know what a spirited girl she was, but went on arguing till he got the father to say fifty pounds, and thinking he had got him so far he said, 'I'll never drop a flap to her unless you give the two heifers.' Julia never said a word, she just sat listening. It was then that the priest came in. And over he goes to Julia; 'And now,' says he, 'aren't you proud to hear that you'll have such a fine fortune, and it's I that'll be glad to see you married, for I can't have any more of your goings-on in my parish. You're the encouragement of the dancing and courting here; but I'm going to put an end to it.' Julia didn't answer a word, and he went over to them that were arguing about the sixty pounds. 'Now why not make it fifty-five?' says he. So the father agreed to that since the priest had said it. And all three of them thought the marriage was settled. 'Now what will you be taking, Father Tom?' says Cahill, 'and you, Michael?' Sorra one of them thought of asking her if she was pleased with Michael; but little did they know what was passing in her mind, and when they came over to the counter to tell her what they had settled, she said, 'Well, I've just been listening to you, and 'tis well for you to be wasting your time talking about me,' and she tossed her head, saying she would just pick the boy out of the parish that pleased her best. And what angered the priest most of all was her way of saying it—that the boy that would marry her would be marrying herself and not the money that would be paid when the book was signed or when the first baby was born. Now it was agin girls marrying according to their fancy that Father Madden had set himself. He had said in his sermon the Sunday before that young people shouldn't be allowed out by themselves at all, but that the parents should make up the marriages for them. And he went fairly wild when Julia told him the example she was going to set. He tried to keep his temper, sir, but it was getting the better of him all the while, and Julia said, 'My boy isn't in the parish now, but maybe he is on his way here, and he may be here to-morrow or the next day.' And when Julia's father heard her speak like that he knew that no one would turn her from what she was saying, and he said, 'Michael Moran, my good man, you may go your way: you'll never get her.' Then he went back to hear what Julia was saying to the priest, but it was the priest that was talking. 'Do you think,' says he, 'I am going to let you go on turning the head of every boy in the parish? Do you think, says he, I'm going to see you gallavanting with one and then with the other? Do you think I'm going to see fighting and quarrelling for your like? Do you think I'm going to hear stories like I heard last week about poor Patsy Carey, who has gone out of his mind, they say, on account of your treatment? No.' says he, 'I'll have no more of that. I'll have you out of my parish, or I'll have you married,' Julia didn't answer the priest, she tossed her head, and went on making up parcels of tea and sugar and getting the steps and taking down candles, though she didn't want them just to show the priest that she didn't mind what he was saying. And all the while her father trembling, not knowing what would happen, for the priest had a big stick, and there was no saying that he wouldn't strike her. Cahill tried to quiet the priest, he promising him that Julia shouldn't go out any more in the evenings, and bedad, sir, she was out the same evening with a young man and the priest saw them, and the next evening she was out with another and the priest saw them, nor was she minded at the end of the month to marry any of them. Then the priest went down to the shop to speak to her a second time, and he went down again a third time, though what he said the third time no one knows, no one being there at the time. And next Sunday he spoke out, saying that a disobedient daughter would have the worst devil in hell to attend on her. I've heard tell that he called her the evil spirit that set men mad. But most of the people that were there are dead or gone to America, and no one rightly knows what he did say, only that the words came pouring out of his mouth, and the people when they saw Julia crossed themselves, and even the boys who were most mad after Julia were afraid to speak to her. Cahill had to put her out."

"Do you mean to say that the father put his daughter out?"

"Sure, didn't the priest threaten to turn him into a rabbit if he didn't, and no one in the parish would speak to Julia, they were so afraid of Father Madden, and if it hadn't been for the blind woman that I was speaking about a while ago, sir it is to the Poor House she'd have to go. The blind woman has a little cabin at the edge of the bog—I'll point it out to you, sir; we do be passing it by—and she was with the blind woman for nearly two years disowned by her own father. Her clothes wore out, but she was as beautiful without them as with them. The boys were told not to look back, but sure they couldn't help it.

"Ah, it was a long while before Father Madden could get shut of her. The blind woman said she wouldn't see Julia thrown out on the road-side, and she was as good as her word for wellnigh two years, till Julia went to America, so some do be saying, sir, whilst others do be saying she joined the fairies. But 'tis for sure, sir, that the day she left the parish Pat Quinn heard a knocking at his window and somebody asking if he would lend his cart to go to the railway station. Pat was a heavy sleeper and he didn't get up, and it is thought that it was Julia who wanted Pat's cart to take her to the station; it's a good ten mile; but she got there all the same!"

"You said something about a curse?"

"Yes, sir. You'll see the hill presently. A man who was taking some sheep to the fair saw her there. The sun was just getting up and he saw her cursing the village, raising both her hands, sir, up to the sun, and since that curse was spoken every year a roof has fallen in, sometimes two or three."

I could see he believed the story, and for the moment I, too, believed in an outcast Venus becoming the evil spirit of a village that would not accept her as divine.

"Look, sir, the woman coming down the road is Bridget Coyne. And that's her house," he said, and we passed a house built of loose stones without mortar, but a little better than the mud cabins I had seen in Father MacTurnan's parish.

"And now, sir, you will see the loneliest parish in Ireland."

And I noticed that though the land was good, there seemed to be few people on it, and what was more significant than the untilled fields were the ruins for they were not the cold ruins of twenty, or thirty, or forty years ago when the people were evicted and their tillage turned into pasture—the ruins I saw were the ruins or cabins that had been lately abandoned, and I said:

"It wasn't the landlord who evicted these people."

"Ah, it's the landlord who would he glad to have them back, but there's no getting them back. Everyone here will have to go, and 'tis said that the priest will say Mass in an empty chapel, sorra a one will be there but Bridget, and she'll he the last he'll give communion to. It's said, your honour, that Julia has been seen in America, and I'm going there this autumn. You may be sure I'll keep a lookout for her."

"But all this is twenty years ago. You won't know her. A woman changes a good deal in twenty years."

"There will be no change in her, your honour. Sure hasn't she been with the fairies?"

Further Readings on George Moore

Bibliography

English Literature in Transition (formerly, *Fiction in Transition*). Annual bibliography, 1959–.

Gerber, Helmut E. "George Moore." In *Anglo-Irish Literature: A Review of Research,* edited by R. J. Finneran, 138–66. New York: Modern Language Association, 1976.

Gilcher, Edwin. *A Bibliography of the Writings of George Moore.* DeKalb, Ill.: Northern Illinois University Press, 1970.

———, et al. *Supplement to a Bibliography of George Moore.* Gerrards Cross, UK: Colin Smythe, 1987.

Langenfeld, Robert. *George Moore: An Annotated Secondary Bibliography of Writings about Him.* New York: AMS Press, 1987.

Selected Works

Collected Works. Carra Edition. 22 vols. New York: Boni and Liveright, 1922–1926.

Diarmuid and Grania. With W. B. Yeats. Edited by A. Farrow. Chicago: DePaul University Press, 1974.

Esther Waters. 1894. Reprint, London: Everyman's Library, 1983.

George Moore on Parnassus: Letters (1900–1933). Edited by Helmut E. Gerber and O. M. Brack. Newark, Del.: University of Delaware Press, 1988.

Hail and Farewell (*Ave* [1911]; *Salve* [1912]; *Valve* [1914]). 1914. Reprint, Atlantic Highlands, N.J.: Humanities Press, 1980.

In Minor Keys: The Uncollected Short Stories. Edited by D. Eakin and H. Gerber. Syracuse, N.Y.: Syracuse University Press, 1985.

The Lake. 1905. Reprint, Gerrards Cross, UK: Colin Smythe, 1981.

The Untilled Field. 1903. Reprint, Freeport, N.Y.: Books for Libraries, 1970.

The Works of George Moore. Uniform Edition. 20 vols. London: Heinemann, 1924–33.

Biography and Criticism

Brown, Malcolm. *George Moore: A Reconsideration.* Seattle: University of Washington Press, 1955.

Dunleavy, Janet Egleson. *George Moore: The Artist's Vision, The Storyteller's Art.* Lewisburg, Pa.: Bucknell, 1973.

————, ed. *George Moore in Perspective*. Naas, Ireland: Malton Books, 1984.

Farrow, Anthony. *George Moore*. Boston: Twayne, 1978.

Frazier, Adrian Woods. *George Moore, 1852–1933*. New Haven: Yale University Press, 2000.

Gray, Tony. *A Peculiar Man: A Life of George Moore*. London: Sinclair-Stevenson, 1996.

Grubgeld, Elizabeth. *George Moore and the Autogenous Self: The Autobiography and Fiction*. Syracuse, N.Y.: Syracuse University Press, 1994.

Hone, Joseph. *The Life of George Moore*. New York: Macmillan, 1936.

Hughes, Douglas A., ed. *The Man of Wax: Critical Essays on George Moore*. New York: New York University Press, 1971.

Jeffares, A. Norman. *George Moore*. London: Longmans, 1965.

Oliver St. John Gogarty

(1878–1957)

It has been Gogarty's burden that he is better known for what others have said of him than for what he has said or written himself. He was the model for the character of Buck Mulligan in James Joyce's *Ulysses,* and his name was borrowed for the protagonist of George Moore's *The Lake* (1905). One of the most crowded pubs in the Temple Bar, Dublin's fashionable nightclub district, is named—almost mockingly—the Oliver St. John Gogarty. In life Gogarty was a colorful conversationalist and wit whose words survive in a half-dozen memoirs. Gogarty was also a man of action and athletic prowess, with great skills as a swimmer and cyclist; when his life was threatened in the Civil War, he made a daring escape by swimming the Liffey. After the signing of the Anglo-Irish Treaty in 1922, Gogarty was appointed to the Free State Senate, later becoming a bitter opponent of the Republican leadership, especially of Eamon de Valera. By profession Gogarty was a medical doctor, but his writing output was large, diverse, and distinguished. He wrote dramas in youth, novels in maturity, and poetry all his life, as well as lively volumes of memoir and autobiography. Gogarty's poetry has little in common with the Eliot/Pound-inspired metaphysical taste of many of his contemporaries but harks back instead to Elizabethan and classical models. After losing a libel suit over his memoir, *As I was Going Down Sackville Street,* Gogarty emigrated to the United States in 1939, where he published much more prose in the last two decades of his life.

His best-known poem, "Ringsend," is an ironic response to reading Leo Tolstoy (or Tolstoi), the Russian novelist who recommended spiritual renewal through a peasant-like rejection of middle-class values and comforts. (Ringsend is a neighborhood south and east of Dublin, adjacent to the harbor.)

The title of Gogarty's memoir, *As I Was Going Down Sackville Street,* is taken from a traditional ballad. Sackville Street, now called O'Connell Street, is Dublin's principal commercial thoroughfare. A revised version published after Gogarty's loss of the libel suit was retitled *As I Was Walking Down Sackville Street.*

Ringsend

AFTER READING TOLSTOI

I will live in Ringsend
With a red-headed whore,
And the fan-light gone in
Where it lights the hall-door;
And listen each night
For her querulous shout,
As at last she streels in
And the pubs empty out.
To soothe that wild breast
With my old-fangled songs,
Till she feels it redressed
From inordinate wrongs,
Imagined, outrageous,
Preposterous wrongs,
Till peace at last comes,
Shall be all I will do,
Where the little lamp blooms
Like a rose in the stew;
And up the back-garden
The sound comes to me
Of the lapsing, unsoilable,
Whispering sea.

The Crab Tree *(Ireland)*

Here is the crab tree,
Firm and erect,
In spite of the thin soil,
In spite of neglect.
The twisted root grapples
For sap with the rock.
And draws the hard juice
To the succulent top:
Here are wild apples,
Here's a tart crop!

No outlandish grafting
That ever grew soft
In a sweet air of Persia,
Or safe Roman croft;
Unsheltered by steading,
Rock-rooted and grown,
A great tree of Erin,
It stands up alone,
A forest tree spreading
Where forests are gone.

Of all who pass by it
How few in it see
A westering remnant
Of days when Lough Neagh
Flowed up the long dingles
Its blossom had lit,
Old days of glory
Time cannot repeat;
And therefore it mingles
The bitter and sweet.

It takes from the West Wind
The thrust of the main;
It makes from the tension
Of sky and of plain,
Of what clay enacted,
Of living alarm,
A vitalised symbol
Of earth and of storm,
Of Chaos contracted
To intricate form.

Unbreakable wrestler!
What sapling or herb
Has core of such sweetness
And fruit so acerb?
So grim a transmitter
Of life through mishap,

That one wonders whether
If that in the sap,
Is sweet or is bitter
Which makes it stand up.

Further Readings on Oliver St. John Gogarty

Bibliography

Carens, James F. "Oliver St. John Gogarty." In *Anglo-Irish Literature: A Review of Research*, edited by R. J. Finneran, 452–59. New York: Modern Language Association, 1976.

Selected Works

As I Was Going Down Sackville Street. 1937. Reprint, New York: Harvest Books of Harcourt Brace, 1965. Rev. ed., *As I Was Walking Down Sackville Street.* 1939. Reprint, London: Sphere, 1988.
Blight, the Tragedy of Dublin. With Joseph O'Connor (under the pseudonyms Alpha and Omega). Dublin: Talbot, 1971. Reprinted in *The Plays of Oliver St. John Gogarty,* edited by J. F. Carens. Newark, Del.: Proscenium, 1972.
Collected Poems. Prefaces by W. B. Yeats, "AE," and Horace Reynolds. London: Constable, 1951.
I Follow St. Patrick. 1938. Rev. ed., London: Constable, 1939.
It Isn't This Time of Year at All: An Unpremeditated Autobiography. 1954. Reprint, London: Sphere, 1983.
Poems and Plays of Oliver St. John Gogarty. Edited by A. Norman Jeffares. Gerrards Cross, UK: Colin Smythe, 2001.
Tumbling in the Hay: A Novel. 1939. Reprint, Dublin: O'Brien Press, 1996.
William Butler Yeats: A Memoir. Dublin: Dolmen Press, 1963.

Biography and Criticism

Carens, James F. *Surpassing Wit: Oliver St. John Gogarty, His Poetry and His Prose.* Dublin: Gill and Macmillan, 1979.
Jeffares, A. Norman, "Oliver St. John Gogarty." *Proceedings of the British Academy,* 46:73–98.
Lyons, J. B. *Oliver St. John Gogarty.* Lewisburg, Pa.: Bucknell University Press, 1976.
O'Connor, Ulick. *The Times I've Seen: Oliver St. John Gogarty, A Biography.* 1963. Reprinted as *Oliver St. John Gogarty: A Poet and His Times.* Dublin: O'Brien Press, 1999.

Pádraic Ó Conaire

(1882–1928)

A Galway landmark is Albert Power's statue of a small man sitting on a wall with his hand holding his lapel and his hat on the back of his head. The figure is that of Pádraic Ó Conaire, who traveled the roads of the west of Ireland with a donkey and cart and who is remembered in F. R. Higgins's poem as well as in Power's stone:

> Dear Pádraic of the wide and sea-cold eyes—
> So lovable, so courteous and noble,
> The very West was in his soft replies.

Ó Conaire was the first significant writer in modern Irish. Stephen McKenna described him in 1925 as "absolutely the only writer you can imagine a European reading." Later, the best Irish-language prose writer of his generation, Máirtín Ó Cadháin, judged him the "most successful exponent in Irish," and went on to point out that "this is no mean praise in a country which is world famous for its short-story writers."

Ó Conaire was not a native speaker of Irish; he went to his uncle's house in Rosmuc in the Connemara Gaeltacht as a schoolboy of eleven. He spent fifteen years as a minor clerk in London before he became involved with the Gaelic League. Most of his best stories, as well as his novel *Deoraídheacht* (In Exile), were written before he returned to Ireland in 1914.

"An Bhean a Ciapadh" (The Woman Who Was Made to Suffer), entitled "Put to the Rack" in this translation, criticizes the old *cleamhnas* or matchmaking system with its sympathetic portrait of a young woman married off to a prosperous middle-aged farmer who has returned to Ireland from America. George Moore's "Julia Cahill's Curse" treats the same theme, as does Liam O'Flaherty's "The Touch," William Carleton's *The Emigrants of Ahadarra* and many folk songs that encourage young people to marry for love rather than for money. Ó Conaire's story not only discloses a heartbroken young girl facing a "made" marriage, but digs deep into the reality of that loveless arrangement: the isolation, the lack of communication, and the inutterable loneliness.

Insight into attitudes about America

Put to the Rack

from Gaelic literally Translated The woman who was made to suffer

Next month in the City of Galway a judge and jury will try an action for slander. Burke of Knockmore and Andrew Finnerty are the parties to the dispute and as judgment will have been given before these words are in print, it is no harm to tell the whole story fully.

Trial = frame of tale

One day, after his return from America, when Burke was sitting on the ditch where the idlers foregather in the City of Galway, he saw coming up the road towards him a girl who walked with the lightest tread and who had the finest bearing he had ever seen. She appeared to be not more than eighteen, but so dainty were her feet that the marks of her footsteps on the muddy street seemed to be those of a child of twelve.

Burke fell in love with the girl of the tiny feet as she passed him by humming an air to herself. He had a piece of chewing gum in his mouth, but he ejected it through a gap in his upper teeth and it fell circling into the water. *author's judgement*

"Who is that young woman?" said he to a hulk of a fellow who sat on the ditch.

"What woman?"

"The little light-footed woman."

"She is a daughter of Andrew Finnerty's, who keeps the shop near the dock."

"Andrew Finnerty?" repeated Burke with deliberation.

"Is he a tall dark man?" he inquired, suddenly.

"He is."

"And has he a mole under his left ear?"

"He has, indeed, and a big one too."

"And has he lost the top of his right thumb?"

"You know all about him, it seems."

Burke jumped off the ditch, seized his umbrella, and made off at top speed. He crossed the bridge in a great hurry and never cried halt until he reached the dock.

Finnerty's shop was stocked mostly with boating gear, and the stranger paused a bit outside looking at the shop and trying to think what he had best buy in such a place.

He walked in.

"Sixpence worth of mackerel hooks," he said.

The proprietor himself was present and he handed them to him.

"Isn't it queer that you don't know your old friend? What a bad memory you have!" said Burke.

The shopkeeper scrutinised him closely.

"It can't be that you are James Burke—you are very like him."

"I'm the same man."

Finnerty gave him a hearty welcome. They had not met for twenty-seven years, since both were working together in the States.

The stranger was invited into the room behind the shop. The two old comrades sat down, glasses were filled, and they began to chat.

"How long is it since we were in Panama?" asked the shopkeeper.

"Twenty-seven years this Christmas."

"And I suppose you got married?"

"I didn't. I never had time."

"I suppose you have made a tidy bit of money, James?"

"I have some."

They heard a sailor in the shop asking for a couple of fathoms of cord. The shopkeeper went to the door, told him to sit down and said he would not keep him long. He filled the glasses again.

"As for you," said Burke, "I needn't ask you."

"No. I'm a widower with a houseful of children. All daughters, except one son."

"Do you say so?"

The sailor in the shop was getting impatient and the shopkeeper had to go out and serve him. When he had gone, Burke began to think. Why should he go away again? Hadn't he made enough money? Wasn't a rest good after such strenuous work? And where could he find a nicer place to spend the rest of his life in than the place where he was born? When leaving the States he had intended to pay only a short visit to Ireland, but as the days and the months slipped by his desire to return became less and less. The old enchantment! The old call of the blood!

When Finnerty came back from the shop his friend said to him—

"I came home to get married, Andrew! I am tired of the life over there."

"One of the Blakes has a fine farm for sale over at Knockmore, if you know the place. You'd get it for a thousand pounds. He wants twelve hundred, and there is as fine a house on it as you ever saw."

"Have you a car?"

"I have."

"Yoke the horse at once, and let us go and look at it."

While the horse was being harnessed, they spoke as follows:

"You have a very bad memory, Andrew!" said Burke. "Don't you remember the Christmas night long ago when we gave our word that one of us wouldn't want for a wife so long as the other had a daughter?"

"I do remember it, and I'll keep my promise if what you tell me about the money is true."

"If she herself is willing."

"Why shouldn't she be?"

"Women nowadays are astonishing. Look at them in England. There's no limit to what they'll do."

Before the car reached the door the match was agreed upon.

A few nights afterwards Mary Finnerty and her father were together. He told her about the match. She was not satisfied with her proposed husband and said she would never marry him. Her father insisted that she should. Mary swore that she would not.

All the same they were married.

It is true that they had a fine house in Knockmore and everything in keeping with it. The house had been built for a gentleman, but in the course of time he became impoverished, and he had to sell out and go away. No wonder the people thought it a fine match for Miss Finnerty. What had the Finnertys ever had even at their best? And even if her husband was getting on in years, who would realise that he was nearing fifty? Was there a young man in the Parish of Knockmore who could work like him? Where was there anyone with the same "go" in him? Wouldn't it delight your heart to see him working? And he was so fond of her! The insignificant little thing without energy, or health, or anything!

The neighbors were right. He was a vigorous man. He was fond of drink, and he was very fond of the little woman he married. But she was not content, and her dissatisfaction was due to the queer way in which he showed his affection. He was a bit rough. Perhaps this was due to his life in America, to the grinding work there and to all he had seen. Anyway, she trembled a little when he came near her for fear he would prove too loving. A little shudder of goose-flesh passed over her as he touched her.

She would not confess to this feeling for anything in the world. She thought it would be a great sin to do so, but nevertheless, she was pleased in spite of herself when he told her that he was going to such and such a fair and would be away for a few days. She could not help her feelings. She could not possibly love him in the way a woman loves a man, and as soon as he had departed she tried to find out whether many women of her acquaintance were in a similar plight.

He did not understand how matters were with her. He was clever, intelligent and vigorous-minded. In a bargain he would certainly not come off second best. He was well-informed in business matters and on political questions, but he failed to understand people who had not his own rough outlook. What was the cause of this? His life in the States, his incessant labour, his strenuous existence, and the scramble for money? Or was it a natural warp in his temperament?

Often when his wife was discontented and out of sorts, and when an appropriate word would have made her all right, he would say something rough that would make her worse. He often noticed her in this way, but he did not understand the cause of it. He had never met a woman like that before. The women whom he had come across in the big cities of America liked nothing better than flattery and presents.

He resolved to give his wife a beautiful present in the hope that it would dispel her queer moods. He went to Galway for the sole purpose of buying this present. He visited all the shops and he finally decided on a fine dress of glacé silk made in the latest fashion. In addition he bought her a large gold brooch. He was always most generous to her, but in the purchase of these articles he went somewhat beyond measure. It was of no consequence, however. Wouldn't she be delighted when she saw them?

And she was delighted. She had never seen such a lovely dress and its style was perfect. When her husband held it up to show it to her it seemed so dainty that it would not fit even the most slender woman.

His wife took it to put it on.

"I am most grateful to you, James! Most grateful indeed," said she.

She put on the dress and it was too small for her. He told her so.

"I'd prefer it that way, James! I'll be in the fashion."

"But in a month or two you won't be able to put it on at all." He said a great deal more to her that I will not mention. It displeased her and when he would not stop she burst into tears and fled to her own room.

He was sorry for having spoken to her in that way. He knew that she did not like such language and he knocked at the door to go in and apologise to her. She would not let him, however.

"Open the door," he said.

"I won't," she answered.

He was getting angry.

"The longer you stay outside the better I'll be pleased," said she.

She opened the door slightly, and flung out the dress.

"And if you want to give a present in future," she said, "give it to some-body else."

He was very angry. He stood for a few minutes at the door between two minds. He would have liked to put his shoulder to the door, to break it in and to thrash her soundly. He did not do it, however, but he took up the fine dress from the floor and threw it into the fire.

"The devil take her!" he said, "but I'll teach her manners," and with that he flung out of the house, rode off on a white horse of his, and never stopped till he reached the town.

He was seen that night on the road swearing terribly and beating his poor horse unmercifully. When her baby boy was born it never saw the light. Two doctors from Galway were called in, but the child was born dead, and the doctors expressed the opinion that if she had another child she would not survive. *[still born child]*

When she got better her husband took practically no notice of her. About this time he commenced going from fair to fair buying cattle to fatten on Knockmore, and often she did not see him or hear from him for a week. She did not mind this in the least. Even when he was at home they spoke but sel-dom. He got up, ate his breakfast, went out to look after the stock and she would not see him till dinner time. Almost every night he had company in the kitchen and spent a good part of the night playing cards and carousing. He had always drunk a fair share, but he was as strong as a bull and was well able to stand it. But his bad habits were gradually getting the upper hand of him, and it was often daylight before he went to bed. Oftener still he did not speak to his wife for a whole day or two days on end unless to ask whether she had done this or that, or whether she wanted money for household expenses.

She was of opinion that he had no longer any respect for her, and where there is no respect there is no love. She was pleased that this was so. She would have been content, or half-content, if he had left her alone except for the nec-essary few words. She would have a wretched life tied to a man whom she hated, but how could she escape it?

He had bought out his land completely and one night that he came home drunk from the fair of Galway his wife learned something of what was trou-bling him. *[She learns what's troubling him]*

"He won't get it whoever gets it," said he to himself as he sat by the fire while she got ready the supper.

"He won't get it, the fool, the cursed knave, the rogue!" said he not noticing the presence of his wife.

Land crazy

It was not long until she knew what was in his mind.

"He knows that none of my people are living, but neither he, nor his people will get it. I'd rather sell the land and throw the money into the sea."

He raised his head and saw his wife. It was very late and she had got up to let him in for fear he might be killed on the flags outside. If he had met his end far from home and unknown to her she would not have cared. When he raised his head and when she looked at him she thought that she had never seen, and hoped that she would never see again, a human face so ugly. She tried to get away from him and get to her own room, but with a coarse remark he caught her by the shoulder.

She succeeded in shaking him off he had so much drink taken, and he fell on to the floor and remained on the cold flags till morning.

He rode the white horse from fair to fair and from town to town, and man and horse were frequently seen travelling the road at midnight—the rider in a drunken sleep and the horse guiding him itself. His wife was at home and any night she expected him she could not sleep till he arrived. She remained up not because of any remnant of affection for him, but she sat at the window listening for the horse's hoofs on the road, hoping she might never hear them and that the rider would drink that last drop that would precipitate him from the saddle on his head on the road.

And visions came before her eyes. She saw her husband being brought home some morning dead. The neighbours would condole with her on the loss of a good husband, and she thought of what she would say to them, or whether she could mourn his loss.

She was, however, a good pious woman, and such thoughts came to her in spite of herself. She never willingly harboured them.

Then she would hear the horse, far away, trotting on the hard road, and she would strain her ears to catch the sound of her husband's voice and to learn from it in what state he was, for she knew how drunk he was by his voice and her terror varied with its sound. When he came home in a maudlin state and showed her affection in his rough way she tried to elude him, but seldom succeeded. How she hated him! How she loathed him as she felt his heavy drunken breath on her cheek! She was a timid little thing by nature and she would never have taken any steps if it were not for something he said to her one morning at breakfast. He made it clear to her that he had no respect for her and that he could not think much of such a woman—who had not given him an heir.

Before he left the house he said a lot more that troubled her greatly. She saw him go down the road on the white horse, and she prayed that he might never return.

she was told she would die if she had another child

But the same night she was at her post at the window listening for the horse. It did not come. Midnight passed, and one, two and three o'clock and no sign. She had time to think of the wretched life she was leading, but what pained her most was what he had said to her that morning and the manner in which he had said it. It was a bright moonlit night, and a sudden desire seized her to go out.

She left the house, and no sooner was she outside than she resolved never to return. She drew her cloak round her, and, setting out to walk to Galway, she did not halt until, before dawn, she stood on her father's hearth.

After three days Burke went to Galway to her. He found Finnerty at home, and he was taken into the room behind the shop.

His glass was filled, as was always done.

"This is a very bad business," said Finnerty.

"She herself is to blame," replied Burke.

Her father had heard only part of her story. The young woman had been ashamed to tell him the worst, and even if she had done so he would not have understood aright. He thought that it was nothing but a young woman's whim, and that it could be easily remedied. He had advised her to go back to her husband, but she refused. This was, in his opinion, only youthful nonsense, but he thought it well to teach her husband a lesson and to give him a fright. He had been too long indulging in drink and late hours.

"I suppose you have come for her," said Finnerty.

"And so she is here?"

He had suspected that she was not.

"Where else would she be? And she says that here she will stay."

"Not here. I am her husband."

Burke assumed a bold attitude. Right was on his side, he thought.

"You've been drinking and carousing too much for the past year," said Finnerty. "I wouldn't blame a man for taking a drink now and again, but every night in the year! Wherever I go I hear nothing but 'did you hear what Burke of Knockmore did lately?' or 'isn't he a terrible drinker?' It's a shame, man! It's a shame!"

"I don't care a straw what they say. I know my own business best—but where is Mary?"

"You know your own business all right, but my daughter is married to you!"

"If they haven't the truth they will tell lies."

"And the truth is bad enough."

"Yes," said Burke in a hesitating tone, as he tried to guess how much of the truth had been told to his old friend.

"Make it up in God's name," said Finnerty, "and don't let the world be laughing at us. I'll call her."

He called her and she came in hurriedly. She bowed to the two men.

"If you have come for me, James!" she said to her husband, "your journey has been in vain."

"You will have to come with me. I am your husband."

"Oughtn't you take advice?" interposed her father. "However wise you are you cannot understand everything."

"I was terribly foolish when I gave in to you both at first, but I have bought sense since then, and I have bought it dearly, and you both know that I have had a hard teacher."

she is em- boldened

She went on to speak, and the two men were surprised at the vigour and boldness of her remarks.

"Is it go back to that fine house in Knockmore and live there with that man who has insulted me every day—that man who is so coarse that he doesn't even know when he is insulting! The man who never wanted anything but to satisfy his unbridled appetite!"

Her father tried to stop her. He had not thought that things were so bad. If he had known perhaps he would not have advised her to go back.

But now she had put aside all shyness and timidity. She would speak her mind out whatever would be the consequence. The two men were at either side of the table and she stood at the head, but she was so excited that she had, at times, to take hold of a chair to steady herself.

"I would far rather spend my life and my health begging from door to door than spend a single night in the same house with you, James Burke!"

Her father made a quiet remark. He was rather afraid of her.

"And I am far from being grateful to you," she said to him. "You only wanted to get me a husband and you didn't care a jot what sort of a man he was so long as he had a little money. To sell me—that is all you wanted. There are some men and God shouldn't give them daughters. There are others and it is a great crime for them to get wives—"

"Stop, woman! Be silent, I say," shouted Burke in a threatening tone. "I have only one word to say," he continued. "You are my wife, and where I am you are, and unless you come home willingly with me, I'll find other means."

He attempted to take hold of her, but Finnerty went between them, and for a moment it looked as if there was going to be a struggle.

"You had better go home to-night, Burke!" said her father. "The matter is not going to be settled in that way."

Burke went away.

That night two men—one in Galway and one in Knockmore—thought long and deeply on the surprises of woman's soul.

A week afterwards Burke was astonished to get a letter from his wife saying that she was willing to return if he would come for her.

He came and on their return home on the car it occurred to Burke to ask her why she had given in. He was proud that he had brought her to reason.

"There was no use in your tormenting yourself," he said. "Didn't you know that you would have to come back? I suppose your father told you that he couldn't keep you at home with his big family."

"That isn't the reason why I am here with you now," she answered. "If he had only a second bit in the house he'd give me one."

"Why, then, have you given in?"

"Whisper," she said, and she spoke a word in his ear known only to him and her.

It was nightfall. The old white horse was ambling along in his own way. There was not a breath of air. The birds had ceased their song. The couple on the car heard no sound except that made by the horse and car. One thought was troubling them both. Burke looked at his wife. She was sad and deep in thought, and her hand lay wearily on the well of the car. He put his hand on her hand and stroked it gently, fearing in his heart that she might draw it away. She did not withdraw it.

"Mary! Mary!" he exclaimed, but could say nothing else.

She bore a son, but died at its birth.

. . . .

Some time after this a young man was walking the road near Knockmore when he heard a car behind him. Burke was on the car, and as the young man knew his late wife and her father he gave him a lift. Burke was on for talking, and the young man contented himself with listening.

"He'll pay dearly for it," said Burke. "The idea of saying that I killed her, considering how fond of her I was! But there is law in the land still, and I'll show him that he cannot call me a murderer."

They were passing Knockmore Cemetery.

"She is buried there," said Burke. "There is her grave."

He stopped the horse.

"We may as well go in and say a prayer for her soul."

The two men knelt over her grave, and when they had prayed for her soul, Burke said:

"I thank you, God! that you did not lay too heavy a hand on me, and even if you have taken away the woman I loved since first I saw her, she has left me an heir."

A feeling of disgust seized the young man at the thought that the other man did not care what had happened to his wife so long as he had a son, and he let him continue his journey alone.

Further Readings on Pádraic Ó Conaire

Bibliography

Ní Cnionnaith, An tSr. Eibhlín. "Pádraic Ó Conaire: Liosta Saothair" *Pádraic Ó Conaire. Léachtaí Cuimhneacháin*, 65–83. Indreabháin: Cló Chonamara, 1983.

Selected Works

Aistí Phádraic Uí Chonaire. Edited by Gearóid Denvir. RosMuc: Cló Chois Fharraige, 1978.
Deoraíocht. Dublin: Cló Talbot, 1974.
Field and Fair. Translated by Cormac Breathnach. 1929. Reprint, Dublin: Cló Talbot, 1974.
15 Short Stories. Dublin: Poolbeg, 1982.
Scothscéalta le Pádraic Ó Conaire. Edited by Tomás de Bhaldraithe. Dublin: Sáirséal agus Dill, 1956.
Seacht mBua Éirí Amach. Baile Átha Cliath: Maunsel, 1918.
The Woman at the Window. Translated by Eamonn O'Neill. Illustrated by Mícheál MacLiammóir. Dublin: Talbot Press, n.d.

Biography and Criticism

Denvir, Gearóid. *Pádraic Ó Conaire: Léachtaí Cuimhneacháin*. Indreabháin: Cló Chonamara, 1983.
Higgins, F. R. "An Appreciation." In *Field and Fair*, 11–15. Dublin: Talbot Press, 1929.
Jordan, John. "On *Deoraíocht*." In *The Pleasures of Gaelic Literature*, edited by John Jordan. Cork: Mercier Press, 1972.
MacGrianna, Seosamh. "Pádraic O'Conaire." In *Pádraic O'Conaire agus Aistí Eile*. 1936. Reprint, Baile Átha Cliath: Oifig an tSolathair, 1969.

Murphy, Maureen. "The Short Story in Irish." *Mosaic* 12:81–89.

Ó Cadháin, Máirtin. "Irish Prose in the Twentieth Century." In *Literature in Celtic Countries,* edited by J. E. Caerwyn Williams. Cardiff: University of Wales Press, 1971.

Ó Maille, Pádraic. "Pádraic O'Conaire—Prince of Storytellers." *The Ireland-American Review* 1:379–88.

Ó Néill, Séamus. "Gaelic Writing." *Irish Writing* 33:7–10.

James Stephens

(1880[82?]–1950)

James Stephens was often called a leprechaun of literature during his lifetime. Not only was he short, standing only four feet ten inches, but his writing, both in poetry and prose, displays a charged mixture of fantasy and athletic verve. He did not, however, look away from the sometimes sordid reality of everyday Irish life. One of his earliest works, *The Charwoman's Daughter* (1912), is a fantasy set amid the poverty of a Dublin Stephens had known well in his childhood. Stephens is probably best remembered today for his imaginative retellings of Old Irish stories that reveal his personal vision of youth and of a world beyond the senses. These include *The Crock of Gold* (1912), *The Demi-Gods* (1914), *Irish Fairy Tales* (1920), *Deirdre* (1923), and *In the Land of Youth* (1924). The American musical *Finian's Rainbow* (1947) might also be cited as a work by Stephens, as it is an adaptation of *The Crock of Gold.*

Stephens was not so much interested in making old stories accessible to the modern reader as in recreating distinctively Irish stories in his own way. His own way included borrowings from Eastern philosophies as well as from the writings of the English mystical poet William Blake, with whom he is often compared. While not a nationalist in the conventional sense, Stephens was greatly moved by the Easter Rising of 1916 and wrote an eyewitness account of it. Later, he was unhappy with the changes wrought by revolution and so emigrated to England in 1924. Late in life, with his best works behind him, Stephens achieved some of his widest popularity as a commentator and storyteller for the British Broadcasting Corporation. Although Stephens appealed to a popular readership, his writing enjoyed the esteem of some of his most demanding contemporaries. James Joyce, for example, found Stephens to be a kindred spirit, and asked that he be ready to complete the incomparably abstruse work, *Finnegans Wake,* should the author be unable to. Joyce believed that he and Stephens were born on the same day, February 2, 1882—an assertion not supported, however, by birth records.

Stephens wrote poetry throughout his career, and it became his dominant concern in the years following the disappointing reception of *In the Land of Youth.* In *Irish Fairy Tales,* the youthful Fionn speaks for Stephens's aesthetic.

From The Insurrection in Dublin

MONDAY

On the way home I noticed that many silent people were standing in their doorways—an unusual thing in Dublin outside the back streets. The glance of a Dublin man or woman conveys generally a criticism of one's personal appearance, and is a little hostile to the passer. The look of each person as I passed was steadfast, and contained an enquiry instead of a criticism. I felt faintly uneasy, but withdrew my mind to a meditation which I had covenanted with myself to perform daily, and passed to my house.

There I was told that there had been a great deal of rifle firing all the morning, and we concluded that the military recruits or Volunteer [i.e., rebel] detachments were practising that arm. My return to business was by the way I had already come. At the corner of Merrion Row I found the same silent groups, who were still looking in the direction of the Green, and addressing each other occasionally with the detached confidence of strangers. Suddenly, and on the spur of the moment, I addressed one of these silent gazers.

"Has there been an accident?" said I.

I indicated the people standing about.

"What's all this for?"

He was a sleepy, rough-looking man about forty years of age, with a blunt red moustache, and the distant eyes which one sees in sailors. He looked at me, stared at me as at a person from a different country. He grew wakeful and vivid.

"Don't you know?" said he.

And then he saw that I did not know.

"The Sinn Feiners have seized the city this morning."

"Oh!" said I.

He continued with the savage earnestness of one who has amazement in his mouth:

"They seized the city at eleven o'clock this morning, The Green there is full of them. They have captured the Castle. They have taken the Post Office."

"My God!" said I, staring at him, and instantly I turned and went running towards the Green.

TUESDAY

There had been looting in the night about Sackville Street, and it was current that the Volunteers had shot twenty of the looters.

The shops attacked were mainly haberdashers, shoe shops, and sweet shops. Very many sweet shops were raided, and until the end of the rising, sweet shops were the favourite mark of the looters. There is something comical in this looting of sweet shops—something almost innocent and child-like. Possibly most of the looters are children who are having the sole gorge of their lives. They have tasted sweetstuffs they had never toothed before, and will never taste again in this life, and until they die the insurrection of 1916 will have a sweet savour for them.

WEDNESDAY

Today the *Irish Times* was published. It contained a new military proclamation, and a statement that the country was peaceful, and told that in Sackville Street some houses were burned to the ground.

On the outside railings a bill proclaiming martial law was posted.

Into the newspaper statement that peace reigned in the country one was inclined to read more of disquietude than truth, and one said: Is the country so extraordinarily peaceful that it can be dismissed in three lines? There is too much peace or too much reticence, but it will be some time before we hear from outside of Dublin.

Meanwhile the sun was shining. It was a delightful day, and the streets outside and around the areas of fire were animated and even gay. In the streets of Dublin there were no morose faces to be seen. Almost everyone was smiling and attentive, and a democratic feeling was abroad, to which our city is very much a stranger; for while in private we are a social and talkative people, we have no street manners or public ease whatever. Every person spoke to every other person, and men and women mixed and talked without constraint.

FRIDAY

Many English troops have been landed each night, and it is believed that there are more than sixty thousand soldiers in Dublin alone, and that they are supplied with every offensive contrivance which military art has invented.

Merrion Square is strongly held by the soldiers. They are posted along both sides of the road at intervals of about twenty paces, and their guns are continually barking up at the roofs which surround them in the great square. It is said that these roofs are held by the volunteers from Mount Street Bridge to the Square, and that they hold in like manner wide stretches of the city.

They appear to have mapped out the roofs with all the thoroughness that had hitherto been expended on the roads, and upon these roofs they are so mobile and crafty and so much at home that the work of the soldiers will he exceedingly difficult as well as dangerous.

Still, and notwithstanding, men can only take to the roofs for a short time. Up there, there can be no means of transport, and their ammunition, as well as their food, will very soon be used up. It is the beginning of the end, and the fact that they have to take to the roofs, even though that be in their programme, means that they are finished.

From the roof there comes the sound of machine guns. Looking towards Sackville Street one picks out easily Nelson's Pillar, which towers slenderly over all the buildings of the neighbourhood. It is wreathed in smoke. Another towering building was the D.B.C. Café. Its Chinese-like pagoda was a landmark easily to be found, but today I could not find it. It was not there, and I knew that, even if all Sackville Street was not burned down, as rumour insisted, this great Café had certainly been curtailed by its roof and might, perhaps, have been completely burned.

On the gravel paths I found pieces of charred and burnt paper. These scraps must have been blown remarkably high to have crossed all the roofs that lie between Sackville Street and Merrion Square.

At eleven o'clock there is continuous firing, and snipers firing from the direction of Mount Street, and in every direction of the city these sounds are being duplicated.

In Camden Street the sniping and casualties are said to have been very heavy. One man saw two Volunteers taken from a house by the soldiers. They were placed kneeling in the centre of the road, and within one minute of their capture they were dead. Simultaneously there fell several of the firing party.

An officer in this part had his brains blown into the roadway. A young girl ran into the road, picked up his cap and scraped the brains into it. She covered this poor debris with a little straw, and carried the lot piously to the nearest hospital in order that the brains might be buried with their owner.

From Irish Fairy Tales

FIONN'S FAVORITE MUSIC

Once, as they rested on a chase, a debate arose among the Fianna-Finn as to what was the finest music in the world.

"Tell us that," said Fionn, turning to Oisín.

"The cuckoo calling from the tree that is highest in the hedge," cried his merry son.

"A good sound," said Fionn. "And you, Oscar," he said, "what is to your mind the finest of music?"

"The top of music is the ring of a spear on a shield," cried the stout lad.

"It is a good sound," said Fionn.

And the other champions told their delight: the belling of a stag across water, the baying of a tuneful pack heard in the distance, the song of a lark, the laugh of a gleeful girl, or the whisper of a moved one.

"They are good sounds all," said Fionn.

"Tell us, chief," one ventured, "what you think?"

"The music of what happens," said great Fionn, "that is the finest music in the world."

Further Readings on James Stephens

Bibliography

Bramsbäck, Birgit. *James Stephens: A Literary and Bibliographical Study.* Uppsala: Lundequist, 1959.

Carens, James F. "James Stephens." In *Anglo-Irish Literature: A Review of Research,* edited by R. J. Finneran, 459–69. New York: Modern Language Association, 1976.

Selected Works

The Charwoman's Daughter. 1912. Reprint, Dublin: Gill and Macmillan, 1972.
Collected Poems. 2nd ed. London: Macmillan, 1954.
Crock of Gold, The. London: Macmillan, 1912; Mineola, N.Y.: Dover, 1997.
Deirdre. London: Macmillan, 1923.
The Demi-Gods. London: Macmillan, 1914.
The Insurrection in Dublin. 1916. Reprint, New York: Barnes and Noble, 1999.
In the Land of Youth. London: Macmillan, 1924.

Irish Fairy Tales. 1920. Reprint, New York: Macmillan, 2001.

James, Seumas and Jacques: Unpublished Writings by James Stephens. Edited by Lloyd Frankenberg. London: Macmillan, 1964.

James Stephens: A Selection. Edited by Lloyd Frankenberg. London: Macmillan, 1962. Under the title *A James Stephens Reader,* New York: Macmillan, 1962.

Letters of James Stephens. Edited by Richard J. Finneran. London: Macmillan, 1974.

Traditional Irish Fairy Tales. New York: Dover, 1996.

Uncollected Prose. Edited by Patricia A. McFate, New York: St. Martin's, 1983.

Biography and Criticism

Journal of Irish Literature 4 (1975). A James Stephens Number.

Martin, Augustine. *James Stephens: A Critical Study.* Dublin: Gill and Macmillan, 1977.

McFate, Patricia A. *The Writings of James Stephens: Variations on a Theme of Love.* London: Macmillan, 1979.

Pyle, Hilary. *James Stephens: His Works and an Account of His Life.* London: Routledge and Kegan Paul, 1965.

The Poets of 1916

The single most electrifying moment in twentieth-century Irish history was the armed seizure of the General Post Office—the "G.P.O."—during Easter Week, April 24–29, 1916. The building itself was of small consequence, but it represented British imperial power on Dublin's main commercial thoroughfare, then called Sackville Street. Sentiment for independence had been diffused before Easter Week, especially since so many Irishmen were off fighting for Britain in World War I. But after the Rising, and especially after the executions of most of its leaders in the first weeks of May, the popular will for freedom solidified, never to be broken.

Among the seven signers of the Proclamation of the Irish Republic were three poets: Padraic Pearse, Thomas MacDonagh, and Joseph Plunkett. Men of action as well as of letters, the three played leading roles in the Rising. Viewed from a global perspective, the Easter Rising in Ireland is distinct for having been led by poets, rather than by soldiers, lawyers, or political ideologues.

P[atrick] H[enry] (or Padraic) Pearse (1879–1916) committed his life to the cause of Ireland from the time he joined the Gaelic League when he was sixteen. Although born of an English father, his knowledge of the Irish language was so proficient that he edited a journal in the language, *An Claidheamh Soluis* (The Sword of Light), and published collections of Irish-language short stories as well (*Íosagán* [1907]). The most important crucible for revolutionary activity as far as Pearse was concerned was the bilingual school, St. Enda's *(Scoil Énna),* which had attracted a wide range of partisan support after its foundation in 1908. A play written for students of the school, *The Singer,* was a literary analogue for the Easter Rising. Some of Pearse's most famous sentiments are to be found in his August 1, 1915, oration at the burial of Jeremiah O'Donovan Rossa (1831–1915), a Fenian leader who advocated armed action for independence. Pearse was executed May 4, 1916.

Thomas MacDonagh (1878–1916) was closely associated with Pearse on many projects, but retained his own distinctive poetic voice. Steeped in both Irish and non-Irish tradition, MacDonagh's poetry shows the influence of such diverse writers as Walt Whitman and A. E. Housman. In an early play, *When the Dawn Is Come* (1908), he envisioned an Ireland free of Britain. Like Pearse, he became proficient in the Irish language and worked at St. Enda's School. With Padraic Colum and Mary Maguire later, Colum's wife, he founded the influential journal, *The Irish Review* (1911–15), which published some of the most significant writers of his generation. Even as the revolutionary fires were rising, MacDonagh was working on his critical history, *Literature in Ireland,* which would be published posthumously. A son, Donagh MacDonagh (1912–68), was also a poet and playwright of distinction. Thomas MacDonagh was executed May 3, 1916.

Joseph Mary Plunkett (1887–1916) died before his poetic style fully matured. Always in ill health, Plunkett spent much of his short life abroad in the warmer, drier climates of Italy, Algeria, and Egypt. He assisted Thomas MacDonagh with *The Irish Review.* In the months before the Rising, he helped Sir Roger Casement (1864–1916) in the thwarted attempt to smuggle German arms into Ireland. On the Good Friday before Easter, Plunkett was hospitalized for throat surgery, and so had to rise from a sickbed in order to enter the fray. He was executed May 4, 1916.

Proclamation of the Irish Republic

Ireland depicted as female again

Irishmen and Irishwomen: In the name of God and of the dead generations from which she receives her old tradition of nationhood, Ireland, through us, summons her children to her flag and strikes for her freedom.

Having organised and trained her manhood through her secret revolutionary organisation, the Irish Republican Brotherhood, and through her open military organisations, the Irish Volunteers and the Irish Citizen Army, having patiently perfected her discipline, having resolutely waited for the right moment to reveal itself, she now seizes that moment, and, supported by her exiled children in America and by gallant allies in Europe, but relying in the first on her own strength, she strikes in full confidence of victory.

We declare the right of the people of Ireland to the ownership of Ireland, and to the unfettered control of Irish destinies, to be sovereign and indefeasible. The long usurpation of that right by a foreign people and government has not extinguished the right, nor can it ever be extinguished except by the destruction of the Irish people. In every generation the Irish people have asserted their right to national freedom and sovereignty; six times during the past three hundred years they have asserted it in arms. Standing on that fundamental right and again asserting it in arms in the face of the world, we hereby proclaim the Irish Republic as a Sovereign Independent State, and we pledge our lives and the lives of our comrades-in-arms to the cause of its freedom, of its welfare, and of its exaltation among the nations.

The Irish Republic is entitled to, and hereby claims, the allegiance of

[handwritten margin notes at top: what is being sought in the war for independence ① Ownership of Ireland ② right to national freedom + sovereignty ③ religious liberty ④ equal opportunities for all]

every Irishman and Irishwoman. The Republic guarantees religious and civil liberty, equal rights and equal opportunities to all its citizens, and declares its resolve to pursue the happiness and prosperity of the whole nation and of all its parts, cherishing all the children of the nation equally, and oblivious of the differences carefully fostered by an alien government, which have divided a minority from the majority in the past.

Until our arms have brought the opportune moment for the establishment of a permanent National Government, representative of the whole people of Ireland and elected by the suffrages of all her men and women, the Provisional Government, hereby constituted, will administer the civil and military affairs of the Republic in trust for the people.

We place the cause of the Irish Republic under the protection of the Most High God, Whose blessing we invoke upon our arms, and we pray that no one who serves that cause will dishonour it by cowardice, inhumanity, or rapine. *[handwritten: plunder]* In this supreme hour the Irish nation must, by its valour and discipline and by the readiness of its children to sacrifice themselves for the common good, prove itself worthy of the august destiny to which it is called.

Signed on Behalf of the Provisional Government,

THOMAS J. CLARKE,

SEAN MACDIARMADA, THOMAS MACDONAGH,
P. H. PEARSE, EAMONN CEANNT,
JAMES CONNOLLY. JOSEPH PLUNKETT.

P. H. *Pearse* (1879–1916)

[handwritten: — creator of Irish republic read Pearse read the Ulster Cycle as an allegory of the story of Calvary Cuchulainn = Christ figure]

I Am Ireland

[handwritten margin: Personification of Ireland]

I am Ireland:
I am older than the Old Woman of Beare. *[handwritten: Peninsula]*

Great my glory:
I that bore Cuchulainn the valiant.

Great my shame:
My own children that sold their mother. *[handwritten: Those aligning with themselves British]*

I am Ireland:
I am lonelier than the Old Woman of Beare.

[handwritten: Pearse's poetry was an allegory of his own tortured imagination]

Ideal, or Renunciation

Naked I saw thee,
O beauty of beauty! *[handwritten: Ireland]*
And I blinded my eyes
For fear I should flinch. *[handwritten: aisling]*

I heard thy music,
O sweetness of sweetness!
And I shut my ears
For fear I should fail. *[handwritten: (Ireland — history of failed revolution)]*

I kissed thy lips
O sweetness of sweetness!
And I hardened my heart
For fear of my ruin.

I blinded my eyes
And my ears I shut,
I hardened my heart
And my love I quenched.

I turned my back
On the dream I had shaped,
And to this road before me
My face I turned.

I set my face
To the road here before me, *[handwritten: Moves to pres. Tense. To him, death is a glorious thing]*
To the work that I see,
To the death that I shall meet.

The Rebel *[handwritten: — more speech than poem]*

I am come of the seed of the people, the people that sorrow,
That have no treasure but hope,
No riches laid up but a memory
Of an Ancient glory.

My mother bore me in bondage, in bondage my mother was born,
    I am of the blood of serfs;
Britain The children with whom I have played, the men and women with whom
    I have eaten,
Have had masters over them, have been under the lash of masters,
    And, though gentle, have served churls;
The hands that have touched mine, the dear hands whose touch is
    familiar to me,
Have worn shameful manacles, have been bitten at the wrist by
    manacles,
Have grown hard with the manacles and the task-work of strangers,
I am flesh of the flesh of these lowly, I am bone of their bone,
    I that have never submitted;
I that have a soul greater than the souls of my people's masters,
I that have vision and prophecy and the gift of fiery speech,
I that have spoken with God on the top of His holy hill.

And because I am of the people, I understand the people,
I am sorrowful with their sorrow, I am hungry with their desire:
My heart has been heavy with the grief of mothers,
My eyes have been wet with the tears of children,
I have yearned with old wistful men,
And laughed or cursed with young men;
Their shame is my shame, and I have reddened for it,
*Blushed
in
shame* Reddened for that they have served, they who should be free,
Reddened for that they have gone in want, while others have been full,
Reddened for that they have walked in fear of lawyers and of their jailors
With their writs of summons and their handcuffs,
Men mean and cruel!
I could have borne stripes on my body rather than this shame of my
    people.

And now I speak, being full of vision;
I speak to my people, and I speak in my people's name to the masters of
    my people.
I say to my people that they are holy, that they are august, despite their
    chains,
That they are greater than those that hold them, and stronger and purer,
That they have but need of courage, and to call on the name of their
    God,

God the unforgetting, the dear God that loves the peoples
For whom He died naked, suffering shame.
And I say to my people's masters: Beware,
Beware of the thing that is coming, beware of the risen people,
Who shall take what ye would not give. Did ye think to conquer the
    people,
Or that Law is stronger than life and than men's desire to be free?
We will try it out with you, ye that have harried and held,
Ye that have bullied and bribed, tyrants, hypocrites, liars!

To Death

I have not gathered gold;
    The fame that I won perished;
In love I found but sorrow,
    That withered my life.

Of wealth or of glory
    I shall leave nothing behind me
(I think it, O God, enough!)
    But my name in the heart of a child.

At the Grave of O'Donovan Rossa

It has seemed right, before we turn away from this place in which we have laid the mortal remains of O'Donovan Rossa, that one among us should, in the name of all, speak the praise of that valiant man, and endeavour to formulate the thought and the hope that are in us as we stand around his grave. And if there is anything that makes it fitting that I, rather than some other, I rather than one of the grey-haired men who were young with him and shared in his labour and in his suffering, should speak here, it is perhaps that I may be taken as speaking on behalf of a new generation that has been re-baptised in the Fenian faith, and that has accepted the responsibility of carrying out the Fenian programme. I propose to you then that, here by the grave of this unrepentant Fenian, we renew our baptismal vows; that, here by the grave of this unconquered and unconquerable man, we ask of God, each one for himself, such unshakable purpose, such high and gallant courage, such unbreakable strength of soul as belonged to Donovan Rossa.

Deliberately here we avow ourselves, as he avowed himself in the dock, Irishmen of one allegiance only. We of the Irish Volunteers, and you others who are associated with us in today's task and duty, are bound together and must stand together henceforth in brotherly union for the achievement of the freedom of Ireland. And we know only one definition of freedom: it is Tone's definition, it is Mitchel's definition, it is Rossa's definition. Let no man blaspheme the cause that the dead generations of Ireland served by giving it any other name and definition than their definition.

We stand at Rossa's grave not in sadness but rather in exaltation of spirit that it has been given to us to come thus into so close a communion with that brave and splendid Gael. Splendid and holy causes are served by men who are themselves splendid and holy. O'Donovan Rossa was splendid in the proud manhood of him, splendid in the heroic grace of him, splendid in the Gaelic strength and clarity and truth of him. And all that splendour and pride and strength was compatible with a humility and a simplicity of devotion to Ireland, to all that was olden and beautiful and Gaelic in Ireland, the holiness and simplicity of patriotism of a Michael O'Clery or of an Eoghan O'Growney. The clear true eyes of this man almost alone in his day visioned Ireland as we of today would surely have her: not free merely, but Gaelic as well; not Gaelic merely, but free as well.

In a closer spiritual communion with him now than ever before or perhaps ever again, in a spiritual communion with those of his day, living and dead, who suffered with him in English prisons, in communion of spirit too with our own dear comrades who suffer in English prisons today, and speaking on their behalf as well as our own, we pledge to Ireland our love, and we pledge to English rule in Ireland our hate. This is a place of peace, sacred to the dead, where men should speak with all charity and with all restraint; but I hold it a Christian thing, as O'Donovan Rossa held it, to hate evil, to hate untruth, to hate oppression, and, hating them, to strive to overthrow them. Our foes are strong and wise and wary; but, strong and wise and wary as they are, they cannot undo the miracles of God who ripens in the hearts of young men the seeds sown by the young men of a former generation. And the seeds sown by the young men of '65 and '67 are coming to their miraculous ripening today. Rulers and Defenders of Realms had need to be wary if they would guard against such processes. Life springs from death; and from the graves of patriot men and women spring living nations. The Defenders of this Realm have worked well in secret and in the open. They think that they have pacified Ireland. They think that they have purchased half of us and intimidated the other half. They think that they have foreseen everything, think that they have provided against everything; but the fools the fools, the fools!—they have left us our Fenian dead, and while Ireland holds these graves, Ireland unfree shall never be at peace.

Thomas MacDonagh (1878–1916)

[handwritten: Influence of Houseman & Whitman]

The Man Upright

[handwritten: Result of British oppression]

I once spent an evening in a village
Where the people are all taken up with tillage,
Or do some business in a small way
Among themselves, and all the day
Go crooked, doubled to half their size,
Both working and loafing, with their eyes
Stuck in the ground or in a board,—
For some of them tailor, and some of them hoard
Pence in a till in their little shops,
And some of them shoe-soles—they get the tops
Ready-made from England, and they die cobblers—
All bent up double, a village of hobblers
And slouchers and squatters, whether they straggle
Up and down, or bend to haggle
Over a counter, or bend at a plough,
Or to dig with a spade, or to milk a cow,
Or to shove the goose-iron stiffly along
The stuff on the sleeve-board or lace the thong
In the boot on the last, or to draw the wax-end
Tight cross-ways—and so to make or to mend
What will soon be worn out by the crooked people.
The only thing straight in the place was the steeple,
I thought at first. I was wrong in that;
For there past the window at which I sat
Watching the crooked little men
Go slouching, and with the gait of a hen
An odd little woman go pattering past,
And the cobbler crouching over his last
In his window opposite, and next door
The tailor squatting inside on the floor—

While I watched them, as I have said before,
And thought that only the steeple was straight,
There came a man of a different gait—
A man who neither slouched nor pattered,
But planted his steps as if each step mattered;
Yet walked down the middle of the street
Not like a policeman on his beat,
But like a man with nothing to do
Except walk straight upright like me and you.

The Yellow Bittern

The yellow bittern that never broke out
  In a drinking bout, might as well have drunk;
His bones are thrown on a naked stone
  Where he lived alone like a hermit monk.
O yellow bittern! I pity your lot.
  Though they say that a sot like myself is curst—
I was sober a while, but I'll drink and be wise
  For I fear I should die in the end of thirst.

It's not for the common birds that I'd mourn,
  The black-bird, the corn-crake, or the crane,
But for the bittern that's shy and apart
  And drinks in the marsh from the long bog-drain.
Oh! if I had known you were near your death,
  While my breath held out I'd have run to you,
Till a splash from the Lake of the Son of the Bird
  Your soul would have stirred and waked anew.

My darling told me to drink no more
  Or my life would o'er in a little short while;
But I told her 'tis drink gives me health and strength
  And will lengthen my road by many a mile.
You see how the bird of the long smooth neck
  Could get his death from the thirst at last
Come, son of my soul, and drain your cup,
  You'll get no sup when your life is past.

In a wintering island by Constantine's halls
  A bittern calls from a wineless place,

And tells me that hither he cannot come
  Till the summer is here and the sunny days.
When he crosses the stream there and wings o'er the sea
  Then a fear comes to me he may fail in his flight—
Well, the milk and the ale are drunk every drop,
  And a dram won't stop our thirst this night.

from the Irish of Cathal Buidhe Mac Giolla Ghunna

Of a Poet Patriot

His songs were a little phrase
  Of eternal song,
Drowned in the harping of lays
  More loud and long.

His deed was a single word,
  Called out alone
In a night when no echo stirred
  To laughter or moan.

But his song new souls shall thrill
  The loud harp's dumb
And his deed the echoes fill
  When the dawn is come.

Joseph Mary Plunkett (1887–1916)

The Little Black Rose Shall Be Red at Last

Because we share our sorrows and our joys
And all your dear and intimate thoughts are mine
We shall not fear the trumpets and the noise
Of battle, for we know our dreams divine,
And when my heart is pillowed on your heart
And ebb and flowing of their passionate flood
Shall beat in concord love through every part
Of brain and body—when at last the blood
O'erleaps the final barrier to find
Only one source wherein to spend its strength.
And we two lovers, long but one in mind

And soul, are made only flesh at length;
Praise God if this my blood fulfils the doom
When you, dark rose, shall redden into bloom. (Blood)

This Heritage to the Race of Kings

This heritage to the race of kings
Their children and their children's seed
Have wrought their prophecies in deed
Of terrible and splendid things.

The hands that fought, the hearts that broke
In old immortal tragedies,
These have not failed beneath the skies,
Their children's heads refuse the yoke.

And still their hands shall guard the sod
That holds their father's funeral urn,
Still shall their hearts volcanic burn
With anger of the sons of God.

No alien sword shall earn as wage
The entail of their blood and tears,
No shameful price for peaceful years
Shall ever part this heritage.

Further Readings on the Poets of 1916

Bibliography

O'Hegarty, P. S. *A Bibliography of Books Written by Thomas MacDonagh and Joseph Mary Plunkett*. Dublin: A. Thom, 1931.
———. "P. H. Pearse." *Dublin Magazine* 6:3, 44–49. Reprint, Dublin: Thom, 1931.

Selected Works

MacDonagh, Thomas. *When the Dawn is Come*. 1908. Reprint, Chicago: DePaul University. 1973.
———. *Literature in Ireland: Studies in Irish and Anglo-Irish*. Dublin: Talbot Press, 1916.

———. *Poetical Works.* 1916. Reprint, New York: AMS Press, 1978.

Pearse, P. H. *Collected Works.* 3 vols. Dublin: Maunsel, 1917–22.

———. *Collected Works.* 5 vols. Dublin: Phoenix, 1924.

———. *The Letters of P. H. Pearse.* Edited by Séamus Ó Buachalla. Gerrards Cross, UK: Colin Smythe, 1980.

———. *Literary Writings.* Edited by Séamas Ó Buachalla. Dublin: Mercier Press, 1979.

———. *Rogha Dánta/Selected Poems.* Edited by Dermot Bolger. Dublin: New Island Books, 1993.

———. *Scríbhinní: Collected Works in Gaelic.* Dublin: Maunsel, 1919.

———. *Short Stories.* Cork: Mercier Press, 1968.

Plunkett, Joseph Mary. *Poems.* 1916. Reprint, New York: AMS Press, 1978.

———. *Sword* [poems]. Dublin: Maunsel, 1911.

Ryan, Desmond, ed. *The 1916 Poets.* 1963. Reprint, Dublin: Gill and Macmillan, 1995.

Biography and Criticism

Coffey, Thomas M. *Agony at Easter.* New York: Macmillan, 1969.

Edwards, Ruth Dudley. *Patrick Pearse: The Triumph of Failure.* London: Gollancz, 1977.

Greaves, C. Desmond. *The Easter Rising in Song and Ballad.* London: Kahn and Averill (for the Workers' Music Association), 1980.

Loftus, Richard J. *Nationalism in Modern Anglo-Irish Poetry.* Madison: University of Wisconsin Press, 1964.

Martin, F. X., ed. *Leaders and Men of the Easter Rising: Dublin 1916.* London: Methuen, 1967.

McCay, Hedley. *Padraic Pearse: A New Biography.* Cork: Mercier Press, 1966.

Moran, Seán Farrell. *Patrick Pearse and the Politics of the Easter Rising, 1916.* Washington, D.C.: Catholic University Press, 1994.

Norstedt, Johann. *Thomas MacDonagh: A Critical Biography.* Charlottesville: University Press of Virginia, 1980.

Parks, Edd Winfield, and Aileen Wells Parks. *Thomas MacDonagh: The Man, the Patriot, the Writer.* Athens: University of Georgia Press, 1967.

Porter, Raymond. *P. H. Pearse.* New York: Twayne, 1973.

Ryan, Desmond. *The Rising,* 4th ed. Dublin: Golden Eagle Books, 1966.

Thompson, William Irwin. *The Imagination of an Insurrection: Dublin, Easter 1916.* New York: Oxford University Press, 1967.

PART THREE

Ireland Since Independence

Repetetive themes) of fiction
writers, 1923 - 40 regarding
disillusionment & disaffection.
3 problems of 19th + early 20th
cent ~~Irish history~~:
① The Church ② nationalism
③ The Land
An entire subgenre of fiction
about the Civil War +
how it destroyed the
illusions of national virtue
held over from the past
(see DVD)
Nationalism ~~& fantasy~~
— Important sub-genre
of the 20's
Great fantasy of the period
was Joyce's Finnegan's Wake
the novel is a dream — a complex
blend of the trivial + archetypal,
a history of the human race.

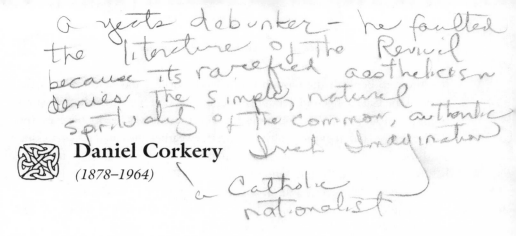

a Yeats debunker - he faulted the literature of the Revival because its rarefied aestheticism denies the simple, natural spirituality of the common, authentic Irish Imagination

a Catholic nationalist

Daniel Corkery
(1878–1964)

Readers of Frank O'Connor's autobiography, *An Only Child,* will remember the young teacher whose passion for the Irish language as an expression of Irish national identity inspired his young students. A versatile artist-playwright as well as novelist, water-colorist as well as writer—Daniel Corkery was mentor to a generation that included Seán O'Faoláin as well as O'Connor. Describing his influence, O'Faoláin wrote: "In the boredom of Cork I do not know what I would have done without his friendly door."

A national teacher who was Professor of English at University College, Cork, from 1931 to 1947, and a member of the Seanad Éireann (1951–54), Corkery is best known for *The Hidden Ireland: A Story of Gaelic Munster in the Eighteenth Century,* a study of the poets of West Cork. A controversial and somewhat simplistic view of Irish history, it nevertheless introduces the reader to the work of such major Munster poets as Aogán Ó Rathaille and Eoghan Rua Ó Suilleabháin. These figures were models for the character of Eoghan Mor O'Donovan in "Solace," Corkery's fictional portrayal of a dispossessed poet. Indeed, Eoghan Mor's song reminds one of Aogán Ó Rathaille's "Cabhair ní ghairfead" (Help I'll Not Call).

Solace

TIME: THE EIGHTEENTH CENTURY

When Eoghan Mor O'Donovan, poet, stooped down and came in over his threshold he saw in spite of the gloom that his son Diarmuid, who all day long had been with him leading the cow at the ploughing, had eaten his evening meal of potatoes and milk, and in his exhaustion had leant his head down on the deal table and fallen asleep. The boy's unkempt head was almost buried in the potato refuse. No one else the poet found before him in the cabin; and the only light was the glow of the broad lire of turf sods. Looking on the weary figure of the boy, in a flash of thought the poet beheld more plainly than when he had stood in it, the stone-strewn patch of mountainside they had been trying to soften up beneath the plough that bitter February day, and he, with the pride of the Gael in his soul, felt more deeply than ever before the hopelessness of his position, the slavery and indignity. Yes, there it was before his eyes: the dark-coloured patch of turfy hillside, with the weather-bleached rocks sticking up through its surface and piled upon them the stones and shale his bleeding hands had gathered from it winter after winter. But the vision made his voice gentle, whereas the living sight of it would have filled him with anger.

"Where's your mother, lad?" he said, laying his earthy, toil-thickened fingers on the boy's shoulder, not without gentleness and warm love in the touch. Diarmuid struggled with his sleepiness.

"Father?" he said, having failed to catch the question.

"Your mother, lad, where has she gone?"

"As I came in she was crying out angrily at a stranger, and he was laughing, mocking her, as he went away."

At the words the weariness fell from the poet's limbs. He was again a strong, gaunt peasant, his voice harsh:

"Is it of Tadhg Smith the Bailiff you are speaking?" he asked, his eyes on fire.

"It is."

The poet wheeled and made passionately for the door. He stared a moment into the gathering night. Then he returned. And weariness was again in his limbs, making them heavy and awkward. Without a word he seated himself listlessly on the settle, and, a hand on either knee, stared helplessly before him. The sound of waters falling among the rocks outside, the roaring of a far-off bull on a mountain ledge, and, occasionally, the stir of the turf sods as they fell on the flagstone were the only sounds until he spoke:

"We might have left our ploughing till to-morrow—or the day after." he said.

The boy was blinking at him. The sleep had brought back some fullness to his eyes; but they were still jaded-looking.

"Yes!" he answered, not having caught all the meaning in his father's words, and " 'Tis yes! indeed," replied the poet, with a return of the gentleness the first glance at the spent figure had inspired.

The boy's head went slowly down among the refuse again.

"And I might have left my new song till to-morrow or the next day," the poet added, half to himself.

But though he said the words as if he saw and felt what a foolish thing it was that he should have slipped unknowingly into the making of one more vision-song while this storm was gathering above his weed-tattered roof of scraps, the power of song was already surging up within him; and a riot of words, golden and flashing with fire and sound and colour, was already taking his brain captive, making it reel for very bliss. But it was not the words of his half-made vision-song were rioting within him now; that song was definitely done with; in the deeper inspiration the bursting of the storm had unloosed, the half-made song seemed but an idle, cold-hearted thing indeed. A new song had leaped within him, leaped with such a strength as made him reckless of the smaller things of life.

His wife entering found him as still as a tree in the evening. She too had had time to shed the first madness of despair: she spoke calmly:

"We will be saying farewell to Gortinfliuch," she said; "you have ploughed the ground for a stranger."

He was sensitive; but his song was struggling within him, growing from moment to moment, its promise vast and great: his spirit was on the heights:

"Gortinfliuch!" he said, with earnest scorn—" 'tis a poor place for such as you to dwell in."

She was in the act of shaking Diarmuid from his sleep, fearing some fever was overcoming him; but she paused and looked at Eoghan; though always a wildly earnest man, it was not often he had spoken in such a strain.

"One would think you were one of those poets who teach school, like Eoghan Ruadh," she replied, "wanderers, with whom one place is as good as another."

"One would think," he answered, in the same tone of sad earnestness, "your name had never been put into a song."

Whatever look was in his face it made her recollect the many songs he and other poets had sung to her name; she guessed that the same phrases of these old songs as were in her brain now, were singing also in his. And so she drew quietly away from the sleeping boy and, her hood still hiding her face and head, seated herself on a sugawn chair before the flameless glow; she turned to speak, but speech failed her, she could see that her husband's thoughts were gone far away. Through the one dim little pane of glass the poet saw the white stars sparkling in the sky, the night-blue of which appeared deepened and enriched by reason of the red turf-glow with which the cabin was filled. He thought of the clods in the new-ploughed field as crumbling under the touch of the keen frost—a thing that had happened ever since the beginning of the world, that would continue until the end, whatever woe befell the world of the Gael.

"God's will be done!" he said aloud out of his thoughts, and bent his head.

"Amen, O Lord," his wife answered.

They both sank again into themselves; and the silence was again deep, except when the boy would stir or snort in his sleep, but at last the woman began to rock herself, and wail in a low and constrained and unnatural tone that had but little resemblance to human speech. Uch! Uch! Ochone! she would cry at the opening of each phrase of her keening; and the name Gortinfliuch was sure to come into every sentence of it: about that homely word she was gathering up the most intimate memories in traditional phrases of woe. One would think that Gortinfliuch was a pleasant, sunny place, and a soil of good heart, instead of being what it was. And she keened old chieftains of the O'Donovans and old dynasties of the MacCarthys, the MacCarthys who once were overlords of all those bleak uplands, their sunken rivers and hidden woodlands.

To that long-continued wail of sorrow, the poet gave no heed. An odd phrase would strike on his ear and stir memories or flash landscapes on his eye. But just then the keening was of no more moment to him than all the other sorrows of men's life; the keen was a part of that life which his spirit was shaping anew, at its own imperious will. He gave no sign when her voice died away into a long litany of the saints of the Gael, and finished with the name of the Mother of God. There was then a deeper silence than before: the poet was conscious of its breadth, its grandeur. The wheeling of the night's great shield of stars had carried that heart-broken keen away with it, as it had done with a hundred others from the same stricken land; and that great shield of blue and gold had dipped its eastern rim in the western sea before any other sound except the regular breathing of the boy disturbed the fire-lit gloom.

Silent but not asleep as yet, the woman's mind was dulled and tired; her grief had spent itself; her spirit had reached that tranquil shore which lies beyond a flood of tears. Her eyes were wide, cold-lidded, piteous; and the fire of anger was entirely quenched in them. The poet's eyes were different: in them was an ever-increasing glow, but it was the heat of great energy of creation, not of anger. Except for the eyes and the tense brows, the man's tall and haggard frame might have been asleep. All day long his body had lurched and swung to the timber plough, as it skirted the rocks; now his body was having its waking rest, while his mind had taken up the ploughing—ploughing of another sort. And the fierce labour held him until at last the grey dawn touched the beams of the hut with its wan light; at which moment it seemed his song came finally to perfection. The triumphant "ceangal," or envoi, his first enraptured line had aspired to was reached just as the last star drew back into the spreading light of the sky. He rose silently up and stretched himself and appeared to notice for the first time the uneasy attitude of his only child, his head resting on the table, the uneasy attitude of his wife, her head fallen low on her breast. Looking at their pathetic figures, for the first time he became conscious of how the night had passed; and conscious too that a new day was come upon the uplands. There was indignity in either thought, a sense of uncomeliness, of fear; and his hut looked miserable in the cold light of morning; the golden song within his brain, however, he soon recollected, was lavish recompense not alone for this night of stormy wailing, this unhappy dawn, but for all the abiding sorrows he and his had ever wrestled with, only to be at last overthrown. It was more than recompense. It was they themselves—these sorrows of his years—crystallised, transfigured, recreated—the same in elements, the self-same, yet a solace instead of a despair, rest instead of worry, triumph instead of defeat! He had often wondered at the miracle of song; the immediate needs of his spirit bade him now not to wonder but to accept. Because he had accepted his face was calm.

Fearing to awaken his little clan, it was on tip-toe he stepped from the room into the haggard. From a brad he took down a huge, clumsy-handled mall. As if still pursued with the fear of waking the sleepers, he stepped gently towards the tumble-down cow-house where their one beast—their whole wealth—had passed the night. He undid the wood bolt, stooped his head, and entered the close-smelling, brown-hued darkness in a gush of lovely sunbeams. The cow was lying lazily on her belly, staring up at him with mild eyes that blinked in the sudden glare. This the poet saw. Without a moment's delay, he raised the mall, swung it and struck one swift, smashing blow at the animal's skull above the eyes. The mall sank in a little way. It was withdrawn, swung again, and there was again the sound of crunching bone, less sudden, less loud. A quiver that began at the hind feet travelled through the animal's frame like a wave, another, yet another; then the life went out, and there on the floor was a high mass of bones and flesh. The poet went for his butcher's knife to let the blood run from the veins.

After a short time he re-entered his hut: his wife, his boy still slept. He wondered a moment at the silence. Then in a voice of authority, and speaking the Irish of the Bardic Schools, most classical of tongues. he cried out: "Maire, the daughter of Kearney, and Diarmuid, the son of Eoghan Mor of the Aislings, awaken! Awaken and order the house for feasting and revelling—the house of Eoghan Mor of the vision songs. Before the coming of night some of them will have gathered at our threshold—the poets of Muskerry and Carbery, Iveleary, and Iveragh and Uibhrathach, of Slieve Luchra and Corkaguiney, of Imokilly and Deise; and it will not be long until they will all have come. After the feasting I will silence them and recite, so that they may know it for ever, the song I have made in the night that has passed over us."

The glow of triumph in his appearance was more radiant than his wife had ever seen there before; yet she made bold to answer, speaking with reverence however, and as one who would urge a necessary consideration, and in the common language of the people:

"The feasting will not last for long; the poets will leave us in the end as desolate as we are now in this dawning: when at last it comes to the nailing up of the door there will be few except ourselves to behold it. Have you thought of the days that will follow on the feasting?"

"Woman," he answered her, "the sorrow that has made us desolate has this night given birth to a song that will live for ever; because of it my name and your name and our son's name, which are woven into its *amhrán* metre, will not pass: were I given my choice this moment to choose between Gortin-fliuch and my song, to which would I reach my hand? This trouble that has come to our doors is as nothing to the rapture in this song of mine!"

That day the poet went east and around by the north; and his son went north and around by the west; and other messengers went in other directions announcing the Bardic Sessions that were to be held at the house of Eoghan Mor O'Donovan, and as they sped, the messengers could not refrain from hinting at a new song that had just been made which was thought to excel even Egan O'Rahilly's "Gile na Gile."

In the eighteenth century a certain traveller, an Englishman, wrote a book of his experiences in the south of Ireland. In one chapter he deals both with Carbery and Iveragh—in neither of which he found much to dwell on. He tells how as he left Carbery and made northwards he came to a curious scene:

As my servant—the droll-spoken Hibernian I have previously made mention of—and myself rode through the mountain pass we became aware that some gathering must be about to take place farther on towards the west. We over-took and passed several knots of those tatterdemalion figures without which no Irish landscape seems complete; and these little groups—some of the way-farers curiously excited in appearance, wildly gesticulating, which seems to be a national characteristic—were all making, we observed, in the one direction. Over the mountains we would notice other groups coming to swell the gath-ering: it was not wonderful therefore that one in whom curiosity is ever alive, as it seems to be in all those who travel much, more especially if their wanderings take them into foreign lands—should set his horse's head in the same path as these turbulent-looking figures. As daylight failed we came on a miserable hut on the fringe of a bleak upland. Several peat-fires, which had been used apparently for the cooking of huge meals, had begun to die: but their relics still encircled the house and set it apart from the one or two others in the same district. The house itself, a miserable cabin, was crowded to the door with wild and picturesque figures. We heard no language but the Gaelic. In the midst of the assembly, as I took trouble to note, a huge gaunt man was reciting what was apparently a very violent poem—to judge by the excitement under which he laboured. I can recall but two lines which run (by the way my guide offered to translate the whole poem into Latin, as he did not seem satisfied that he could appositely render it in such English as he knew):

Till through my coffin-wood white blossoms start to grow
No grace I'll beg from one of Cromwell's crew.

It was a strange scene to come on in the midst of lonely mountains at the close of the day; but I could not help reflecting that these strong-bodied, though ill-clad peasants, might have found better employment on an evening admirably suited for ploughing. I noticed in a patch of bogland not far from the hut some ploughing gear lying haphazardly in a half-length of furrow, as if some peasant had flung it down on hearing a call to join the curious throng. But such reflections come into the mind of the observant traveller at every hand's turn in this strange land.

Further Readings on Daniel Corkery

Bibliography

Saul, George Brandon. *Daniel Corkery*. Lewisburg, Pa.: Bucknell University Press, 1973.

Selected Works

The Hounds of Banba. New York: Viking Press, 1922.
A Munster Twilight. Cork: Mercier Press, 1963.
Nightfall and Other Stories. Edited by Francis Michael Doherty. Belfast: Blackstaff Press, 1988.
The Stormy Hills. London: Jonathan Cape, 1929.
The Threshold of Quiet. New York: Stokes, 1918.

The Wager and Other Stories. New York: Devin-Adair, 1950.
The Yellow Bittern and Other Plays. Dublin: Talbot Press, 1920.

Studies

The Fortunes of the Irish Language. Dublin: At the Sign of the Three Candles, 1954.
The Hidden Ireland: A Study of Gaelic Munster in the Eighteenth Century. 1925.
    Reprint, Dublin: Gill and Macmillan, 1975.
Synge and Anglo-Irish Literature: A Study. Dublin: Gill, 1931.

Biography and Criticism

Cullen, L. M. "The Hidden Ireland: Reassessment of a Concept." *Studia Hibernica* 9
    (1969): 7–47.
Kiely, Ben. "Chronicle by Rushlight: Daniel Corkery's Quiet Desperation." *Irish
    Bookman* 2 (January 1948): 23–35.
Larkin, Emmet. "A Reconsideration: Daniel Corkery and His Ideas on Irish Cultural
    Nationalism." *Éire-Ireland* 8, no. 1 (Spring 1973): 42–51.
McCaffrey, Lawrence. "Daniel Corkery and Irish Cultural Nationalism." *Éire-Ireland*
    8, no. 1 (Spring 1973): 35–41.
Maume, Patrick. *Life That is Exile: Daniel Corkery and the Search for Irish Ireland.*
    Belfast: Institute for Irish Studies, Queen's University, 1993.
———. *The Rise and Fall of Irish Ireland: D. P. Moran and Daniel Corkery.* Coleraine,
    Northern Ireland: University of Ulster, 1996.
O'Connor, Frank. *An Only Child.* New York: Alfred A. Knopf, 1961. Reprint, Dublin:
    Pan Books, 1970.
O'Faoláin, Seán. "Daniel Corkery." *Dublin Magazine* 11 (April-June 1936): 49–61.
———. *Vive Moi,* pp. 168–73. Boston: Little, Brown and Co., 1964.
Ó Tuama, Seán. "Dónal Ó Corcora agus Filíocht na Gaeilge." *Studia Hibernica* 5
    (1965): 29–41.
Saul, George Brandon. *Daniel Corkery.* Lewisburg, Pa.: Bucknell University Press,
    1973.
Walsh, Patrick. *Strangers: Reflections on a Correspondence Between Daniel Corkery and
    John Hewitt.* Coleraine: University of Ulster, 1996.

[Handwritten note:] Characteristic strengths of modern Irish fiction: (1) a sense that significant meaning lies just beyond the edge of ordinary experience; & its logical extension (2) Great importance of community

Seán O'Faoláin *[handwritten:]* last great survivor of his generation
(1900–1991)

Though best known as one of his country's premier short-story writers, Seán O'Faoláin was a writer of many parts whose career spanned more than sixty years. Born John Whelan, O'Faoláin took the Irish form of his name in response to the Easter Rising of 1916; it is pronounced "oh fwa-LOIN." Often, he wrote as if he were the spokesman for the soul of modern Ireland. This was especially so during his six-year tenure, beginning in 1940, as editor of the influential quarterly, *The Bell,* as he fought censorship and provincialism, championed higher critical standards, and furthered the careers of a number of younger writers. His short book, *The Irish* (1947), continues to be one of the most widely read introductions to the national culture. O'Faoláin's deep knowledge of Irish history and politics was demonstrated in his five biographies, including those of Eamon de Valera, Countess Markievicz, Daniel O'Connell, and the sixteenth-century leader Hugh O'Neill. O'Faoláin produced distinguished literary criticism, including *The Short Story* (1948) and *The Vanishing Hero* (1956), in addition to travel literature, autobiography, translations, plays, and poetry. Success with the novel eluded him, however, as he published only four of the eight he wrote, and none of these to either critical or popular acclaim.

At once nationalist and cosmopolitan, O'Faoláin's career embraced many contrasts. In the course of one year in his twenties, for instance, he both served as a private in the Irish Republican Army and was introduced to a member of the British royal family as a Commonwealth scholarship winner. He studied the Irish language among peasants in the *Gaeltacht* (Irish-speaking areas), yet always acknowledged his debt to the Russian writers Turgenev and Chekhov and to the French novelist Stendhal. Although O'Faoláin earned a degree at Harvard University, he spent more of his adult career in Ireland than did many of his contemporaries. And while O'Faoláin led the quiet private life of a good Catholic layman, he was published frequently in *Playboy* magazine while in his seventies and eighties.

"The Fur Coat" dates from the late 1940s, when O'Faoláin had achieved his mature style: bemused and detached but forgiving. His wide social experience gave him empathy with the discomfort of unvarnished country people facing the demands of rising responsibilities following independence from Imperial Britain. Although the author never intended it so, the following story contributes to the discussion of postcolonialism in Ireland.

The Fur Coat

When Maguire became parliamentary secretary to the minister for roads and railways his wife wound her arms around his neck, lifted herself on her toes, gazed into his eyes and said, adoringly:

"Now, Paddy, I must have a fur coat."

"Of course, of course, me dear," Maguire cried, holding her out from him admiringly; for she was a handsome little woman still, in spite of the greying hair and the first hint of a stoop, "Get two fur coats! Switzer's will give us any amount of tick from now on."

Molly sat back into her chair with her fingers clasped between her knees and said, chidingly:

"You think I'm extravagant!"

"Indeed, then, I do not. We've had some thin times together and it's about time we had a bit of comfort in our old age. I'd like to see my wife in a fur coat. I'd love to see my wife take a shine out of some of those straps in Grafton Street—painted jades that never lifted a finger for God or man, not to as much as mention the word *Ireland*. By all means get a fur coat. Go down to Switzer's tomorrow morning," he cried with all the innocence of a warm-hearted, inexperienced man, "and order the best fur coat that money can buy."

Molly Maguire looked at him with affection and irritation. The years had polished her hard—politics, revolution, husband in and out of prison, children reared with the help of relatives and Prisoners' Dependents' funds. You could see the years on her finger tips, too pink, too coarse, and in her diamond-bright eyes.

"Paddy, you big fool, do you know what you'd pay for a mink coat? Not to mention a sable? And not as much as to whisper the word broadtail?"

"Say a hundred quid," said Paddy, manfully. "What's a hundred quid? I'll be handling millions of public money from now on. I have to think big."

She replied in her warm Limerick singsong; sedately and proudly as befitted a woman who had often, in her father's country store, handled thousands of pound notes.

"Do you know, Paddy Maguire, what a really bang-up fur coat could cost you? It could cost you a thousand guineas, and more."

"One thousand guineas? For a coat? Sure, that's a whole year's salary."

"It is."

Paddy drew into himself. "And," he said, in a cautious voice, "is that the kind of coat you had in mind?"

She laughed, satisfied at having taken him off his perch.

"Yerrah, not at all. I thought I might pick up a nice little coat for, maybe, thirty or forty or, at the outside, fifty quid. Would that be too much?"

"Go down to Switzer's in the morning and bring it home on your back."

But, even there, she thought she detected a touch of the bravo, as if he was still feeling himself a great fellow. She let it pass. She said she might have a look around. There was no hurry. She did not bring up the matter again for quite fifteen minutes.

"Paddy! About that fur coat. I sincerely hope you don't think I'm being *vulgar*?"

"How could you be vulgar?"

"Oh, sort of *nouveau riche*. I don't want a fur coat for show-off." She leaned forward eagerly. "Do you know the reason why I want a fur coat?"

"To keep you warm. What else?"

"Oh, well, that too, I suppose, yes," she agreed shortly. "But you must realize that from this on we'll be getting asked out to parties and receptions and so forth, And—well—I haven't a rag to wear!"

"I see," Paddy agreed; but she knew that he did not see.

"Look," she explained, "what I want is something I can wear any old time. I don't want a fur coat for grandeur." (This very scornfully.) "I want to be able to throw it on and go off and be as well dressed as anybody. You see, you can wear any old thing under a fur coat."

"That sounds a good idea." He considered the matter as judiciously as if he were considering a memorandum for a projected by-pass. She leaned back, contented, with the air of a woman who has successfully laid her conscience to rest.

Then he spoiled it all by asking, "But, tell me, what do all the women do who haven't fur coats?"

"They dress."

"Dress? Don't ye all dress?"

"Paddy, don't be silly. They think of nothing else but dress, I have no time for dressing, I'm a busy housewife and, anyway, dressing costs a lot of money." (Here she caught a flicker in his eye which obviously meant that forty quid isn't to be sniffed at either.) "I mean they have costumes that cost twenty-five pounds. Half a dozen of 'em. They spend a lot of time and thought over it. They live for it. If you were married to one of 'em you'd soon know what it means to dress. The beauty of a fur coat is that you can just throw it on and you're as good as the best of them."

"Well, that's fine! Get the ould coat."

He was evidently no longer enthusiastic. A fur coat, he had learned, is not a grand thing—it is just a useful thing, He drew his brief case towards him. There was that pier down in Kerry to be looked at. "Mind you," he added, "it'd be nice and warm, too. Keep you from getting a cold."

"Oh, grand, yes, naturally, cosy, yes, all that, yes, yes!"

And she crashed out and banged the door after her and put the children to bed as if she were throwing sacks of turf into a cellar. When she came back he was poring over maps and specifications. She began to patch one of the boy's pyjamas. After a while she held it up and looked at it in despair. She let it sink into her lap and looked at the pile of mending beside her.

"I suppose when I'm dead and gone they'll invent plastic pyjamas that you can wash with a dishcloth and mend with a lump of glue."

She looked into the heart of the turf fire. A dozen pyjamas . . . underwear for the whole house . . .

"Paddy!"

"Huh?"

"The last thing that I want anybody to start thinking is that I, by any possible chance, could be getting grand notions."

She watched him hopefully. He was lost in his plans.

"I can assure you, Paddy, that I loathe—I simply loathe all this modern show-off."

"That's right."

"Those wives that think they haven't climbed the social ladder until they've got a fur coat!"

He grunted at the map of the pier.

"Because I don't care what you or anybody else says, Paddy, there *is* something vulgar about a fur coat. There's no shape to them. Especially musquash. What I was thinking of was black Indian lamb, Of course, the real thing would be ocelot. But they're much too dear. The real ones. And I wouldn't be seen dead in an imitation ocelot."

He glanced sideways from the table. "You seem to know a lot about fur." He leaned back and smiled benevolently. "I never knew you were hankering all this time after a fur coat."

"Who said I'm hankering! I am *not*. What do you mean? Don't be silly, I just want something decent to wear when we go out to a show, or to wear over a dance frock, that's all. What do you mean—hankering?"

"Well, what's wrong with that thing you have with the fur on the sleeves? The shiny thing with the what-do-you-call-'ems—sequins, is it?"

"That! Do you mean *that*? For heaven's sake, don't be talking about what you don't know anything about. I've had *that* for fourteen years. It's like something me grandmother wore at her own funeral."

He laughed. "You used to like it."

"Of course, I liked it when I got it. Honestly, Paddy Maguire, there are times when . . ."

"Sorry, sorry, sorry. I was only trying to be helpful. How much is an ocelot?"

"Eighty-five or ninety—at the least."

"Well, why not?"

"Paddy, tell me honestly. Honestly, now! Do you seriously think that I could put eighty-five pounds on my back?"

With his pencil Maguire frugally drew a line on the map, reducing the pier by five yards, and wondered would the county surveyor let him get away with it.

"Well, the question is: will you be satisfied with the Indian lamb? What colour did you say it is? Black? That's a very queer lamb."

Irritably he rubbed out the line. The wretched thing would be too shallow at low water if he cut five yards off it.

"It's dyed. You could get it brown, too," she cried. "You could get all sorts of lamb. Broadtail is the fur of unborn Persian lambs."

That woke him up: the good farmer stock in him was shocked.

"Unborn lambs!" he cried. "Do you mean to say that they . . ."

"Yes, isn't it awful? Honest to Heaven, Paddy, anyone that'd wear broadtail ought to be put in prison, Paddy, I've made up my mind. I just couldn't buy a fur coat. I just won't buy it. That's the end of it."

She picked up the pyjamas again and looked at them with moist eyes. He turned to devote his full attention to her problem.

"Molly, darling, I'm afraid I don't understand what you're after. I mean, do you or do you not want a fur coat? I mean, supposing you didn't buy a fur coat, what else could you do?"

"Just exactly what do you mean?"—very coldly.

"I mean, it isn't apparently necessary that you should buy a fur coat. I mean, not if you don't really want to, There must be some other way of dressing besides fur coats? If you have a scunner against fur coats, why not buy something else just as good? There's hundreds of millions of other women in the world and they all haven't fur coats."

"I've told you before that they dress! And I've no time to dress. I've explained all that to you."

Maguire got up. He put his back to the fire, his hands behind him, a judicial look on him. He addressed the room.

"All the other women in the world can't all have time to dress. There must be some way out of it. For example, next month there'll be a garden party up at the President's house, How many of all these women will be wearing fur coats?" He addressed the armchair. "Has Mrs de Valera time to dress?" He turned and leaned over the turf basket. "Has Mrs General Mulcahy time to dress? There's ways and means of doing everything." (He shot a quick glance at the map of the pier; you could always knock a couple of feet off the width of it.) "After all, you've told me yourself that you could purchase a black costume for twenty-five guineas. Is that or is that not a fact? Very well then," triumphantly, "why not buy a black costume for twenty-five guineas?"

"Because, you big fathead, I'd have to have shoes and a blouse and hat and gloves and a fur and a purse and everything to match it, and I'd spend far more in the heel of the hunt, and I haven't time for that sort of thing and I'd have to have two or three costumes—Heaven above, I can't appear day after day in the same old rig, can I?"

"Good! Good! That's settled, Now, the question is: shall we or shall we not purchase a fur coat? Now! What is to be said for a fur coat?" He marked off the points on his fingers. "Number one: it is warm. Number two: it will keep you from getting cold. Number three . . ."

Molly jumped up, let a scream out of her, and hurled the basket of mending at him.

"Stop it! I told you I don't want a fur coat! And you don't want me to get a fur coat! You're too mean, that's what it is! And, like all the Irish, you have the peasant streak in you, You're all alike, every bloody wan of ye. Keep your rotten fur coat. I never wanted it . . ."

And she ran from the room sobbing with fury and disappointment.

"Mean?" gasped Maguire to himself. "To think that anybody could say that I . . . Mean!"

She burst open the door to sob:

"I'll go to the garden party in a mackintosh. And I hope that'll satisfy you!" and ran out again.

He sat miserably at his table, cold with anger. He murmured the hateful word over and over, and wondered could there be any truth in it. He added ten yards to the pier. He reduced the ten to five, and then, seeing what he had done, swept the whole thing off the table.

It took them three days to make it up. She had hit him below the belt and they both knew it. On the fourth morning she found a cheque for a hundred and fifty pounds on her dressing table. For a moment her heart leaped. The next moment it died in her. She went down and put her arms about his neck and laid the cheque, torn in four, into his hand.

"I'm sorry, Paddy," she begged, crying like a kid. "You're not mean. You never were. It's me that's mean."

"You! Mean?" he said, fondly holding her in his arms.

"No, I'm not mean, It's not that. I just haven't the heart, Paddy, It was knocked out of me donkeys' years ago." He looked at her sadly. "You know what I'm trying to say?"

He nodded. But she saw that he didn't. She was not sure that she knew herself. He took a deep, resolving breath, held her out from him by the shoulders, and looked her straight in the eyes. "Molly, tell me the truth, You want this coat?"

"I do. O God, I do!"

"Then go out and buy it."

"I couldn't, Paddy. I just couldn't."

He looked at her for a long time. Then he asked:

"Why?"

She looked straight at him and, shaking her head sadly, she said in a little sobbing voice:

"I don't know."

Further Readings on Seán O'Faoláin

Selected Works

And Again? A Novel. New York: Carol, 1989.
The Collected Short Stories of Sean O'Faolain. 3 vols. London: Constable, 1980–83; Boston: Little, Brown, 1983.
Constance Markievicz: or, The Average Revolutionary. 1934. Revised edition, London: Sphere Books, 1968 and London: Cresset Women's Voices, 1987.
De Valera. Harmondsworth: Penguin, 1939.
Foreign Affairs and Other Stories. 1982. Reprint, London: Penguin, 1986.

The Great O'Neill: A Biography of Hugh O'Neill, Earl of Tyrone, 1550–1616. London: Longmans, and New York: Duell, Sloan, Pearce, 1942.

The Irish. West Drayton: Penguin, 1947. Under the title *The Irish: A Character Study,* New York: Devin-Adair, 1949; revised edition, Harmondsworth: Penguin, 1969.

King of Beggars: A Life of Daniel O'Connell, The Irish Liberator. 1938. Reprint, Dublin: Allen Figgis, 1970.

Midsummer Night Madness. 1932. Reprint, London: Penguin, 1986.

A Purse of Coppers. London: Jonathan Cape, 1937; Viking, 1938.

Selected Stories. Boston: Little, Brown, 1978.

Short Stories: A Study in Pleasure. Boston: Little, Brown, 1961.

The Short Story. London and Toronto: Collins, 1948; New York: Devin-Adair, 1951.

The Vanishing Hero: Studies in the Novelists of the Twenties. London: Eyre and Spottiswoode, 1956; Boston: Little, Brown, 1957.

Biography and Criticism

Arndt, Marie. *A Critical Study of Sean O'Faolain's Life and Work.* Lewiston, N.Y.: E. Mellen, 2001.

Bonaccorso, Richard. *Sean O'Faolain's Irish Vision.* Albany: State University of New York Press, 1987.

Butler, Pierce. *Sean O'Faolain: A Study of the Short Fiction.* New York: Twayne, 1993.

Doyle, Paul A. *Seán O'Faoláin.* New York: Twayne, 1968.

Harmon, Maurice. *Seán O'Faoláin: A Critical Introduction.* South Bend, Ind.: University of Notre Dame Press, 1967.

Harmon, Maurice. *Seán O'Faoláin.* London: Constable, 1994.

Irish University Review 6, no. 1 (Spring/Summer 1976). Special issue on Seán O'Faoláin.

Rippier, Joseph Storey. *The Short Stories of Seán O'Faoláin: A Study in Descriptive Technique.* Gerrards Cross, UK: Colin Smythe, 1976.

Writing soon after the deaths of year of Joyce, he was as well as a benefactor as a critic of the Literary Review.

He was a Republican in the civil war. He became a prisoner of Free State Army

Frank O'Connor

(1903–1966)

A powerful critic of Irish public life *of Irish public life* *no writer of his time came closer to understanding middle class Catholic Ireland*

Although born in poverty and self-educated, Frank O'Connor became one of the most accomplished short-story writers in Ireland, as well as a gifted translator and discerning critic. (Born Michael O'Donovan, he used the pseudonym Frank O'Connor throughout his career.) Critical recognition came immediately and persisted through his thirty-year-long career. The success of his first collection, *Guests of the Nation* (1931), helped to win him the position of artistic director of the Abbey Theatre and a working relationship with Yeats from 1935 to 1939. In his last years, his stories appeared regularly in the *New Yorker,* America's most prestigious short-story journal.

O'Connor did less well with the novel, as his two efforts, *The Saint and Mary Kate* (1932) and *Dutch Interior* (1940), are usually ranked among his lesser works. More impressive are his various books dealing with Irish tradition and Old Irish literature. His *Irish Miles* (1947) is both a personal travelogue and an argument for the preservation of early buildings and monuments. A series of lively translations from the Irish (or Gaelic) helped to introduce that literature to a wide international readership; among the most important of these are *The Midnight Court* (1945), from the eighteenth-century poet Brian Merriman; *Kings, Lords, and Commons* (1959); and *The Golden Treasury of Irish Poetry* (1967). O'Connor wrote extensively on literature, and some of his studies have been much admired, especially *Mirror on the Roadway* (1956), on the art of the novel, and *The Lonely Voice* (1962), on the art of the short story. In the years before his death he wrote a personalized history of Irish literature, *The Backward Look* (1967)—the only work of its kind ever attempted by a significant Irish writer. Finally, his two volumes of autobiography, *An Only Child* (1961) and *My Father's Son* (1968), are often ranked with the finest work produced by any Irish writer in the last century.

During most of his career O'Connor was a scourge of Irish provincialism and puritanism, a fact that prompted the government to ban some of his books. Nevertheless, Ireland remained his principal concern, although he did not always wish to live there. He was affiliated with the British Broadcasting Corporation in the 1940s before emigrating to the United States in 1951, where he lectured at several universities, including Harvard and Stanford. One of his many students in America was Ken Kesey, author of *One Flew Over the Cuckoo's Nest* (1962). After suffering a stroke in 1961, O'Connor returned to Ireland.

"The Long Road to Ummera" (1940), one of O'Connor's best-known stories, first appeared in *The Bell,* a quarterly periodical edited by his friend and fellow Corkman, Seán O'Faoláin.

The Long Road to Ummera

Stay for me there. I will not fail
To meet thee in that hollow vale.

Always in the evenings you saw her shuffle up the road to Miss O's for her little jug of porter, a shapeless lump of an old woman in a plaid shawl, faded to the color of snuff, that dragged her head down on to her bosom where she clutched its folds in one hand; a canvas apron and a pair of men's boots without laces. Her eyes were puffy and screwed up in tight little buds of flesh and her rosy old face that might have been carved out of a turnip was all crumpled with blindness. The old heart was failing her, and several times she would have to rest, put down the jug, lean against the wall, and lift the weight of the shawl off her head. People passed; she stared at them humbly; they saluted her; she turned her head and peered after them for minutes on end. The rhythm of life had slowed down in her till you could scarcely detect its faint and sluggish beat. Sometimes from some queer instinct of shyness she turned to the wall, took a snuffbox from her bosom, and shook out a pinch on the back of her swollen hand. When she sniffed it it smeared her nose and upper lip and spilled all over her old black blouse. She raised the hand to her eyes and looked at it closely and reproachfully, as though astonished that it no longer served her properly. Then she dusted herself, picked up the old jug again, scratched herself against her clothes, and shuttled along close by the wall, groaning aloud.

When she reached her own house, which was a little cottage in a terrace, she took off her boots, and herself and the old cobbler who lodged with her turned out a pot of potatoes on the table, stripping them with their fingers and dipping them in the little mound of salt while they took turn and turn about with the porter jug. He was a lively and philosophic old man called Johnny Thornton.

After their supper they sat in the firelight, talking about old times in the country and long-dead neighbors, ghosts, fairies, spells, and charms. It always depressed her son, finding them together like that when he called with her

[handwritten: Her well-to-do son | Pat dislikes the "old talk"]

monthly allowance. He was a well-to-do businessman with a little grocery shop in the South Main Street and a little house in Sunday's Well, and nothing would have pleased him better than that his mother should share all the grandeur with him, the carpets and the china and the chiming clocks. He sat moodily between them, stroking his long jaw, and wondering why they talked so much about death in the old-fashioned way, as if it was something that made no difference at all.

"Wisha, what pleasure do ye get out of old talk like that?" he asked one night.

"Like what, Pat?" his mother asked with her timid smile.

"My goodness," he said, "ye're always at it. Corpses and graves and people that are dead and gone."

"Arrah, why wouldn't we?" she replied, looking down stiffly as she tried to button the open-necked blouse that revealed her old breast. "Isn't there more of us there than here?"

"Much difference 'twill make to you when you won't know them or see them!" he exclaimed.

"Oye, why wouldn't I know them?" she cried angrily. "Is it the Twomeys of Lackroe and the Driscolls of Ummera?"

"How sure you are we'll take you to Ummera!" he said mockingly.

"Och aye, Pat," she asked, shaking herself against her clothes with her humble stupid wondering smile, "and where else would you take me?"

"Isn't our own plot good enough for you?" he asked. "Your own son and your grandchildren?"

"Musha, indeed, is it in the town you want to bury me?" she shrugged herself and blinked into the fire, her face growing sour and obstinate. "I'll go back to Ummera, the place I came from." *[handwritten: Her wish to be buried at her birth place]*

"Back to the hunger and misery we came from," Pat said scornfully.

"Back to your father, boy."

"Ay, to be sure, where else? But my father or grandfather never did for you what I did. Often and often I scoured the streets of Cork for a few ha'pence for you."

"You did, amossa, you did, you did," she admitted, looking into the fire and shaking herself. "You were a good son to me."

"And often I did it and the belly falling out or me with hunger," Pat went on, full of self-pity.

"'Tis true for you," she mumbled, " 'tis, 'tis, 'tis true. 'Twas often and often you had to go without it. What else could you do and the way we were left?"

"And now our grave isn't good enough for you," he complained. There was real bitterness in his tone. He was an insignificant little man and jealous of the power the dead had over her.

She looked at him with the same abject, half-imbecile smile, the wrinkled old eyes almost shut above the Mongolian cheekbones, while with a swollen old hand, like a pot-stick, it had so little life in it, she smoothed a few locks of yellow-white hair across her temples—a trick she had when troubled.

"Musha, take me back to Ummera, Pat," she whined. "Take me back to my own. I'd never rest among strangers. I'd be rising and drifting."

"Ah, foolishness, woman!" he said with an indignant look. "That sort of thing is gone out of fashion."

"I won't stop here for you," she shouted hoarsely in sudden, impotent fury, and she rose and grasped the mantelpiece for support.

"You won't be asked," he said shortly.

"I'll haunt you," she whispered tensely, holding on to the mantelpiece and bending down over him with a horrible grin.

"And that's only more of the foolishness," he said with a nod of contempt. "Haunts and fairies and spells."

She took one step towards him and stood, plastering down the two little locks of yellowing hair, the half-dead eyes twitching and blinking in the candlelight, and the swollen crumpled face with the cheeks like cracked enamel.

"Pat," she said, "the day we left Ummera you promised to bring me back. You were only a little gorsoon that time. The neighbors gathered round me and the last word I said to them and I going down the road was: 'Neighbors, my son Pat is after giving me his word and he'll bring me back to ye when my time comes.' . . . That's true as the Almighty God is over me this night. I have everything ready." She went to the shelf under the stairs and took out two parcels. She seemed to be speaking to herself as she opened them gloatingly, bending down her head in the feeble light of the candle. "There's the two brass candlesticks and the blessed candles alongside them. And there's my shroud aired regular on the line."

"Ah, you're mad, woman," he said angrily. "Forty miles! Forty miles into the heart of the mountains!"

She suddenly shuffled towards him on her bare feet, her hand raised clawing the air, her body like her face blind with age. Her harsh croaking old voice rose to a shout.

"I brought you from it, boy, and you must bring me back. If 'twas the last shilling you had and you and your children to go to the poorhouse after, you must bring me back to Ummera. And not by the short road either! Mind what

[handwritten: Pat must take her by the long road.]

I say now! The long road! The long road to Ummera round the lake, the way I brought you from it. I lay a heavy curse on you this night if your bring me the short road over the hill. And ye must stop by the ash tree at the foot of the boreen where ye can see my little house and say a prayer for all that were ever old in it and all that played on the floor. And then—Pat! Pat Driscoll! Are you listening? Are you listening to me, I say?"

She shook him by the shoulder, peering down into his long miserable face to see how was he taking it. *[handwritten: be]*

"I'm listening," he said with a shrug. *[handwritten: Promise to be kept.]*

"Then"—her voice dropped to a whisper—"you must stand up overnight the neighbors and say—remember now what I'm telling you!—"Neighbors, this is Abby, Batty Heige's daughter, that kept her promise to ye at the end of all.' " *[handwritten: *]*

She said it lovingly, smiling to herself, as if it were a bit of an old song, something she went over and over in the long night. All West Cork was in it: the bleak road over the moors to Ummera, the smooth gray pelts of the hills with the long spider's web of the fences ridging them, drawing the scarecrow fields awry, and the whitewashed cottages, poker-faced between their little scraps of holly bushes looking this way and that out of the wind. *[handwritten: Poetic sensibility of peasant]*

"Well, I'll make a fair bargain with you," said Pat as he rose. Without seeming to listen she screwed up her eyes and studied his weak melancholy face. "This house is a great expense to me. Do what I'm always asking you. Live with me and I'll promise I'll take you back to Ummera." *[handwritten: Pat tries to bargain]*

"Oye, I will not," she replied sullenly, shrugging her shoulders helplessly, an old sack of a woman with all the life gone out of her.

"All right," said Pat. " 'Tis your own choice. That's my last word; take it or leave it. Live with me and Ummera for your grave, or stop here and a plot in the Botanics." *[handwritten: Pat's ultimatum]*

She watched him out the door with shoulders hunched about her ears. Then she shrugged herself, took out her snuffbox and took a pinch.

"Arrah. I wouldn't mind what he'd say," said Johnny. "A fellow like that would change his mind tomorrow."

"He might and he mightn't," she said heavily, and opened the back door to go out to the yard. It was a starry night and they could hear the noise of the city below hem in the valley. She raised her eyes to the bright sky over the back wall and suddenly broke into a cry of loneliness and helplessness.

"Oh, oh, oh, 'tis far away from me Ummera is tonight above any other night, and I'll die and be buried here, far from all I ever knew and the long roads between us."

[handwritten: Pat portrayed as weak compared to Abby his mother]

Of course old Johnny should have known damn well what she was up to the night she made her way down to the cross, creeping along beside the railings. By the blank wall opposite the lighted pub Dan Regan, the jarvey, was standing by his old box of a covered car with his pipe in his gob. He was the jarvey all the old neighbors went to. Abby beckoned to him and he followed her into the shadow of a gateway overhung with ivy. He listened gravely to what she had to say, sniffing and nodding, wiping his nose in his sleeve, or crossing the pavement to hawk his nose and spit in the channel, while his face with its drooping mustaches never relaxed its discreet and doleful expression.

Johnny should have known what that meant and why old Abby, who had always been so open-handed, sat before an empty grate sooner than light a fire, and came after him on Fridays for the rent, whether he had it or not, and even begrudged him the little drop of porter which had always been give and take between them. He knew himself it was a change before death and that it all went into the wallet in her bosom. At night in her attic she counted it by the light of her candle and when the coins dropped from her lifeless fingers he heard her roaring like an old cow as she crawled along the naked boards, sweeping them blindly with her palms. Then he heard the bed creak as she tossed about in it, and the rosary being taken from the bedhead, and the old voice rising and falling in prayer; and sometimes when a high wind blowing up the river roused him before dawn he could hear her muttering: a mutter and then a yawn; the scrape of a match as she peered at the alarm clock—the endless nights of the old—and then the mutter of prayer again.

But Johnny in some ways was very dense, and he guessed nothing till the night she called him and, going to the foot of the stairs with a candle in his hand, he saw her on the landing in her flour-bag shift, one hand clutching the jamb of the door while the other clawed wildly at her few straggly hairs.

"Johnny!" she screeched down at him, beside herself with excitement. "He was here."

"Who was there?" he snarled back, still cross with sleep.

"Michael Driscoll, Pat's father."

"Ah, you were dreaming, woman," he said in disgust. "Go back to your bed in God's holy name."

"I was not dreaming," she cried. "I was lying broad awake, saying my beads, when he come in the door, beckoning me. Go down to Dan Regan's for me, Johnny."

"I will not, indeed, go down to Dan Regan's for you. Do you know what hour of night it is?"

" 'Tis morning."

" 'Tis. Four o'clock! What a thing I'd do! . . . Is it the way you're feeling bad?" he added with more consideration as he mounted the stairs. "Do you want him to take you to hospital?"

"Oye, I'm going to no hospital," she replied sullenly, turning her back on him and thumping into the room again. She opened an old chest of drawers and began fumbling in it for her best clothes, her bonnet and cloak.

"Then what the blazes do you want Dan Regan for?" he snarled in exasperation.

"What matter to you what I want him for?" she retorted with senile suspicion. "I have a journey to go, never you mind where."

"Ach, you old oinseach, your mind is wandering," he cried. "There's a divil of a wind blowing up the river. The whole house is shaking. That's what you heard. Make your mind easy now and go back to bed."

"My mind is not wandering," she shouted. "Thanks be to the Almighty God I have my senses as good as you. My plans are made. I'm going back now where I came from. Back to Ummera."

"Back to where?" Johnny asked in stupefaction.

"Back to Ummera."

"You're madder than I thought. And do you think or imagine Dan Regan will drive you?"

"He will drive me then," she said, shrugging herself as she held an old petticoat to the light. "He's booked for it any hour of the day or night."

"Then Dan Regan is madder still."

"Leave me alone now," she muttered stubbornly, blinking and shrugging. "I'm going back to Ummera and that was why my old comrade came for me. All night and every night I have my beads wore out, praying the Almighty God and His Blessed Mother not to leave me die among strangers. And now I'll leave my old bones on a high hilltop in Ummera."

Johnny was easily persuaded. It promised to be a fine day's outing and a story that would delight a pub, so he made tea for her and after that went down to Dan Regan's little cottage, and before smoke showed from any chimney on the road they were away. Johnny was hopping about the car in his excitement, leaning out, shouting through the window of the car to Dan and identifying big estates that he hadn't seen for years. When they were well outside the town, himself and Dan went in for a drink, and while they were inside the old woman dozed. Dan Regan roused her to ask if she wouldn't take a drop of something and at first she didn't know who he was and then she asked where they were and peered out at the public-house and the old dog sprawled asleep in the sunlight before the door. But when next they halted she had fallen asleep again, her mouth hanging open and her breath coming in noisy gusts. Dan's face grew gloomier. He looked hard at her and spat. Then he took a few turns about the road, lit his pipe and put on the lid.

"I don't like her looks at all, Johnny," he said gravely. "I done wrong. I see that now. I done wrong."

After that, he halted every couple of miles to see how she was and Johnny, threatened with the loss of his treat, shook her and shouted at her. Each time Dan's face grew graver. He walked gloomily about the road, clearing his nose and spitting in the ditch. "God direct me!" he said solemnly. " 'Twon't be wishing to me. Her son is a powerful man. He'll break me yet. A man should never interfere between families. Blood is thicker than water. The Regans were always unlucky."

When they reached the first town he drove straight to the police barrack and told them the story in his own peculiar way.

"Ye can tell the judge I gave ye every assistance," he said in a reasonable brokenhearted tone. "I was always a friend of the law. I'll keep nothing back— a pound was the price agreed. I suppose if she dies 'twill be manslaughter. I never had hand, act or part in politics. Sergeant Daly at the Cross knows me well."

When Abby came to herself she was in a bed in the hospital. She began to fumble for her belongings and her shrieks brought a crowd of unfortunate old women about her.

"Whisht, whisht, whisht!" they said. "They're all in safe-keeping. You'll get them back."

"I want them now," she shouted, struggling to get out of bed while they held her down. "Leave me go, ye robbers of hell! Ye night-walking rogues, leave me go. Oh, murder, murder! Ye're killing me."

At last an old Irish-speaking priest came and comforted her. He left her quietly saying her beads, secure in the promise to see that she was buried in Ummera no matter what anyone said. As darkness fell, the beads dropped from her swollen hands and she began to mutter to herself in Irish. Sitting about the fire, the ragged old women whispered and groaned in sympathy. The Angelus rang out from a nearby church. Suddenly Abby's voice rose to a shout and she tried to lift herself on her elbow.

"Ah, Michael Driscoll, my friend, my kind comrade, you didn't forget me after all the long years. I'm a long time away from you but I'm coming at last. They tried to keep me away, to make me stop among foreigners in the town, but where would I be at all without you and all the old friends? Stay for me, my treasure! Stop and show me the way. . . . Neighbors," she shouted, pointing into the shadows, "that man there is my own husband, Michael Driscoll. Let ye see he won't leave me to find my way alone. Gather round me with yeer lanterns, neighbors, till I see who I have. I know ye all. 'Tis only the sight that's weak on me. Be easy now, my brightness, my own kind loving comrade. I'm coming. After all the long years I'm on the road to you at last. . . ."

It was a spring day full of wandering sunlight when they brought her the long road to Ummera, the way she had come from it forty years before. The lake was like a dazzle of midges; the shafts of the sun revolving like a great millwheel poured their cascades of milky sunlight over the hills and the little whitewashed cottages and the little black mountain cattle among the scarecrow fields. The hearse stopped at the foot of the lane that led to the roofless cabin just as she had pictured it to herself in the long nights, and Pat, looking more melancholy than ever, turned to the waiting neighbors and said:

Setting

"Neighbors, this is Abby, Batty Heige's daughter, that kept her promise to ye at the end of all."

Priest has persuaded Pat

Further Readings on Frank O'Connor

Bibliography

Sheehy, Maurice. "Towards a Bibliography of Frank O'Connor's Writing." In *Michael/Frank: Studies on Frank O'Connor,* ed. M. Sheehy, 168–99. Dublin: Gill and Macmillan, and New York: Knopf, 1969.

Selected Works

The Backward Look: A Survey of Irish Literature. London: Macmillan, 1967. Under the title *A Short History of Irish Literature: A Backward Look.* New York: Putnam, 1967.
Collected Stories. New York: Knopf, 1981.
Dutch Interior. New York: Macmillan, 1940. Reprint, Dublin: Millington, 1973.
A Frank O'Connor Reader. Edited by Michael Steinman. Syracuse, N.Y.: Syracuse University Press, 1994.
The Golden Treasury of Irish Poetry. Edited, with David Greene. London: Macmillan, 1967.
Guests of the Nation. London: Macmillan, 1931. Reprint, Swords, Republic of Ireland: Poolbeg, 1979.
Happiness of Getting It Right: Letters of Frank O'Connor and William Maxwell, 1945–1966. Edited by Michael Steinman. New York: Knopf, 1996.
Irish Miles. London: Macmillan, 1947.

Kings, Lords, and Commons. New York: Knopf, 1959; London: Macmillan, 1961.

The Lonely Voice. Cleveland, Ohio: World, 1962; London: Macmillan, 1963.

The Midnight Court. A Rhythmical Bacchanalia from the Irish of Bryan Merriman. Dublin: Fridberg, 1947.

The Mirror in the Roadway. New York: Knopf, 1956; London: Hamish Hamilton, 1957.

My Father's Son. London: Macmillan, 1968; New York: Knopf, 1969. Reprint, Syracuse, N.Y.: Syracuse University Press, 1999.

An Only Child. New York: Knopf, 1961; London: Macmillan, 1962. Reprint, Syracuse, N.Y.: Syracuse University Press, 1997.

The Saint and Mary Kate. London: Macmillan, 1932.

Biography and Criticism

Evans, Robert C., and Richard Harp, eds. *Frank O'Connor: New Perspectives.* West Cornwell, Conn.: Locust Hill Press, 1998.

Hildebidle, John. *Five Irish Writers.* Cambridge: Harvard University Press, 1989.

Matthews, James H. *Frank O'Connor.* Lewisburg, Pa.: Bucknell University Press, 1976.

———. *Voices: A Life of Frank O'Connor.* New York: Atheneum, 1983.

McKeon, Jim. *Frank O'Connor: A Life.* Edinburgh: Mainstream, 1998.

Sheehy, Maurice, ed. *Michael/Frank: Studies on Frank O'Connor.* Dublin. Gill and Macmillan; New York: Knopf, 1969.

Steinman, Michael. *Frank O'Connor at Work.* Syracuse, N.Y.: Syracuse University Press, 1990.

Tomory, William M. *Frank O'Connor.* Boston: Twayne, 1980.

Wohlgelernter, Maurice. *Frank O'Connor: An Introduction.* New York: Columbia University Press, 1977.

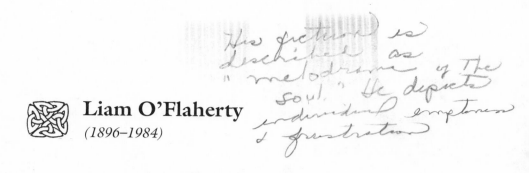

His fiction is described as "melodrama of the soul." He depicts individual emptiness & frustration

Liam O'Flaherty
(1896–1984)

Liam O'Flaherty's best-known work is *The Informer* (1925), a novel about betrayal set in Dublin during the 1920s. John Ford made it into a film and Victor McLaglen won an Academy Award for his role as Gypo Nolan. It is Irish rural life, however, especially life on the Aran Islands where he was born, that provides the theme and setting for most of O'Flaherty's fiction—stories of islanders and their creatures, stories set in a grim world of rock, sea, and sky and told with simplicity and dignity.

O'Flaherty's own story would provide the plots for several novels. By his account, he studied to be a priest, served in the Irish Guards in World War I, led an army of unemployed into the Rotunda Hospital in Dublin, joined the Republicans during the Civil War, shipped out as a merchant sailor, cut lumber in Canada, intrigued in the Balkans, taught in Rio, and stumped for the Irish Communist Party. He then settled down to a writing career that produced more than a dozen novels and several volumes of short stories, as well as two autobiographies, a biography, social and political commentary, an appreciation of Joseph Conrad, and a play. In 1953, O'Flaherty published *Dúil,* a collection of stories that first appeared in English. It was praised by a number of Irish critics, including Seán Ó Riordáin, who wrote in his diary that reading the stories was like holding a live robin in his hands.

"Going into Exile" describes the poignant leave-taking of two Aran teenagers who are going to America. Here, the writer may have drawn on the departure of his own brother, since Tom Flaherty's autobiography tells a similar story, although one focused on the restrained but deeply felt relationship between father and son.

Going into Exile   *Aran Islands*

Patrick Feeney's cabin was crowded with people. In the large kitchen men, women, and children lined the walls, three deep in places, sitting on forms, chair, stools, and on one another's knees. On the cement floor three couples were dancing a jig and raising a quantity of dust, which was, however, soon sucked up the chimney by the huge turf fire that blazed on the hearth. The only clear space in the kitchen was the corner to the left of the fireplace, where

Pat Mullaney sat on a yellow chair, with his right ankle resting on his left knee, a spotted red handkerchief on his head that reeked with perspiration, and his red face contorting as he played a tattered old accordion. One door was shut and the tins hanging on it gleamed in the firelight. The opposite door was open and over the heads of the small boys that crowded in it and outside it, peering in at the dancing couples in the kitchen, a starry June sky was visible and, beneath the sky, shadowy grey crags and misty, whitish fields lay motionless, still and sombre. There was a deep, calm silence outside the cabin and within the cabin, in spite of the music and dancing in the kitchen and the singing in the little room to the left, where Patrick Feeney's eldest son Michael sat on the bed with three other young men, there was a haunting melancholy in the air.

The people were dancing, laughing and singing with a certain-forced and boisterous gaiety that failed to hide from them the real cause of their being there, dancing, singing and laughing. For the dance was on account of Patrick Feeney's two children, Mary and Michael, who were going to the United States on the following morning.

Feeney himself, a black-bearded, red-faced, middle-aged peasant, with white ivory buttons on his blue frieze shirt and his hands stuck in his leather waist belt, wandered restlessly about the kitchen, urging the people to sing and dance, while his mind was in agony all the time, thinking that on the following day he would lose his two eldest children, never to see them again perhaps. He kept talking to everybody about amusing things, shouted at the dancers and behaved in a boisterous and abandoned manner. But every now and then he had to leave the kitchen, under the pretence of going to the pigsty to look at a young pig that was supposed to be ill. He would stand, however, upright against his gable and look gloomily at some star or other, while his mind struggled with vague and peculiar ideas that wandered about in it. He could make nothing at all of his thoughts, but a lump always came up his throat, and he shivered, although the night was warm.

Then he would sigh and say with a contraction of his neck: "Oh, it's a queer world this and no doubt about it. So it is." Then he would go back to the cabin again and begin to urge on the dance, laughing, shouting and stamping on the floor.

Towards dawn, when the floor was crowded with couples, arranged in fours, stamping on the floor and going to and fro, dancing the "Walls of Limerick," Feeney was going out to the gable when his son Michael followed him out. The two of them walked side by side about the yard over the grey sea pebbles that had been strewn there the previous day. They walked in silence and yawned without need, pretending to be taking the air. But each of them was very excited. Michael was taller than his father and not so thickly built, but the shabby blue serge suit that he had bought for going to America was too narrow for his broad shoulders and the coat was too wide around the waist. He moved clumsily in it and his hands appeared altogether too bony and big and red, and he didn't know what to do with them. During his twenty-one years of life he had never worn anything other than the homespun clothes of Inverara, and the shop-made clothes appeared as strange to him and as uncomfortable as a dress suit worn by a man working in a sewer. His face was flushed a bright red and his blue eyes shone with excitement. Now and again he wiped the perspiration from his forehead with the lining of his grey tweed cap.

At last Patrick Feeney reached his usual position at the gable end. He halted, balanced himself on his heels with his hands in his waist belt, coughed and said, "It's going to be a warm day." The son came up beside him, folded his arms and leaned his right shoulder against the gable.

"It was kind of Uncle Ned to lend the money for the dance, father," he said, "I'd hate to think that we'd have to go without something or other, just the same as everybody else has. I'll send you that money the very first money I earn, father . . . even before I pay Aunt Mary for my passage money. I should have all that money paid off in four months, and then I'll have some more money to send you by Christmas."

And Michael felt very strong and manly recounting what he was going to do when he got to Boston, Massachusetts. He told himself that with his great strength he would earn a great deal of money. Conscious of his youth and his strength and lusting for adventurous life, for the moment he forgot the ache in his heart that the thought of leaving his father inspired in him.

The father was silent for some time. He was looking at the sky with his lower lip hanging, thinking of nothing. At last he sighed as a memory struck him. "What is it?" said the son. "Don't weaken, for God's sake. You will only make it hard for me." "Fooh!" said the father suddenly with pretended gruffness. "Who is weakening? I'm afraid that your new clothes make you impudent." Then he was silent for a moment and continued in a low voice: "I was thinking of that potato field you sowed alone last spring the time I had the influenza. I never set eyes on that man that could do it better. It's a cruel world that takes you away from the land that God made you for."

"Oh, what are you talking about, father?" said Michael irritably. "Sure what did anybody ever get out of the land but poverty and hard work and potatoes and salt?"

"Ah, yes," said the father with a sigh, "but it's your own, the land, and

over there"—he waved his hand at the western sky—"you'll be giving your
sweat to some other man's land, or what's equal to it."

"Indeed," muttered Michael, looking at the ground with a melancholy
expression in his eyes, "it's poor encouragement you are giving me."

They stood in silence fully five minutes. Each hungered to embrace the
other, to cry, to beat the air, to scream with excess of sorrow. But they stood
silent and sombre, like nature about them, hugging their woe. Then they
went back to the cabin. Michael went into the little room to the left of the
kitchen, to the three young men who fished in the same curragh with him and
were his bosom friends. The father walked into the large bedroom to the right
of the kitchen.

The large bedroom was also crowded with people. A large table was laid
for tea in the centre of the room and about a dozen young men were sitting at
it, drinking tea and eating buttered raisin cake. Mrs. Feeney was bustling
about the table, serving the food and urging them to eat. She was assisted by
her two younger daughters and by another woman, a relative of her own. Her
eldest daughter Mary, who was going to the United States that day, was sitting
on the edge of the bed with several other young women. The bed was a large
four poster bed with a deal canopy over it, painted red, and the young women
were huddled together on it. So that there must have been about a dozen of
them there. They were Mary Feeney's particular friends, and they stayed with
her in that uncomfortable position just to show how much they liked her. It
was a custom.

Mary herself sat on the edge of the bed with her legs dangling. She was a
pretty, dark-haired girl of nineteen, with dimpled, plump, red cheeks and ru-
minative brown eyes that seemed to cause little wrinkles to come and go in her
little low forehead. Her nose was soft and small and rounded. Her mouth was
small and the lips were red and open. Beneath her white blouse that was frilled
at the neck and her navy blue skirt that outlined her limbs as she sat on the
edge of the bed, her body was plump, soft, well-moulded and in some manner
exuded a feeling of freshness and innocence. So that she seemed to have been
born to be fondled and admired in luxurious surroundings instead of having
been born a peasant's daughter, who had to go to the United States that day
to work as a servant or maybe in a factory.

And as she sat on the edge of the bed crushing her little handkerchief between her palms, she kept thinking feverishly of the United States, at one moment with fear and loathing, at the next with desire and longing. Unlike her
brother she did not think of the work she was going to do or the money that
she was going to earn. Other things troubled her, things of which she was half

ashamed, half afraid, thoughts of love and of foreign men and of clothes and of houses where there were more than three rooms and where people ate meat every day. She was fond of life, and several young men among the local gentry had admired her in Inverara. But . . .

She happened to look up and she caught her father's eyes as he stood silently by the window with his hands stuck in his waist belt. His eyes rested on hers for a moment and then he dropped them without smiling, and with his lips compressed he walked down into the kitchen. She shuddered slightly. She was a little afraid of her father, although she knew that he loved her very much and he was very kind to her. But the winter before he had whipped her with a dried willow rod, when he caught her one evening behind Tim Hernon's cabin after nightfall, with Tim Hernon's son Bartly's arms around her waist and he kissing her. Ever since, she always shivered slightly when her father touched her or spoke to her.

"Oho!" said an old peasant who sat at the table with a saucer full of tea in his hand and his grey flannel shirt open at his thin, hairy, wrinkled neck. "Oho! indeed, but it's a disgrace to the island of Inverara to let such a beautiful woman as your daughter go away, Mrs. Feeney. If I were a young man, I'll be flayed alive if I'd let her go."

There was a laugh and some of the women on the bed said: "Bad cess to you, Patsy Coyne, if you haven't too much impudence, it's a caution." But the laugh soon died. The young men sitting at the table felt embarrassed and kept looking at one another sheepishly, as if each tried to find out if the others were in love with Mary Feeney.

"Oh, well, God is good," said Mrs. Feeney, as she wiped her lips with the tip of her bright, clean, check apron. "What will be must be, and sure there is hope from the sea, but there is no hope from the grave. It is sad and the poor have to suffer, but . . ." Mrs. Feeney stopped suddenly, aware that all these platitudes meant nothing whatsoever. Like her husband she was unable to think intelligently about her two children going away. Whenever the reality of their going away, maybe for ever, three thousand miles into a vast unknown world, came before her mind, it seemed that a thin bar of some hard metal thrust itself forward from her brain and rested behind the wall of her forehead. So that almost immediately she became stupidly conscious of the pain caused by the imaginary bar of metal and she forgot the dread prospect of her children going away. But her mind grappled with the things about her busily and efficiently, with the preparation of food, with the entertaining of her guests, with the numerous little things that have to be done in a house where there is a party and which only a woman can do properly. These little things, in a manner, saved her, for the moment at least, from bursting into tears whenever she looked at her daughter and whenever she thought of her son, whom she loved most of all her children, because perhaps she nearly died giving birth to him and he had been very delicate until he was twelve years old. So she laughed down in her breast a funny laugh she had that made her heave where her check apron rose out from the waist band in a deep curve. "A person begins to talk," she said with a shrug of her shoulders sideways, "and then a person says foolish things."

"That's true," said the old peasant, noisily pouring more tea from his cup to his saucer.

But Mary knew by her mother laughing that way that she was very near being hysterical. She always laughed that way before she had one of her fits of hysterics. And Mary's heart stopped beating suddenly and then began again at an awful rate as her eyes became acutely conscious of her mother's body, the round, short body with the wonderful mass of fair hair growing grey at the temples and the fair face with the soft liquid brown eyes, that grew hard and piercing for a moment as they looked at a thing and then grew soft and liquid again, and the thin-lipped small mouth with the beautiful white teeth and the deep perpendicular grooves in the upper lip and the tremor that always came in the corner of the mouth, with love, when she looked at her children. Mary became acutely conscious of all these little points, as well as of the little black spot that was on her left breast below the nipple and the swelling that came now and again in her legs and caused her to have hysterics and would one day cause her death. And she was stricken with horror at the thought of leaving her mother and at the selfishness of her thoughts. She had never been prone to thinking of anything important but now, somehow for a moment, she had a glimpse of her mother's life that made her shiver and hate herself as a cruel, heartless, lazy, selfish wretch. Her mother's life loomed up before her eyes, a life of continual misery and suffering, hard work, birth pangs, sickness and again hard work and hunger and anxiety. It loomed up and then it fled again, a little mist came before her eyes and she jumped down from the bed, with the jaunty twirl of her head that was her habit when she set her body in motion.

"Sit down for a while, mother," she whispered, toying with one of the black ivory buttons on her mother's brown bodice. "I'll look after the table." "No, no," murmured the mother with a shake of her whole body, "I'm not a bit tired. Sit down, my treasure. You have a long way to travel to-day."

And Mary sighed and went back to the bed again.

At last somebody said: "It's broad daylight." And immediately everybody looked out and said: "So it is, and may God be praised." The change from the starry night to the grey, sharp dawn was hard to notice until it had arrived. People looked out and saw the morning light sneaking over the crags silently, along the ground, pushing the mist banks upwards. The stars were growing dim. A long way off invisible sparrows were chirping in their ivied perch in some distant hill or other. Another day had arrived and even as the people looked at it, yawned and began to search for their hats, caps and shawls preparing to go home, the day grew and spread its light and made things move and give voice. Cocks crew, blackbirds carolled, a dog let loose from a cabin by an early riser chased madly after an imaginary robber, barking as if his tail were on fire. The people said goodbye and began to stream forth from Feeney's cabin. They were going to their homes to see to the morning's work before going to Kilmurrage to see the emigrants off on the steamer to the mainland. Soon the cabin was empty except for the family.

All the family gathered into the kitchen and stood about for some minutes talking sleepily of the dance and of the people who had been present. Mrs. Feeney tried to persuade everybody to go to bed, but everybody refused. It was four o'clock and Michael and Mary would have to set out for Kilmurrage at nine. So tea was made and they all sat about for an hour drinking it and eating raisin cake and talking. They only talked of the dance and of the people who had been present.

There were eight of them there, the father and mother and six children. The youngest child was Thomas, a thin boy of twelve, whose lungs made a singing sound every time he breathed. The next was Bridget, a girl of fourteen, with dancing eyes and a habit of shaking her short golden curls every now and then for no apparent reason. Then there were the twins, Julia and Margaret, quiet, rather stupid, flat-faced girls of sixteen. Both their upper front teeth protruded slightly and they were both great workers and very obedient to their mother. They were all sitting at the table, having just finished a third large pot of tea, when suddenly the mother hastily gulped down the remainder of the tea in her cup, dropped the cup with a clatter to her saucer and sobbed once through her nose.

"Now mother," said Michael sternly, "what's the good of this work?"

"No, you are right, my pulse," she replied quietly. "Only I was just thinking how nice it is to sit here surrounded by all my children, all my little birds in my nest, and then two of them going to fly away made me sad." And she laughed, pretending to treat it as a foolish joke.

"Oh, that be damned for a story," said the father, wiping his mouth on his sleeve; "there's work to be done. You Julia, go and get the horse. Margaret,

you milk the cow and see that you give enough milk to the calf this morning."
And he ordered everybody about as if it were an ordinary day of work.

But Michael and Mary had nothing to do and they sat about miserably
conscious that they had cut adrift from the routine of their home life. They no
longer had any place in it. In a few hours they would be homeless wanderers.
Now that they were cut adrift from it, the poverty and sordidness of their
home life appeared to them under the aspect of comfort and plenty.

So the morning passed until breakfast time at seven o'clock. The
morning's work was finished and the family was gathered together again. The
meal passed in a dead silence. Drowsy after the sleepless night and conscious
that the parting would come in a few hours, nobody wanted to talk. Everybody had an egg for breakfast in honour of the occasion. Mrs. Feeney, after
her usual habit, tried to give her egg first to Michael, then to Mary, and as each
refused it, she ate a little herself and gave the remainder to little Thomas who
had the singing in his chest. Then the breakfast was cleared away. The father
went to put the creels on the mare so as to take the luggage into Kilmurrage.
Michael and Mary got the luggage ready and began to get dressed. The
mother and the other children tidied up the house. People from the village
began to come into the kitchen, as was customary, in order to accompany the
emigrants from their home to Kilmurrage.

At last everything was ready. Mrs. Feeney had exhausted all excuses for
moving about, engaged on trivial tasks. She had to go into the big bedroom
where Mary was putting on her new hat. The mother sat on a chair by the
window, her face contorting on account of the flood of tears she was keeping
back. Michael moved about the room uneasily, his two hands knotting a big
red handkerchief behind his back. Mary twisted about in front of the mirror
that hung over the black wooden mantelpiece. She was spending a long time
with the hat. It was the first one she had ever worn, but it fitted her beautifully,
and it was in excellent taste. It was given to her by the schoolmistress, who was
very fond of her, and she herself had taken it in a little. She had an instinct for
beauty in dress and deportment.

But the mother, looking at how well her daughter wore the cheap navy
blue costume and the white frilled blouse, and the little round black hat with
a fat, fluffy, glossy curl covering each ear, and the black silk stockings with blue
clocks in them, and the little black shoes that had laces of three colours in
them, got suddenly enraged with . . . She didn't know with what she got enraged. But for the moment she hated her daughter's beauty, and she remembered all the anguish of giving birth to her and nursing her and toiling for her,
for no other purpose than to lose her now and let her go away, maybe to be

ravished wantonly because of her beauty and her love of gaiety. A cloud of mad jealousy and hatred against this impersonal beauty that she saw in her daughter almost suffocated the mother, and she stretched out her hands in front of her unconsciously and then just as suddenly her anger vanished like a puff of smoke, and she burst into wild tears, wailing: "My children, oh, my children, far over the sea you will be carried from me, your mother." And she began to rock herself and she threw her apron over her head.

Immediately the cabin was full of the sound of bitter wailing. A dismal cry rose from the women gathered in the kitchen. "Far over the sea they will be carried," began woman after woman, and they all rocked themselves and hid their heads in their aprons. Michael's mongrel dog began to howl on the hearth. Little Thomas sat down on the hearth beside the dog and, putting his arms around him, he began to cry, although he didn't know exactly why he was crying, but he felt melancholy on account of the dog howling and so many people being about.

In the bedroom the son and daughter, on their knees, clung to their mother, who held their heads between her hands and rained kisses on both heads ravenously. After the first wave of tears she had stopped weeping. The tears still ran down her cheeks, but her eyes gleamed and they were dry. There was a fierce look in them as she searched all over the heads of her two children with them, with her brows contracted, searching with a fierce terror-stricken expression, as if by the intensity of her stare she hoped to keep a living photograph of them before her mind. With her quivering lips she made a queer sound like "im-m-m-m" and she kept kissing. Her right hand clutched at Mary's left shoulder and with her left she fondled the back of Michael's neck. The two children were sobbing freely. They must have stayed that way a quarter of an hour.

Then the father came into the room, dressed in his best clothes. He wore a new frieze waistcoat, with a grey and black front and a white back. He held his soft black felt hat in one hand and in the other hand he had a bottle of holy water. He coughed and said in a weak gentle voice that was strange to him, as he touched his son: "Come now, it is time."

Mary and Michael got to their feet. The father sprinkled them with holy water and they crossed themselves, Then, without looking at their mother, who lay in the chair with her hands clasped on her lap, looking at the ground in a silent tearless stupor, they left the room. Each hurriedly kissed little Thomas, who was not going to Kilmurrage, and then, hand in hand, they left the house. As Michael was going out the door he picked a piece of loose whitewash from the wall and put it in his pocket. The people filed out after them, down the yard and on to the road, like a funeral procession. The mother was left in the house with little Thomas and two old peasant women from the village. Nobody spoke in the cabin for a long time.

Then the mother rose and came into the kitchen. She looked at the two women, at her little son and at the hearth, as if she were looking for something she had lost. Then she threw her hands into the air and ran out into the yard. "Come back," she screamed; "come back to me."

She looked wildly down the road with dilated nostrils, her bosom heaving. But there was nobody in sight. Nobody replied. There was a crooked stretch of limestone road, surrounded by crags grey that were scorched by the sun. The road ended in a hill and then dropped out of sight. The hot June day was silent. Listening foolishly for an answering cry, the mother imagined she could hear the crags simmering under the hot rays of the sun. It was something in her head that was singing.

The two old women led her back into the kitchen. "There is nothing that time will not cure," said one, "Yes. Time and patience," said the other.

Further Readings on Liam O'Flaherty

ends with message of resignation like "orden to The Sea"

Bibliography

Doyle, Paul A. *Liam O'Flaherty*. Troy: Whitston Publishing, 1972.

———. "A Liam O'Flaherty Checklist." *Twentieth Century Literature* 13, no. 1 (April 1967): 49–51.

Jefferson, George. *Bibliography of the Writings of Liam O'Flaherty*. Dublin: Privately Published, 1988.

———. *Liam O'Flaherty: A Descriptive Bibliography of His Works*. Dublin: Wolfhound Press, 1993.

Zneimer, John. *The Literary Vision of Liam O'Flaherty*. Syracuse, N.Y.: Syracuse University Press, 1970.

Selected Works

The Black Soul. 1924. Reprint, Bath: Lythway Press, 1972.

Dúil. Baile Átha Cliath: Sáirséal agus Dill, 1953.

Ecstasy of Angus. London: Joiner and Steel, 1931; reprint, Dublin: Wolfhound Press, 1978.

Famine. London: Landsborough Publications, 1966.

The Informer. 1925. Reprint, New York: Harcourt Brace, 1980.

Land. London: Victor Gollancz; New York: Random House, 1946.

Letters of Liam O'Flaherty. Edited by A. A. Kelly. Dublin: Wolfhound Press, 1996.

Liam O'Flaherty: The Collected Stories, 3 vols. Edited by A. A. Kelly. New York: St. Martin's Press, 1999.

The Pedlar's Revenge and Other Stories. Dublin: Wolfhound Press, 1976.

Spring Sowing. 1924. Reprint, London: Travellers' Library, 1935.

The Short Stories of Liam O'Flaherty. London: Four Square Books, 1966.

The Stories of Liam O'Flaherty. Introduction by Vivian Mercier. New York: Devin-Adair, 1956.

Biography and Criticism

Cahalan, James M. *Liam O'Flaherty: A Study of the Short Fiction.* Boston: Twayne, 1991.

de Bhaldraithe, Tomás. "Ó Flaithearta—Aistritheoir" (O'Flaherty—Translator). *Comhar* 25 (1967): 35–37.

Doyle, Paul. *Liam O'Flaherty.* New York: Twayne Publishers, 1971.

Fridberg, Hedda. *The Old Order and a New: The Split World of Liam O'Flaherty's Novels.* Uppsala, Sweden: Uppsala University, 1996.

Hildebidle, John. *Five Irish Writers.* Cambridge, Mass.: Harvard University Press, 1989.

Kelleher, John V. "Irish Literature Today." *Atlantic Monthly* 176 (1945): 70–76.

Kelly, A. A. *Liam O'Flaherty The Storyteller.* London: Macmillan, 1976.

Murray, Michael H. "Liam O'Flaherty and the Speaking Voice." *Studies in Short Fiction,* 5 (1968): 154–62.

O'Brien, James H. *Liam O'Flaherty.* Bucknell University Press, 1973.

O'Faoláin, Seán. "Don Quixote O'Flaherty." *London Mercury* 37 (December 1937): 170–75.

Saul, George Brandon. "A Wild Sowing: The Short Stories of Liam O'Flaherty." *A Review of English Literature* 4, no. 3 (July 1963): 108–13.

Sheeran, Patrick F. *The Informer.* Analysis of John Ford's 1935 film adaptation. Cork: Cork University Press, 2002.

———. *The Novels of Liam O'Flaherty: A Study of Romantic Realism.* Dublin: Wolfhound Press, 1976.

Zneimer, John. *The Literary Vision of Liam O'Flaherty.* Syracuse, N.Y.: Syracuse University Press, 1970.

Poets from the Post-Independence Generation

The treaty signed with Great Britain in 1922 changed Ireland as had no other document in its history. However, while it ended the Anglo-Irish War, it did not bring peace. Former comrades in arms fought a civil war over the terms of the treaty, which provided for the division of Ireland into a twenty-six-county Free State, with six counties remaining in the United Kingdom. *÷ Ireland*

Despite the bloodshed and attendant economic decline, however, a generation of younger poets found distinctive voices. They were at once more national and less parochial. The great international prestige of William Butler Yeats brought the attention of new readers in distant lands, even as it sometimes proved a burden for younger writers. At the same time, technological and economic transformations that led to a shrinking of distances often placed Irish writers in new environments: John Hewitt lived much of his life in England. Even those writers who "stayed home" sought new meaning from Irish traditions. Austin Clarke, a lapsed Catholic, could write a verse "sermon" on a Protestant Dubliner of the eighteenth century—Jonathan Swift.

Forming no discrete school of their own, the poets of this generation often found themselves divided by new definitions of politics and religion. John Hewitt and others became citizens of the six-county province united with Great Britain, while most became citizens of the Irish Free State. In many cases, though, the poets of this generation made bonds with foreign poets as diverse as Ezra Pound, W. H. Auden, and Robert Penn Warren.

F[rederick] R[obert] Higgins (1896–1941) is probably best remembered today as W. B. Yeats's closest friend among the poets of his generation. The child of a Protestant, Unionist, Ascendancy family, he was nonetheless passionately interested in Irish folk tradition, and became an official of the Irish labor movement. As manager of the Abbey Theatre during the thirties, he encouraged new plays. Higgins also produced five volumes of poetry, of which only *Arable Holdings* (1933) has been reprinted in recent years.

Austin Clarke (1896–1974) published more than thirty works of poetry, drama, fiction, and autobiography in a career that spanned fifty-seven years (minus a seventeen-year "silence," 1938–1955). Often compared to Yeats in his youth, Clarke lost the older poet's favor and sought new directions, including many experiments with Gaelic prosody in English. Clarke founded a society to promote spoken verse and helped to produce plays at various Dublin theaters as well as programs on Irish radio. In his later years, Clarke saw his critical prestige rise: while receiving an honorary degree in 1966 he heard himself described as "the outstanding literary figure in modern Ireland."

John Hewitt (1907–1987) spent much of his working career in England, where he was the director of the Herbert Art Gallery and Museum in Coventry. He nonetheless remained closely associated with his native Belfast and drew deeply from the Ulster Protestant experience. Through his association with two journals, *Lagan* and *Threshold,* he helped to foster an Ulster regional literary consciousness that would be continued in the next generation by such poets as Seamus Heaney, Michael Longley, and Derek Mahon.

F. R. Higgins (1896–1941)

Father and Son

Only last week, walking the hushed fields
Of our most lovely Meath, now thinned by November,
I came to where the road from Laracor leads
To the Boyne river—that seemed more lake than river,
Stretched in uneasy light and stript of reeds.

And walking longside an old weir
Of my people's, where nothing stirs—only the shadowed
Leaden flight of a heron up the lean air—
I went unmanly with grief, knowing how my father,
Happy though captive in years, walked last with me there.

Yes, happy in Meath with me for a day
He walked, taking stock of herds hid in their own breathing;
And naming colts, gusty as wind, once steered by his hand,
Lightnings winked in the eyes that were half shy in greeting
Old friends—the wild blades, when he gallivanted the land.

For that proud, wayward man now my heart breaks—
Breaks for that man whose mind was a secret eyrie,
Whose kind hand was sole signet of his race,
Who curbed me, scorned my green ways, yet increasingly loved me
Till Death drew its grey blind down his face.

And yet I am pleased that even my reckless ways
Are living shades of his rich calms and passions—
Witnesses for him and for those faint namesakes
With whom now he is one, under yew branches,
Yes, one in a graven silence no bird breaks.

Padraic Ó Conaire, Gaelic Storyteller

They've paid the last respects in sad tobacco
And silent is this wakehouse in its haze;
They've paid the last respects; and now their whiskey
Flings laughing words on mouths of prayer and praise;
And so young couples huddle by the gables,
O let them grope home through the hedgy night—
Alone I'll mourn my old friend, while the cold dawn
Thins out the holy candlelight.

Respects are paid to one loved by the people;
Ah, was he not—among our mighty poor—
The sudden wealth cast on those pools of darkness,
Those bearing, just, a star's faint signature;
And so he was to me, close friend, near brother,
Dear Padraic of the wide and sea-cold eyes—
So lovable, so courteous and noble,
The very West was in his soft replies.

They'll miss his heavy stick and stride in Wicklow—
His story-talking down Winetavern Street,
Where old men sitting in the wizen daylight
Have kept an edge upon his gentle wit;
While women on the grassy streets of Galway,
Who hearken for his passing—but in vain,
Shall hardly tell his step as shadows vanish
Through archways of forgotten Spain.

Ah, they'll say: Padraic's gone again exploring;
But now down glens of brightness. O he'll find
An alehouse overflowing with wise Gaelic
That's braced in vigour by the bardic mind,
And there his thoughts shall find their own forefathers—
In minds to whom our heights of race belong,
In crafty men, who ribbed a ship or turned
The secret joinery of song.

Alas, death mars the parchment of his forehead;
And yet for him, I know, the earth is mild—
The windy fidgets of September grasses
Can never tease a mind that loved the wild;
So drink his peace—this grey juice of the barley
Runs with a light that ever pleased his eye—
While old flames nod and gossip on the hearthstone
And only the young winds cry.

Austin Clarke (1896–1974)

Aisling

At morning from the coldness of Mount Brandon,
The sail is blowing half-way to the light:
And islands are so small, a man may carry
Their yellow crop in one cart at low tide.
Sadly in thought, I strayed the mountain grass
To hear the breezes following their young
And by the furrow of a stream, I chanced
To find a woman airing in the sun.

Coil of her hair, in cluster and ringlet,
Had brightened round her forehead and those curls—
Closer than she could bind them on a finger—
Were changing gleam and glitter. O she turned
So gracefully aside, I thought her clothes
Were flame and shadow while she slowly walked,

Or that each breast was proud because it rode
The cold air as the wave stayed by the swan.

But knowing her face was fairer than in thought,
I asked of her was she the Geraldine—
Few horsemen sheltered at the steps of water?
Or that Greek woman, lying in a piled room
On tousled purple, whom the household saved,
When frescoes of strange fire concealed the pillar:
The white coin all could spend? Might it be Niav

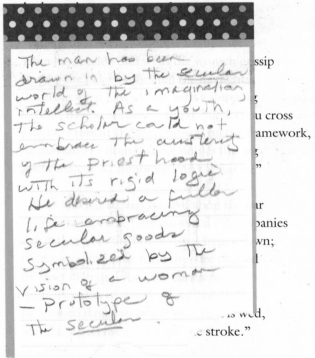

"Shall I, too, find at dark of rain," I cried,
"Neighbours around a fire cast up by the ocean
And in that shining mansion hear the rise
Of companies, or bide among my own—
Pleasing a noble ear? O must I wander
Without praise, without wine, in rich strange lands?"
But with a smile the secret woman left me,
At morning in the coldness of Mount Brandon.

[handwritten: persona poem]

The Straying Student

[handwritten: Explores love, chastity, religion, clericalism, art, faith, intell., reason, pitting one against another in this portrait of an 18th cent. Irish scholar from Inishmore who'd gone to Salamanca to study for the priesthood, but was sent home a failure.]

On a holy day when sails were blowing southward,
A bishop sang the Mass at Inishmore, *[handwritten: largest of Aran island]*
Men took one side, their wives were on the other
But I heard the woman coming from the shore:
And wild in despair my parents cried aloud
For they saw the vision draw me to the doorway.

[handwritten: rep. secular world]

Long had she lived in Rome when Popes were bad,
The wealth of every age she makes her own, *[handwritten: materialism that corrupted the church]*
Yet smiled on me in eager admiration,
And for a summer taught me all I know,
Banishing shame with her great laugh that rang
As if a pillar caught it back alone.

I learned the prouder counsel of her throat,
My mind was growing bold as light in Greece;
And when in sleep her stirring limbs were shown,
I blessed the noonday rock that knew no tree:
And for an hour the mountain was her throne,
Although her eyes were bright with mockery.

They say I was sent back from Salamanca
And failed in logic, but I wrote her praise
Nine times upon a college wall in France.
She laid her hand at darkfall on my page *[handwritten: Imagination]*
That I might read the heavens in a glance
And I knew every star the Moors had named.

Awake or in my sleep, I have no peace now,
Before the ball is struck, my breath has gone, *[handwritten: when age & scholarly brings the wisdom & experience, the fears that in the end the physical & secular will desert him.]*
And yet I tremble lest she may deceive me
And leave me in this land, where every woman's son
Must carry his own coffin and believe,
In dread, all that the clergy teach the young.

Post WWII Ireland

Humorously catches the speed of the Irish-american priests sojourn with a telegraphic technique

Irish-American Dignitary

Glanced down at Shannon from the sky-way
With his attendant clergy, stayed night
In Dublin, but whole day with us
To find his father's cot, now dust
And rubble, bless new church, school buildings
At Glanworth, drive to Spangle Hill
And cut first sod, hear, answer, fine speeches,
Accept a learned gown, freedom
Of ancient city, so many kissing
His ring—God love him!—almost missed
The waiting liner: that day in Cork
Had scarcely time for knife and fork.

an expatriot Irishman who has become a mechanized robot.

Burial of an Irish President

(DR. DOUGLAS HYDE)

The tolling from St. Patrick's
Cathedral was brangled, repeating
Itself in top-back room
And alley of the Coombe,
Crowding the dirty streets,
Upbraiding all our pat tricks
Tricoloured and beflowered,
Coffin of our President,
Where fifty mourners bowed,
Was trestled in the gloom
Of arch and monument,
Beyond the desperate tomb
Of Swift. Imperial flags,
Corunna, Quatre Bras,
Inkermann, Pretoria,
Their pride turning to rags,
Drooped, smoke-thin as the booming
Of cannon. The simple word
From heaven was vaulted, stirred
By candles. At the last bench

note use of puns — a powerful comment on poisonous effects of religious intolerance on Irish life.

Two Catholics, the French
Ambassador and I, knelt down.
The vergers waited. Outside.
The hush of Dublin town,
Professors of cap and gown,
Costello, his Cabinet,
In Government cars, hiding
Around the corner, ready
Tall hat in hand, dreading
Our Father in English. Better
Not hear that "which" for "who"
And risk eternal doom.

A Sermon on Swift

Friday, 11.30 A.M. April 28th, 1967

Gentle of hand, the Dean of St. Patrick's guided
My silence up the steps of the pulpit, put around
My neck the lesser microphone.
                              "I feel
That you are blessing me, Mr. Dean."
                              Murmur
Was smile.
                In this first lay sermon, must I
Not speak the truth? Known scholars, specialists,
From far and near, were celebrating the third
Centenary of our great satirist.
They spoke of the churchman who kept his solemn gown,
Full-bottom, for Sunday and the Evening Lesson,
But hid from lectern the chuckling rhymster who went,
Bald-headed, into the night when modesty
Wantoned with beau and belle, his pen in hand.
Dull morning clapped his oldest wig on. He looked from
The Deanery window, spied the washerwomen
Bundling along, the hay carts swaying from
The Coombe, dropping their country smells, the hackney—
Clatter on cobbles—ready to share a quip
Or rebus with Sheridan and Tom Delaney,

Read an unfinished chapter to Vanessa
Or Stella, then rid his mind of plaguey curling—
Tongs, farthingales and fal-de-lals. A pox on
Night-hours when wainscot, walls, were dizziness,
Tympana, maddened by inner terror, celled
A man who did not know himself from Cain.
A Tale of a Tub, Gulliver's Travels, fables
And scatological poems, I pennied them on
The Quays, in second-hand book-stalls, when I was young,
Soon learned that humour, unlike the wit o' the Coffee
House, the Club, lengthens the features, smile hid by
A frown.
                Scarce had I uttered the words,
                                    "Dear Friends,
Dear Swiftians"—
                            when from the eastern window
The pure clear ray, that Swift had known, entered the
Shady church and touched my brow. So blessed
Again, I gathered 'em up, four-letter words,
Street-cries, from the Liberties.
                                        Ascend,
Our Lady of Filth, Cloacina, soiled goddess
Of paven sewers. Let Roman fountains, a-spay
with themselves, scatter again the imperious gift
Of self-in-sight.
                        Celia on a close-stool
Stirs, ready to relace her ribs. Corinna,
Taking herself to pieces at midnight, slips from
The bed at noon, putting together soilures
And soft sores. Strephon half rouses from a dream
Of the flooding Tiber on his marriage-night,
When Chloe stoops out unable to contain her
Twelve cups of tea. Women are unsweet at times,
No doubt, yet how can willynilly resist
The pleasures of defaulting flesh?
                                        My Sermon
Waits in the plethora of Rabelais, since
March veered with the rusty vane of Faith. I had reached
The house of Aries. Soon in the pure ray,

I am aware of my ancestor, Archbishop
Browne, hastily come from Christ Church, to dispel
Error and Popish superstition. He supped
Last night with Bishop Bale of Ossory,
Robustious as his plays, and, over the talk
And malmsey, forgot the confiscated wealth
Of abbeys.
     In prose, plain as pike, pillory.
In octosyllabic verse turning the two-way
Corner of rhyme, Swift wrote of privy matters
That have to be my text. The Lilliputian
March-by or the crack regiments saluting
On high the double pendulosity
Of Gulliver, glimpsed through a rent in his breeches:
The city square in admiration below. But who
Could blame the Queen when that almighty
Man hosed the private apartments of her palace,
Hissed down the flames of carelessness, leaving
The royal stables unfit for Houyhnhnms, or tell (in
A coarse aside) what the gigantic maidens
Of Brobdignab did in their playfulness with
The tiny Lemuel when they put him astride
A pap, broader than the mizzen mast of his
Wrecked ship, or hid him in the tangle below?

Reasonable century of Bolingbroke,
Hume, hundred-quilled Voltaire. Satyr and nymph
Disported in the bosk, prim avenues
Let in the classical sky. The ancient temples
Had been restored. Sculptures replaced the painted
Images of the saints. Altars were fuming,
And every capital was amaranthed.
Abstraction ruled the decumana of verse,
Careful caesura kept the middle silence
No syllable dared to cross.
                Swift gave his savings
To mumbling hand, to tatters. Bare kibes ran after
Hoof as he rode beside the Liffey to sup
At Celbridge, brood with Vanessa in a star-bloomed

Bower on Tory politics, forget
Queen Anne, stride from a coffee-house in Whitehall
And with his pamphlets furrow the battle-fields
Of Europe once more, tear up the blood-signed contracts
Of Marlborough, Victualler of Victories;
While in St. Patrick's Cathedral the candling clerk
Shifted the shadows from pillar to pillar, shuffling
His years along the aisles with iron key.
Last gift of an unwilling patriot, Swift willed
To us a mansion of forgetfulness. I lodged
There for a year until Erato led me
Beyond the high-walled garden of Memory,
The Fountain of Hope, to the rewarding Gate,
Reviled but no longer defiled by harpies. And there
In Thomas Street, night to the busy stalls,
Divine Abstraction smiled.

My hour, above.

Myself draws to an end. Satiric rhymes
Are safe in the Deanery. So I must find
A moral, search among my wits.

I have

It.
In his sudden poem *The Day of Judgment*
Swift borrowed the allegoric bolt of Jove,
Damned and forgave the human race, dismissed
The jest of life. Here is his secret belief
For sure: the doctrine of Erigena,
Scribing his way from West to East, from bang
Of monastery door, click o' the latch,
His sandals worn out, unsoled, a voice proclaiming
The World's mad business—Eternal Absolution.

John Hewitt (1907–1987)

The Glens

Groined by deep glens and walled along the west
by the bare hilltops and the tufted moors,

this rim of arable that ends in foam
has but to drop a leaf or snap a branch
and my hand twitches with the leaping verse
as hazel twig will wrench the straining wrists
for untapped jet that thrusts beneath the sod.

Not these my people, of a vainer faith
and a more violent lineage. My dead
lie in the steepled hillock of Kilmore
in a fat country rich with bloom and fruit.
My days, the busy days I owe the world,
are bound to paved unerring roads and rooms
heavy with talk of politics and art.
I cannot spare more than a common phrase
of crops and weather when I pace these lanes
and pause at hedge gap spying on their skill,
so many fences stretch between our minds.

I fear their creed as we have always feared
the lifted hand against unfettered thought,
I know their savage history of wrong
and would at moments lend an eager voice,
if voice avail, to set that tally straight.

And yet no other corner in this land
offers in shape and colour all I need
for sight to torch the mind with living light.

An Irishman in Coventry

A full year since, I took this eager city,
the tolerance that laced its blatant roar,
its famous steeples and its web of girders,
as image of the state hope argued for,
and scarcely flung a bitter thought behind me
on all that flaws the glory and the grace
which ribbons through the sick, guilt-clotted legend
of my creed-haunted, Godforsaken race.
My rhetoric swung round from steel's high promise

to the precision of the well-gauged tool,
tracing the logic in the vast glass headlands, *} England*
the clockwork horse, the comprehensive school. *}*

shift

Then, sudden, by occasion's chance concerted,
in enclave of my nation, but apart,
the jigging dances and the lilting fiddle
stirred the old rage and pity in my heart. *Homesickness yet criticism of his native land*
The faces and the voices blurring round me,
the strong hands long familiar with the spade,
the whiskey-tinctured breath, the pious buttons,
called up a people endlessly betrayed
by our own weakness, by the wrongs we suffered
in that long twilight over bog and glen,
by force, by famine and by glittering fables
which gave us martyrs when we needed men, *✗*
by faith which had no charity to offer,
by poisoned memory, and by ready wit,
with poverty corroded into malice,
to hit and run and howl when it is hit.

This is our fate: eight hundred years' disaster,
crazily tangled as the Book of Kells; *✗ Simile*
the dream's distortion and the land's division,
the midnight raiders and the prison cells. *allusion*
Yet like Lir's children banished to the waters
our hearts still listen for the landward bells.
Hope

see "O Country people" in supplement

Further Readings on Poets from the Post-Independence Generation

Bibliography

MacManus, M. J. "A Bibliography of F. R. Higgins." *Dublin Magazine* 12 (1937): 61–67

Lyne, Gerard. "Austin Clarke: A Bibliography." *Irish University Review* 4, no. 1 (Spring 1974): 137–55.

Miller, Liam. "The Books of Austin Clarke. A Checklist." In *A Tribute to Austin Clarke on his Seventieth Birthday, 9 May 1966,* ed. Liam Miller and John Montague. Dublin: Dolmen; Chester Springs, Pa.: Du Four, 1966.

Selected Works

Clarke, Austin. *The Bright Temptation* [prose]. London: Allen and Unwin, 1932. Reprint, Dublin: Dolmen, 1965.

————. *Collected Poems.* London: Allen and Unwin, 1936.

————. *Poetry in Modern Ireland.* Dublin: Cultural Relations Committee, 1961.

————. *Collected Plays.* Dublin: Dolmen, 1963.

————. *A Sermon on Swift and Other Poems.* Dublin: Bridge, 1968.

————. *Collected Poems.* Dublin: Dolmen, 1974.

————. *Selected Poems.* Edited by Hugh Maxton. Dublin: Lilliput; Winston-Salem, N.C.: Wake Forest, 1991.

————. *Selected Poems.* Edited by W. J. McCormack. London: Penguin, 1991.

————. *Reviews and Essays.* Edited by Gregory A. Schirmer. Lanham, Md.: Barnes and Noble, 1992.

Hewitt, John. *Ancestral Voices.* Edited by Tom Clyde. Belfast: Blackstaff Press, 1987.

————. *Collected Poems of John Hewitt.* Edited by Frank Ormsby. Belfast: Blackstaff Press, 1991.

Higgins, F. R. *The Dark Breed.* London: Macmillan, 1927.

————. *The Gap of Brightness.* London and New York: Macmillan, 1940.

————. *Arable Holdings.* Dublin: Cuala, 1933; reprint, Shannon: Irish University Press, 1971.

————. *39 Poems.* Edited by R. Dardis Clarke. Dublin: Ridge Press, 1992.

Biography and Criticism

Clarke, R. Dardis, and Seamus Heaney. *Austin Clarke Remembered.* Dublin: Bridge Press, 1996.

Dawe, Gerald, and Longley, Edna, eds. *Across a Roaring Hill: The Protestant Imagination in Modern Ireland: Essays in Honour of John Hewitt.* Belfast: Blackstaff Press, 1985.

Halpern, Susan. *Austin Clarke, His Life and Works.* Dublin: Dolmen, 1974.

Harmon, Maurice. *Austin Clarke, 1896–1974: A Critical Introduction.* Dublin: Wolfhound Press, 1988.

————, ed. *Irish Poetry After Yeats: Seven Poets.* Boston: Little, Brown, 1979.

Heaney, Seamus. "The Poetry of John Hewitt." *Threshold* 22 (Summer 1969): 73–77.

Irish University Review 4, no. 1 (Spring 1974). Austin Clarke Issue.

Loftus, Richard J. *Nationalism in Modern Anglo-Irish Poetry.* Madison: University of Wisconsin Press, 1964.

Miller, Liam, and Montague, John, eds. *A Tribute to Austin Clarke on his Seventieth Birthday, 9 May 1966.* Dublin: Dolmen; Chester Springs, Pa.: DuFour, 1966.

Ricigliano, Lorraine. *Austin Clarke: A Reference Guide.* New York: G. K. Hall, 1993.

Schirmer, Gregory. *The Poetry of Austin Clarke*. Mountrath, Ireland: Dolmen; South Bend, Ind.: University of Notre Dame Press, 1983.

Tapping, G. Craig. *Austin Clarke: A Study of His Writings*. Totowa, N.J.: Barnes and Noble, 1981.

Taylor, Geoffrey. "The Poetry of F. R. Higgins," *The Bell* 13, no. 2: 122–29.

Walsh, Patrick. *Strangers: Reflections on a Correspondence Between Daniel Corkery and John Hewitt*. Coleraine: University of Ulster, 1996.

The 1940s — a bad time to be an Irish writer, like others, Kavanagh suffered. Most turned caustically critical after nationalist myths dissolved. Kavanagh liberated Irish poetry from ghosts of the past — Yeats in particular

Austin Clarke & Kavanagh were to prove important connectors between the Renaissance & contemporary poetry in Ireland. Each became preceding figures over the Irish poetry of our time.

Patrick Kavanagh
(1904–1967)

(Movement from rural impressionism and angry satire to life-affirming lyricism)

S eamus Heaney has called Patrick Kavanagh the "twice born" poet. The son of a cobbler and small farmer in County Monaghan, Kavanagh worked at farming and poetry until 1939, when he left Inniskeen for a journalist's life in Dublin. There, he wrote and reviewed for *The Irish Times, The Irish Press* and *The Standard*.

The publication of the first part of his long poem, "The Great Hunger," in *Horizon* (1942) caused that magazine to be taken off the stands, (The poem was published the same year by the Cuala Press.) In April 1952, Kavanagh, with his brother's backing, launched his own paper, *Kavanagh's Weekly*, which ran to thirteen issues, Later that year, the poet initiated a libel action against the *The Leader* for an unsigned article titled "Profile: Mr. Patrick Kavanagh." The case went to trial in 1954 and *The Leader* was found not guilty. The decision was appealed, and the matter finally settled out of court.

Kavanagh's early poems, particularly "The Great Hunger" (its title alludes to the famine of a century before), describes the poverty and isolation of rural Ireland in the thirties and forties; other rural poems, such as "In Memory of My Mother," are nostalgic. Kavanagh's rebirth, after surgery for lung cancer in 1955, is celebrated in the sonnet "Canal Bank Walk," with its lyrical opening: "leafy with-love." The poem, a personal as well as a poetic achievement, marked Kavanagh's last years—years that brought him the happiness of a late marriage, the comforts of a secure reputation, and the satisfaction of knowing he was a major influence on a new generation of Irish poets.

Shancoduff

childhood farm — a "wonderland" that enriched his imagination all his life; consisted of 7 watery hills

My black hills have never seen the sun rising,
Eternally they look north towards Armagh.
Lot's wife would not be salt if she had been
Incurious as my black hills that are happy
When dawn whitens Glassdrummond chapel.

My hills hoard the bright shillings of March
While the sun searches in every pocket.
They are my Alps and I have climbed the Matterhorn
With a sheaf of hay for three perishing calves
In the field under the Big Forth of Rocksavage.

The sleety winds fondle the rushy beards of Shancoduff
While the cattle-drovers sheltering in the Featherna Bush
Look up and say: "Who owns them hungry hills
That the water-hen and snipe must have forsaken?
A poet? Then by heavens he must be poor."
I hear and is my heart not badly shaken?

Epic

I have lived in important places, times
When great events were decided, who owned
That half a rood of rock, a no-man's land
Surrounded by our pitchfork-armed claims.
I heard the Duffys shouting "Damn your soul"
And old McCabe stripped to the waist, seen
Step the plot defying blue cast-steel—
"Here is the march along these iron stones"
That was the year of the Munich bother. Which
Was more important? I inclined
To lose my faith in Ballyrush and Gortin
Till Homer's ghost came whispering to my mind
He said: I made the Iliad from such
A local row. Gods make their own importance.

Monaghan 1934

Pegasus

My soul was an old horse
Offered for sale in twenty fairs.
I offered him to the Church—the buyers
Were little men who reared his unusual airs.
One said: "Let him remain unbid
In the wind and rain and hunger

Of sin and we will get him—
With the winkers thrown in—for nothing."

Then the men of State looked at
What I'd brought for sale.
One minister, wondering if
Another horse-body would fit the tail
That he'd kept for sentiment—
The relic of his own soul—
Said, "I will graze him in lieu of his labour."
I lent him for a week or more
And he came back a hurdle of bones,
Starved, overworked, in despair.
I nursed him on the roadside grass
To shape him for another fair.

I lowered my price. I stood him where
The broken-winded, spavined stand
And crooked shopkeepers said that he
Might do a season on the land—
But not for high-paid work in towns.
He'd do a tinker, possibly.
I begged, "O make some offer now,
A soul is a poor man's tragedy.
He'll draw your dungiest cart," I said,
"Show you short cuts to Mass,
Teach weather lore, at night collect
Bad debts from poor men's grass."
    And they would not.

    Where the
Tinkers quarrel I went down
With my horse, my soul.
I cried, "Who will bid me half a crown?"
From their rowdy bargaining
Not one turned. "Soul," I prayed,
"I have hawked you through the world
Of Church and State and meanest trade.
But this evening, halter off,

Never again will it go on.
On the south side of ditches
There is grazing of the sun.
No more haggling with the world. . . ."

As I said these words he grew
Wings upon his back. Now I may ride him
Every land my imagination knew.

In Memory of My Mother

I do not think of you lying in the wet clay
Of a Monaghan graveyard; I see
You walking down a lane among the poplars
On your way to the station, or happily

Going to second Mass on a summer Sunday—
You meet me and you say:
"Don't forget to see about the cattle—"
Among your earthiest words the angels stray.

And I think of you walking along a headland
Of green oats in June,
So full of repose, so rich with life—
And I see us meeting at the end of a town

On a fair day by accident, after
The bargains are all made and we can walk
Together through the shops and stalls and markets
Free in the oriental streets of thought.

O you are not lying in the wet clay,
For it is a harvest evening now and we
Are piling up the ricks against the moonlight
And you smile up at us—eternally.

[handwritten: One of his Canal Poems series — Poems of rebirth]

Canal Bank Walk *(Sonnet)*

[handwritten right margin: Kavanagh was a poet of satiric outburst until his lung operation — changed to a poet of reflection + wisdom]

Leafy-with-love banks and the green waters of the canal
Pouring redemption for me, that I do
The will of God, wallow in the habitual, the banal,
Grow with nature again as before I grew.
The bright stick trapped, the breeze adding a third
Party to the couple kissing on an old seat,
And a bird gathering materials for the nest for the Word
Eloquently new and abandoned to its delirious beat.
O unworn world enrapture me, enrapture me in a web
Of fabulous grass and eternal voices by a beech,
Feed the gaping need of my senses, give me ad lib
To pray unselfconsciously with overflowing speech

[handwritten: Petition (Christian belief in God)]

For this soul needs to be honoured with a new dress woven
From green and blue things and arguments that cannot be proven.

Lines Written on a Seat on the Grand Canal, Dublin, "Erected to the Memory of Mrs Dermot O'Brien"

[handwritten: (Thus the sculpture)]

(Sonnet)

O commemorate me where there is water,
Canal water preferably, so stilly
Greeny at the heart of summer. Brother
Commemorate me thus beautifully.
Where by a lock Niagarously roars

[handwritten: ref to Niagara Falls]

The falls for those who sit in the tremendous silence
Of mid-July. No one will speak in prose
Who finds his way to these Parnassian islands. *[handwritten: Greek ref.]*
A swan goes by head low with many apologies,
Fantastic light looks through the eyes of bridges—
And look! a barge comes bringing from Athy
And other far-flung towns mythologies.
O commemorate me with no hero-courageous
Tomb—just a canal-bank seat for the passer-by. *[handwritten: ✗]*

Further Readings on Patrick Kavanagh

Bibliography

Kavanagh, Peter. *Garden of the Golden Apples. A Bibliography of Patrick Kavanagh.* New York: Peter Kavanagh Hand Press, 1972.
Nemo, John. "A Bibliography of Writings by and about Patrick Kavanagh." *Irish University Review* 3:80–106. Reprinted in Nemo's *Patrick Kavanagh,* 159–61. Boston: Twayne, 1979. (Secondary sources are annotated.)

Selected Works

By Night Unstarred: An Autobiographical Novel by Patrick Kavanagh. Edited by Peter Kavanagh. The Curragh, Republic of Ireland: Goldsmith Press, 1977.
Collected Poems. 1964. Reprint, New York: W. W. Norton and Co., 1973.
Collected Prose. London: MacGibbon and Kee, 1967.
Come Dance with Kitty Stobling and Other Poems. Philadelphia: Dufour, 1960.
The Complete Poems of Patrick Kavanagh. Collected, arranged, and edited by Peter Kavanagh. 1972. Reprint, New York: Peter Kavanagh Hand Press, 1996.
The Great Hunger: Poem. London: MacGibbon and Kee, 1967.
The Great Hunger: Poem Into Play. Adapted by Tom MacIntyre. Mullingar, Ireland: Lilliput Press, 1988.
The Green Fool. 1938. Reprint, London: Penguin, 2001.
Kavanagh's Weekly: A Journal of Literature and Politics. 7 vols. (12 April–5 July 1952). Dublin: Peter Kavanagh, 1952.
Lapped Furrows: Correspondence 1933–1967 between Patrick and Peter Kavanagh. Edited by Peter Kavanagh. New York: Peter Kavanagh Hand Press, 1969.
No Earthly Estate: God and Patrick Kavanagh, An Anthology. Edited by Tom Stack. Blackrock, Ireland: Columba Press, 2002.
A Poet's Country: Selected Prose. Edited by Antoinette Quinn. Dublin: Lilliput Press, 2003.
Selected Poems. Edited by Antoinette Quinn. London, New York: Penguin, 1996.
Self Portrait. Dublin: Dolmen Press, 1964.
A Soul for Sale. London: Macmillan, 1947.
Tarry Flynn. 1948. Reprint, Harmondsworth: Penguin, 1978.

Biography and Criticism

Agnew, Una. *Mystical Imagination of Patrick Kavanagh.* Blackrock, Ireland: Columba Press, 1998.
Allison, Jonathan. *Patrick Kavanagh: A Reference Guide.* New York: G. K. Hall, 1996.

Garratt, Robert F. "Patrick Kavanagh and the Killing of the Irish Revival." *Colby Library Quarterly* 17:170–83.

Johnston, Dillon. *Irish Poetry after Joyce,* 121–66. Montrath: Dolmen Press, 1985.

Kavanagh, Peter. *Beyond Affection: An Autobiography.* New York: Peter Kavanagh Hand Press, 1977.

———. *A Guide to Patrick Kavanagh Country.* New York: Peter Kavanagh Hand Press, 1978.

———. *Patrick Kavanagh: 1904–1967, A Life Chronicle.* New York: Kavanagh Hand Press, 2000.

———, ed. *Patrick Kavanagh, Man and Poet.* Orono, Me.: National Poetry Foundation, 1986.

———. *Sacred Keeper: A Biography of Patrick Kavanagh.* The Curragh, Republic of Ireland: Goldsmith Press, 1979.

Nemo, John. *Patrick Kavanagh.* Boston: Twayne, 1979.

O'Brien, Darcy. *Patrick Kavanagh.* Lewisburg, Pa.: Bucknell University Press, 1975.

"Poetry Since Yeats: An Exchange of Views—Stephen Spender, Patrick Kavanagh, Thomas Kinsella, W. D. Snodgrass." *Tri-Quarterly* 4:100–111.

Quinn, Antoinette. *Patrick Kavanagh: A Biography.* Dublin: Gill and Macmillan, 2001.

———. *Patrick Kavanagh: Born-Again Romantic.* Dublin: Gill and Macmillan, 1991; also known as *Patrick Kavanagh: A Critical Study.* Syracuse, N.Y.: Syracuse University Press, 1991.

Warner, Alan. *Clay is the Word: Patrick Kavanagh, 1904–1967.* Dublin: Dolmen Press, 1983.

Flann O'Brien

(1911–1966)

a great parodist
a punster
post modern writer before his Time

The novelist usually known as Flann O'Brien was a man of many parts and many names. Born Brian O'Nolan (or Nolan), the writer used a series of pseudonyms in connection with his various literary efforts. Like many of his contemporaries, he sometimes used the Irish (or Gaelic) form of his name, Brian Ó Nualláin. He was best known in his lifetime as Myles na Gopaleen (or sometimes gCopaleen), the regular if idiosyncratic columnist of "Cruiskeen Lawn" for the *Irish Times*. At other times he appeared as Brother Barnabas, James John Doe, George Knowall, Matt Duffy, and Count O'Blather. But he is best remembered today for the five volumes of fiction he wrote under the name Flann O'Brien.

Despite the prestige he enjoys posthumously, O'Brien's career had longer periods of disappointment than success. A brilliant young linguist and debater, O'Brien published his greatest work, *At Swim-Two-Birds* (1939), when he was only twenty-eight. Despite the acclaim from writers as diverse as Graham Greene and Dylan Thomas, *At Swim-Two-Birds* was a commercial failure. O'Brien's next novel, *The Third Policeman,* was rejected by a series of publishers and did not appear until 1967, after the author's death. Meanwhile, under the pseudonym Myles na Gopaleen, he had begun writing the "Cruiskeen Lawn" column, which continued for almost twenty-five years, until his death.

At different times the author offered jokes in Old Irish, cross-linguistic puns, phonetic transcriptions from Homeric Greek, and a continuing series of shaggy-dog stories about the adventures of Keats and his friend Chapman. O'Brien continued to write stories and plays, but in his view as well as those of later critics, he did not realize his early promise. He loathed his principal occupation as a minor bureaucrat in the Department of Local Government, from which he retired in 1953. Thus, by the early sixties he appeared to many to be an embittered failure who happened to write a curious newspaper column. But then *At Swim-Two-Birds* was rediscovered and republished, bringing a second period of activity that produced the comic novels *The Hard Life* (1961) and *The Dalkey Archive* (1964)—the latter adapted for the stage by Hugh Leonard as *When the Saints Go Cycling In* (1965).

The action of *At Swim-Two-Birds* begins as an unnamed narrator, a layabout student at University College, Dublin, tells the story of Dermot Trellis, a tenant in the seedy Red Swan Hotel, who has begun to write a novel. Trellis, with a more limited imagination than the student, borrows characters from pulp fiction as well as Old Irish tradition, notably the hero Finn MacCool (Fionn mac Cumhaill). However, Trellis's characters soon tire of his banality and begin to tell a story about him. The passage excerpted here cuts through different levels of narration. At first, the student narrator converses with his friend Brinsley on the art of fiction, voicing the most frequently cited line from the work: ". . . a satisfactory novel should be a self-evident sham." The action then proceeds to the premises of the Red Swan Hotel. At no point in the entire novel does anyone explain the significance of the title "At Swim-Two-Birds," a translation of the medieval Irish placename, *Snámh-dá-éan*, which appears in *Buile Suibhne* (The Frenzy [Or Madness] of Sweeney).

The unprecedented satire *An Béal Bocht* (The Poor Mouth) (1941) cuts many ways. Outwardly it is a spoof of the Irish language autobiographies popular with nationalists in the early days of independence, like Tomás Ó Criomhthain's *An tOileánach* (The Islandman) (1929), portraying dignified hard work in a rainy, cold climate. At the same time the Irish phrase *béal bocht* may mean "grumbling" as well as a pretense of poverty in order to gain advantage, as from creditors, just as the translation "poor mouth" does in English. The passages here, from the third chapter, take the point of view of an Irish speaker confused by the larger and encroaching English-speaking world. A boy who thought his name was Séamas Ó Domhnaill is bewildered to be addressed by an English name he has never heard before. And if a reward is offered to a child willing to break away from Irish, maybe the family pig can grunt the incomprehensible lingo just as well.

From At Swim-Two-Birds

[handwritten: Considered one of the great comic novels of the century]

I withdrew my elbow and fell back again as if exhausted by my effort. My talk had been forced, couched in the accent of the lower or working-classes. Under the cover of the bed-clothes I poked idly with a pencil at my navel. Brinsley was at the window giving chuckles out.

Nature of chuckles: Quiet, private, averted.

What are you laughing at? I said.
You and your book and your porter, he answered.
Did you read that stuff about Finn, I said, that stuff I gave you?

Oh, yes, he said, that was the pig's whiskers. That was funny all right.

This I found a pleasing eulogy. The God-big Finn. Brinsley turned from the window and asked me for a cigarette. I took out my "butt" or half-spent cigarette and showed it in the hollow of my hand.

That is all I have, I said, affecting a pathos in my voice.

By God you're the queer bloody man, he said.

He then brought from his own pocket a box of the twenty denomination, lighting one for each of us.

There are two ways to make big money, he said, to write a book or to make a book.

It happened that this remark provoked between us a discussion on the subject of Literature—great authors living and dead, and character of modern poetry, the predilections of publishers and the importance of being at all times occupied with literary activities of a spare-time or recreative character. My dim room rang with the iron of fine words and the names of great Russian masters were articulated with fastidious intonation. Witticisms were canvassed, depending for their utility on a knowledge of the French language as spoken in the medieval times. Psycho-analysis was mentioned—with, however, a somewhat light touch, I then tendered an explanation spontaneous and unsolicited concerning my own work, affording an insight as to its aesthetic, its daemon, its argument, its sorrow and its joy, its darkness, its sun-twinkle clearness.

Nature of explanation offered: It was stated that while the novel and the play were both pleasing intellectual exercises, the novel was inferior to the play inasmuch as it lacked the outward accidents of illusion, frequently inducing the reader to be outwitted in a shabby fashion and caused to experience a real concern for the fortunes of illusory characters. The play was consumed in wholesome fashion by large masses in places of public resort; the novel was self-administered in private. The novel, in the hands of an unscrupulous writer, could be despotic. In reply to an inquiry, it was explained that a satisfactory novel should be a self-evident sham to which the reader could regulate at will the degree of his credulity. It was undemocratic to compel characters to be uniformly good or bad or poor or rich. Each should be allowed a private life, self-determination and a decent standard of living. This would make for self-respect, contentment and better service. It would be incorrect to say that it would lead to chaos. Characters should be interchangeable as between one book and another. The entire corpus of existing literature should be regarded as a limbo from which discerning authors could draw their characters as required, creating only when they failed to find a suitable existing puppet. The modern novel should be largely a work of reference. Most authors spend their time saying what has been said before—usually said much better. A wealth of references to existing works would acquaint the reader instantaneously with the nature of each character, would obviate tiresome explanations and would effectively preclude mountebanks, upstarts, thimbleriggers and persons of inferior education from an understanding of contemporary literature. Conclusion of explanation.

That is all my bum, said Brinsley.

But taking precise typescript from beneath the book that was at my side, I explained to him my literary intentions in considerable detail—now reading, now discoursing, oratio recta and oratio obliqua. [direct speech and indirect speech]

Extract from Manuscript as to nature Red Swan premises, oratio recta: The Red Swan premises in Lower Leeson Street are held in fee farm, the landlord whosoever being pledged to maintain the narrow lane which marks its eastern boundary unimpeded and free from nuisance for a distance of seventeen yards, that is, up to the intersection of Peter Place. New Paragraph. A terminus of the Cornelscourt coach in the seventeenth century, the hotel was rebuilt in 1712 and afterwards fired by the yeomanry for reasons which must be sought in the quiet of its ruined garden, on the three-perch stretch that goes by Croppies' Acre. Today, it is a large building of four storeys. The title is worked in snow-white letters along the circumference of the fanlight and the centre of the circle is concerned with the delicate image of a red swan, pleasingly conceived and carried out by a casting process in Birmingham delf. Conclusion of the foregoing.

Further extract descriptive of Dermot Trellis rated occupier of the Red Swan Hotel, oratio recta: Dermot Trellis was a man of average stature but his person was flabby and unattractive, partly a result of his having remained in bed for a period of twenty years. He was voluntarily bedridden and suffered from no organic or other illness. He occasionally rose for very brief periods in the evening to pad about the empty house in his felt slippers or to interview the slavey in the kitchen on the subject of his food or bedclothes. He had lost all physical reaction to bad or good weather and was accustomed to trace the seasonal changes of the year by inactivity or virulence of his pimples. His legs were puffed and affected with a prickly heat, a result of wearing his woollen undertrunks in bed. He never went out and rarely approached the windows.

Tour de force by Brinsley, vocally interjected, being a comparable description in the Finn canon: The neck to Trellis is house-thick and house-rough and is guarded by night and day against the coming of enemies by his old watchful boil. His bottom is the stern of a sea-blue schooner, his stomach is its mainsail with a filling of wind. His face is snowfall on old mountains, the feet are fields.

There was an interruption, I recall, at this stage, My uncle put his head through the door and looked at me in a severe manner, his face flushed from walking and an evening paper in his hand. He was about to address me when he perceived the shadow of Brinsley by the window.

Well, well, he said. He came in in a genial noisy manner, closed the door with vigour and peered at the form of Brinsley. Brinsley took his hands from his pockets and smiled without reason in the twilight.

Good evening to you, gentlemen, said my uncle.

Good evening, said Brinsley.

This is Mr Brinsley, a friend of mine, I said, raising my shoulders feebly from the bed, I gave a low moan of exhaustion.

My uncle extended an honest hand in the grip of friendship.

Ah, Mr Brinsley, how do you do? he said. How do you do, Sir? You are a University man, Mr Brinsley?

Oh yes.

Ah, very good, said my uncle. It's a grand thing, that—a thing that will stand to you. It is certainly. A good degree is a very nice thing to have. Are the masters hard to please, Mr Brinsley?

Well, no. As a matter of fact they don't care very much.

Do you tell me so! Well it was a different tale in the old days. The old schoolmasters believed in the big stick. Oh, plenty of that boyo.

He gave a laugh here in which we concurred without emotion.

The stick was mightier than the pen, he added, laughing again in a louder way and relapsing into a quiet chuckle. He paused for a brief interval as if examining something hitherto overlooked in the interior of his memory.

And how is our friend? he inquired in the direction of my bed.

Nature of my reply: Civil, perfunctory, uninformative.

My uncle leaned over towards Brinsley and said to him in a low, confiden-
tial manner:

Do you know what I am going to tell you, there is a very catching cold
going around. Every second man you meet has got a cold. God preserve us,
there will be plenty of 'flu before the winter's out, make no mistake about
that. You would need to keep yourself well wrapped up.

As a matter of fact, said Brinsley in a crafty way, I have only just recovered
from a cold myself.

You would need to keep yourself well wrapped up, rejoined my uncle, you
would, faith.

Here there was a pause, each of us searching for a word with which it
might be broken.

Tell me this, Mr Brinsley, said my uncle, are you going to be a doctor?

I am not, said Brinsley.

Or a schoolmaster?

Here I interposed a shaft from my bed.

He hopes to get a job from the Christian Brothers, I said, when he gets
his B.A.

That would be a great thing, said my uncle. The Brothers, of course, are
very particular about the boys they take. You must have a good record, a clean
sheet.

Well I have that, said Brinsley.

Of course you have, said my uncle. But doctoring and teaching are two
jobs that call for great application and love of God. For what is the love of God
but the love of your neighbour?

He sought agreement from each of us in turn, reverting a second to
Brinsley with his ocular inquiry.

It is a grand and a noble life, he said, teaching the young and the sick and
nursing them back to their God-given health. It is, faith. There is a special
crown for those that give themselves up to that work.

It is a hard life, but, said Brinsley.

A hard life? said my uncle. Certainly so, but tell me this: Is it worth your
while?

Brinsley gave a nod.

Worth your while and well worth it, said my uncle. A special crown is a
thing that is not offered every day of the week. Oh, it's a grand thing, a grand

life. Doctoring and teaching, the two of them are marked out for special graces and blessings.

He mused for a while, staring at the smoke of his cigarette. He then looked up and laughed, clapping his hand on the top of the washstand.

But long faces, he said, long faces won't get any of us very far. Eh, Mr Brinsley? I am a great believer in the smile and the happy word.

A sovereign remedy for all our ills, said Brinsley.

A sovereign remedy for all our ills, said my uncle. Very nicely put. Well . . .

He held out a hand in valediction.

Mind yourself now, he said, and mind and keep the coat buttoned up, The 'flu is the boy I'd give the slip to.

He was civilly replied to. He left the room with a pleased smile but was not gone for three seconds till he was back again with a grave look, coming upon us suddenly in the moment of our relaxation and relief.

Oh, that matter of the Brothers, he said in a low tone to Brinsley, would you care for me to put in a word for you?

Thanks very much, said Brinsley, but—

No trouble at all, said my uncle. Brother Hanley, late of Richmond Street, he is a very special friend of mine, No question of pulling strings, you know. Just a private word in his ear. He is a special friend.

Well, that is very good of you, said Brinsley.

Oh, not in the least, said my uncle. There is a way of doing things, you understand. It is a great thing to have a friend in court. And Brother Hanley, I may tell you privately, is one of the best—Oh, one of the very best in the world. It would be a pleasure to work with a man like Brother Hanley. I will have a word with him tomorrow.

The only thing is, but, said Brinsley, it will be some time before I am qualified and get my parchment.

Never mind, said my uncle, it is always well to be in early. First come, first called.

At this point he assembled his features into an expression of extreme secrecy and responsibility:

The Order, of course, is always on the look-out for boys of education and character. Tell me this, Mr Brinsley, have you ever.

I never thought of that, said Brinsley in surprise.

Do you think would the religious life appeal to you?

I'm afraid I never thought much about it.

Brinsley's tone was of a forced texture as if he were labouring in the stress of some emotion.

It is a good healthy life and a special crown at the end of it, said my uncle. Every boy should consider it very carefully before he decides to remain out in the world. He should pray to God for a vocation.

Not everybody is called, I ventured from the bed.

From An Béal Bocht (The Poor Mouth)

I was seven years old when I was sent to school. I was tough, small and thin, wearing grey-wool breeches[1] but otherwise unclothed above and below. Many other children besides me were going to school that morning with the stain of the ashes still on the breeches of many of them. Some of them were crawling along the road, unable to walk. Many were from Dingle, some from Gweedore, another group floated in from Aran. All of us were strong and hearty on our first school day. A sod of turf was under the armpit of each one of us. Hearty and strong were we!

The master was named Osborne O'Loonassa. He was dark, spare and tall and unhealthy with a sharp, sour look on his face where the bones were protruding through the yellow skin. A ferocity of anger stood on his forehead as permanent as his hair and he cared not a whit for anyone.

We all gathered into the schoolhouse, a small unlovely hut where the rain ran down the walls and everything was soft and damp. We all sat on benches, without a word or a sound for fear of the master. He cast his venomous eyes over the room and they alighted on me where they stopped. By jove! I did not find his look pleasant while these two eyes were sifting me. After a while he directed a long yellow finger at me and said:

~ Phwat is yer nam?

I did not understand what he said nor any other type of speech which is practised in foreign parts because I had only Gaelic as a mode of expression and as a protection against the difficulties of life. I could only stare at him, dumb with fear. I then saw a great fit of rage come over him and gradually increase exactly like a rain-cloud. I looked around timidly at the other boys. I heard a whisper at my back:

~ Your name he wants!

My heart leaped with joy at this assistance and I was grateful to him who prompted me. I looked politely at the master and replied to him:

~ Bonaparte, son of Michelangelo, son of Peter, son of Owen, son of Thomas's Sarah, grand-daughter of John's Mary, grand-daughter of James, son of Dermot . . . [2]

Before I had uttered or half-uttered my name, a rabid bark issued from the master and he beckoned to me with his finger. By the time I had reached him, he had an oar in his grasp. Anger had come over him in a flood-tide at this stage and he had a businesslike grip of the oar in his two hands. He drew it over his shoulder and brought it down hard upon me with a swish of air, dealing me a destructive blow on the skull. I fainted from that blow but before I became totally unconscious I heard him scream:

~ Yer nam, said he, is Jams O'Donnell![3]

Jams O'Donnell? These two words were singing in my ears when feeling returned to me. I found that I was lying on my side on the floor, my breeches, hair and all my person saturated with the streams of blood which flowed from the split caused by the oar in my skull. When my eyes were in operation again, there was another youngster on his feet being asked his name. It was apparent that this child lacked shrewdness completely and had not drawn good beneficial lessons for himself from the beating which I had received because he replied to the master, giving his common name as I had. The master again brandished the oar which was in his grasp and did not cease until he was shedding blood plentifully, the youngster being left unconscious and stretched out on the floor, a bloodied bundle. And during the beating the master screamed once more:

~ Yer nam is Jams O'Donnell!

He continued in this manner until every creature in the school had been struck down by him and all had been named *Jams O'Donnell*. No young skull in the countryside that day remained unsplit. Of course, there were many unable to walk by the afternoon and were transported home by relatives. It was a pitiable thing for those who had to swim back to Aran that evening and were without a bite of food or a sup of milk since morning.

When I myself reached home, my mother was there boiling potatoes for the pigs and I asked her for a couple for lunch. I received them and ate them with only a little pinch of salt. The bad situation in the school was bothering me all this time and I decided to question my mother.

~ Woman, said I, I've heard that every fellow in this place is called *Jams O'Donnell*. If that's the way it is, it's a wonderful world we have and isn't O'Donnell the wonderful man and the number of children he has?

~ 'Tis true for you, said she.

~ If 'tis true itself, said I, I've no understanding of that same truth.

~ If that's the way, said she, don't you understand that it's Gaels that live in this side of the country and that they can't escape from fate? It was always said and written that every Gaelic youngster is hit on his first school day because he doesn't understand English and the foreign form of his name and that no one has any respect for him because he's Gaelic to the marrow. There's no other business going on in school that day but punishment and revenge and the same fooling about *Jams O'Donnell*. Alas! I don't think that there'll ever be any good settlement for the Gaels but only hardship for them always. The Old-Grey-Fellow was also hit one day of his life and called *Jams O'Donnell* as well.

~ Woman, said I, what you say is amazing and I don't think I'll ever go back to that school but it's now the end of my learning!

~ You're shrewd, said she, in your early youth.

. . . .

I had no other connection with education from that day onwards and therefore my Gaelic skull has not been split since. But seven years afterwards (when I was seven years older), it came to pass that wonderful things happened in our neighbourhood, things connected with the question of learning and, for this reason, I must present some little account of them here.

The Old-Fellow was one day in Dingle buying tobacco and tasting spirits, when he heard news which amazed him. He did not believe it because he never trusted the people of that town. The next day he was selling herrings in the Rosses and had the same news from them there; he then half-accepted the story but did not altogether swallow it. The third day he was in Galway city and the story was there likewise. At last he believed it believingly and when he returned, drenched and wet (the downpour comes heavily on us unfailingly each night), he informed my mother of the matter (and me also who was eavesdropping in the end of the house!).

~ Upon me soul, said he, I hear that the English Government is going to do great work for the good of the paupers here in this place, safe and saved may everyone be in this house! It is fixed to pay the likes of us two pounds a skull for every child of ours that speaks English instead of this thieving Gaelic. Trying to separate us from the Gaelic they are, praise be to them sempiternally! I don't think there'll ever be good conditions for the Gaels while having small houses in the corner of the glen, going about in the dirty ashes, constantly fishing in the constant storm, telling stories at night about the hardships and hard times of the Gaels in sweet words of Gaelic is natural to them.

~ Woe is me! exclaimed my mother, and I with only the one son; this dying example here that's on his backside over on the floor there.

~ If that's the way, said the Old-Fellow, you'll have more children or else you're without resource!

During the following week, a staunch black gloom came over the Old-Grey-Fellow, a portent that his mind was filled with difficult complicated thoughts while he endeavoured to solve the question of the want of children. One day, while in Cahirciveen, he heard that the new scheme was under way; that the good foreign money had been received already in many houses in that district and that an inspector was going about through the countryside counting the children and testing the quality of English they had. He also heard that this inspector was an aged crippled man without good sight and that he lacked enthusiasm for his work as well. The Old-Fellow pondered all that he heard and when he returned at night (drenched and wet), he informed us that there is no cow unmilkable, no hound unraceable and, also, no money which cannot be stolen.

~ Upon me soul, said he, we'll have the full of the house before morning and everyone of them earning two pounds for us.

~ It's a wonderful world, said my mother, but I'm not expecting anything of that kind and neither did I hear that a house could be filled in one night.

~ Don't forget, said he, that Sarah is here.

~ Sarah, indeed! said my startled mother.

Amazement leaped up and down through me when I heard the mention of the sow's name.

~ The same lady exactly, said he. She has a great crowd of a family at present and they have vigorous voices, even though their dialect is unintelligible to us. How do we know but that their conversation isn't in English. Of course, youngsters and piglets have the same habits and take notice that there's a close likeness between their skins.

~ You're reflective, replied my mother, but they must have suits of clothes made for them before the inspector comes to look at them.

~ They must indeed, said the Old-Grey-Fellow.

~ It's a wonderful world these days, said I from the back-bed at the end of the house.

~ Upon me soul, but 'tis wonderful, said the Old-Fellow, but in spite of the payment of this English money for the good of our likes, I don't think there'll ever be good conditions for the Gaels.

The following day we had these particular residents within, each one wearing a grey-wool clothing while squealing, rooting, grunting and snoring in the rushes in the back of the house. A blind man would know of their presence from the stench there. Whatever the condition of the Gaels was at that time, our own condition was not at all good while these fellows were our constant company.

We kept a good vigil for the inspector's arrival. We were obliged to wait quite a while for him but, as the Old-Fellow said, whatever is coming will come. The inspector approached us on a rainy day when there was bad light everywhere and a heavy twilight in the end of our house where the pigs were. Whoever said that the inspector was old and feeble, told the truth. He was English and had little health. the poor fellow! He was thin, stooped and sour-faced. He cared not a whit for the Gaels—no wonder!—and never had any desire to go into the cabins where they lived. When he came to us, he stopped at the threshold and peered short-sightedly into the house. He was startled when he noticed the smell we had but did not depart because he had much experience of the habitations of the true Gaels. The Old-Grey-Fellow stood respectfully and politely near the door in front of the gentleman, I beside him and my mother was in the back of the house caring and petting the piglets. Occasionally, a piglet jumped into the centre of the floor and without delay returned to the twilight. One might have thought that he was a strong male youngster, crawling through the house because of the breeches which he wore. A murmur of talk arose all this time from my mother and the piglets; it was difficult to understand because of the noise of wind and rain outside. The gentleman looked sharply about him, deriving but little pleasure from the stench. At last he spoke:

~ How many?

~ Twalf, sor![4] said the Old-Grey-Fellow courteously.

~ Twalf?

The other man threw another quick glance at the back of the house while he considered and attempted to find some explanation for the speech he heard.

~ All spik Inglish?

~ All spik, sor, said the Old-Fellow.

Then the gentleman noticed me standing behind the Old-Grey-Fellow and he spoke gruffly to me:

~ Phwat is yer nam? said he.

~ Jams O'Donnell, sor!

It was apparent that neither I nor my like appealed to this elegant stranger but this answer delighted him because he could now declare that he questioned the young folk and was answered in sweet English; the last of his labours was completed and he might now escape freely from the stench. He departed amid the rain-showers without word or blessing for us. The Old-Grey-Fellow was well satisfied with what we had accomplished and I had a fine meal of potatoes as a reward from him. The pigs were driven out and we were

all quiet and happy for the day. Some days afterwards the Old-Grey-Fellow received a yellow letter and there was a big currency note within it. That is another story and I shall narrate it at another time in this volume.

When the inspector had gone and the pigs' odour cleared from the house,
it appeared to us that the end of that work was done and the termination of
that course reached by us. But, alas! things are not what they seem and if a
stone be cast, there is no foreknowledge of where it may land. On the following day, when we counted the pigs while divesting them of their breeches, it
appeared that we were missing one. Great was the lamentation of the Old-
Grey-Fellow when he noticed that both pig and suit of clothes had been
snatched privily from him in the quiet of the night. It is true that he often stole
a neighbour's pig and he often stated that he never slaughtered one of his own
but sold them all, although we always had half-sides of bacon in our house.
Night and day there was constant thieving in progress in the parish—paupers
impoverishing each other—but no one stole a pig except the Old-Fellow. Of
course, it was not joy which flooded his heart when he found another person
playing his own tune.

~ Upon me soul, said he to me, I'm afraid they're not all just and honest
around here. I wouldn't mind about the young little pig but there was a fine
bit of stuff in that breeches.

~ Everyone to his own opinion, my good man, said I, but I don't think
that anyone took that pig or the breeches either.

~ Do you think, said he, that fear would keep them from doing the steal-
ing?

~ No, I replied, but the stench would.

~ I don't know, son, said he, but that you're truly in the right. I don't
know but that the pig is off rambling?

~ It's an unfragrant rambling if 'tis true for you, my good man, said I.

That night the Old-Fellow stole a pig from Martin O'Bannassa and killed
it quietly in the end of the house. It happened that the conversation had reminded him that our bacon was in short supply. No further discussion concerning the lost pig took place then.

A new month called March was born; remained with us for a month and
then departed. At the end of that time we heard a loud snorting one night in
the height of the rain. The Old-Fellow thought that yet another pig was being
snatched from him by force and went out. When he returned, his companion
consisted of none other than our missing pig, drenched and wet, the fine
breeches about him in saturated rags. The creature seemed by his appearance
to have trudged quite an area of the earth that night. My mother arose will-

ingly when the Old-Fellow stated that it was necessary to prepare a large pot of potatoes for the one who had after all returned. The awakening of the household did not agree too well with Charlie and, having lain awake, looking furious during the talking and confusion, he suddenly arose and charged out into the rain. The poor creature never favoured socialising much. God bless him!

The return in darkness of the pig was amazing but still more amazing was the news which he imparted to us when he had partaken of the potatoes, having been stripped of the breeches by the Old-Grey-Fellow. The Old-Fellow found a pipe with a good jot of tobacco in one pocket. In another he found a shilling and a small bottle of spirits.

~ Upon me soul, said he, if 'tis hardship that's always in store for the Gaels, it's not that way with this creature. Look, said he, directing his attention to the pig, where did you get these articles, sir?

The pig threw a sharp glance out of his two little eyes at the Old-Fellow but did not reply.

~ Leave the breeches on him, said my mother. How do we know but that he'll be coming to us every week and wonderful precious things in his pockets—pearls, necklaces, snuff and maybe a money-note—wherever in Ireland he can get them. Isn't it a marvellous world today altogether?

~ How do we know, said the Old-Grey-Fellow in reply to her, that he will ever again return but live where he can get these good things and we'd be for ever without the fine suit of clothes that he has?

~ True for you, indeed, alas! said my mother.

The pig was now stark naked and was put with the others.

Notes

1. *grey-wool breeches:* In Gaelic *"brístí de ghlas na gcaorach,"* this phrase occurs in books written by writers such as Máire. The wool is undyed. The Gaelic writers generally refer only to the breeches as if the child wore nothing else!

2. *Bonaparte . . . :* In Gaelic this occurs as *"Bonapáirt Mícheálangaló Pheadair Eoghain Shorcha Thomáis Mháire Sheáin Shéamais Dhiarmada . . ."* This is more euphonious than the translation but Gaelic here has the advantage because of the possibility of using genitive cases for each word after the first one.

3. *Jams O'Donnell:* In Máire's novel, *Mo Dhá Róisín,* the author speaks of a pupil hearing himself called by his official name *James Gallagher* on his first schoolday. He had never heard it before! Myles seems to use the name as a generic term for the Gaeltacht man as seen by those outside his boggy rainy ghetto.

4. *sor:* In D. this spelling appears for *sir.* The Gaelic pun is untranslatable—*sor* means "louse" in English!

Further Readings on Flann O'Brien

Bibliography

Powell, David. "A Checklist of Brian O'Nolan." *Journal of Irish Literature* 3:104–12.

Selected Works

As Brian Ó Nualláin:

An Béal Bocht. Dublin: An Press Náisiunta, 1941. Reprint, Cork: Mercier, 1999. Translated by Patrick C. Power as *The Poor Mouth*. 1973. Reprint, Normal, Ill.: Dalkey Archive, 1996.

As Flann O'Brien:

At Swim-Two-Birds. 1939. Reprint, Normal, Ill.: Dalkey Archive, 1998.

The Dalkey Archive. 1964. Reprint, Normal, Ill.: Dalkey Archive, 1993.

Flann O'Brien At War: Myles na gCopaleen, 1940–1945. Edited by John Wyse Jackson. London: Duckworth, 1999.

The Hard Life. 1961. Reprint, London: Flamingo, 1995.

King of Ireland: The First Translation of the Writings in Irish. London: Gibson Square, 2003.

Myles Before Myles: A Selection of the Earlier Writings of Brian O'Nolan. Edited by John Wyse Jackson. London: Grafton, 1988.

Rhapsody in Stephen's Green: The Insect Play. Edited by Robert Tracy. Dublin: Lilliput, 1994.

Stories and Plays by Flann O'Brien. 1974. Reprint, London: Grafton, 1991.

The Third Policeman. 1967. Reprint, London: Flamingo, 2001.

As Myles na Gopaleen:

The Best of Myles. 1968. Reprint, Normal, Ill.: Dalkey Archive, 1999.

Cruiskeen Lawn. Dublin: Cahill, 1943.

Faustus Kelly: A Play in Three Acts. Dublin: Cahill, 1943.

Further Cuttings: From Cruiskeen Lawn. London: Paladin, 1989; Normal, Ill.: Dalkey Archive, 2000.

The Hair of the Dogma: A Further Selection from "Cruiskeen Lawn." London: Paladin, 1989.

Myles Away from Dublin: Being a Selection from the Column Written or the Nationalist and Leinster Times, Carlow, Under the Name George Knowall. Edited by Martin Green. 1985. Reprint, London: Flamingo, 1993.

Various Lives of Keats and Chapman and the Brother. 1976. London: Paladin, 1990.

Biography and Criticism

Asbee, Sue. *Flann O'Brien*. Boston: Twayne, 1991.

Booker, M. Keith. *Flann O'Brien, Bakhtin, and Menippean Satire*. Syracuse: Syracuse University Press, 1995.

Clissmann, Anne. *Flann O'Brien: A Critical Introduction to His Writing*. Dublin: Gill and Macmillan, 1975.

Clune, Anne. *Flann O'Brien: A Critical Introduction to His Writings: The Story-Teller's Book-Web*. Dublin: Gill and Macmillan, 1975.

————— and Tess Hurson, eds. *Conjuring the Complexities: Essays on Flann O'Brien*. Belfast: Institute for Irish Studies, 1997.

Costello, Peter, and Peter Van de Kamp. *Flann O'Brien: An Illustrated Biography*. London: Bloomsbury, 1987.

Cronin, Anthony. *No Laughing Matter: The Life and Times of Flann O'Brien*. London: Grafton, 1989.

Gallagher, Monique. *Flann O'Brien: Myles from Dublin*. Gerrards Cross, UK: Colin Smythe, 1991.

Hopper, Keith. *Flann O'Brien: A Portrait of the Artist as a Young Post-Modernist*. Cork: Cork University Press, 1995.

Imhof, Rüdiger. *Alive Alive O! Flann O'Brien's At Swim-Two-Birds,* Dublin: Wolfhound Press Press, 1986.

Journal of Irish Literature 3, no. 1 (January 1974). Flann O'Brien Special Issue.

Lanters, José. *Unauthorized Versions: Irish Menippean Satire, 1919–1952*. Washington: Catholic University Press, 2000.

O'Keefe, Timothy, ed. *Myles: Portraits of Brian O'Nolan*. London: Martin Brian and O'Keefe, 1973.

Ó Nualláin, Ciarán. *Early Years of Brian O'Nolan, Flann O'Brien, Myles na gCopaleen*. Dublin: Lilliput, 1998.

Shea, Thomas F. *Flann O'Brien's Exorbitant Novels*. Lewisburg, Pa.: Bucknell University Press, 1992.

Wäppling, Eva. *Four Irish Legendary Figures in At Swim-Two-Birds*. Uppsala: Academia Upsaliensis, 1984.

Began publishing
in the heyday of
O'Connor + O'Faolain

 # Mary Lavin
(1912–1996)

For more than forty years, Mary Lavin's fiction appeared on both sides of the Atlantic, a phenomenon that mirrored her own Irish and American roots. Massachusetts-born, her parents moved back to Ireland when she was ten. After earning her B.A. and M.A. degrees at University College, Dublin, she abandoned an academic career to write. Since "Miss Holland" (1939), she produced eleven collections of short stories and two novels, as well as children's books and even a couple of poems. She was honored with prizes and fellowships, including an honorary D.Litt. from the National University of Ireland in 1972.

A. A. Kelly called Lavin the "quiet rebel," a reference perhaps to the way that Lavin was able to develop her own voice while accommodating Irish middle-class sensibility. "Happiness" is one of a series of autobiographical stories. Like the protagonist, Vera Traske, Lavin was widowed with three young daughters, was responsible for an elderly mother, and was tireless in her efforts to keep a Dublin house going as well as a working farm near Bective Abbey, County Meath. Vera's celebration of those who joyously respond to life, in contrast to those who deny life by being narrow, selfish, and demanding, is a favorite Lavin theme in such stories as "Frail Vessel" and "A Happy Death."

Happiness

Mother had a lot to say. This does not mean she was always talking but that we children felt the wells she drew upon were deep, deep, deep. Her theme was happiness; what it was, what it was not; where we might find it, where not; and how, if found, it must be guarded. Never must we confound it with pleasure. Nor think sorrow its exact opposite.

"Take Father Hugh," Mother's eyes flashed as she looked at him. "According to him, sorrow is an ingredient of happiness—a *necessary* ingredient, if you please!" And when he tried to protest she put up her hand. "There may be a freakish truth in the theory—for some people. But not for me. And not, I hope, for my children." She looked severely at us three girls. We laughed.

None of us had had much experience with sorrow. Bea and I were children and Linda only a year old when our father died suddenly after a short illness that had not at first seemed serious. "I've known people to make sorrow a *substitute* for happiness," Mother said.

Father Hugh protested again. "You're not putting me in that class, I hope?"

Father Hugh, ever since our father died, had been the closest of anyone to us as a family, without being close to any one of us in particular—even to Mother. He lived in a monastery near our farm in County Meath, and he had been one of the celebrants at the Requiem High Mass our father's political importance had demanded. He met us that day for the first time, but he took to dropping in to see us, with the idea of filling the crater of loneliness left at our centre. He did not know that there was a cavity in his own life, much less that we would fill it. He and Mother were both young in those days, and perhaps it gave scandal to some that he was so often in our house, staying till late into the night and, indeed, thinking nothing of stopping all night if there was any special reason, such as one of us being sick. He had even on occasion slept there if the night was too wet for tramping home across the fields.

When we girls were young, we were so used to having Father Hugh around that we never stood on ceremony with him but in his presence dried our hair and pared our nails and never minded what garments were strewn about. As for Mother—she thought nothing of running out of the bathroom in her slip, brushing her teeth or combing her hair, if she wanted to tell him something she might otherwise forget. And she brooked no criticism of her behaviour. "Celibacy was never meant to take all the warmth and homeliness out of their lives." she said.

On this point, too, Bea was adamant. Bea, the middle sister, was our oracle. "I'm so glad he *has* Mother," she said, "as well as her having him, because it must be awful the way most women treat them—priests, I mean—as if they were pariahs. Mother treats him like a human being—that's all."

And when it came to Mother's ears that there had been gossip about her making free with Father Hugh, she opened her eyes wide in astonishment. "But he's only a priest!" she said.

Bea giggled. "It's a good job he didn't hear *that.*" she said to me afterwards." It would undo the good she's done him. You'd think he was a eunuch."

"Bea!" I said. "Do you think he's in love with her?"

"If so, he doesn't know it." Bea said firmly. "It's her soul he's after! Maybe he wants to make sure of her in the next world!"

But thoughts of the world to come never troubled Mother. "If anything ever happens to me, children," she said, "suddenly, I mean, or when you are not near me, or I cannot speak to you, I want you to promise you won't feel bad. There's no need! Just remember that I had a happy life—and that if I had to choose my kind of heaven I'd take it on this earth with you again, no matter how much you might annoy me!"

You see, annoyance and fatigue, according to Mother, and even illness and pain, could coexist with happiness. She had a habit of asking people if they were happy at times and in places that—to say the least of it—seemed to us inappropriate. "But are you happy?" she'd probe as one lay sick and bathed in sweat, or in the throes of a jumping toothache. And once in our presence she made the inquiry of an old friend as he lay upon his death bed.

"Why not?" she said when we took her to task for it later. "Isn't it more important than ever to be happy when you're dying? Take my own father! You know what he said in his last moments? On his deathbed, he defied me to name a man who had enjoyed a better life. In spite of dreadful pain, his face *radiated* happiness!" Mother nodded her head comfortably. "Happiness drives out pain, as fire burns out fire."

Having no knowledge of our own to pit against hers, we thirstily drank in her rhetoric. Only Bea was sceptical. "Perhaps you *got* it from him, like spots, or fever," she said. "Or something that could at least be slipped from hand to hand."

"Do you think I'd have taken it if that were the case!" Mother cried. "Then, when he needed it most?"

"Not there and then!" Bea said stubbornly. "I meant as a sort legacy."

"Don't you think in *that* case," mother said, exasperated, "he would have felt obliged to leave it to your grandmother?"

Certainly we knew that in spite of his lavish heart our grandfather had failed to provide our grandmother with enduring happiness. He had passed that job on to Mother. And Mother had not made too good a fist of it, even when Father was living and she had him—and later, us children—to help.

As for Father Hugh, he had given our grandmother up early in the game. "God Almighty couldn't make that woman happy," he said one day, seeing Mother's face, drawn and pale with fatigue, preparing for the nightly run over to her own mother's flat that would exhaust her utterly.

There were evenings after she came home from the library where she worked when we saw her stand with the car keys in her hand, trying to think which would be worse—to slog over there on foot, or take out the car again. And yet the distance was short. It was Mother's day that had been too long.

Weren't you over to see her this morning?" Father Hugh demanded.

"No matter!" said Mother. She was no doubt thinking of the forlorn face our grandmother always put on when she was leaving. ("Don't say good night, Vera," Grandmother would plead. "It makes me feel too lonely. And you never can tell—you might slip over again before you go to bed!")

"Do you know the time?" Bea would say impatiently, if she happened to be with Mother. Not indeed that the lateness of the hour counted for anything, because in all likelihood Mother *would* go back, if only to pass by under the window and see that the lights were out, or stand and listen and make sure that as far as she could tell all was well.

"I wouldn't mind if she was happy," Mother said.

"And how do you know she's not?" we'd ask.

"When people are happy, I can feel it. Can't you?"

We were not sure. Most people thought our grandmother was a gay creature, a small birdy being who even at a great age laughed like a girl, and—more remarkably—sang like one, as she went about her day. But beak and claw were of steel. She'd think nothing of sending Mother back to a shop three times if her errands were not exactly right. "Not sugar like that—that's *too* fine; it's not castor sugar I want. But *not* as coarse as *that,* either. I want an in-between kind."

Provoked one day, my youngest sister, Linda, turned and gave battle. "You're mean!" she said. "As a girl, I used to be called Miss Imperious."

And Miss Imperious she remained as long as she lived, even when she was a great age. Her orders were then given a wry twist by the fact that as she advanced in age she took to calling her daughter Mother, as we did.

There was one great phrase with which our grandmother opened every sentence: "if only." "If only," she'd say, when we came to visit her—"if only you'd come earlier, before I was worn out expecting you!" Or if we were early, then if only it was later, after she'd had a rest and could enjoy us, be *able* for us. And if we brought her flowers, she'd sigh to think that if only we'd brought them the previous day she'd have had a visitor to appreciate them, or say it was a pity the stems weren't longer. If only we'd picked a few green leaves, or included some buds, because, she said disparagingly, the poor flowers we'd brought were already wilting. We might just as well not have brought them! As the years went on, Grandmother had a new bead to add to her rosary: if only her friends were not all dead! By their absence, they reduced to nil all *real* enjoyment in anything. Our own father—her son-in-law—was the one person who had ever gone close to pleasing her. But even here there had been a snag. "If only he was my real son!" she used to say with a sigh.

Mother's mother lived on through our childhood and into our early maturity (though she outlived the money our grandfather left her), and in our minds she was a complicated mixture of valiance and defeat. Courageous and generous within the limits of her own life, her simplest demand was yet enormous in the larger frame of Mother's life, and so we never could see her with the same clarity of vision with which we saw our grandfather, or our own father. Them we saw only through Mother's eyes.

"Take your grandfather!" she'd cry, and instantly we'd see him, his eyes burning upon us—yes, upon *us*, although in his day only one of us had been born: me. At another time, Mother would cry, "Take your own father!" and instantly we'd see *him*—tall, handsome, young, and much more suited to marry one of us than poor bedraggled Mother.

Most fascinating of all were the times Mother would say "Take me!" By magic then, staring down the years, we'd see blazingly clear a small girl with black hair and buttoned boots, who, though plain and pouting, burned bright, like a star. "I was happy, you see," Mother said. And we'd strain hard to try and understand the mystery of the light that still radiated from her. "I used to lean along a tree that grew out of the river," she said, "and look down through the grey leaves at the water flowing past below, and I used to think it was not the stream that flowed but me, spread-eagled over it, who flew through the air! Like a bird! That I'd found the secret!" She made it seem there might *be* such a secret, just waiting to be found. Another time she'd dream that she'd be a great singer.

"We didn't know you sang, Mother!"

She had to laugh. "Like a crow," she said.

Sometimes she used to think she'd swim the Channel.

"Did you swim *that* well, Mother?"

"Oh, not really—just the breast stroke," she said. "And then only by the aid of two pig bladders blown up by my father and tied around my middle. But I used to throb—yes, throb—with happiness."

Behind Mother's back, Bea raised her eyebrows.

What was it, we used to ask ourselves—that quality that she, we felt sure, misnamed? Was it courage? Was it strength, health, or high spirits? Something you could not give or take—a conundrum? A game of catch-as-you-can?

"I know," cried Bea. "A sham!"

Whatever it was, we knew that Mother would let no wind of violence from within or without tear it from her. Although, one evening when Father Hugh was with us, our astonished ears heard her proclaim that there might be a time when one had to slacken hold on it—let go—to catch at it again with a surer hand. In the way, we supposed, that the high-wire walker up among the painted stars of his canvas sky must wait to fling himself through the air until the bar he catches at has started to sway perversely from him. Oh no, no! That downward drag at our innards we could not bear, the belly swelling to the shape of a pear. Let happiness go by the board. "After all, lots of people seem to make out without it," Bea cried. It was too tricky a business. And might it not be that one had to be born with a flair for it?

"A flair would not be enough," Mother answered. "Take Father Hugh. He, if anyone, had a flair for it—a natural capacity! You've only to look at him when he's off guard, with you children, or helping me in the garden. But he rejects happiness! He casts it from him."

"That is simply not true, Vera," cried Father Hugh, overhearing her. "It's just that I don't place an inordinate value on it like you. I don't think it's enough to carry one all the way. To the end, I mean—and after."

"Oh, don't talk about the end when we're only in the middle," cried Mother. And, indeed at that moment her own face shone with such happiness it was hard to believe that earth was not her heaven. Certainly it was her constant contention that of happiness she had had a lion's share, This, however, we, in private, doubted. Perhaps there were times when she had had a surplus of it—when she was young, say, with her redoubtable father, whose love blazed circles around her, making winter into summer and ice into fire. Perhaps she did have a brimming measure in her early married years. By straining hard, we could find traces left in our minds from those days of milk and honey. Our father, while he lived, had cast a magic over everything, for us as well as for her. He held his love up over us like an umbrella and kept off the troubles that afterwards came down on us, pouring cats and dogs!

But if she did have more than the common lot of happiness in those early days, what use was that when we could remember so clearly how our father's death had ravaged her? And how could we forget the distress it brought on us when, afraid to let her out of our sight, Bea and I stumbled after her everywhere, through the woods and along the bank of the river, where, in the weeks that followed, she tried vainly to find peace.

The summer after Father died, we were invited to France to stay with friends, and when she went walking on the cliffs at Fécamp our fears for her grew frenzied, so that we hung on to her arm and dragged at her skirt, hoping that like leaded weights we'd pin her down if she went too near to the edge. But at night we had to abandon our watch, being forced to follow the conventions of a family still whole—a home still intact—and go to bed at the same time as the other children. It was at that hour, when the coast guard was gone from his rowing boat offshore and the sand was as cold and grey as the sea, that Mother liked to swim. And when she had washed, kissed, and left us, our hearts almost died inside us and we'd creep out of bed again to stand in our bare feet at the mansard and watch as she ran down the shingle, striking out when she reached the water where, far out, wave and sky and mist were one, and the greyness closed over her. If we took our eyes off her for an instant, it was impossible to find her again.

"Oh, make her turn back, God, please!" I prayed out loud one night.

Startled, Bea turned away from the window, "She'll *have* to turn back sometime, won't she? Unless . . . ? "

Locking our damp hands together, we stared out again, "She wouldn't!" I whispered. "It would he a sin!"

Secure in the deterring power of sin, we let out our breath. Then Bea's breath caught again. "What if she went out so far she used up all her strength? She couldn't swim back! It wouldn't be a sin then!"

"It's the intention that counts," I whispered.

A second later, we could see an arm lift heavily up and wearily cleave down, and at last Mother was in the shallows, wading back to shore.

"Don't let her see us!" cried Bea. As if our chattering teeth would not give us away when she looked in at us before she went to her own room on the other side of the corridor, where, later in the night, sometimes the sound of crying would reach us.

What was it worth—a happiness bought that dearly.

Mother had never questioned it. And once she told us, "On a wintry day, I brought my own mother a snowdrop. It was the first one of the year—a bleak bud that had come up stunted before its time—and I meant it for a sign. But do you know what your grandmother said? 'What good are snowdrops to me now?' Such a thing to say! What good is a snowdrop at all if it doesn't hold its value always, and never lose it! Isn't that the whole point of a snowdrop? And that is the whole point of happiness, too! What good would it be if it could be erased without trace? Take me and those daffodils!" Stooping, she buried her face in a bunch that lay on the table waiting to be put in vases. "If they didn't hold their beauty absolute and inviolable, do you think I could bear the sight of them after what happened when your father was in hospital?"

It was a fair question. When Father went to hospital, Mother went with him and stayed in a small hotel across the street so she could be with him all day from early to late. "Because it was so awful for him—being in Dublin!" she said. "You have no idea how he hated it."

That he was dying neither of them realized. How could they know, as it rushed through the sky, that their star was a falling star! But one evening when she'd left him asleep Mother came home for a few hours to see how we were faring, and it broke her heart to see the daffodils out all over the place—in the woods, under the trees, and along the sides of the avenue. There had never been so many, and she thought how awful it was that Father was missing them. "You sent up little bunches to him, you poor dears!" she said. "Sweet little bunches, too—squeezed tight as posies by your little fists! But stuffed into vases they couldn't really make up to him for not being able to see them growing!"

So on the way back to the hospital she stopped her car and pulled a great bunch—the full of her arms. "They took up the whole back seat," she said, "and I was so excited at the thought of walking into his room and dumping them on his bed—you know—just plomping them down so he could smell them, and feel them, and look and look! I didn't mean them to be put in vases, or anything ridiculous like that—it would have taken a rainwater barrel to hold them. Why, I could hardly see over them as I came up the steps; I kept tripping. But when I came into the hall, that nun—I told you about her—that nun came up to me, sprang out of nowhere it seemed, although I know now that she was waiting for me, knowing that somebody had to bring me to my senses. But the way she did it! Reached out and grabbed the flowers, letting lots of them fall—I remember them getting stood on. 'Where are you going with those foolish flowers, you foolish woman?' she said. 'Don't you know your husband is dying? Your prayers are all you can give him now!'

"She was right. I *was* foolish. But I wasn't cured. Afterwards, it was nothing but foolishness the way I dragged you children after me all over Europe. As if any one place was going to be different from another, any better, any less desolate. But there was great satisfaction in bringing you places your father and I had planned to bring you—although in fairness to him I must say that he would not perhaps have brought you so young. And he would not have had an ulterior motive. But above all, he would not have attempted those trips in such a dilapidated car."

"Oh, that car! It was a battered and dilapidated red sports car, so depleted of accessories that when, eventually, we got a new car Mother still stuck out her hand on bends, and in wet weather jumped out to wipe the windscreen with her sleeve. And if fussed, she'd let down the window and shout at people, forgetting she now had a horn. How we had ever fitted into it with all our luggage was a miracle.

"You were never lumpish—any of you!" Mother said proudly. "But you were very healthy and very strong." She turned to me. "Think of how you got that car up the hill in Switzerland!"

"The Alps are not hills, Mother!" I pointed out coldly, as I had done at the time, when, as actually happened, the car failed to make it on one of the inclines. Mother let it run back until it wedged against the rock face, and I had to get out and push till she got going again in first gear. But when it got started it couldn't be stopped to pick me up until it got to the top, where they had to wait for me, and for a very long time.

"Ah, well," she said, sighing wistfully at the thought of those trips. "You got something out of them, I hope. All that travelling must have helped you with your geography and your history."

We looked at each other and smiled, and then Mother herself laughed. "Remember the time," she said, "when we were in Italy, and it was Easter, and all the shops were chock-full of food? The butchers' shops had poultry and game hanging up outside the doors, fully feathered, and with their poor heads dripping blood, and in the windows they had poor little lambs and suckling pigs and young goats, all skinned and hanging by their hindfeet." Mother shuddered. "They think so much about food. I found it revolting. I had to hurry past. But Linda, who must have been only four then, dragged at me and stared and stared. You know how children are at that age; they have a morbid fascination for what is cruel and bloody. Her face was flushed and her eyes were wide. I hurried her back to the hotel. But next morning she crept into my room. She crept up to me and pressed against me. 'Can't we go back, just once, and look again at that shop?' she whispered. 'The shop where they have the little children hanging up for Easter!' It was the young goats, of course, but I'd said 'kids,' I suppose. How we laughed." But her face was grave. "You were *so* good on those trips, all of you," she said. "You were really very good children in general. Otherwise I would never have put so much effort into rearing you, because I wasn't a bit maternal. You brought out the best in me! I put an unnatural effort into you, of course, because I was taking my standards from your father, forgetting that this might not have remained so inflexible if he had lived to middle age and was beset by life, like other parents."

"Well, the job is nearly over now, Vera," said Father Hugh. "And you didn't do so badly."

"That's right, Hugh," said Mother, and she straightened up, and put her hand to her back the way she sometimes did in the garden when she got up

[handwritten: Happiness achieved through resistance to self pity]

from her knees after weeding. "I didn't go over to the enemy anyway! We survived!" Then a flash of defiance came into her eyes. "And we were happy. That's the main thing!"

Father Hugh frowned. "There you go again!" he said.

Mother turned on him. "I don't think you realize the onslaughts that were made upon our happiness! The minute Robert died, they came down on me—cohorts of relatives, friends, even strangers, all draped in black, opening their arms like bats to let me pass into their company. 'Life is a vale of tears,' they said. 'You are privileged to find it out so young!' Ugh! After I staggered on to my feet and began to take hold of life once more, they fell back defeated. And the first day I gave a laugh—pouff, they were blown out like candles. They weren't living in a real world at all; they belonged to a ghostly world where life was easy: all one had to do was sit and weep. It takes effort to push back the stone from the mouth of the tomb and walk out."

Effort. Effort. Ah, but that strange-sounding word could invoke little sympathy from those who had not learned yet what it meant. Life must have been hardest for Mother in those years when we older ones were at college—no longer children, and still dependent on her. Indeed, we made more demands on her than ever then, being moved into new areas of activity and emotion. And our friends! Our friends came and went as freely as we did ourselves, so that the house was often like a café—and one where pets were not prohibited but took their places on our chairs and beds, as regardless as the people. And anyway it was hard to have sympathy for someone who got things into such a state as Mother. All over the house there was clutter. Her study was like the returned-letter department of a post-office, with stacks of paper everywhere, bills paid and unpaid, letters answered and unanswered, tax returns, pamphlets, leaflets. If by mistake we left the door open on a windy day, we came back to find papers flapping through the air like frightened birds. Efficient only in that she managed eventually to conclude every task she began, it never seemed possible to outsiders that by Mother's methods anything whatever could be accomplished. In an attempt to keep order elsewhere, she made her own room the clearing house into which the rest of us put everything: things to be given away, things to be returned—even things to be thrown out! By the end of the year, the room resembled an obsolescence dump. And no one could help her; the chaos of her life was as personal as an act of creation—one might as well try to finish another person's poem.

As the years passed, Mother rushed around more hectically. And although Bea and I had married and were not at home any more, except at holiday time and for occasional weekends, Linda was noisier than the two of us put together had been, and for every follower we had brought home she brought twenty. The house was never still. Now that we were reduced to being visitors, we watched Mother's tension mount to vertigo, knowing that, like a spinning top, she could not rest till she fell. But now at the smallest pretext Father Hugh would call in the doctor and Mother would be put on the mail boat and dispatched for London. For it was essential that she get far enough away to make phoning home every night prohibitively costly.

Unfortunately, the thought of departure often drove a spur into her and she redoubled her effort to achieve order in her affairs. She would be up until the early hours ransacking her desk. To her, as always, the shortest parting entailed a preparation as for death. And as it were her end that was at hand, we would all be summoned, although she had no time to speak a word to us, because five minutes before departure she would still be attempting to reply to letters that were the acquisition of weeks and would have taken whole days to dispatch.

"Don't you know the taxi is at the door, Vera?" Father Hugh would say, running his hand through his grey hair and looking very dishevelled himself. She had him at times as distracted as herself. "You can't do any more. You'll have to leave the rest till you come back."

"I can't, I can't!" Mother would cry. "I'll have to cancel my plans."

One day, Father Hugh opened the lid of her case, which was strapped up in the hall, and with a swipe of his arm he cleared all the papers on the top of the desk pell-mell into the suitcase. "You can sort them on the boat," he said, "or the train to London."

Thereafter, Mother's luggage always included an empty case to hold the unfinished papers on her desk. And years afterwards a steward on the Irish Mail told us she was a familiar figure, working away at letters and bills nearly all the way from Holyhead to Euston. "She gave it up about Rugby or Crewe," he said. "She'd get talking to someone in the compartment." He smiled. "There was one time coming down the train I was just in time to see her close up the window with a guilty look. I didn't say anything, but I think she'd emptied those papers of hers out the window!"

Quite likely. When we were children, even a few hours away from us gave her composure. And in two weeks or less, when she'd come home, the well of her spirit would be freshened. We'd hardly know her—her step so light, her eyes so bright, and her love and patience once more freely flowing. But in no time at all the house would fill up once more with the noise and confusion of too many people and too many animals, and again we'd be fighting our corner with cats and dogs, bats, mice, bees and even wasps. "Don't kill it!" Mother would cry if we raised a hand to an angry wasp. "Just catch it, dear, and put it outside. Open the window and let it fly away!" But even this treatment could at times be deemed too harsh. "Wait a minute. Close the window!" she'd cry. "It's too cold outside. It will die. That's why it came in, I suppose! Oh dear, what will we do?" Life would be going full blast again.

There was only one place Mother found rest. When she was at breaking point and fit to fall, she'd go out, into the garden—not to sit or stroll around but to dig, to drag up weeds, to move great clumps of corms or rhizomes, or indeed quite frequently to haul huge rocks from one place to another. She was always laying down a path, building a dry wall, or making compost heaps as high as hills. However jaded she might be going out, when dark forced her in at last her step had the spring of a daisy. So if she did not succeed in defining happiness to our understanding, we could see that whatever it was, she possessed it to the full when she was in her garden.

One of us said as much one Sunday when Bea and I had dropped round for the afternoon. Father Hugh was with us again. "It's an unthinking happiness, though," he cavilled. We were standing at the drawing-room window, looking out to where in the fading light we could see Mother on her knees weeding, in the long border that stretched from the house right down to the woods. "I wonder how she'd take it if she were stricken down and had to give up that heavy work!" he said. Was he perhaps a little jealous of how she could stoop and bend? He himself had begun to use a stick. I was often a little jealous of her myself, because although I was married and had children of my own, I had married young and felt the weight of living as heavy as a weight of years. "She doesn't take enough care of herself," Father Hugh said sadly. "Look at her out there with nothing under her knees to protect her from the damp ground." It was almost too dim for us to see her, but even in the drawing-room it was chilly. "She should not be let stay out there after the sun goes down."

"Just you try to get her in then!" said Linda, who had come into the room in time to hear him. "Don't you know by now anyway that what would kill another person only seems to make Mother thrive?"

Father Hugh shook his head again. "You seem to forget it's not younger she's getting!" He fidgeted and fussed, and several times went to the window to stare out apprehensively. He was really getting quite elderly.

"Come and sit down, Father Hugh," Bea said, and to take his mind off Mother she turned on the light and blotted out the garden. Instead of seeing through the window, we saw into it as into a mirror, and there between the flower-laden tables and lamps it was ourselves we saw moving vaguely. Like

Father Hugh, we, too, were waiting for her to come in before we called an end to the day.

"Oh, this is ridiculous!" Father Hugh cried at last. "She'll have to listen to reason." And going back to the window he threw it open. "Vera!" he called. "Vera!"—sternly, so sternly that, more intimate than an endearment, his tone shocked us. "She didn't hear me," he said, turning back blinking at us in the lighted room. "I'm going out to get her." And in a minute he was gone from the room. As he ran down the garden path, we stared at each other, astonished; his step, like his voice, was the step of a lover. "I'm coming, Vera!" he cried.

Although she was never stubborn except in things that mattered, Mother had not moved. In the wholehearted way she did everything, she was bent down close to the ground. It wasn't the light only that was dimming; her eyesight also was failing, I thought, as instinctively I followed Father Hugh.

But halfway down the path I stopped. I had seen something he had not: Mother's hand that appeared to support itself in a forked branch of an old tree peony she had planted as a bride was not in fact gripping it but impaled upon it. And the hand that appeared to be grubbing in the clay in fact was sunk into the soft mould. "Mother!" I screamed, and I ran forward, but when I reached her I covered my face with my hands. "Oh Father Hugh!" I cried. "Is she dead?"

It was Bea who answered hysterical. "She is! She is!" she cried, and she began to pound Father Hugh on the back with her fists, as if his pessimistic words had made this happen.

But Mother was not dead. And at first the doctor even offered hope of her pulling through. But from the moment Father Hugh lifted her up to carry her into the house we ourselves had no hope, seeing how effortlessly he, who was not strong, could carry her. When he put her down on her bed, her head hardly creased the pillow. Mother lived for four more hours.

Like the days of her life, those four hours that Mother lived were packed tight with concern and anxiety. Partly conscious, partly delirious, she seemed to think the counterpane was her desk, and she scrabbled her fingers upon it as if trying to sort out a muddle of bills and correspondence. No longer indifferent now, we listened, anguished, to the distracted cries that had for all our lifetime been so familiar to us. "Oh, where is it? Where is it? I had a minute ago! Where on earth did I put it?"

"Vera, Vera, stop worrying," Father Hugh pleaded, but she waved him away and went on sifting through the sheets as if they were sheets of paper. "Oh, Vera!" he begged. "Listen to me. Do you not know—"

Bea pushed between them. "You're not to tell her!" she commanded. "Why frighten her?"

"But it ought not to frighten her," said Father Hugh. "This is what I was always afraid would happen—that she'd be frightened when it came to the end."

At that moment, as if to vindicate him, Mother's hands fell idle on the coverlet, palm upward and empty. And turning her head she stared at each of us in turn, beseechingly. "I cannot face it," she whispered. "I can't! I can't! I can't!"

"Oh, my God!" Bea said, and she started to cry.

"Vera. For God's sake listen to me," Father Hugh cried, and pressing his face to hers, as close as a kiss, he kept whispering to her, trying to cast into the dark tunnel before her the light of his own faith.

But it seemed to us that Mother must already be looking into God's exigent eyes. "I can't!" she cried. "I can't!"

Then her mind came back from the stark world of the spirit to the world where her body was still detained, but even that world was now a whirling kaleidoscope of things which only she could see. Suddenly her eyes focussed, and, catching at Father Hugh, she pulled herself up a little and pointed to something we could not see. "What will be done with them?" Her voice was anxious. "They ought to be put in water anyway," she said, and leaning over the edge of the bed, she pointed to the floor. "Don't step on that one!" she said sharply. Then more sharply still, she addressed us all. "Have them sent to the public ward," she said peremptorily. "Don't let that nun take them; she'll only put them on the altar. And God doesn't want them! He made them for *us*—not for Himself!"

It was the familiar rhetoric that all her life had characterized her utterances. For a moment we were mystified. Then Bea gasped. "The daffodils!" she cried. "The day Father died!" And over her face came the light that had so often blazed over Mother's. Leaning across the bed, she pushed Father Hugh aside. And, putting out her hands, she held Mother's face between her palms as tenderly as if it were the face of a child. "It's all right, Mother. You don't *have* to face it! It's over!" Then she who had so fiercely forbade Father Hugh to do so blurted out the truth. "You've finished with this world, Mother," she said, and, confident that her tidings were joyous, her voice was strong.

Mother made the last effort of her life and grasped at Bea's meaning. She let out a sigh, and, closing her eyes, she sank back, and this time her head sank so deeply into the pillow that it would have been dented had it been a pillow of stone.

Further Readings on Mary Lavin

Bibliography

Doyle, Paul A. "Mary Lavin: a Checklist." *Papers of the Bibliographical Society of America* 63:317–21.

Krawchak, Ruth and Mahlke, Regina. *Mary Lavin: A Checklist*. Berlin: Hildebrand, 1979.

Selected Works

The Becker Wives and Other Stories. 1946. Reprint, New York: New American Library, 1971.

Collected Stories. Introduction by V. S. Pritchett. Boston: Houghton Mifflin, 1971.

Family Likeness and Other Stories, A. London: Constable, 1985.

The House in Clewe Street. 1945. London: Virago, 1987.

In a Café: Selected Stories. Dublin: Town House, 1995.

In the Middle of the Field and Other Stories. New York: Macmillan, 1967.

A Likely Story. 1957. Reprint, Dublin: Poolbeg, 1990. [Juvenile fiction.]

Mary O'Grady. 1950. Reprint, London: Virago, 1986.

A Memory and Other Stories. London: Constable, 1973.

Selected Stories. Introduction by the author. London: Macmillan, 1959.

Selected Stories. Harmondsworth: Penguin, 1981.

The Shrine and Other Stories. London: Constable, 1977.

The Stories of Mary Lavin: I. London: Constable, 1964.

The Stories of Mary Lavin: II. London: Constable, 1974.

Tales from Bective Bridge. Introduction by Lord Dunsany. 1942. Reprint, Dublin: Town House, 1996.

Biography and Criticism

Bowen, Zack. *Mary Lavin*. Lewisburg, Pa.: Bucknell University Press, 1975.

Chauvire, Roger. "The Art of Mary Lavin." *The Bell* 11:600–609.

Dunleavy, Janet E. "The Fiction of Mary Lavin: Universal Sensibility in a Particular Milieu." *Irish University Review* 7:222:36.

———. "The Making of Mary Lavin's *A Memory*." *Éire-Ireland* 12:90–99.

Faucet, Eileen. *Studies in the Fiction of Jennifer Johnston and Mary Lavin*. Fort Lauderdale, Fla.: Working Papers in Irish Studies, 1998.

Harmon, Maurice. "The Landscape of Mary Lavin." *Ireland of the Welcomes* 18:34–37.

Kelly, A. A. *Mary Lavin: Quiet Rebel: A Study of Her Short Stories.* Dublin: Wolfhound
  Press Press, 1980.

Kiely, Benedict. "Green Island, Red South." *Kilkenny Magazine,* 18:18–39.

Levenson, Leah. *Four Seasons of Mary Lavin.* Dublin: Marino Books, 1998.

Martin, Augustine. "A Skeleton Key to the Stories of Mary Lavin." *Studies*
  52:393–406.

Meszaros, Patricia K. "Woman as Artist: The Fiction of Mary Lavin." *Critique: Studies
  in Modern Fiction* 24:39–54.

Murphy, Catherine A. "The Ironic Vision of Mary Lavin." *Mosaic* 12:69–79.

O'Connor, Frank. "The Girl at the Gaol Gate." *A Review of English Literature*
  1:25–33.

Peterson, Richard F. *Mary Lavin.* Boston: Twayne Publisher, 1978.

Reynolds, Lorna. "Mary Lavin: An Appreciation." *Hibernia* 34:14.

Contemporary Poets in Irish and English

Máirtín Ó Direáin (1910–1988)

The most prolific poet writing in the Irish language in the last century was Máirtín Ó Direáin, whose first book of lyrics, *Coinnle Geala* (1942), played a pioneering role in the development of Modern Irish poetry. His autobiographical *Feamainn Bhealtaine* (1961) describes his boyhood on Aran, a life he abandoned at eighteen when he went to work in Galway.

While Ó Direáin spent his entire adult life away from Aran, it is a major theme in his poetry. "Honesty" speaks not only to the integrity of landscape, but also to that intensity of feeling that is essential to lyric poetry. "The Dignity of Sorrow" reveals the depth of his feeling about exile; however, it is borne with the stoicism one finds in other Aran Islands literature: Synge's "Riders to the Sea" and O'Flaherty's "Going into Exile," for example. The poem illustrates the association of emigration with death that was so common in the Irish countryside, where the ritual of departure parodied the ritual of death. An emigrant from Aran, he observed with sadness, sometimes even with bitterness, the changes in traditional life.

Honesty

A great poet once said
an island and a woman's love
are the matter and reason for my poems,
It is truth you speak, my brother.

I'll keep the island — *Aran*
another while in my poem
because of the integrity
that is in stone, rock and strand.

trans. Maureen Murphy

The Dignity Of Sorrow

Once I was shown
The great dignity of sorrow
On seeing two women
Walk out from the crowd.
In their clothes of mourning
Not speaking a word,
Dignity went with them
In the murmur of the crowd.

There was a tender at quayside
From the liner in the bay,
And everyone was busy
With noise and loud talk,
But two there were quiet,
Who walked out by themselves;
In their clothes of mourning,
Dignity went with them.

> *trans. Maureen Murphy*

Memories

Their memory lives in my mind
White flannel and bright shirts
Blue shirts and grey vests
Trousers' tweed of homespun frieze
Worn by men of venerable age
On Sunday morning going to mass
Travelling the long way by foot
That in my youth inspired thoughts
Of purity, freshness—
Always of blessedness.

Their memory lives in my mind
Long Sunday skirts of crimson hue
Blue skirts dyed with indigo
Heavy handsome Galway shawls

On comely women, tidy, trim
Going to mass as they've always done
And though they're going out of fashion
Their memory lives in my mind
It will live there surely—
Till I'm in the ground.

    trans. Maureen Murphy

Further Readings on Máirtín Ó Direáin

Bibliography

Prút, Liam. "Saothar le Máirtín Ó Direáin," *Máirtín Ó Direáin. File Tréadúil*. Maigh Nuad: An Sagart Maigh Nuad, 1982, 119–21.

Selected Works

Dánta 1939–1979. Baile Átha Cliath: Clóchomhar, 1980.
Feamainn Bhealtaine. Baile Átha Cliath: An Clóchomhar, 1961.
Four Poems. Translated by Timothy Engelland. Deerfield, Mass.: Deerfield Press, 1980.
Máirtín Ó Direáin: Dánta 1939–1979. Dublin: Clóchomhar, 1980.
Ó Mórna, agus Dánta Eile. Dublin: Cló Morainn, 1957.
Selected Poems: Tacar Dánta. Translated by Tomás mac Síomóin and Douglas Sealy. Newbridge, County Kildare: Goldsmith Press, 1984.

Biography and Criticism

MacConghail, Muiris. "Ré Dhearóil Mháirtín Uí Dhireáin." *Feasta* 19:13–20.
Murphy, Maureen. "Elegy for Aran: The Poetry of Máirtín Ó Direáin." In *Contemporary Irish Writing*, ed. James D. Brophy and Raymond J. Porter, 143–56. Boston: Iona College Press, 1983.
Ní Riain, Isobel. *Carraig agus Cathair: Ó Direáin*. Dublin: Cois Life Teo, 2002.
O'Brien, Frank. *Filíocht Ghaeilge na Linne Seo*. Baile Átha Cliath: An Clóchomhar, 1968.
Ó hUanacháin, Mícheál. "Máirtin O'Direáin." In *The Pleasure of Gaelic Poetry*, ed. Sean MacRéamoinn, 145–60. London: Allen Lane, 1982.
Prút, Liam. *Máirtín Ó Direáin. File Treadúil*. Maynooth, Ireland: An Sagart Maigh Nuad, 1982.
Sewell, Frank. *Modern Irish Poetry: A New Alhambra*. Oxford: Oxford University Press, 2000.

Seán Ó Ríordáin (1916–1977)

Uncertainty was Ó Ríordáin's life. He left the West Cork Gaeltacht of Baile Bhúirne (Ballyvorney) where he had been born upon the death of his Irish-speaking father in 1926. His family settled outside Cork city, where he was educated and where he worked as a local government clerk from 1937 to 1965. He spent seven of the thirteen years between 1938 and 1951 in a tuberculosis sanatorium, and for the rest of his life he was haunted by the specter of that dread illness. Another blow was the death of his mother in 1945, an experience he nevertheless turned into his first important poem, "Adhlacadh mo Mháthar" (My Mother's Burying).

Ó Ríordáin spent his last years teaching at University College, Cork, and writing a weekly column for *The Irish Times*. An honorary degree from the National University of Ireland formally recognized his influence as a shaping force in modern Irish poetry. His diary, sections of which have been published posthumously, may well provide a similar direction for Irish prose.

This selection of poems offers a contrast between the happiness and innocence of "Cúl an Tí" (The Back of the House), a poem which may recall the early years in Baile Bhúirne, and the loneliness and death of "Reo" (Frozen) and "Adhlacadh mo Mháthar" (My Mother's Burying).

The Back of the House

At the back of the house is the Land of Youth,
a beautiful, untidy land,
where four-footed folk wend their way,
without shoes or shirt,
without English or Irish.

But a cloak grows on every back
in this untidy land,
and a language is spoken at the back of the house,
that no man knew but Aesop,
and he is in the clay now.

There are hens there and a clutch of chickens,
and a sluggish unsophisticated duck
and a great black dog like a foe in the land,

snarling at everybody,
and a cat milking the sun.

At the western corner is a bank of refuse,
containing the wonders of the world,
a chandelier, buckles, an old straw hat,
a trumpet dumb but elegant,
and a white goose-like kettle.

It is hither the tinkers come,
saintly and untidy,
they are germane to the back of the house,
and they are accustomed to beg
at the back of every house in Ireland.

I would wish to be at the back of the house,
when it is dark and late,
that I might see on a moonlight visit
the tiny professor Aesop,
that scholarly fairy.
        trans. Seán Ó Ríordáin

Frozen

On a frosty morning I went out
And a handkerchief faced me on a bush,
I reached to put it in my pocket
But it slid from me for it was frozen.
No living cloth jumped from my grasp
But a thing that died last night on a bush
And I went searching in my mind
Till I found the occasion's equivalent—
The day I kissed a woman of my kindred
And she in the coffin, frozen, stretched.
        trans. Valentin Iremonger

My Mother's Burying

A June sun in an orchard.
    A rustle in the silk of afternoon,
The droning of an ill-natured bee
    Loudly ripping the film of evening.

Reading an old dog-eared letter,
    with every tearful word I drank in
A raging pain stabbed my side.
    Every word forced out its own tear.

I remembered the hand that did the writing
    A hand as familiar as a face,
A hand that dispersed kindness like an old Bible,
    A hand that was like the balsam and you ill.

And June toppled backwards into Winter.
    The orchard became a white graveyard by a river.
In the midst of the dumb whiteness all around me,
    The dark hole screamed loudly in the snow.

The white of a young girl the day of her First Communion,
    The white of the holy water Sunday on the altar,
The white of milk slowly issuing from the breasts:
    When they buried my mother—the white of the sward.

My mind was screwing itself endeavouring
    To comprehend the interment to the full
When through the white tranquility gently flew
    A robin, unconfused and unafraid,

It waited over the grave as though it knew
    That the reason why it came was unknown to all
Save the person who was waiting in the coffin
    And I was jealous of the unusual affinity.

The air of Heaven descended on that graveside,
    A marvellous holy joy possessed the bird.

I was outside the mystery, a layman.
    The grave before me in the distance.

My debauched soul was bathed in the waters of sorrow,
    A snow of purity fell on my heart.
Now I will bury my heart so made clean
    The memory of the woman who carried me three seasons in her
        womb.

The gravediggers came with the rough noises of shovels
    And vigorously swept the clay into the grave.
I looked the other way, a man was brushing his knees.
    I looked at the priest, in his face was worldliness.

A June sun in an orchard,
    A rustle in the silk of afternoon.
The droning of an ill-natured bee
    Loudly ripping the film of evening.

Lame little verses being written by me.
    I would like to catch a robin's tail.
I would like to rout the spirit of those knee-brushers.
    I would like to journey sorrowfully to the day's end.
    trans. Valentin Iremonger

Further Readings on Seán Ó Ríordáin

Bibliography

Ó Coileáin, Seán, *Seán Ó Ríordáin. Beatha agus Saothar.* Dublin: An Clóchomhar, 1982.

Selected Works

Brosna. Dublin: Sáirséal agus Dill, 1964.
Eireball Spideoige. Dublin: Sáirséal agus Dill, 1952.
Línte Liombó. Dublin: Sáirséal agus Dill, 1971.
Scáthán Véarsai: Rogha Dáta le Seán Ríordáin. Dublin: Sáirséal agus Ó Marcaigh, 1985.
Tar éis mo Bháis. Dublin: Sáirséal agus Dill, 1978.

Biography and Criticism

MacCana, Proinseas. *Literature in Irish.* Dublin: Department of Foreign Affairs, 1980, 60–61.

O'Brien, Frank. *Filíocht Ghaeilge na Linne Seo.* Dublin: An Clóchomhar, 1968, 301–35.

Ó Dúshláine, Tadhg. *Paidir File.* Indreabhán, Ireland: Cló Iar-Chonnachta, 1993.

Ó Tuama, Seán. "Seán Ó Ríordáin." In *Filí faoi Screimhle.* Dublin: Oifig an tSolathair, 1978, 1–80.

———. "Seán Ó Ríordáin." In *The Pleasures of Gaelic Poetry,* ed. Seán MacRéamoinn. London: Allen Lane, 1982, 129–41.

Scríobh 3. Edited by Seán Ó Mordha. Dublin: An Clóchomar, 1978.

Sewell, Frank. *Modern Irish Poetry: A New Alhambra.* Oxford: Oxford University Press, 2000.

Máire Mhac an tSaoi (b. 1922)

Máire Mhac an tSaoi (pronounced Maurya WOK an Tee) was born in Dublin; however, she spent much of her childhood in Dunquin in the Kerry Gaeltacht. Her father, Seán MacEntee, was Táiste or deputy prime minister, in the de Valera and Lemass governments. After she completed her degree from University College, Dublin, Mhac an tSaoi studied in Paris, returned to the Dublin Institute for Advanced Studies for further work in Celtic Studies, trained for the Irish Bar, and finally entered the foreign service. She is married to the diplomat and journalist Conor Cruise O'Brien, who served as minister for post and telegraph during the Cosgrave government (1973–77).

A scholar as well as a poet, Mhac an tSaoi's authoritative essays and reviews provide lucid commentary on poetry in Irish from Gaelic society to the present day. *Margadh na Saoire* (Market of Bargains), a collection of poems written over the course of twenty years, has been praised for its sense of craft, its command of Munster Irish, and its erudition. Like the best examples of Early Irish lyrics, Mhac an tSaoi's poetry is spare and compressed. She frequently speaks of loss in her poems: both historical loss, which observes the passing of traditional life, and personal loss—especially lost or hopeless love, "Inquisitio 1584" probably refers to the Desmond Rising in Munster that was suppressed in 1583; the plantation of the province followed and the Irish lands were confiscated. Séamus Ennis, subject of the "Lament for Séamus Ennis," was Ireland's premier piper until his death in 1984.

Inquisitio 1584

In that year of the age of Our Lord
Fifteen hundred and eighty
Or some few short years after
Sean MacEdmund MacUlick
Hard by Shannon was hanged.

Hard by the shoals of Shannon
In Limerick, history's city,
Sean MacEdmund MacUlick
Come west from the parish of Marrhan
Who was chieftain of Balleneenig.

Treason his crime, his lands
Were given in hand of the stranger
And now around Mount Marrhan
His name is not even remembered
Nor is his kindred known there.

Undisturbed be your sleep
Sean MacEdmund MacUlick
On the banks of the mighty Shannon
When the wind blows in from the sea
From the west and from your own country.

For Sheila

I remember a room on the seaward side—
The squall caught it from the south-west—
And the rain a tattoo on the window
Unslackening since the fall of night,
And I remember that you were there, Sheila,
    Sitting low by the fire,
    The gold ring on your childlike finger.
You gave us a heartbroken song,
And your voice was the music of flutes,
Love's catalogue brought here from France—

The fairness of your head was like the meadowsweet
Under the light of the lamp set on the table. . . .

What do they matter more, little dear one, between us,
Separation of years and aversions bred of friendship?
It was my lot to know you at that time.

Finit

By chance I learned from them the marriage-contract
And wondered at this check on the wind's lightness;
You were so unpredictable, spontaneous,
Untamed like it, and lonely, I remember.

Know now the lot of all is yours henceforward,
Hardship and commonplace each following season,
Slipping from memory as turns the quarter—
We doubt you or your like ever existed.

But that there will be tunes I'll not hear ever
Without your being again there in the corner,
Waiting, "music" to hand, before the dancing,
Your eyes the mystery of the night outside.

Lament for Séamus Ennis,
Late Champion Piper of Ireland (Slow Air)

Shee-people wheening, wintry their wail;
Fairy wives keening near and away
West to the dune's edge:
Donn,* spread the tale.

Make the drum's roar a flail—
    Lay on great strokes,
Redoubling each in train,
    Hammers of woe;

* "Donn of the dune" was the Old Irish god of death.

This prince, the music waned,
    Seeks his clay home.

Wizards of liss and fort, hosts of the air,
Panicked and routed go, each from his lair;
Boyne's* airy pleasure-dome, rainstorm lays bare.

Desert and harpless,
    Tara is grass;
Yet we had argued
    Even such pass
No mortal harm meant—
    No more, alas!

White flowers of repentance the barren staff knew;
The pillar-stones danced to hear Orpheus' tunes;
But, King-piper of Ireland, voice is withheld from you—Ever!
    trans. and elaborated by Máire Mhac an tSaoi
    from a first draft by Canon Coslett Quinn

Further Readings on Máire Mhac an tSaoi

Selected Works: Poetry

Codhladh an Ghaiscígh. Dublin: Sáirséal agus Dill, 1973.
An Galar Dubhach. Dublin: Sáirséal agus Dill, 1980.
A Heart Full of Thought. Dublin: Dolmen Press, 1959. [Translations from the Irish.]
Margadh na Saoire. 1956. Reprint, Dublin: Sáirséal agus Dill, 1971.
Shoa agus Dánta Eile. Dublin: Sáirséal agus Ó Marcaigh, 1999.
Trasládáil: Dánta Gaeilge Roghnaithe agus Aistrithe Ag. Belfast: Lagan Press, 1997.

Selected Works: Studies

Dhá Sgéal Artúraíochta: Mar atá Eachtra Mhelóra agus Orlando agus Céilidhe Iosgaise Léithe. Dublin: Dublin Institute for Advanced Studies, 1946.
[As O'Brien, Máire Cruise]. "The Female Principle in Gaelic Poetry." *Canadian Journal of Irish Studies* 8:26–37.

---

* Prehistoric tombs on the Boyne were believed to be the palaces of the old god.

"An tOileánach." In *The Pleasures of Gaelic Literature,* ed. John Jordan, 25–38. Dublin: Mercier Press, 1977.

"The Role of the Poet in Gaelic Society." In *The Celtic Consciousness,* ed. Robert O'Driscoll, 63–201. New York: Braziller, 1982.

Biography and Criticism

Davitt, Michael. "Comhrá le Máire Mhac an tSaoi," *Innti* 8:38–59.

O'Brien, Frank. *Filíocht Ghaeilge na Línne Seo,* 163–201. Dublin: An Clochomhar, 1968.

Thomas Kinsella (b. 1928)

able to write modernist in a manner w/o losing his identity

A major Irish poet since the publication of *Another September* (1958), Thomas Kinsella is at once the most serious and the most experimental of the contemporary Irish poets. His lyrical, formally structured early work, with its debt to such modern poets as Auden, contrasts with the dense, difficult style of his later poetry—a poetry marked by fragmentation, absorption in a private world, and a dark, brooding tone. It is a poetry that reflects the philosophy expressed in his prose preface to *Wormwood* (1966): "Maturity and peace are to be sought through ordeal after ordeal."

Born to a working-class Dublin family, Kinsella attended the Inchicore Model School and studied science at University College, Dublin, before entering the civil service in 1946 as a clerk for the Congested District Board. In 1965 he resigned from his post as a senior officer in the Department of Finance to teach in America—first at Southern Illinois University and later at Temple University, where he directed their spring program in Dublin. Long associated with the Dolmen Press, Kinsella now has his own publishing company, called Peppercanister Press.

Kinsella is well known for his translations from the Irish as well as for his own poetry. His highly praised *The Táin* (The Cattle Raid of Cooley, 1969) was followed in 1981 by translations for *An Duanaire* (An Irish Anthology), a collection of Modern Irish poetry edited by Seán Ó Tuama. "The Poet Egan O'Rahilly, Homesick in Old Age," Kinsella's tribute to one of the most distinguished poets in the collection, observes O'Rahilly (Aogán Ó Rathaille) the artist who nourished the spirit of his starving countrymen, the poet in a hostile landscape. "Sisters" refers to the suicide of two Irish women: Deirdre, who kills herself at the end of "The Fate of the Children of Uisnech" when Conchobar gives her to Eógan son of Durthacht; and Sybil Ferriter, who, according to tradition, killed herself after her poet husband was hanged in Killarney in 1653 for his support of the Irish cause in the 1641 rising. Another rising, the 1798 rebellion in Wicklow, provides the setting—Vinegar Hill, the Slaney—for "In the Ringwood," Kinsella's version of an Irish street ballad in which the poet's bride is transformed into "Sorrow's daughter."

In the Ringwood

[handwritten: Treatment of poisoned romance]

As I roved out impatiently
Good Friday with my bride
To drink in the rivered Ringwood
The draughty season's pride
A fell dismay held suddenly
Our feet on the green hill-side.

The yellow Spring on Vinegar Hill,
The smile of Slaney water,
The wind that swept the Ringwood,
Grew dark with ancient slaughter.
My love cried out and I beheld her
Change to Sorrow's daughter.

[handwritten marginalia: overlooks the Slaney river in Co. Wexford - The scene of one of the more savage episodes in Ireland's past when insurrectionaries of 1798 were butchered by British soldiers. The blood in the air becomes assoc. in the poet's mind with the passion of Christ and the mortality of human love.]

"Ravenhair, what rending
Set those red lips a-shriek,
And dealt those locks in black lament
Like blows on your white cheek,
That in your looks outlandishly
Both woe and fury speak?"

As sharp a lance as the fatal heron
There on the sunken tree
Will strike in the stones of the river
Was the gaze she bent on me,
O her robe into her right hand
She gathered grievously.

"Many times the civil lover
Climbed that pleasant place,
Many times despairing
Died in his love's face,

His spittle turned to vinegar,
Blood in his embrace.

"Love that is every miracle
Is torn apart and rent.
The human turns awry
The poles of the firmament.
The fish's bright side is pierced
And good again is spent.

"Though every stem on Vinegar Hill
And stone on the Slaney's bed
And every leaf in the living Ringwood
Builds till it is dead
Yet heart and hand, accomplished,
Destroy until they dread.

"Dread, a grey devourer,
Stalks in the shade of love.
The dark that dogs our feet
Eats what is sickened of.
The End that stalks Beginning
Hurries home its drove."

I kissed three times her shivering lips.
I drank their naked chill.
I watched the river shining
Where the heron wiped his bill.
I took my love in my icy arms
In the Spring on Ringwood Hill.

Handclasp at Euston

The engine screams and Murphy, isolate
—Chalk-white, comedian—in the smoky glare,
Dwindles among the churns and tenders. Weight,
Person, race, the human, dwindle there.
I bow to the cases cluttering the rack,
Their handles black with sweat of exile. Wales,

Wave and home; I close my eyes. The track
Swerves to a greener world: sea-rock, thigh-scales.

Sisters

Grim Deirdre sought the stony fist, her grief
Capped at last by insult, Pierce's bride,
Sybil Ferriter, fluttered like a leaf
And fell in courtly love to stain the tide.
Each for a murdered husband—hanged in silk
Or speared in harness—threw her body wide,
And offered treachery a bloody milk;
Each cast the other's shadow when she died.

The Poet Egan O'Rahilly, Homesick in Old Age

He climbed to his feet in the cold light, and began
The decrepit progress again, blown along the cliff road,
Bent with curses above the shrew his stomach.

The salt abyss poured through him, more raw
with every laboured, stony crash of the waves:
His teeth bared at their voices, that incessant dying.

Iris leaves bent on the ditch, unbent,
Shivering in the wind: leaf-like spirits
Chattered at his death-mark as he passed.

He pressed red eyelids; aliens crawled
Breaking princely houses in their jaws;
Their metal faces reared up, chewing at light.

"Princes overseas, who slipped away
In your extremity, no matter where I travel
I find your great houses like stopped hearts.

"Likewise your starving children—though I nourish
Their spirit, and my own, on the lists of praises
I make for you still in the cooling den of my craft.

"Our enemies multiply. They have recruited the sea:
Last night, the West's rhythmless waves destroyed my sleep;
This morning, winkle and dogfish persisting in the stomach . . ."

Further Readings on Thomas Kinsella

Bibliography

Woodbridge, Hensley C. "Thomas Kinsella. A Bibliography." *Éire-Ireland* 2, no. 2 (Summer 1967): 122–33.

Selected Works

Another September. Dublin: Dolmen Press, 1958.
Citizen of the World. Dublin: Dedalus, 2000.
Collected Poems, 1956–1994. Oxford: Oxford University Press, 1996.
Collected Poems, 1956–2001. Manchester: Carcanet, 2001.
Downstream. Dublin: Dolmen Press: 1962.
The Dual Tradition: An Essay on Poetry and Politics in Ireland. Manchester: Carcanet, 1995.
Fifteen Dead. Dublin: Dolmen Press: 1979.
Godhead. Manchester: Carcanet, 1999.
Her Vertical Smile. Dublin: Peppercanister Press, 1985.
New Poems. 1973. Dublin: Dolmen Press, 1973.
Nightwalker and Other Poems. New York: Alfred Knopf, 1968.
Peppercanister Poems, 1972–1978. Winston-Salem, N.C.: Wake Forest University Press, 1979.
Poems, 1956–1973. Winston-Salem, N.C.: Wake Forest University Press, 1979.
Poems and Translations. New York: Atheneum, 1961.
Poems from Centre City. Dublin: Dedalus Press, 1990.
Songs of the Psyche. Dublin: Peppercanister Press, 1985.

Translations

An Duanaire, An Irish Anthology 1600–1900: Poems of the Dispossessed. edited by Seán Ó Tuama. Philadelphia: University of Pennsylvania Press, 1981.
The Táin. Illustrated by Louis le Brocquy. 1969. Reprint, Philadelphia: University of Pennsylvania Press, 2002.

Biography and Criticism

Abbate Badin, Donatella. *Thomas Kinsella*. New York: Twayne: 1996.

Bendient, Calvin. "Thomas Kinsella." In *Eight Contemporary Poets,* 119–38. London: Oxford University Press, 1974.

Garratt, Robert F. "Fragilities and Structures: Poetic Strategy in Thomas Kinsella's 'NightWalker' and 'Phoenix Park.'" *Irish University Review* 13, no. 1 (1983): 88–102.

Harmon, Maurice. *The Poetry of Thomas Kinsella*. Dublin: Wolfhound Press, 1974.

———. "The Poetry of Thomas Kinsella (1972–1983)." *Studies* 72:57–66.

Jackson, Thomas H. *The Whole Matter: The Poetic Evolution of Thomas Kinsella*. Dublin: Lilliput, 1995.

John, Brian. *Reading the Ground: The Poetry of Thomas Kinsella*. Washington: Catholic University Press, 1996.

Johnston, Dillon. *Irish Poetry after Joyce*. Mountrath: Dolmen Press, 1985.

Longley, Edna. "Searching the Darkness: Richard Murphy, Thomas Kinsella, John Montague and James Simmons." In *Two Decades of Irish Writing: A Critical Survey,* edited by Douglas Dunn, 118–53. Cheadle, Cheshire: Carcanet Press, 1975.

O'Hara, Daniel. "An Interview with Thomas Kinsella." *Contemporary Poetry: A Journal of Criticism* 4:1–18.

"Poetry Since Yeats: An Exchange of Views—Stephen Spender, Patrick Kavanagh, Thomas Kinsella, W. D. Snodgrass." *Tri-Quarterly* 4:100–111.

The Southern Review. A Special Issue: Contemporary Irish Poetry and Criticism. 31, no. 3 (Summer 1995).

Turbridy, Derval. *Thomas Kinsella: The Peppercanister Poems*. Dublin: University College Dublin Press, 2000.

John Montague (b. 1929)

John Montague was born in Brooklyn, New York, but he was raised in Garvaghey (Irish *garbh acaidh,* "rough field,' pronounced GAREV-ah-he), County Tyrone, by a pair of maiden aunts. After taking his degree at University College, Dublin, he became a journalist before devoting himself to writing and teaching. He is a member of the English faculty at University College, Cork; however, he is equally at home at colleges and universities in France and in the United States.

Montague has been concerned from his first collection, *Poisoned Lands* (1961), with Ireland past and present—or, as Montague puts it, "Ireland's past in present"; his poem "Like Dolmens Round my Childhood the Old People" explores the mythic qualities of those who represent a vanishing rural Ireland to him. Many of Montague's early poems have been incorporated into his long poem, *The Rough Field*

(1972, rev. ed.), an ambitious meditation on Ulster history that combines archaeology, biography, history, literature, and mythology in a format that includes documents, letters, religious tracts, riddles, rhymes, and reproductions of old woodcuts. "The Flight of the Earls" links the loss of Ulster's Gaelic language and culture with the dispossession and exile of the O'Neills, one of the great Northern families. Finally, "A Grafted Tongue," a poem about the imposition of English on the Irish-speaking countryside, recalls Montague's own humiliation as a stammering child.

Have students take stanza — read aloud

Like Dolmens Round My Childhood, the Old People

Like dolmens round my childhood, the old people.

(explores mythic quality of those who repres a vanishing rural Ireland,

Montague here is sketching out a mythic, prehistoric hinterland

I

Jamie MacCrystal sang to himself,
A broken song without tune, without words;
He tipped me a penny every pension day,   *Dan*
Fed kindly crusts to winter birds,
When he died, his cottage was robbed,
Mattress and money box torn and searched,
Only the corpse they didn't disturb.

Old people are brought into line with the megalith makers,

II

Maggie Owens was surrounded by animals,
A mongrel bitch and shivering pups,
Even in her bedroom a she-goat cried.
She was a well of gossip defiled,   *Tracy*
Fanged chronicler of a whole countryside;
Reputed a witch, all I could find
Was her ravening need to deride.

Alienated from the region of his childhood, he would . repossess it . imaginatively

III

The Nialls lived along a mountain lane
Where heather bells bloomed, clumps of foxglove.
All were blind, with Blind Pension and Wireless,   *Alexa*
Dead eyes serpent-flicked as one entered
To shelter from a downpour of mountain rain.

Crickets chirped under the rocking hearthstone
Until the muddy sun shone out again.

IV

Mary Moore lived in a crumbling gatehouse,
Famous as Pisa for its leaning gable.
Bag apron and boots, she tramped the fields
Driving lean cattle from a miry stable.
A by-word for fierceness, she fell asleep
Over love stories, Red Star and Red Circle,
Dreamed of gypsy love rites, by firelight sealed.

V

Wild Billy Harbison married a Catholic servant girl
When all his Loyal family passed on:
We danced round him shouting "To Hell with King Billy,"
And dodged from the arc of his flailing blackthorn.
Forsaken by both creeds, he showed little concern
Until the Orange drums banged past in the summer
And bowler and sash aggressively shone.

VI

Curate and doctor trudged to attend them,
Through knee-deep snow, through summer heat,
From main road to lane to broken path,
Gulping the mountain air with painful breath.
Sometimes they were found by neighbours,
Silent keepers of a smokeless hearth,
Suddenly cast in the mould of death.

VII

Ancient Ireland indeed! I was reared by her bedside,
The rune and the chant, evil eye and averted head,
Formorian fierceness of family and local feud.

Gaunt figures of fear and of friendliness,
For years they trespassed on my dreams,
Until once, in a standing circle of stones,
I felt their shadows pass

Into that dark permanence of ancient forms.

A Grafted Tongue (Group)

Harks back to poets own childhood... imposing English on Irish-speaking countryside

    (Dumb,
bloodied, the severed
head now chokes to
speak another tongue:—

    As in
a long suppressed dream,
some stuttering garb-
led ordeal of my own)

    An Irish
child weeps at school
repeating its English.
After each mistake

autobiographical

    The master
gouges another mark
on the tally stick
hung about its neck

Intermittent rhyme

    Like a bell
on a cow, a hobble
on a straying goat.
To slur and stumble

simile

    In shame
the altered syllables
of your own name;
to stray sadly home

and find
the turf cured width
of your parent's hearth
growing slowly alien:

In cabin
and field, they still
speak the old tongue,
You may greet no one.

To grow
a second tongue, as
harsh a humiliation
as twice to be born.

Decades later
that child's grandchild's
speech stumbles over lost
syllables of an old order.

The Flight of the Earls

The fiddler settles in
to his playing so easily:
rosewood box tucked under
      chin,
saw of rosined bow
& angle of elbow
that the mind elides
for a while what he plays:
hornpipe or reel to warm
us up well, heel or toecap
twitching in tune

till the sound expands
in the slow climb of a lament.
As by some forest campfire
listeners draw near, to honour
a communal loss

This was a distinguished crew for one
ship; for it is indeed certain that the sea
had not supported, and the winds had
not wafted from Ireland, in modern
times, a party of one ship who would
have been more illustrious, or noble in
point of genealogy, or more renowned
for deeds, valour or high
achievements. . . .

Annals of the Four Masters

We have killed, burnt and despoiled all
along the Lough to within four miles of
Dungannon . . . in which journeys we
have killed above a hundred of all sorts,
besides such as we have burned, how

& a shattered procession
of anonymous suffering
files through the brain:
burnt houses, pillaged farms,
a province in flames.

With an intricate
& mournful mastery
the thin bow glides & slides,
assuaging like a bardic poem,
our tribal pain—

Disappearance & death
of a world, as down Lough
    Swilly
the great ship, encumbered with
    nobles,
swells its sails for Europe:
The Flight of the Earls.

many I know not. We spare none, of
what quality or sex soever, and it had
bred much terror in the people who
heard not a drum nor saw not a fire of
long time.

Chichester to Mountjoy
Spring 1701
Is uaigneach Éire

[handwritten marginal note: ref to Ulster Earls took ship Sept. 4, 1607 continent. The Earls had been the last hope of effective resistance to swelling English power.]

Further Readings on John Montague

Selected Works

About Love: Poems. Riverdale-on-Hudson, N.Y.: Sheep Meadow Press, 1993.

Bitter Harvest: An Anthology of Contemporary Irish Verse. (ed.) New York: Scribner, 1989.

Born in Brooklyn: John Montague's America. With David Lampe. Fredonia, N.Y.: White Pine Press, 1991.

A Chosen Light. Chicago: Swallow, 1967.

Collected Poems. Winston-Salem, N.C.: Wake Forest University Press, 1995.

Company: A Chosen Life. London: Duckworth, 2001.

The Dead Kingdom. Winston-Salem N.C.: Wake Forest University Press, 1984.

Death of a Chieftain and Other Stories. 1957. Rev. ed., Dublin: Dolmen Press, 1977; reprint, Dublin: Wolfhound Press, 1998.

The Faber Book of Irish Verse. (ed.) London: Faber and Faber, 1974.

The Figure in the Cave, and Other Essays. With Antoinette Quinn. Dublin: Lilliput, 1989.

Forms of Exile: Poems. Dublin: Dolmen Press, 1958.

The Great Cloak. Dublin: Dolmen Press, 1978.

A Love Present and Other Stories. Dublin: Wolfhound Press, 1997.

Mount Eagle. Winston-Salem, N.C.: Wake Forest University Press, 1989.

New Selected Poems. Oldcastle, Ireland: Gallery Press, 1989.

Patriotic Suite. Dublin: Dolmen Press, 1966.

Poisoned Lands and Other Poems. 1961. New. ed., London: Oxford University Press, 1977.

The Rough Field, 1961–1971. 1972. 5th ed., Oldcastle, Ireland: Gallery Press, 1989.

Selected Poems. Winston-Salem, N.C.: Wake Forest University Press, 1982.

Selected Poems. London: Penguin, 2001.

A Slow Dance. London: Oxford University Press, 1975.

Smashing the Piano. Oldcastle: Gallery Press, 1999.

Time in Armagh. Oldcastle: Gallery Press, 1993.

Biography and Criticism

Frazier, Adrian. "Pilgrim Haunts: Montague's *The Dead Kingdom* and Heaney's *Station Island.*" *Éire-Ireland* 20:134–43.

Johnston, Dillon, *Irish Poetry after Yeats.* Mountrath, Ireland: Dolmen Press, 1985.

Kersnowski, Frank. *John Montague.* Lewisburg, Pa.: Bucknell University Press, 1975.

The Southern Review. A Special Issue: Contemporary Irish Poetry and Criticism. 31, no. 3 (Summer 1995).

Welch, Robert. *The Structure of Process: John Montague's Poetry.* Coleraine, Northern Ireland: Cranagh Press, 1999.

Seamus Heaney (b. 1939)

[handwritten: roots, digging, burial + recovery are recurring metaphors in his early work.]

With the winning of the Nobel Prize for Literature in 1995, Seamus Heaney went from being an admired Irish poet to being the most esteemed living poet writing in English. During the 1990s, he divided the academic year between two honorary positions, one at Oxford University, the other at Harvard University. Still soft-spoken with modest country manners, Heaney is a beloved public figure in Ireland. His image graces the walls of Shannon Airport, a welcome to visitors. In 1997 he had to refuse a popular appeal that he be made president of the Republic of Ireland, a largely ceremonial position.

Heaney was born on a farm in Mossbawn, County Derry, a place he has described as "fifty acres between bog and big house." He was educated at St. Columb's College in Derry, Queen's University, Belfast, and at St. Joseph's College of Education. A popular lecturer and gifted teacher, Heaney taught in secondary school and at colleges and universities in both Ireland and America before accepting the Boylston Chair at Harvard University in 1981.

Heaney's poems about his childhood, among them "Digging" and "Mossbawn: Two Poems in Dedication," pay careful attention to folkways, describing traditional skills and naming the tools for cutting turf, smithing, bread-making, and preparing seed. In the concluding stanza of "Digging," Heaney addresses his own trade with the same sense of craftsmanship and in doing so reconciles the distance that education and his own vocation have interposed between his rural roots and himself.

Heaney's major poetic theme has been history. As he said in a 1972 *Irish Times* interview: "I have been writing poems out of history. It is the hump we live off. I have my tap root in personal and racial memory. The Famine, the '98 Rebellion, things like that have surfaced in my imagination and they are a living language here." One aspect of history as language—the relationship between Irish and English—is the subject of "Traditions."

Many of the poems in *North* (1975) are informed by Heaney's interest in the perfectly preserved bodies of ancient people found in the bogs of northern Denmark. The collection expands on the concept of the bog as the "memory of landscape" that he explored in "Bogland" (*Death of a Naturalist,* 1966). In "Punishment," the body of a young woman hanged in Jutland for adultery inspires a meditation on tribal justice: the poet sees its modern counterpart in the shaved and tarred heads of the young women in Northern Ireland humiliated for fraternizing with British soldiers. In "Exposure," the last poem in *North,* Heaney broods about living away from his troubled native province. *Station Island* (1985) marked a new development: a long poem on the penitential pilgrimage to Lough Derg, County Donegal, that is much favored by Northern Catholics. Like Dante, the poet meets the dead: family, friends, and such literary forebears as Carleton, Kavanagh, and Joyce.

Some of Heaney's most affecting poetry is personal. His "A Brigid's Girdle" is addressed to Adele Dalsimer (1939–2000), an American academic who had just been diagnosed with cancer.

Digging

Between my finger and my thumb
The squat pen rests; snug as a gun.

Under my window, a clean rasping sound
When the spade sinks into gravelly ground:
My father, digging. I look down

Till his straining rump among the flowerbeds
Bends low, comes up twenty years away

Stooping in rhythm through potato drills
Where he was digging.

The coarse boot nestled on the lug, the shaft
Against the inside knee was levered firmly.
He rooted out tall tops, buried the bright edge deep
To scatter new potatoes that we picked
Loving their cool hardness in our hands.

By God, the old man could handle a spade.
Just like his old man.

My grandfather cut more turf in a day
Than any other man on Toner's bog.
Once I carried him milk in a bottle
Corked sloppily with paper. He straightened up
To drink it, then fell to right away

Nicking and slicing neatly, heaving sods
Over his shoulder, going down and down
For the good turf. Digging.

The cold smell of potato mould, the squelch and slap
Of soggy peat, the curt cuts of an edge
Through living roots awaken in my head.
But I've no spade to follow men like them.

Between my finger and my thumb
The squat pen rests.
I'll dig with it.

Traditions

for Tom Flanagan

I

Our guttural muse
was bulled long ago

by the alliterative tradition,
her uvula grows

[handwritten annotation: fleshy mass of tissue suspended from center of soft palate back of tongue]

vestigial, forgotten
like the coccyx
or a Brigid's Cross
yellowing in some outhouse

while custom, that "most
sovereign mistress,"
beds us down into *[handwritten: irony]*
the British isles.

II

we are to be proud
of our Elizabethan English:
"varsity," for example,
is grass-roots stuff with us;

we "deem" or we "allow"
when we suppose
and some cherished archaisms
are correct Shakespearean.

Not to speak of the furled
consonants of lowlanders
shuttling obstinately
between bawn and mossland.

III

MacMorris, gallivanting
round the Globe, whinged
to courtier and groundling
who had heard tell of us

as going very bare
of learning, as wild hares,

as anatomies of death:
"What ish my nation?"

And sensibly, though so much
later, the wandering Bloom
replied, "Ireland," said Bloom,
"I was born here. Ireland."

[handwritten: Leopold Bloom Protagonist of Ulysses]

Mossbawn: Two Poems in Dedication

[handwritten: region where he grew up]

for Mary Heaney

[handwritten: Heaney's mother — Honors her memory with many poems]

1. SUNLIGHT

There was a sunlit absence.
The helmeted pump in the yard
heated its iron,
water honeyed

[handwritten: Throughout his work memory is a Trigger + release.]

in the slung bucket
and the sun stood
like a griddle cooling
against the wall

of each long afternoon.
So, her hands scuffled
over the bakeboard,
the reddening stove

sent its plaque of heat
against her where she stood
in a floury apron
by the window.

Now she dusts the board
with a goose's wing,
now sits, broad-lapped,
with whitened nails

and measling shins:
here is a space
again, the scone rising
to the tick of two clocks.

And here is love   *Lovely final*
like a tinsmith's scoop   *simile*
sunk past its gleam
in the meal-bin.

2. THE SEED CUTTERS

They seem hundreds of years away. <u>Breughel,</u>   *Flemish painter*
You'll know them if I can get them true.   *famous for*
They kneel under the hedge in a half-circle   *portraits of*
Behind a windbreak wind is breaking through.   *peasant*
They are the seed cutters. <u>The tuck and frill</u>   *folk*
<u>Of leaf-sprout is on the seed potatoes</u>   *culture*
Buried under that straw. With time to kill
They are taking their time. Each sharp knife goes
Lazily halving each root that falls apart
In the palm of the hand: a milky gleam,
And, at the centre, a dark watermark.
O calendar customs! Under the broom
Yellowing over them, <u>compose the frieze</u>   *Poet becomes*
With all of us there, our anonymities.   *part of the scene*

Act of Union

I

Tonight, a first movement, a pulse,
As if the rain in bogland gathered head
To slip and flood: a bog-burst,
A gash breaking open the ferny bed.
Your back is a firm line of eastern coast
And arms and legs are thrown
Beyond your gradual hills. I caress

The heaving province where our past has grown.
I am the tall kingdom over your shoulder
That you would neither cajole nor ignore.
Conquest is a lie. I grow older
Conceding your half-independent shore
Within whose borders now my legacy
Culminates inexorably.

II

And I am still imperially
Male, leaving you with the pain,
The rending process in the colony,
The battering ram, the boom burst from within.
The act sprouted an obstinate fifth column
Whose stance is growing unilateral.
His heart beneath your heart is a wardrum
Mustering force. His parasitical   *England*
And ignorant little fists already
Beat at your borders and I know they're cocked
At me across the water. No treaty
I foresee will salve completely your tracked   *addressee*
And stretchmarked body, the big pain   *Ireland*
That leaves you raw, like opened ground, again.

Exposure

It is December in Wicklow:
Alders dripping, birches   *Broods about*
Inheriting the last light,   *living away from*
The ash tree cold to look at.   *his troubled*
                                     Province native
A comet that was lost
Should be visible at sunset,
Those million tons of light
Like a glimmer of haws and rose-hips,

And I sometimes see a falling star.
If I could come on meteorite!

Instead I walk through damp leaves,
Husks, the spent flukes of autumn,

Imagining a hero
On some muddy compound,
His gift like a slingstone
Whirled for the desperate.

How did I end up like this?
I often think of my friends'
Beautiful prismatic counselling
And the anvil brains of some who hate me

As I sit weighing and weighing
My responsible *tristia*.
For what? For the ear? For the people?
For what is said behind-backs?

Rain comes down through the alders,
Its low conducive voices
Mutter about let-downs and erosions
And yet each drop recalls

The diamond absolutes.
I am neither internee nor informer;
An inner émigré, grown long-haired
And thoughtful; a wood-kerne

Escaped from the massacre,
Taking protective colouring
From bole and bark, feeling
Every wind that blows;

Who, blowing up these sparks
For their meagre heat, have missed
The once-in-a-lifetime portent,
The comet's pulsing rose.

> Final image
Prophecy of the
comet

[handwritten: Group]

Punishment

[handwritten: Ryan's Daughter theme]

[handwritten: Body preserved in ancient bog]

I can feel the tug
of the halter at the nape
of her neck, the wind
on her naked front.

[handwritten: Ritualized murder of young woman accused of adultery (violence of clan life)]

It blows her nipples
to amber beads,
it shakes the frail rigging
of her ribs.

I can see her drowned
body in the bog,
the weighing stone,
the floating rods and boughs.

Under which at first
she was a barked sapling
that is dug up
oak-bone, brain-firkin:

her shaved head
like a stubble of black corn,
her blindfold a soiled bandage,
her noose a ring

[handwritten: Relates plight of woman here (adulteress) to that of a woman in N. Ireland humiliated (sometimes tarred + feathered) for fraternizing with British soldiers]

to store
the memories of love.
Little adulteress,
before they punished you

you were flaxen-haired,
undernourished, and your
tar-black face was beautiful.
My poor scapegoat,

I almost love you
but would have cast, I know,

[handwritten: would have expected followed of the custom of the community]

the stones of silence.
I am the artful voyeur

of your brain's exposed
and darkened combs,
your muscles' webbing
and all your numbered bones:

I who have stood dumb
when your betraying sisters,
cauled in tar, —→ *recent history*
wept by the railings,

who would connive
in civilized outrage
yet understand the exact
and tribal, intimate revenge.

From Station Island

XII [JAMES JOYCE]

Like a convalescent, I took the hand
stretched down from the jetty, sensed again
an alien comfort as I stepped on ground

Journey like Dante's
Pilgrimage to Lough
Derg, Co. Donegal

to find the helping hand still gripping mine,   *like Virgil*
fish-cold and bony, but whether to guide
or to be guided I could not be certain

for the tall man in step at my side
seemed blind, though he walked straight as a rush
upon his ashplant, his eyes fixed straight ahead.

Then I knew him in the flesh
out there on the tarmac among the cars,
wintered hard and sharp as a blackthorn bush.

His voice eddying with the vowels of all rivers
came back to me, though he did not speak yet,
a voice like a prosecutor's or a singer's,

cunning, narcotic, mimic, definite
as a steel nib's downstroke, quick and clean,
and suddenly he hit a litter basket

with his stick, saying, 'Your obligation
is not discharged by any common rite.
What you do you must do on your own.

The main thing is to write
for the joy of it. Cultivate a work-lust
that imagines its haven like your hands at night

[handwritten: Joyce's words to advise the Pilgrim]

dreaming the sun in the sunspot of a breast.
You are fasted now, light-headed, dangerous.
Take off from here. And don't be so earnest,

so ready for the sackcloth and the ashes.
Let go, let fly, forget.
You've listened long enough. Now strike your note.'

It was as if I had stepped free into space
alone with nothing that I had not known
already. Raindrops blew in my face

as I came to and heard the harangue and jeers
going on and on. 'The English language
belongs to us. You are raking at dead fires,

rehearsing the old whinges at your age.
That subject people stuff is a cod's game,
infantile, like this peasant pilgrimage.

You lose more of yourself than your redeem
doing the decent thing. Keep at a tangent.
When they make the circle wide, it's time to swim

out on your own and fill the element
with signatures on your own frequency,
echo-soundings, searches, probes, allurements,

elver-gleams in the dark of the whole sea.'
The shower broke in a cloudburst, the tarmac
fumed and sizzled. As he moved off quickly

the downpour loosed its screens round his straight walk.

Sweeney Redivivus

I stirred wet sand and gathered myself
to climb the steep-flanked mound,
my head like a ball of wet twine
dense with soakage, but beginning
to unwind.
    Another smell
was blowing off the river, bitter
as night airs in a scutch mill.
The old trees were nowhere,
the hedges thin as penwork
and the whole enclosure lost
under hard paths and sharp-ridged houses.

And there I was, incredible to myself,
among people far too eager to believe me
and my story, even if it happened to be true.

A Brigid's Girdle

for Adele   — a teaching friend diagnosed with cancer

Last time I wrote I wrote from a rustic table
Under magnolias in South Carolina
As blossoms fell on me, and a white gable
As clean-lined as the prow of a white liner

Bisected sunlight in the sunlit yard.
I was glad of the early heat and the first quiet
I'd had for weeks. I heard the mocking bird
And a delicious, articulate

Flight of small plinkings from a dulcimer
Like feminine rhymes migrating to the north
Where you faced the music and the ache of summer
And earth's foreknowledge gathered in the earth.

Now it's St Brigid's Day and the first snowdrop
In County Wicklow, and this a Brigid's Girdle
I'm plaiting for you, an airy fairy hoop
(Like one of those old crinolines they'd trindle),

Twisted straw that's lifted in a circle
To handsel and to heal, a rite of spring
As strange and lightsome and traditional
As the motions you go through going through the thing.

Tollund

That Sunday morning we had travelled far.
We stood a long time out in Tollund Moss:
The low ground, the swart water, the thick grass
Hallucinatory and familiar.

A path through Jutland fields. Light traffic sound.
Willow bushes; rushes; bog-fir grags
In a swept and gated farmyard; dormant quags.
And silage under wraps in its silent mound.

It could have been a still out of the bright
'Townland of Peace', that poem of dream farms
Outside all contention. The scarecrow's arms
Stood open opposite the satellite

Dish in the paddock, where a standing stone
Had been resituated and landscaped,
With tourist signs in *futhark* runic script
In Danish and in English. Things had moved on.

It could have been Mulhollandstown or Scribe.
The by-roads had their names on them in black

And white; it was user-friendly outback
Where we stood footloose, at home beyond the tribe,

More scouts than strangers, ghosts who'd walked abroad
Unfazed by light, to make a new beginning
And make a go of it, alive and sinning,
Ourselves again, free-willed again, not bad.
  September 1994

Postscript

And some time make the time to drive out west
Into County Clare, along the Flaggy Shore,
In September or October, when the wind
And the light are working off each other
So that the ocean on one side is wild
With foam and glitter, and inland among stones
The surface of a slate-grey lake is lit
By the earthed lightning of a flock of swans,
Their feathers roughed and ruffling, white on white,
Their fully grown headstrong-looking heads
Tucked or cresting or busy underwater.
Useless to think you'll park and capture it
More thoroughly. You are neither here nor there,
A hurry through which known and strange things pass
As big soft buffetings come at the car sideways } *final affecting image*
And catch the heart off guard and blow it open. }

Further Readings on Seamus Heaney

Bibliography

Durkan, Michael J., and Rand Brandes. *Seamus Heaney: A Reference Guide*. New York: G. K. Hall, 1996.

Selected Works

Beowulf: A New Verse Translation. London: Faber and Faber; 2000.
The Cure at Troy: A Version of Sophocles' Philoctetes. New York: Noonday Press, 1991.

Crediting Poetry: The Nobel Lecture. New York: Farrar, Straus and Giroux, 1996.

Death of a Naturalist. London: Faber and Faber, 1966.

Door into the Dark. London: Faber and Faber, 1969.

Electric Light. London: Faber and Faber, 2001.

Field Work. London: Faber and Faber, 1979.

Finders Keepers: Selected Prose, 1971–2001. London: Faber and Faber, 2002.

The Government of the Tongue: The 1986 T. S. Eliot Memorial Lectures and Nine Other Critical Writings. London: Faber and Faber, 1988.

The Haw Lanterns. London: Faber and Faber, 1987. [Prose.]

The Midnight Verdict. Oldcastle, Ireland: Gallery Press, 2000. [Translation of *Cúirt an Mheadhon Oídhche.*]

North. London: Faber and Faber, 1975.

Opened Ground: Selected Poems, 1966–1996. London: Faber and Faber, 1998.

The Place of Writing. Atlanta, Ga.: Scholars Press, 1989.

Preoccupations: Selected Prose, 1968–1978. New York: Farrar, Straus and Giroux, 1980.

The Rattle Bag: An Anthology of Poetry. London: Faber and Faber, 1982. (As editor with Ted Hughes.)

The Redress of Poetry. London: Faber and Faber, 1995.

Seeing Things. London: Faber and Faber, 1991.

Selected Poems, 1965–1975. New York: Farrar, Straus and Giroux, 1980.

Selected Poems, 1966–1987. London: Faber and Faber, 1990.

The Spirit Level. London: Faber and Faber, 1996.

Station Island. New York: Farrar, Straus and Giroux, 1985.

Sweeney Astray. A Version from the Irish. New York: Farrar, Straus and Giroux, 1984. (As translator.)

Wintering Out. New York: Oxford University Press, 1972.

Biography and Criticism

Allen, Michael. *Seamus Heaney.* New York: St. Martin's, 1997.

Andrews, Elmer. *The Poetry of Seamus Heaney: All The Realms of Whisper.* Basingstoke: Macmillan, 1988.

Bloom, Harold. *Seamus Heaney.* 1986. Reprint, New Haven: Chelsea House, 2002.

———. *Seamus Heaney: Comprehensive Research and Study Guide.* Philadelphia: Chelsea House, 2003.

Burris, Sidney. *The Poetry of Resistance: Seamus Heaney and the Pastoral Tradition.* Athens, Ohio: Ohio University Press, 1990.

Broadbridge, Edward, ed. *Seamus Heaney.* Copenhagen: Danmarks Radio, 1977.

Buttel, Robert. *Seamus Heaney.* Lewisburg, Pa.: Bucknell University Press, 1975.

Corcoran, Neil. *Seamus Heaney.* 1986. Reprint, London: Faber and Faber, 1998.

Curtis, Tony. *The Art of Seamus Heaney.* 1982. Reprint, Brigend, Wales: Seren, 2001.

Deane, Seamus. "Unhappy and at Home: Interview with Seamus Heaney." *The Crane Bag* 1:61–67.

Foster, John Wilson. *The Achievement of Seamus Heaney.* Dublin: Lilliput, 1995.

Foster, Thomas C. *Seamus Heaney.* Boston: Twayne, 1989.

Garratt, Robert F., ed. *Critical Essays on Seamus Heaney.* New York: G. K. Hall; London: Prentice-Hall International, 1995.

Hart, Henry. *Seamus Heaney, Poet of Contrary Progressions.* Syracuse: Syracuse University Press, 1992.

Kennedy-Andrews, Elmer. *The Poetry of Seamus Heaney.* 1988. Reprint, New York: Columbia University Press, 1998.

——, ed. *Seamus Heaney: A Collection of Critical Essays.* New York: St. Martin's, 1992.

Longley, Edna. "Stars and Horses, Pigs and Trees." *The Crane Bag* 3:54–60.

Malloy, Catharine, and Phyllis Carey. *Seamus Heaney: The Shaping Spirit.* Newark, Del.: University of Delaware Press, 1996.

Molino, Michael R. *Questioning Tradition, Language, and Myth: The Poetry of Seamus Heaney.* Washington: Catholic University Press, 1994.

Morrison, Blake. *Seamus Heaney.* London: Methuen, 1982.

O'Brien, Eugene. *Seamus Heaney and the Place of Writing.* Gainesville: University Press of Florida, 2002.

——. *Seamus Heaney: Creating Irelands of the Mind.* Dublin: Liffey Press, 2002.

——. *Seamus Heaney's Prose: Searches for Answers.* London: Pluto, 2003.

Parker, Michael. *Seamus Heaney: The Making of a Poet.* Dublin: Gill and Macmillan, 1993.

Tamplin, Ronald. *Seamus Heaney.* Milton Keynes, UK: Open University Press, 1989.

Thomas, Harry. *Talking with Poets.* New York: Handsel Books, 2002.

Tobin, Daniel. *Passage to the Center: Imagination and the Sacred in the Poetry of Seamus Heaney.* Lexington: University of Kentucky Press, 1999.

Vendler, Helen Hennessy. *Seamus Heaney.* Cambridge, Mass.: Harvard University Press, 1998.

Michael Longley (b. 1939)

A Trinity-trained classicist, Michael Longley taught school before settling in his native Belfast to work for the Arts Council of Northern Ireland. He retired as Combined Arts Director to devote himself to writing and teaching. His *Selected Poems* appeared in 1999.

Longley's lyrics reveal his concern for form—for the way that experience shapes syntax and stanza. His economy of form, his striking imagery, and his frequent themes—the natural world; love—are qualities he shares with the poet Emily

Dickinson. "In Memoriam" describes Longley's father as a young soldier in a Scottish regiment on the Western Front. A classical love poem, "The Linen Industry" sets love in the landscape of Northern Ireland.

Emily Dickinson

Emily Dickinson, I think of you ~~A~~
Wakening early each morning to write, ~~B~~
Dressing with care for the act of poetry. ~~C~~
Yours is always a perfect progress through ~~A~~
Such cluttered rooms to eloquence, delight, ~~B~~ *Rhyme*
To words—your window on the mystery. ~~C~~ *scheme*

In your house in Amherst Massachusetts,
Though like love letters you lock them away,
The poems are ubiquitous as dust.
You sit there writing while the light permits—
While you grow older they increase each day,
Gradual as flowers, gradual as rust.

The Linen Industry   *N. Ireland*

Pulling up flax after the blue flowers have fallen
And laying our handfuls in the peaty water
To rot those grasses to the bone, or building stooks
That recall the skirts of an invisible dancer,

We become a part of the linen industry
And follow its processes to the grubby town
Where fields are compacted into window-boxes
And there is little room among the big machines.

But even in our attic under the skylight
We make love on a bleach green, the whole meadow
Draped with material turning white in the sun
As though snow reluctant to melt were our attire.

What's passion but a battering of stubborn stalks,   *metaphor making*
Then a gentle combing out of fibres like hair   *of making love and processing linen*

also death (grieving)

And a weaving of these into christening robes,
Into garments for a marriage or funeral?

Since it's like a bereavement once the labour's done
To find ourselves last workers in a dying trade,
Let flax be our matchmaker, our undertaker,
The provider of sheets for whatever the bed—

And be shy of your breasts in the presence of death,
Say that you look more beautiful in linen
Wearing white petticoats, the bow on your bodice
A butterfly attending the embroidered flowers.

In Memoriam

My father, let no similes eclipse
where crosses like some forest simplified
Sink roots into my mind; the slow sands
Of your history delay till through your eyes
I read you like a book. Before you died,
Re-enlisting with all the broken soldiers
You bent beneath your rucksack, near collapse,
In anecdote rehearsed and summarised
These words I write in memory. Let yours
And other heartbreaks play into my hands.

Now I see in close-up, in my mind's eye,
The cracked and splintered dead for pity's sake.
Each dismal evening predecease the sun,
You, looking death and nightmare in the face
With your kilt, harmonica and gun,
Grow older in a flash, but none the wiser
(Who, following the wrong queue at The Palace,
Having joined the London Scottish by mistake),
Your nineteen years uncertain if and why
Belgium put the kibosh on the Kaiser.

Between the corpses and the soup canteens
You swooned away, watching your future spill.

But, as it was, your proper funeral urn
Had mercifully smashed to smithereens,
To shrapnel shards that sliced your testicle.
That instant I, your most unlikely son,
In No Man's Land was surely left for dead,
Blotted out from your far horizon.
As your voice now is locked inside my head,
I yet was held secure, waiting my turn.

Finally, that lousy war was over.
Stranded in France and in need of proof
You hunted down experimental lovers,
Persuading chorus girls and countesses:
This, father, the last confidence you spoke.
In my twentieth year your old wounds woke
As cancer. Lodging under the same roof
Death was a visitor who hung about,
Strewing the house with pills and bandages,
Till he chose to put your spirit out.

Though they overslept the sequence of events
Which ended with the ambulance outside,
You lingering in the hall, your bowels on fire,
Tears in your eyes, and all your medals spent,
I summon girls who packed at last and went
Underground with you. Their souls again on hire,
Now those lost wives as recreated brides
Take shape before me, materialise.
On the verge of light and happy legend
They lift their skirts like blinds across your eyes.

Further Readings on Michael Longley

Selected Works

Baucis and Philemon, after Ovid. Hatch End, UK: Poet and Printer, 1993.
Broken Dishes. Belfast: Abbey Press, 1998.
Causeway. (ed.) The Arts in Ulster. Belfast: Arts Council, 1971.
No Continuing City: Poems, 1963–1968. Dublin: Gill and Macmillan, 1969.

The Echo Gate. London: Secker and Warburg, 1979.

An Exploded View: Poems, 1968–1972. London: Victor Gollancz, 1973.

The Ghost Orchid. London: Cape Poetry, 1995.

Gorse Fires. London: Seeker and Warburg, 1991.

Man Lying on a Wall. London: Victor Gollancz, 1976.

Out of the Cold: Drawings and Poems for Christmas. With Sarah Longley. Newry, Northern Ireland: Abbey Press, 1999.

Poems. Dublin: Gallery Press, 1985.

Poems 1963–1983. 1985. Reprint, London: Secker and Warburg, 1991.

Selected Poems, 1963–1980. Winston-Salem, N.C.: Wake Forest University Press, 1981.

Selected Poems. London: Cape Poetry, 1999.

The Ship of the Wind: Eight Poems. Dublin: Poetry Ireland, 1997.

Tuppeny Stung: Autobiographical Chapters. Belfast: Lagan, 1994.

20th-Century Irish Poems. London: Faber and Faber, 2002.

The Weather in Japan. London: Jonathan Cape, 2000.

Biography and Criticism

Johnston, Dillon. "Interview with Michael Longley." *Irish Literary Supplement* 5:2.

"Michael Longley." *Contemporary Literary Criticism.* 29:291–97.

Peacock, Alan J., and Kathleen Devine. *The Poetry of Michael Longley.* Gerrards Cross, UK: Colin Smythe, 2000.

The Southern Review. A Special Issue: Contemporary Irish Poetry and Criticism. 31, no. 3 (Summer 1995).

Storey, Mark. "Michael Longley: A Precarious Act of Balancing." *Fortnight* 194:21–22.

Derek Mahon (b. 1941)

Derek Mahon started writing poetry as a schoolboy. He won the Eric Gregory Prize for Poetry while an undergraduate at Trinity College, Dublin, for poems which would become part of *Night-Crossing* (1968). Five collections followed, with *Poems 1962–1978* appearing in 1979. Translator as well as poet, Mahon has published versions of Nerval's *Les Chimères* and Molière's *The School for Husbands*. His *Selected Poems* appeared in 1991.

Mahon is one of the most elegant poets of his generation; his poems have been praised for their wit and polish. Critics have described the mood of much of Mahon's poetry as "detached," noting that he often uses images of windows as distancing devices, as in "The Snow Party," where the falling snow silences the sounds of the violent world beyond. Similarly, "A Disused Shed in Co. Wexford" speaks for those silenced. Referring to the image of the mushrooms straining through the darkness toward the shaft of light coming through the keyhole, another poet, Seamus Heaney, has written: "It is about the need to love and be known, the need for selfhood, recognition in the eye of God and the eye of the world."

Mahon has spent much of his maturity in the United States, where he has received continuing recognition, including the award of a Guggenheim Fellowship. In "Imbolc: JBY," he examines his attitudes toward returning to Ireland by comparing himself with another Irish Protestant exile, painter John Butler Yeats (1839–1922), who remained in the United States and is buried on the property of a wealthy patron near Lake George, New York. John Butler Yeats was the father of poet William Butler Yeats, whom he referred to as "Willie." Imbolc is the Old Irish name for a festival held 1 February, at the first intimations of spring, now Christianized as St. Brigid's Day.

A Disused Shed in Co. Wexford

> *Let them not forget us, the weak souls among the asphodels.*
> —Seferis, "Mythistorema
> for J. G. Farrell"

Even now there are places where a thought might grow—
Peruvian mines, worked out and abandoned
To a slow clock of condensation,
An echo trapped for ever, and a flutter of
Wildflowers in the lift-shaft,
Indian compounds where the wind dances
And a door bangs with diminished confidence,
Lime crevices behind rippling rainbarrels,
Dog corners for shit burials;
And in a disused shed in Co. Wexford,

Deep in the grounds of a burnt-out hotel,
Among the bathtubs and the washbasins
A thousand mushrooms crowd to a keyhole.
This is the one star in their firmament
Or frames a star within a star.
What should they do there but desire?
So many days beyond the rhododendrons
With the world waltzing in its bowl of cloud,

They have learnt patience and silence
Listening to the crows querulous in the high wood.

They have been waiting for us in a foetor of
Vegetable sweat since civil war days,
Since the gravel-crunching, interminable departure
Of the expropriated mycologist.
He never came back, and light since then
Is a keyhole rusting gently after rain.
Spiders have spun, flies dusted to mildew,
And once a day, perhaps, they have heard something—
A trickle of masonry, a shout from the blue
Or a lorry changing gear at the end of the lane.

There have been deaths, the pale flesh flaking
Into the earth that nourished it;
And nightmares born of these and the grim
Dominion of stale air and rank moisture.
Those nearest the door grow strong—
Elbow room! Elbow room!
The rest, dim in a twilight of crumbling
Utensils and broken pitchers, groaning
For their deliverance, have been so long
Expectant that there is left only the posture.

A half century, without visitors, in the dark—
Poor preparation for the cracking lock
And creak of hinges, Magi, moonmen,
Powdery prisoners of the old regime,
Web-throated, stalked like triffids, racked by drouth
And insomnia, only the ghost of a scream
At the flash-bulb firing squad we wake them with
Shows there is life yet in their feverish forms.
Grown beyond nature now, soft food for worms,
They lift frail heads in gravity and good faith.

They are begging us, you see, in their wordless way,
To do something, to speak on their behalf
Or at least not to close the door again.

Lost people of Treblinka and Pompeii!
Save us, save us, they seem to say,
Let the god not abandon us
Who have come so far in darkness and in pain.
We too had our lives to live.
You with your light meter and relaxed itinerary,
Let not our naive labours have been in vain!

The Snow Party

for Louis Asekoff

Basho, coming
To the city of Nagoya,
Is asked to a snow party.

There is a tinkling of china
And tea into china,
There are introductions.

Then everyone
Crowds to the window
To watch the falling snow.

Snow is falling on Nagoya
And farther south
On the tiles of Kyoto.

Eastward, beyond Irago,
It is falling
Like leaves on the cold sea.

Elsewhere they are burning
Witches and heretics
In the boiling squares,

Thousands have died since dawn
In the service
Of barbarous kings—

But there is silence
In the houses of Nagoya
And the hills of Ise.

Imbolc: JBY

There is something vulgar in all success; the greatest men fail, or seem to have failed.
—Oscar Wilde

The Good has nothing to do with purpose, indeed it excludes the idea of purpose . . . The
only genuine way to be good is to be good "for nothing."
—Iris Murdoch, *The Sovereignty of Good*

A roof over my head, protected from the rain,
I'm reading, 'pilgrim father,' your letters to your son
and wondering if, unlike you, I should head for home.
Escaping the turbulence of this modern Rome
in a flurry of skyline views and exploding foam,
I can see that 747 in flight over Nova Scotia,
over Shannon and Limerick, snoring back to the fuchsia,
to that land of the still-real I left in '91,
of Jennifer Johnston and Seosaimhín Ní Gabhráin;
I can see a united Ireland from the air,
its meteorological gaiety and despair,
some evidence of light industry and agriculture,
familiar contours, turf-smoke on field and town;
I can even hear the cabin crew's soft *'failte'*
and the strains of 'My Lagan Love' as we touch down.
A recovering Ulster Protestant like you from Co. Down,
I shall walk the Dublin lanes as the days grow shorter,
I who once had a poem in *The New Yorker,*
and spend old age, if any, in an old mac
with the young audibly sneering behind my back,
deafened by gulls and the heart-breaking cries
of children—ourselves, once—by perilous seas
where nightingale never yet dared raise its voice.
Now, listening to the *rus-in-urbe,* spring-in-winter noise
of late-night diners, while the temperatures rise
and the terrible wind-chill factor abates, I realize
the daffodils must be out in ditch and glen

and windows soon flung wide to familiar rain;
and marvel how, a figure out of the past,
'an old man in a hurry,' you stuck it here to the last, *WB yeats*
the rightful Duke of Ormonde housed like Willie's Bedouin
with only 'an iron bedstead, an old rug' and, of course,
your easel getting the pale north-light, while you
for whom art was never prey to commercial rage
nor beauty sacrificed to a ruthless mortgage
read Shakespeare, Keats and the Russian novelists
(dachas, troika troilism, the endless versts . . .),
negotiating the ice-fields of Eighth Avenue
on your way home past the Blarney Stone and the White Rose, *— Pubs in NYC*
to die on West 29th of the Asian 'flu—
leaving us, since you never *could* 'do hands,'
your unfinished self-portrait just as it stands,
'more sketch than picture' (nothing is ever 'done').
    . . . But first you met by chance at the riverside
a young woman with a sick child she tried to hide
(not out of shame, you felt, but anguished pride), *Keats allusion*
soft-spoken, 'from Donnybrook,' amid the alien corn.
'It pained me that her bright image should fade.'
Thus your epiphany, and you wrote to explain:
'The nightingale sings with its breast against a thorn,
it's out of pain that personality is born'
(same thing for the sedge-warbler and the yellow bittern);
and, knowing that we must suffer to be wise
unless, 'like Raphael,' we avert our eyes
from a dying infant or an unhappy wife,
you recommended 'the poetry of life.'
Things you understood: children, the human face,
'something finer than honesty,' the loneliness
of beautiful women, the priority of the real.
Things that puzzled you: economy, fear,
the argument from design, the need to feel secure,
the belief in another world besides this one here.
Despite your rationalism, did it ever occur
(the obvious next step for a quixotic who
preferred the Virgin to the Dynamo)
that the universe might be *really* 'magical,' sir,

and you yourself a showing-forth of that soul?
'Art is dreamland.' When you rejoined the whole
under most of the same stars, and closed your voyage
in a woman friend's family vault beside Lake George,
what glimpse was given to you in the black hole?
Now, to 'Yeats, Artist and Writer,' may we add
that you were at home here and in human nature?
—But also, in your own words, lived and died
like all of us, then as now, 'an exile and a stranger'?

'To Mrs. Moore at Inishannon'

*The statue's sculptor, Frédéric-Auguste Bartholdi, reacted with horror to the prospect of
immigrants landing near his masterpiece; he called it 'a monstrous plan.' So much for
Emma Lazarus . . . I wanted to do homage to the ghosts.*
—Mary Gordon, *Good Boys and Dead Girls*

No. 1, Fifth Avenue, New York City, Sept. 14th, 1895
—and Mother, dear, I'm glad to be alive
after a whole week on the crowded *Oceanic*—
tho' I got here all right without being sick.
We boarded in the rain, St. Colman's spire
shrinking ashore, a few lamps glimm'ring there
('Will the last to leave please put out the lights?'),
and slept behind the engines for six nights.
A big gull sat at the masthead all the way
from Roche's Point to Montock, till one day
it stagger'd up and vanish'd with the breeze
in the mass'd rigging by the Hudson quays . . .
Downtown, dear God, is like a glimpse of Hell
in a 'hot wave': drunken men, the roaring 'El',
the noise and squalour indescribable.
(Manners are rough and speech indelicate;
more teeming shore than you cd. shake a stick at.)
However, the Kellys' guest-house; church and tram;
now, thanks to Mrs. O'Brien, here I am
at last, install'd amid the kitchenware
in a fine house a short step from Washington Square.
Protestants, mind you, and a bit serious

[handwritten marginal notes: "Rhyme scheme"; "Takes on persona of immigrant Brigit Moore (writes to her mother in Ireland)"]

much like the Bandon sort, not fun like us,
the older children too big for their britches
tho' Sam, the 4-yr.-old, has me in stitches:
in any case, the whole country's under age.
I get each Sunday off and use the privilege
to explore Broadway, the new Brooklyn Bridge
or the Statue of Liberty, copper torch on top
which, wd. you believe it, actually lights up,
and look at the Jersey shore-line, blue and gold:
it's all fire and sunlight here in the New World.
Eagles and bugles! Curious their simple faith
that stars and stripes are all of life and death—
as if Earth's centre lay in Central Park
when we both know it runs thro' Co. Cork.
Sometimes at night, in my imagination,
I hear you calling me across the ocean;
but the money's good, tho' I've had to buy new clothes
for the equatorial climate. I enclose
ten dollars, more to come (here, for God's sake,
the fling the stuff around like snuff at a wake).
'Bye now; and Mother, dear, you may be sure
I remain
    yr. loving daughter,
    —Bridget Moore.

Further Readings on Derek Mahon

Selected Works

Antarctica. Dublin: Gallery Press, 1985.

The Bacchae: After Euripides. Oldcastle, Ireland: Gallery, 1991.

Courtyards in Delft. Dublin: Gallery Press, 1981.

The Hudson Letter. Loughcrew: Gallery, 1995.

The Hunt by Night. 1972. Reprint, Winston-Salem, N.C.: Wake Forest University Press, 1995.

Journalism: Selected Prose 1970–1995. Edited by Terence Brown. Loughcrew, Ireland, 1996.

Lives. New York: Oxford University Press, 1972.

Night-Crossing. London: Oxford University Press, 1968.

Poems 1962–1978. London: Oxford University Press, 1979.

Selected Poems. Oldcastle, Ireland: Gallery Press, 1991.
The Snow Party. London: Oxford University Press, 1975.
The Sphere Book of Modern Irish Poetry. London: Sphere, 1972. (As editor.)
The Yaddo Letter. Loughcrew, Ireland: Gallery Press, 1992.
The Yellow Book: A Selection of Poems. Loughcrew, Ireland: Gallery Press, 1997.

Biography and Criticism

Brown, Terence. "An Interview with Derek Mahon." *Poetry Ireland Review* 14:11–19.
Byrne, John. "Derek Mahon: A Commitment to Change." *The Crane Bag* 6:62–72.
"Derek Mahon." *Contemporary Literary Criticism* 27:286–93.
Howe, Irving, ed. "Unaccommodated Mahon: An Ulster Poet." *The Hollins Critic* 17, no. 5 (December 1980): 1–16.
Johnston, Dillon. *Irish Poetry after Joyce,* 224–46. South Bend, Ind.: University of Notre Dame Press, 1985; 2nd ed., Syracuse, N.Y.: Syracuse University Press, 1997.
Kelly, Willie. "Each Poem for Me a New Beginning." Interview in *Cork Review* 2:10–12.
Kennedy-Andrews, Elmer. *The Poetry of Derek Mahon.* Gerrards Cross, UK: Colin Smythe, 2002.
Sewell, Frank. *"Where Paradoxes Grow": The Poetry of Derek Mahon.* Coleraine, Northern Ireland: Cranagh Press, 2000.
The Southern Review. A Special Issue: Contemporary Irish Poetry and Criticism. 31, no. 3 (Summer 1995).

Caitlín Maude (1941–1982)

Born near Casla in the Connemara Gaeltacht, Maude was educated at University College, Dublin, where she was active in the student drama society and in the Taibhdhearc, Galway's Irish-language theater. Her role as Máire in the 1964 Damer production of Máiréad Ní Ghráda's *An Triail* (The Trial) established her reputation as an actress. An accomplished traditional singer, her album *Caitlín* was released on the Gael-linn label in 1975. While Maude wrote drama and fiction, she is remembered primarily as a poet. Her collection *Dánta* (poems), edited by Ciarán Ó Coigligh, was published posthumously.

Maude's untitled elegy for Bobby Sands (1954–1981) commemorates the first of ten Republicans to die on hunger strike at Long Kesh Prison.

Untitled

[handwritten annotation: Elegy for Bobby Sands from his POV]

In my own place in the North
life is like the stormy weather
far more rain than sun.
But there was a sun-burst over my cot, *[handwritten: during hunger strike at Long Kesh Prison]*
and I never gave in to the dark skies.
Look at me—
not able to find rest in my own country,
nor could any saint.
I walloped stones *[handwritten: Throwing stones at Brits]*
along with the very schoolboy,
Understanding that it wasn't a street game at all— *[handwritten: elected to Brutish Parliament during strike]*
And I was the Indian.

[handwritten: Oppression of native people]

> *trans. Maureen Murphy*

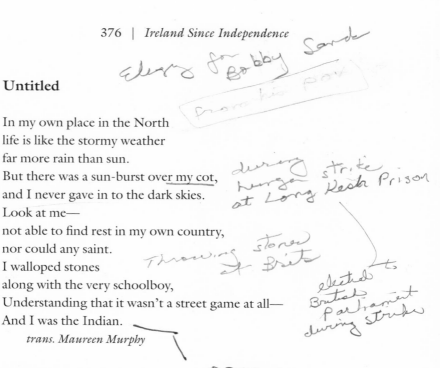

Further Readings on Caitlín Maude

Selected Works

Caitlín Maude: Dánta. Edited by Ciarán Ó Coighligh. Dublin: Coiscéim, 1984.
Caitlín Maude: Dramaíocht agus Prós. Edited by Ciarán Ó Coigligh. Dublin: Coiscéim, 1988.

Biography and Criticism

Murphy, Maureen. "The Elegiac Tradition in the Poetry of Máire Mhac an tSaoi, Caitlín Maude and Nuala Ní Dhomhnaill." In *New Irish Writing,* edited by James Brophy and Eamomon Grennan, 141–51. New York: Twayne, 1989.
Ni Ghrádha, Mairéad. *Breithiúnas.* Dublin: Oifig an tSoláthair, 1978.
Weekes, Ann Owens. "Caitlín Maude." In *Unveiling Treasures,* 221–22. Dublin: Attic Press, 1993.

Eiléan Ní Chuilleanáin (b. 1942)

Eiléan Ní Chuilleanáin's first formal recognition as a poet was the *Irish Times* Award for Poetry, which she received in 1966 while a graduate student at Lady Margaret Hall, Oxford, on a traveling studentship from the National University of Ireland. An

English Renaissance scholar, she has lectured in English at Trinity since 1966. She is also a founding editor of *Cyphers*.

The scholar-poet role rests easily with Ní Chuilleanáin, since she grew up the daughter of the professor of Irish at University College, Cork, and the novelist Éilis Dillon. She is married to Macdara Woods, a poet and fellow *Cyphers* editor.

Her work has been praised for its sense of history, and the poet for the quality of her imagination, her clarity of image, and her precise diction. The O'Rourke betrayed in "Waterfall" is an allusion to Brian na Múrtha (Brian of the Ramparts), who was hanged as felon in London in 1591 for having aided the shipwrecked survivors of the Spanish Armada.

The Second Voyage

Odysseus rested on his oar and saw
The ruffled foreheads of the waves
Crocodiling and mincing past: he rammed
The oar between their jaws and looked down
In the simmering sea where scribbles of weed defined
Uncertain depth, and the slim fishes progressed
In fatal formation, and thought
    If there was a single
Streak of decency in these waves now, they'd be ridged
Pocked and dented with the battering they've had
And we could name them as Adam named the beasts,
Saluting a new one with dismay, or a notorious one
with admiration: they'd notice us passing
And rejoice at our shipwreck, but these
Have less character than sheep and need more patience.

I know what I'll do he said;
I'll park my ship in the crook of a long pier
(And I'll take you with me he said to the oar)
I'll face the rising ground and walk away
From tidal waters, up riverbeds
Where herons parcel out the miles of stream,
Over gaps in the hills, through warm
Silent valleys, and when I meet a farmer
Bold enough to look me in the eye
With "where are you off to with that long

Winnowing fan over your shoulder?"
There I will stand still
And I'll plant you for a gatepost or a hitching-post
And leave you as a tidemark. I can go back
And organise my house then.
    But the profound
Unfenced valleys of the ocean still held him:
He had only the oar to make them keep their distance;
The sea was still frying under the ship's side.

He considered the water-lilies, and thought about fountains
Spraying as wide as willows in empty squares,
The sugarstick of water clattering into the kettle,
The flat lakes bisecting the rushes. He remembered spiders and frogs
Housekeeping at the roadside in brown trickles floored with mud,
Horsetroughs, the black canal, pale swans at dark:
His face grew damp with tears that tasted
Like his own sweat or the insults of the sea.

Waterfall

This airy afternoon, warm and free,
My head lies against the bridge,
The vibrant coping-stones
Arching the green insistent waterfall;
My cheek feels the cold
Bricks of the cistern where Vercingetorix
Died in Rome, the dark earth of London
Where blood fell from O'Rourke betrayed
    1591,
The cool grass of White Island
Monastic, long ruined and freshly springing
In between broken walls,
Carved and scattered stones.

[handwritten annotation: allusion to The Brian of the Ramparts who was hanged in 1591 for aiding shipwrecked survivors of Sp. Armada]

Old Roads

[handwritten annotation: Imagery-rich depicting fresh rural land-scape]

Missing from the map, the abandoned roads
Reach across the mountain, threading into

Clefts and valleys, shuffle between thick
Hedges of flowery thorn.
The grass flows in to tracks of wheels,
Mowed evenly by the careful sheep;
Drenched, it guards the gaps of silence
Only trampled on the pattern day.

And if, an odd time, late
At night, a cart passes
Splashing in a burst stream, crunching bones,
The wavering candle hung by the shaft
Slaps light against a single gable
Catches a flat tombstone
Shaking a nervous beam in a white face

Their arthritic fingers
Their stiffening grasp cannot
Hold long on the hillside—
Slowly the old roads lose their grip.

personification

J'ai Mal à Nos Dents

in memory of Anna Cullinane (Sister Mary Antony)

The Holy Father gave her leave
To return to her father's house
At seventy-eight years of age.

When young in the Franciscan house at Calais
She complained to the dentist, *I have a pain in our teeth*
—Her body dissolving out of her first mother,
Her five sisters aching at home.

Her brother listened to news
Five times in a morning on Radio Éireann
In Cork, as the Germans entered Calais.
Her name lay under the surface, he could not see her
Working all day with the sisters,
Stripping the hospital, loading the sick on lorries,

While Reverend Mother walked the wards and nourished them
With jugs of wine to hold their strength.
J'étais à moitié saoûle. It was done,
They lifted the old sisters on to the pig-cart
And the young walked out on the road to Desvres,
The wine still buzzing and the planes over their heads.

Je mangerai les pissenlits par les racines.
A year before she died she lost her French accent
Going home in her habit to care for her sister Nora
(Une malade à soigner une malade).
They handed her back her body,
Its voices and its death.

St Mary Magdalene Preaching at Marseilles

Now at the end of her life she is all hair—
A cataract flowing and freezing—and a voice
Breaking loose from the loose red hair,
The secret shroud of her skin:
A voice glittering in the wilderness.
She preaches in the city, she wanders
Late in the evening through shaded squares.

The hairs on the back of her wrists begin to lie down
And she breathes evenly, her elbows leaning
On a smooth wall. Down there in the piazza,
The boys are skimming on toy carts, warped
On their stomachs, like breathless fish.

She tucks her hair around her,
Looking beyond the game
To the suburban marshes.

Out there a shining traps the sun.
The waters are still clear,
Not a hook or a comma of ice
Holding them, the water-weeds

Lying collapsed like hair
At the turn of the tide;

They wait for the right time, then
Flip all together their thousands of sepia feet.

Further Readings on Eiléan Ní Chuilleanáin

Selected Works

Acts and Monuments. Dublin: Gallery Press, 1972.

The Brazen Serpent. Oldcastle, Ireland: Gallery Press, 1994.

The Girl Who Married the Reindeer. Oldcastle, Ireland: Gallery Press, 2001.

The Magdalene Sermon and Earlier Poems. Oldcastle, Ireland: Gallery Press, 1989.

The Rose Geranium. Dublin: Gallery Press, 1980.

The Second Voyage. 1977. Reprint, Winston-Salem, N.C.: Wake Forest University Press, 1991.

Site of Ambush. Dublin: Gallery Books, 1975.

The Water Horse: Poems in Irish. With Nuala Ní Dhomhnaill and Medbh McGuckian. Oldcastle, Ireland: Gallery Press, 1999.

Studies

"As I Was Among the Captives": Joseph Campbell's Prison Diary, 1922–23. Cork: Cork University Press, 2001. (As editor.)

"Gaelic Ireland Rediscovered: Courtly and Country Poetry." In *Irish Poets in English, The Pleasures of Gaelic Poetry,* edited by Sean Lucy. Cork: Mercier Press, 1973.

Irish Women: Image and Achievement. Dublin: Arlen House, 1985.

"Love and Friendship." In *The Pleasures of Gaelic Poetry,* edited by Sean MacReamoinn. London: Allen, Lane, 1982.

Noble and Joyous Histories: English Romances, 1375–1650, Dublin: Irish Academic Press, 1993. (As editor with J. D. Pheifer.)

The Wilde Legacy. Dublin: Four Courts, 2003.

Biography and Criticism

Browne, Joseph. "Eiléan Ní Chuilleanáin." In *Dictionary of Literary Biography*. Vol. 40, *Poets of Great Britain and Ireland Since 1960*, edited by Vincent B. Sherry. Detroit: Gale, 1985.

Eiléan Ní Chuilleanáin and Nuala Ní Dhomhnaill in Conversation with Dillon Johnston. Sante Fe, N.M.: Lannan Foundation, 1997, 1999. VHS Videorecording.

Gellert, Elisabeth. *Poetry Criticism: Excerpts from Criticism of the Works of the Most Significant and Widely Studied Poets of World Literature*, vol. 34. Farmington Hills, Mi.: Gale, 2002.

Haberstroh, Patricia Boyle. *Women Creating Women: Contemporary Irish Women Poets*. Syracuse, N.Y.: Syracuse University Press, 1996.

The Southern Review. A Special Issue: Contemporary Irish Poetry and Criticism 31, no. 3 (Summer 1995).

Eavan Boland (b. 1944)

Eavan Boland, the youngest child of diplomat Frederick Boland and painter Frances Kelly, was educated in Dublin, London, and New York. (Her poem "After a Childhood Away from Ireland" speaks to that temporary exile.) After a brilliant undergraduate career at Trinity, she returned there to lecture in 1967–1968. Boland has won a number of awards, including the Irish American Cultural Institute's prize.

Many of her early poems, such as "The Winning of Etain," are rooted in Irish tradition; others, like "Athene's Song," draw from other mythologies. Marriage to novelist Kevin Casey and the birth of children brought poems about domesticity and motherhood—poems that extend her range from the wit of "The New Pastoral" to the passionate restraint of "Child of Our Time," her moving elegy for her child.

Athene's Song

for my father

From my father's head I sprung
Goddess of the war, created
Partisan and soldiers' physic—
My symbols boast and brazen gong—
Until I made in Athens wood
Upon my knees a new music.

When I played my pipe of bone,
Robbed and whittled from a stag,
Every bird became a lover
Every lover to its tone
Found the truth of song and brag;
Fish sprung in the full river.

Peace became the toy of power
When other noises broke my sleep.
Like dreams I saw the hot ranks
And heroes in another flower
Than any there; I dropped my pipe
Remembering their shouts, their thanks.

Beside the water, lost and mute,
Lies my pipe and like my mind
Remains unknown, remains unknown
And in some hollow taking part
With my heart against my hand
Hold its peace and holds its own.

Requiem for a Personal Friend

(ON A HALF-EATEN BLACKBIRD)

A striped philistine with quick
Sight, quiet paws, today—
In gorging on a feathered prey—
Filleted our garden's music.

Such robbery in such a mouthful!
Here rests, shovelled under simple
Vegetables, my good example—
Singing daily, daily faithful.

No conceit and not contrary—
My best colleague, worst of all,
Was half-digested, his sweet whistle
Swallowed like a dictionary.

Little victim, song for song—
Who share a trade must share a threat—
So I write to cheat the cat
Who got your body, of my tongue.

After a Childhood Away from Ireland

[handwritten: father, a diplomat whose work took him + family to England]

One summer
we slipped in at dawn
on plum-coloured water
in the sloppy quiet.

[handwritten: Return to homeland]

The engines
of the ship stopped.
There was an eerie
drawing near,
a noiseless, coming head-on
of red roofs, walls,
dogs, barley stooks.
Then we were there.
Cobh. ← *[handwritten: Pron. Cove]*

Coming home.
I had heard of this:
the ground the emigrants
resistless, weeping
laid their cheeks to,
put their lips to kiss.
Love is also memory.
I only stared.
What I had lost
was not land
but the habit
of land,
whether of growing out of

or settling back on
or being defined by.
I climb
to your nursery.

I stand listening
to the dissonances

of the summer's day ending.
I bend to kiss you.
Your cheeks are brick pink.
They store warmth like clay.

Child of Our Time

for Aengus —— *Her lost child*

Yesterday I knew no lullaby
But you have taught me overnight to order
This song, which takes from your final cry
Its tune, from your unreasoned end its reason;
Its rhythm from the discord of your murder
Its motive from the fact you cannot listen.

We who should have known how to instruct
With rhymes for your waking, rhythms for your sleep,
Names for the animals you took to bed,
Tales to distract, legends to protect,
Later an idiom for you to keep
And living, learn, must learn from you, dead.

To make our broken images rebuild
Themselves around your limbs, your broken
Image, find for your sake whose life our idle
Talk has cost, a new language. Child
Of our time, our times have robbed your cradle.
Sleep in a world your final sleep has woken.

Further Readings on Eavan Boland

Selected Works

Against Love Poetry. New York: Norton, 2001.
Code. Manchester, UK: Carcanet, 2001.

A Dozen Lips. Dublin: Attic, 1994.
Collected Poems. Manchester, UK: Carcanet, 1995.
In a Time of Violence. New York: Norton, 1994.
In Her Own Image. Dublin: Arlen House, 1980.
Introducing Eavan Boland: Poems. Princeton, Ont.: Ontario Review Press, 1981.
The Journey and Other Poems. Manchester, UK: Carcanet, 1987.
The Lost Land: Poems. New York: Norton, 1998.
The Making of a Poem: A Norton Anthology of Poetic Forms. New York: Norton, 2000.
    (As editor with Mark Strand.)
New Territory. Dublin: Allen Figgis, 1967.
Night Feed. Dublin: Arlen House, 1982.
Object Lessons: The Life of the Woman and the Poet in Our Time. New York: Norton, 1995.
An Origin like Water: Collected Poems, 1967–1987. New York: Norton, 1996.
Outside History: Selected Poems, 1980–1990. New York: Norton, 1990.
The War Horse. London: Victor Gollancz, 1975.
The Younger Irish Poets. Belfast: Blackstaff Press, 1982.

Biography and Criticism

Browne, Joseph. "Eavan Boland." In *Dictionary of Literary Biography. Vol. 40, Poets of Great Britain and Ireland Since 1960,* edited by Vincent B. Sherry, 36–41. Detroit: Gale, 1985.
Griggs, Dan. *Eavan Boland.* Los Angeles: The Foundation, 1994. VHS video-recording.
Haberstroh, Patricia Boyle. *Women Creating Women: Contemporary Irish Woman Poets.* Syracuse, N.Y.: Syracuse University Press, 1996.
———, ed. *My Self, My Muse: Irish Women Poets Reflect on Life and Art.* Syracuse, N.Y.: Syracuse University Press, 2001.
Kennelly, Brendan. "Eavan Boland." In *Dictionary of Irish Literature,* edited by Robert Hogan, 112–14. Westport, Conn.: Greenwood Press, 1979.
Roche, Anthony. *Eavan Boland.* Dublin: Irish University Press, 1993.

Ciarán Carson (b. 1948)

Athough born in Belfast, Carson spoke only Irish until he was four, when he began picking up English from the street. After graduating from Queen's University, he worked briefly as a teacher before becoming a civil servant for the Arts Council, responsible both for literature and the "traditional arts." A skilled singer-musician, he has long championed Irish traditional music and has published widely on it.

After publication of *The New Estate* (1976), containing adaptations of early Irish nature lyrics, it was eleven years before Carson produced a second volume, *The Irish for No* (1987). His new aesthetic combined the urgency of traditional music with storytelling. His mature poetry sets him apart from his contemporaries on two counts. One is his taste for long lines, often combining common language with traditional forms. The second is his nightmare vision of his native city under relentless threat of violence. *First Language* (1993) shows a poet at the height of his powers, equally concerned with the roots of language and of conflict.

The Bomb Disposal

[handwritten: Question]

[handwritten: Ref. to Troubles / The Belfast / in]

Is it just like picking a lock
with the slow deliberation of a funeral,
hesitating through a darkened nave
until you find the answer?

Listening to the malevolent tick
of its heart, can you read
the message of the threaded veins
like print, its body's chart?

The city is a map of the city,
its forbidden areas changing daily,
I find myself in a crowded taxi
making deviations from the known route,

ending in a cul-de-sac
where everyone breaks out suddenly
in whispers, noting the boarded windows,
the drawn blinds

Gate

Passing *Terminus* boutique the other day, I see it's got a bit of flak:
    The *T* and the *r* are missing, leaving *e minus*, and a sign saying,
    MONSTER
CLOSING DOWN SALE. It opened about six months back, selling
    odd-job-lots,
Ends of ranges. Before that it was Burton's, where I bought my wedding
    suit.

Which I only wear for funerals, now, *Gone for a Burton,* as the saying
    goes.

The stopped clock of *The Belfast Telegraph* seems to indicate the time
    Of the explosion—or was that last week's? Difficult to keep track:
    Everything's a bit askew, like the twisted pickets of the security gate,
    the wreaths
That approximate the spot where I'm told the night patrol went
    through.

Last Orders

Squeeze the buzzer on the steel mesh gate like a trigger, but
It's someone else who has you in their sights. Click. It opens.
    Like electronic
Russian roulette, since you never know for sure who's who, or
    what
You're walking into. I, for instance, could be anybody. Though
    I'm told
Taig's written on my face. See me, would *I* trust appearances?

Inside a sudden lull. The barman lolls his head at us. We order
    Harp—
Seems safe enough, everybody drinks it. As someone looks
    daggers at us
From the *Bushmills* mirror, a penny drops: how simple it would
    be for someone
Like ourselves to walk in and blow the whole place, and
    ourselves, to Kingdom Come.

Further Readings on Ciarán Carson

Selected Works

The Alexandrine Plan: Versions of Sonnets by Baudelaire, Mallarmé, and Rimbaud.
    Winston-Salem, N.C.: Wake Forest University Press, 1998.
Ballad of HMS Belfast, The: A Compendium of Belfast Poems. Oldcastle, Ireland:
    Gallery Press, 1999.
Belfast Confetti. Oldcastle, Ireland: Gallery Press, 1989.

Breaking News. Winston-Salem, N.C.: Wake Forest University Press, 2003.
Ciarán Carson: Selected Poems. Winston-Salem, N.C.: Wake Forest University Press, 2001.
First Language: Poems. Oldcastle, Ireland: Gallery Press, 1994.
Fishing for Amber: A Long Story. London: Granta, 2000.
The Inferno. Dante Alighieri, (tr.). London: Granta, 2002.
The Irish for No. Winston-Salem, N.C.: Wake Forest University Press, 1987
Irish Traditional Music. Belfast: Appletree Press, 1986.
Last Night's Fun: A Book About Irish Traditional Music. London: Jonathan Cape, 1996.
Letters from the Alphabet. Oldcastle, Ireland: Gallery Press, 1995.
The New Estate and Other Poems. Belfast: Blackstaff Press, 1976; Oldcastle, Ireland: Gallery Press, 1988.
Opera et Cetera. Oldcastle, Ireland: Gallery Press, 1996.
Shamrock Tea. London, New York: Granta, 2001.
The Star Factory. London: Granta, 1997.
The Twelfth of Never. Oldcastle, Ireland: Gallery Press, 1998.

Biography and Criticism

Andrews, Elmer, ed. *Contemporary Irish Poetry: A Collection of Critical Essays.* Basingstoke, UK: Macmillan, 1990.
Houen, Alex. *Terrorism and Modern Literature, from Joseph Conrad to Ciarán Carson.* Oxford: Oxford University Press, 2002.

Medbh McGuckian (b. 1950)

Medbh McGuckian was educated at Queen's University, Belfast, studying English under Seamus Heaney. She won the Poetry Society competition in 1979 for "The Flitting," and the following year received an Eric Gregory Award. *The Flower Master* (1982) won both the Rooney Prize and the Alice Hunt Barlett Award.

Known for her stunning and often startling imagery and sensual language, she treats two quintessential McGuckian subjects in two poems from *The Flower Master* (1982): the natural landscape and sexuality. "The Mast Year" describes a stand of trees, a beechwood whose deeply shaded floor allows but little growth, with the res003ult that it produces a rich leaf mold. (Lammas, the Anglo-Saxon name for August 1, is still used in the north of Ireland; however, it sometimes refers to Lughnasa, the Celtic harvest festival.) The erotic "Soil Map" suggests a reading of Kinsella's translation of *The Táin* in its two allusions to Medb (Modern Irish Medbh) of Connacht:

she was said never to have been "without one man in the shadow of another," and it was she who offered the "friendship of her thighs" to Dáire mac Fiachna if he would lend her the Brown Bull of Cuailnge.

The Mast Year

Some kinds of trees seem ever eager
To populate new ground, the oak or pine.
Though beech can thrive on many soils
And carve itself an empire, its vocation
Is gentler: it casts a shade for wildflowers
Adapted to the gloom, which feed
Like fungus on its rot of bedstraw leaves.

It makes an awkward neighbour, as the birch
Does, that lashes out in gales, and fosters
Intimacy with toadstools, till they sleep
In the benevolence of each other's smells,
Never occupying many sites for long:
The thin red roots of alder vein
The crumbled bank, the otter's ruptured door.

Bee-keepers love the windbreak sycamore.
The twill of hanging flowers that the beech
Denies the yew—its waking life so long
It lets the stylish beechwood
Have its day, as winded oaks
Lay store upon their Lammas growth,
The thickening of their dreams.

The Soil-Map

I am not a woman's man, but I can tell,
By the swinging of your two-leaf door,
You are never without one man in the shadow
Of another; and because the mind
Of a woman between two men is lighter
Than a spark, the petalled steps to your porch
Feel frigid with a lost warmth. I will not

Take you in hardness, for all the dark cage
Of my dreaming over your splendid fenestration,
Your moulded sills, your slender purlins,

The secret woe of your gutters. I will do it
Without niggardliness, like food with one
Generous; a moment as auspicious
And dangerous as the christening of a ship,
My going in to find the settlement
Of every floor, the hump of water
Following the moon, and her discolouring,
The saddling derangement of a roof
That might collapse its steepness
Under the sudden strain of clearing its name.

For anyone with patience can divine
How your plasterwork has lost key, the rendering
About to come away. So like a rainbird,
Challenged by a charm of goldfinch,
I appeal to the god who fashions edges
Whether such turning-points exist
As these saltings we believe we move
Away from, as if by simply shaking
A cloak we could disbud ourselves,
Dry out, and cease to live there?

I have found the places on the soil-map,
Proving it possible once more to call
Houses by their names, Annsgift or Mavisbank,
Mount Juliet or Bettysgrove; they should not
Lie with the gloom of disputes to interrupt them
Every other year, like some disease
Of language making humorous the friendship
Of the thighs. I drink to you as Hymenstown,
(My touch of fantasy) or First Fruits,
Impatient for my power as a bride.

Vanessa's Bower

I will tell you words which you will
Probably soon afterwards throw out of
Your head, where everything is in order,
And in bloom, like the bird-cherry reading
In a frostless climate, or the cheerfulness
Of ships being wooed by the sea away from
My possessive arm. Dear owner, you write,
Don't put me into your pocket: I am not
A willow in your folly-studded garden
Which you hope will weep the right way:
And there are three trains leaving, none
Of which connects me to your E-shaped
Cottage. Alas, I have still the feeling,
Half fatherly, half different, we are
Travelling together in the train with this letter,
Though my strange hand will never be your sin.

Further Readings on Medbh McGuckian

Selected Works

Captain Lavender. Winston-Salem, N.C.: Wake Forest University Press, 1995.
Drawing Ballerinas. Oldcastle, Ireland: Gallery Press, 2001.
The Face of the Earth. Oldcastle, Ireland: Gallery Press, 2002.
The Flower Master. 1982. Rev. ed. as *The Flower Master and Other Poems.* Oldcastle,
    Ireland: Gallery Press, 1993.
Had I a Thousand Lives. Oldcastle, Ireland: Gallery Press, 2003.
Horsepower Pass By!: A Study of the Car in the Poetry of Seamus Heaney. Coleraine,
    Northern Ireland: Cranagh Press, 1999.
Marconi's Cottage. Oldcastle, Ireland: Gallery Press, 1991.
On Ballycastle Beach. 1988; Oldcastle, Ireland: Gallery Press, 2000.
Portrait of Joanna. Belfast: Ulsterman, 1980.
Selected Poems, 1978–1994. Oldcastle, Ireland: Gallery Press, 1997.
Shelmalier. Oldcastle, Ireland: Gallery Press, 1998.
The Soldiers of the Year II. Winston-Salem, N.C.: Wake Forest University Press, 2002.
Trio 2: Damian Gorman, Medbh McGuckian, Douglas Marshall. Belfast: Blackstaff
    Press, 1980.

Two Women, Two Shores: Poems. With Nuala Archer. Baltimore: New Poets Series, 1989.

Venus and the Rain. Oxford: Oxford University Press, 1984.

The Water Horse: Poems in Irish. With Nuala Ní Dhomhnaill and Eiléan Ní Chuilleanáin. Oldcastle, Ireland: Gallery Press, 1999.

The Younger Irish Poets. Belfast: Blackstaff Press, 1982.

Biography and Criticism

Burgoyne-Johnson, Jolanta. *Bleeding the Boundaries: The Poetry of Medbh McGuckian*. Coleraine, Northern Ireland: Cranagh Press, 1999.

Haberstroh, Patricia Boyle. *Women Creating Women: Contemporary Irish Women Poets*. Syracuse, N.Y.: Syracuse University Press, 1996.

Henigan, Robert. "Contemporary Woman Poets in Ireland." *Concerning Poetry* 18:103–15.

Salas, Susan, and Laura A. Wisner-Broyles, eds. *Poetry Criticism: Excerpts from Criticism of the Works of the Most Significant and Widely Studies Poets in World Literature*, vol. 27. Detroit: Gale Group, 2000.

Sered, Danielle. *The Destination of a Rhyme: Elusiveness and Theft in the Poetry of Medbh McGuckian*. Fort Lauderdale, Fla.: Working Papers in Irish Studies, 2001.

The Southern Review. A Special Issue: Contemporary Irish Poetry and Criticism. 31, no. 3 (Summer 1995).

Wills, Clair. *Improprieties: Politics and Sexuality in Northern Irish Poetry*. Oxford: Clarendon Press, 1993.

Peter Fallon (b. 1951)

Born in Germany in 1951 and raised in rural County Meath, Peter Fallon makes his home on a small farm in Loughcrew. When he was eighteen, he founded The Gallery Press, Ireland's preeminent poetry press. The Gallery Press's twenty-fifth year was marked with a gala reading at the Abbey Theatre, where President Mary Robinson paid tribute to Fallon's contribution ". . . to the diverse and challenging voices in Ireland."

Poet as well as publisher, Fallon received the 1993 O'Shaugnessy Poetry Award from the Irish American Cultural Institute. Among the poets who praised Fallon's work, Ted Hughes said, "Peter Fallon's poetry has become very tough and alive, like a just-cut holly stick. Snappy and weighty. Very strong, sharp savour—and where do you find that these days?"

The Lost Field

for Tanya and Wendell Berry

Somewhere near Kells in County Meath
a field is lost, neglected, let by common law.

When the Horse Tobin went to the bad
and sold a farm and drank the money
there was outlying land we couldn't find.

The maps weren't marked.
My people farmed the farm.
They looked and asked about.
They kept an ear to the ground.

They asked the Horse himself.
He handed out handfuls of fivers,
cups of whiskey, and sang dumb.

His sister said, he's fearless but no fool.
He has a fame for fighting
and carried far from himself
caused cases for the County Nurse.
I can't help you. I pray to God
he'll come back to his senses.

Then I came home from Dublin
to take my place.
My part in this is reverence.

Think of all that lasts. Think of land.
The things you could do with a field.
Plough, pasture or re-claim. The stones
you'd pick, the house you'd build.

Don't mind the kind of land,
a mess of nettles even,
for only good land will grow nettles.

I knew a man shy from a farm
who couldn't find a weed
to tie the pony to.

Imagine the world
the place your own windfalls could fall.

I'm out to find that field, to make it mine.

Fostering

[handwritten: sheep]

He was lost in the blizzard of himself
and lay, a cold white thing, in a drift
of afterbirth. Another stood to drink dry spins.
I put him with the foster ewe who sniffed

and butted him from his birthright, her milk.
I took the stillborn lamb and cleft
with axe on chopping-block its head,
four legs, and worked the skin apart with deft

·skill and rough strength. I dressed the living lamb
in it. It stumbled with the weight, all pluck,
towards the ewe who sniffed and smelled and licked
rainment she recognized. Then she gave suck—

and he was Esau's brother and I Isaac's wife
working kind betrayals in a field blessed for life.

[handwritten: Biblical ref.]

Further Readings on Peter Fallon

Co-Incidence of Flesh. Dublin: Gallery Press, 1972.

Eye to Eye. Oldcastle, Ireland: Gallery Press, 1992.

The First Affair. Dublin: Gallery Press, 1974.

A Gentler Birth. Deerfield, Mass.: Deerfield Press, 1976.

The News and Weather. Dublin: Gallery Press, 1987.

News of the World: Selected Poems. Winston-Salem, N.C.: Wake Forest University Press, 1993.

News of the World: Selected and New Poems. Oldcastle, Ireland: Gallery Press, 1998.

Soft Day. Notre Dame: Notre Dame University Press, 1980. (As editor with Seán Golden.)

The Speaking Stones. Dublin: Gallery Press, 1978.

Winter Work. Dublin: Gallery Press, 1983.

The Writers: A Sense of Ireland: New Works by 44 Irish Writers. Dublin: O'Brien, 1980. (As editor with Andrew Carpenter.)

Paul Muldoon (b. 1951)

[handwritten: see supplement meeting the British]

Any mention of Paul Muldoon usually includes a comment about his precocious-ness, for he was only twenty-one when he published *New Weather* (1973), his stylish first book of lyrics. Born in south Armagh and educated in Belfast, he is sometimes called the youngest of that generation of Queen's University, Belfast, poets of whom Seamus Heaney is preeminent. For several years, Muldoon was a producer for BBC in Belfast.

Muldoon has often drawn on Old Irish sources. His narrative poem, the mock-heroic "Immran," is a search for a lost father written in the language of Raymond Chandler. It is based on *Imram Mael Dúin* (The voyage of Mael Dúin), an early Irish tale of a son's journey to avenge his father. "Neither one thing or the other," a line from the title poem "Mules," speaks to all mixed marriages in that volume. "The Boundary Commission," an allusion to the commission set up after the treaty to set the geographical boundary between Northern Ireland and the Republic, also speaks to the problem of identity in Northern Ireland.

Muldoon's witty, pun-loving post-modernist sensibility sets him apart from his contemporaries. Some puns are merely teasing, like linking the County Armagh of Muldoon's native Northern Ireland and the biblical Armageddon. Others surpass those of James Joyce in *Finnegans Wake.* Muldoon's translations from the Irish-language poet Nuala Ní Dhomhnaill, *The Astrakhan Cloak,* link Ní Dhomhnaill's Turkish-born husband and the Irish word for translation, *aistriúchán.*

After many years as writer-in-residence at Princeton University, Muldoon won the 2003 Pulitzer Prize for his collection *Moy Sand and Gravel.*

Mules

Should they not have the best of both worlds?

Her feet of clay gave the lie
To the star burned in our mare's brow.

Would Parsons' jackass not rest more assured
That cross wrenched from his shoulders?

We had loosed them into one field.
I watched Sam Parsons and my quick father
Tense for the punch below their belts,
For what was neither one thing or the other.

[handwritten: ret to mixed marriages]

It was as though they had shuddered
To think of their gaunt, sexless foal
Dropped tonight in the cowshed.

We might yet claim that it sprang from earth
were it not for the afterbirth
Trailed like some fine, silk parachute,
That we would know from what heights it fell.

The Boundary Commission

[handwritten: Bet N. Ireland & the Republic]

You remember that village where the border ran
Down the middle of the street,
With the butcher and baker in different states?
Today he remarked how a shower of rain

Had stopped so cleanly across Golightly's lane
It might have been a wall of glass
That had toppled over. He stood there, for ages,
To wonder which side, if any, he should be on.

Moy Sand and Gravel

[handwritten: his home town]

To come out of the Olympic Cinema and be taken aback
by how, in the time it took a dolly to travel
along its little track
to the point where two movie stars' heads
had come together smackety-smack
and their kiss filled the whole screen,

those two great towers directly across the road
at Moy Sand and Gravel

had already washed, at least once, what had flowed
or been dredged from the Blackwater's bed
and were washing it again, load by load,
as if washing might make it clean.

The Ancestor

The great-grandmother who bears down on us, as if beholding the mote
in our eye, from a nineteenth-century Hungarian portrait
on our library wall is no relation. Not even remote.
The straw-hatted man in a daguerreotype, though he and I may share
the trait

of putting two fingers to the little carbuncle
on our right chin, is no more of my blood than I am
consanguineous with Cromwell. Our Webster's is inscribed "Philip. Best
uncle."

Our napkins bear an unfamiliar monogram.

Yet how familiar all become. Shaving mug, gymkhana rosette, five
charms
from a charm bracelet—all those heirlooms
to which we're now the heirs are at once more presentable and

more present than our own. This great-grandmother with folded arms
who lurches and looms
across the library may not be so unreasoning in her reprimand.

The Stoic

This was more like it, looking up to find a burlapped fawn
halfway across the iced-over canal, an Irish navvy who'd stood there for
an age

with his long-tailed shovel or broad griffawn,
whichever foot he dug with showing the bandage

that saved some wear and tear, though not so much that there wasn't a

leak

of blood through the linen rag, a red picked up nicely by the turban
he sported, those reds lending a little brilliance to the bleak
scene of suburban or—let's face it—*urban*

sprawl, a very little brilliance. This was more like the afternoon last

March

when I got your call in St. Louis and, rather than rave
as one might rant and rave at the thought of the yew
from Deirdre's not quite connecting with the yew from Naoise's grave,

rather than shudder like a bow of yew or the matchless Osage orange
at the thought of our child already lost from view
before it had quite come into range,
I steadied myself under the Gateway Arch

and squinted back, first of all, through an eyelet of bone
to a point where the Souris
had not as yet hooked up with the Assiniboine,
to where the Missouri

had not as yet been swollen by the Osage,
then ahead to where—let's face it—there are now *two* fawns
on the iced-over canal, two Irish navvies who've stood there for a

veritable age

with their long-tailed shovels or broad griffawns.

One Last Draw of the Pipe

Heard a piece of Roscommon folklore the other night. At some village or other, they lay pipes full of tobacco on the graves of the new buried in case they may like a draw of the pipe. A wild American Indian kind of business it seems.
—A Letter from W. B. Yeats to Douglas Hyde, October 1889

Even though it happened as long ago as the late fifties, I could still draw
you a picture of the place. A little draw

through which we were helping a neighbor draw
green hay when we would suddenly draw

level with a freshly dug hole. He must have been torn between one last
                                                                    draw
of the pipe and hurriedly trying to draw

a veil of thatch and pine boughs over the hole before having to
                                                            withdraw,
that ghost who may even now draw

a bead on me. On the day Sitting Bull was shot, his old trick pony (once
                                                                such a draw
in Buffalo Bill's circus because he was given to dance
attendance
when he heard a volley of shots) would automatically draw

himself up and raise one hoof.
Even now I hear it coming down. I hear it coming down on my yew-
                                                        bough roof.

The Breather

Think of this gravestone
as a long, low chair
strategically placed
at a turn in the stair.

Further Readings on Paul Muldoon

Selected Works

The Annals of Chile. London: Faber and Faber, 1994.

The Astrakhan Cloak. Poems from the Irish by Nuala Ní Dhomhnaill. Oldcastle: Gallery Press, 1992. (As translator.)

Bandanna: An Opera in Two Acts and a Prologue. With Daron Hagen. London: Faber and Faber, 1999.

The Faber Book of Contemporary Irish Poetry. London: Faber and Faber, 1985.

Hay. New York: Farrar, Straus and Giroux, 1998.

Kerry Slides. Oldcastle, Ireland: Gallery Press, 1996.

Madoc: A Mystery. London: Faber and Faber, 1990.

Meeting the British. London: Faber and Faber, 1987.

Moy Sand and Gravel. London: Faber and Faber, 2001.

Mules. Winston-Salem, N.C.: Wake Forest University Press, 1977.

Mules and Earlier Poems. Winston-Salem, N.C.: Wake Forest University Press, 1985.

New Selected Poems, 1968–1994. London: Faber and Faber, 1996.

New Weather. Winston-Salem, N.C.: Wake Forest University Press, 1973.

Poems, 1968–1998. London: Faber and Faber, 2001.

The Prince of the Quotidian. Winston-Salem, N.C.: Wake Forest University Press, 1994.

Quoof. Winston-Salem, N.C.: Wake Forest University Press, 1983.

Selected Poems, 1968–1983. London: Faber and Faber, 1986.

Selected Poems, 1968–1986. New York: Ecco Press, 1987.

Shining Brow. With Daron Hagen. London: Faber and Faber, 1993.

Six Honest Serving Men. Oldcastle, Ireland: Gallery Press, 1995.

To Ireland, I. Oxford: Oxford University Press, 2000, 2001.

Vera of Las Vegas. Oldcastle, Ireland: Gallery Press, 2001.

Why Brownlee Left. Winston-Salem, N.C.: Wake Forest University Press, 1980.

The Wishbone. Dublin: Gallery Press, 1984.

Biography and Criticism

Frazier, Adrian. "Juniper, Otherwise Known: Poems by Paulin and Muldoon." *Éire-Ireland* 19:123–33.

Johnston, Dillon. *Irish Poetry after Joyce*, 263–72. South Bend, Ind.: University of Notre Dame Press, 1975.

Kendall, Tim. *Paul Muldoon.* Bridgend, Wales: Seren, 1996.

Wills, Claire. *Improprieties: Politics and Sexuality in Northern Irish Poetry.* Oxford: Clarendon Press, 1993.

———. *Reading Paul Muldoon.* Newcastle upon Tyne, UK: Bloodaxe, 1998.

Nuala Ní Dhomhnaill (b. 1952)

Born in Lancashire to Irish physicians, Nuala Ní Dhomhnaill (pronounced "NOO-la nee GHON-al," with a guttural "GH") was sent back at the age of five to an aunt's household in Cahiratrant, a village in the Corca Dhuibhne Gaeltacht near Ventry, County Kerry. After studying English and Irish at University College, Cork, she became acquainted with the coterie publishing the magazine *Innti,* interested in reviving Irish-language poetry while fully immersed in popular culture and American Beat poetry. Her marriage to Turkish geologist Dogan Leflef prompted moves to the Netherlands and Turkey before she returned to the Kerry Gaeltacht.

From her first collection, *An Dealg Droighin* (1981), Ní Dhomhnaill has united a deep understanding of folklore and mythology with a distinctly contemporary awareness of political issues, ecology, nationalism, and especially gender. She has reshaped folk traditions of the Munster fertility goddess known as Mór. In *Feis* (1991), a title using a widely known Irish word usually translated as "festival," she traces the root of the word to the Old Irish *fo-aid*: "sleeping with." The joyous acceptance of the sensual, commonplace in early Irish culture but repressed for centuries, is reborn in her work.

Allusions in her poetry here may be explained in passages from our first chapter. "Great Queen" is a translation of the name of Mórrígan, who confronts Cúchulainn, or Cú Chulainn, in the *Táin Bó Cuailnge*. Her literary character is drawn in part from Mór, the Munster goddess. Muirghil is the cook in the household who allows Suibne, or Sweeny, a drink of milk if he takes it from a hole poked in a mound of dung.

Although Ní Dhomhnaill deals with everyday matters in English, she composes poetry in Irish. In a memorable essay for the *New York Times* she explained why this remains her preference, describing Irish as "The Corpse that Sits Up and Talks Back." After translating some of her early work, she has since preferred to leave that task for others. The finest English-language poets among her contemporaries have readily taken the assignment: Michael Hartnett, Ciarán Carson, Michael Longley, Paul Muldoon, and Seamus Heaney. Unlikely as it may seem, Ní Dhomhnaill is much in demand for readings of her poetry before audiences in America and Europe who know no Irish. A skilled reader with an expressive, dramatic voice, as well as distinctive, long red hair, she can make audiences feel they know the poem before they hear the translation. To Irish speakers she is known affectionately as *"Nuala rua"* or "red Nuala."

Deepfreeze

Cornucopia of the age, the magic casket
from which we draw the best of food and drink,
every delicacy that your mouth might water after
and no two mouthfuls of quite the same taste.

Miscellany of household needs, healing well
of our ancestral hungers which neither increase nor

go away.
We adore its cairn of plenty.
There are no limits to its icy
streams of milk and honey, peaches, apples,
Irish stews, french fries,
quarters of beef already minced,
desserts, sweet cakes, two whole sheep.

There are five loaves here and two fishes
to feed the multitude of neighbours (if they ever come).
And who chucked this dead cat in amongst the spinach?
—Jimín Mháire Thadhg, I'll complain you to your Mam!

Seated victorious in the heart of every kitchen
is this basic metaphor of our civilisation.
The faerie music of the world ringing in our ears
is reduced to its contented hum, high velocity purr of electricity

A *memento mori,* par excellence, if I
ever saw one, awesome reminder of the ditch
we come from and to which we are going,
graven images everything we hamster there
—dead and hard and as cold as the grave.

Inside Out

Like the full moon
in grand array
you sail
into the room to me.
Master indeed
of all you survey,—
the shine on the furniture, the swellbeat
of my trembling, apprehensive heart.

Let's say you are "well on,"
your head is in a spin,
your gestures and your jests
grandiloquent

you don't even notice
that your white jersey
is crumpled
and inside out on you.

You are so careful
of your waistline,
so dapper and so nifty
in your dressing,—
what else is left for me
to do but go out in the garden
and sit on the lawn
and howl my anguish at the moon.

Because, *ochón*, my sorrow,
but there is truth in the old saw
that there are three smiles
more bitter than death itself:
the grin of a treacherous hound,
the beam of melting snow,
and the smirk of your lover
who has just slept with another woman.

    trans. Nuala Ní Dhomhnaill

Annunciations

She remembered to the very end
the angelic vision
in the temple:
the flutter of wings
about her—
noting the noise of doves,
sun-rays raining
on lime-white walls—
the day she got the tidings.

He—
he went away
and perhaps forgot

what grew from his loins—
two thousand years
of carrying a cross
two thousand years
of smoke an[...]
of rows that [...]
than all the [...]

Remember [...]
o most tenc[...]
that never v[...]
that a man [...]
in the darkness alone,
his feet bare, his teeth white
and roguery swelling in his eyes.

   trans. Michael Hartnett

Marvellous Grass

When you were a holy priest
in the middle of Mass in your purple robes
your linen mantle, your stole, your chasuble.
you saw my face in the crowd
approaching you for communion
and you dropped the blessed host.

I—I said nothing.
I was ashamed.
My lips were locked.
But still it lay on my heart
like a mud-thorn until
it penetrated my insides.
From it I nearly died.

Not long till I took to my bed:
medical experts came in hundreds
doctors, priests and friars—
not one could cure me
they abandoned me for death.

Go out, men:
take with you spades and scythes
sickles, hoes and shovels.
Ransack the ruins
cut the bushes, clear the rubble,
the rank growth, the dust, the misery
that grows on my tragic grassland.

And in the place where fell
the sacred host you will see
among the useless plants
a patch of marvellous grass.

Let the priest come and with his fingers
take dexterously the sacred host.
And it's given to me: on my tongue
it will melt and I will sit up in the bed
as healthy as I was when young.

  trans. Michael Hartnett

The Great Queen Speaks. Cú Chulainn Listens.

I came to you
as a queen
colourfully clothed
beautifully formed
to grant you power
and kingdoms
all the internal country
all the territory of the soul
in one second
power over all this
and much glory
for it was given to me
to bestow on whom I wish
I brought you jewellery
and chattels.
But when I slipped

Drawn + from adapted Ulster Cycle stories

into bed with you
you said "Get off!"
This is no time for fun
I'm not here on behalf
of a woman's bum!
The wide world was yet
to be deafened
by your great deeds
your skills had yet
to be improved
and you gave me the back of your hand
if you didn't a closed fist.
All right, so—
it's a bargain—
please yourself.
But it will be worse for you
when I'm amongst your enemies
I will creep up on you
will await you at the ford
I'll be a grey wolf
who'll drive the herds
to stampede you
I'll be an eel
to trip you
I will be a polly cow
at the herd's head—
hard for God even
to save you from our hooves.
There's my hot harangue for you
Cú Chulainn.
    trans. Michael Hartnett

Muirghil Castigates Sweeny

"I dent with my heel
the cow-dung:
I pour milk in.
This is where you die."

These days
he can spend the hours
looking out the window
his eyes wide with fright—
if you come on him quick
"widdershins" as he thinks.
He drinks tea from a saucer,
he hasn't a tosser
'twas easy knowing
he'd end up a beggar.

"Whirr in—
drink my milk.
Whirr out again."

He complains about pains
in his bones, doctor—
I say 'don't mind about pains
in your bones—
wait until they get to your head!'
I do be only jokin', like.
Still he's brazen enough
to take to the beach
in his bare feet.
I f he wore the leg-warmers
I knitted for him
I wouldn't mind
but *no*—they're not good enough!
Oh, he's the boy, thanks very much—
don't thank me very much!

"Come home, home,
drink my milk
your season's done
your race is run"

I don't know how to tell you, Father—
he told me to send for no priest
—it's hard to explain on the phone—

he's out in the garden
since morning
tied to a tree by a horse-hair rope.
I never realised there was anything up
'til he got a crick in his neck
and a chough got up on his shoulder
I'm killed from him, Father—
he's driving me mad.

"I dented with my heel
the cow's dung:
I pour milk in.
This is where you die."

trans. Michael Hartnett

Parthenogenesis

Once, a lady of the Ó Moores
(married seven years without a child)
swam in the sea in summertime.
She swam well, and the day
was fine as Ireland ever saw
not even a puff of wind in the air
all the day calm, all the sea smooth—
a sheet of glass—supple, she struck out
with strength for the breaking waves
and frisked, elated by the world.
She ducked beneath the surface and there saw
what seemed a shadow, like a man's
And every twist and turn she made
the shadow did the same
and came close enough to touch.
Heart jumped and sound stopped in her mouth
her pulses ran and raced, sides near burst
The lower currents with their ice
pierced her to the bone
and the noise of the abyss numbed all her limbs
then scales grew on her skin . . .

the lure of the quiet dreamy undersea . . .
desire to escape to sea and shells . . .
the seaweed tresses where at last
her bones changed into coral
and time made atolls of her arms,
pearls of her eyes in deep long sleep,
at rest in a nest of weed,
secure as feather beds . . .
But stop!
Her heroic heritage was there,
she rose with speedy, threshing feet
and made in desperation for the beach:
with nimble supple strokes she made the sand.

Near death until the day,
some nine months later
she gave birth to a boy.
She and her husband so satisfied,
so full of love for this new son
forgot the shadow in the sea
and did not see what only the midwife saw—
stalks of sea-tangle in the boy's hair
small shellfish and sea-ribbons
and his two big eyes
as blue and limpid as lagoons.
A poor scholar passing by
who found lodging for the night
saw the boy's eyes never closed
in dark or light and when all the world slept
he asked the boy beside the fire
'Who are your people?' Came the prompt reply
"Sea People."

This same tale is told in the West
but the woman's an Ó Flaherty
and 'tis the same in the South
where the lady's called Ó Shea:
this tale is told on every coast.
But whoever she was I want to say
that the fear she felt
when the sea-shadow followed her

is the same fear that vexed
the young heart of the Virgin
when she heard the angel's sweet bell
and in her womb was made flesh
by all accounts
the Son of the Living God.
   trans. Michael Hartnett

The Language Issue

I place my hope on the water
in this little boat
of the language, the way a body might put
an infant

in a basket of intertwined
iris leaves,
its underside proofed
with bitumen and pitch,

then set the whole thing down amidst
the sedge
and the bulrushes by the edge
of a river

only to have it borne hither and thither,
not knowing where it might end up;
in the lap, perhaps,
of some Pharaoh's daughter.
   trans. Paul Muldoon

The Shannon Estuary
Welcoming the Fish

The leap of the salmon
in darkness,
naked blade
shield of silver.
I am welcoming, full of nets,
inveigling

slippery with seaweed,
quiet eddies
and eel-tails.

This fish
is nothing but meat
with very few bones
and very few entrails;
twenty pounds of muscle tauted,
aimed
at its nest in the mossy place.

And I will sing a lullaby
to my lover
wave on wave,
stave upon half-stave,
my phosphorescence as bed-linen under him,
my favourite, whom I, from afar have chosen.
      trans. Michael Hartnett

Further Readings on Nuala Ní Dhomhnaill

Bibliography

A Catalogue of the Manuscripts, Typescripts, and Correspondence of Nuala Ní Dhomh-naill. Galway, Ireland: Kenny's Bookshop and Art Gallery, 1994.

Selected Works

An Dealg Droighin. Cork: Mercier, 1981.
The Astrakhan Cloak. Translation by Paul Muldoon. Winston-Salem, N.C.: Wake Forest University Press, 1993.
Cead Aighis. Daingean, Ireland: An Sagart, 1998.
Ceist na Teangan: The Language Issue. Translated by Paul Muldoon. Carbondale, Ill.: Southern Illinois University Press, 1994.
Féar Suaithinseach. Maynooth, Ireland: An Sagart, 1984
Feis. Maynooth, Ireland: An Sagart, 1991.
In the Heart of Europe: Poems for Bosnia. Dublin: Amnesty International, 1998.
Jumping Off Shadows: Selected Contemporary Irish Poets. Cork: Cork University Press, 1995. (As editor with Greg Delanty.)

Pharaoh's Daughter. Oldcastle, Ireland: Gallery, 1990; Winston-Salem, N.C.: Wake Forest University Press, 1993.

RTÉ 100 Years: Ireland in the 20th Century. With Yseult Thornley. Dublin: Townhouse, 2001.

Selected Poems: Rogha Dánta. Translated by Michael Hartnett. 1986. Rprint, Dublin: New Island Books, 2000.

Spíonáin is Róiseanna: Compánach don Chaiséad CIC L21. Inverin, Ireland: Cló Iar-Chonnachta, 1993.

The Water Horse: Poems in Irish. With Medbh McGuckian, Eiléan Ní Chuilleanáin. Oldcastle, Ireland: Gallery Press, 1999.

"Why I Choose to Write in Irish, the Corpse That Sits Up and Talks Back," *New York Times Book Review* (January 8, 1995), 3. Reprinted in *Representing Ireland: Gender, Class, Nationality,* edited by Susan Shaw Sailer. Gainesville, Fla.: University Press of Florida, 1997.

Biography and Criticism

Eiléan Ní Chuilleanáin and Nuala Ní Dhomhnaill in Conversation with Dillon Johnston. Sante Fe, N.M.: Lannan Foundation, 1999. VHS videorecording.

Haberstroh, Patricia Boyle, ed. *My Self, My Muse: Irish Women Poets Reflect on Life and Art.* Syracuse, N.Y.: Syracuse University Press, 2003.

———. *Women Creating Women: Contemporary Irish Women Poets.* Syracuse, N.Y.: Syracuse University Press, 1996.

O'Connor, Mary. *Sex Lies and Sovereignty: Nuala Ní Dhomhnaill's Re-vision of the Táin.* Boston: Working Papers in Irish Studies, 1992.

Sewell, Frank. *Modern Irish Poetry: A New Alhambra.* Oxford: Oxford University Press, 2000.

The Southern Review. A Special Issue: Contemporary Irish Poetry and Criticism. 31, no. 3 (Summer 1995).

Paula Meehan (b. 1955)

Dubliner poet and playwright Paula Meehan was educated at Trinity College, Dublin, and Eastern Washington University. She won the Irish American Cultural Institute's Butler Award for Poetry in 1998; her play *Cell* was short-listed for the *Irish Times* Theatre Award from the Irish Arts Council. In her foreword to *The Man Who Was Marked by Winter,* poet Eavan Boland described Meehan's poetry as the work of a woman "who is restarting the Irish poem in terms of new initiatives and perspectives."

Meehan's poem "The Statue of the Virgin at Granard Speaks" is based on the death of an Irish teenaged girl who died alone and unaided after giving birth, in January 1984, at the foot of the grotto of Mary. The story became a call for more compassion and support for unmarried mothers. Meehan sets her poem on All Souls' Night, the feast of the Catholic Church that remembers the dead. The statue/speaker alludes to the Marian theology: that Mary was born free of original sin (Immaculate Conception) and that she was taken to heaven in her human form. A keen *(caoine)* is a lament for the dead.

The Statue of the Virgin at Granard Speaks

It can be bitter here at times like this,
November wind sweeping across the border.
Its seeds of ice would cut you to the quick.
The whole town tucked up safe and dreaming,
even wild things gone to earth, and I
stuck up here in this grotto, without as much as
star or planet to ease my vigil.

The howling won't let up. Trees
cavort in agony as if they would be free
and take off—ghost voyagers
on the wind that carries intimations
of garrison towns, walled cities, ghetto lanes
where men hunt each other and invoke
the various names of God as blessing
on their death tactics, their night manoeuvres.
Closer to home the wind sails over
dying lakes. I hear fish drowning.
I taste the stagnant water mingled
with turf smoke from outlying farms.

They call me Mary—Blessed, Holy, Virgin,
They fit me to a myth of a man crucified:
the scourging and the falling, and the falling again,
the thorny crown, the hammer blow of iron
into wrist and ankle, the sacred bleeding heart.
They name me Mother of all this grief
though mated to no mortal man.

They kneel before me and their prayers
fly up like sparks from a bonfire
that blaze a moment, then wink out.

It can be lovely here at times. Springtime,
early summer. Girls in Communion frocks
pale rivals to the riot in the hedgerows
of cow parsley and haw blossom, the perfume
from every rushy acre that's left for hay
when the light swings longer with the sun's push north.

Or the grace of a midsummer wedding
when the earth herself calls out for coupling
and I would break loose of my stony robes,
pure blue, pure white, as if they had robbed
a child's sky for their color. My being
cries out to be incarnate, incarnate,
maculate and tousled in a honeyed bed.

Even an autumn burial can work its own pageantry.
The hedges heavy with the burden of fruiting
crab, sloe, berry, hip; clouds scud east,
pear scented, windfalls secret in long
orchard grasses, and some old soul is lowered
to his kin. Death is just another harvest
scripted to the season's play.

But on this All Souls' Night there is
no respite from the keening of the wind.
I would not be amazed if every corpse came risen
from the graveyard to join in exaltation with the gale,
a cacophony of bone imploring sky for judgement
and release from being the conscience of the town.

On a night like this I remember the child
who came with fifteen summers to her name,
and she lay down alone at my feet
without midwife or doctor or friend to hold her hand
and she pushed her secret out into the night,

far from the town tucked up in little scandals,
bargains struck, words broken, prayers, promises,
and though she cried out to me in extremis
I did not move,
I didn't lift a finger to help her,
I didn't intercede with heaven,
nor whisper the charmed word in God's ear.

On a night like this I number the days to the solstice
and the turn back to the light. *(Pagan belief)*
   O sun,
center of our foolish dance,
burning heart of stone,
molten mother of us all,
hear me and have pity.

Further Readings on Paula Meehan

Selected Works

Cell: A Play in Two Acts for Four Actors and a Voice. Dublin: New Island Books, 2000.
Dharmakaya. Manchester, UK: Carcanet Press, 2000.
The Man Who Was Marked by Winter. Oldcastle, Ireland: Gallery Press, 1991.
Mysteries of the Home. Newcastle upon Tyne, UK: Bloodaxe Books, 1996.
Pillow Talk. Oldcastle, Ireland: Gallery Press, 1994.
Reading the Sky. Dublin: Beaver Row Press, 1985.
Return and No Blame. Dublin: Beaver Row Press, 1984.

Biography and Criticism

Dorgan, Theo. "An Interview with Paula Meehan." *Colby Quarterly* 28, no. 4 (December 1992): 265–69.
Weekes, Ann Owens. *Unveiling Treasures: The Attic Guide to the Published Works of Irish Women Literary Writers,* 224–26. Dublin: Attic Press, 1993.

Moya Cannon (b. 1956)

After a childhood in remote Dunfanaghy, County Donegal, Moya Cannon completed honors degree in history and politics at University College, Dublin, and a graduate degree at Corpus Christi College, Cambridge University. Most of her professional career has been spent as a teacher in the west of Ireland, most recently at a school for Travellers, the Irish class most discriminated against. She has also been a writer-in-residence at Trent University, Peterborough, Ontario, and has served as the editor of *Poetry Ireland Review*.

Her relatively small output of poetry has been enthusiastically received. Her first collection, *Oar* (1990), won the Brendan Behan Memorial Prize, and her poems were broadcast on British (BBC) and Irish (RTÉ) radio and television. Composer Jane O'Leary set several of her poems to music. Her poetry unites great themes with personal experience and makes extensive use of distinctive Irish landscapes, such as the three-hundred-square-kilometer region of County Clare known as the Burren, a limestone moonscape with wildflowers and archaeological ruins.

ck. out her poems on The Burren

Night

Coming back from Cloghane
in the sudden frost
of a November night,
I was ambushed
by the river of stars.

Disarmed by lit skies
I had utterly forgotten
this arc of darkness,
this black night
where the frost-hammered stars
were notes thrown from a chanter,
crans of light.

So I wasn't ready
for the dreadful glamour of Orion
as he struck out over Barr dTrí gCom
in his belt of stars.

At Gleann na nGealt
his bow of stars
was drawn against my heart.

What could I do?

Rather than drive into a pitch-black ditch
I got out twice,
leaned back against the car
and stared up at our windy, untidy loft
where old people had flung up old junk
they'd thought might come in handy,
ploughs, ladles, bears, lions, a clatter of heroes,
a few heroines, a path for the white cow, a swan
and, low down, almost within reach,
Venus, completely unfazed by the frost.

Further Readings on Moya Cannon

Selected Works

Cúm: An Anthology of New Writing from Co. Kerry. Tralee, Ireland: Kerry County
    Council, 1996.
Oar. Galway, Ireland: Salmon Publishing, 1990.
The Parchment Boat. Oldcastle, Ireland: Gallery Press, 1997.

Biography and Criticism

Denman, Peter. "Recent Verse." *Irish Literary Supplement* (Fall 1995): 9.
Haberstroh, Patricia Boyle, ed. *My Self, My Muse: Irish Women Poets Reflect on Life and
    Art.* Syracuse, N.Y.: Syracuse University Press, 2003.
McRedmond, Louis, ed. *Modern Irish Lives.* Dublin: Gill and Macmillan, 1996.
Sullivan, Moynagh. "Three From Gallery Press." *Irish Literary Supplement* (Spring,
    1999): 21–22.

Cathal Ó Searcaigh (b. 1956)

Born in the Donegal Gealtacht in 1956, Ó Searcaigh was educated at the National
Institute for Higher Education at Limerick (now the University of Limerick) and at
Maynooth College, where he read Celtic studies. After periods first in London and
then in Dublin, he entered Irish broadcasting, RTÉ. There he hosted a bilingual program, *Aisling Gheal* (Bright Vision) for three years. He then returned to farming in
the Gaeltacht at Gort a' Choirce (Gortahork Cottage) so that he might devote all his
artistic energies to writing in the Irish language. He has described the process as
"repossessing tongue and tradition."

His poetry reflects seemingly contradictory influences, from eighteenth- and nineteenth-century Irish-language poets on the one hand, to popular culture, American beat poetry, Eastern philosophy, and a nonorthodox form of spirituality on the other. On a trip to the Himalayas, he adopted a Nepalese boy, Prem Timalsina, whom he raised to maturity. His finely crafted poetry is known for its lyric intensity and sensuality and has won many awards. He composes poetry only in Irish but has found a distinguished array of translators, among them Gabriel Rosenstock, John F. Deane, and Seamus Heaney. From 1992 to 1995, Ó Searcaigh served as writer-in-residence at University College, Cork, and Queen's University, Belfast.

The Well

FOR MÁIRE MHAC AN tSAOI

" 'Twill put a stir in you, and life,"
says old Bridget, spark in her eyes
profferring in a bowl of spring-water
from the purest well in Gleann an Atha,
a well that was tended lovingly
from generation to generation, the precious
heritage of the household
snugly sheltered in a nook,
a ditch around it for protection,
a flagstone on its mouth.

When I was growing up
here in the early 'sixties
there wasn't a house in the neighborhood
without its like,
for everyone was proud then
of how wholesome and pure
they kept the family well:
they wouldn't let it become murky or slimy
and at the first trace of red-rust
it was bailed-out with a tin bucket;
every season it was purified with kiln-lime.

Lively, living water, pellucid spring-water
gushed forth from our family well.

In tin-cans and pitchers
they drew it daily
and in the devouring thirst
of sweltering summer
it slaked and cooled them
in field and bog.
It was a tonic, too,
that made them throb with delight
and for their ablutions
it served from cradle to grave.

But, this long time, piped water from distant hills
sneaks into every kitchen
on both sides of the glen;
water spurts from a tap,
mawkish, without sparkle,
zestless as slops
and among my people
the springwell is being forgotten.

" 'Tis hard to find a well nowadays,"
says Bridget filling the bowl again.
"They're hidden in rushes and grass,
choked by green scum and ferns,
but, despite the neglect,
they've lost none of their true mettle.
Seek out your own well, my dear,
for the age of water is near:
There will have to be a going back to sources."
        trans. Gabriel Fitzmaurice

Beyond

In your sleep you raise
Neither fort nor sanctuary

At night I pace
That other world behind your eyes

Of a clearer blue, truer
Than the sash of the Virgin Mary.

On the other side of words
Lies a world of that same clarity.

trans. Rosita Boland

Further Readings on Cathal Ó Searcaigh

Selected Writings

Ag Tnúth leis an tSolas: 1975-2000. Inverin, Ireland: Cló Iar-Chonnachta, 2000.
Caiseal na gCorr. With Jan Voster. Inverin, Ireland: Cló Iar-Chonnachta, 2002.
Cré na Cuimhne. Cast in Clay. Belfast: HU Publications, 1997.
Homecoming: Selected Poems. An Bealach 'na Bhaile. Translated by Gabriel Fitzmaurice. Inverin, Ireland: Cló Iar-Chonnachta, 1993.
Miontraigéide Cathrach. Falcara, Ireland: Cló Uí Chuirreáin, 1975.
Na Buachailli Bána. Inverin, Ireland: Cló Iar-Chonnachta, 1996.
Out in the Open. Translated by Frank Sewell. Inverin, Ireland: Cló Iar-Chonnachta, 1997.
Seal in Neípeal. Inverin, Ireland: Cló Iar-Chonnachta, 2003.
Suibhne. Dublin: Coiscéim, 1987.
Súile Shuibhne. Dublin: Coiscéim, 1983.

Biography and Criticism

Brown, John, ed. "Interviewing Cathal Ó Searcaigh," *In the Chair: Interviews with Poets from Northern Ireland*. Cliffs of Moher, Ireland: Salmon Publishing, 2002.
Doan, James, and Frank Sewell, eds. *On the Side of Light: Critical Essays on the Poetry of Cathal Ó Searcaigh*. Galway: Arlen House, 2002.
Dorgan, Theo, ed. *Irish Poetry Since Kavanagh*. Blackrock, Ireland: Four Courts, 1996.
O'Carroll, Íde, and E. Collins, eds. *Lesbian and Gay Visions of Ireland: Towards the Twenty-First Century*. London: Cassell, 1995.
Sewell, Frank. *Modern Irish Poetry: A New Alhambra*. Oxford: Oxford University Press, 2000.
Walshe, Éibhear, ed. *Sex, Nation and Dissent in Irish Writing*. Cork: Cork University Press, 1997.

Greg Delanty (b. 1958)

Greg Delanty was born and educated in Cork, where he took his degree in English and history and trained for teaching. He was awarded the Patrick Kavanagh Memorial Award in 1983. He is the youngest poet represented in *The Field Day Anthology of Irish Literature,* vols. 1–3.

Since 1987, Delanty has been a member of the faculty of English at St. Michael's College. His American experience has informed his poems, especially those that explore the complexity of the emigrant experience. The Heritage Center in Cobh is located in the old railroad station where about two and one-half million Irish arrived to meet their emigrant ships. "To President Mary Robinson," is Delanty's ironic riposte to a memorable phrase in the president's inaugural address in 1990—her promise to put a light in the window of the Aras an Uachtarán, the Irish White House.

The Heritage Centre, Cobh 1993

The Cobh train might be a time machine
transporting us from the smog-shrouded city.
Chemical plants surrounding the Lee
& harbour flick by into the future.
We enter the simulated coffin ship,
& peruse dioramas of papier-mâché emigrants
poised in various stages of travail,
accompanied by the canned clamour
of goodbyes, hooters & sailors rigging mast.

We are back doing Lent's Stations
from convict ship to the grand finale
of the *Lusitania* and *Titanic,* buried
in the sea's unopened sepulcher.
The *Titanic*'s washed-up spyglass
is too rusted to extend further.
Turned the wrong way around
and everything diminishes & goes far off

just as our own world goes further
from what we want each day: a place

But I keep doomsaying theatrics to myself,
afraid I'll sound like that diver's commentary
down for the first televised time in the *Titanic,*
dramatising the merest chink at every stage,
from first-class cabin, below to the dark,
fathomless eternity of the gashed steerage.

To President Mary Robinson

Yes, we're moved by the light in your window
    but, returning on another brief holiday
    from England, Australia or the USA,
we can't help feel somewhat mocked by its glow.
For though we know full well we are no
    Holy Family, we're still turned away
    to settle in the unfamiliar, cold hay.

Further Readings on Greg Delanty

Selected Work

American Wake. Belfast: Blackstaff Press, 1995.
The Blind Stitch: Poems. Manchester, UK: Carcanet, 2001.
Cast in the Fire. Portlaoise, Ireland: Dolmen, 1986.
The Hellbox. Oxford: Oxford University Press, 1998.
Jumping Off Shadows: Selected Contemporary Irish Poets. Cork: Cork University Press,
    1995. (As editor with Nuala Ní Dhomhnaill.)
Leper's Walk. Burlington, Vt.: Private published, 2000.
Southward: Poems. Dublin: Dedalus Press, 1992.
Striped Ink. With Paulette Myers-Rich. Minneapolis: Traffic Street Press, 2000.

PART FOUR

Late Twentieth-Century Fiction and Drama

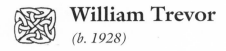

William Trevor
(b. 1928)

County Cork–born William Trevor has produced more than forty works, including short-story collections, novels, dramas, filmscripts, anthologies, travel pieces, memoirs, and edited anthologies. Although much esteemed for his novels, several of which have been filmed, he has achieved even greater critical acclaim for his short stories, which appear regularly in the *New Yorker*. He is, uncommonly, one of the few living short story writers to reach a wide market, his massive, 1261-page *Collected Stories* racking up substantial sales in a Penguin paperback.

Trevor was born William Trevor Cox, the name under which he began to publish in 1958. Although the son of a Protestant bank official, Trevor did not grow up in privilege. As he has said, he could have been a boy hired to fetch tennis balls on the estate of another Cork Protestant, Elizabeth Bowen (1899–1973), with whom he is sometimes compared. Like Bowen, Trevor has set his fiction in both England and Ireland, although since he left Ireland in the 1950s, his Irish fiction has tended to be set only before that time.

Quite a bit of Trevor's Irish fiction deals with political violence, especially the way it has affected innocent, apolitical persons. Examples include the novels *Fools of Fortune* and *In the Garden* and the short stories "The News From Ireland," "Beyond the Pale," and "Attracta."

Both his English and Irish fiction are characterized by Trevor's dark, satirical humor. He often shows sympathy for marginal or rejected figures, including the perverted and insane. His novel *Felicia's Journey* (1994) deals with a girl from the Irish Midlands who migrates to Britain, where she falls into the hands of a sexual psychopath, Mr. Hilditch, an outwardly gentle and likable fellow.

Trevor's humor has mellowed somewhat over the years. Perhaps his best-known story, "The Ballroom of Romance" (1972), shows a gentler mode of Trevor's dark comedy. Feminist commentators have praised Trevor for his empathy with a single woman in a male-dominated society. Trevor adapted the story for Pat O'Connor's fifty-two-minute film version for BBC-TV; released in 1982 and starring Brenda Fricker, John Kavanagh, and Cyril Cusack, it has been available from select agencies.

The Ballroom of Romance

On Sundays, or on Mondays if he couldn't make it and often he couldn't, Sunday being his busy day, Canon O'Connell arrived at the farm in order to hold a private service with Bridie's father, who couldn't get about any more, having had a leg amputated after gangrene had set in. They'd had a pony and cart then and Bridie's mother had been alive: it hadn't been difficult for the two of them to help her father on to the cart in order to make the journey to Mass. But two years later the pony had gone lame and eventually had to be destroyed; not long after that her mother had died. "Don't worry about it at all," Canon O'Connell had said, referring to the difficulty of transporting her father to Mass. "I'll slip up by the week, Bridie."

The milk lorry called daily for the single churn of milk, Mr Driscoll delivered groceries and meal in his van, and took away the eggs that Bridie had collected during the week. Since Canon O'Connell had made his offer, in 1953, Bridie's father hadn't left the farm.

As well as Mass on Sundays and her weekly visits to a wayside dance-hall Bridie went shopping once every month, cycling to the town early on a Friday afternoon. She bought things for herself, material for a dress, knitting wool, stockings, a newspaper, and paper-backed Wild West novels for her father. She talked in the shops to some of the girls she'd been at school with, girls who had married shop-assistants or shopkeepers, or had become assistants themselves. Most of them had families of their own by now. "You're lucky to be peaceful in the hills," they said to Bridie, "instead of stuck in a hole like this." They had a tired look, most of them, from pregnancies and their efforts to organize and control their large families.

As she cycled back to the hills on a Friday Bridie often felt that they truly envied her her life, and she found it surprising that they should do so. If it hadn't been for her father she'd have wanted to work in the town also, in the tinned-meat factory maybe, or in a shop. The town had a cinema called the Electric, and a fish-and-chip shop where people met at night, eating chips out of newspaper on the pavement outside. In the evenings, sitting in the farmhouse with her father, she often thought about the town, imagining the shop-windows lit up to display their goods and the sweet-shops still open so that people could purchase chocolates or fruit to take with them to the Electric cinema. But the town was eleven miles away, which was too far to cycle, there and back, for an evening's entertainment.

"It's a terrible thing for you, girl," her father used to say, genuinely troubled, "tied up to a one-legged man." He would sigh heavily, hobbling back from the fields, where he managed as best he could. "If your mother hadn't died," he'd say, not finishing the sentence.

If her mother hadn't died her mother could have looked after him and the scant acres he owned, her mother could somehow have lifted the milk-churn on to the collection platform and attended to the few hens and the cows. "I'd be dead without the girl to assist me," she'd heard her father saying to Canon O'Connell, and Canon O'Connell replied that he was certainly lucky to have her.

"Amn't I as happy here as anywhere?" she'd say herself, but her father knew she was pretending and was saddened because the weight of circumstances had so harshly interfered with her life.

Although her father still called her a girl, Bridie was thirty-six. She was tall and strong: the skin of her fingers and her palms were stained, and harsh to touch. The labour they'd experienced had found its way into them, as though juices had come out of vegetation and pigment out of soil: since childhood she'd torn away the rough scotch grass that grew each spring among her father's mangolds and sugar beet; since childhood she'd harvested potatoes in August, her hands daily rooting in the ground she loosened and turned. Wind had toughened the flesh of her face, sun had browned it; her neck and nose were lean, her lips touched with early wrinkles.

But on Saturday nights Bridie forgot the scotch grass and the soil. In different dresses she cycled to the dance-hall, encouraged to make the journey by her father. "Doesn't it do you good, girl?" he'd say, as though he imagined she begrudged herself the pleasure. "Why wouldn't you enjoy yourself?" She'd cook him his tea and then he'd settle down with the wireless, or maybe a Wild West novel. In time, while still she danced, he'd stoke the fire up and hobble his way upstairs to bed.

The dance-hall, owned by Mr Justin Dwyer, was miles from anywhere, a lone building by the roadside with treeless boglands all around and a gravel expanse in front of it. On pink pebbled cement its title was painted in an azure blue that matched the depth of the background shade yet stood out well, unfussily proclaiming *The Ballroom of Romance*. Above these letters four coloured bulbs—in red, green, orange and mauve—were lit at appropriate times, an indication that the evening rendezvous was open for business. Only the façade of the building was pink, the other walls being a more ordinary grey. And inside, except for pink swing-doors, everything was blue.

On Saturday nights Mr Justin Dwyer, a small, thin man, unlocked the metal grid that protected his property and drew it back, creating an open mouth from which music would later pour. He helped his wife to carry crates of lemonade and packets of biscuits from their car, and then took up a position in the tiny vestibule between the drawn-back grid and the pink swing-doors. He sat at a card-table, with money and tickets spread out before him. He'd made a fortune, people said: he owned other ballrooms also.

People came on bicycles or in old motor-cars, country people like Bridie from remote hill farms and villages. People who did not often see other people met there, girls and boys, men and women. They paid Mr Dwyer and passed into his dance-hall, where shadows were cast on pale-blue walls and light from a crystal bowl was dim. The band, known as the Romantic Jazz Band, was composed of clarinet, drums and piano. The drummer sometimes sang.

Bridie had been going to the dance-hall since first she left the Presentation Nuns, before her mother's death. She didn't mind the journey, which was seven miles there and seven back: she'd travelled as far every day to the Presentation Nuns on the same bicycle, which had once been the property of her mother, an old Rudge purchased originally in 1936. On Sundays she cycled six miles to Mass, but she never minded either: she'd grown quite used to all that.

"How're you, Bridie?" inquired Mr Justin Dwyer when she arrived in a new scarlet dress one autumn evening. She said she was all right and in reply to Mr Dwyer's second query she said that her father was all right also, "I'll go up one of these days," promised Mr Dwyer, which was a promise he'd been making for twenty years.

She paid the entrance fee and passed through the pink swing-doors. The Romantic Jazz Band was playing a familiar melody of the past, "The Destiny Waltz." In spite of the band's title, jazz was not ever played in the ballroom: Mr Dwyer did not personally care for that kind of music, nor had he cared for various dance movements that had come and gone over the years. Jiving, rock and roll, twisting and other such variations had all been resisted by Mr Dwyer, who believed that a ballroom should be, as much as possible, a dignified place. The Romantic Jazz Band consisted of Mr Maloney, Mr Swanton, and Dano Ryan on drums. They were three middle-aged men who drove out from the town in Mr Maloney's car, amateur performers who were employed otherwise by the tinned-meat factory, the Electricity Supply Board and the County Council.

"How're you, Bridie?" inquired Dano Ryan as she passed him on her way to the cloakroom. He was idle for a moment with his drums, "The Destiny Waltz" not calling for much attention from him.

"I'm all right, Dano," she said. "Are you fit yourself? Are the eyes better?" The week before he'd told her that he'd developed a watering of the eyes that must have been some kind of cold or other. He'd woken up with it in the morning and it had persisted until the afternoon: it was a new experience, he'd told her, adding that he'd never had a day's illness or discomfort in his life.

"I think I need glasses," he said now, and as she passed into the cloakroom she imagined him in glasses, repairing the roads, as he was employed to do by the County Council. You hardly ever saw a road-mender with glasses, she reflected, and she wondered if all the dust that was inherent in his work had perhaps affected his eyes.

"How're you, Bridie?" a girl called Eenie Mackie said in the cloakroom, a girl who'd left the Presentation Nuns only a year ago.

"That's a lovely dress, Eenie," Bridie said. "Is it nylon, that?"

"Tricel actually. Drip-dry."

Bridie took off her coat and hung it on a hook. There was a small wash-basin in the cloakroom above which hung a discoloured oval mirror. Used tissues and pieces of cotton-wool, cigarette-butts and matches covered the concrete floor. Lengths of green-painted timber partitioned off a lavatory in a corner.

"Jeez, you're looking great, Bridie," Madge Dowding remarked, waiting for her turn at the mirror. She moved towards it as she spoke, taking off a pair of spectacles before endeavouring to apply make-up to the lashes of her eye. She stared myopically into the oval mirror, humming while the other girls became restive.

"Will you hurry up, for God's sake!" shouted Eenie Mackie. "We're standing here all night, Madge."

Madge Dowding was the only one who was older than Bridie. She was thirty-nine, although often she said she was younger. The girls sniggered about that, saying that Madge Dowding should accept her condition—her age and her squint and her poor complexion—and not make herself ridiculous going out after men. What man would be bothered with the like of her anyway? Madge Dowding would do better to give herself over to do Saturday-night work for the Legion of Mary: wasn't Canon O'Connell always looking for aid?

"Is that fellow there?" she asked now, moving away from the mirror. "The guy with the long arms. Did anyone see him outside?"

"He's dancing with Cat Bolger," one of the girls replied. "She has herself glued to him."

"Lover boy," remarked Patty Byrne, and everyone laughed because the person referred to was hardly a boy any more, being over fifty it was said, a bachelor who came only occasionally to the dance-hall.

Madge Dowding left the cloakroom rapidly, not bothering to pretend she wasn't anxious about the conjunction of Cat Bolger and the man with the long arms. Two sharp spots of red had come into her checks, and when she stumbled in her haste the girls in the cloakroom laughed. A younger girl would have pretended to be casual.

Bridie chatted, waiting for the mirror. Some girls, not wishing to be delayed, used the mirrors of their compacts. Then in twos and threes, occasionally singly, they left the cloakroom and took their places on upright wooden chairs at one end of the dance-hall, waiting to be asked to dance. Mr Maloney, Mr Swanton and Dano Ryan played "Harvest Moon" and "I Wonder Who's Kissing Her Now" and "I'll Be Around."

Bridie danced. Her father would be falling asleep by the fire; the wireless, tuned in to Radio Éireann, would be murmuring in the background. Already he'd have listened to *Faith and Order* and *Spot the Talent*. His Wild West novel, *Three Rode Fast* by Jake Matall, would have dropped from his single knee on to the flagged floor. He would wake with a jerk as he did every night and, forgetting what night it was, might be surprised not to see her, for usually she was sitting there at the table, mending clothes or washing eggs. "Is it time for the news?" he'd automatically say.

Dust and cigarette smoke formed a haze beneath the crystal bowl, feet thudded, girls shrieked and laughed, some of them dancing together for want of a male partner. The music was loud, the musicians had taken off their jackets. Vigorously they played a number of tunes from *State Fair* and then, more romantically, "Just One of Those Things." The tempo increased for a Paul Jones, after which Bridie found herself with a youth who told her he was saving up to emigrate, the nation in his opinion being finished. "I'm up in the hills with the uncle," he said, "labouring fourteen hours a day. Is it any life for a young fellow?" She knew his uncle, a hill farmer whose stony acres were separated from her father's by one other farm only. "He has me gutted with work," the youth told her. "Is there sense in it at all, Bridie?"

At ten o'clock there was a stir, occasioned by the arrival of three middle-aged bachelors who'd cycled over from Carey's public house. They shouted and whistled, greeting other people across the dancing area. They smelt of stout and sweat and whiskey.

Every Saturday at just this time they arrived, and, having sold them their tickets, Mr Dwyer folded up his card-table and locked the tin box that held the evening's takings: his ballroom was complete.

"How're you, Bridie?" one of the bachelors, known as Bowser Egan, inquired. Another one, Tim Daly, asked Patty Byrne how she was. "Will we take the floor?" Eyes Horgan suggested to Madge Dowding, already pressing the front of his navy-blue suit against the net of her dress. Bridie danced with Bowser Egan, who said she was looking great.

The bachelors would never marry, the girls of the dance-hall considered: they were wedded already, to stout and whiskey and laziness, to three old mothers somewhere up in the hills. The man with the long arms didn't drink but he was the same in all other ways: he had the same look of a bachelor, a quality in his face.

"Great," Bowser Egan said, feather-stepping in an inaccurate and inebriated manner. "You're a great little dancer, Bridie."

"Will you lay off that!" cried Madge Dowding, her voice shrill above the sound of the music. Eyes Horgan had slipped two fingers into the back of her dress and was now pretending they'd got there by accident. He smiled blearily, his huge red face streaming with perspiration, the eyes which gave him his nickname protuberant and bloodshot.

"Watch your step with that one," Bowser Egan called out, laughing so that spittle sprayed on to Bridie's face. Eenie Mackie, who was also dancing near the incident, laughed also and winked at Bridie. Dano Ryan left his drums and sang. "Oh, how I miss your gentle kiss," he crooned, "and long to hold you tight."

Nobody knew the name of the man with the long arms. The only words he'd ever been known to speak in the Ballroom of Romance were the words that formed his invitation to dance. He was a shy man who stood alone when he wasn't performing on the dance-floor. He rode away on his bicycle afterwards, not saying good-night to anyone.

"Cat has your man leppin' tonight," Tim Daly remarked to Patty Byrne, for the liveliness that Cat Bolger had introduced into foxtrot and waltz was noticeable.

"I think of you only," sang Dano Ryan. "Only wishing, wishing you were by my side."

Dano Ryan would have done, Bridie often thought, because he was a different kind of bachelor: he had a lonely look about him, as if he'd become tired of being on his own. Every week she thought he would have done, and during the week her mind regularly returned to that thought. Dano Ryan would have done because she felt he wouldn't mind coming to live in the farmhouse while her one-legged father was still about the place. Three could live as cheaply as two where Dano Ryan was concerned because giving up the wages he earned as a road-worker would be balanced by the saving made on what he paid for lodgings. Once, at the end of an evening, she'd pretended that there was a puncture in the back wheel of her bicycle and he'd concerned himself with it while Mr Maloney and Mr Swanton waited for him in Mr Maloney's car. He'd blown the tyre up with the car pump and had said he thought it would hold.

It was well known in the dance-hall that she fancied her chances with Dano Ryan. But it was well known also that Dano Ryan had got into a set way of life and had remained in it for quite some years. He lodged with a widow called Mrs Griffin and Mrs Griffin's mentally affected son, in a cottage on the outskirts of the town. He was said to be good to the affected child, buying him sweets and taking him out for rides on the crossbar of his bicycle. He gave an hour or two of his time every week to the Church of Our Lady Queen of Heaven, and he was loyal to Mr Dwyer. He performed in the two other rural dance-halls that Mr Dwyer owned, rejecting advances from the town's more sophisticated dance-hall, even though it was more conveniently situated for him and the fee was more substantial than that paid by Mr Dwyer. But Mr Dwyer had discovered Dano Ryan and Dano had not forgotten it, just as Mr Maloney and Mr Swanton had not forgotten their discovery by Mr Dwyer either.

"Would we take a lemonade?" Bowser Egan suggested. "And a packet of biscuits, Bridie?"

No alcoholic liquor was ever served in the Ballroom of Romance, the premises not being licensed for this added stimulant. Mr Dwyer in fact had never sought a licence for any of his premises, knowing that romance and alcohol were difficult commodities to mix, especially in a dignified ballroom. Behind where the girls sat on the wooden chairs Mr Dwyer's wife, a small stout woman, served the bottles of lemonade, with straws, and the biscuits, and crisps. She talked busily while doing so, mainly about the turkeys she kept. She'd once told Bridie that she thought of them as children.

"Thanks," Bridie said, and Bowser Egan led her to the trestle table. Soon it would be the intermission: soon the three members of the band would cross the floor also for refreshment. She thought up questions to ask Dano Ryan.

When first she'd danced in the Ballroom of Romance, when she was just sixteen, Dano Ryan had been there also, four years older than she was, playing the drums for Mr Maloney as he played them now. She'd hardly noticed him then because of his not being one of the dancers: he was part of the ballroom's scenery, like the trestle table and the lemonade bottles, and Mrs Dwyer and Mr Dwyer. The youths who'd danced with her then in their Saturday-night blue suits had later disappeared into the town, or to Dublin or Britain, leaving behind them those who became the middle-aged bachelors of the hills. There'd been a boy called Patrick Grady whom she had loved in those days. Week after week she'd ridden away from the Ballroom of Romance with the image of his face in her mind, a thin face, pale beneath black hair. It had been different, dancing with Patrick Grady, and she'd felt that he found it different dancing with her, although he'd never said so. At night she'd dreamed of him and in the daytime too, while she helped her mother in the kitchen or her father with the cows. Week by week she'd returned to the ballroom, delighting in its pink façade and dancing in the arms of Patrick Grady. Often they'd stood together drinking lemonade, not saying anything, not knowing what to say. She knew he loved her, and she believed then that he would lead her one day from the dim, romantic ballroom, from its blueness and its pinkness and its crystal bowl of light and its music. She believed he would lead her into sunshine, to the town and the Church of Our Lady Queen of Heaven, to marriage and smiling faces. But someone else had got Patrick Grady, a girl from the town who'd never danced in the wayside ballroom. She'd scooped up Patrick Grady when he didn't have a chance.

Bridie had wept, hearing that. By night she'd lain in her bed in the farmhouse, quietly crying, the tears rolling into her hair and making the pillow damp. When she woke in the early morning the thought was still naggingly with her and it remained with her by day, replacing her daytime dreams of happiness. Someone told her later on that he'd crossed to Britain, to Wolverhampton, with the girl he'd married, and she imagined him there, in a place she wasn't able properly to visualize, labouring in a factory, his children being born and acquiring the accent of the area. The Ballroom of Romance wasn't the same without him, and when no one else stood out for her particularly over the years and when no one offered her marriage, she found herself wondering about Dano Ryan. If you couldn't have love, the next best thing was surely a decent man.

Bowser Egan hardly fell into that category, nor did Tim Daly. And it was plain to everyone that Cat Bolger and Madge Dowding were wasting their time over the man with the long arms. Madge Dowding was already a figure of fun in the ballroom, the way she ran after the bachelors; Cat Bolger would end up the same if she wasn't careful. One way or another it wasn't difficult to be a figure of fun in the ballroom, and you didn't have to be as old as Madge Dowding: a girl who'd just left the Presentation Nuns had once asked Eyes Horgan what he had in his trouser pocket and he told her it was a penknife. She'd repeated this afterwards in the cloakroom, how she'd requested Eyes Horgan not to dance so close to her because his penknife was sticking into her. "Jeez, aren't you the right baby!" Patty Byrne had shouted delightedly; everyone had laughed, knowing that Eyes Horgan only came to the ballroom for stuff like that. He was no use to any girl.

"Two lemonades, Mrs Dwyer," Bowser Egan said, "and two packets of Kerry Creams. Is Kerry Creams all right, Bridie?"

She nodded, smiling. Kerry Creams would be fine, she said.

"Well, Bridie, isn't that the great outfit you have!" Mrs Dwyer remarked. "Doesn't the red suit her, Bowser?"

By the swing-doors stood Mr Dwyer, smoking a cigarette that he held cupped in his left hand. His small eyes noted all developments. He had been aware of Madge Dowding's anxiety when Eyes Horgan had inserted two fingers into the back opening of her dress. He had looked away, not caring for the incident, but had it developed further he would have spoken to Eyes Horgan, as he had on other occasions. Some of the younger lads didn't know any better and would dance very close to their partners, who generally were too embarrassed to do anything about it, being young themselves. But that, in Mr Dwyer's opinion, was a different kettle of fish altogether because they were decent young lads who'd in no time at all be doing a steady line with a girl and would end up as he had himself with Mrs Dwyer, in the same house with her, sleeping in a bed with her, firmly married. It was the middle-aged bachelors who required the watching: they came down from the hills like mountain goats, released from their mammies and from the smell of animals and soil. Mr Dwyer continued to watch Eyes Horgan, wondering how drunk he was.

Dano Ryan's song came to an end, Mr Swanton laid down his clarinet, Mr Maloney rose from the piano. Dano Ryan wiped sweat from his face and the three men slowly moved towards Mrs Dwyer's trestle table.

"Jeez, you have powerful legs," Eyes Horgan whispered to Madge Dowding, but Madge Dowding's attention was on the man with the long arms, who had left Cat Bolger's side and was proceeding in the direction of the men's lavatory. He never took refreshments. She moved, herself, towards the men's lavatory, to take up a position outside it, but Eyes Horgan followed her. "Would you take a lemonade, Madge?" he asked. He had a small bottle of whiskey on him: if they went into a corner they could add a drop of it to the lemonade. She didn't drink spirits, she reminded him, and he went away.

"Excuse me a minute," Bowser Egan said, putting down his bottle of lemonade. He crossed the floor to the lavatory. He too, Bridie knew, would have a small bottle of whiskey on him. She watched while Dano Ryan, listening to a story Mr Maloney was telling, paused in the centre of the ballroom, his head bent to hear what was being said. He was a big man, heavily made, with black hair that was slightly touched with grey, and big hands. He laughed when Mr Maloney came to the end of his story and then bent his head again, in order to listen to a story told by Mr Swanton.

"Are you on your own, Bridie?" Cat Bolger asked, and Bridie said she was waiting for Bowser Egan. "I think I'll have a lemonade," Cat Bolger said.

Younger boys and girls stood with their arms still around one another, queuing up for refreshments. Boys who hadn't danced at all, being nervous because they didn't know any steps, stood in groups, smoking and making jokes. Girls who hadn't been danced with yet talked to one another, their eyes wandering. Some of them sucked at straws in lemonade bottles.

Bridie, still watching Dano Ryan, imagined him wearing the glasses he'd referred to, sitting in the farmhouse kitchen, reading one of her father's Wild West novels. She imagined the three of them eating a meal she'd prepared, fried eggs and rashers and fried potato-cakes, and tea and bread and butter and jam, brown bread and soda and shop bread. She imagined Dano Ryan leaving the kitchen in the morning to go out to the fields in order to weed the mangolds, and her father hobbling off behind him, and the two men working together. She saw hay being cut, Dano Ryan with the scythe that she'd learned to use herself, her father using a rake as best he could. She saw herself, because of the extra help, being able to attend to things in the farmhouse, things she'd never had time for because of the cows and the hens and the fields. There were bedroom curtains that needed repairing where the net had ripped, and wallpaper that had become loose and needed to be stuck up with flour paste. The scullery required white-washing.

The night he'd blown up the tyre of her bicycle she'd thought he was going to kiss her. He'd crouched on the ground in the darkness with his ear to the tyre, listening for escaping air. When he could hear none he'd straightened up and said he thought she'd be all right on the bicycle. His face had been quite close to hers and she'd smiled at him. At that moment, unfortunately, Mr Maloney had blown an impatient blast on the horn of his motor-car.

Often she'd been kissed by Bowser Egan, on the nights when he insisted on riding part of the way home with her. They had to dismount in order to push their bicycles up a hill and the first time he'd accompanied her he'd contrived to fall against her, steadying himself by putting a hand on her shoulder. The next thing she was aware of was the moist quality of his lips and the sound of his bicycle as it clattered noisily on the road. He'd suggested then, regaining his breath, that they should go into a field.

That was nine years ago. In the intervening passage of time she'd been kissed as well, in similar circumstances, by Eyes Horgan and Tim Daly. She'd gone into fields with them and permitted them to put their arms about her while heavily they breathed. At one time or another she had imagined marriage with one or other of them, seeing them in the farmhouse with her father, even though the fantasies were unlikely.

Bridie stood with Cat Bolger, knowing that it would be some time before Bowser Egan came out of the lavatory. Mr Maloney, Mr Swanton and Dano Ryan approached, Mr Maloney insisting that he would fetch three bottles of lemonade from the trestle table.

"You sang the last one beautifully," Bridie said to Dano Ryan. "Isn't it a beautiful song?"

Mr Swanton said it was the finest song ever written, and Cat Bolger said she preferred "Danny Boy," which in her opinion was the finest song ever written.

"Take a suck of that," said Mr Maloney, handing Dano Ryan and Mr Swanton bottles of lemonade. "How's Bridie tonight? Is your father well, Bridie?"

Her father was all right, she said.

"I hear they're starting a cement factory," said Mr Maloney. "Did anyone hear talk of that? They're after striking some commodity in the earth that makes good cement. Ten feet down, over at Kilmalough."

"It'll bring employment," said Mr Swanton. "It's employment that's necessary in this area."

"Canon O'Connell was on about it," Mr Maloney said. "There's Yankee money involved."

"Will the Yanks come over?" inquired Cat Bolger. "Will they run it themselves, Mr Maloney?"

Mr Maloney, intent on his lemonade, didn't hear the questions and Cat Bolger didn't repeat them.

"There's stuff called Optrex," Bridie said quietly to Dano Ryan, "that my father took the time he had a cold in his eyes. Maybe Optrex would settle the watering, Dano."

"Ah sure, it doesn't worry me that much—"

"It's terrible, anything wrong with the eyes. You wouldn't want to take a chance. You'd get Optrex in a chemist, Dano, and a little bowl with it so that you can bathe the eyes."

Her father's eyes had become red-rimmed and unsightly to look at. She'd gone into Riordan's Medical Hall in the town and had explained what the trouble was, and Mr Riordan had recommended Optrex. She told this to Dano Ryan, adding that her father had had no trouble with his eyes since. Dano Ryan nodded.

"Did you hear that, Mrs Dwyer?" Mr Maloney called out. "A cement factory for Kilmalough."

Mrs Dwyer wagged her head, placing empty bottles in a crate. She'd heard references to the cement factory, she said: it was the best news for a long time.

"Kilmalough won't know itself," her husband commented, joining her in her task with the empty lemonade bottles.

" 'Twill bring prosperity certainly," said Mr Swanton. "I was saying just there, Justin, that employment's what's necessary.'

"Sure, won't the Yanks—" began Cat Bolger, but Mr Maloney interrupted her.

"The Yanks'll be in at the top, Cat, or maybe not here at all—maybe only inserting money into it. It'll be local labour entirely."

"You'll not marry a Yank, Cat," said Mr Swanton, loudly laughing. "You can't catch those fellows."

"Haven't you plenty of homemade bachelors?" suggested Mr Maloney. He laughed also, throwing away the straw he was sucking through and tipping the bottle into his mouth. Cat Bolger told him to get on with himself. She moved towards the men's lavatory and took up a position outside it, not speaking to Madge Dowding, who was still standing there.

"Keep a watch on Eyes Horgan," Mrs Dwyer warned her husband, which was advice she gave him at this time every Saturday night, knowing that Eyes Horgan was drinking in the lavatory. When he was drunk Eyes Horgan was the most difficult of the bachelors.

"I have a drop of it left, Dano," Bridie said quietly. "I could bring it over on Saturday. The eye stuff."

"Ah, don't worry yourself, Bridie—"

"No trouble at all. Honestly now—"

"Mrs Griffin has me fixed up for a test with Dr Cready. The old eyes are no worry, only when I'm reading the paper or at the pictures. Mrs Griffin says I'm only straining them due to lack of glasses."

He looked away while he said that, and she knew at once that Mrs Griffin was arranging to marry him. She felt it instinctively: Mrs Griffin was going to marry him because she was afraid that if he moved away from her cottage, to get married to someone else, she'd find it hard to replace him with another lodger who'd be good to her affected son. He'd become a father to Mrs Griffin's affected son, to whom already he was kind. It was a natural outcome, for Mrs Griffin had all the chances, seeing him every night and morning and not having to make do with weekly encounters in a ballroom.

She thought of Patrick Grady, seeing in her mind his pale, thin face. She might be the mother of four of his children now, or seven or eight maybe. She might be living in Wolverhampton, going out to the pictures in the evenings, instead of looking after a one-legged man. If the weight of circumstances hadn't intervened she wouldn't be standing in a wayside ballroom, mourning the marriage of a road-mender she didn't love. For a moment she thought she might cry, standing there thinking of Patrick Grady in Wolverhampton. In her life, on the farm and in the house, there was no place for tears. Tears were a luxury, like flowers would be in the fields where the mangolds grew, or fresh whitewash in the scullery. It wouldn't have been fair ever to have wept in the kitchen while her father sat listening to *Spot the Talent:* her father had more right to weep, having lost a leg. He suffered in a greater way, yet he remained kind and concerned for her.

In the Ballroom of Romance she felt behind her eyes the tears that it would have been improper to release in the presence of her father. She wanted to let them go, to feel them streaming on her cheeks, to receive the sympathy of Dano Ryan and of everyone else. She wanted them all to listen to her while she told them about Patrick Grady who was now in Wolverhampton and about the death of her mother and her own life since. She wanted Dano Ryan to put his arm around her so that she could lean her head against it. She wanted him to look at her in his decent way and to stroke with his road-mender's fingers the backs of her hands. She might wake in a bed with him and imagine for a moment that he was Patrick Grady. She might bathe his eyes and pretend.

"Back to business," said Mr Maloney, leading his band across the floor to their instruments.

"Tell your father I was asking for him," Dano Ryan said. She smiled and she promised, as though nothing had happened, that she would tell her father that.

She danced with Tim Daly and then again with the youth who'd said he intended to emigrate. She saw Madge Dowding moving swiftly towards the man with the long arms as he came out of the lavatory, moving faster than Cat Bolger. Eyes Horgan approached Cat Bolger. Dancing with her, he spoke earnestly, attempting to persuade her to permit him to ride part of the way home with her. He was unaware of the jealousy that was coming from her as she watched Madge Dowding holding close to her the man with the long arms while they performed a quickstep. Cat Bolger was in her thirties also.

"Get away out of that," said Bowser Egan, cutting in on the youth who was dancing with Bridie. "Go home to your mammy, boy." He took her into his arms, saying again that she was looking great tonight. "Did you hear about the cement factory?" he said. "Isn't it great for Kilmalough?"

She agreed. She said what Mr Swanton and Mr Maloney had said: that the cement factory would bring employment to the neighbourhood.

"Will I ride home with you a bit, Bridie?" Bowser Egan suggested, and she pretended not to hear him. "Aren't you my girl, Bridie, and always have been?" he said, a statement that made no sense at all.

His voice went on whispering at her, saying he would marry her tomorrow only his mother wouldn't permit another woman in the house. She knew what it was like herself, he reminded her, having a parent to look after: you couldn't leave them to rot, you had to honour your father and your mother.

She danced to "The Bells Are Ringing," moving her legs in time with Bowser Egan's while over his shoulder she watched Dano Ryan softly striking one of his smaller drums, Mrs Griffin had got him even though she was nearly fifty, with no looks at all, a lumpish woman with lumpish legs and arms. Mrs Griffin had got him just as the girl had got Patrick Grady.

The music ceased, Bowser Egan held her hard against him, trying to touch her face with his. Around them, people whistled and clapped: the evening had come to an end. She walked away from Bowser Egan, knowing that not ever again would she dance in the Ballroom of Romance. She'd been a figure of fun, trying to promote a relationship with a middle-aged County Council labourer, as ridiculous as Madge Dowding dancing on beyond her time.

"I'm waiting outside for you, Cat," Eyes Horgan called out, lighting a cigarette as he made for the swing-doors.

Already the man with the long arms—made long, so they said, from carrying rocks off his land—had left the ballroom. Others were moving briskly. Mr Dwyer was tidying the chairs.

In the cloakroom the girls put on their coats and said they'd see one another at Mass the next day. Madge Dowding hurried. "Are you OK, Bridie?" Patty Byrne asked and Bridie said she was. She smiled at little Patty Byrne, wondering if a day would come for the younger girl also, if one day she'd decide that she was a figure of fun in a wayside ballroom.

"Good-night so," Bridie said, leaving the cloakroom, and the girls who were still chatting there wished her good-night. Outside the cloakroom she paused for a moment. Mr Dwyer was still tidying the chairs, picking up empty lemonade bottles from the floor, setting the chairs in a neat row. His wife was sweeping the floor. "Good-night, Bridie," Mr Dwyer said. "Good-night, Bridie," his wife said.

Extra lights had been switched on so that the Dwyers could see what they were doing. In the glare the blue walls of the ballroom seemed tatty, marked with hair-oil where men had leaned against them, inscribed with names and initials and hearts with arrows through them. The crystal bowl gave out a light that was ineffective in the glare; the bowl was broken here and there, which wasn't noticeable when the other lights weren't on.

"Good-night so," Bridie said to the Dwyers. She passed through the swing-doors and descended the three concrete steps on the gravel expanse in front of the ballroom. People were gathered on the gravel, talking in groups, standing with their bicycles. She saw Madge Dowding going off with Tim Daly. A youth rode away with a girl on the crossbar of his bicycle. The engines of motor-cars started.

"Good-night, Bridie," Dano Ryan said.

"Good-night, Dano," she said.

She walked across the gravel towards her bicycle, hearing Mr Maloney, somewhere behind her, repeating that no matter how you looked at it the cement factory would be a great thing for Kilmalough. She heard the bang of a car door and knew it was Mr Swanton banging the door of Mr Maloney's car because he always gave it the same loud bang. Two other doors banged as she reached her bicycle and then the engine started up and the headlights went on. She touched the two tyres of the bicycle to make certain she hadn't a puncture. The wheels of Mr Maloney's car traversed the gravel and were silent when they reached the road.

"Good-night, Bridie," someone called, and she replied, pushing her bicycle towards the road.

"Will I ride a little way with you?" Bowser Egan asked.

They rode together and when they arrived at the hill for which it was necessary to dismount she looked back and saw in the distance the four coloured bulbs that decorated the façade of the Ballroom of Romance. As she watched, the lights went out, and she imagined Mr Dwyer pulling the metal grid across the front of his property and locking the two padlocks that secured it. His wife would be waiting with the evening's takings, sitting in the front of their car.

"D'you know what it is, Bridie," said Bowser Egan, "you were never looking better than tonight." He took from a pocket of his suit the small bottle of whiskey he had. He uncorked it and drank some and then handed it to her. She took it and drank. "Sure, why wouldn't you?" he said, surprised to see her drinking because she never had in his company before. It was an unpleasant taste, she considered, a taste she'd experienced only twice before, when she'd taken whiskey as a remedy for toothache. "What harm would it do you?" Bowser Egan said as she raised the bottle again to her lips. He reached out a hand for it, though, suddenly concerned lest she should consume a greater share than he wished her to.

She watched him drinking more expertly than she had. He would always be drinking, she thought. He'd be lazy and useless, sitting in the kitchen with the *Irish Press*. He'd waste money buying a secondhand motor-car in order to drive into the town to go to the public houses on fair-days.

"She's shook these days," he said, referring to his mother. "She'll hardly last two years, I'm thinking." He threw the empty whiskey bottle into the ditch and lit a cigarette. They pushed their bicycles. He said:

"When she goes, Bridie, I'll sell the bloody place up. I'll sell the pigs and the whole damn one and twopence worth." He paused in order to raise the cigarette to his lips. He drew in smoke and exhaled it. "With the cash that I'll get I could improve some place else, Bridie."

They reached a gate on the left-hand side of the road and automatically they pushed their bicycles towards it and leaned them against it. He climbed over the gate into the field and she climbed after him. "Will we sit down here, Bridie?" he said, offering the suggestion as one that had just occurred to him, as though they'd entered the field for some other purpose.

"We could improve a place like your own one," he said, putting his right arm around her shoulders. "Have you a kiss in you, Bridie?" He kissed her, exerting pressure with his teeth. When his mother died he would sell his farm and spend the money in the town. After that he would think of getting married because he'd have nowhere to go, because he'd want a fire to sit at and a woman to cook food for him. He kissed her again, his lips hot, the sweat on his cheeks sticking to her. "God, you're great at kissing," he said.

She rose, saying it was time to go, and they climbed over the gate again. "There's nothing like a Saturday," he said. "Good-night to you so, Bridie."

He mounted his bicycle and rode down the hill, and she pushed hers to the top and then mounted it also. She rode through the night as on Saturday nights for years she had ridden and never would ride again because she'd reached a certain age. She would wait now and in time Bowser Egan would seek her out because his mother would have died. Her father would probably have died also by then. She would marry Bowser Egan because it would be lonesome being by herself in the farmhouse.

Further Readings on William Trevor

Bibliography

Rees, David. *Muriel Spark, William Trevor, Ian McEwan: A Bibliography of Their First Editions*. London: Colophon, 1992.

Selected Works

Angels at the Ritz and Other Stories. London: Bodley Head, 1975.
The Ballroom of Romance and Other Stories. New York: Viking, 1972.
Beyond the Pale and Other Stories. London: Bodley Head, 1981.
Children of Dynmouth. London: Bodley Head, 1976.
Collected Stories. New York: Viking, 1992.
The Day We Got Drunk on Cake and Other Stories. London: Bodley Head, 1967.
Excursion in the Real World: Memoirs. New York: Knopf, 1994.
Felicia's Journey. New York: Viking, 1994.
Fools of Fortune. New York: Viking, 1983.
The Hill Bachelors. New York: Viking, 2000.
The Love Department. London: Bodley Head, 1966.
Lovers of Their Times and Other Stories. New York: Viking, 1978.
News from Ireland and Other Stories. New York: Viking, 1986.
Nights at the Alexandra. New York: Harper, 1997; reprinted, Random House, 2001.
The Old Boys. New York: Viking, 1964.
Other People's Worlds. London: Bodley Head, 1980.
The Silence in the Garden. New York: Viking, 1988.
Standard of Behaviour. London: Hutchinson, 1958.
The Story of Lucy Gault. New York: Viking, 2002.
Two Lives. New York: Viking, 1991.

Biography and Criticism

Fitzgerald-Hoyt, Mary. *William Trevor: Re-imaging Ireland*. Dublin: Liffey Press, 2003.

MacKenna, Dolores. *William Trevor: The Writer and His Work*. Dublin: New Island, 1999.

Morrison, Kristin. *William Trevor*. New York: Twayne, 1993.

Paulson, Suzanne Morrow. *William Trevor: A Study of the Short Fiction*. New York: Twayne, 1993.

Schirmer, Gregory A. *William Trevor: A Study of His Fiction*. New York: Routledge, 1990.

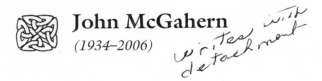

The Dark (in lib) was banned in Ireland for its alleged pornographic content. (implied clerical sexual abuse)

John McGahern
(1934–2006)

writes with detachment

The phrase "greatest Irish short-story writer since Joyce" was a tagline that followed John McGahern, although he never sought it. Other writers have consciously modeled themselves on Joyce, while McGahern did not. His meticulously crafted stories, without one word wasted, scrutinize the desperation of otherwise ordinary people, just as those in *Dubliners* do. While McGahern has some stories set in the capital or outside Ireland, most take place in the rural West Midlands around the fictional town of Oakport. His Ireland is often a prison for the human soul. The action of "Korea" takes place among the last of the freshwater eel-fisherman in the 1950s, but persons and locales here appear in other stories and novels, sometimes in other decades.

Born in Dublin, McGahern grew up in Cootehill, County Cavan, scene of his earliest fiction, where his father was a local policeman. After graduating from St. Patrick's Training College, Drumcondra, and University College, Dublin, McGahern taught for several years at St. John the Baptist National School in suburban Clontarf. Publication of his second novel, *The Dark* (1965), thrust him into an angry public controversy; after the book was banned and McGahern was dismissed by the clerical administration, he moved abroad for some years, living in England, Spain, and the United States. In 1974 he returned to Ireland, settling at Mohill, County Leitrim. Writing was his first profession, but he was a welcome writer-in-residence at many universities, including Durham and Newcastle in the United Kingdom and Colgate in upstate New York.

McGahern was known to be an extremely careful writer and an obsessive reviser. In 1984 he took the extraordinary step of revising the second half of his novel *The Leavetaking* (1974), adding a preface with penetrating authorial self-analysis. Some of his highest praise has come from other writers, such as the American John Updike, who allowed that McGahern "writes well, and for the usual reasons: he observes well, hears faithfully, and feels keenly."

The resonant but very short story "Korea" served as the basis of Cathal Black's feature film of the same name, released in 1995 with Donal Donnelly playing the father and Andrew Scott the son. Scriptwriters Joe O'Byrne and John D'Alton borrowed narrative materials from McGahern's novel *Amongst Women* (1990) to produce a ninety-minute film. Although it won prizes at festival competitions, *Korea* did not receive wide commercial release.

Korea

[handwritten: made into a film by Cathal Black (1996)]

"You saw an execution then too, didn't you?" I asked my father, and he started to tell as he rowed. He'd been captured in an ambush in late 1919, and they were shooting prisoners in Mountjoy as reprisals at that time. He thought it was he who'd be next, for after a few days they moved him to the cell next to the prison yard. He could see out through the bars. No rap to prepare himself came to the door that night, and at daybreak he saw the two prisoners they'd decided to shoot being marched out: a man in his early thirties, and what was little more than a boy, sixteen or seventeen, and he was weeping. They blindfolded the boy, but the man refused the blindfold. When the officer shouted, the boy clicked to attention, but the man stayed as he was, chewing very slowly. He had his hands in his pockets.

"Take your hands out of your pockets," the officer shouted again, irritation in the voice.

The man slowly shook his head.

"It's a bit too late now in the day for that," he said.

The officer then ordered them to fire, and as the volley rang, the boy tore at his tunic over the heart, as if to pluck out the bullets, and the buttons of the tunic began to fly into the air before he pitched forward on his face.

The other heeled quietly over on his back: it must have been because of the hands in the pockets.

The officer dispatched the boy with one shot from the revolver as he lay face downward, but he pumped five bullets in rapid succession into the man, as if to pay him back for not coming to attention.

"When I was on my honeymoon years after, it was May, and we took the tram up the hill of Howth from Sutton Cross," my father said as he rested on the oars. "We sat on top in the open on the wooden seats with the rail around that made it like a small ship. The sea was below, and smell of the sea and furze-bloom all about, and then I looked down and saw the furze pods bursting, and the way they burst in all directions seemed shocking like the buttons when he started to tear at his tunic. I couldn't get it out of my mind all day. It destroyed the day."

"It's a wonder their hands weren't tied?" I asked him as he rowed between the black navigation pan and the red where the river flowed into Oakport.

"I suppose it was because they were considered soldiers."

"Do you think the boy stood to attention because he felt that he might still get off if he obeyed the rules?"

"Sounds a bit highfalutin' to me. Comes from going to school too long," he said aggressively, and I was silent. It was new to me to hear him talk about his own life at all. Before, if I asked him about the war, he'd draw fingers across his eyes as if to tear a spider web away, but it was my last summer with him on the river, and it seemed to make him want to talk, to give of himself before it ended.

Hand over hand I drew in the line that throbbed with fish; there were two miles of line, a hook on a lead line every three yards. The licence allowed us a thousand hooks, but we used more. We were the last to fish this freshwater for a living.

As the eels came in over the side I cut them loose with a knife into a wire cage, where they slid over each other in their own oil, the twisted eel hook in their mouths. The other fish—pike choked on hooked perch they'd tried to swallow, bream, roach—I slid up the floorboards towards the bow of the boat. We'd sell them in the village or give them away. The hooks that hadn't been taken I cleaned and stuck in rows round the side of the wooden box. I let the line fall in its centre. After a mile he took my place in the stern and I rowed. People hadn't woken yet, and the early morning cold and mist were on the river. Outside of the slow ripple of the oars and the threshing of the fish on the line beaded with running drops of water as it came in, the river was dead silent, except for the occasional lowing of cattle on the banks.

"Have you any idea what you'll do after this summer?" he asked.

"No. I'll wait and see what comes up," I answered.

"How do you mean *what comes up?*"

"Whatever result I get in the exam. If the result is good, I'll have choices. If it's not, there won't be choices. I'll have to take what I can get."

"How good do you think they'll be?"

"I think they'll be all right, but there's no use counting chickens, is there?"

"No," he said, but there was something calculating in the face; it made me watchful of him as I rowed the last stretch of the line. The day had come, the distant noises of the farms and the first flies on the river, by the time we'd lifted the large wire cage out of the bulrushes, emptied in the morning's catch of eels, and sunk it again.

"We'll have enough for a consignment tomorrow," he said.

Each week we sent the live eels to Billingsgate in London.

"But say, say even if you do well, you wouldn't think of throwing this country up altogether and going to America?" he said, the words fumbled for as I pushed the boat out of the bulrushes after sinking the cage of eels, using the oar as a pole, the mud rising a dirty yellow between the stems.

"Why America?"

"Well, it's the land of opportunity, isn't it, a big, expanding country? There's no room for ambition in this poky place. All there's room for is to make holes in pints of porter."

I was wary of the big words. They were not in his own voice.

"Who'd pay the fare?"

"We'd manage that. We'd scrape it together somehow."

"Why should you scrape for me to go to America if I can get a job here?"

"I feel I'd be giving you a chance I never got. I fought for this country. And now they want to take away even the licence to fish. Will you think about it anyhow?"

"I'll think about it," I answered.

Through the day he trimmed the brows of ridges in the potato field while I replaced hooks on the line and dug worms, pain of doing things for the last time as well as the boredom the knowledge brings that soon there'll be no need to do them, that they could be discarded almost now. The guilt of leaving came: I was discarding his life to assume my own, a man to row the boat would eat into the decreasing profits of the fishing, and it was even not certain he'd get renewal of his licence. The tourist board had opposed the last application. They said we impoverished the coarse fishing for tourists—the tourists who came every summer from Liverpool and Birmingham in increasing numbers to sit in aluminium deck-chairs on the riverbank and fish with rods. The fields we had would be a bare living without the fishing.

I saw him stretch across the wall in conversation with the cattle-dealer Farrell as I came round to put the worms where we stored them in clay in the darkness of the lavatory. Farrell leaned on the bar of his bicycle on the road. I passed into the lavatory thinking they were talking about the price of cattle, but as I emptied the worms into the box, the word *Moran* came, and I carefully opened the door to listen. It was my father's voice. He was excited.

"I know. I heard the exact sum. They got ten thousand dollars when Luke was killed. Every American soldier's life is insured to the tune of ten thousand dollars."

"I heard they get two hundred and fifty dollars a month each for Michael and Sam while they're serving," he went on.

"They're buying cattle left and right," Farrell's voice came as I closed the door and stood in the darkness, in the smell of shit and piss and the warm fleshy smell of worms crawling in too little clay.

The shock I felt was the shock I was to feel later when I made some social blunder, the splintering of a self-esteem and the need to crawl into a lavatory to think.

Luke Moran's body had come from Korea in a leaden casket, had crossed the stone bridge to the slow funeral bell with the big cars from the embassy behind, the coffin draped in the Stars and Stripes. Shots had been fired above the grave before they threw in the clay. There were photos of his decorations being presented to his family by a military attaché.

He'd scrape the fare, I'd be conscripted there, each month he'd get so many dollars while I served, and he'd get ten thousand if I was killed.

In the darkness of the lavatory between the boxes of crawling worms before we set the night line for the eels I knew my youth had ended.

I rowed as he let out the night line, his fingers baiting each twisted hook so beautifully that it seemed a single movement. The dark was closing from the shadow of Oakport to Nutley's boathouse, bats made ugly whirls overhead, the wings of ducks shirred as they curved down into the bay.

"Have you thought about what I said about going to America?" he asked, without lifting his eyes from the hooks and the box of worms.

"I have."

The oars dipped in the water without splash, the hole whorling wider in the calm as it slipped on the stern seat.

"Have you decided to take the chance, then?"

"No. I'm not going."

"You won't be able to say I didn't give you the chance when you come to nothing in this fool of a country. It'll be your own funeral."

"It'll be my own funeral," I answered, and asked after a long silence, "As you grow older, do you find your own days in the war and jails coming much back to you?"

"I do. And I don't want to talk about them. Talking about the execution disturbed me no end, those cursed buttons bursting into the air. And the most I think is that if I'd conducted my own wars, and let the fool of a country fend for itself, I'd be much better off today. I don't want to talk about it."

I knew this silence was fixed for ever as I rowed in silence till he asked, "Do you think, will it be much good tonight?"

"It's too calm," I answered.

"Unless the night wind gets up," he said anxiously.

"Unless a night wind," I repeated.

As the boat moved through the calm water and the line slipped through his fingers over the side I'd never felt so close to him before, not even when he'd carried me on his shoulders above the laughing crowd to the Final. Each move he made I watched as closely as if I too had to prepare myself to murder.

Further Readings on John McGahern

Bibliography

Rees, David. *Brian Moore, Alasdair Gray, John McGahern: A Bibliography of Their First Editions.* London: Colophon Press, 1991.

Selected Works

Amongst Women. New York: Viking, 1990.
The Barracks. London: Faber and Faber, 1964.
By the Lake. New York: Knopf, 2002; published in the UK as *That They May Face the Rising Son.* London: Faber and Faber, 2002.
The Collected Stories. London: Faber and Faber, 1992.
The Dark. 1965. Reprint, London: Penguin, 2002.
Getting Through. London: Faber and Faber, 1978.
High Ground. London: Faber and Faber, 1985.
The Leavetaking. 1974. Reprint, London: Faber and Faber, 2001.
Nightlines. London: Faber and Faber, 1971.
The Pornographer. London: Faber and Faber, 1979.
The Power of Darkness. London: Faber and Faber, 1991. [Stage play.]

Biography and Criticism

Canadian Journal for Irish Studies. Special John McGahern Issue. Edited by Denis Sampson. Vancouver: Canadian Association for Irish Studies, 1991.
Corcoran, Neil. *After Yeats and Joyce: Reading Modern Irish Literature.* Oxford: Oxford University Press, 1997.
Dunn, Douglas, ed. *Two Decades of Irish Writing.* Manchester, UK: Carcanet, 1975.
Imhof, Rüdiger, ed. *Contemporary Irish Novelists.* Tübingen: Gunter Narr, 1990.

Kalasky, Drew, ed. *Short Story Criticism: Excerpts from Works of Short Fiction Writers.* Vol. 17. Detroit: Gale Research, 1995.

Lloyd, Richard Burr. *The Symbolic Mass: Thematic Resolution in the Irish Novels of John McGahern.* Emporia, Kans.: Emporia State University Press, 1987.

Rafroidi, Patrick and Terence Brown, eds. *The Irish Short Story.* Gerrards Cross, UK: Colin Smythe, 1979.

Rogers, Lori. *Feminine Nation: Performance, Gender and Resistance in the Works of John McGahern and Neil Jordan.* Lanham, Md.: University Press of America, 1998.

Sampson, Denis. *Outstaring Nature's Eye: The Fiction of John McGahern.* Dublin: Lilliput, 1993.

Updike, John. *Hugging the Shore: Essays and Criticism.* New York: Knopf, 1983.

Whyte, James. *History, Myth, and Ritual in the Fiction of John McGahern: Strategies of Transcendence.* Lewiston, N.Y.: Edwin Mellen Press, 2002.

Éilís Ní Dhuibhne
(b. 1954)

Immersion in the Irish language does not always imply living in some remote rural Gaeltacht. Éilís Ní Dhuibhne (pronounced "AY-leesh nee GHIV-neh," with a guttural "GH") was born to a family of Irish-language enthusiasts in Dublin. Although always conversant with English, she has never used the English language equivalent of her name. As a child she spent summers in the west of the country speaking only Irish, experiences she drew on for *The Dancers Dancing* (1999). She has made her reputation in English-language fiction but continues to publish in Irish, mostly fiction about Dublin's professional class.

By training, Ní Dhuibhne is a medievalist and folklorist, having earned degrees in Old and Middle English from University College, Dublin, and undertaken further study at the University of Copenhagen. She has been a curator at the National Library of Ireland and has lectured widely on folklore, literature, and related topics. She is married to leading folklorist Bo Almqvist. At the same time, Ní Dhuibhne has many connections with popular culture. She has contributed scripts to RTÉ's *Glenroe,* Irish television's most popular soap opera, and to Irish-language television's *Ros na Rún.*

Ní Dhuibhne's fiction is set in an Ireland that has become a prosperous member of the European Union. In her "Love, Hate and Friendship," the protagonist, Fiona, flies to France for a conference on Literature in European Minority Languages. One hundred years have passed since Douglas Hyde's "The Necessity for the De-Anglicization of Ireland." Yet the theme of the story is hardly cultural politics. Ní Dhuibhne finds the heart a less charted territory.

Love, Hate and Friendship

Fiona is flying to France. She is going to attend a one-day conference on Literature in European Minority Languages, to be held in Bordeaux. She is not especially interested in this conference and has never planned to see Bordeaux, although its associations with wine, of which she has always been aware, and with Rome, of which she became aware last night when she looked at a holiday brochure the conference organisers had sent to her office, are certainly attractive. She decided only a week ago, however, to use all her conference allowance on this trip, because just then she felt a pressing need to escape from Ireland. She believed if she placed herself in a fresh environment, even for a day or two, she would change the relationship she was having with the empirical world in general.

The plane is filled with holiday-makers, returning home after trips to Ireland; their tourist status manifests itself in the bags they carry, plastic, stuffed with woollen jumpers and bottles of whiskey.

The girl sitting next to Fiona has an Aran jumper folded on her lap. Her boyfriend's hand is in the jumper, fondling its ropy hairiness, whenever he takes a break from fondling the girl's shoulders, bare arms, face. The face is soft and loose, the sort of face for which the word *louche* might have been coined. It has, however, a perverse attractiveness, dimly perceived by Fiona. Its very flabbiness and laziness, its carelessness about the standard rules for beauty, lend it a power which brighter, more alert faces could not achieve. Her awful clothes have the same odd appeal. They might have been selected with a view to killing the French reputation for chic once and for all, although Fiona has noticed before that many French people depart radically from the national stereotype in their dress. The girl wears a print frock in some shiny synthetic material, shapeless in cut and of that length which reveals all flaws but is determinedly unsexy. Its colours are brown and purple. Around her shoulders hangs a thin cardigan in one of the murkier shades of pink, rather dirty. The Aran jumper is clearly destined for another day, or another wearer.

Fiona herself has a tidy, well-structured face, and an expression which is simultaneously sweet—or perhaps just shy—and penetrating. Her blond hair, freshly tinted by the hairdresser, is cropped close to the head with only a ragged fringe softening the harsh style, popular at the time. Fiona hopes it suggests femininity, but, of course, what it implies is something different: childishness, or even vulnerability. Her clothes, by contrast, could not be smarter. She has a short grey skirt, a grey, collarless, Chanel-type jacket, a stiff, crisp, snow white blouse. She has read in a novel that grey is correct for Paris and hopes that what is correct for Paris will also be correct for Bordeaux. Besides, grey and white suit her. Edward liked her in her grey dress. "You look like a Quaker," he said, whenever she wore it. He liked girls to look like Quakers. "It's lovely." He has not seen this suit, and perhaps will not.

They are practically making love, that pair. Both their faces wear the oblivious, abandoned expression of people who have recently enjoyed blissful sexual union. Fiona sighs enviously. Tears prick her eyes. She thinks if she were another type of person, a more noble and altruistic person, or maybe just a slightly older person, she would be pleased by this frank manifestation of love. She would smile benignly and avert her eyes, recalling fondly, without rancour, that as they are now so was she, once. More than once, to be honest, and with more than one man. True love is rare, but not as rare as you believe when you are in it. Even if she could accept that much with her whole heart, she would probably be less irritated than she is at this moment.

She closes her book, which she has been unable to concentrate on, and takes a writing pad and Biro out of her bag. She starts a letter to Edward. She has no trouble at all in concentrating on that.

She met Edward Matthews at a prize-giving ceremony for novelists a little over a year ago. She was not getting a prize; she was there because of her job as a public relations officer for a publisher of books in Irish (she edits, typesets, keeps accounts, and drives around the country with piles of books on the back seat of the car, as well as being public relations officer). Edward is not a writer, either, but a literary agent from London. Fiona had met him a few times before, at book launches and similar events, but he did not remember that.

He approached Fiona and a woman she was talking to, a protégée of his, called Carol. Carol was very dramatically dressed that evening—as, indeed, she usually was—in a long, clinging purple dress. She had several strings of imitation diamonds wound around her neck and her lips were painted a startling scarlet.

"You look like a cardinal," said Edward.

Carol immediately moved away and joined another group.

"Would you look at that man!" said Edward to Fiona. He had had three glasses of wine and was indulging his habit of staring at people and passing remarks on their appearance, a habit which Fiona shared. Fiona wondered why he and Carol did not get on. "Can you believe that he is fifty-eight?"

Fiona turned her gaze to the novelist who had won the award. He was tall, with a trim white beard and matching hair. "Well," she said. "What age are you?"

Edward was slim and not very big. He had an intriguing fringe of gingery hair falling over his forehead, and a thin veil of greyish hair bravely scraped across his naked crown. "Take off twelve years or so," he said sheepishly.

"Those Americans!" said Fiona. "They all look like that. I used to think they got face lifts but now I believe it's the kind of cornflakes they eat. They send the dross to Europe. All that stuff about riboflavin and vitamin B is just a cover-up. That's what I've heard."

"Get away!" Edward smiled and his eyes met hers. Behind his glasses, his eyes were a surprising shade of green, moss colour. His skin was very clean. Fiona understood that he did not think she looked like a cardinal.

"It's true. And I don't like that man's looks, either. I think he looks as if he lives in Salem, Massachusetts. I think his name could be Judge Hathorne."

Edward moved an inch closer to her.

"I can picture him sending old women called Goody this and Goody that to the stake, can't you?"

He did not take Fiona home that night. He couldn't, because his wife was at the reception, too, circulating in the crowd. But two days later he rang her office and asked her to have lunch with him. He wanted to discuss a few ventures on which they might cooperate to their mutual advantage. Fiona knew what the invitation meant. She knew, because her stomach gave a little silly flip of pleasure when she heard his voice. And also because the one kind of Irish literature Edward, or any London agent, could have no interest whatsoever in was the kind she published, Irish literature which is not written in English.

The air hostesses bring around trays of food. Dinner, even though it is four o'clock in the afternoon. The couple had stopped kissing when Fiona had started writing her letter, casting uneasy, suspicious glances at her writing pad. Now they fall upon the little bits of salmon and potato salad with gusto, picking up things and examining them in the light, commenting on the taste of every item. Fiona eats, too. She is not hungry, but she does not know when she will get an opportunity to have a meal again. So she munches her way through everything, from baby tomatoes to blackcurrant tart, and begins to think about the food that will be available in Bordeaux. Food with a taste. It will be good to eat food with a taste, the kind you get in France. Surely that will change her perspective.

The couple begin to have a quarrel. The boy has spilt some red wine on the Aran jumper, and the girl is berating him. She is not shouting, but talking in a fast, furious whisper, while she rubs at the wine with a tissue. Rubbing it in.

"Try some salt." Fiona leans over. She does not like this girl but she can't resist giving advice. Before she worked for the publisher she was a teacher.

The girl looks at her angrily. Her face is not louche now. It looks alert and edgy. Like an Irish face.

"Du sel!" says Fiona, picking up a little white package and dangling it in front of the girl's nose.

"Fuck off!" says the girl.

She is still fighting with the boy when the plane lands in Paris and when Fiona sees the last of her she is stomping out of the baggage reclaim area dragging an enormous suitcase, without wheels, across the floor, while he waits nonchalantly for his bag to appear on the carousel.

Fiona arrives at her hotel at about ten o'clock that night. She checks in, puts her bag in her room, and has a shower. The room is tiny and functional. Its only decorations are two framed tracts on the walls. Maxims by La Rochefoucauld. Funny things to put on walls, but cheap hotels often express eccentricity in this way, she has noticed before. "Love and Hatred are more akin to one another than Friendship" is in one frame. "We can forgive those who bore us, but we never forgive those whom we bore," the second proclaims. Fiona wonders if somebody else has used that, after La Rochefoucauld. Oscar Wilde or somebody?

She takes off the grey suit. The only other outfit in her bag is a pair of black velvet leggings and a long blue silk shirt, put in at the last minute, in the event she would need them for some exciting and unplanned social event. Fiona has been abroad on trips of this kind often enough to know that such occasions seldom arise. She has never, on a plane or at an airport, met a wonderful, charming, delightful man who has invited her to dinner. Not since she was about twenty, anyway (and then she mistrusted them, quite sensibly). But she always travels with clothes to date in, something silk or something velvet. Just in case. Now she puts on these things in order to go for a solitary walk. She cannot bear to go to bed before she has had a look at the neighbourhood. This impatient curiosity she recognises as a good sign, and its indulgence well worth the risk of rape or murder, which for all she knows she may be taking, wandering around this strange city in the middle of the night.

The hotel is situated on a seedy street lined with office blocks. Like most office buildings, they present at street level a variety of shaded foyers, dark entries, secluded porticoes. And in some of these threatening caves Fiona notices stirrings and signs of life. A drunk snoring with his back to a pillar. A young, dark-skinned man emerging suddenly from a porch and diving into a taxi.

This part of the walk is unenjoyable but soon she is in a much better part of town: the old part, where the houses are flat fronted and locked up or else pedimented with brightly lit cafés, from which strains of music and talk emerge onto the pavement. She examines a menu or two, peers into interiors with oilcloth and candles on the tables, sees Chinese faces, Algerian, Turkish and French (she thinks). Soon she arrives at what has to be the cathedral. It is a big medieval chunk of a building, shaped like a brick and made of crumbly blocks of sandstone which are the colour of tabby cats in the floodlights. She walks right around it, looking at the statues which project from the pavement, taking pleasure in the big wooden doors, barred with iron, like the doors of a fortress. She imagines mail clad soldiers galloping up to these doors, hammering on them with their swords. We are the king's men. And the reply, from the shadowy, cosy sanctuary: We are all the king's men.

The cathedral is dedicated to a saint whose name reminds her of Edward's. That is not the reason for Fiona's impatience to see it. She believes. On the contrary, that coincidence puts her off. She is surprised that she can look at this cathedral and enjoy its unpretentious contours, its friendly medieval air, even though it has this association. Surprised, and glad. His power must be diminishing, as she hoped it would, now that she has put water between them.

Edward colonised her territory. Everywhere she looked in Ireland reminded her of him. He had taken over every place and every object in her life.

First he did this systematically. "I want to know everything about you, everything!" he said, eagerly. "Do you have glass in your hall door? Do you drink red or white? Do you shave under your arms?"

All too soon his curiosity was satisfied. What there was to know, he knew. It is hard to resist men like Edward, men who overwhelm you initially with the intensity of their need for you. It is hard to resist them even if you know from experience that such men will, and must, cool off just as abruptly, and almost as emphatically, and there will be nothing you can do about it. Because there was nothing you did in the first place, either, to start the whole thing off. Except acquiesce. Gladly, in this case—which means the acquiescence was more than that. Edward was so attractive. This cliché suited him eminently well. Summed up the mixture of gentle manners, good humour, clean skin and light colours that constituted him. Summed up his easy gossipy conversational style, his interest in everything that was ordinary: clothes and people and food. Talking to Edward was like talking to a woman. It was that easy and that intimate. And at the same time you could sense that there was some hard and masculine characteristic at his centre, some barrier you would have to crack in order to reach him.

She could not remember when she had stopped thinking he was monkish and started thinking he was sexy. She could not remember when she stopped indulging him and started needing him. She could not remember when she had started loving him more than he loved her. She could not remember when he had stopped loving her altogether. Or if he had. She was tired. Not of him, but of the way he claimed her world, the world that should have been her own.

First, when he loved her and she did not quite love him, she saw everything exaggerated and crystallised. Objects acquired a hard, polished look; they were like reflections in a highly buffed mirror. She moved through this looking-glass world like a high, haughty queen, letting her hand flutter along surfaces, not condescending to touch anything.

Then, when she loved him and he still loved her, the world disappeared. She was not dismissive of it, she just didn't see it. Not at all. There were only two people. Everything else became a blurry, dim backdrop for the reality that they represented. Time disappeared then, too. This was the flash-of-lightening phase, the road to Damascus. The gate opens, just a chink, but that is enough to eliminate everything that is ugly in the world.

The third phase was the bad one. Is the bad one, because it is still going on. When Edward became complacent, then indifferent. Her attempts to hold him met with polite but stunning rebuffs: that hard masculine part of him was no longer a secret centre, but a suit of armour which gleamed menacingly whenever she saw him, through the feminine polish of his chatter.

She saw him less and less often. But his absence was more powerful than his presence. It drained all objects and at the same time invested them with an astonishing potential to inflict pain. Trains, trees, cups and saucers stabbed her. She could look at the sun shining on a field and think, Oh God, I can't bear it. She could not stand the sight of flowers, dustbins, children playing in the street. Young lovers, mothers, elderly, tottering couples.

Self-pity, this sort of thing is called. Fiona knows its name. She knows its nature, too, and she knows it will eventually pass. But none of this makes it easier to put up with the onslaughts when they are at their worst. They are at their worst when Edward says he will phone her, and does not, or when he can't at the last minute make it to a lunch date, and leaves her waiting for him in a restaurant or on the side of the street. He has done this more than once. She has let him away with it. She has no self-respect where he is concerned. Even when she decides that she can't take it any more, she gives in. His excuses always seem reasonable. And he is always so penitent, there can be no question, as she suspects when she is standing in the porch of some pub, her stomach gristled with rage and despair, that he is trying to get her to leave him. After standing her up, he reverts to being just what he was in the early days. To being desperately in love with her, clinging like a child who has been naughty and needs absolute forgiveness. She strokes his hair. She brushes his warm, light skin. She grants him absolution.

She knows the line of thinking which maintains that this is self-destructive and masochistic and the line of thought which maintains it's plain silly. But she feels, at these undignified, pride-shattering times, that she is getting to know Edward's secret. It is at these times, only at these times, that he seems to let her in.

She dreams that she is standing on a beach, watching the waves approach the shore. They are large navy blue breakers, and she enjoys looking at them. One wave, in the middle distance, gets bigger than the others. It swells and swells as it rolls in. She stares, unable to believe that it is really getting so huge, on what is a little, familiar, predictable Irish beach. Suddenly she notices that it is dangerously high, higher than a house, a great tidal wave of a thing. She runs away behind the beach, stands in a car park among sand dunes, waiting for it to crash. The wave pursues her, sweeps over the edge of the high dunes, splashes down around her and the cars, drenching everything but not harming her.

The dream does not frighten her. It is accompanied by a pleasant sense of security and delight, and she wakes from it smiling.

The conference is not taking place in the city, but on the coast, about twenty miles away. Delegates are transported there in a bus. The bus deposits them in a car-park in a big evergreen forest. The conference centre turns out to be a variety of marquees, dotted like mushrooms in a clearing. Fiona begins to wander from tent to tent. There are a number of lectures going on simultaneously, and, it seems, more than one conference. Fiona notices a crowd of men in cotton suits tasting wine, another crowd watching videos of Donald Duck: that tent has a sign saying "Vidéothèque" outside. Most of them do not have any signs, however. You are supposed to be divinely inspired, it seems, or else just to check out everything until you find what it is you should be at.

The ground is covered with pine needles and here and there are huge, outsized cones. Fiona picks up one, then throws it away when a big insect creeps out of it. She is feeling very hot. The grey suit is not at all correct, it could not be more inappropriate for this suntrap. Everyone else is wearing shorts, or little strappy dresses. It is only ten o'clock in the morning but the sun is throbbing in the sky. Fiona feels her head begin to swim.

She retreats from the clearing where the tents are pitched and goes into the forest. The trees from which those huge cones fall are themselves huge. They stretch like skyscrapers into the burnt blue heavens. Their scent is strong and sweet, and the wind hisses and roars through their branches. Everything here is big, and energetic; there is a sense of tremendous fertility. The trees, the tables in the cafés groaning with food, the vines bent by their thick loads of fruit. Loads of sun and light and growing things. You can't ignore the world here, because it is bigger than you. It is a giant which stoops over you, overwhelms you. Not like the little, watery, cool nature of Ireland, totally dependent on the observer. Being human seems less of a big deal, here, and is probably more fun in consequence.

If you're dressed for it. It is horribly hot. She takes off her stockings, shoes, and her jacket, and puts them under a stone by a tree. Then she walks through the forest along a little path. She comes to a signpost which says "Plage." It does not mention a distance, so she assumes it is not far away. And sure enough, after about ten minutes she reaches a stretch of water.

It is not the sea, but a lake. The beach is a little shelf of shingle. Lake water flirts with it, lapping against the shore with lacy gestures, butterfly strokes. She had been thinking she would find herself up against the Atlantic. She had been thinking of huge navy blue breakers, pounding against the shore, ranting and raving in her ears. The lake is big but it sounds like a baby. Its baby waves plash on the sand. Plup plup. Gurgle.

What type of man is Edward? It is unreasonable to classify people, but Fiona, who wants to think about him all the time, anyway, finds it comforting to categorise him. Labelling gives her the illusion of control, a control she feels she lacks entirely in reality. He is this type: a childish man, with a child's enthusiasm for new things and a child's diffidence. And a child's dependence. He is the type of man who falls rapidly in love, pursues the beloved with utmost energy, almost with aggression, and then, just as quickly, falls out of love again. After that a few things can happen. If the circumstances are right, and if the woman wants it, he could marry her. If the circumstances are not right, or if she doesn't want him desperately enough, he won't bother. He is not going to push himself, one way or the other. He is not going to raise storms, shatter lives. Or even rock any boats.

He will not leave his wife and marry Fiona, because his wife wouldn't like that. But he will not leave Fiona, not if she doesn't want him to, and not if nothing unpleasant happens. For instance, if his wife finds out, he will probably abandon Fiona. He will then feel that hers is the lesser right. But if she doesn't, or if she does and doesn't mind too much, he won't abandon her.

Fiona has not seen Edward for more than a month. He has probably not been in Ireland during that time. Sometimes his work takes him there one week out of three, sometimes less frequently. An absentee landlord. Still, her imagination has surrendered her places to him, territory which he certainly doesn't want. Half the streets of Dublin are in his fiefdom. That is why she needed to get out, to fly to France, a wild goose. (Which reminded her of something else: get some of that Château Lynch wine when the shops open, for her boss, Molly Lynch. She liked to get drunk on wine bearing her own name on the label, and so did Fiona.)

She could ring Edward herself. If she does, he will be gentle and understanding. He will ring her soon anyway, even if she doesn't get in touch with him. When he visits Ireland again, when he feels he should check to see that she is all right. He is a considerate man—too considerate, if anything. Why should it be so hard to forget all this romantic stuff and simply accept his friendship?

She walks into the water. It is warm, as she hoped it would be. Not warm like a bath, of course, not even quite lukewarm, but much, much warmer than any natural water in Ireland, or any place she has been before. She paddles around, enjoying the comfort of it on her feet, watching the motor boats rip through the lake. It would be lovely to swim, to feel this warm soft water all over her skin, to wallow in the south, in its generosity, its blessedness. But there are people not far away, and she has no swimsuit, no towel, nothing to wear except that hot grey skirt and starched blouse. So she keeps paddling around, letting her toes have a holiday.

Further Readings on Éilís Ní Dhuibhne

Selected Fiction

Blood and Water. Dublin: Attic Press, 1988.
The Bray House. Dublin: Attic Press, 1990.
Cailíní Beaga Ghlean na mBláth. Dublin: Cois Life Teoranta, 2003.
The Dancers Dancing. Belfast: Blackstaff Press, 1999.

Dúnmharú sa Daingean. Dublin: Cois Life Teo, 2000.
Eating Women Is Not Recommended. Dublin: Attic Press, 1991.
The Inland Ice and Other Stories. Belfast: Blackstaff Press, 1997.
Midwife to the Fairies: New and Selected Stories. Cork: Attic Press, 2003.
Milseog an tSamhraidh; Dún na mBan trí Thine. Dublin: Cois Life Teoranta, 1997.
The Pale Gold of Alaska and Other Stories. Belfast: Blackstaff Press, 2000.
Singles. Dublin: Basement Press, 1994.
The Voices on the Wind: Women Poets of the Celtic Twilight. ed. Dublin: New Island, 1995.

Studies

Viking Ale: Studies on Folklore Contacts Between the Northern and the Western Worlds. With Bo Almqvist and Séamas Ó Catháin. Aberystwyth, Wales: Boethius Press, 1991.

Biography and Criticism

Moloney, Caitriona, and Helen Thompson, eds. *Irish Women Writers Speak Out.* Syracuse, N.Y.: Syracuse University Press, 2003.
Perry, Donna Marie. *Backtalk: Women Writers Speak Out: Interviews.* New Brunswick, N.J.: Rutgers University Press, 1997.

Tom/Thomas Murphy

(b. 1935)

The appearance of Tom Murphy's *On the Outside* in 1959 was a harbinger of what was to become a great flowering of Irish drama, surpassing the glory of the Irish renaissance dramatists, William Butler Yeats, John Millington Synge, and Lady Gregory. Murphy and his contemporaries—Brian Friel, Frank McGuinness, Marina Carr, Thomas Kilroy, Tom MacIntyre, Sebastian Barry, Marie Jones, and Hugh Leonard, among many—not only have won acclaim in their own country, but find their works regularly performed on stages in London, New York, and elsewhere around the world. So great has been the esteem for recent Irish drama that it is now commonplace for actors training in Britain or North America to be required to master Irish accents, since they are highly likely to be called upon to use them. Murphy's interest in one-act plays, however, is not shared by many of the others.

Born the youngest of ten children in Tuam, County Galway, Murphy did not seem destined for a life in the arts. A trained metalfitter, he was teaching in a vocational school when he became involved in local amateur theatricals. In *On the Outside,* which Murphy wrote with Noel O'Donoghue at age twenty-four, the rage of those excluded from the Paradise dance hall drew on his own and his students' experiences. Murphy cites the American Tennessee Williams as an influence, but commentators have suggested parallels with Samuel Beckett's *Waiting for Godot.*

Within the next two years Murphy submitted two full-length plays to the national theater in Dublin, the Abbey. They were *A Whistle in the Dark,* now usually regarded as his greatest play, and *The Fooleen,* later retitled *A Crucial Week in the Life of a Grocer's Assistant.* Ernst Blythe, then the director of the Abbey—a figure now routinely reviled for his narrowness and poor judgment—rejected and denounced both. At this Murphy emigrated to Britain, where *A Whistle in the Dark* became a great if controversial success. He also became a full-time professional writer, producing original scripts for the British Broadcasting Company.

In 1968, after the Abbey built its new facility and Ernst Blythe retired as director, Murphy's three-part *Famine,* epic theater influenced by Bertolt Brecht, appeared in the experimental Peacock Theatre, part of the Abbey complex. Two years after that, Murphy returned to Ireland, where he has since written prolifically for both the stage and television. Many of his works have explored the gulf between the ideals of the founders of the Irish state alongside the Catholic Church and the actual mental and emotional lives of people in contemporary life. In both theme and language he has often broken new ground. His first novel, *The Seduction of Morality* (1994), deals with an Irish woman who returns from a life of prostitution in New York to take over an inherited family business in Ireland.

On the Outside

WRITTEN WITH NOEL O'DONOGHUE

A quiet country road outside a dancehall. The dancehall, in the background, is an austere building suggesting, at first glance, a place of compulsory confinement more than one of entertainment. Then, through a small window, high up on the wall, can be seen the glow of the ballroom lights, and, occasionally, to complement the more romantic numbers, a revolving crystal ball, tantalizing and tempting to anyone on the outside without the wherewithal to gain admission. Popular music of the time (late fifties) played badly by the band, continues throughout the play, except from time to time when a dance ends. Then follows some half-hearted applause, and this in turn is followed by the faint buzz of voices. The usual dance-hall noises.

A placard is placed somewhere against the dancehall wall, and its message reads: "I.N.T.O. DANCE TONIGHT, 8–12. MUSIC BY THE MARVEL-TONES ORCHESTRA. ADMISSION 6/–."

There are two girls on the stage when the lights come up: Kathleen and Anne. Anne is the younger, about twenty, very naive and anxious to be conventional. She is sincere but rather stupid; the words of a popular song are the true expression of the human spirit. Kathleen, on the other hand, is two years older and more so-phisticated. She has, perhaps, worked in Dublin or England for a time. She has less romantic illusions, is more neutral and even cynical at times. But that is not to say that she is unromantic. She simply has a better idea than Anne of what it is all in aid of.

When we first see them, Anne is rather dejected, looking off towards the main road half-hopefully. Kathleen is walking up and down. She has a cardigan pulled tightly over her shoulders. They have obviously been waiting for a long time. Kathleen stops and looks at Anne.

KATHLEEN. It's late. (*Pause.*) Well, don't you think you've waited long enough? We're here I-don't-know-how-long.

ANNE. Just another few minutes.

KATHLEEN (*to herself*). Just another few . . . It's late!

ANNE. He'll be here any second now. I'm sure of it.

KATHLEEN. Yes, when the dance is over; I suppose. And that won't be very long at all now. Lord, I'm frozen.

ANNE. It's not that cold.

KATHLEEN. And I left off that heavy vest too. I hope my mother doesn't find it under the pillow. And will you look at the cut of my shoes! Oh, come on in. It's silly waiting any longer.

ANNE. Ah, Kathleen, a few seconds more.

KATHLEEN. He's not coming.

ANNE. But why? He said he would. It was he wanted to. He said to meet him here outside the hall.

KATHLEEN (*impatiently*). Yes—yes, but he's kind of late, isn't he? (*There is a short pause;* KATHLEEN *sees she is having no effect.*) What's his name anyway, Frank what?

ANNE. . . . But he's very nice though.

KATHLEEN. Are you sure his first name is Frank even? . . . What does he do? What kind of job has he?

ANNE. Ah, Kathleen.

KATHLEEN. Oh, you never can tell. I was going with a fella last year in Dublin. Not bad looking either. And, of course, fool here was real struck. I liked him. Richard Egan. And then one night we met—yeh know Mary O'Brien nursing in the Mater? And later she took me aside. "Do you not know who he is?" she said. "No." "He's the porter at the hospital." The shagging porter. *And* his name wasn't Richard.

ANNE. What was it?

KATHLEEN. Declan . . . I don't remember what he told me he was. The Civil Service I suppose. Taught me a lot I can tell you . . . What did this Frank tell you he was?

ANNE. He said he was—he didn't say.

KATHLEEN. What?

ANNE. He isn't like that. He really is very nice.

KATHLEEN. Tck!

ANNE. We—talked to each other.

KATHLEEN. Talk! They're all the same. (*Moving to a better vantage point.*) . . . Wait on: someone coming now.

ANNE. Is it him?

KATHLEEN. I can't make him out so well. It might be.

ANNE. Oh, what'll I say? What'll I do?

KATHLEEN. Up near the car park.

ANNE. Come on in, Kathleen—We're going in—We're not waiting a second longer—Come on.

KATHLEEN (*still looking off Right*). Oh, it's not him at all. He's gone up the other way.

ANNE (*disappointed*). Are you sure?

KATHLEEN. Some old drunk. They're everywhere. Well, we might as well go in so.

ANNE. Ah, Kathleen.

KATHLEEN. What's wrong with you now? You were mad to go in a few seconds ago.

ANNE. I can't understand it.

KATHLEEN. He's forgotten, he's with someone else, he's drinking. In some pub.

ANNE. I don't like men who drink.

KATHLEEN. The dance is half-over—

ANNE. I asked him and he smokes alright—

KATHLEEN. He isn't coming—

ANNE. But he doesn't drink, he said.

KATHLEEN. You're only a fool.

ANNE. . . . But why?

KATHLEEN. For god's sake, don't take him so seriously: You've only seen him once before . . . Look, I'm sure he's very nice, but he'll hardly come tonight now. There's thousands of them in there! Maybe you'll meet someone with a car.

ANNE (*childishly*). I don't want a car . . . I don't agree . . . I don't care what he does.

KATHLEEN (*giving up*). I don't know, I'm a worse fool to be waiting here with you at all.

ANNE. Do you think . . . could he . . . have come, maybe, and didn't see us here and gone in, thinking, maybe, I wasn't coming?

KATHLEEN (*to herself*). In the name of—! (*Seeing her chance.*) Yes. That's what happened. We'll go in and see. Come on. Well, come on.

ANNE (*reluctantly*). Alright.

KATHLEEN (*as they exit*). Good job you brought your own money with you.

The stage is empty. There is a short pause. Then JOE *comes in. He looks at the hall entrance.*

For the record, JOE *is about twenty-two and employed as an apprentice to some trade, as indeed is* FRANK. *He is immature and irresponsible but not bad.*

JOE (*calling softly off*). Alright, sham, they're gone.

FRANK *enters. He is a stronger personality than* JOE. *Same age as* JOE *and works at the same trade. He is old enough, however, to be aware of the very rigid class distinctions that pervade a small, urban-rural community and resents "them" with the cars and money because he has not got the same. It is hard to say how far he is really bad and how far he is only an intelligent product of his environment.*

JOE. Blazes, I thought they'd never go. I've cramps all over from being stuck back there.

FRANK. What did you think of her? Not bad, is she?

JOE. Not too bad for this hole, I suppose.

FRANK. Ah, she's alright now.

JOE. Wait'll you see the one I'll get. (*Starts to move towards door.*)

FRANK. Stall, sham, take it easy a while. We don't want to land in right after them.

JOE. Hey, what are you going to say to her? . . . You kept her waiting all night . . . Tell her you're an automatic scientist and you were ducking communists all night. If she's a bit innocent, she'll swallow anything.

FRANK. Stall it, stall it.

JOE. Tell her the truth so. I was hiding behind the wall all night watching you because I hadn't got the price of two tickets. That'll go down well.

FRANK. Pity I didn't work the see-you-inside act, but she thinks I'm loaded. The car we came in broke down and we only got here now.

JOE. And she'll say: "Who did you come with?" And you'll say—oh, Mickey Ford or someone, And she'll say: "Oh, de Mickey de Ford or someone: we saw de Mickey de Ford going in at nine o'clock." What's all the fuss about this one for anyway, she's only a mul.

FRANK. I just want something she'll believe. I wouldn't mind hanging on to her for a while. What would you tell her?

JOE. Slap her down.

FRANK. I'll tell her what I like and she'll believe me. And I'll be narked she didn't wait for me.

FRANK *breaks into song.* JOE *dances, then stops when he sees the poster.*

JOE. Hey!

FRANK. What?

JOE. How much is this dance tonight, did you say?

FRANK. Four bob.

JOE (*points at poster*). The poster. Admission is six bob.

FRANK. Six what!

JOE. Six shillings. You and your four bob dance. Where did you get that from?

FRANK. It's robbery. (*Laughing.*) Six bob!

JOE. Just because there's no other dance on around here tonight.

FRANK. Well, we'll just have to pay up since we came this far. Give us two bob till Friday.

JOE (*laughs*). What? And how do you think I'm fixed?

FRANK. You'll get it back Friday.

JOE. Give you hell. I've four and six. Four and a lousy kick. And I borrowed that just before I came out here.

FRANK. Are you coddin' me?

JOE. Where would I get it?

FRANK. Great, that's great, that's just deadly now, I've just the bare four bob. (*Pause.*) The quare one in the box-office?

JOE. Will I give her a twirl? (*"try-her"*). Give us your money.

FRANK. Offer her half-a-dollar apiece first: we might get in for four then.

JOE (*adjusting his tie*). We might get in for choicer (*nothing*) yet.

FRANK. Okay, Elvis, go to it.

JOE *moves up the steps into the hall.* FRANK *takes out his cigarettes immediately.* JOE *has disappeared, and lights one. Noises are heard off stage and the* DRUNK *enters. He is a small, labouring man, aged about fifty. He shuffles on stage, sees* FRANK *and approaches him.* FRANK *treats him in a very off-hand manner.*

DRUNK. Excuse me. Excuse me—Sir! (FRANK *ignores him.*) Excuse me. Give us a light, will you? (*He has a cigarette in his hand.* FRANK *still ignores him.*) Could you oblige a gentleman with a light, Sir? (FRANK *gives him a light.*) Thanks. Much obliged. Thank you. (*Notices music in background.*) What's on?

FRANK. Dance.

DRUNK. Hah? A dance? Oh, a dance! . . . Who's playing it? Who's playing the music?

FRANK. Marveltones.

DRUNK. Marbletones—Mar—Marvel (*Laughs.*) I thought you said the Marvel—Marble—tones. (*He laughs.*) How much is it?

FRANK. Six bob.

DRUNK. Hah?

FRANK. Six bob. Six shillings.

DRUNK (*still unaware of* FRANK's *annoyance*). Hah?

FRANK. One, two, three, four, five, six shillings.

DRUNK (*looking at him seriously for a second in silence*). No need to be smart, young fellah. No need at all. You can answer a civil question when it's put to you.

FRANK. Go away.

DRUNK. No need for that. No need.

FRANK (*controlling himself*). Right, no need, Now will you clear before I call the guards or something. Go home to your wife. Go home.

DRUNK. Home? Anything but the death! (*He grins.*)

FRANK (*looks at him for a moment, then walks away*). . . . Look, don't be annoying me.

DRUNK. And I've no wife, I'm single. No one in the world but me. No one cares. I don't care! . . . Why did you say—

FRANK. Okay, okay, you've no wife. Now will you go.

DRUNK. Where?

FRANK. Anywhere.

JOE *comes out of the hall.*

FRANK. Any good.

JOE. No good, no luck, no cut: six bob.

FRANK. Bitch.

JOE. If the hall was empty they'd be damn glad to take it.

FRANK. Bloody crowd of robbers.

DRUNK. What's up lads?

JOE. We might try her again later on though.

DRUNK. What's up lads?

JOE. Who's the sham?

DRUNK. How ya goin' on, young fellah?

FRANK. Oh, my pardon. Ten thousand, one hundred and eighteen pardons! This gentlemen here is Mr Narrow-Neck.

JOE. How yeh, Mr Narrow-Neck!

DRUNK. Hah? No—no, I said—I said—

FRANK. You didn't? Sorry about that, sham. I thought the name suited him, didn't you? (*They laugh.*)

DRUNK. No, I said—

JOE. Little-Back, he said. Delighted!

DRUNK. No, I said—

FRANK. No, you didn't. Are you drunk or something?

JOE. You'd better watch out, Mr Little-Back, or you'll be seeing gollies next: Waw—waw—aw!

DRUNK. I said Jim Daly. Jim Daly. Seamus O'Dálaigh.

FRANK *and* JOE *laugh.*

FRANK. Ah, of course. I knew I'd seen you before. Muscles himself: Mr Universe of 1958. Well, Mr Daly, meet my friend here (*Points to* JOE.) Bill Bottle and goodbye now. Scram, do you understand? Scram! Scram! JOE *takes* DRUNK'*s cap and throws it deftly at dancehall door.* DRUNK follows his cap and exits to hall. JOE laughs then becomes silent.

JOE. Well he's in and we're here.

FRANK. Was she anyway promising at all? (*Nodding towards box office.*) Boxy.

JOE. We'll try her again in a while.

FRANK. Who do they think they are with their little post-office books and two and a half per cent, per annum.

JOE. Anno Domini, Annie get your gun.

FRANK. This one ass place.

JOE. And she got her gun. (*Then suddenly.*) We're the asses to come out here miles. Six bob! And the floor like corrugated iron in there.

FRANK. Lord, I'd love to be independent. . . . I have to get in.

JOE. You won't see me paying six bob.

FRANK. What do you think?

JOE. Could we get pass-outs maybe?

FRANK. Yeh . . . (*To himself.*) Yeh, cadge and cadge again.

JOE. There's a good crowd in there. There's bound to be someone leaving soon: jiggy-jiggy in the passion wagons.

While JOE *is saying the last line above,* MICKEY FORD *comes out of the dancehall. He is about the same age as* FRANK *and* JOE. *His suit is better than theirs and he wears a loud American-style tie. He is well off, having a car and no lack of money. He is a tradesman of some kind or at any rate he has a good job. Nevertheless, he is adolescent in many ways. He likes to talk about himself and boast of his exploits in a rather naive way. This smugness and boasting make him very self-confident and lead to an appalling triviality in his conversation. Naturally, neither* FRANK *nor* JOE *can bear him since he represents all that they are not and all that they resent. He affects a slight American accent whenever he thinks of it.*

FRANK *and* JOE watch him go up the road.

FRANK. Oh, look out: there's Handsome himself! Whid (*look at*) the tie he has on.

JOE. How yeh, Mick!

MICKEY. Hi, fellahs! Are you going in?

FRANK. ⎫
JOE. ⎬ Yeh.

MICKEY (*exiting to a shop off*). See you inside. (*They laugh quietly at his disappearing back.*)

JOE. Think would he—would he be any good for the touch?

FRANK. No.

JOE. Well, we can't wait for someone to come along and say, "here, lads, here's three-and-six for ye."

FRANK. And he'll tell half the hall inside we touched him. His money, you know, is real special. He's loaded to the nockers with threepenny bits—legacy stakes.

JOE. Well, I'm going to try him when he comes back. If he tells anyone we touched him we won't give him the money back: Law three hundred and six in the touchers' rule book.

FRANK. Do you see him driving round the town always with one arm sticking out the window? Hail, rain or snow the elbow is out. I don't know how he doesn't get paralyzed with the cold. I'm going to write to Henry Ford.

JOE. Yeh?

FRANK. And tell him to invent a car—great idea—with an artificial arm fixed on and sticking out the window. The hard man car they'll call it. Then fellahs like Mickey can still be dog tough without exposing themselves. Get me?

They laugh.

JOE. Stall it. Brilliantino is coming back.

FRANK. Are you happy at your work?

JOE *whistles furiously in reply.* MICKEY FORD *enters, eating an apple.*

JOE. Oh, there y'are, Mick!

FRANK *nods.*

MICKEY. Hi fellahs! (*He comes over to them.*)

JOE. What's the dance like, Mick?

MICKEY. Not bad. The band's not bad.

JOE. Much women inside?

MICKEY. Loaded, stacked, powerful talent, deadly. Best I've seen for a long while.

FRANK (*dryly*). I bet you've squared already, Mick?

MICKEY. I've my eye on a few but I don't know which I'll bother with yet. There's a Jane in there that's nursing in England home on holidays. What a woman! Full of your arms, you know. (*He winks.*)

JOE. There's nothing like the ones that spend a while in England. Them are the ones to get.

FRANK. And the Protestants.

MICKEY. And she's all talk too. Ah, but I don't think I'll bother.

FRANK (*innocently*). Jay, and I bet you'd be sound there too, sham.

MICKEY. Sure I know. But there's a few others I'm sort of watching.

FRANK. Yeh?

MICKEY. There's a Kelly one in there from round here. I had—

JOE. Anne Kelly?

MICKEY. Do you know her, Joe?

JOE (*looks at* FRANK). Sort of.

MICKEY. I had a dance or two with her. I was thinking about her but—I don't know.

JOE. Why?

MICKEY. Ah—there's not an awful lot of her in it. Do you know her, Frank?

FRANK (*nods*). How's the car going, Mick?

MICKEY. A bird.

JOE. Any accidents or anything?

MICKEY. No, but do you know, I was coming home from work the other evening. Monday. Well you know me—boot down all the time.

FRANK (*dryly*). You were doing over fifty, I suppose?

MICKEY. Fifty? Sixty-five, seventy. I was flying along. All of a sudden I felt the pull to the right. Like a flash, I changed down and slapped on the brakes. The front tyre was gone.

FRANK (*whistles*). Wheeew!

MICKEY. They're tubeless, you know.

FRANK. Go on!

JOE. Jay!

MICKEY. Well, you know yourselves when you're speeding like that and you get a blow-out, the car could go anywhere. Heaven, hell, anywhere. You just want to stay cool and act fast. It's easy enough to get killed nowadays.

JOE. That's if you're not fast enough like you were?

MICKEY. Gee, guys, you want to be fast alright.

FRANK. That's for a blow?

MICKEY. For any emergency, and for a blow-out too. Which reminds me, I'd better blow. (*All laugh.*) I've a real nice bit asked for the next dance.

JOE. Good man, Mick—Oh Mick, a second! You see we're kind of stuck, like, and—

MICKEY. Aw jay, lads, the car is full!

JOE. No. We're okay for getting home: we're stuck for a few shillings.

MICKEY. Aw jay, lads—

JOE. Three and six—

MICKEY. Aw jay, lads—

JOE. Till Friday night—Friday dinner time.

MICKEY. I couldn't. I've—I've only five bob on me and I've to get a gallon of juice for the bus going home. And it might be a roundabout way too. (*He smiles slyly but gets no response.*)

JOE. Maybe you'd manage without the petrol?

MICKEY. I couldn't, honest. She's very low. I had five and sevenpence and I bought the apple. The good stuff costs five bob a gallon.

JOE. If you give us three and six we'll borrow it inside for you. There's a crowd from home in there.

MICKEY. Aw, I couldn't risk it.

JOE. We'd be sure to get it! There's no risk.

MICKEY. Aw, it's too chancey. Look, I'd like to help you but I can't. I've a few odd pence here if that's any use to—

FRANK. Okay.

MICKEY. Jay, sorry now, fellahs.

JOE *is about to try again.*

FRANK. Okay!

JOE. Okay, sham.

MICKEY. Sorry. I'd better go in. Be seeing you.

He goes into the hall.

JOE. You have your glue. Twilix. (*He joins* FRANK). Where did he get that accent. "Hi, fellahs."

FRANK. He has an uncle in America and they get letters at home from him. . . . He'll be all double bases and carburettors and ignition keys inside now with the women.

JOE. And they seem to fall for that kind of bull too. He squares a lot— (*pulls a lot of women.*)

FRANK. I don't know does he square that many. A lot of the women he gets are very thick anyway. The car helps . . . He mustn't give anything up at home at all.

JOE. By God, it's not so with me. That auld fellow would break my back.

FRANK. How much do you give up?

JOE. Half . . . How much do you give up? (FRANK *sighs.*) . . . But they need it.

FRANK (*pause*). And what do you do with the other half? A pound!

JOE. Spend it! (*They laugh.*)

FRANK. Aw but—Jesus!—this bumming around from one end of the week to the other is terrible! Jesus, look at us now! Look at us in that auld job with Dan Higgins. The fags we get out of him—just from soft-soaping an imbecile. Ah, yes, we all get a big laugh but—I don't know.

JOE. Did you see Dan Higgins today going into the boss's office? (*Laughs.*) He nearly tore the head of himself pulling off his cap.

FRANK. But again it's not so funny. No, serious, sham, This old job. Do you know what I think? Do you know what the job is like? Serious, sham.

JOE (*laughing*). What?

FRANK. The bosses are gods and we're only—

JOE (*laughing*). Carney, the transport boss—

FRANK. No, but the job. You know, it's like a big tank. The whole town is like a tank. At home is like a tank. A huge tank with walls running up, straight up. And we're at the bottom, splashing around all week in their Friday night vomit, clawing at the sides all around. And the bosses—and the big-shots—are up around the top, looking in, looking down. You know the look? Spitting. On top of us. And for fear we might climb out someway—Do you know what they're doing?—They smear grease around the walls.

They laugh. Pause.

FRANK. It's pushing on. We'd better do something quick.

JOE. Will I try Mary Jane in the office again?

FRANK. I don't think so.

JOE. What?

FRANK. . . . Joe.

JOE. Yeh?

FRANK. It's no good standing out here. If one of us went in he could borrow money for the other.

JOE. Or if he had a date inside he could go off with her.

FRANK. Look, sham, give us two bob and I'll get it for you inside. This Anne Kelly—look, sham, if I don't get in there I'm finished with her.

JOE. So what?

FRANK. I'll get the money for you inside.

JOE. Who'll give it to you?

FRANK. I'll get it.

JOE. Do you think I'm going to be standing around out here, frozen, on my tod?

FRANK. I'll only be a second.

JOE. No.

FRANK. It's the only chance we have. Listen, I have to go in there: You heard Ford yourself: He has his eye on her.

JOE. Alright so. I'll go in and borrow the money for you. Give me one and six.

FRANK. No, I've a better chance.

JOE. I don't see that.

He exits for a few moments to investigate the possibility of getting in by means of a back way. Noises and voices arguing are heard from the box-office. JOE *returns.*

JOE. Hey, what's up?

FRANK. It must be a ladies choice: the women are charging Ford!

JOE. It's a bull and cow! (*A row.*)

They move to a better vantage point as dancehall door opens and BOUNCER *appears pushing* DRUNK *out of the hall.*

BOUNCER. Out! Out!

DRUNK. Come out, come out! Come on out, you and all the other bastards in there!

BOUNCER. You watch your language around here now, Daly.

He exits returning to dancehall.

DRUNK. I want my bottle back! No one takes anything from me and gets away with it! I'll show yeh! (*To himself.*) Mr Tough. God, I'd kill him. Steal their lousy booze. (*He sees* FRANK *and* JOE.) Did you see that? I'm telling you he's lucky I didn't—Did you see that?

FRANK. I thought you'd tear him to pieces.

DRUNK. I would too. (*Shouts.*) And I will!

JOE. What were you going on with the girl for anyway?

DRUNK. Hah? What girl? There was no girls.

JOE. At your age, too, McGoo.

DRUNK. No, no, the booze was—

FRANK. What were you doing to her?

DRUNK. It was the booze.

JOE. Come off it!

DRUNK. No! I had a bottle of stout in my pocket and I was just having a quiet slug when up comes Tough. Mr Big Tough comes up and says I stole it. I didn't. 'Twasn't me.

JOE. Stole what? Your bottle?

DRUNK. Naw! The band's booze. Someone stole it, all of it—the whole

case of it! But 'twasn't me. They blamed me. They put me out and said it
was me.

FRANK. That band is failing alright.

DRUNK (*puzzled*). Hah?

FRANK. Right, we'll see you to-morrow.

They ignore DRUNK. DRUNK *begins to move away. He tugs up his trousers
and money rattles.* FRANK *and* JOE *look at each other.*

FRANK. Oh, Jim?

DRUNK. Hah?

FRANK. That chucker-out wants his ears pinned back alright.

DRUNK. And I told him. I told him I never set eyes on it.

FRANK. Sure—

DRUNK. I'm not one for drinking that much—a case of it!

JOE. Sure.

FRANK. Jim, old stock, you know the three of us should stick together.
Pals.

DRUNK. Pals.

FRANK. Joe, that chucker-out can't get away with insulting people like
that. I'll tell you, we'll go in and get stuck in him.

JOE. Cripes, we will. Come on. Oh, how much is the dance?

DRUNK. I don't know. I paid—

FRANK. It's six bob.

JOE. I've only four and six.

FRANK. Wait a minute. (*Produces his money.*) Four lousy bob.

JOE. We're only short three and six. Just three and six.

FRANK. That's all that's stopping us from Chucker-head. A lousy three
and six.

DRUNK. Short of cash, lads?

JOE. Three and six.

DRUNK (*mournfully*). Lousy three and six.

FRANK. A friend is what we need now.

DRUNK. Well, I'm your pal, amn't I?

JOE. Sure!

DRUNK. Well, I'm your pal, amn't I?

FRANK. The best, Jim. You won't see us stuck.

DRUNK. I wo'ont. How much do ye want?

JOE. Three and six.

DRUNK. Three and six. (*He takes some coins from his pocket and hands them
to* JOE.) Here.

FRANK (*to* JOE). How much is in it?

JOE. Hang on.

DRUNK. Here's more. Take it. (Handing more coins.)

FRANK. How much is in it?

JOE (*to* DRUNK). Is that all you have? (*To* FRANK.) Sixpence halfpenny.

FRANK. What?

DRUNK (*still searching*). That's all. All gone now, pals. Have ye enough? Then don't worry. We'll get him. We'll wait here till Mr Tough comes out after the dance to get him.

FRANK. Go home.

DRUNK. Hah?

JOE. Get home!

DRUNK (*as he exits*). Home. Scram, Pals. Well, I'm not going home. . . .

JOE (*turns to look after* DRUNK). Jays, like a stray dog! . . . What brought us out here? What clown told you it was a four bob dance?

FRANK. Stall—Wait—two coming out now.

A couple, man and a girl, anywhere between twenty and thirty years of age, come out from dance and start to move off. They have been given passes by the BOUNCER *in case they want to go back again.*

GIRL. I thought we were going to the shop?

MAN. I just want to get something in the car for a minute.

JOE. Hey, any pass-outs?

MAN. No. Not a soul fainted. (*He grins proudly. The girl laughs.*)

FRANK. ⎫ Haw-haw! Funny man! Big joke! Pity about your face!

JOE. ⎭ Makum joke for squaw! Waw! Buff! The wit! Half wit!

FRANK. Great old fun wasn't he?

JOE. God bless him.

FRANK *begins to whistle idly.* JOE *rattles the money in his pocket and idly takes out a box of matches, looks at them and quickly replaces them. He moves up and down giving an occasional kick to the ground.*

JOE. Oh, to have a lickle house, to own the hearth and stool and all, in the dear little, sweet little emerald Isle, in the county of Mayo.

Pause.

"Break down the bridge six warriors rushed,

and the storm was shot and they shat in the storm!

FRANK. And Sarsfield strung up by the nockers behind them! (*Pause.*) Look, let me go in and borrow the money for you.

JOE. Now don't start that again.

FRANK. It's the only sensible thing to do.

JOE. Will I try the quare one in the office again.

FRANK. I'll try her.

FRANK *exits into hall.* JOE *takes out cigarettes and lights one quickly. He takes several deep pulls furiously in order to make the cigarette smaller. The couple (that just exited) re-enter, the girl in a minor huff adjusting her clothing. At the same time,* BOUNCER *appears in dancehall doorway, ejecting* FRANK.

BOUNCER. Out! Out!

FRANK. No need to break my effing arm!

BOUNCER. What's that?

FRANK (*walking away*). Okay, Jim.

BOUNCER. You watch your filthy tongue and keep away from here if you know what's good for you.

Couple and BOUNCER *exit to hall.*

JOE. What happened?

FRANK. Boxy in the office got ratty and called the bouncer. Jim. (*Roughly.*) Give us a fag.

JOE. It's only a butt, I had, sham.

FRANK *gropes in his pockets and produces a butt. A second couple come out of the hall. The girl is* KATHLEEN. JOE *runs over to them.*

JOE. Are you going back again?

SECOND MAN (*curtly*). No.

JOE. Any chance of your pass-outs?—We'll buy them.

KATHLEEN. That your friend over there?

JOE. Yeh.

KATHLEEN. Is he Frank?

JOE (*doubtfully*). Yes.

KATHLEEN. I was with a girl tonight who was waiting for him.

JOE. Is that—ah—so? (*He does not know how to handle the situation.*) Frank! Come here, a minute, sham. This here is a friend of Anne Kelly's.

FRANK. Oh, hello. Oh yes.

THIRD MAN. What's up?

KATHLEEN. Just a minute. (*To* FRANK.) She was very disappointed when you didn't come.

FRANK. Yes? Is that so? You see, we were held up. I was disappointed too. Is she inside?

KATHLEEN. She waited an awful long time for you.

FRANK. Yeh? Well. She shouldn't have waited so long.

JOE. In the cold too.

FRANK. I hope she wasn't mad at me.

KATHLEEN. I don't know. Maybe she'll understand. You're going in aren't you?

Slight pause.

JOE. Well, if you give us the—

FRANK (*cutting in quickly*). We were playing a football match. Oh, only a sort of a street league, you know. But they take that kind of thing so seriously, you see? And the match started late too. I was vexed but what could I do—you know?—togged out there—I just couldn't—you know?

JOE. And it was nearly eight o'clock when—

FRANK (*cutting in again*). Yeh. And then to crown it all—you know how before a match you've no right place to put your clothes—and I gave my money to one of the crowd to hold for me and—well, the match finishing so late I just fired on my clothes and dashed out here and forgot all about the money. I knew Anne would be waiting and I didn't want to keep her that long, so—

KATHLEEN. Then you haven't any—

FRANK. Oh, any other time, you know—you couldn't forget to collect a thing like that—but it was so late and it never entered my head and I didn't want to keep Anne so long.

KATHLEEN. So you haven't any money?

JOE. That's why we want pass-outs.

SECOND MAN. Well, you can have ours. (*He gives them to* JOE.)

JOE. Thanks.

FRANK. Thanks very much. I hate to—

SECOND MAN. That's alright. So long. (*He's trying to get away.*)

KATHLEEN. Oh, you'd better hurry.

FRANK. Yes?

KATHLEEN. Competition.

FRANK. Me? Who?

KATHLEEN. Bye.

SECOND MAN. Bye.

KATHLEEN *and* SECOND MAN *exit.*

JOE. So long.

FRANK. So I've competition.

JOE. Wonder who it is.

FRANK. Ford. Well, we'll soon take care of that. Come on. Give me one of those passes. Act casual-like now, like as if you were in before.

They go into the hall. The stage is empty. Slight pause.

JOE'S VOICE. We were in before!

BOUNCER'S VOICE. Get out! You weren't in before!

FRANK'S VOICE. We were!

BOUNCER'S VOICE. Outside the two of you! Quick now! I've had enough of you all night.

BOUNCER, FRANK *and* JOE *appear at the door.*

FRANK (*holding up his pass-out*). And what are these things meant to be for?

BOUNCER. You watch your filthy tongue!

JOE. What are pass-outs for?

BOUNCER. Give them to me. (*Takes* JOE'S.) They're not transferable.

FRANK (*pleads*). Aw, Jim. We'll slip you eight bob.

BOUNCER. You don't know me, don't use my name therefore. (*Pushes them away.*) Now clear.

JOE (*an undertone*). Now clear before Johnny MacBrown swallows his false tooth.

BOUNCER. What? . . . Did you pass a remark? . . . (*To* JOE.) Are you a good man? . . . (*To* FRANK.) Are you? . . . Maybe you're two good men, hah? . . . Townies . . . Clear. (*His challenge not accepted, he exits to hall.*)

JOE. . . . Will we blow?

FRANK. These buffers will soon object to us walking on the roads. He wouldn't be so tough in town.

JOE. I thought earlier the pass-outs wouldn't work.

FRANK. Yeh-yeh-yeh-yeh-yeh, you knew it all. (FRANK *regrets the remark, he takes out his last two cigarettes; he would like to smoke one and give the other to* JOE: *the futility of it. He puts cigarettes back in his pocket.*) God, these buffers! (MICKEY FORD *enters. They do not see him.*) Like as if we were dirt.

JOE. . . . Will we blow?

MICKEY. Hi, fellahs.

JOE. ⎫
FRANK. ⎬ Hi!

MICKEY. Gee, guys, hot in there. Girl inside talking about you, Frank. Anne Kelly.

FRANK. Yeh?

MICKEY. You had a—sort of a date with her.

FRANK. Sort of?

MICKEY. Are you thinking of going with her?

FRANK. What business is that of yours?

MICKEY. I mean—She knows you're out here.

FRANK. How does she know? Did you—

MICKEY. I didn't tell her. I—

FRANK. Mouth! Listen Ford, no one else would have told her.

MICKEY. I didn't—I just came out to—

FRANK. Ah, shut up. You'd better keep well away from me from now on because I'd love to hurt that handsome face.

MICKEY. God, I'd give you more than you'd want anytime. (FRANK *gives a short derisive laugh.*) But I have my brothers inside tonight—

FRANK. Your brothers—Your big brothers—The crankshaft family! You give me a pain in my royal differential arse!

MICKEY. They're inside. And you remember you have a long way to go home.

FRANK. And you remember they're only home on holidays, and in a week or two nice little Mickey-bags will go home some night with his Florida Beach tie all blood. (*He grabs at* MICKEY'S *tie and gives it a tug.*)

MICKEY. God, you won't try anything like that on with me. Think back what happened with you and your auld drunken auld layabout auld fella last year: oh, didn't quiet, cunning Frank stand beside him kicking in the shop window, and stand beside him wanting to take on the town. The priest saved you from being arrested but he mightn't bother a second time.

FRANK. How many girls have you squared tonight, sham?

MICKEY. I've Anne Kelly squared. Do you think she'd have anythin' to do with you now?

FRANK *moves towards him.*

MICKEY. You'd better to stay where you are.

FRANK. Pity about his head—isn't it, Joe?

MICKEY. I'll be out in a—

FRANK. Tell us about the blow-out again, sham.

MICKEY. I'll be out in a minute with her. If you know what's good for you, you'll—well, you know what's best to do. Remember my brothers will be just inside the door. (*Exits quickly into hall.*)

FRANK. I'll get him. I'll get him.

JOE. Not tonight, Frank.

FRANK. I'll get him, I'll kick the day-lights out of him.

JOE. Take it easy—

FRANK. I'll make him sorry.

JOE. The brothers. Four of them.

FRANK. I'm not an eejit. They'll be back in England in a week or two.

JOE. What's so special about this Kelly one anyway.

FRANK. . . . Ah, she can go to hell. I'm not sticking around here much longer. England. I'm bailing out of that lousy job. Lousy few bob a week. Twenty-two years old and where does it get me? Yes, sir—I'm a pig, sir—if you say so, sir! (*Suddenly.*) Well, he's not getting away with her that easy.

JOE. But—

FRANK. Don't worry—don't worry.

JOE. But he'll call the brothers—

FRANK. No. By now, he'll have told her how hard a man he is—how he can break a fellah's back with a spit. I'll chat her up when she comes out. (*He stands watching the door.*)

JOE. Let's blow, sham.

DRUNK *enters.*

FRANK (*to* DRUNK *intensely*). You! Keep away from me!

JOE (*to* FRANK). You want to chat her up? Here she is.

MICKEY *and* ANNE come out.

FRANK. Anne. Anne! (ANNE *stops.*)

MICKEY (*nervously*). Leave her alone.

FRANK. I can explain. Honest to God, I was playing football. Honest to . . . No. I hadn't the money. Am I leaving you home?

MICKEY. What about all the lies you told her? Pick on someone your own class now.

FRANK. Ford, there's nothing surer but I'll get you.

MICKEY. Now, Miss Kelly—there's Frank Mooney. What do you think of him? (ANNE *is crying now.*)

FRANK. Am I taking you home? Anne?

ANNE. . . . . You're only a liar. I wouldn't have anything to do with you. (*As she exits.*) Are you coming, Mickey?

MICKEY *exits after her.*

FRANK (*quietly*). . . . Shout at them.

JOE. What?

FRANK. Shout, shout, shout at them!

JOE (*roars*). Spark-plug face! Handsome! Glue-bags!

FRANK. Torn mouth!

JOE. Carburettor head! Cop on yank!

FRANK. Torn mouth!—Torn mouth!—Torn mouth! (*Laughing harshly, drawing* DRUNK *into their company.*) Wait, he's in top gear now!—She's not tickin' over so good. Valve timing out, I'd say—condenser is faulty. Going round a corner, bootin' her to the last, doin' seventy three and a half miles an hour and do you know what happened him?—Do you know what happened to him? A cock of hay fell on top of him! (*They laugh harshly.*) Oh,

484 | *Late Twentieth-Century Fiction and Drama*

this—this damn place, this damn hall, people, those lousy women! I could—I could—

> *He rushes over to the poster and hits it hard with his fist. He kicks it furiously.*
> JOE. Come on out of here to hell.

They exit. The band plays on. DRUNK *is giving a few impotent kicks to the poster as the lights fade.*

Further Readings on Tom Murphy

Selected Published Works

Bailegangaire: The Story of Bailegangaire and How It Came by Its Appellation. Dublin: Gallery Press, 1986.

A Crucial Week in the Life of a Grocer's Assistant. Dublin: Gallery Press, 1978.

Famine. Dublin: Gallery Press, 1977.

The Fooleen. Early version of *A Crucial Week.* . . . Dixon, Calif.: Proscenium Press, 1968.

The Gigli Concert. Dublin: Gallery Press, 1984.

The Morning After Optimism. Cork: Mercier, 1973.

On the Inside. Dublin: Gallery Press, 1976.

On the Outside. With Noel O'Donoghue. Dublin: Gallery, 1984.

On the Outside/On the Inside. Dublin: Gallery Press, 1976.

The Orphans. Newark, Del.: Proscenium Press, 1974.

The Sanctuary Lamp. Dublin: Poolbeg, 1976.

The Seduction of Virtue. Prose fiction. Boston: Little, Brown, 1994.

Too Late for Logic. London: Methuen, 1990.

A Whistle in the Dark: A Play in Three Acts. 1970. Reprint, Dublin, Gallery Press, 1984.

Produced, Unpublished Plays

The Blue Macushla. Dublin: Abbey Theatre, 1980.

Epitaph under Ether. One act. Dublin: Abbey Theatre, 1979.

Famine Trilogy. I. *The Moral Force.* II. *The Policy.* III. *Relief.* Dublin: Radio Telefís Éireann, 1973.

The Fly Sham. London: British Broadcasting Corporation, 1963. [Television play.]

The J. Arthur McGinnis Story: The First 36,525 Days. Dublin: Pavillion Theatre, 1977.

Snakes and Reptiles. London: British Broadcasting Corporation, 1968.[Television play.]

Speeches of Farewell. Dublin: Radio Telefís Éireann, 1977. [Television play.]

Veronica. London: British Broadcasting Corporation, 1963. [Television play.]
The White House. Dublin: Abbey Theatre, 1972.
Young Man in Trouble. London: Thames, 1970. [Television play.]

Biography and Criticism

Murray, Christopher, ed. "Tom Murphy Special Issue." Special issue, *Irish University Review* 16 (Spring 1987).
O'Toole, Fintan. *The Politics of Magic: The Work and Times of Tom Murphy*. Dublin: Raven Arts, 1987.

Glossary

Words, Places, Persons, Allusions

a bouchal. (Ir. *a bhuachaill*) boy.

acanthus. Decorative representation of a leaf at the top of a Corinthian column in classical architecture.

a-chuisle. (Lit. "Oh pulse [of my heart])," pron. a-KOOSH-la) Dear one, darling, a conventional term of endearment.

Act of Union. In 1800, dissolution of the Irish Parliament and the imposed pretense that Ireland was part of the United Kingdom with representation in Westminster; perceived by nationalists as a disaster for Ireland.

Aeneas. *See* pious Aeneas.

Aeval, Eevel. Anglicizations of *Aibell* (Mod. Ir. *Aoibheall*), fairy queen of north Munster whose name was cited for more than a thousand years.

agra. (Ir. *a ghrá*, pron. a-GRAW) My love, my dear.

Aife. (Mod. Ir. *Aoife*) (pron. EE-fa) Name from early Irish tradition, also used as a translation for the name of the biblical Eve. Borne by dozens of females, including the cruel stepmother in the "Children of Lir" story and the Amazonian chieftainess whose affair with Cúchulainn produces Connla, called Conlaoch by Lady Gregory.

Ailill. (pron. AL-il) Medb's husband and king of Connacht.

Ainnle. Brother of Noíse, Deirdre's lover.

aisling. (pron. ASH-ling) A kind of vision poetry that flourished in eighteenth-century Munster, usually with political implications. The aisling formula consists of three parts: (1) the poet, out walking, meets a lady; (2) he describes her appearance, often employing rose and lily imagery; (3) the poet begins a conversation with her. (The woman is a personification of Ireland.)

Alanna. (Ir. *a leanbh,* pron. a-LAN-ev) My child. Term of endearment.

Alban, Alba. Poetic name for Scotland.

Alexander (356–323 B.C.). Commonly called Alexander the Great, Macedonian ruler of Greece who extended his kingdom as far as India.

amadán. See oinseach.

ambrán. (pron. aw-RAWN) Meter, song meter; the meter of Irish poetry from 1600 and after that gave up the strict rules of bardic schools in favor of the natural accent of the vowel and vowel sounds.

amossa. (Ir. *muise, mhuise!* meaning "well, well!") An exclamation, sometimes without stress in the sentence. *Cf.* musha.

Angus, Angus Óg. Pre-Christian god of poetry. G. W. Russell perceived him to be a counterpart of the Greek Eros, god of love.

Anne, Queen. Queen of Great Britain and Ireland, 1702–1714.

Annie Get Your Gun. Broadway music by Irving Berlin (1946) based on the life of vaudeville sharpshooter Annie Oakley (1860–1926).

Antrim, County. One of the six counties of Northern Ireland still a part of Great Britain. It is situated just north of Belfast.

Aoife. Modern Irish spelling for Aífe.

Apollo. Classical god of poetry, music, and the fine arts.

Aran Islands. Chain of small islands at the mouth of Galway Bay, between counties Clare and Galway: Inishmore (or Aranmore), Inishmaan, and Inisheer. As the Islands are still Irish-speaking, many nationalists have felt, perhaps wrongly, that they are the most Irish parts of Ireland.

d'Arbois de Jubainville, Marie-Henri (1827–1910). French Celticist whose many publications were influential in the development of Celtic and Irish studies.

Árd Cuillean. Placename in the *Táin* identified with Crossakeel, County Westmeath.

Ardan. Brother of Noíse, Deirdre's lover.

Aries. Zodiacal sign of the Ram (March 21 to April 20).

arrah. (Ir. *ara*) Well, indeed. An interjection that is often deprecatory.

ashplant. A walking stick; rather, the word favored for a walking stick in James Joyce's *Ulysses* (1922).

Ascoli, Graziadio I. (1829–1907). Italian linguist who helped to define the place of Celtic languages within the Indo-European family.

Assiniboine. A Sioux-speaking tribe of Native Americans residing in the northern plains states; also a river of eastern Saskatchewan joining the Red River at Winnipeg.

Áth Mór. (Ir. "big ford") Placename in the *Táin* identified with the modern town of Athlone, County Westmeath, which controls the Shannon crossing between Leinster and Connacht. Medb's army crossed the Shannon at Áth Mór on its return.

Athene, Athena. Greek goddess of wisdom.

Athy. Market town in County Kildare on the River Barrow.

Aughrim. (pron. AWK-rim). Village in Galway, site of the decisive defeat of the Jacobite-Williamite War, making it the last time an Irish army opposed English forces in the field, 12 July 1691.

[Saint] Augustine (A.D. 354–430). Bishop, philosopher, one of the Latin Fathers of the Church and seminal thinker in early Christianity, known especially for his self-searching autobiography, *Confessions*.

avick. (Ir. *a mhic*) My son, my boy.

avourneen. (Ir. *a mhuirnín*) My darling, my dear.

Baile's Strand. The seashore around Dundalk and the mouth of the Boyne River.

Bailey, the. Well-known pub in downtown Dublin, frequented by writers.

bailiff. An agent of an estate.

Ballyrush. Townland in the parish of Inniskeen, Cavan, Patrick Kavanagh's birthplace.

Ballyvaughan. Fishing village in north Clare.

Bann. River in County Antrim that divides the industrialized east from the rural hinterlands to the west.

bardic session. Public gathering of bardic poets to demonstrate their craft.

Barr dTrí gCom. Irish form of a Dingle place name, lit. "High point of the three coombs, cirques, or recesses."

Barrow. River in southeastern Ireland that empties into Waterford Harbour. The Barrow valley was a center for stone carving; the high crosses of Castledermot and Moone are among this group.

bawn. Protective walls within which settlers made their homes during the British plantation of Ulster.

Beare. Peninsula in southwest Ireland, between Bantry Bay and the Kenmare River estuary in counties Cork and Kerry. Haunt of the Old Woman of Beare, a personification of Ireland.

Beaumont, Francis (1584–1616). English dramatist.

bedad. Disguised oath, comparable to "by gosh," for "by God"; *cf.* begobs.

Beg-Innish. Transliteration of the Irish for Little Island (Ir. *beag inis*). Synge's citation may refer to what is now called Beginish in Valentia Harbour, Kerry.

begobs. A disguised oath, comparable to "by gosh," for "by God"; *cf.* bedad.

Bert, the big-foot. Hungarian princess who became the mother of Charlemagne (eighth century). Subject of romantic legends in France as Berthe au Grand Pied. So named for her club foot.

Billingsgate. London's major fish market.

Binn os Gaoith. (pron. binn os GEE) Placename meaning cliff or peak above the wind.

Blackwater. Name for several rivers in Ireland and the British Isles. Paul Muldoon cites the one in County Tyrone running into Lough Neagh, Northern Ireland.

Blarney Stone. An Irish bar in Manhattan, and, by implication, a generic name for such a bar.

Bloom. Leopold Bloom, hero of James Joyce's *Ulysses* (1922).

bob. Slang for shilling.

bohereen, boreen. (Ir. *bóithrín*, small road) Narrow country road or lane, especially in hilly country.

Bolingbroke, [Viscount] Henry St. John (1678–1751). Conservative rationalist English statesman and historian.

Book of Kells. Most famous of all early Irish illuminated manuscripts, an illustrated text of the Gospels named for the town of Kells, where it was found.

boreen. *See* bohereen.

bouchal. *See a bouchal.*

Boyne. Most important river of eastern Ireland. Seventy miles long, it empties into the Irish Sea near Drogheda. Site of William of Orange's important defeat of James II and the Catholic cause, 1 July, 1690.

Brandon, Mount. Peak 2764 feet high on the north coast of the Dingle Peninsula, Kerry.

Breagh. Variant spelling for the Latin *Bregia. See* following entry.

Bregia. Placename in the *Táin.* A plain in eastern Ireland between the Liffey and Boyne Rivers, County Meath. Ir. *Mag Breg:* Plain of Bray.

Breughel, Pieter (1520?–1569). Flemish painter known for his depictions of peasant life and landscapes.

Brian Boru. Irish historical king who defeated the Norse at the Battle of Clontarf in A.D. 1014.

Brigid, Brigit, St. Sixth-century nun of County Kildare, one of the three patron saints of Ireland, sometimes called "Mary of the Gael"; sometimes linked with pre-Christian fire goddess of the same name. *See also* Imbolc.

Brigid's Cross. A cross woven of rushes and considered to be a protective charm for a house.

Brigid's Girdle. Small hoop made of rushes, thought to encourage healing.

Brobdignab. Kingdom of the giants in Swift's *Gulliver's Travels* (1726).

Browne, Archbishop George. Authorized first use of the Anglican *Book of Common Prayer* in Dublin, 1551.

Bruno, Giordano (*c.* 1548–1600). Italian philosopher burned at the stake for heresy.

Buffalo Bill. William Frederick Cody (1846–1917). American scout and frontiersman, better known in later life as a showman and circus owner.

buffer. A self-important person.

bulled. Reference to Adrian IV's papal bull, *Laudabiliter,* which provided the authorization for Henry II's invasion of Ireland in 1171.

Burke, William (1792–1829). The "bodysnatcher." Worked with William Hare murdering by suffocation, in order to sell victims' bodies to scientists for dissection. Burke was hanged after Hare turned King's evidence.

Burns, Robert (1759–1796). Lowland Scottish poet who often wrote in dialect. First poet born of the peasantry in the British Isles to achieve wide acclaim.

Bushmills. Whiskey distilled in Northern Ireland; a preference for it is sometimes perceived as Protestant or Unionist.

Caesar, Gaius Julius (100–44 B.C.). Roman general and statesman. Cleopatra, Caesar's mistress, bore him a son, Cesarion.

Cahirciveen. Town in southwestern County Kerry on the picturesque route known as the "Ring of Kerry," often perceived as one of the most Irish of Irish towns.

Cairbré. (Normative Cairbre) Name borne by many figures of early Irish history and legend, notably Cairbre Lifechair ("of the Liffey," "Liffey-Lover"), a king in the Fenian Cycle.

cairn. (Ir. *carn*) Pile of stones used as a marker, often a memorial.

caoine. (pron. KEEN) Cry for the dead, often, an extempory elegy. *See also* keen.

capernosity. Peevishness, ill temper.

Carbery, Muskerry, Iveleary, etc. The names of baronies, administrative units in the province of Munster.

Carlow, County. A southern, rural county of Leinster, almost midway between Dublin and Cork.

Carrick. (Ir. *carraig*) Rock. Common in place names.

Casement, Sir Roger (1864–1916). Irish patriot, captured while smuggling German arms into Ireland and executed August 3, 1916.

Cassandra. Princess and prophetess of Troy, seized by the Greeks after the fall of her city.

Cassandra [Salviata]. An heiress of Blois, beloved by French poet Pierre de Ronsard (1524–1585), subject of a sequence of poems, who nonetheless rejected him. This is the Cassandra of J. M. Synge's "Queens."

Castle, the. *See* Dublin Castle.

Cathbad. (pron. KATH-vadh, KAFF-a) Chief druid of Ulster and a leading figure of the Ulster Cycle; among many distinctions, he foretells the fate of Deirdre and serves as a teacher to Cúchulainn.

Cathleen Ní Houlihan. *See* Kathleen Ní Houlihan.

Cavan, County. Rural, dominantly Roman Catholic southern county of the province of Ulster, about eighty miles southwest of Belfast. It is today a part of the Republic of Ireland.

Cawdor. Macbeth was prophesied to be the Thane of Cawdor in Shakespeare's play.

ceangal. (pron. CAN-gul) Tie or binding, as in prosody. Name given to a stanza that serves a postscript to a poem.

Ceannt, Eamonn (1881–1916). (pron. CANT) Revolutionary, athlete, and musician who participated in the Howth gun running, July 1914 and commanded the South Dublin Union during Easter week, 1916. Executed May 8, 1916.

Celbridge. Village in Kildare, about ten miles west of Dublin. A favorite retreat of Jonathan Swift.

Celia. An idealization of feminine beauty, especially as immortalized in the poetry of Ben Jonson (1572–1637).

Cervantes, Miguel de (1547–1616). Spanish novelist, author of *Don Quixote*.

chip man. Man who cooks fish and *chips,* i.e., deep-fried potatoes.

Chloe. Stock name for a shepherdess in pastoral romances.

chucker out. An ejected or chucked out person.

Clan Colam, Conaill, Creide. Rolleston's variant spellings for several heroic families of Ireland. The Clan Conaill (or *Cenél* Conaill) occupied Tirconnel in what is now Donegal.

Clan Jansen. *See* Jansen.

Clare, County. A Munster county north of the Shannon estuary on the west coast. Anciently called Thomond, it is associated with the O'Brien family.

Clarke, Thomas J. (1857–1916). Fenian, revolutionary leader, and publisher of the anti-English journal, *Irish Freedom.* At the request of the other leaders, he was the first signer of the Proclamation of the Republic. Executed May 3, 1916.

Cloacina. Ironic feminine personification of a sewer or drain (Latin: *cloaca*).

Cloghane. Fishing village in the west of County Kerry, twenty-one miles west of Tralee, on Brandon Bay.

Clongowes Wood. Jesuit boarding school for boys in Kildare, attended by James Joyce from 1888 to 1891.

Clonmacnois, Clonmacnoise. Important monastic site, now a ruin, on the east bank of the Shannon, four miles north of Shannonbridge, Offaly. Founded by St. Ciarán (or Kieran) A.D. 545, the monastery is perhaps best known for the compilation of the great codex of early Irish literature, *Lebor na hUidre:* The Book of the Dun Cow.

Clontarf. Site of battle where the Irish under Brian Boru defeated the Norse A.D. 1014. It is north of the modern city of Dublin.

Cnogba na Rig. Place name in the *Táin* identified with Knowth, County Meath, the site of an important megalithic tomb.

Cobh. (pron. COVE) Southern port near Cork city. Formerly called Queenstown, it was the major embarcation point for those emigrating to America.

Colam. *See* Clan Colam.

"Colleen dhas crotha na mbo." (Ir. *cailín deas crúite na mbó,* pron. COLL-een DYASS CRU-te na MO) Literally, "A pretty girl milking her cow." Irish folk song thought to be unlucky since it had once distracted a priest on his way to a sick call, causing him to arrive too late.

Collins, Michael (1890–1922). Revolutionary leader and one of the originators of modern guerrilla warfare, using a system of cadres he called "Flying Columns." Killed in ambush, August 22, 1922.

Combe, The. A back street near St. Patrick's Cathedral, Dublin.

compositum. Latin: Something made of parts joined together.

Conaill, Clan. People of Donegal, western Ulster.

Conall. A leading Ulster hero, foster-brother of Cuchulainn and avenger of his death. His name often carries the cognomen *Cernach,* or "of the victories."

Conchobar mac Nessa, Conchubar, Conor MacNessa (pron. KON-or). Legendary king of Ulster throughout much of the Ulster cycle. Although usually a heroic figure, he is less attractive when he appears as the lover of Deirdre.

Conn "the Hundred-Fighter," or "of the Hundred Battles" (Ir. *Cetchathach*). Legendary ancestor of the kings of Ireland, and of many important families.

Connacht, Connaught. The most westerly of the four ancient provinces of Ireland, running roughly from the Shannon Valley to the west coast of the island.

Connemara. Region of west County Galway, home of the largest population of Irish speakers. Many find the stark treeless beauty of the landscape to be uniquely Irish.

Connolly, James (1868–1916). Labor leader, political theorist, and a leader in the seizure of the General Post Office in Easter Week, 1916. Executed May 12, 1916.

Cootehill. Market town in County Cavan that takes its name from the Coote family who settled there in the seventeenth century.

Corinna. An idealization of feminine beauty, specifically: (1) a Greek poetess who gave instruction to Pindar (522–442 B.C.); (2) a character in the poetry of Robert Herrick (1591–1674).

Cormac Conloingeas. Ulster warrior, son of Conchobar.

Corunna [La Caruna]. Site of an important British imperial battle (1809). Others cited by Austin Clarke evoke the Crimean War (Inkermann, 1854) and the Boer War (Pretoria).

Costello, John A. (1891–1976). Prime Minister *(Taoiseach)* of the Republic of Ireland, 1948–1951 and 1954–1957.

Coventry. English industrial city. To be "put in Coventry" is to be shunned by one's fellow workers.

Craglee. Anglicization of *Craigh Liath,* a forty-foot rock about one mile south of Killaloe, County Clare, with rich associations in Irish folklore. Possible residence of Aeval/Aíbell.

Crashaw, Richard (*c.* 1612–1649). English poet known for religious works showing devotional ecstasy.

crathur. Pronounced as in the Irish, *créatúr* (CRAY-toor). Creature. Usually an expression of sympathy, as "the poor crathur," though occasionally used contemptuously. Also used to mean a drop of whiskey.

creels. Wicker baskets.

Creide. *See* Clan Creide.

Crivelli, Lucrezia. Mistress of the Milanese prince Ludovico Sforza, painted by Leonardo da Vinci (1495); through misattribution, the painting is sometimes known as *La Belle Ferronière*.

Cromwell, Oliver (1599–1658). English general and statesman. While Lord Lieutenant of Ireland, Cromwell arrived in 1649 to begin a campaign to subdue the Irish. His massacres at Drogheda and Wexford established a reputation for cruelty that continues to smolder in folk memory.

Cruachan. Royal seat of Medb, warrior queen of Connacht; the site, three miles from Tulsk, Roscommon, is known today at Rathcroghan.

Cruithne. Irish name for the Picts, aboriginal inhabitants of the British Isles. The Picts are of disputed cultural originals, perhaps non-Indo-European.

Cúchulainn, Cúchulain, Cú Chulainn, etc. (pron. koo-KHULL-in) Hero of the Old Irish Ulster Cycle and principal figure of the epic *Táin Bó Cuailnge* [Cattle raid of Cooley]. His name means "Hound of Culann."

Cúil Silinni. Placename in the *Táin*, Tulsk, Roscommon.

dacha. A Russian country retreat.

Dál nAraide. In *The Madness of Suibhne,* Suibhne's home in southern Antrim, near Lough Neagh.

Dana. Great mother goddess of pre-Christian Ireland, patroness of the Tuatha Dé Danann. Also spelled Ana.

Dante Alighieri (1265–1321). Italian poet and author of the *Divine Comedy,* which includes an oft-cited vision of the afterlife.

decumana. A large portion, literally—the largest from among ten.

Debrett's Peerage and Baronetage. Guide to the history of noble and landowning families.

Deirdre. Tragic lover of the Ulster Cycle.

Derg. *See* Lough Derg.

Derry. Modern city in Derry, Northern Ireland, founded on the site of a monastery established by St. Columcille in A.D. 546. Also called Doire Choluim Cille (Columcille's Oak Grove) and Londonderry by Unionists.

de Valera, Éamon (1882–1975). American-born leader of the 1916 Uprising who escaped execution, opposed the 1922 Treaty, founded the Fianna Fáil Party, and served as prime minister and later president of Ireland.

Diana. Roman deity identified with the Greek Artemis. Goddess of the moon, as well as of hunting, archery, and running.

disjecta membra. Latin: scattered fragments.

dolmen. Type of megalithic monument still seen in the Irish countryside. A tripod of stone, its large capstone is sometimes called "the bed of Diarmait and Gráinne."

Donegal, County. A mountainous and thinly populated county in western Ulster, in the far northwest of Ireland.

Donnybrook. Area southwest of Dublin, cite of a nineteenth-century country fair, known for its riotousness, now a fashionable residential neighborhood.

Down, County. One of the six counties of Northern Ireland, south of Belfast; one of the most Protestant of Irish counties.

doxy, a tinker's. The mistress or whore of a travelling person, Ireland's pariah class.

Drogheda (pron. DRAW-hed-a). Small port town near the mouth of the Boyne River, 32 miles north of Dublin. The name of the city lives in Irish history as the site of the slaughter of Irish men, women, and children by Cromwellian troops in 1649.

druid. Pre-Christian priestly class among the Celts.

Dublin Castle. Imposing building in downtown Dublin whose foundations date from thirteenth century. Seat of British government in Ireland before 1922.

Dubthach, Dubhthach. (pron. DUV-thach, DUFF-ach). Ulster warrior noted for his evil disposition.

Dundealgan. Dundalk, coastal town in Louth, midway between Dublin and Belfast.

Dungloe, Donglow. Fishing village in County Donegal.

Dunleary. (Ir. *Dún Laoghaire,* doon-LEARY). Literally, Leary's fort. Formerly, Kingstown. Port city southeast of Dublin, embarkation point for Irish leaving by boat train for Britain.

Dunquin. Parish in western Kerry, seven miles west of Dingle.

Dun Scathach. Anglicization of *Dún Scáthaig* [Scáthach's fort], a poetic name for the Isle of Skye; implicitly the ruined fortress of Dunscaith, six miles west of Oronsay. Also linked to the amazonian Scáthach.

Dun Sobairche. Placename in the *Táin* identified with Dunseverick, County Antrim.

Durrow. Abbey four miles from Tullamore, Offaly, founded by St. Columcille, A.D. 551. The Book of Durrow, an illuminated manuscript of the Gospels, is in the library of Trinity College, Dublin.

Du sel! French for "some salt!"

Earls, Flight of. *See* Flight of Earls.

eejit. Phonetic spelling of *idiot.*

Elmo's Fire, [Saint]. A bright ball of fire, a natural phenomenon formerly seen to play among the masts of ships.

Emain Macha (pron. EV-in MAH-cha). Political center of Ulster in Old Irish literature. Identified with a site known as Navan Fort, near the modern town of Armagh.

Ennis. The principal town in county Clare.

Eochu Feidlech. (pron. OCH-oo FAYTH-lech) Father of Medb.

Eogan son of Durthacht. (pron. OWEN) Noíse's killer.

Erato. Muse of erotic poetry in classical mythology.

Erigena, Johannes Scotus (*c.* 810–*c.* 870). Irish-born cleric and philosopher. One of the initiators of Scholastic philosophy, and, by implication, the first Irish intellectual.

Erne. River of northwestern Ireland, emptying into Donegal Bay. Site of many heroic adventures in Old Irish literature.

Étaín. (pron. ay-TOYN or ay-TEEN) Name of several romantically beautiful women in Old Irish literature.

Euston. London railroad station, terminus for the Irish boat train.

fags. Cigarettes.

fal-de-lals. Gaudy or trifling ornaments or trinkets.

fan lights. Distinctive decorative windows found in many Dublin houses, above the doors of both elegant townhouses and tenements. A semicircle of long glass triangles in roughly the shape of a fan.

Fand. Mythic queen of Old Irish literature, closely associated with the powers of the sea.

Feakle. Village in north east County Clare, 7.5 miles northeast of Tulla.

Fedlimid. (pron. FAYTH-lim-ith or FAY-lim-id) Deirdre's mother.

Fenian Cycle. One of three cycles of Old Irish literature, centering on Fionn mac Cumhaill, Oisín (or Ossian), and Oscar. (The other two cycles are the Ulster and the Mythological.)

Fenians. Alternate name for the Irish Republican Brotherhood in the British Isles and North America, especially during the 1860s. At other times the word Fenian may refer to any Irish nationalist.

Ferdiad, Fer Diad. (pron. fer-DEE-adh) Friend of Cuchulainn who fought with the men of Connacht in the *Táin*. Later slain by Cuchulainn in single combat.

Fergus mac Róich. Anglicized as Fergus son of Roech. A king of Ulster. He took the Connacht side in the *Táin* after learning he had been tricked by Conchobar into betraying the sons of Usnach.

Ferriter, Pierce or **Piaras** (*c.* 1600–1653). Kerry soldier and poet who supported the Irish cause in 1641. Hanged 1653.

Fian, Fians (Ir. pl. of *Fianna*). Roving bands of hunter-warriors, sometimes but not always identical with the followers of Fionn.

Fianna, Fianna Éireann, Fianna-Finn. Followers of Fionn in the Fenian Cycle.

Fianna Fáil. Political party founded in opposition to the 1922 Treaty with Great Britain, dominated by Éamon de Valera in much of the twentieth century. Often in opposition to the Fine Gael party.

Fine Gael. Political party founded in support of the 1922 Treaty with Great Britain. Often in opposition to the Fianna Fáil party.

Finn. *See* Fionn.

Fionn mac Cumhaill, Fin MacCool, etc. Hero of Old Irish Fenian Cycle whose stories have continued in the oral tradition in modern times.

firkin. A small wooden barrel for butter.

Flight of the Earls. After the Irish defeat at the battle of Kinsale (1603), the old Gaelic order was broken. In 1607, the Great Ulster Earls of Tirconnell (O'Donnell) and Tyrone (O'Neill) left for the Continent with their followers. Their departure left Ulster without leadership, facilitating the plantation of that province with Protestant settlers from Scotland and England.

footy. Poor, insignificant.

France, Anatole (1844–1924). French novelist and critic.

frieze coat. A coat made of shaggy, long-haired wool.

futhark. Alphabet used by the North Germanic peoples between the third and seventeenth centuries A.D. The name is taken from the first six letters of that alphabet. Also called runic.

Gae Bulg. Spear of Cuchulainn.

Gaeltacht. (pron. GOIL-tahk) Areas of Ireland, especially along the western coast, where the Irish language (or Gaelic) is still the first language of most of the population.

gaiks. Instrument that mechanically lifts a churn staff.

Gall. Not a Gael, i.e., a foreigner living in Ireland, a Norman, Anglo-Norman, Dane, or Englishman.

Galway. (1) A county in western Ireland, the western portion of which is Connemara. (2) The shire town or county seat of County Galway, a large town (pop. *c.* 35,000) and important port. (3) A bay on the west coast of Ireland, thirty miles long and twenty-three miles across, adjacent to the Aran Islands.

Gateway Arch. The famous St. Louis, Missouri, landmark, on the banks of the Mississippi.

Gauls. Ancient inhabitants of what is now France, cultural cousins of the Gaelic Irish.

Gaza. An area of ancient Palestine where the blinded Samson went into exile.

geis. (Ir. *geis,* pron. gesh) Taboo or prohibition; binding obligation; magic spells.

Gentleman Jim. Nickname of James J. Corbett (1866–1933), Irish-American heavyweight boxing champion.

Georgian. Pertaining to the reigns of Kings George I, II, III, and IV, 1714–1830, especially as the era is reflected in the urban architecture of Dublin and some other Irish cities.

Geraldine. Conglomerate name for the group of interconnecting Catholic families who led the "Geraldine Rebellion" against English rule, 1565–1583.

Giraldus Cambrensis. (*c.* 1146–1223). Welsh clergyman. His observations of Ireland shortly after the Anglo-Norman conquest (1170) are detailed and unfriendly.

Glanworth. A village in County Cork with a small woolen manufacturing industry.

Gleann na nGealt. Valley in the Dingle Peninsula, County Kerry, whose name translates as "Valley of the Mad," from the archaic folk belief that waters of a spring there would cure insanity. Cited in *Buile Shuibhne.*

Glen Dubh. Literally, "Dark Glen." A figurative placename.

Glencree. Rivulet and valley in north Wicklow.

Glenmacnass. Valley and waterfall in Wicklow near the monastic site of Glendalough.

glims. Lights.

Glorianna. Poetic name for Elizabeth I (1533–1603).

glue, you have your. You have your rejection.

gob. (Ir. "beak" or "bill") Mouth.

gollies. Short for golliwogs: comic, grotesque apparitions.

Gonne, Maud (1866–1953). Patriot and revolutionary, remembered today principally for the unrequited love W. B. Yeats bore for her.

gorse. Furze; plant covered with dark-green spines.

Gortin. (Ir. "the little field") Townland in Inniskeen parish, County Cavan.

Gortinfliuch. Irish, "the little wet field."

gossoon. (Ir. *garsún,* a small boy; Fr. *garçon*) A boy.

Grafton Street. Running south from St. Stephen's Green to Trinity College, the more fashionable of Dublin's two shopping areas, the other being O'Connell Street.

Granard. A small market town in eastern County Longford.

Grangegorman. A Dublin mental hospital.

Granuaile, Gran Uaile. A poetic name for Ireland, cast heroically. Contains an allusion to Gráinne (or Grace) ni Mhaille (or O'Malley), *c.* 1530–1603, an Irish pirate widely celebrated in story and song. For more information, see Anne Chambers, *Granuaile, the Life and Times of Grace O'Malley.* Dublin: Wolfhound Press, 1983.

Great Queen. Mórrígan within the context of the *Táin Bó Cuailnge;* a translation of her name.

Green or **Greene, Robert** (*c.* 1560–1592). Elizabethan wit, poet, playwright, and pamphleteer.

Green, the. *See* St. Stephen's Green.

griffawn, griffaun. A sturdy hoe used for cutting turf or peat. Irish *grafán:* hoe, grub-axe.

Griffith, Arthur (1871–1922). Journalist. Founder of the nationalist movement *Sinn Féin,* and first president of the Irish Free State.

Grosvenor Square, London. A fashionable address for wealthy absentee landlords.

Guinea. In Irish and English currency before decimalization (1971), a measurement of one pound and one shilling, or 5 percent more than a pound. Often used in calculating the price of such luxury items as *objets d'art.*

Gweedore. Village on the west coast of Donegal.

gymkhana. Originally a place for athletic display, latterly more specifically for competition between horse riders or car drivers.

Harp. Lager beer brew brewed in the Republic of Ireland; ordering in Northern Ireland implies Catholic or nationalist sentiments.

harpies. Monstrous creatures of classical mythology, part bird and part woman, who contaminated what they could not eat.

Hibernia. Roman name for Ireland.

Hibernian. A person from Ireland.

hob. Projection on the far side of a fireplace on which something, such as food, can be kept warm.

Houlihan. *See* Kathleen.

Hound of Cuailnge. Translation of the name Cuchulainn. Sometimes written as Hound of Culann.

House of the Red Branch. Alternative name for the warriors of the Ulster Cycle.

Houynhnms. The horses (and embodiments of rationality) in Book 4 of Swift's *Gulliver's Travels* (1726).

Howth. Rocky peninsula north of Dublin Bay, now a distant suburb; the end of the tram line. Pronounced "HOH-th."

Hume, David (1711–1776). Scottish philosopher.

Hungry Grass. (Ir. *fĕar gortach*) According to Irish folk belief, a field of grass that will induce insatiable hunger in all who walk upon it.

Imbolc. Old Irish name for the feast celebrated 1 February, Christianized as St. Brigid's Day, the first signs of spring. Pronounced "im-bol-ek." Modern Irish *Óimelc*.

I.H.S. A monogram for the name of Jesus, derived from Greek letters.

Inishmore. Largest of the Aran Islands off Ireland's west coast. Also known as Aranmore.

Inkermann. *See* Corunna.

Iraird Cuillenn. (pron. IR-erd QUILL-in) Placename in the *Táin*, Crossakeel, County Westmeath.

Irish Press. Former daily newspaper that represented the interests of the nationalist Fianna Fáil party in general and the de Valera family in particular.

Irish Volunteers. Name for the military force that seized British buildings in Dublin during Easter week, April 1916. Founded November 1913, by Eoin MacNeill, the Irish Volunteers reached its peak of two hundred thousand men in August 1914, at which time an ideological split divided the membership, when John Redmond pledged to volunteer for World War I.

Is uaigneach Eire. (pron. iss WIG-nach AIR-eh) Literally, "It's lonely, Ireland."

Jansen, Clan, Jansenism. A puritanical movement within Roman Catholicism that denied free will. Originating in seventeenth-century Holland and France, the movement persisted in rural Ireland until the twentieth century. Named for Cornelis Jansen (1585–1638).

jarvey. Driver of a horse-drawn hackney or taxi.

Jay! Short for Jesus! An oath.

jobber. A middleman who deals with stocks and securities among stockbrokers. In Devlin's implication, an affluent businessman.

Johnston, Jennifer. (b. 1930) Irish novelist, often deals with the decline of the Protestant upper class or ascendancy.

John the Blind. St. John the apostle and evangelist who, according to tradition, composed the last book of the New Testament, Revelation (Protestant) or Apocalypse (Roman Catholic), while in exile on Patmos.

Joyce, Patrick Weston (1827–1914). Historian, collector of folk music, scholar, and author of *Origin and History of Irish Names of Places* (1869) and other works.

Jubainville. *See* d'Arbois de Jubainville.

Judith. Heroine of the book of the Apocrypha that bears her name. The Apocrypha was regarded by some to be a part of the Bible, but is rejected by Protestants because it was not first written in Hebrew.

Jutes. Germanic invaders of fifth-century Britain, along with the Angles and Saxons. The Jutes settled in the southeastern county of Kent.

Jutland. Peninsula composing mainland Denmark, region where most of the two-thousand-year-old bodies were found, subjects of Heaney poetry.

Kateen-beug. Little Kate. Synge's name for any Irish peasant girl.

Kathleen Ní Houlihan, Cathleen Ní Houlihan. A romantic personification of Ireland.

Kead millia Failta ghud. (Ir. *céad míle failte dhuit,* pron. KAYD MEAL-a FALL-te'ud) One hundred thousand welcomes to you (traditional greeting).

keen. (Anglicization of *caoine*) A wailing lamentation for the dead.

Kells. *See* Book of Kells.

Kent. Southeastern county of England, settled by Jutes in the fifth century.

kerne. Armed foot soldier: medieval Irish infantryman.

khafir, kafir. (Arabic, "infidel"). Derisive term for a non-Muslim.

kibosh. (Ir. *caidhp bháis,* pron. KY-bosh) Literally, the cap of death. The expression has come to mean put an end to something, stop it finally.

Kieran, Saint. (Ir. *Ciarán*) Founder (A.D. 545) of the great monastery at Clonmacnois.

Kilmainham. Jail at the junction of South Circular Road and Inchicore Road on the western side of Dublin. Site of the ancient church for which it is named. Used for political prisoners from the eighteenth through the twentieth centuries, including Parnell, Pearse, Plunkett, and MacDonagh.

Kilmallock. A small market town twenty miles south of Limerick.

Kilmore. (Ir. "big monastic church") Although more than twenty Irish locations bear this name, Hewitt implies the one in County Antrim, four miles from Cushendall.

Kyoto, Nagoya, Irago. Cities on the island of Honshu, Japan.

Láeg. Cúchulainn's faithful charioteer.

Lake George. Upstate New York, north of Albany, where John Butler Yeats is buried.

Lammas, Lammas Day. Outwardly Christian festival, 1 August, commemorating St. Peter's deliverance from prison, actually rooted in the pre-Christian festival of Lughnasa.

Land League. Agrarian movement founded by Michael Davitt and others in 1879 to win rights for small farmers, especially tenant farmers. The Land League organized history's first "boycott" by refusing to provide services to the landlord of that name.

Laracor. Village in western Meath, two miles south of Trim. Jonathan Swift once lived here.

La Rochefoucauld, Duc François de. French author (1613–1680) of memoirs and sardonic maxims.

Leborcham. (pron. LE-vor-cham) Deirdre's guardian.

Lebor Gabála Éirenn. [Ir. book of the taking of Ireland] Twelfth-century text in five volumes, often known in English as the *Book of Invasions* or the *Book of Conquests*. It is an ecclesiastical attempt to synchronize Irish myths, legends and genealogies within the framework of Biblical exegesis, thus a "pseudo-history."

Lebor na hUidre [Book of the Dun Cow]. Oldest manuscript written entirely in Irish, compiled at the great monastic center of Clonmacnois on the Shannon before A.D. 1106.

Leinster. (pron. LEN-ster) The easternmost of the four ancient provinces of Ireland, running roughly from the Shannon Valley to the eastern coast of the Island.

Leitrim, County (pron. LEE-trim). A rural county in northernmost Connacht. One of the poorest and least populous of all Irish counties.

Lemuel. First name of Gulliver in Swift's *Gulliver's Travels* (1726).

lickle. Little.

Liffey. A river, fifty miles long, that flows through Dublin.

Lir. A sea god of old Irish mythology. The exile of his children and their transformation into swans is one of the best-known stories in Old Irish literature.

Liss. (Ir. *lios*) Ringed-fort or enclosed space. Fairy mound.

Londonderry. *See* Derry.

Longford, County. Rural county in central Ireland on the east bank of the Shannon River.

louche. French for "suspicious."

Lough Carra. Lake in County Mayo seven miles from Balintubber. Moore Hall, George Moore's family home, overlooks Lough Carra, which is described in the opening pages of *The Lake* (1905).

Lough Derg. Place of pilgrimage. Also known as "St. Patrick's Purgatory," since the saint was thought to have fasted and had a vision of the next world there. Known since the Middle Ages: the lough (lake) itself, one of several of this name, is located between counties Fermanagh and Donegal in western Ulster.

Lough Neagh. A 153-square-mile lake in Ulster, northeastern Ireland. The largest body of fresh water in the British Isles.

Lough Swilly. Bay in northern County Donegal. The Earls of Tírconnel and Tyrone left Lough Swilly in 1607, and Wolfe Tone was captured there aboard a French ship, part of the expeditionary force in 1798.

Lug Lámfhota. Anglicized as Lug or Lugh of the Long Arms. Divine hero of the Mythological Cycle and divine father of Cúchulainn.

Lyon. Large city in eastern France. France's "second city."

MacCarthy, John G. (1829–1892). Land commissioner, author, and pro-Home Rule Member of Parliament at Westminster.

MacCarthys. Family that ruled Desmond from Cashel after defeating the Anglo-Irish at the Battle of Callan near Kenmare, County Kerry, in 1261.

MacDiarmada, Seán (1884–1916). Revolutionary, organizer for Irish Republican Brotherhood, and despite being crippled by polio, participant in the seizing of the General Post Office, Easter week, 1916. Executed May 12, 1916.

Macha, Plain of. Area in what is today County Armagh. A home territory of the Ulster warriors. It includes Emain Macha *(q.v.)*.

Macha na Bo. (pron. MACH-ah na BOW) Cow's pasture.

MacMorris. Shakespeare's only Irishman *(Henry V)*.

MacNessa, Conor. *See* Conchobar mac Nessa.

MacSwiney, Terence (1879–1920). Lord Mayor of Cork who died on a hunger strike in Brixton prison protesting British policies.

Maeve. Anglicization of Medb *(q.v.)* and Medbh.

Mag Aí. Plains around Cruachan, County Roscommon. Placename in the *Táin*.

Maginn, William (1794–1842). Journalist and wit who died after having been imprisoned for debt.

Malin Head. A promontory in southwest County Donegal, one of the westernmost points in Ulster.

malt. Liquor made from malt, including beer or ale.

Mannan mac Lir, normative **Mannanán mac Lir.** Principal sea god of pre-Christian Ireland, unrelated to Lir, the father of the swan children.

Maritain, Jacques (1882–1973). French Catholic philosopher, a leading interpreter of St. Thomas Aquinas in the twentieth century.

Marlborough, Duke of (1650–1744). English general and statesman who defeated the French at Blenheim in 1704.

Marot, Clement (1496–1544). French poet, known for his sonnets, pastorals, and translations of the Psalms.

Maurya Jude. Maurya, Daughter of Jude. Synge's name for any Irish peasant girl.

Maynooth. Town in County Kildare, fifteen miles west of Dublin. Site of St. Patrick's College (founded 1795). The college, usually known as "Maynooth," is the principal seminary of the nation, and has traditionally been associated with political conservatism. The College of St. Patrick is today part of the National University of Ireland.

Mazzini, Giuseppe (1805–1872). Italian nationalist and writer. His movement, Young Italy (1831), sought to unify Italy, and was a model for Irish nationalists.

Meath, County. A flat county north and west of Dublin, containing many of the most important archaeological sites in Ireland, including Tara (q.v.)

Medb. (Mod. Ir. Medbh, anglicized Maeve) Warrior queen of Connacht, adversary of Cúchulainn in the **Táin Bó Cuailnge.**

memento mori. Lat.: Remember that you must die.

Merovingian. Dynasty of kings in what is now France, *c.* A.D. 500–751. Associated with the post-Roman spread of Christianity.

Meyer, Kuno (1858–1919). German Celticist who edited and translated many texts. He helped to found the School for Irish Learning, and edited its scholarly journal, *Ériu* (1904).

Milesian. The last in a series of invaders of Ireland, and therefore identical with the early Gaels, according to the *Lebor Gabála* [The Book of Invasions]. Also, the early Irish as perceived heroically.

minerals. Carbonated soft drinks, soda pop.

Monna Lisa. J. M. Synge's spelling for Mona Lisa, Leonardo da Vinci's famous painting.

Mórrígan, Morrígu, etc. (Ir. great queen) A war goddess of pre-Christian Ireland, part of a trio known as Mórrígna. An adversary of Cúchulainn in the *Táin Bó Cuailnge.*

mossa. *See* musha.

Mossbaun. The Heaney family farm in south east County Derry.

Mount Jerome. A Protestant cemetery in Dublin.

Mountjoy. A prison, formerly the most famous in Ireland. *See also* Kilmainham.

Moy. Small town in County Tyrone, Northern Ireland, on the banks of the Backwater River. Name comes from the Irish *mag* or *magh* for "plain" or "field."

Muighil. Cook in the household of St. Moling who gives slight comfort to Suibne: milk held in a hole in a pile of dung.

Muirtheimne, Muirthe. (pron. MUR-hev-na) Homeland or domain of Cuchulainn in northeast County Louth, a plain north of the mouth of the River Boyne.

Mulcahy, General Richard (1886–1971). Soldier and politician, supporter of the 1922 Treaty with Great Britain, affiliated with the Fine Gael party.

Munich bother. Munich was the site of the 1938 meeting between Neville Chamberlain (England), Édouard Daladier (France), Benito Mussolini (Italy) and Adolf Hitler (Gemany) that resulted in the partition of Czechoslovakia. The word Munich has come to be a symbol for appeasement.

Munster. Largest and most southerly of the four ancient provinces of Ireland. It stretches from Waterford in the east to Kerry in the west, and includes Cork and the Shannon estuary.

musha, mossa. (Ir. *muise*) An assertive interjection used at the opening of a sentence: well; indeed. A milder form is *wisha.*

musquash. Variant form for muskrat, a less expensive fur.

"My Lagan Love." Plaintive, traditional love song, much associated with Northern Ireland.

nancy boys. Effeminate young men or homosexuals.

Naoise, Noisi. Modern Irish forms for Noíse.

Nash or Nashe, Thomas (1567–1601). Elizabethan satirist and writer who introduced the novel of adventure into England.

National University of Ireland. Public higher education in Ireland. Before the year 2000, individual branches, e.g. Dublin, were known as University College, Dublin, or "UCD."

Nelson's Pillar. Imposing monument to British Admiral Horatio Nelson that formerly stood on Dublin's O'Connell Street (Sackville Street before 1922). Long resented by Irish nationalists, the Pillar was destroyed by a bomb blast in 1966.

Newtownmountkennedy. Village in northeast County Wicklow, twenty-two miles south of Dublin.

Niav. Anglicization of the Irish name Niamh, borne by many female figures in Old and Middle Irish—especially the beautiful woman who led Oisín to the land of eternal youth, Tir na nÓg, beyond the waves.

Ninety-eight. Short for 1798, a year of rebellion in Ireland: risings in Leinster and Ulster by the United Irishmen in May and June. A small French force in support of the Irish landed in Connacht in August. All were unsuccessful.

nob. Head.

nockers. The cleft of the buttocks.

noggin. Small drinking vessel, less than a pint.

Noíse, Naoise, Naoisi. Lover of Deirdre. Pronounced "NEE-sha." He and his brothers Ainnle and Ardan are the "Sons of Usnach."

Nore. River that runs through the southeastern lowlands of Ireland past Kilkenny, where it meets the Barrow and empties into Waterford Harbor.

O'Brien, Dermot (1866–1945). President of the Royal Hibernian Academy and grandson of William Smith O'Brien *(q.v.)*.

O'Brien, William Smith (1803–1864). Parliamentarian and later a leader of the Young Ireland rebellion of 1848. After the failure of the rebellion, O'Brien was exiled to Tasmania (1849–1856).

ochón, Irish for "alas"; a cry of lament.

O'Clery, Mícheál [Ó Cléirigh, Micheal] (1575–1643). Franciscan monk who served as the chief compiler of the Annals of the Four Masters (1632–1636), a chronicle of Irish history from earliest days down to 1616.

O'Connell Street. Dublin's widest boulevard, running north of the Liffey River, known as Sackville Street before independence. Includes prominent General Post Office, the "G.P.O.," seized in the 1916 Rising.

Odi atque amo. Lat.: I hate and I love.

Odysseus. Greek hero of the Trojan War. His adventures en route home provide the subject of Homer's Odyssey.

Óg. (pron. Ohg) Young.

ogham. A system of reproducing the Irish and Pictish languages dating from about the fourth century and lasting until the early seventh century. It used sets of grooves and notches, usually at the corners of standing stones.

O'Growney, Eugene (1863–1899). Priest and Irish language revival leader. His *Simple Lessons in Irish* (1894) was for many years a standard introductory textbook on the subject.

oinseach. (Ir. *óinseach*) Stupid or foolish woman; fool. A male fool is an *amadán*.

Oisín. Son of Fionn mac Cumhaill, and a leading character of the Fenian Cycle.

Old Woman of Beare. (Ir. *Cailleach Bhéirre*) A sovereignty figure and personification of Ireland, thought to reside on the Beare peninsula, in counties Cork and Kerry, southwestern Ireland.

O'Moore [O'More], Rory (d. c. 1652). Leader of an unsuccessful rebellion against the English, 1641–49.

Orange, Orange Lodge. An organization of Protestant men, largely working-class, who favor union with Great Britain and are therefore anti-nationalist.

oratio obliqua. Lat.: indirect speech; reported speech.

oratio recta. Lat.: direct speech; quoted speech.

Orion. Constellation named for the hunter of classical mythology; the most clearly defined in the Northern Hemisphere, it contains Sirius, the brightest star in the heavens, as well as Betelgeuse and Rigel.

Ormond, Ormonde. Anglicized name for a region in East Munster, *Aurmumu,* coextensive with County Kilkenny and north Tipperary.

Orphic egg. According to the ancient cult of Orphism, contemporary with early Christianity, the world was egg-shaped, and was hatched from an egg made by the Creator.

Osage. River of Missouri and Kansas, named for a Sioux-speaking tribe of native Americans.

Osage orange. An inedible, orange-like fruit native to North America.

Oscar. Grandson of Fionn in the Fenian Cycle. An admirable and heroic figure, he is sometimes called the Galahad of the Cycle.

Ossian. Anglicized spelling for Oisín, the son of Fionn mac Cumhaill. In James Macpherson's partially bogus translations, *The Poems of Ossian* (1760–1763), Ossian is the narrator of a heroic Gaelic past.

Ossory. A diocese in County Kilkenny coextensive with the ancient kingdom of Osraighe.

Pan. Greek and Roman god of the countryside, poetry, and music.

Paris. Trojan prince who had to select the fairest from among the Greek goddesses Hera, Aphrodite, and Athena. He chose Aphrodite, thus sowing the first seeds of the Trojan War.

Parnassian Islands. Islands in the Parnassus range, which terminates at the Corinthian Gulf.

Parnell, Charles (1846–1891). Powerful leader of the Irish Party at Westminster. His fall from power with the revelation of his adulterous affair with Kitty O'Shea in 1890 is often perceived as one of the milestones in Irish political and intellectual life in the years preceeding the Irish Renaissance.

Paschal. Easter or Passover season.

Patmos. Island in Aegean Sea, where, according to legend, St. John the Divine wrote the last book of The New Testament—Revelation (Protestant) or Apocalypse (Roman Catholic).

Peelers. Irish constabulary founded by Sir Robert Peel (1788–1850), who also gave his name to London Bobbies.

penal times. Period following the Treaty of Limerick (1691) when the rights of the native Irish (as well as those of the Roman Catholic Church) were severely curtailed.

pension day. The pension is an Irish government subsidy to the elderly. For country people, therefore, pension day is a day in town.

pietà. (Italian: pity). In painting and sculpture, a representation of the Virgin Mary mourning the body of Christ that she holds in her arms.

pike. Weapon used by Irish rebels in 1798, consisting of a shaft and a steel head. Precursor of the bayonet.

pious Aeneas. Hero of the Roman epic, *The Aeneid*. Called "pious" for his loyalty to his family and to the gods.

plage. French for "beach."

polly, polly cow. Hornless cow.

Pompeii. City located at the foot of Vesuvius, destroyed in A.D. 79 by a volcanic eruption.

porter. Dark brown malt liquor, resembling ale, especially popular in Ireland.

Posidonius. (*c.* 135–*c.* 51 B.C.) Syrian-born Roman philosopher, the most thorough of ancient commentators on the Celts.

potato drills. Potatoes sown in a light furrow or trench.

poteen. (pron. PUT-SHEEN) Anglicization of *poitín:* little pot; home-distilled (illegal) whiskey; moonshine.

praskeen. (Ir. *práiscín*) Rag.

Pretoria. *See* Corunna.

Prometheus. Titan of Greek mythology who defied the gods to steal fire for the benefit of mankind.

Quartre Bras. *See* Corunna.

Quays, The. (pron. KEYS) Commercial streets built on embankments lining the sides of the river Liffey in central Dublin.

Rabelais, François (*c.* 1494–*c.* 1553). French humorist and satirist, known for his bawdy and boisterous novel *Gargantua*.

Radio Telefís Éireann (RTÉ). The Irish national broadcasting service.

Raphael. (1483–1520) Renaissance Italian painter.

rasher. A slice of bacon.

Red Branch Cycle. Another name for the Ulster Cycle. (The name is taken from the hall of the Ulstermen.)

Red Dan Sally, Red Dan Philly. Names evocative of the peasantry.

Redmond, John Edward (1856–1918). Political leader and súpporter of C. S. Parnell. Redmond headed the pro-Parnell minority in the Irish Party at Westminster after that leader's fall from power in 1890. Redmond supported the British cause in World War I, and was surprised by the Rising of Easter Week 1916.

rémscél. (Mod. Ir. *réimscéal*)A fore-tale or prologue to a longer narrative, such as the *Táin Bó Cuailnge*. It pertains to the greater text, even when not containing characters or themes from it.

riastrad. Irish name for Cúchulainn's transforming battle-fury or warp spasm.

ricks. Stacks or piles of grain, straw, or hay in the fields.

Ringsend. Working-class neighborhood southeast of Dublin, adjacent to the harbor.

Ronsard, Pierre de (1524–1584). French lyric poet, principal figure of a group of poets known as the Pleiade.

Rossa, Jeremiah O'Donovan (1831–1915). Journalist and leader of the Irish Republican Brotherhood or Fenians. After having been jailed from 1865 to 1871, he spent his later life in the United States, where his many publications counseled violent action in the cause of Irish independence. P. H. Pearse delivered a famous panegyric at Rossa's grave, August 1, 1915.

The Rosses. Area of rocks and small lakes in western County Donegal.

RTÉ. *See* Radio Telefís Éireann.

rus-in-urbe. Latin: country in the city, a contradiction.

Sackville Street. Former name of Dublin's principal commercial thoroughfare. Now called O'Connell Street.

Saint—. *See* cited name, as Kieran, etc.

Saint Patrick's Cathedral. Largest church ever built in Ireland, serving worshippers from the Church of Ireland, which is comparable to the Anglican (UK) or Episcopal (U.S.A.) faiths.

St. Stephen's Green. One of Dublin's large squares, now a public park.

Salamanca. Spanish university. Irish clerics were trained here when Catholic education was outlawed in the British Isles.

Samhain. (pron. SOW-en) Old Irish calendar feast beginning the dark or deathly half of the year. Counterpart of Halloween.

Sarsfield, Patrick. Irish military hero (d. 1693) who defended Limerick twice, 1690 and 1691.

Sartor Resartus. Thomas Carlyle's discussion of philosophical systems, disguised as a philosophy of clothes. Published in *Fraser's Magazine*, 1833–1834.

scoil. (pron. skull) School.

settle. Long wooden bench with a high back.

shagging. Although *shag* means "copulate," as does the American f-word, this is a less intense expletive.

sham. Slang term for a townie; slightly derogatory. Also a mate or a friend, especially one from Tuam, County Galway.

"Shan Van Vocht." (Ir. *Sean Bhean Bhocht:* poor old woman) Title of a song associated with the rebellion of the United Irishmen in 1798. The Poor Old Woman is a personification of Ireland, and the song named for her is a kind of Irish *Marseillaise.*

Shannon. (1) The principal river of Ireland, following 224 miles through the central and western portions of the island. (2) The principal international airport of Ireland, adjacent to the Shannon River estuary in south County Clare.

Sheba, Queen of. Woman mentioned in the Old Testament as having known Solomon (1 Kings 10).

shee. Anglicization of *sídh (q.v.).*

Shelley, Percy Bysshe (1792–1822). English poet. His works include *Prometheus Unbound* (1818).

Sheridan, Thomas (1719–1822). Irish actor, elocutionist, and lexicographer. He was the godson of Jonathan Swift and the father of playwright Richard Brinsley Sheridan.

shillelagh. An oak stick, named for the place famous for such oak.

shilling. Before decimalization (1971), twelve pence, or 1/20 of a pound. Although its value may not have been exactly twenty-five cents, it served as the equivalent of the North American quarter.

Shule Aroon. (Ir. walk, treasure) Familiar from the verse: Walk, walk, walk, treasure! / Walk calmly and walk quietly. / Walk to the door and steal off with me / And may you go safely my darling.

sídh. *Sídhe* (gen. and pl.), anglicized as *shee.* Name for a fairy mound, many of which are misunderstood archaeological sites, and by extension the realm of the otherworld.

Sigerson, George (1836–1925). Scientist and man of letters who wrote on both medicine and early Irish literature. His translations, *Bards of the Gael and Gall* (1897), were especially influential.

simony. The buying or selling of ecclesiastical offices in the Church—a sin that a child would know of only by studying a catechism.

Sinn Féin. (Irish: we ourselves) A political (non-military) movement founded in 1905 by Arthur Griffith and others to promote non-violent economic independence. Although Sinn Féin did not support the Easter Rising or 1916, the phrase "Sinn Féin" nevertheless denoted all Irish nationalist groups in the popular mind.

Sitting Bull (*c.* 1834–1890). Native American victor at the battle of Little Big Horn (1876), who spent his declining years working in a Wild West circus.

6/–. Notation for six shillings before decimalization.

six bob. Six shillings.

skivvy. A scullery maid; an unappreciated female drudge of low social station. A term of derogation.

Slane. Village in County Meath, on the north bank of the River Boyne.

sloe. The fruit of the blackthorn.

Smith, Goldwin (1823–1910). English historian and journalist, known for his liberal, anti-imperalistic views.

Smyrna. Former Greek name for a port city on the east shore of the Aegean. (The current Turkish name is Izmir.)

Snám Dá Én. (Mod. Ir. *snámh dhá eán*)[Swim Two Birds] A small church near Clonmacnoise where Suibne makes a memorable stop in his travels.

sneezer. Drink.

Sorcha. Mythical land that can be identified with almost any distant place, perhaps Syria.

Souris. A river of Saskatchewan and North Dakota that flows into the Assiniboine.

spiv. Fancy swindler or corrupt dandy.

squeezer. Gallows.

Stella. Nickname given to Esther Johnson (1681–1728) by Jonathan Swift, who addressed love poems to her.

Stephens, James (1825–1901). Political leader who founded the Irish Republican Brotherhood, or Fenians, during the 1850's, but parted company with that body when he failed to lead a rising in 1865. (Note: Should be distinguished from the poet and storyteller of the same name [1880–1950].)

stooks. Shocks of flax. Also, a step in the linen-making process.

storeen. (Ir. *stór:* treasure, riches) Little treasure, dear one—a conventional term of endearment.

stout. A strong, very dark porter or ale.

streels. Strolls, saunters, drags, trails. In Gogarty's "Ringsend," this makes a pun with another word in Irish-English, the noun *streel* (from *straoilleog:* slattern, slut).

Strephon. A stock name for a rustic lover in pastoral poetry.

Sualtam. (pron. SOOL-tam) Cúchulainn's mortal father.

sugawn. (Ir. *sugán*) Straw rope. Also, a chair with a seat woven of sugawn.

Suir. River that rises in Tipperary and flows southeast, emptying into Waterford Harbor.

Sullivan, John L. (1858–1918). Irish-American heavyweight boxing champion.

Susanna. Beautiful and virtuous woman in the Old Testament, proved innocent of adultery by Daniel.

Sutton Cross. Suburb of Dublin, a tram stop on the way to Howth.

sweated their duds. Pawned their clothes.

Swim Two Birds. *See* Snám Dá Én.

Switzer's. Department store on Dublin's O'Connell Street, known for value rather than high fashion.

taig, teague, etc. Insulting term for an Irish Catholic or nationalist, especially in Northern Ireland. From the once common male name Tadhg ("poet").

Tandy, (James) Napper (1740–1803). Dublin orator and politician. Instrumental in founding the United Irishmen in Dublin (1791) with Wolfe Tone.

tanner. Sixpence (before Irish and British money was decimalized [1971]).

Tara. Hill in County Meath, about twenty-five miles northwest of Dublin; site of the ritual coronation of Irish high kings. The nineteenth-century assumption that Tara was once a palace is not supported by modern archaeology. Also written *Teamhair, Temair,* etc.

Teffia. Anglicization of *Tethba, Tethbae,* the name of a region in pre-Norman Ireland coextensive with the modern counties of Longford and Westmeath, east of the Shannon.

Thanam o'n dhoul. (Ir. *D'anam don diabhal,* pron. HAN-am un DOWL) Go to the devil!

theosophy. Any of several systems of philosophy that seek direct knowledge of the divine through contemplation or spiritual ecstasy.

Thig im thu shinn? Thigum. Thigum. (Ir. *An dtuigeann tú sin?* pron. DIG-in too shin? HIG-im. HIG-im) Do you understand that? I understand. I understand.

Thomond. Former name of north Munster, especially County Clare.

three and six. Before decimalization (1971), three shillings and six pence.

throttler. One who chokes or suffocates another; the hangman.

tinker. Superseded term, now thought insulting, for traveller or itinerant population, Ireland's pariah class.

titan. Greek divinity representing an elemental force of nature. (When a titan is referred to as *the* Titan, it is usually Prometheus.)

Titian (*c.* 1477–1576). Italian painter.

Titian's lady with amber belly. One of many nudes by the painter, perhaps his *Venus del Prado.*

tod, on my. All alone.

Tollund. Archaeological site in Denmark where the fully preserved body of a two-thousand-year-old man was discovered in the mid-twentieth century; inspiration for many Seamus Heaney poems.

toucher. Someone likely to ask for a small loan.

trap-case. Coffin.

Treblinka. Major German concentration camp located sixty-two miles northeast of Warsaw, Poland. Treblinka 2, the extermination camp that operated between July 1942 and October 1943, killed an estimated 731,000 Jews.

tricolour. The Irish flag since 1922, of green, white, and orange.

tristia. Sadness; gloom.

troika. Russian carriage pulled by three horses.

"Troubles, the." Colloquial name for the civic unrest in Ireland, 1916–1926. The Easter Rising and the taking of the GPO on Sackville Street occurred in April 1916; the Anglo-Irish War, or "Black and Tan War," was 1919–1922; the Civil War, between pro-Treaty or Free State Forces and anti-Treaty or Republican forces, was 1922–1923.

Tuam. Small market town in eastern County Galway, seat of both a Roman Catholic archdiocese and a Protestant diocese.

Tuatha Dé Danann. Semi-divine invaders of Ireland in the pseudo-history, *Lebor Gabála.* They arrive before the mortal Milesians, the last invaders.

Tubber. (Ir. *tobar:* well, spring, fountain) Name of several Irish hamlets.

turf. Partially carbonized vegetable materials, chiefly mosses, found in bogs in Ireland; although usually saturated with water, it can be cut, dried, and turned into a fuel, one with a distinctive odor. Known as peat in North America.

Turloch Caille Móire. Placename in the *Táin,* north of Knowth.

twenty-two and sixpence. 22 shillings and 6 pence, or 1 pound, 2½ shillings.

Tyler, Watt (d. 1381). Leader of an unsuccessful peasants' revolt in England; killed by the lord mayor of London while speaking with King Richard II.

Tyrone, County. Anciently, the homeland of the O'Neill family, County Tyrone in central Ulster, is one of the six counties still united with Great Britain.

Uch, Uch, Ochone! (Ir. *ochón*) Alas! Cry, wail.

Uisnech, sons of. Noíse, the lover of Deirdre, and his brothers Ainnle and Ardan (Usnach is a hill in County Westmeath).

Ulaid. Men of Ulster.

Ulster. The most northeasterly of the four ancient provinces of Ireland. Although comprised of nine counties, Ulster is sometimes wrongly thought to refer only to the six counties still united to Great Britain.

Ulster Cycle. One of the three heroic cycles of Old Irish literature, sometimes described as the most "aristocratic" of the three. Leading figures include Cúchulainn, Deirdre, Conchobar, and Maeve. Also known as the Red Branch Cycle."

Ummera. Fictional place name; cf Mod. Ir. *úmmera:* ridge.

Una, Úna, Oona. Wife of Finnbheara, one of several claimants to be king of the fairies.

Unionist. One who favors or supports the Act of Union (1800), making Ireland a part of the United Kingdom of Great Britain. In much of the twentieth century, "Unionist" has been a political term for a person who supports the union of the six counties of North Ireland with Great Britain. *Cf.* West Briton.

Vanessa. Nickname given to Esther Vanhomrigh (1687–1723) by Jonathan Swift, who wrote poems about her but eventually denied her love.

Vercingetorix. Leader of the rebellion that started the Gallic War.

Vico, Giovanni Battista (1668–1744). Italian philosopher, whose theory of history influenced James Joyce.

Villon, François (1431–*c*. 1463). French poet.

Vinegar Hill. Site of the battle between the United Irishmen and the English during the rising of 1798. After a bloody battle, the Irish were defeated. It is near Enniscorthy, County Wexford.

Virgin . . . Dynamo. Choice posed by American writer Henry Adams (1838–1918) representing tradition vs. modernity.

Voltaire. Pseudonym of F. M. Arouet (1694–1778), French wit and philosopher.

Volunteers. *See* Irish Volunteers.

West Briton. A disparaging term for an Irishperson who apes British manners and denies Irish identity. Cf. Unionist.

"which" for "who." Pronouns used in Protestant and Roman Catholic translations of the Lord's Prayer, the Our Father.

whisht. (Ir. *thoist*) Silence! hush! be quiet!

Whitehall. The former royal palace of English monarchs, near Westminster Abbey, where government offices are located.

White Rose. An Irish bar in Manhattan.

Wickow County. A mountainous county of eastern Leinster, just south of Dublin. J. M. Synge spent much of his childhood here.

Wild Geese. Irish soldiers who fled their native country after the defeats of 1689–1691 to serve in foreign armies.

William, King, William of Orange. Dutch prince who helped to vanquish Irish national aspiration, 1698–1691, and later served as king, first in conjunction with his wife Mary and later as William III. Known derisively as "King Billy" by Irish nationalists.

Williamite. A follower or admirer of William of Orange, King William III. More recently, "Williamite" refers to someone who has come from England or Scotland to exploit Ireland's economic weakness.

Windisch, Ernst (1844–1918). German scholar of Sanskrit and early Celtic languages who compiled an important Old Irish grammar and dictionary, as well as translated many texts.

winkers. Horse's blinders.

wisha. (Ir. *mhuise*) Well! indeed! An interjection. A milder form of musha, mossa (q.v.).

workhouse. Poorhouse, in nineteenth-century Ireland.

Wotan. Named used in early England for Odin, old Germanic sky god.

Yeats, John Butler (1839–1922). Irish painter, father of the poet William Butler Yeats. Lived later years in the United States.

Young Ireland. Nationalist movement led by Thomas Davis. Young Ireland supported the unsuccessful rebellion of 1848 led by William Smith O'Brien and
others.

Zeuss, Johann Kaspar (1806–1856). German Celticist whose *Grammatica Celtica*
(1853) opened the field of ancient Celtic philology to scientific inquiry.

Zimmer, Heinrich (1851–1910). German Celticist, known for his daring and imaginative theories that sought to explain the early history of Ireland.

Selected Background Readings

Adams, Michael. *Censorship: The Irish Experience.* University, Ala.: University of Alabama Press, 1968.

Allen, Michael, and Angela Wilcox, eds. *Critical Approaches to Anglo-Irish Literature.* Gerrards Cross, UK: Colin Smythe, 1988.

Andrews, Elmer, ed. *Contemporary Irish Poetry: A Collection of Essays.* Basingstoke, UK: Macmillan, 1990.

Ardagh, John. *Ireland and the Irish: Portrait of a Changing Society.* London: Penguin Books, 1995.

Bardon, Jonathan. *A History of Ulster.* Belfast: Blackstaff Press, 1992.

Barry, Sebastian, ed. *The Inherited Boundaries: Younger Poets of the Republic of Ireland.* Portlaoise, Ireland: Dolmen Press, 1986.

Beckett, J. C. *The Anglo-Irish Tradition.* London: Faber and Faber, 1976.

Bell, Sam Hanna. *The Theatre in Ulster.* Dublin: Gill and Macmillan, 1972.

Boland, Eavan. *A Kind of Scar: The Woman Poet in a National Tradition.* Dublin: Attic Press, 1989.

Bolger, Dermot, ed. *The Bright Wave: Poetry in Irish Now/An Tonn Gheal.* Dublin: Raven Arts, 1986.

Boylan, Henry. *A Dictionary of Irish Biography.* Dublin: Gill and Macmillan, 1978.

Bradley, Anthony, ed. *Contemporary Irish Poetry,* rev. ed. Berkeley, Calif.: University of California Press, 1989.

——— and Maryann Gialanella Valiulis, eds. *Gender and Sexuality in Modern Ireland.* Amherst: University of Massachusetts, 1997.

Brady, Anne M., and Brian Cleeve. *A Biographical Dictionary of Irish Writers.* New York: St. Martin's Press, 1985.

Bramsbäck, Birgit, and Martin Croghan, eds. *Anglo-Irish and Irish Literature: Aspects of Language and Culture.* Papers from the 1986 IASAIL Conference. Stockholm: Almqvist and Wiksell, 1988.

Brophy, James D., and Raymond J. Porter, eds. *Contemporary Irish Writing.* New Rochelle: Iona College Press, 1983.

———. *New Irish Writing.* New York: Twayne, 1989.

Brown, Malcolm. *The Politics of Irish Literature.* Seattle: University of Washington Press, 1972.

Brown, Terence. *Ireland: A Social and Cultural History, 1922 to the Present.* Ithaca: Cornell University Press, 1985.

———. *Ireland's Literature: Selected Essays.* Dublin: Lilliput Press, 1988.

———, and Nicholas Grene, eds. *Tradition and Influence in Anglo-Irish Poetry.* Basingstoke, UK: Macmillan, 1989.

Butler, Hubert. *Independent Spirit: Essays.* New York: Farrar, Straus and Giroux, 1996.

Byrne, Terry. *Power in the Eye: An Introduction to Contemporary Irish Film.* Lanham, Md.: Scarecrow Press, 1997.

Cahalan, James M. *Double Visions: Women and Men in Modern and Contemporary Irish Fiction.* Syracuse, N.Y.: Syracuse University Press, 1999.

———. *The Irish Novel: A Critical History.* Boston: Twayne, 1988.

Cairns, David, and Shaun Richards. *Writing Ireland: Colonialism, Nationalism and Culture.* Manchester: Manchester University Press, 1988.

Canadian Journal of Irish Studies. Montreal: 1974—.

Carlson, Julia, ed. *Banned in Ireland: Censorship and the Irish Writer.* Athens, Ga.: University of Georgia Press, 1990.

Carney, James, ed. *Early Irish Poetry.* Cork: Mercier, 1965.

———. *Early Irish Literature.* New York: Barnes and Noble, 1966. This is a reprint of Gerard Murphy, *Saga and Myth in Early Ireland* (Dublin: At the Sign of the Three Candles, 1955); *The Ossianic Lore and Romantic Tales of Medieval Ireland* (Dublin: At the Sign of the Three Candles, 1961); and Eleanor Knott, *Irish Classical Poetry* (Dublin: At the Sign of the Three Candles, 1955).

Carpenter, Andrew, and Peter Fallon, eds. *The Penguin Book of Contemporary Irish Poetry.* London: Penguin, 1990.

Carty, Ciaran, and Dermot Bolger, eds. *The Hennessy Book of Irish Fiction.* Dublin: New Island Books, 1995.

Casey, Daniel J., and Linda Casey, eds. *Stories by Contemporary Irish Women.* Syracuse, N.Y.: Syracuse University Press, 1990.

———, and Robert E. Rhodes, eds. *Views of the Irish Peasantry, 1800–1916.* Hamden, Conn.: Archon Books, 1977.

Collins, Kevin. *The Cultural Conquest of Ireland.* Dublin: Mercier, 1990.

Comhar. Dublin: 1942—. [Irish-language journal.]

Connolly, Peter, ed. *Literature and the Changing Ireland.* Gerrards Cross, UK: Colin Smythe, 1982.

Corcoran, Neil. *After Yeats and Joyce: Reading Modern Irish Literature.* Oxford: Oxford University Press, 1997.

———, ed. *The Chosen Ground: Essays on Contemporary Poetry of Northern Ireland.* Brigend, Wales: Seren, 1991.

Corkery, Daniel. *The Hidden Ireland: A Study of Gaelic Munster in the Eighteenth Century.* 1925. Reprint, Gill and Macmillan, 1967.

Costello, Peter. *The Heart Grown Brutal.* Dublin: Gill and Macmillan, 1975.

Craig, Patricia, ed. *The Raffle of the North: An Anthology of Ulster Prose*. Belfast: Blackstaff Press, 1993.

Cronin, Anthony. *Heritage Now: Irish Literature in English Language*. Dingle, Co. Kerry: Brandon Books, 1982.

Cronin, John. *The Anglo-Irish Novel*, 2 vols. Belfast: Appletree Press, 1980.

———. *Irish Fiction: 1900–1940*. Belfast: Appletree Press, 1992.

Cronin, Michael, and Cormac Ó Cuilleanáin, eds. *The Languages of Ireland*. Dublin: Four Courts Press, 2003.

Cross, Tom Peete. *Motif Index of Early Irish Literature*. Bloomington, Ind.: Indiana University Press, 1952.

Crotty, Patrick, ed. *Modern Irish Poetry: An Anthology*. Belfast: Blackstaff Press, 1996.

Cullingford, Elizabeth Butler. *Yeats, Ireland and Fascism*. New York: New York University Press, 1981.

Curtis, L. Perry. *Apes and Angels: The Irishman in Victorian Caricature*, 2nd ed. Washington: The Smithsonian, 1997.

Dawe, Gerald, ed. *The New Younger Irish Poets*. Belfast: Blackstaff Press, 1991.

Dawe, Gerald, and Edna Longley. *Across a Roaring Hill: The Protestant Imagination in Modern Ireland*. Belfast: Blackstaff Press, 1985.

Deane, John F., ed. *Irish Poetry of Faith and Doubt: The Cold Heaven*. Dublin: Wolfhound Press, 1991.

Deane, Seamus. *Celtic Revivals*. London: Faber and Faber, 1985.

———. *A Short History of Irish Literature*. London: Hutchinson, 1986.

———. *Strange Country: Modernity and Nationhood Since 1790*. New York: Oxford University Press, 1997.

———, et al., eds. *Ireland's Field Day*. Notre Dame, Ind.: University of Notre Dame Press, 1986.

Delanty, Greg, and Nuala Ní Dhomhnaill, eds. *Jumping Off Shadows*. Cork: Cork University Press, 1995.

Dillon, Myles. *The Cycles of Kings*. London: Oxford University Press, 1946.

———. *Early Irish Literature*. Chicago: University of Chicago Press, 1948.

———, ed. *Early Irish Sagas*. Cork: Mercier, 1968.

Dolan, Terence Patrick, comp. *A Dictionary of Hiberno-English*. Dublin: Gill and Macmillan, 1999.

Donoghue, Denis. *We Irish: Essays on Irish Literature and Society*. New York: Knopf, 1986.

Donovan, Katie, A. Norman Jeffares, and Brenda Kennelly, eds. *Ireland's Women: Writing Past and Present*. New York: Norton, 1995.

Dorgan, Theo, ed. *Irish Poetry since Kavanagh*. Blackrock, Ireland: Four Courts Press, 1996.

Duffy, Noel, and Theo Dorgan, eds. *Watching the River Flow: A Century in Irish Poetry*. Dublin: Poetry Ireland, 1999.

Dunn, Douglas, ed. *Two Decades of Irish Writing*. Manchester, UK: Carcanet, 1975.

Eager, Alan R. *A Guide to Irish Bibliographical Material: A Bibliography of Irish Bibliographies and Sources of Information*. Rev. ed., London: Library Association, 1980.

Eagleton, Terry. *Heathcliff and the Great Hunger: Studies in Irish Culture*. New York: Verso, 1995.

Éire-Ireland. Morristown, N.J.: 1966—. [Irish studies journal.]

Eglinton, John [pseudonym of William K. Magee], W. B. Yeats, George Russell, William Larminie. *Literary Ideals in Ireland*. London: Unwin, 1889; rpt. New York: Lemma, 1973.

Etherton, Michael. *Contemporary Irish Dramatists*. Basingstoke, UK: Macmillan Education, 1989.

Études irlandaises. Caen, Lille, Reims and Rennes: 1972—. [Literary, history, and arts journal.]

Eyler, Audrey S., and Robert F. Garratt. *The Uses of the Past: Essays on Irish Culture*. Newark, Del.: University of Delaware Press, 1988.

Fallis, Richard. *The Irish Renaissance*. Syracuse, N.Y.: Syracuse University Press, 1977.

Field Day Anthology of Irish Writing. 3 vols. Edited by Seamus Deane, Andrew Carpenter, et al. Derry: Field Day, 1991.

Field Day Anthology of Irish Writing. Irish Women's Writing and Traditions. 2 vols. Edited by Angela Bourke, et al. Cork: Cork University Press, 2002.

Finneran, Richard, ed. *Anglo-Irish Literature: A Review of Research*. New York: Modern Language Association, 1976.

———, ed. *Recent Research on Anglo-Irish Writers*. New York: Modern Language Association, 1983.

Fitz-Simon, Christopher. *The Irish Theatre*. London: Thames and Hudson, 1983.

Fitz-Simon, Christopher, and Sanford Sternlicht. *New Plays from the Abbey Theatre*. Vol. 1, *1993–1995*. Syracuse, N.Y.: Syracuse University Press, 1996.

Fitzmaurice, Gabriel, ed. *Irish Poetry Now: Other Voices*. Dublin: Wolfhound Press, 1993.

Flanagan, Thomas. *The Irish Novelists, 1800–1850*. New York: Columbia University Press, 1959.

Flannery, James W. *W. B. Yeats and the Idea of a Theatre: The Early Abbey Theatre in Theory and Practice*. New Haven: Yale University Press, 1976.

Flower, Robin. *The Irish Tradition*. Oxford: Clarendon, 1947.

Foster, John Wilson. *Colonial Consequences: Essays in Irish Literature and Culture*. Dublin: Lilliput, 1991.

———. *Fictions of the Irish Literary Revival: A Changeling Art*. Syracuse, N.Y.: Syracuse University Press, 1987.

———. *Forces and Themes in Ulster Fiction*. Dublin: Gill and Macmillan, 1974.

Foster, R. F. *Modern Ireland, 1600–1972*. London: Penguin, 1988.

————. *Paddy and Mr. Punch: Connections in Irish and English History*. New York: Penguin, 1993.

Friel, Judy, and Sanford Sternlicht, eds. *New Plays from the Abbey Theatre*. Vol. 2, *1996–1998*. Syracuse, N.Y.: Syracuse University Press, 1999.

————, eds. *New Plays from the Abbey Theatre*. Vol. 3, *1999–2001*. Syracuse, N.Y.: Syracuse University Press, 2002.

Gallagher, S. F., ed. *Woman in Irish Legend, Life and Literature*. Gerrards Cross, UK: Colin Smyth, 1983.

Garratt Robert. *Modern Irish Poetry: Tradition and Continuity from Yeats to Heaney*. Berkeley: University of California Press, 1986.

Gibbons, Luke. *Transformation in Irish Culture*. Notre Dame, Ind.: University of Notre Dame Press, 1996.

Gillespie, Michael Patrick. *James Joyce and the Fabrication of an Irish Identity*. Amsterdam, Atlanta, Ga.: Rodopi, 2001.

Haberstroh, Patricia Boyle, ed. *My Self: My Muse: Irish Women Poets Reflect on Love and Art*. Syracuse, N.Y.: Syracuse University Press, 2001.

————. *Women Creating Women: Contemporary Irish Women Poets*. Syracuse, N.Y.: Syracuse University Press, 1996.

Hall, Wayne E. *Shadowy Heroes: Irish Literature of the 1890s*. Syracuse, N.Y.: Syracuse University Press, 1980.

Harkness, David. *Ireland in the Twentieth Century: Divided Island*. London: Macmillan, 1996.

Harmon, Maurice, ed. *The Irish Writer and the City*. Gerrards Cross, UK: Colin Smythe, 1984.

Harrington, John P., ed. *Modern Irish Drama*. New York: Norton, 1991.

————, and Elizabeth J. Mitchell, eds. *Politics and Performance in Contemporary Northern Ireland*. Amherst: University of Massachusetts Press, 1999.

Harte, Liam, and Michael Parker, eds. *Contemporary Irish Fiction: Themes, Tropes, Theories*. New York: St. Martin's, 2000.

Hayes, Richard J. *Manuscript Sources for the History of Irish Civilization*. 11 vols. Boston: G. K. Hall, 1970.

————. *Sources for the History of Irish Civilization*. 9 vols. Boston: G. K. Hall, 1965.

Hennessey, Thomas. *A History of Northern Ireland, 1920–1996*. Dublin: Gill and Macmillan, 1997.

Henry, P. L., ed. *Dánta Ban: Poems of Irish Women, Early and Modern*. Cork: Mercier Press, 1991.

Herr, Cheryl. *For the Land They Loved: Irish Political Melodramas, 1890–1925*. Syracuse, N.Y.: Syracuse University Press, 1991.

Hildebidle, John. *Five Irish Writers: The Errands of Keeping Alive*. Cambridge: Harvard University Press, 1989.

Hill, John, Martin McLoone, and Paul Hainsworth, eds. *Border Crossings: Film in Ireland, Britain and Europe*. Belfast: Institute for Irish Studies, 1994.

Hogan, Robert. *Dictionary of Irish Literature*. Westport, Conn.: Greenwood Press, 1979.

Holloway, Joseph. *Joseph Holloway's Abbey Theatre*. Carbondale: University of Southern Illinois Press, 1967.

The Honest Ulsterman. Portrush, Northern Ireland: 1968—. [Literary magazine.]

Hooley, Ruth, ed. *The Female Line: Northern Irish Women Writers*. Belfast: Women's Rights Movement, 1985.

Hunt, Hugh. *The Abbey: Ireland's National Theatre*. Dublin: Gill and Macmillan, 1979.

Hussey, Gemma. *Ireland Today: Anatomy of a Changing State*. Dublin: Townhouse, 1993.

Imhof, Rüdiger, ed. *Contemporary Irish Novelists*. Tübingen: Gunter Narr, 1990.

Innes, C. L. *Women and Nation in Irish Literature and Society, 1880–1935*. Athens, Ga.: University of Georgia Press, 1993.

Irish Literary Supplement. Selden, N.Y.: 1982—.

The Irish Review. Cork: 1986—.

Irish Studies Review. Bath, UK: 1992—.

Irish University Review. Dublin: 1970—.

Jackson, Kenneth H. *Studies in Celtic Nature Poetry*. Cambridge: Cambridge University Press, 1935.

———. *The Oldest Irish Tradition: A Window on the Iron Age*. Cambridge: Cambridge University Press, 1964.

James Joyce Quarterly. Tulsa, Okla.: 1963—.

Johnson, Toni O'Brien, and David Cairns, eds. *Gender and Irish Writing*. Milton Keynes, UK: Open University Press, 1991.

Johnston, Dillon. *Irish Poetry after Joyce*. South Bend, Ind.: University of Notre Dame Press, 1985; 2nd ed. Syracuse, N.Y.: Syracuse University Press, 1997.

Jordan, John, ed. *The Pleasures of Gaelic Literature*. Cork: Mercier, 1977.

Kearney, Richard, ed. *The Irish Mind: Exploring Intellectual Traditions*. Dublin: Wolfhound Press, 1985.

———. *Postnationalist Ireland: Politics, Culture, Philosophy*. New York: Routledge, 1997.

Kelleher, John V. *Selected Writings of John V. Kelleher on Ireland and Irish-America*, ed. Charles Fanning. Carbondale. Ill.: University of Southern Illinois Press, 2002.

Kelly, A. A., ed. *Pillars of the House: An Anthology of Verse by Irish Women from 1690 to the Present*. Dublin: Wolfhound Press, 1987.

Kenneally, Michael, ed. *Cultural Contexts and Literary Idioms in Contemporary Irish Literature*. Totowa, N.J.: Barnes and Noble, 1988.

———. *Irish Literature and Culture*. Gerrards Cross, UK: Colin Smythe, 1992.

Kiberd, Declan. *Inventing Ireland: The Literature of the Modern Nation*. London: Jonathan Cape, 1995.

————. *Irish Classics.* Cambridge, Mass.: Harvard University Press, 2001.

————. *Synge and the Anglo-Irish Language.* London: Macmillan, 1979.

————, and Gabriel Fitzmaurice, eds. *An Crann Faoi Bhláth/The Flowering Tree: Contemporary Irish Poetry with Verse Translations.* Dublin: Wolfhound Press, 1991.

King, Kimball. *Ten Modern Irish Playwrights: A Comprehensive Annotated Bibliography.* New York: Garland, 1979.

Kinsella, Thomas. *The Dual Tradition: An Essay on Poetry and Politics in Ireland.* Manchester: Cancarnet, 1995.

————, ed. *The New Oxford Book of Irish Verse.* Oxford: Oxford University Press, 1986.

Knott, Eleanor. *Irish Classical Poetry.* Dublin: At the Sign of the Three Candles, 1955; reprint in *Early Irish Literature,* ed. James Carney. New York, 1966.

Kosok, Heinz, ed. *Studies in Anglo-Irish Literature.* Bonn: Bouvier, 1982.

Krause, David. *The Profane Book of Irish Comedy.* Ithaca: Cornell University Press, 1982.

————. *Revisionary Views: Some Counter-Statements about Irish Life and Literature.* Dublin: Maunsel, 2002.

Kreilkamp, Vera. *The Anglo-Irish Novel and the Big House.* Syracuse, N.Y.: Syracuse University Press, 1998.

Lanters, José. *Unauthorized Versions: Irish Menippean Satire, 1919–1952.* Washington: Catholic University Press, 2000.

Leerssen, Joseph Th. *Mere Irish and fior-gheal: Studies in the Idea of Irish Nationality, Its Development and Literary Expression Prior to the Nineteenth Century.* Amsterdam: Benjamins, 1986; reprint, Cork: Cork University Press, 1996.

Lloyd, David. *Anomalous States: Irish Writing and the Post-Colonial Moment.* Durham: Duke University Press, 1993.

————. *Nationalism and Minor Literature: James Clarence Mangan and the Emergence or Irish Cultural Nationalism.* Berkeley: University of California Press, 1987.

Loftus, Richard J. *Nationalism in Modern Anglo-Irish Poetry.* Madison, Wis.: University of Wisconsin Press, 1964.

Longley, Edna. *The Living Stream: Literature and Revisionism in Ireland.* Newcastle upon Tyne: Bloodaxe Books, 1994.

————. *Poetry in the Wars.* Newcastle upon Tyne: Bloodaxe Books, 1986.

————, and Declan Kiberd. *Multi-Culturalism: The View from the Two Irelands.* Cork: Cork University Press, 2001.

Lyons, F. S. L. *Culture and Anarchy in Ireland, 1890–1939.* Oxford: Oxford University Press. 1979.

————. *Ireland since the Famine.* New York: Charles Scribner's, 1971.

McBreen, Joan, ed. *The White Page/An Bhligeog Bhán: Twentieth Century Irish Women Poets.* Cliffs of Moher, Ireland: Salmon Press, 1999.

McConnell, Michael. *Changed Utterly: Ireland and the New Irish Psyche*. Dublin: Liffey, 2002.

McCormack, W. J. *Ascendancy and Tradition in Anglo-Irish Literary History from 1798 to 1939*. Oxford: Clarendon Press, 1985.

McHugh, Roger, and Maurice Harmon, eds. *Short History of Anglo-Irish Literature: From Its Origin to the Present Day*, Dublin: Wolfhound Press, 1982.

McIlroy, Brian. *Shooting to Kill: Filmmaking and the "Troubles" in Northern Ireland*. Wiltshire, UK: Flicks Books, 2001.

———. *World Cinema 4: Ireland*. Trowbridge, UK: Flicks Books, 1988. Also known as *Irish Cinema: An Illustrated History*. Dun Laoghaire, Ireland: Anna Livia Press, 1988.

McKenna, Brian. *Irish Literature, 1800–1875: A Guide to Information Sources*. Detroit: Gale Research, 1978.

MacKillop, James. *Dictionary of Celtic Mythology*. Oxford: Oxford University Press, 1998.

———. *Fionn mac Cumhaill: Celtic Myth in English Literature*. Syracuse, N.Y.: Syracuse University Press, 1986.

———. *Penguin Guide to Celtic Mythology*. London: Penguin, 2006.

———, ed. *Contemporary Irish Cinema: From* The Quiet Man *to* Dancing at Lughnasa. Syracuse, N.Y.: Syracuse University Press, 1999.

McLoone, Martin. *Irish Film: The Emergence of a Contemporary Cinema*. London: British Film Institute, 2000.

McMinn, Joseph, ed. *The Internationalism of Irish Literature and Drama*. Gerrards Cross, UK: Colin Smythe, 1992.

MacNeill, Máire. *The Festival of Lughnasa: A Study of the Survival of the Celtic Festival olthe Beginning of the Harvest*. Oxford: Oxford University Press, 1962; reprint, Dublin: Comhairle Bhéaloideas Éireann, 1982.

Martin, Augustine, ed. *Forgiveness: Ireland's Best Contemporary Short Stories*. Peterborough, UK: Ryan, 1989.

———. *The Genius of Irish Prose*. Cork: Mercier, 1984.

Maxwell, D. E. S. *A Critical History of Modern Irish Drama, 1891–1980*. Cambridge: Cambridge University Press, 1984.

Mercier, Vivian. *The Irish Comic Tradition*. Oxford: Clarendon Press, 1962.

Moloney, Caitriona, and Helen Thompson, eds. *Irish Women Writers Speak Out: Voices from the Field*. Syracuse, N.Y.: Syracuse University Press, 2003.

Morash, Christopher. *A History of Irish Theatre, 1601–2000*. Cambridge: Cambridge University Press, 2002.

Moynahan, Julian. *Anglo-Irish: The Literary Imagination in a Hyphenated Culture*. Princeton: Princeton University Press, 1995.

Muldoon, Paul, ed. *Faber Book of Contemporary Irish Poetry*. London: Faber and Faber, 1986.

Murphy, Gerard. *Saga and Myth in Ancient Ireland*. Dublin: At the Sign of the Three

Candles, 1955; reprinted in *Early Irish Literature,* edited by James Carney. Cork: Mercier, 1966.

———. *The Ossianic Lore and Romantic Tales of Medieval Ireland.* Dublin: At the Sign of the Three Candles, 1961; reprinted in *Early Irish Literature,* edited by James Carney. Cork: Mercier, 1966.

Murray, Christopher. *Twentieth-Century Irish Drama: Mirror up to Nation.* Manchester, UK: Manchester University Press, 1997.

Ní Dhuibhne, Éilís, ed. *Voices on the Wind: Women Poets of the Celtic Twilight.* Dublin: New Island Books. 1995.

O'Brien, Peggy, ed. *The Wake Forest Book of Irish Women's Poetry, 1967–2000.* Winston-Salem, N.C.: Wake Forest University Press, 2000.

O'Carroll, Íde, and E. Collins, eds. *Lesbian and Gay Visions of Ireland: Towards the Twenty-First Century.* London: Cassell, 1995.

O'Connor, Frank. *The Backward Look: A Survey of Irish Literature.* London: Macmillan. 1967. Retitled as *A Short History of Irish Literature.* New York: Putnam's, 1967.

O'Connor, Theresa. *Comic Tradition of Irish Women Writers.* Gainesville, Fla.: University Press of Florida, 1997.

O'Connor, Ulick. *All the Olympians.* New York: Atheneum, 1984.

O'Faolain, Seán. *The Irish.* [London]: Penguin, 1947. Retitled as *The Irish: A Character Study.* New York, Old Greenwich: 1949, 1956.

Ó hAodha, Micheál. *Theatre in Ireland.* Oxford: Blackwell; Totowa, N.J.: Rowman and Littlefield, 1974.

O'Leary, Philip. *The Prose Literature of the Gaelic Revival, 1881–1921: Ideology and Innovation.* University Park: Pennsylvania State University Press, 1994.

O'Malley, William T. *Anglo-Irish Literature: A Bibliography of Dissertations, 1873–1989.* Westport, Conn.: Greenwood Press, 1990.

Ó Muirithe, Diamaid. *The Words We Use.* Dublin: Four Courts, 1996.

———. *A Dictionary of Anglo-Irish.* Dublin: Four Courts, 1999.

O'Rahilly, T. F. *Early Irish History and Mythology.* Dublin: Dublin Institute for Advanced Studies, 1946.

Ormsby, Frank, ed. *Poets from the North Ireland.* Belfast: Blackstaff Press, 1979.

———. *A Rage for Order: Poetry of the Northern Ireland Troubles.* Belfast: Blackstaff Press, 1992.

O'Toole, Fintan. *After the Ball: Ireland after the Boom.* Dublin: New Island, 2003.

———. *Black Hole, Green Card: The Disappearance of Ireland.* Dublin: New Island Books, 1994.

———. *The Ex-Isle of Erin: Images of a Global Ireland.* Dublin: New Island Books, 1997.

———. *The Lie of the Land: Irish Identities.* Dublin: New Island Books, 1998.

———. *A Mass for Jesse James: A Journey Through 1980's Ireland.* Dublin: Raven Arts, 1990.

Ó Tuama, Seán. *Repossessions: Selected Essays on the Irish Literary Experience*. Cork: Cork University Press, 1991.

———, ed., and Thomas Kinsella, tr. *An Duanaire, 1600–1900: Poems of the Dispossessed*. Portlaoise, Ireland: Dolmen Press, 1981, 1985.

Paulin, Tom. *Ireland and the English Crisis*. Newcastle upon Tyne: Bloodaxe Books, 1984.

Pettitt, Lance. *Screening Ireland: Film and Television Representation*. Manchester: Manchester University Press, 2000.

Poetry Ireland Review. Dublin: 1981—.

Power, Patrick. *A Literary History of Ireland*. Cork: Mercier, 1969.

———. *The Story of Anglo-Irish Poetry*. Cork: Mercier, 1967.

Rafroidi, Patrick, and Maurice Harmon, eds. *The Irish Novel in Our Time*. Lille: Université de Lille, 1976.

———, and Terence Brown, eds. *The Irish Short Story*. Gerrards Cross, UK: Colin Smythe, 1979.

Robinson, Lennox. *Ireland's Abbey Theatre*. London: Sidgewick and Jackson, 1951.

Rockett, Kevin. *The Irish Filmography: Fiction Films, 1896–1996*. Dublin: Red Mountain, 1996.

———. *Ten Years After: The Irish Film Board, 1993–2003*. Dublin: Irish Film Board, 2003.

———. *Still Irish: A Century of the Irish in Film*. Dublin: Red Mountain, 1995.

———, Luke Gibbons, and John Hill. *Cinema and Ireland*. Beckenham, UK: Croom Helm; Syracuse, N.Y.: Syracuse University Press, 1988.

Sailer, Susan Shaw, ed. *Representing Ireland: Gender, Class, Nationality*. Gainesville, Fla.: University Press of Florida, 1997.

Sekine, Masaru, ed. *Irish Writers and Society at Large*. Gerrards Cross, UK: Colin Smythe, 1985.

Sewell, Frank. *Modern Irish Poetry: A New Alhambra*. Oxford: Oxford University Press, 2000.

Share, Bernard. *Slanguage: A Dictionary of Slang and Colloquial English in Ireland*. Dublin: Gill and Macmillan. 1997.

Sloan, Barry. *The Pioneers of Anglo-Irish Fiction, 1800–1850*. Gerrards Cross, UK: Colin Smythe, 1986.

Smyth, Ailbhe, ed. *Wildish Things: An Anthology of New Irish Women's Writing*. Dublin: Attic Press, 1989.

Storey, Mark. *Poetry and Ireland since 1800, a Source Book*. London: Routledge, 1988.

Studia Hibernica. Dublin: 1961—.

Studies: An Irish Quarterly Review. Dublin: 1912—.

Threshold. Belfast: 1957—.

Thuente, Mary Helen. *The Harp Restrung: The United Irishmen and the Rise of Irish Literary Nationalism*. Syracuse, N.Y.: Syracuse University Press, 1994.

Todd, Loreto. *The Language of Irish Literature*. Blasingstoke: Macmillan, 1989.

Trevor, William. *A Writer's Ireland: Landscape in Literature.* London: Thames and Hudson, 1984.

Trotter, Mary. *Ireland's National Theaters: Political Performance and the Origin of the Irish Dramatic Movement.* Syracuse, N.Y.: Syracuse University Press, 2001.

Tymoczko, Maria. *Translation in a Postcolonial Context: Early Irish Literature in English Translation.* Manchester: St. Jerome, 1999.

———, and Colin Ireland, eds. *Language and Tradition in Ireland: Continuities and Displacements.* Amherst: University of Massachusetts Press, 2003.

Valiulis, Maryann, and Mary O'Dowd. *Women and Irish History.* Dublin: Wolfhound Press, 1997.

Vance, Norman. *Irish Literature: A Social History. Tradition, Identity and Difference.* Oxford: Blackwell, 1990.

———. *Irish Literature since 1800.* London: Longman, 2002.

Vorm, William, ed. *Paddy No More: Modern Irish Short Stories.* Dublin: Wolfhound Press, 1978.

Wall, Richard, ed. *Medieval and Modern Ireland.* Gerrards Cross, UK: Colin Smythe, 1988.

Walshe, Éibhear, ed. *Sex, Nation and Dissent in Irish Writing.* Cork: Cork University Press, 1997.

Waters, Maureen. *The Comic Irishman.* Albany: State University of New York Press, 1983.

Weekes, Ann Owens. *Irish Women Writers: An Uncharted Tradition.* Lexington, Ky.: University of Kentucky Press, 1990.

Welch, Robert. *Changing States: Transformations in Modern Irish Writing.* London: Routledge, 1993.

———. *The History of Verse Translation from the Irish, 1789–1897.* Gerrards Cross, UK: Colin Smythe, 1988.

———. *Irish Poetry from Moore to Yeats.* Gerrards Cross, UK: Colin Smythe, 1980.

———. *The Oxford Companion to Irish Literature.* Oxford: Oxford University Press, 1996.

Williams, J. E. Caerwyn, and Patrick K. Ford. *The Irish Literary Tradition.* Cardiff: University of Wales Press, 1992.

Wills, Clair. *Improprieties: Politics and Sexuality in Northern Irish Poetry.* Oxford: Clarendon Press, 1993.

Worth, Katharine. *The Irish Drama of Europe from Yeats to Beckett.* London: Athlone, 1978.

Index